CISTERCIAN STUDIES SERIES: NUMBER ONE HUNDRED THIRTY-FIVE

BERNARDUS MAGISTER

CISTERCIAN STUDIES SERIES: NUMBER ONE HUNDRED THIRTY-FIVE

BERNARDUS MAGISTER

Papers Presented at the Nonacentenary
Celebration of the Birth of
Saint Bernard of Clairvaux,
Kalamazoo, Michigan

Sponsored by the Institute of Cistercian Studies
Western Michigan University
10–13 May 1990

edited by
John R. Sommerfeldt

Cistercian Publications
&
Cîteaux: Commentarii Cistercienses
1992

The work of Cistercian Publications is made possible in part
by support from Western Michigan University to
The Institute of Cistercian Studies

Available in North America from
Cistercian Publications
Saint Joseph's Abbey
Spencer, MA 01562
USA

Available in Britain and Europe from
Cîteaux: Commentarii Cistercienses
Abbaye de Cîteaux
21700 Saint-Nicolas-lès-Cîteaux
France

Library of Congress Cataloguing in Publication Data

Bernardus Magister : in celebration of the nonacentenary of the birth of Saint
Bernard of Clairvaux : 1090–1990 / edited by John R. Sommerfeldt.
    p. cm. — (Cistercian studies series : 135)
   ISBN 0-87907-635-6 (alk. paper).   — ISBN 0-87907-735-2 (pbk. : alk.
paper)
    1. Bernard of Clairvaux, Saint, 1090 or 91-1153.   2. Cistercians—History.
I. Sommerfeldt, John R.   II. Series: Cistercian studies series ; no. 135.
BX4700.B5B48   1992
271'.1202—dc20   92-13334
[B]   CIP

Printed in the United States of America

TABLE OF CONTENTS

5

TABLE OF ABBREVIATIONS

General Abbreviations

ASOC   *Analecta Sacri Ordinis Cisterciensis*; *Analecta Cisterciensia*. Rome, 1945–.

BGPTM   *Beiträge zur Geschichte der Philosophie und Theologie des Mittelalters*. Münster, 1891–.

CC   *Corpus Christianorum*. Turnhout, Belgium, 1953–.

CCCM   *Corpus Christianorum, Continuatio Mediaevalis*. Turnhout, Belgium, 1971–.

CF   *Cistercian Fathers*. Spencer, Massachusetts; Washington, D.C.; Kalamazoo, Michigan, 1969–.

Cîteaux *Cîteaux in de Nederlanden*; *Cîteaux: Commentarii cistercienses*. Westmalle, Belgium; Saint-Nicholas-lès-Cîteaux, France, 1950–.

Coll.   *Collectanea o.c.r.*; *Collectanea cisterciensia*. Rome, 1934–.

CS   *Cistercian Studies* (series). Spencer, Massachusetts; Washington, D.C.; Kalamazoo, Michigan, 1969–.

CSt   *Cistercian Studies* (periodical). Chimay, Belgium, 1961–.

DSp   *Dictionnaire de Spiritualité*. Paris, 1932–.

James   Bruno Scott James (trans.). *The Letters of St. Bernard of Clairvaux*. London: Burns Oates, [1953].

Luddy   *St. Bernard's Sermons for the Seasons & Principal Festivals of the Year*. Trans. A Priest of Mount Melleray [Ailbe J. Luddy]. Reprint, Westminster, Maryland: The Carroll Press, 3 vols., 1950.

PL   J.-P. Migne (ed.). *Patrologia latina*. Paris, 221 vols., 1844–1864.

RB   *Regula monachorum sancti Benedicti*.

RSPT   *Revue des sciences philosophiques et théologiques*. Paris; Kain, Belgium, 1907–.

9

RSV   Revised Standard Version of the Bible.
RTAM   *Recherches de théologie ancienne et médiévale.* Louvain, 1929–.
SAn   *Studia Anselmiana.* Rome, 1933–.
SCh   *Sources chrétiennes.* Paris, 1941–.

The Works of Bernard of Clairvaux

SBOp   Jean Leclercq *et al.* (edd.). *Sancti Bernardi opera.* Rome: Editiones Cisterciensis, 8 vols. in 9, 1957–1977.
Abb   *Sermo ad abbates.*
Abael   *Epistola in erroribus Abaelardi.*
Adv   *Sermo in adventu Domini.*
Ann   *Sermo in annuntiatione dominica.*
Apo   *Apologia ad Guillelmum abbatem.*
Asc   *Sermo in ascensione Domini.*
Asspt   *Sermo in assumptione B.V.M.*
Bapt   *Epistola de baptismo.*
Ben   *Sermo in natali sancti Benedicti.*
Circ   *Sermo in circumcisione Domini.*
Conv   *Sermo ad clericos de conversione.*
Csi   *De consideratione.*
Ded   *Sermo in dedicatione ecclesiae.*
Dil   *De diligendo Deo.*
Div   *Sermo de diversis.*
Ep   *Epistola.*
Epi   *Sermo in epiphania Domini.*
Gra   *De gratia et libero arbitrio.*
IV HM   *Sermo in feria IV hebdomadae sanctae.*
Hum   *De gradibus humilitatis et superbiae.*
Humb   *Sermo in obitu Domni Humberti.*
Lab   *Sermo in labore messis.*
Miss   *Homilia super 'Missus est' in laudibus Virginis Matris.*
Mor   *Epistola de moribus et officiis episcoporum.*
Nat   *Sermo in nativitate Domini.*
Nat B.V.M. *Sermo in nativitate B.V.M.I.*
I Nov   *Sermo in dominica I novembris.*
OPasc   *Sermo in octava paschae.*
OS   *Sermo in festivitate omnium sanctorum.*
Palm   *Sermo in ramis palmarum.*
Par   *Parabola.*

Pasc	*Sermo in die paschae.*
Pent	*Sermo in die pentecostes.*
Pre	*De precepto et dispensatione.*
PP	*Sermo in festo ss. Apostolorum Petri et Pauli.*
Pur	*Sermo in purificatione B.V.M.*
QH	*Sermo super psalmum 'Qui habitat'.*
Quad	*Sermo in quadragesima.*
SC	*Sermo super Cantica canticorum.*
Sent	*Sententia.*
Sept	*Sermo in septuagesima.*
S Mal	*Sermo de sancto Malachia.*
Tpl	*Ad milites Templi de laude novae militiae.*
Vict	*Sermo in natali sancti Victoris.*
V Mal	*Vita sancti Malachiae.*
V Nat	*Sermo in vigilia nativitatis Domini.*

Biblical Abbreviations

Ac	Acts.
Ba	Baruch.
1 Co	1 Corinthians.
2 Co	2 Corinthians.
Col	Colossians.
Dn	Daniel.
Eph	Ephesians.
Ex	Exodus.
Ga	Galatians.
Gn	Genesis.
Heb	Hebrews.
Ho	Hosea.
Is	Isaiah.
Jb	Job.
Jl	Joel.
Jn	John.
1 Jn	1 John.
2 K	2 Kings.
Lk	Luke.
Lm	Lamentations.
Lv	Leviticus.
Mk	Mark.
Mt	Matthew.

Nb	Numbers.
Ph	Phillipians.
Pr	Proverbs.
Ps	Psalm.
Rm	Romans.
Sg	Song of Songs.
Si	Ecclesiasticus; Sirach.
Tb	Tobit.
1 Th	1 Thessalonians.
1 Tm	1 Timothy.
2 Tm	2 Timothy.
Tt	Titus.
Ws	Wisdom.

INTRODUCTION

EACH MAY, an annual Cistercian Studies Conference, sponsored by the Institute of Cistercian Studies of Western Michigan University, is held in Kalamazoo, Michigan, in conjunction with the International Congress on Medieval Studies, convened each year by the Medieval Institute of the University. At the May 1985 meeting, Professor E. Rozanne Elder (who combines—and successfully executes—the roles of Editorial Director of Cistercian Publications and Director of the Institute of Cistercian Studies) pointed ahead to the 1990 nonacentenary of Bernard of Clairvaux' birth. The result was that several scholars were charged with the program for the american 1990 celebration—I among them. I must confess that I was somewhat taken aback by the length of the preparation period, but Professor Elder proved more farsighted than I. It took all of the five years alloted to prepare the program.

The celebration proved a great success. Some ninety-one papers were presented by scholars from all over the world. Moreover, some additional, rich offerings were presented. Chrysogonus Waddell, of Gethsemani Abbey, led us in singing the twelfth-century cistercian vespers; the bishop of Kalamazoo, Paul V. Donovan, presided—with the assistance of the abbot-general of the strict observance Cistercians, Ambrose Southey. Professor Audrey Davidson of Western Michigan University led her Society for Old Music in a splendid concert of cistercian music of the twelfth through the twentieth centuries, a program prepared by her and Chrysogonus Waddell. Basil Pennington, of St Joseph's Abbey, offered two evening presentations: one, a practical exercise in disposing oneself for contemplation; the other, a tour, through a slide

13

presentation, of cistercian monasteries in the United States. Additionally, our eyes feasted on an exhibit of manuscripts and rare books from the Obrecht Collection, Gethsemani Abbey, now on permanent loan to the Institute of Cistercian Studies and arranged by the Institute's librarian, Beatrice Beech.

The nonacentenary celebration combined the efforts of the Society for the Studies of the Crusades and the Latin East (six sessions), the International Center of Medieval Art (four sessions arranged by Professor Meredith Parsons Lillich of Syracuse University), and the Institute of Cistercian Studies (eighteen sessions arranged by Professor Elder and me). Only the papers presented in the sessions sponsored by the Institute are included in this volume. The others are being published under the auspices of their sponsoring societies.

In inviting the submission of papers for the nonacentenary program, I had but a modest goal: to present a brief survey of Bernard's most significant contributions and then examine the impact of his thought on subsequent generations. I expected only summaries of the status of current scholarship. The contributors went far beyond my modest expectations. To single out but one example, Professor Raymond DiLorenzo's paper on Dante and Bernard constitutes a revolutionary reading of Dante's *Divine Comedy*, based on a thorough appreciation and appropriation—by both Dante and DiLorenzo—of Bernard's *On Grace and Free Will*.

Unfortunately, not all the papers presented could be fitted within this festschrift, and some of those not included will see publication elsewhere. There are, however, two papers, by Jean Leclercq and Adriaan Bredero, slated to be read, but not presented, at the celebration.

Nuns, monks, friars, secular clergy, and lay folk from Australia, Canada, China, Denmark, France, Germany, Indonesia, Israel, Italy, the Netherlands, the United Kingdom, and Uruguay did take their place at the podium, along with their sisters and brothers from the United States. How many additional countries were represented by their audience, I cannot tell. But it was truly an international gathering of scholars who taught and learned much about the twelfth-century monk who sometimes resided at Clairvaux.

I hope that the joint publication of this volume by Cistercian Publications and *Cîteaux: Commentarii cistercienses* will enlarge the number of those who will profit from our 1990 celebration. I am deeply grateful to Rozanne Elder and Jean-François Holthof, the editorial directors of those two sources of cistercian wisdom, for their generous cooperation and supervision. I am also grateful to Professor Hella Hennessee and

Professor J. Stephen Maddux for their important contributions to the editorial process. The person who bore the brunt of the labor in producing this volume is Jeri Guadagnoli, whose patient and precise typing has won praise from many of the authors. She surely has mine—along with deep gratitude for her generous gift of her many talents.

John R. Sommerfeldt
The University of Dallas

PART I
IN QUEST OF BERNARD

TOWARD A SOCIOLOGICAL INTERPRETATION
OF THE VARIOUS SAINT BERNARDS

Jean Leclercq
Abbaye St-Maurice, Clervaux

WHY ARE WE HERE? That is the great question which comes to mind when we consider this gathering at Kalamazoo. For, indeed, the fact that you have flocked here so eagerly to celebrate the memory of Saint Bernard of Clairvaux certainly poses a sociological problem. Why is it that so many people have gathered here to remember him and to speak about him—either criticizing him or praising him—and to celebrate him in one way or another? What sort of man was he that he should cause such a stir? That too is a sociological problem. Many learned papers are scheduled for this event; they will scrutinize Bernard from every angle and examine a host of historical and doctrinal problems. But if we are to have an exact understanding of the *raison d'être* of the display of so much learning and scholarship on so many different issues connected with him, history and theology will not suffice. We need to have recourse to interdisciplinary study, and, specifically, to socio-history—that is to say, to sociology as it is currently applied to certain facts and people of the past and present.

We are faced with no easy task, for there are now, as there always have been, as it were, several Bernards. There is the historical Bernard, the man who can be pinpointed as he really existed against the background of his own time. Then we have the legendary Bernard depicted by the many stories which began to be woven around his person even before his death and have continued to be woven right up to our own day. And many of these have been circulated through the medium of iconography. We also have Bernard as portrayed in his writings. These are being constantly examined from every point of view. Finally we have the Bernard of historians, many of whom have conjured up their own Bernard. Thus, we can hardly fail to be intrigued and to wonder what sociological fact lies at the root of the variety and durability of the 'Bernard phenomenon'.

THE HISTORICAL BERNARD

Saint Bernard of Clairvaux has always been a paradox. He was so for himself, and he continues to be so for anyone attempting to interpret his role in Church and society. He summed up the dilemma in a few short words written to a bishop: 'What are we, who am I, that I should write to a bishop?'[1] He knew that, socially, he was nothing; he had no social standing comparable with that of the dignity and authority of bishops. Even so, he did not hesitate to write to them, for them, and about them. Where shall we find the key to understanding this role? How does it fit in with the society of his time?

One of the key-concepts of Max Weber, the founder of sociology as a science, can enlighten us in our approach to these questions. Indeed, in writing at the turn of the century, Weber frequently used the category of what he termed 'charisma',[2] and this word—in its Greek form as here, rather than in the anglicized form 'charism'—has come to be part of the vocabulary of English-speaking sociologists.[3] Weber used it to designate those forms of power which go beyond the everyday forms and are, thus, out of the ordinary, extraordinary. He applied it particularly to that form of power which has always been a typical characteristic of certain political leaders claiming to exert a certain ascendancy or domination over people. But the use of the category charisma has been extended beyond the political realm and is applied to any person gifted with this power of ascendancy in whatever realm.

---

[1]Mor; SBOp 7:100.

[2]Max Weber, *Wirtschaft und Gesellschaft* (4th ed., Tübingen, 1952) II, 252–55, 685, etc. Weber's application of the category charisma to political power has been criticized, for example in works reviewed by Jean Séguy, 'Sociologie religieuse et sociologie générale', *Archives des Sciences sociales des religions* 59 (1985) 205–213. Here I shall retain Weber's general categories, as they suit the purpose.

[3]For example, B. R. Wilson, *The Noble Savages: The Primitive Origins of Charisma and Its Contemporary Survivals* (Berkeley, 1975). See also the work of Roy Wallis in the following publications: 'The Social Construction of Charisma', *Social Compass* 29 (1982) 25–39; *Charisma and Sacred Biography* (Ohio, [California]: Scholar Press, 1982); *Millenarism and Charisma* (Belfast, 1982).

Weber made a useful distinction between functional or institutional charisma and personal charisma. But, be it functional or personal, charisma must be recognized and, consequently, in some way legitimized by the social group in which the charismatic leader exercises his or her power. Functional or institutional charisma is received from the institution itself and can therefore be transmitted within the institutional framework. Personal charisma, on the contrary, is peculiar to an individual person and dies with him or her.

Bernard's charisma was not granted him by society, for he was not a member of the upper aristocracy. Nor did it come to him from monastic society, for he was not a founder but merely the young abbot of a newly established monastery without the prestige enjoyed by ancient and prosperous abbeys such as Saint Denys, Fleury, Cluny, or Monte Cassino. He had received no special designation of appointment from a church authority. He had no other ritual approval apart from his priestly ordination.

He was not even the self-appointed leader of a specific group, except of the small group of companions he brought with him to Cîteaux. They became members of that community, followed him when he was sent to found Clairvaux, and then became heads of the foundations made by him. But both he and they remained members of the Order of Cîteaux, and he never pretended to act as their representative. Finally, we may say that, though very early on he played a general and even an universal role, that role was in no way rooted in a functional charisma. His was a truly personal charisma, an inherent attribute of his nature, a God-given grace. And he very soon became aware of this gift, this capacity for ascendancy, for influence.

The tone of many of Bernard's letters, in which he warns, rebukes, or begs those to whom he is writing, gives us a glimpse of his irresistibly winning ways, the power of persuasion he had exerted over the other young men and adults he took with him to Cîteaux. He was not the eldest of his family or the senior among his companions, but they all gave way to his charisma, surrendered to his charm, let themselves be convinced by him, and gave way to his demands. At the end of his life, when he was a wandering crusade preacher in germanic territories, a witness relates that his words were immediately translated into the regional tongue. What the translator had to say roused no interest, but when Bernard himself was speaking in the romance tongue, which no one understood, the crowds became enthusiastic and rallied to his words.[4] This journey, and others too, especially those in Italy and in Languedoc, would provide us with some interesting data of a sociological nature. These journeys were triumphs! There was something fascinating about his whole person and his speech. Throughout his life, most people who met him and heard him were won over by his charm. Many with political power or ecclesiastical status consulted him or bowed to his wishes—wishes which were sometimes nothing short of direct orders. Bernard could hardly fail to notice his ascendancy.

However, such personal charisma needs to be accepted and confirmed by the social group in order to acquire and maintain legitimacy.[5] This recognition of authenticity is what medieval people called 'canonization' —before this term came to be reserved to the act of putting someone on the official ecclesiastical record of saints. Bernard acquired this approval by the very fact that he was left free to exert his ascendancy, was even requested to do so, for the furthering of many a good cause and in many business matters of the day. This influence was a gift, as we have seen, but it responded to the social needs of the people who turned to him.[6] When the Second Crusade was being planned and prepared, a bavarian abbot wrote about Bernard: 'He can do more than others.'[7] He had the ability to play such a role, and he was asked, even begged, to do so.

However, this situation caused two sorts of conflict: one, exterior to Bernard himself, when, naturally or because it was expected of him, he clashed with princes or prelates invested with a charisma of function. It was inevitable, too, that he should be the cause of jealousy, especially among men in the papal entourage. But there was also an inner conflict, stemming from the contrast between the fact that he was invested with no institutional authority but was, even so, requested to intervene in many matters.

Bernard was no dupe. He was well aware of this tension in and around

[4]Geoffrey of Auxerre, *Vita prima sancti Bernardi* 3.3; PL 185: 307.

[5]Jean Séguy, 'Charisme, prophétie, religion populaire', *Archives des Sciences sociales des religions* 57 (1984) 160; Alphose Dupont, *Du sacré: Croisades et pèlerinages: Images et langages* (Paris, 1987) pp. 533–36: 'Le Saint: sa reconnaissance collective'. Some examples of the old use of the word *canonizo* are cited in Prinz (ed.), *Mittellateinishes Wörterbuch* (Munich, 1969) II, col. 183.

[6]In 'S. Bernard écrivain, I, Pourquoi S. Bernard écrit-il?', forthcoming in the acts of the nonacentenary congress held at Lyon in June 1990, I have quoted several formulas in which Bernard says that he was asked to write, that people insisted he should do so, and why he agreed.

[7]Letter of Adalbert, abbot of the regular canons of Ellwangen, edited in Jean Leclercq, *Recueil d'études sur saint Bernard et ses écrits*, II (Rome, 1966) p. 337.

him, and we find his awareness expressed in his own writings. He was conscious of his place in the Church: *meum in Ecclesia locum*. He was a negligible quantity: 'How small I am'; *quantulus ego in populo christiano*. That was what he wrote to the abbot of an important benedictine abbey who insisted (*instas*) and urged (*urges*) him, with the support of several others (*alios precatores*), to compose a liturgical office.[8] To the archbishop of Sens, a high-ranking prelate who had ordered (*iubetis*) him to write a treatise on the way bishops should conduct themselves, Bernard sent the answer already quoted: *Quid enim nos sumus ut scribamus episcopis?*; 'What are we, who am I, that I should write to a bishop?'[9]

On the other hand, Bernard realized that, if people had urged him to write, it was because he was qualified to do so by reason of his personal charisma. He did occasionally protest that he had but little talent: *Aut quantulum mihi ingenii eloquium facultas*; 'How little talent and facility of expression I have!' With consummate art, and no little humor, he confessed to the onsets of anxiety which resulted:

> As for me, unhappy man that I am, naked and poor, it is my lot of labor. An unfledged nestling, I am obliged to spend most of my time out of my nest exposed to the tempests and troubles of the world. I am shaken and upset like a drunken man, and cares devour my conscience.[10]

Is this merely rhetoric? Whatever the answer to that question, apart from exceptional cases which will presently be described, Bernard did not refuse to put his charisma at the service of institutional causes with which he found himself connected, sometimes in spite of himself.

We sometimes get the impression that, by being forced to play successive roles in the institution, Bernard's activity integrated progressively with his personality and became part of him. One might think he acquired the equivalent of a public function. In the majority of cases, he was effective in carrying out these duties. In a word, he was a success. One cannot help thinking that the greatest temptations constantly assailing him were those which menace most, if not all political leaders: the fascination of power, complacency in personal influence. Did Bernard give way to this *hybris* in seeking after domination? Some failures and repudiations served to put him on his guard. Thus, for example, in 1143, Innocent II,

---

[8]Ep 398.1–2; SBOp 8:377–78.
[9]Mor; SBOp 7:100.
[10]Ep 398.2; SBOp 8:378.

for whom Bernard had worked so hard during the schism of Anacletus, influenced by men in his entourage, showed disapproval of Bernard in connection with some matters with which he had had nothing to do. Bernard began his answer to the pope with these words: 'I knew I was not worth much [*aliquid vel modicum*], but now I have been reduced to nothing [*ad nihilum redactus sum*].' And he went on to wonder why, in spite of his nothingness, this *nihilum* which he stressed, the same pope called on him so much for help.[11] Whatever the reason, he went on to say that he could 'easily mend his ways', cover his mouth, and talk less. A similar situation came up under Eugenius III, one of Bernard's former monks. But for all that, Bernard never lost his ardor or his serenity. He remained ardent and calm to his dying day. Bernard's greatness, and, in Christian terms, I would dare say his holiness, was that he had in mind the service of the Church, as he perceived it, and not his own personal success or promotion. He could have acceded to a charisma of function; more than once he was chosen bishop. But he stayed a monk.

However, his personal charisma had its limits, and he accepted them with lucidity: 'Who am I that I should write to a bishop?' Write and act: he did both, but not always or in every sphere. The subjects on which he felt compelled to write, as by force of some 'pulsion' (*pulsor*),[12] were subjects related to morals and to spirituality: the contemplation of the mysteries of salvation, the manner in which one should behave, act, govern in keeping with christian principles. The greater part of his written work—treatises and sermons—stems from the contemplative in him. And so do most of his letters, especially the longer ones. However, there was one sphere in which he refused, several times, to intervene: that of doctrinal controversy. He only did so when he was persuaded that the opinions being debated were dangerous to the integrity of the faith.

Bernard's opposition to Abelard is frequently brought up. But it began only in 1139, after more than twenty years of silent observation on Bernard's side. He had been informed of Abelard's ideas in 1118 by William of Saint-Thierry, and they were condemned in 1121 at Soissons. The most recent expert on William has said of him: 'He only decided to break his silence about Abelard, a silence which he would have preferred to keep, because of the incompetence of the authorities. . . .' William of Saint-Thierry, who took part in several public controversies, always did so 'in spite of himself and with a reticence which became increasingly

[11]Ep 218; SBOp 8:78–79.
[12]Ep 11.10; SBOp 7:60, l. 12.

obvious.'[13] This is the true attitude of a monk, and it was Bernard's attitude when William urged him to write against Abelard, and even drew up a dossier to help him. Bernard was at first reluctant, but finally threw himself into the fray with characteristic ardor.

Bernard received similar requests from other people. For example, Matthew, bishop of Cracow, asked him to refute the Ruthenian Orthodox; Gerhoh, provost of the regular canons of Reichersberg, addressing him as 'the oracle of the godhead', asked him to re-establish the truth on different points of christology.[14] William of Saint-Thierry, once more, asked him to take a stand against certain teachings of William of Conches.[15] Finally, Peter the Venerable wanted him to do the same against the Muslims.[16] Bernard also refused to get involved in a controversy about the Eucharist,[17] and in another concerning the validity of sacraments administered by simoniacs.[18]

These examples go to prove that Bernard was in control of his personal charisma, which tended—in spite of himself, as he said—to become a charisma of function. Deep down in the ground of his being, he was a contemplative and a reformer, endowed with the fervor proper to contemplatives and the energy proper to reformers.

And, finally, in Bernard we see the confirmation of one of the laws formed by sociology on the basis of observation of a great number of data, namely, that the influence of a charismatic leader rarely survives his death. Bernard seems to have foreseen what has been called 'the rapid decline of the Cistercian Order',[19] which did continue to expand, but not always along the lines Bernard would have wished. This was also the fate of St Francis of Assisi in the century after Bernard's: the Franciscan Order spread far and wide, but with an observance of poverty greatly different from the ideal of Francis who, before his death, said sadly, but

[13]M. Lemoine, *Guillelmus de Sancto-Theodorico, Guillaume de Saint-Thierry, De natura corporis et animae* (Paris, 1988) p. 29.

[14]In 'S. Bernard et le mystère de l'Ascension', Coll. 15 (1955) 81–88, I have quoted and discussed this text and Bernard's reply.

[15]Text edited in *Recueil*, IV (Rome, 1987) pp. 357–69.

[16]*Bernard de Clairvaux* (Paris, 1953) p. 397.

[17]*Bernard de Clairvaux*, p. 269; and F. Gastadelli, 'I primi vent'anni di S. Bernardo: Problemi e interpretazioni', ASOC 43 (1987) 140.

[18]*Bernard de Clairvaux*, p. 269.

[19]The expression is used by Jean de la Croix Bouton, in *Bernard de Clairvaux*, p. 611.

with no bitterness: 'If only the brothers had believed me. . . .'[20] But, at least, the model left to posterity by these two great men has never ceased being a point of reference for their successors and their admirers,[21] or an object of criticism for their few enemies. Saint Bernard was also a master in theological doctrine. And it is thus that he is still at work among us, and for us, with astonishing reality. We must now evoke this survival.

THE LEGENDARY BERNARD

In all that is covered by the word history, applied to a person of the past, it is possible to distinguish three sorts of fact. At the origin, there is what we might call *real history*, that is to say, the set of acts and moods of the person in question. At the end, there is *history-science*, the most objective and true knowledge which it has been possible for scholars of successive generations to acquire from the examination of the facts of the past. Between the two, we have *history-tradition*, made up of constant re-readings of the facts, re-readings practiced in the past-present, so to speak, of successive generations and for the benefit of people living in each of those time sequences. Thus we have imagined history, past reality as it was imagined in varying times and places. For, it is true to say, past history is dynamic, active in giving self-understanding to the present. Such history-tradition is the object of scientific research. It is also the seed bed and the specific sphere of legend.

Saint Bernard, Saint Patrick, Saint Francis of Assisi, and many another have been subjected to the process of legend-making, the process by which the transformation of reality acquires greater importance than the reality itself. Why does this phenomenon come about? And to what literary and iconographical projections does it lead?

The question 'why' has its answer in sociology. A recent study carries the title *Les saints et les stars: Le texte hagiographique dans la culture populaire*.[22] For, in fact, the cult of stars today has something in common with the cult of saints in the past. A charisma of function has no need of social recognition; it is legitimized by the institution which confers it. A

---

[20]'Si fratres mihi credidissent'; *Legenda Perusina*, 101; text quoted and discussed by Raoul Manselli, *Nos qui cum eo fuimus: Contributo alla questione franciscana* (Rome, 1980) p. 178.

[21]Guy Philipart, 'Les écrits des compagnons de S. François: Aperçu de la "question franciscaine" des origines à nos jours', *Analecta Bollandiana* 90 (1972) 143–66. Manselli, pp. 3–57, has given an inventory of all these 'legends'.

[22]Ed. Jean-Claude Schmitt (Paris, 1983).

personal charisma, on the other hand, needs this social recognition and acceptance, as we have already seen. And it is the collective conscience which acclaims the star and proclaims the saint. Alphonse Dupront, an expert in the study of the sociology of the sacred, has written that this

> . . . recognition is the reading in an historical reality of marks of holiness. Such reading is often spontaneous and even occurs during the lifetime of the future saint. This amounts to saying that in both popular canonization and in the prudent procedure of the Church, in the institutional disciplining of the irrational fervor of the masses, there exists a latent or explicit set of characteristics typical of holiness. . . .[23]

The religious soul discerns, or foresees, in the saint, the realization of her own spiritual ambition. She rejoices in this and approves of it. Such admiration tends to find expression in veneration taking the form of a cult.

In the tradition of the Church, such a cult can only be celebrated if the charisma has been duly recognized by the competent ecclesiastical authority. In the twelfth century, this authority was that of the bishops. Afterward it was reserved to the pope. And one of the conditions required for official recognition and authorization of a cult by canonization was that it had not existed previously. This is one of the points examined during the process of canonization. This fact alone is sufficient to show that there had been some popular canonizations or other closely allied forms of veneration. I remember seeing a television program in honor of a well-known singer, some years after he had been assassinated. The whole program was virtually a cultic commemoration. In another context, I have heard Thomas Merton referred to as 'Blessed' Thomas Merton.

What happened to Bernard of Clairvaux?[24] He was esteemed, admired, praised much more than he thought he deserved, and he protested: 'I am not what you think I am.'[25] But that did not hinder people from beginning to write a *Life*. Biographies ordinarily turn rapidly into hagiographies. For Bernard, the process was reversed: for, about ten years before he died, one of his admirers, William of Saint-Thierry, started writing the *Life* of Bernard without his knowledge, on the sly, so to speak, because, said William, Bernard 'would have found it unbearable to suffer such

---

[23]Dupront, pp. 533–34.
[24]Geoffrey of Auxerre, *Vita prima* 4.2; PL 185:323.
[25]'Non sum talis qualis putor vel dicor.' Ep 11.10; SBOp 7:60.

praise.'[26] This *Life* was nothing less than hagiography. A similar sort of pre-canonization once happened to Mother Teresa the day after an interreligious meeting at the United Nations Headquarters in New York: the *New York Times* heralded her as 'The Living Saint'. She protested and exclaimed: 'Let me die first!'

Very early, the historical Bernard tended to fade into oblivion and to give place to the Bernard of legend and of theology. It has been said of him that 'he passed into legend before passing into history.' But, it must be realized, William of Saint-Thierry was not writing simply in his own name. He was the spokesman for an entire circle of admirers from whom he collected various elements to help him compose Bernard's *Life*. William gave his reasons: Bernard was a 'servant of God', a 'man of God'. Gregory the Great had already attributed these titles to Saint Benedict, and they had been traditionally reserved for men considered to be saints, examples, models to be followed and imitated. As we would say today, they had an iconic value. Was William a bad hagiographer? Did he give way to facile hagiography? It must be admitted that he produced a beautiful hagiography, written in most elegant style and quite in keeping with the laws of the literary genre of a 'life'. He used traditional themes and thus proposed to his readers an ideal, an icon. His work was didactic. It should be noted too that he projected onto Bernard his own psychological problems, in particular a tendency to anxiety which, according to the most recent research on William, was precisely one of his own personality traits.[27]

The legendary account begun by William was continued after Bernard's death by Arnold of Bonneval, who did not belong to the same circle. This was followed by several other 'lives'. However, the written legend contains facts useful to history-science, and it is only one of the forms of the process of legend-making. Legends bearing on particular points develop and give rise to others. For example, with the extension of devotion to the Virgin Mary in the second half of the twelfth century, Bernard was attributed marvelous manifestations of piety toward her, and mention is made of the response she is said to have made to such piety. So it was that, because he was opposed to the new feast introduced in honor of her conception, he is depicted with a stain on his white

---

[26]That is also why William did not wish the *Life* published before Bernard's death: 'nec edenda vivente ipso, sicut nec scribantur ipso sciente'. *Vita prima* I, praefatio; PL 185:226.

[27]Lemoine, pp. 213–23.

robe. This is a 'silly and spiteful legend', as has been pointed out by an eminent mariologist of our day.[28] But Mary countered this representation of Bernard, and so appeared the legend of the lactation, suggested by the more or less unconscious imaginations of certain circles, the same sort of imaginations to which modern media tend to cater and cultivate. Some of the legends about Bernard gave rise to erroneous devotions which the Church was obliged to forbid.[29] They were also the origin of an iconography which illustrated either the whole supposed life cycle of Bernard or certain aspects of his doctrine, real or imagined. Or, again, they gave birth to those pseudo-Bernards to whom have been attributed more than two hundred writings.[30]

Among the unfounded legends are those which associated Bernard with alchemy, druidic religions, the origins of guilds of architects, the 'frères pontifes' (bridge builders), Free Masons, and so on. As to the 'Saint Bernard Balsam', based on marmot grease and sold in european pharmacies, it is said to be good for sportsmen. Could this be a souvenir of the historical Bernard, who seems to have been an energetic man, or is it in memory of the Bernard who, according to legend, was so sickly? For, let it be said in passing, Saint Bernard's poor health was perhaps not merely a literary theme found in his letters, as in the letters of many other writers. Was it a historical reality, or was it an invention of legend, so that he could be proposed as a model of courage in suffering? In seventeenth-century Europe, when tobacco was a fairly recently imported drug, Bernard's picture and name figured on tobacco grinders—collections of which still exist. Was this meant to be an antidote to the bad effects of smoking? As we see, there are still many obscure points concerning the legendary Bernard.

A CHOICE OF BERNARDS

Between the historical Bernard and the legendary Bernard, we have the Bernard as portrayed by his own writings. It would seem that this is the man we can get to know with the greatest certainty, since he is revealed by authentic texts. However, these texts do raise their own problems. The inventory of their contents is now greatly facilitated

[28]Henri Barré, 'Saint Bernard, Docteur marial', in *Saint Bernard théologien* (Rome, 1953) (=ASOC 9 [1953]) p. 101.

[29]An example is given by A. de Bonhome, 'Dévotions', in DSp 3:783.

[30]According to Leopold Janauschek, *Bibliographia Bernardina* (Vienna, 1891) pp. iv–xiv.

by the computerization of all the words, together with their context, contained in the three thousand pages of the total corpus of his works. The interpretation of these words remains to be done by philologists and psycho-linguists. Certain readers may be tempted to project their own ideas onto Bernard's words, and even go so far as to twist the text to fit their own ideas, in spite of the witness of the manuscript tradition.

On the basis of these three principal Bernards—the Bernard of history, legend, and of his own written works—many others have developed. We can do no more than evoke them here; there exists abundant documentation for the inquiring reader eager to have further information. Let us now name and typify these various Bernards.

First, there is the Bernard of piety in all its devotional manifestations: personal piety based on prayers inspired by his texts and his person, and by countless holy pictures; popular devotion as it is expressed in collective phenomena, for example, in the names given to towns, villages, churches, and chapels placed under his patronage, or by the veneration of objects which came from him. What strata of society have prayed to Saint Bernard? Where and why?

Secondly, there is the Bernard of theology: in the Catholic tradition to Thomas Merton and our own present day, in the Protestant tradition from Luther and Calvin to Karl Barth.

Thirdly, there is the Bernard of inter-religious dialogue. His connections with Judaism have given rise to Jewish legends, but he has also been compared with Rabbi Rashi who commented on the Torah in the rabbinic school of Troyes, not far from Clairvaux. In dialogue between Christians and the far-eastern religions—Buddhism and Hinduism—Bernard is not dominant, but he is to some measure present by his teaching on true self-knowledge and the experience of transcendency.

Then there is the Bernard of intellectual thought, for example, in nineteenth-century positivism, and in the thinking of present-day psychologists who apply to Bernard the theories of Freud, Jung, and others.

And, of course, there is the Bernard of iconography. In the not too distant future, we shall have a complete inventory of the innumerable representations of Saint Bernard. But there is still a great deal to be done in the way of phenomenological and sociological interpretations of these images, along the lines of what has already been done for the iconography of Saint Jerome. It seems fairly certain that the most primitive icon of Bernard, which has been handed down through the centuries, shows him as a Doctor, teaching and holding the Bible on which he commented so well.

Nor should we forget the Bernard beloved by men of letters, poets and romanticists from Dante to Schiller, Goethe and—why not mention him?—Umberto Eco.

Finally, there is the Bernard of historians, working from the start of their scientific methods of research in the seventeenth century to our own day. It must be said that the most clear-sighted of contemporary historians admit that 'history is always subjective'. One historian situates Bernard in the context of the role played by nobility; another sets him against his socio-economic background, the means of production and the miserable conditions of the workers of his day, trying to find in him the verification of the insights of Marx and Engels. The personal tendencies of each historian influence the selection and interpretation he or she makes of Bernard's acts and words, in keeping with his or her own major preoccupation: aesthetics and art, knighthood and combat, or the Holy Land. However, because of the freedom of speech which is enjoyed in many parts of the world, and also by reason of the mutual control exercised by scholars, the Bernard of history and the Bernard of theology contribute most surely to our knowledge of the true Bernard.

But this multiplicity of Bernards, quite often complementary, occasionally contradictory, gives rise to two kinds of questions. First, why do people take so much interest in Saint Bernard? Why was there no process of legend-making for Peter the Venerable, Abelard, or Suger, either during their lifetime or after their death? What surprises us is not so much that Bernard should have been the object of legend-making on the part of his admirers, who compiled legends often put together with borrowings from other legendary figures, but that these legends should have been so widely diffused and even, as it were, imposed. What was it that made, and continues to make, Bernard seem so different to other great men? Did he win lasting fame because he was the builder of magnificent churches, or because he was an intellectual genius, a theologian of outstanding merit, a hero, or an exemplary monk? I think not! He was above all a fervent religious whose spiritual experience found expression in confessions and aspirations with which every religious soul can identify. And the example he gave seems in keeping with his doctrine. The fact is that, in spite of the limitations inherent to every human being and in spite of failings which can be found in every person's life, Bernard is the living realization of an universal archetype: that of a life lived in singleness of purpose and heart, a life soaring far beyond mediocrity.

And to close, let us ask just one more short question. Must we take our pick, and choose one among all these different Bernards? Each of us will have a personal answer to give to this question. But, when all is said and done, if we manage to glimpse at least something of Bernard as he was to himself, in his own eyes, the Bernard of Bernard, then we shall begin to grasp, in spite of his elusiveness, the real Bernard.

ABSTRACTS

Pour éclairer la variété des représentations de saint Bernard, usage est fait de catégories empruntées à la sociologie religieuse de Max Weber. La distinction entre 'charisme personnel' et 'charisme institutionnel' appliquée au cas de l'abbé de Clairvaux peut être utile. L'influence dont il a joui ne relève pas d'un charisme institutionnel mais bien plutôt personnel. Bernard sut très consciemment mettre au service de l'institution ses dons. Mais c'est comme à son insu qu'il acquit cette reconnaissance de l'entourage qu'on peut appeler 'canonisation' au sens sociologique du terme, reconnaissance qui se déploiera dès avant sa mort et jusqu'à nos jours, à travers de multiples approches plus ou moins légendaires. Ainsi la variété des interprétations de saint Bernard déborde la simple réalité événementielle et ne s'explique pas par une influence historique durable, tant il est vrai qu'un charisme personnel ne survit guère à son détenteur. Le nombre et l'impact des interprétatons de saint Bernard indique qu'il est la réalisation personnelle d'un archétype universel.

In order to cast light on the variety of representations of saint Bernard, use is made of categories borrowed from the religious sociology of Max Weber. The distinction between 'personal charism' and 'institutional charism' applied to the case of the abbot of Clairvaux can be useful. The influence he enjoyed is a matter of a personal, rather than an institutional charism. Bernard was able very consciously to put his gifts at the service of the institution. But it is unknowingly, as it were, that he acquired that recognition on the part of those surrounding him which can be termed 'canonization' in the sociological sense of the term, a recognition which unfolded even before his death and up to the present day through multiple, more or less legendary approaches. Thus the variety of interpretations of Saint Bernard goes beyond the mere reality of events and cannot be explained by a lasting historical influence, for true it is that a personal charism does not survive its bearer. The number and impact of interpretations of Saint Bernard indicates that he is the personal realization of a universal archetype.

Um die Vielfalt der Darstellungen des hl. Bernhard zu erhellen, wird von Kategorien Gebrauch gemacht, die der religiösen Soziologie von Max Weber entnommen sind. Die Unterscheidung zwischen 'persönlichem Charisma' und 'institutionellem Charisma', angewandt auf den Fall des Abtes von Clairvaux, kann nützlich sein. Der Einfluss, den er hatte, zeigt nicht ein institutionelles Charisma, sondern eher ein persönliches. Bernhard konnte sehr bewußt seine Begabungen in den Dienst der Institution stellen. Aber gewissermassen ohne sein Wissen erhält er die Anerkennung der Umgebung, die man 'Kanonisierung' im soziologischen Sinne nennen kann, eine Anerkennung, die sich seit vor seinem Tod bis heute durch vielfältige, mehr oder weniger legendäre Annäherungen ausgebreitet hat. So übersteigt die Vielfalt der Interpretationen des hl. Bernhard die einfache Wirklichkeit reiner Darstellung und erklärt sich nicht durch einen dauerhaftern geschichtlichen Einfluß, solange es wahr ist, daß ein persönliches Charisma seinen Besitzer nicht überlebt. Die Abzahl und die Auswirkung der Interpretationen des hl. Bernhard zeigt an, daß er die persönliche Verwirklichung eines universellen Archetyps ist.

THE PRESENCE—AND ABSENCE—OF BERNARD OF CLAIRVAUX IN THE TWELFTH-CENTURY CHRONICLES

Paschal Phillips, OCSO
Our Lady of Guadalupe Abbey

THE THESIS PRESENTED in this paper is a simple one. It is that the domination and influence that Bernard of Clairvaux exercised in his lifetime was, in fact, very different and more restricted than the picture which springs to the modern mind after reading the panegyrics. By concentrating on documentation written during or immediately after Bernard's lifetime, we can place ourselves in the position of his contemporaries, who did not guess his future fame. That documentation presents a level of awareness far below what we have been trained to expect.

In his widely-read history of the Catholic Church, Philip Hughes calmly introduces one of his characters in a way that might startle bernardine scholars, as

> ...one of Gratian's pupils, his first great commentator,...Roland Bandinelli, whose personality was to dominate the second half of the twelfth century, as St Bernard's had dominated the first.[1]

Although bernardine scholars will recognize Roland as Pope Alexander III, they might be startled to find his influence set on an equal footing with that of Bernard in his own generation.

Nor does Hughes have some anti-bernardine axe to grind. In fact, an entire chapter just preceding the above quotation is entitled 'The Age of St Bernard', and the author leaves no question about his position:

---

[1]Philip Hughes, *A History of the Church* (New York: Sheed & Ward, 1949) 2:291.

Above the richly crowded pageant that filled the 30 years after the
triumphant council of 1123, popes, emperors, crusaders, philosophers,
and theologians, one figure stands out in solitary grandeur, St Bernard,
Abbot of Clairvaux. Nothing of importance passed in those years
without his active and often decisive intervention. For a lifetime, he
dominated the whole Christian scene. After 750 years his influence is
still active. . . . [2]

Here we stand on more familiar ground. Statements such as 'Bernard of
Clairvaux dominated the twelfth century as it has been given to few men
to dominate their century' and 'During his lifetime he bestrode the world
like a colossus' are indeed commonplace and appear to rest on the unas-
sailable facts of Bernard's life. We need only think of the vast expansion
of his own monastic family, of his decisive interventions following the
disputed papal election of 1130, the preaching of the Second Crusade, the
controversies with Cluny, Peter Abelard, and Bernard's correspondence.

Too many panegyrics are the cause, not the result of the impression.
The result is a sort of scholarly folk myth, the roots of which go
deep indeed. Geoffrey of Auxerre, at the beginning of the bernardine
phenomenon, could write:

> You were the strongest and most splendid pillar of the church, a mighty
> trumpet of God, the sweet organ of the Holy Spirit whose presence
> was to councils what the sun is to the heavens, whose absence left
> assemblies lifeless and dumb.[3]

This somewhat exaggerated encomium is symbolic of the genesis of our
problem. Geoffrey of Auxerre, of course, was Bernard's confidant and
secretary. Like so many in close contact with Bernard, including modern
scholars, he developed an intense awareness of the greatness of Bernard
of Clairvaux, and thus he in a way initiated the process which, constantly
repeated through the centuries, would maintain Bernard's reputation at
its fullness. At the same time, the forgetfulness of history would reduce
other prominent men around him to ever smaller stature until it has
become all too easy to misjudge the relationship between Bernard and
leading men of his time.

It is hardly surprising that concentration on Bernard as an object of
study, in combination with the enthusiasm and affection that Bernard's

---

[2]Hughes, 2:275.
[3]PL 185:576; quoted in Ailbe Luddy, *Life and Teaching of St Bernard* (Dublin: Gill
& Son, 1927) p. 749.

personality and writings have elicited from the scholars who have read him ever since, tends to exaggerate his role in his own lifetime. If we add to this constant repetition of generous praise a subconscious transfer of modern mass media celebrity processes, the stage is set for serious misunderstanding of Bernard's role in his world, with special reference to the degree of awareness that world had of Bernard's presence. In short, perhaps circumstances have lured us into unquestioningly accepting (and copying) statements about Bernard of Clairvaux that would be closely examined were the same sentiments voiced about, say, Roland Bandinelli.

Let us turn first to the mysterious silence that inspired the title to this paper: the absence of comment concerning Bernard of Clairvaux in the chroniclers roughly contemporaneous with his active life and shortly after his death. It is significant that some of the most careful modern bernardine scholars have not only failed to notice this silence, but from time to time have confessed, at least implicitly, that they had assumed the opposite and are surprised on consulting the available documentation. For example, Adriaan Bredero, writing in 1978:

> When I started this study I took as my point of departure the opinion his contemporaries had about him. It was not my ambition to add a new biography to the many already existing, but I did hope to prepare the way through an investigation into contemporary opinion about him, for a more unbiased interpretation of his significance in the history of his own time. Namely, the first half of the twelfth century. *The result of this investigation was rather meager.* For that reason the report on it remained unwritten. . . . [4]

The meager results Bredero found are even more surprising since medieval chroniclers by definition were writing history, as they understood it, that nearly all were monks, and that their attention was fixed on a relatively small geographical area of northwestern Europe. All of these factors would seem to suggest an easy awareness of Bernard on the part of the chronicler. Yet a careful combing of the works of some twenty-five chroniclers contemporaneous with Bernard, including William of Newburgh, Otto of Freising, William of Malmesbury, Geoffrey of Monmouth, Suger of Saint Denis, Robert of Torigny, John of Salisbury, Peter of Celles, Hugh of Huntington, and Ordericus Vitalis—a good cross section

---

[4]Adriaan Bredero, 'The Conflicting Interpretation of the Relevance of Bernard of Clairvaux to the History of His Own Time', Cîteaux 31 (1980) 53–81. Emphasis added.

of contemporary chroniclers—yields sparse results. Of the list above only three, Ordericus, Otto, and John of Salisbury offer anything beyond a passing reference, the majority of the others (William of Malmesbury, for example) do not mention Bernard of Clairvaux at all! And even when Bernard is mentioned, it is always in a matter of fact way that argues that the author was not consciously aware of anything especially unusual about him.

It is, of course, difficult to give citations quoting silence, so we confine our efforts to the only three chroniclers who have much of anything to say. Their comments are especially relevant since in all three cases we would expect the chronicler to be especially aware of Bernard.

Ordericus is a good example to start with. He died in 1143, so he was almost exactly contemporaneous with Saint Bernard. And he wrote an ecclesiastical history which gives extensive notice to the cistercian phenomenon. In fact, in his ecclesiastical history, Ordericus included an entire chapter on Cîteaux, followed by a chapter on eminent abbots of his day (Bernard is not listed). He was interested in a geographical area heavily influenced by Bernard's activities, and he had a habit of mentioning almost all of the many individuals who crossed his scholarly path.

This last proclivity results in his mentioning seventeen Bernards. Almost all of them are obscure, but some get fairly extensive notice. Bernard de Neuf-Marche, for example, is mentioned five times, whereas Bernard of Clairvaux is noted only once! And this notice itself is instructive because of its routine manner and lack of any apparent sense of unusual significance. In the course of relating a matter of no great historical importance—at least to us—Ordericus recorded the travels of one Abbot Warin, who was seeking to negotiate with an Abbot Natalis of Rebais:

> Natalis told him it was his intention to go to Clairvaux and offered to conduct him there; in consequence they went to Clairvaux with their attendants and were kindly received by the brethren of that monastery, who endeavor to practice the rule of Saint Benedict to the letter. They presented themselves to the Lord Bernard, abbot of that monastery, and conversing with him made many inquiries and were struck with his profound wisdom. He commented with clearness on the Sacred Scriptures, satisfying all their questions and demands. On hearing the claims of the monks of Saint Everaux, he kindly supported Abbot Warin and gave letters of exhortation to the Convent of Rebais: After

Abbot Warin delivered the letter of the venerable Abbot Bernard, which was well received by the chapter of Rebais, and when it was read, they determined to comply with the request.[5]

This incident occurred in the year 1130, the year of the council of Étampes, and of Bernard's interview with Henry I of England concerning the cause of Innocent II. While it is dangerous to rely on silence, it does seem odd that Ordericus would have phrased things the way he did if he had been possessed of a keen awareness that Bernard of Clairvaux was the most important man of the century, and, indeed, its dominating influence.

Otto of Freising is another interesting study in relative silence. After all, Otto was a Cistercian; furthermore his dates are 1111 to 1158, and his fascination with history would suggest that he would surely have experienced Bernard as the most significant individual in his world. But the results are sparse and disappointing. Otto's major work, the world chronicle or *History of the Two Cities*, does not mention Bernard at all, and this in spite of the fact that the seventh book describes events contemporary to himself, and the eighth book includes substantial reference, direct and indirect, to the cistercian phenomenon.

Otto's second work, *The Life of Frederick Barbarossa*, yields several notices of Bernard, some of them quite laudatory, but all of them brief, and most of them are mere matter-of-fact listings of Bernard among other persons. The most meaningful passage is this:

> There was at that time in France a certain abbot of the monastery of Clairvaux named Bernard, venerable in life and character, conspicuous in his religious order, endowed with wisdom and a knowledge of letters, renowned for signs and wonders. The prince decided to have him summoned and to ask of him as of a divine oracle what ought to be done with reference to this matter. . . . The abbot previously named [was a man] who[m] . . . all the peoples of France and Germany regarded as a prophet and apostle. . . . [6]

The passage is certainly impressive in its commendation of Bernard, and well suited to the context which refers to Bernard's role in the Second Crusade. But it is only one paragraph of the whole book, a book crowded

---

[5]*Ecclesiastical History*, 5.10; quoted from *Ecclesiastical History of Ordericus Vitalis*, trans. Thomas Forester (London: Henry Bolen, 1854) 2:318.

[6]Book I, IP XXXV; quoted from *The Deeds of Frederick Barbarossa*, trans. Charles Mierow (New York: Columbia University Press, 1953) p. 70.

with the names of many other important persons, some of them also
spoken of in laudatory terms.

It is also interesting to observe that Otto thought it necessary to identify
Bernard, carefully describing who he was and why people thought him
important. This would suggest that he thought a significant percentage of
his readership would either not know Bernard at all, or would be puzzled
about the importance of his role. Otto's language would be quite difficult
to understand if he knew that everyone in the 'age of Saint Bernard' was
immediately familiar with the man and his works. By contrast, it would
be surprising to find a Frenchman, writing in 1815, beginning with 'There
was a certain politician, Napoleon by name, well known for his military
skills. . . .'

The references to Bernard in Otto's account of the Abelard and Gilbert
de la Porrée affairs are even more disconcerting. The description of both
covers some twenty pages in the standard English translation by Mierow.
No one reading these pages, unless he were preconditioned by other
sources of information, would imagine that Bernard of Clairvaux played
a crucial role. This to such an extent that we may wonder if he really did.
The few mentions of Bernard are primarily just inclusions of his name
in various lists. For example, this quotation from a letter by Innocent II:

> Bishop Innocent, the servant of the servants of God, to the venerable
> brethren the Archbishop Henry of Sens, and Samson of Reims and
> their suffragans and to his very dear son in Christ Bernard, abbot of
> Clairvaux, greeting and apostolic benediction. . . . [7]

If we examine the only two passages of any substance, they are again
disquieting:

> The archdeacons returned to France and induced Bernard, the ab-
> bot previously mentioned, whom they consulted to favor their cause
> against the Bishop [Gilbert]. Now the aforesaid abbot was both zealous
> in his devotion to the christian religion and somewhat credulous in
> consequence of a habitual mildness, so that he had an abhorrence of
> teachers who put their trust in worldly wisdom and clung too much to
> human argument. If anything at variance with the Christian faith were
> told him concerning anybody he would readily give ear. . . . [8]

And a few pages later:

[7]Mierow, p. 71.
[8]Book I, IP XLIX; Mierow, p. 82.

Whether the aforesaid abbot of Clairvaux, in consequence of the frailty of human weakness, being a mere man, was deceived in this matter, or the Bishop, being a very learned gentleman, escaped the condemnation of the Church by shrewdly concealing his view, it is not our task to discuss or to decide. . . . So much for that.[9]

The point here is not that some people vigorously objected to Bernard's zealous but somewhat intemperate partisanship, but that these short notices are virtually awash in a sea of names, events, and persons, all of which and whom seem to have appeared at least as important, and apparently more important, to Otto of Freising than did the supposedly dominating influence of Bernard of Clairvaux.

Otto was interrupted by death before finishing his work on Barbarossa. The last two books were completed by his faithful secretary, Rahewin. So, in effect, we have the testimony of one more author. Here the results provide even less material on which to work. For example, in quoting a letter of Emperor Frederick, Rahewin gives the following lists of persons:

While these things were going on at Rome and we were consulting men of religion, that is, archbishops and bishops, as to what should be done regarding so great a schism, there appeared as though sent by God the Archbishop of Moutiers-en-Tarentaise, the abbot of Clairvaux, the abbot of Morimund, and other abbots to the number of ten, seeking peace for the people of Milan.[10]

Two pages later, Bernard appears again in another list, this time in a decree of the Council of Pavia:

Then the venerable bishops Herman of Verden, and Daniel of Prague, and Otto the count palatine and Herbert the provost, whom the Lord Emperor, on the advice of twenty-two bishops and the abbots of Cîteaux and Clairvaux and other pious men present at this time, had sent to Rome to summon both factions to Pavia to appear before the council. . . . [11]

Of course it could be argued that Bernard's lack of official position as an archbishop or even as head of the cistercian order automatically relegated his name to a lower level of notice in official documents such as those quoted above.

[9]Book I, IP LXI; Mierow, p. 101.
[10]Mierow, p. 319.
[11]Mierow, p. 322.

But we search these chapters by Rahewin in vain looking for substantive comment on Bernard of Clairvaux. Again, we see the recurrence of the phenomenon that Bernard of Clairvaux is mentioned as one of many players on a crowded field. And, in these references as well as in many others, there is no apparent awareness on the author's part that one of those individuals stands head and shoulders above all the others combined.

Perhaps the most instructive of the authors nearly contemporaneous with Bernard is John of Salisbury (1115–1180). If any of the more prolific authors of the day had an opportunity to experience Bernard's importance, John was a candidate for first place. He had studied in Paris under Abelard and at the cathedral school at Chartres, was a tutor in Paris after 1140, knew Gilbert de la Porrée, and was a lifelong friend of Peter of Celles. He attended the Synod of Reims and appears to have been part of the papal court under Eugenius III, a former novice at Clairvaux. In 1154, the year after Bernard's death, John began a twenty-year service as secretary to Theobald, archbishop of Canterbury.

John's extensive writings contain only three passing comments on Bernard. In the *Pontifical History*, we find Bernard mentioned twice. First, in reference to Gilbert's trials and problems:

> Among those present was a man of great sanctity and weighty influence, Bernard Abbot of Clairvaux. . . . Master Gilbert, bishop of Poitiers, was summoned to court to answer the Abbot of Clairvaux, a man of greatest eloquence and highest repute. . . . [12]

John then goes on at some length about how the bishops refused to hear Bernard and is, in fact, critical of Bernard's role. In another section, somewhat later, John writes: 'He [Master Peter Abelard] denounced the abbot whose name is renowned above all others for his many virtues.'[13] These passing references are no more than that, in a work of some length by medieval standards. The pattern repeats itself here: unstinted praise of Bernard, a clear recognition of his outstanding holiness and virtues, and, by implication, an even clearer recognition that he was but one of many influential men of his day.

John's letters, most of them written in his capacity of secretary to Archbishop Theobald, have also been preserved for us. There are three

---

[12]*Memoirs of the Papal Court*, trans. Marjorie Chibnall (London: Nelson, 1956) p. 14.
[13]Chibnall, p. 64.

hundred and twenty-five of them, adressed to a wide variety of persons contemporaneous with Bernard. (They remind us that Bernard was not the only one writing to the prominent leaders of his day. On the contrary, his letters must have been almost lost in the heavy flow of such epistles.) Yet, in that entire collection of John's letters, Bernard is only mentioned twice, each time more or less in passing. The brief passages are so helpful in evaluating Bernard's literary impact that I reserve comment on them for a later page in this essay.

It would be wearisome to report negative results in detail, but it is instructive to notice that many authors whom we would expect to have substantial awareness of Bernard of Clairvaux, did not mention him: William of Malmesbury is an obvious example, and Suger of Saint-Denis too, at least in his major works. One must admit however, that Bernard is the hidden antagonist—unmentioned but nevertheless calling forth Suger's apologia concerning the consecration of the church at the Royal Abbey of Saint Denis.[14]

Before attempting to assess (or, more accurately, to guess) just how much the average man on the street, or even a secular ruler or religious leader, was aware of Bernard's 'domination', we might give sober reflection to one more warning from a historian: a warning somewhat in the line of the quotation concerning Roland Bandinelli, and this time from one of the most renowned specialists on monastic history, David Knowles: 'To think of the age of Saint Bernard as *in any sense* dominated by the monastic ideal would be wholly misleading.'[15] This statement is worth reflection. It occurs in the most respected work of a dedicated monk and scholar, who certainly cannot be accused of minimizing monasticism. Yet, Knowles says, to think of the age of Saint Bernard as 'in any sense' dominated by the monastic ideal would be misleading!

If one assumes that Knowles is right (and the section including the quoted passage makes a strong case), that the monastic ideal itself did not dominate even the religious life of the century, then how much more misleading to imagine that the cistercian phenomenon, within that monastic ideal, dominated the age. It would seem to follow that it would be a further delusion to imagine that one man within that cistercian order, one of the many prominent leaders produced by that movement,

[14]See Erwin Panofsky, *Abbot Suger* (2nd ed., Princeton, New Jersey: Princeton University Press, 1979) introduction, especially p. 15.

[15]David Knowles, *The Monastic Order in England* (Cambridge, England: Cambridge University Press, 1941) p. 217. Emphasis added.

dominated the age. And if he did, how is it possible for highly respected authors on the Middle Ages to write voluminous histories and not mention Bernard of Clairvaux, except in a passing reference or two? Indeed, most general histories of the Middle Ages reserve at best a page or so for Bernard.[16]

The impact of Bernard's career on the awareness of his non-monastic contemporaries may have been still less, because almost every writer in the twelfth century was himself a monk. The reader of medieval sources may be too easily lulled into forgetting that the twelfth century was, after all, ninety-nine percent non-monastic. This may put Knowles' comment into a less surprising context. To transpose the distorting power of this sociological mindset into something analogous to the modern world, let us assume that, after an atomic war, only the records of the military, carefully stored in bomb shelters, remain for historians. In these circumstances, it would be easy for future generations of the latter to grossly over-estimate the importance of military ideals and science in the late twentieth century. Thus, in the case of Saint Bernard, it is too easy to move from the widespread preservation of bernardine manuscripts in monastic circles to the conclusion that the general public had intense awareness of his activity and spirituality. And this conclusion is particularly suspect in view of the relative silence of the monastic writers themselves until at least a decade after Bernard's death.

With these cautions in mind, it seems possible to raise the question as to whether our vision of the stature of Bernard of Clairvaux in his century is not to some extent a so-called 'Whig interpretation of history'. This odd phrase derives from the famous work of that name by Herbert Butterfield.[17] Butterfield's thesis, that the selection of facts is influenced by a preconceived myth in the mind of the historian, has become paradigmatic in modern historical studies, but somehow still fails to be sufficiently noticed by specialists, such as those concentrating on a particular century, movement, or individual. At any rate, a case can be

---

[16]See Previté-Orton, *Cambridge Shorter Medieval History* (Cambridge, England: Cambridge University Press, 2 vols., 1952): fourteen comments on Bernard, but most of them insignificant. Robert S. Lopez, *The Birth of Europe* (London: Phoenix House, 1967). The original french edition is entitled *Naissance de l'Europe* (Paris: Librairie Armand Colin, 1962). The author emphasizes the economic development of Europe but includes ample treatment of ecclesiastical affairs. The Cistercians get only four passing references in 402 pages.

[17]Herbert L. Butterfield, *The Whig Interpretation of History* (London: G. Bell & Sons, 1931, frequently reprinted).

made that the so-called Whig interpretation has profoundly influenced the interpretation of monastic history.[18]

In the paragraphs following, I select, more or less at random, a few aspects of the bernardine history and documentation which illustrate this phenomenon of fact-selection, a selection tending toward an exaggeration in modern minds of Bernard's presence in the early twelfth century. None of these considerations suffice in themselves, but a sober reflection on their cumulative effect may suggest a second look at Bernard's 'dominance'. If the various approaches seem disconnected, their central theme will be found in Butterfield's line of thought, best summarized by the aphorism 'the myth enables us to see the facts, the facts do not enable us to see the myth.'[19]

In the first place, consider the foreshortening of history. Start by eliminating those incidents in Bernard's career, however important in themselves, which would have received little attention beyond the individuals or regions specifically involved: for example, the controversy over the succession to the archdiocese of York, or the affair of Arnold of Brescia. Next discount, if not deduct, events which aroused much monkish furor but probably did not seem too relevant at the time to the average duke, bishop, or fish-monger outside of Burgundy: for example, the controversy with Cluny and Abbot Arnold's irregular departure from Morimund. This should be done without regard for whether or not, at a later time, these controversies were perceived as significant. Further, although we children of a non-theological age are in constant danger of minimizing the theological interests of past ages, it does seem appropriate to question the impact of such incidents as the controversy with Gilbert de la Porrée outside a fairly narrow theological circle.

We end with only three incidents which would have actually brought widespread attention and publicity to Bernard of Clairvaux, even (if we may say so without incongruity) in our modern news-media culture, namely, the double election of Innocent II and Anacletus II (1130 and following), Abelard (1140), and the Second Crusade (1147). Note that the span of these three episodes is seventeen years, and all tended to be centered in France. The usual phrase, 'He dominated European affairs for half a century', seems to call for adjustment when re-calibrated at

---

[18]Paschal Phillips, 'The Whig Interpretation of Monastic History', *American Benedictine Review* 31 (1980) 201.

[19]Benedict Janecko, 'Myth History, God and Jesus', *American Benedictine Review* 23 (1972) 174.

seventeen years and mostly in the section of Europe now occupied by France and western Germany. Further, there are notable gaps of time between these incidents, during which we may suspect that those not specifically interested in the clerical aspect of the culture would have heard little of Bernard of Clairvaux.

Such gaps may well have been a bit more quiet than we are wont to imagine, at least for those of his contemporaries not in correspondence with the great abbot. Take, for example, the facile conclusion that since Bernard of Clairvaux was the heart and soul of the Council of Étampes, which deliberated the double papal election, it must follow that he was at the forefront of everyone's mind and heart during the preparation of that council. This, of course, is not impossible, but, at the very least, it is undocumented. Further, such conclusions also ignore the fact that we really do not know what procedures were involved in the amazing decision by the assembled bishops to constitute Bernard a committee of one to solve their problems. Indeed, the puzzling fact that they had not done such a thing before, and did not do it again, leaves a disquieting suspicion that we know much less than the full story.

Even assuming that the traditional story is true, and that the bishops, out of respect for Bernard's extraordinary sincerity and holiness, delegated their function to him, it does not follow that persons outside the power elite were intensely aware of Bernard's activities and genius. They could have been so aware, of course, but at least this hypothesis is in direct conflict with modern experience. It is true that, before a man is appointed to preside over a prestigious commission or board, there is a preparation consisting of correspondence, meetings, and politicking among a small group of the power elite. But, even in our electronic news-media age, this preparation is largely unnoticed by the public until the moment the candidate is suddenly announced by the head of State or from the balcony of Saint Peter's.

Another approach to the same question is to compare Bernard to the other individuals crowding his horizon. Suger of Saint-Denis has already been noted, and Cardinal Haimeric, chancellor of the roman church, deserves mention in this context. Also, the great cluniac monk, Matthew of Albano, often delegate of the Roman See, was then rising to his peak of influence after the Gregorian Reform. All of these men played roles of high public prominence during the life of Saint Bernard. They too knew kings and abbots; they also were consulted; they also filled crucial roles at the numerous synods, councils, and meetings of ecclesiastical and lay officials. They too spoke for prominent groups and movements in their society, and this to a point that the unfortunate Matthew of Albano has often been caricaturized unmercifully as the ultra-conservative champion. But, as we know from our own world, ultra-conservatives too have their following, their influence, and their apparent importance in the eyes of their contemporaries. Thus the *Chronicon Moriniacense* (PL 180: 159) could report on an assembly of notables gathered with Innocent II at the dedication of an altar:

> Among the venerable persons present at this sacred consecration the better known were the cardinal bishops William of Praeneste, Matthew of Albano, John of Ostia, Guido of the Tiber; and the cardinal priests John of Cremona, Peter Rubeus; the cardinal deacons Romanus of the title of St Mary's, Haimeric the chancellor, deacon cardinal of the title of Saint Mary's the New; Adenulph, abbot of Farfa, Bernard, abbot of Clairvaux, who at that time in Gaul was a most famous preacher of the word of God; Peter Abelard, monk and abbot, and a most religious man, an outstanding teacher of the schools to whom have flocked nearly all those learned in latinity, Girard, an abbot equally learned and devout, and Sauxon, abbot of Saint Lucianus of Belvaco. Henry, archbishop of Sens, was next to the lord pope. Gaudfried the bishop gave the sermon to the people...

It is only scholars of succeeding ages who, with the benefit of hindsight, sort out those actors on the stage of the past into those whose work appears (and Butterfield has well demonstrated that the appearance is deceptive) to be significant to events in the present world and those whose work does not appear significant. This sorting is from hindsight and quite independent of the level of awareness society cherished concerning any given individual during his or her lifetime. In fact, we may surmise that Suger, Haimeric, and Matthew would all have been sore amazed to know they were relegated to the ranks of the 'also-rans'.

To change focus, the rapid diffusion of Bernard's devotional writings is almost always cited as one of the strongest proofs of his enormous influence. There can be no question that he was recognized even during his lifetime as the most influential and persuasive writer of his day. But a careful look at the documentary evidence and some simple calculations will make us wonder just how far Bernard's writings had penetrated society in general before 1153. Spreading literary fame subsequent to that date is excluded from this study.

John of Salisbury has already been noted as one of the few chroniclers to show any awareness of Bernard. In the context of evaluating the impact of the latter's writings on his contemporaries, John's letters offer a unique insight. There are two mentions of Bernard in the three hundred and twenty-five letters. They occur in the same context: two letters of 1157 to Peter of Celles. The relevant quotations are:

> [from *Letter* 97:]: 'Please send me the letters of Bernard. I beg you to have an anthology made of his works and yours and of the Precentor of Troyes.'
>
> [from *Letter 98* :] 'Thanks for sending me the works of Bernard. I persist in my entreaties that you will cause all the best passages from his works to be transcribed for me. . . .'[20]

The author then goes on to ask for relics and various other gifts.

These two rather mundane quotations provide much food for thought. It is entirely possible to use them to show that everyone was clamoring to read the works of Saint Bernard, and there is truth in that. But note some other features. In the first place, the letters are dated 1157, four years after Bernard's death. They are written from the chancery office of the archbishop of Canterbury by an official who had access, certainly, to all the books available in the many cathedrals and monasteries in southern England and access to copyists in number. The author is a highly literate and important person who has moved in the same world as Saint Bernard for twenty-five years. He apparently had no copies of Bernard's works and did not know where to find any locally! Were this in the context of a request for a copy of Bernard's last works, it would still be surprising that a man like John could find no copy six years after publication. At the very least, such a delay would suggest that the diffusion of Bernard's writings was left to the same slow processes as the writings of less known scholars rather than receiving some sort of priority attention. But the letters quoted seem to refer to even the earlier writings, and a twenty-five-year delay in transmittal to southern England is quite significant.

We should now reflect on the slow scribal method of copying books, their expense, and their tendency to be concentrated in certain monastic libraries, and add to this the fact that some of Bernard's most significant works (*De consideratione*) were not completed until the very end of his life, and that others (the *Treatise on Grace and Free Choice*) must

---

[20]Epp 96 and 97; PL 199:87 and 88. Translation, *The Letters of John of Salisbury*, by Miller and Button (Oxford: Clarendon Press, 1986) pp. 51 and 54 (the letters are numbered 31 and 32 in this translation).

have appealed to a limited audience. In such context it may no longer be so obvious that, during Bernard's lifetime, the wide diffusion of his writings brought about the sort of general recognition that popular authors receive today.

Note, also, that this one and only reference to Bernard out of three hundred and twenty-five letters mentions him in the same breath and on the same standing as two other authors who are to us much less important: Peter of Celles and Geboin of Troyes. To us this seems surprising, but the impression is anachronistic. As the old saying goes: 'History is written by the victors.' From hindsight, we can see that, of those three authors, the works of one of them would survive as living entities mostly by reason of Bernard's fire and limpid sincerity. But also, be it remembered, they survived partly by reason of the earnest efforts of his numerous religious family. These future events were unknown to Bernard's contemporaries. To them there would be nothing incongruous at all about urging an anthology of the works of Bernard, Peter, and Geboin. Again, we find that every path of inquiry leads back to the conclusion that Bernard of Clairvaux in his day may have been the most important single figure, but, nevertheless, only one figure of many.

A striking example of a forgotten figure rivalling Bernard in his own day and competing, so to speak, for popular attention, is Saint Peter of Tarentaise, one of the only three Cistercians ever formally canonized. The scholar who has done the most to rescue Peter from total obscurity, Anselme Dimier, does not hesitate to affirm that, in his own days and thereafter, Peter enjoyed 'a notoriety, a glory equal to that of St Bernard.'[21] In many ways the two saints, Peter of Tarentaise and Bernard of Clairvaux, were alike, even though Peter eventually accepted election as an archbishop. Basil Pennington writes:

As Peter's life unfolded, it was indeed similar to Bernard's in many respects. Both were about the same age when they entered small Cistercian communities that were to develop rapidly. Both knew the formative influence of St Stephen Harding; Bernard directly, Peter through his abbot, John of Valence, who was formed at Cîteaux. Both saw much of their family follow in their footsteps. They were both called upon at a relatively young age to lead a new foundation. Their succeeding years saw mounting fame, numerous miracles, extensive travels and missions of reconciliation. In time of schism both stood

[21]Anselme Dimier, *St Pierre de Tarentaise* (Poitiers: Renault, 1935) p. 1.

forcefully and courageously at the side of the man who in the end
was acknowledged to be the true Vicar of Christ. Both were respected
by high and low alike, not excluding the grateful Roman Pontiffs.
And in the midst of all this activity, both longed to be free of it,
to hide themselves in the cloister and live the regular life. Peter's
prolonged visits to the Carthusians in the last years of his life call to
mind Bernard's intimate friend, William of St Thierry, and his visit
to Mount Dieu.[22]

Further, in Bernard's case, his activity was centered almost entirely
between the Rhine and the Pyrenees. We may well wonder whether
the extraordinary influence of french scholars on the study of medieval
church history has not biased our evaluation of just how large a figure
Bernard cut in the busy canvas of twelfth-century Europe taken as
a whole.

Again, one may examine the 'tree' diagrams found in monastic histories and note the numerous filiation of the monastery of Clairvaux. The
fecundity of that house and its daughter houses to the third and fourth
generation is awesome. But to imagine that each such house was a sort
of beachhead of specifically bernardine influence is another matter. After
all, we have virtually no documentation that could be used to prove or
disapprove such a facile assumption. Therefore, we must be on our guard
against too easily assuming an influence that we know 'should' have been
there on the basis of Bernard's importance. We fail to recognize that the
argument is circular. The rapid spread of the Clairvaux filiation proves
the importance of Bernard, and the importance of Bernard explains the
rapid expansion. There may have been other factors at play, especially
in the second or third generation of foundations.

In the absence of any documentation, we can fall back on an analogy
to modern monks. Admittedly, over a period of centuries this analogy
stretches thin because of the accumulation of sociological and cultural
changes. But, in the absence of documentation, it is better than nothing.

In the case of the second generation foundations, Bernard would have
been only the father immediate of the founding community. The modern
trappist-cistercian monk should be keenly aware of the name, influence,
and personality of the father immediate, the abbot of his mother house,
who has certain supervisory rights over each community founded from

[22]Basil Pennington, *The Last of the Fathers* (Still River, Massachusetts: St Bede
Publications, 1983) p. 273.

his own. But, so far as a quick survey reveals, very few modern trappist monks even know the name of the father immediate of their mother house! A quick check at this writer's monastery could find only three monks who could identify that worthy official.

Thus, although the wide branching of the family of Clairvaux is often cited without question as a proof of Bernard's domination of his century, there is much to make us wonder if that phenomenon can be translated without reservation into a wide bernardine influence. Did people in Scotland become more specifically aware of Bernard as a dominant power of the age after the foundation of Melrose (a second generation filiation through Rievaulx)? We must reply with caution.

One of the weaknesses of the Whig interpreter of history is to search for 'roots' in events of the past seen as analogous to the present. The analogy has its base in a present-day realization that certain values and institutions are important, *now*, in the world contemporaneous to the historian. This realization creates an activity which is indeed the very bread and butter of most historical study: the close examination of the origins of movements later understood to be of tremendous importance. This search is legitimate. Jesus Christ made but little impression in his own day, but a vast weight of scholarly research has rightly been expended ever since on every facet of his life and times. The same could be said, on a lesser scale, of Karl Marx, or the founders of the american republic. But, in every such case, including the case of Bernard of Clairvaux, there is an ever present danger of exaggerating the importance of the individual in his own day.

There are indeed some persons who were perceived by their contemporaries as dominant in their own time, but they were usually military conquerors. The seeds of other sorts of greatness tend to grow slowly. The historian can slip out of context by retrospective appreciation for the importance of what was going on under the surface. But this later appreciation is of its nature quite hidden from the man in the street, going about his daily business during the years which scholarly biographers will later dub something like 'Chapter Three, The Crucial Publications' or, perhaps, that ubiquitous chapter heading 'The Age of Saint Bernard'.

My conclusion is that a realistic interpretation of Bernard's world and life demands a sober rethinking of his influence on the life of twelfth-century everyman, or, for that matter, every-bishop or every-baron. Clearly he was influential; clearly, indisputably, he was more in the public eye than any other ecclesiastical individual in his day.

But when all reserve has been made, the impact of Bernard's personality on his age still appears tremendous. Indeed it is difficult to name any other saint in the history of the church whose influence, both on the public life of an epoch and on the conscience of a multitude of individuals, was during his lifetime so profound and so persuasive.[23]

Nevertheless, the documentation stands to remind us that he was but one of many to his contemporaries, surrounded as they were by a multitude of vocal and creative men stirred to action by the internal dynamism of a newly exuberant culture.

To stretch an analogy over eight hundred years, perhaps we might reflect on the present position of Pope John Paul II, who is certainly the most quoted, most photographed, and most controversial ecclesiastical personage in our world. It is even possible that later ages will see his position as pivotal, as setting a course for the next century—in other words, as far more important than he is perceived in the twentieth century. But to us who have not the benefit of hindsight, he remains one impressive and influential figure among many.

We may wonder, if Bernard of Clairvaux had not been canonized and had not been survived by an enormous religious family dedicated to continuing his memory and propagating his spirituality, whether or not we would be mentioning him in the same breath with other leaders and movements that flourished in the twelfth century but, through historical accident, did not leave such vigorous descendants, for example, the Victorines. In view of the scanty documentation, we can only speculate as to what importance we would read into Bernard's role during his own century had it been Richard of Saint Victor rather than Bernard who had been canonized, and if the Cistercians, rather than the Victorines, had suffered extinction in the French Revolution. Somehow it seems evident that our conclusions would be rather different from those bandied about today.

Perhaps such a realization would bring into better focus many of the controversies, the disappointments, and indeed the greatness of Bernard of Clairvaux—and, for that matter, of Roland Bandinelli.

ABSTRACTS

Un tour d'horizon des chroniques monastiques composées du vivant de Bernard et au cours des deux ou trois années qui ont suivi sa mort

---

[23]Knowles, p. 217.

révèle un silence surprenant au sujet de ses activités. Même lorsqu'il y est mentionné, la forme de la notation donne à penser que l'auteur n'est pas conscient d'une importance spéciale ou extraordinaire attachée à la personne de Bernard de Clairvaux. L'analyse de ces textes amène à conclure que le 'public' était beaucoup moins au courant de son existence et de son activité que la plupart des historiens ne l'imaginent. Le profil haut conféré à Bernard par la postérité agit comme un verre déformant qui a grossi son influence et l'impact qu'il exerçait sur ses contemporains. Replacés contre l'arrière-fond d'un entourage ecclésial et social qui lui attribuait en fait un rôle important mais aucunement dominant, bien des épisodes de sa vie paraissent moins étonnants.

A survey of the monastic chronicles written during the lifetime and within the first two or three years after Bernard's death shows a surprising silence concerning his activities. Even when he is mentioned, the notice is in a form which suggests the author is not aware of any special or extraordinary importance attached to Bernard of Clairvaux. An analysis of these texts leads to the conclusion that the public awareness of Bernard and his activity was at a much lower level than most historians imagine. The high profile given him by posterity has created a distorting lens which has magnified Bernard's influence and impact on his own contemporaries. Many incidents in Bernard's life seem less surprising when examined against an ecclesiastical and social ambiance which in fact allocated to Bernard an important but by no means dominant role.

Ein Überblick über die monastischen Chronisten zu Bernhards Lebenszeit und während der ersten zwei oder drei Jahre nach seinem Tod zeigt ein überraschendes Schweigen über seine Aktivitäten. Auch wenn Bernhard erwähnt wird, ist dies in einer Form gehalten, die darauf schließen läßt, daß der Autor nichts von einer speziellen oder außergewöhnlichen Bedeutung Bernhards von Clairvaux weiß. Eine Analyse dieser Texte führt zu der Schlußfolgerung, daß das öffentliche Wissen über Bernhard von Clairvaux und seine Aktivität auf einem viel niedrigeren Stand war, als die meisten Historiker glauben. Das starke Profil, das Bernhard von der Nachwelt gegaben wurde, hat ein verzerrendes Licht auf ihn geworfen, das Bernhards Einfluss und Wirkung auf seine Zeitgenossen verklärte. Viele Ereignisse in Bernhards Leben erscheinen weniger überraschend, wenn sie auf dem Hintergrund einer kirchlichen und sozialen Umgebung gesehen werden, die in der Tat Bernhard eine wichtige, aber keineswegs dominante Rolle zuerkannte.

TOWARD A METHODOLOGY FOR THE *VITA PRIMA*: TRANSLATING THE FIRST LIFE INTO BIOGRAPHY

Michael Casey, OCSO
Tarrawarra Abbey

IT MAY SEEM SURPRISING in a century so fertile in talented historians that Saint Bernard has not yet found a biographer. It is true that this sublime figure who dominated the twelfth century has tempted the pen of many writers, but their attempts are incomplete since in-depth preliminary studies are lacking. In general, source criticism has judged them defective.[1]

Thus, a hundred years ago, Elphège Vacandard began his celebrated biography of Bernard of Clairvaux. In the years that have elapsed since its publication, it has not yet been surpassed. Despite notable advances in bernardine studies, this century is yet to produce a biography which integrates new knowledge and brings Bernard the man into sharper focus. No one has yet done for the abbot of Clairvaux what Peter Brown did for Augustine.[2]

To mark the eighth centenary of Bernard's death in 1953, the Commission d'Histoire de l'Ordre de Cîteaux published a large volume which brought together much of the available historical information about Bernard.[3] It was not a biography, as such, but a vast repository of relevant

---

[1]Elphège Vacandard, *Vie de saint Bernard, Abbé de Clairvaux* (Paris: Librairie Victor Lecoffre, 1895) p. ix.

[2]Peter Brown, *Augustine of Hippo: A Biography* (London: Faber & Faber, 1967).

[3]Commission d'histoire de l'Ordre de Cîteaux (ed.), *Saint Bernard de Clairvaux* (Paris: Editions Alsatia, [1953]).

facts. In general, however, it has not been exploited in a way worthy of its careful compilation. Despite this, despite the labors of Jean Leclercq and others, many biographical outlines of Bernard's career tend to be little more than uncritical adaptations of the *Vita prima*, seasoned with subjective impressions of varying accuracy.

It is this widespread abuse of the *First Life* which makes it imperative that some consensus be reached about the extent to which it may serve as a source of factual information which could provide a sound basis for a modern biography. It is as a preliminary step towards this goal that some reflections on an appropriate methodology may be in order.

TEXT

A first priority is the technical task of producing a widely-accepted critical text which highlights the differences between the two recensions of the *Vita prima* and identifies its major sources and parallels.[4] Not only must such a presentation of the text take into account the problem of multiple authorship and the differences between composition and redaction, it must also take note of the nuancing and expansion to be found in the later *vitae* and in the classical accounts of the saint's life.[5] As with the Bible, there is a problem with unsophisticated literalism. Only when the relevant information is printed *with* the text or translation can one be sure that researchers with basic integrity will at least pause before offering a facile paraphrase of the *Vita prima* as certified historical fact.

Some progress has been made along this way by the studies of Professor Bredero and in the discussion these have generated.[6] Much, however,

---

[4]The elements of such an edition are gradually being assembled. Many areas remain, however, in which primary research is still needed.

[5]It seems sometimes that there were many blameless youths around, clever, good-looking and resistant to the temptations which beset their contemporaries. For example, Wolfgang (PL 146:397ab), Arnulf (PL 174: 1378cd), Matthew of Albano (PL 189:913c), Robert of Molesme (PL 157:1271–1272), Peter of Molesme, the companion of Stephen Harding (PL 185:1257–1258), Malachy as portrayed by Bernard (SBOp 3:309–312), Aelred as presented by Walter Daniel (*The Life of Ailred of Rievaulx*, ed. and trans. F. M. Powicke [London, 1950, rpt 1978] 2–5).

[6]Adriaan Bredero, 'Etudes sur la Vita Prima de S. Bernard', ASOC 17 (1961) 3–72, 215–60; 18 (1962) 3–59. 'San Bernardo di Chiaravalle: Correlazione tra fenomeno cultico e storico', in *Studi su San Bernardo di Chiaravalle nell'ottavo centenario della canonizzazione*, Bibliotheca Cisterciensis 6 (Rome: Editiones Cistercienses, 1975) pp. 23–48. 'The Canonization of St Bernard of Clairvaux', in Basil Pennington (ed.), *Saint Bernard of Clairvaux: Studies Commemorating the Eighth Centenary of his Canonization*, CS 28 (Kalamazoo, Michigan: Cistercian Publications, 1977) pp. 63–100. 'The Canonization of

remains to be done. It seems to me almost inevitable that the hermeneutical level will remain low until we have a good text well annotated.

GENRE

Once the *Vita prima* is identified as hagiography, we can begin to gauge its specific quality by looking at similar works of the same period.[7] Inevitably we are surprised at the number of formal similarities to be found in the accounts of the lives of very dissimilar saints. Without such exposure to other writings of the same literary genre it is almost impossible to reach any appreciation of the specificity of Bernard's *First Life*. It is not enough to know the conventions of hagiography, it is necessary to develop a 'feel' for the genre which enables one sometimes to read between the lines.

The fundamental assertion of the *Vita prima* is that Bernard of Clairvaux was a holy man. The single most important fact which this work mediates is that some of his contemporaries thought sufficiently highly of him to present his career from this perspective. The use of the hagiographical genre is itself indicative. It is possible to debate whether the account of Bernard's holy life was intended primarily to advance the cause of his canonization or whether it was simply to tell his story in such a way that others would hold his memory in veneration, be edified by his life, and feel drawn to imitation.[8] What is certain is that the *Vita prima* is not principally concerned with conserving objective data for the use of future historians. Facts it certainly contains, but they are elaborated selectively. There is a case to present; if suitable facts are available they are exploited. If not they can be expanded or glossed; incidents can be leaned on to yield a favorable interpretation. Where cooperative events are lacking, legends may be used. Through a process of inference or retrojection it is possible to guess about experiences which passed unrecorded, or rebuild them according to the models found in the

St Bernard and the Rewriting of his Life', in J. Sommerfeldt (ed.), *Cistercian Ideals and Reality*, CS 60 (Kalamazoo, Michigan: Cistercian Publications, 1978) pp. 80–105. See also W. E. Goodrich, 'The Reliability of the Vita Prima Sancti Bernardi', CSt 21 (1986) 213–27; ASOC 43 (1987) 153–80.

[7]See Jean Leclercq, *A Second Look at Saint Bernard*, CS 105 (Kalamazoo, Michigan: Cistercian Publications, 1990).

[8]In Bredero's hypothesis, the explicit intention of furthering Bernard's canonization is more marked in Recension B, whereas the earlier version was more generic in its aims. See especially his article 'The Canonization of St Bernard', cited in footnote 5, above.

vitae of other saints, or perhaps close the gap by pure supposition or invention. On the other hand, negative incidents can be simply omitted or so systematically excluded that an *a priori* doubt is created should they be mentioned in another source.

In this way a *vita* was constructed. The danger is that such stratagems can easily backfire for readers of another century who subscribe to a different notion of holiness. We find it difficult to accept as a saint one who is defective in humanity. We do not accept a non-developmental account of a life; for us there is no sanctity without struggle and failure. William's account of Bernard's heroic chastity seems to suggest that a single extreme rejection of concupiscence was sufficient to render him immune for the rest of his life.[9] The story of Bernard's immobility when a naked girl leaped into his bed *palpans et stimulans* does not seem like great virtue to us. We would probably guess that it shows he was undersexed, or that terror had rendered him impotent, or that he was homosexual.[10] If this incident did not happen as described, then a harmless recasting of a story may well lead us to wrong conclusions. Unless we learn to interpret the *Vita prima* in terms of its own presuppositions, we will probably go astray. We will be forced to choose between Bernard's humanity and holiness, on the one hand, and the historical reliability of the *First Life*, on the other.

It is only by reading it as hagiography that we are able to cope with the theological cast given to Bernard's life by the *Vita prima*. Otherwise he appears very ponderous and unreal. We need to recognize that the biblical quotations and theological terms have probably been inserted at the level of interpretation; they are not necessarily indicative of Bernard's own outlook on life; they belong to the authors and editors of the *Vita prima*, not to its unwitting subject.

This interpretative pall covers all the various types of incident which purportedly constitute Bernard's career: 1) the providential confluence of events: his parents, family, friends; his character, opportunities and contacts; 2) the interplay of grace and response in the decisions made which shaped his life; 3) the external works undertaken in giving expression to his basic stance and in response to the calls which came to

---

[9]*Vita prima* [VP] 1.6–7; PL 185:230–31.

[10]Later in life, in refuting the dualist rejection of marriage, Bernard seems to demonstrate some familiarity with the strength of the sexual urge: 'to be always with a woman and not to have sex with her was more difficult than raising the dead.' SC 65.4; SBOp 2:175, 3–4.

him through situations and people; 4) the content of his teaching both in extended discourses and in his occasional responses to those who sought his guidance; 5) the miracles with which he is credited; and 6) the creative impact and influence he is said to have exercised over many persons both at an interpersonal level and by reason of his activities.

Narratives describing each of these categories need to be treated differently. 1) In general we need to recognize that the Middle Ages did not share our passion for absolute accuracy in names, places, and dates.[11] As a result, what we may regard as the elements of a normal biographical outline may be defective. Such *neutral* information as the *Vita prima* contains may be considered probable if it does not clash with other sources. 'Facts' included which are evaluated *positively* must be submitted to methodological doubt. What is interpreted is not necessarily untrue, but its value as history needs to be assayed. 2) Statements about Bernard's spiritual life can ultimately have only one source. Only the saint himself could have communicated such information. Granted Bernard's reticence in this matter, and William of Saint-Thiery's avowed intention to treat only of the *exteriora*,[12] it may be assumed—unless there are indications to the contrary—that such passages represent the author's projections, for example, presuming that the child Bernard had the same values and outlook as the man of mellower years. 3) External events and involvements can sometimes be verified by reference to independent sources. It is to be expected, of course, that the relative prominence of the abbot of Clairvaux may be diminished in more objective sources. 4) Fragments of Bernard's teaching given in the *Vita prima* can be verified by reference to his writings, taking into account the possibility that they may be direct borrowings from the published text. Apart from the content, a study of the vocabulary and style may yield some indication of whether the quotation is Bernard's own or the author's. 5) It seems undeniable that Bernard was believed to have been a miracle-worker by his contemporaries. Our assessment of the factual basis of this reputation will depend on our attitude to miracles. There is no doubt that the authors of *vitae* felt free to improvise in this matter and to read coincidence as causality and to stretch the extraordinary into the miraculous.[13] It

[11]Bernadette Barrière, *Le cartulaire de l'abbaye cistercienne d'Obazine* (Clermont-Ferrand: Publications de l'Institut d'Etudes du Massif Central, 1989) pp. 46–47.

[12]VP *Praefatio*, col. 226b: 'non invisibilem illam vitam viventis et loquentis in eo Christi enarrare proposui, sed exteriora quaedam vitae ipsius experimenta.'

[13]In the Bull of canonization of Saint Robert of Molesme, Honorius IV dismissed without rancor the miracles attributed to the saint by his *vita*: PL 157:1294a. It seems

would seem that a special set of norms is required for dealing with material in the *Vita prima* which falls into this category. 6) The beneficent impact of the saint on those around him is a commonplace of medieval *vitae*. Great caution is needed because reactions are habituaily simplified and schematized. They are presented from the saint's point of view, so that one moment of contact assumes far more importance than the cumulative contributions of a lifetime's experience. It is not unbelievable that Bernard, with his gifts, his reputation, and the enthusiasm around him, may have had an extraordinary effect on people. He seems to have acted as a catalyst in many persons' lives. This, however, does not mean that impact-statements in the *Vita prima* do not have to be qualified. In fact one of the major problems involved in using the *First Life* as a source is its tunnel vision. Its focus is on Bernard. He is presented as the center of events in which he may equally have taken part from the periphery.

This is not to say that the only appropriate attitude to the *Vita prima* is one of profound skepticism. I believe that most incidents it describes have a *fundamentum in re*. The point is that the text needs to be interpreted if it is to yield its factual nucleus, and the only sound basis of such an interpretation is an appreciation of the specific bias of its authors and editors. When this is isolated, it can be neutralized and the residue examined for historical probability.

THE WORK OF GEOFFREY OF AUXERRE

Not all who offer an interpretation of the *Vita prima* are aware of the major contribution made by Geoffrey of Auxerre, the prince of cistercian propagandists. Becoming Bernard's secretary in 1145, he was responsible for the compilation of the *corpus epistolarum* and for the fact that many people's first impression of Bernard comes from his polemical letter to his cousin Robert on the abuses which had been allowed to flourish at Cluny under the thirteen years of Pons de Melgueil's rule. At about the same time, he began collecting the elements of a biography, the *Fragmenta Gaufredi* based on his experiences as Bernard's companion on his journey through Languedoc and on interviews with Clairvaux veterans. This collection served as a source for all the authors of the *First Life*. Geoffrey prevailed on William of Saint-Thierry to undertake the labor of love, as Bernard himself had on behalf of his friend Malachy

that such exaggeration or falsification was accepted as par for the course and no penalty imposed.

of Armagh. William had known Bernard intimately for thirty years, and he was also a competent writer and a man of prestige, whose participation would enhance the credibility of the project. On William's death, Arnold of Bonneval was selected to cover the increasingly public life of Bernard from 1130 until the point at which Geoffrey himself could assume the narrator's role. For the most part, Arnold was not familiar with the domestic details of Bernard's interaction at Clairvaux. Perhaps, as a Black Monk, he was chosen as a more independent witness, and one less likely to criticize Bernard for meddling in affairs beyond his jurisdiction. The remaining three books were written by Geoffrey himself. The book was put together and submitted to the judgement of certain prelates who had been friends of the saint and who gathered at Clairvaux in 1155-1156. This process of revision resulted in Recension A. About ten years later, during Geoffrey's brief period as abbot of Clairvaux, Recension B was produced. Geoffrey's sermon for the tenth anniversary of Bernard's death indicates that he may have considered himself the keeper of the flame.[14] Despite the participation of many in the process of producing the *Vita prima*, the controlling hand was Geoffrey's. The Bernard we learn about from the *First Life* is one who conforms to Geoffrey's vision. Bernard's sanctity is presented according to the way in which Geoffrey perceived holiness. To interpret the *Vita prima*, we need to know a lot more about the attitudes and values of its principal collaborator.

Geoffrey's Bernard is a serious man without much in the way of lightheartedness or spontaneity:

> He was serene of countenance and modest in bearing, cautious in speech, fearful in action, zealous in meditating on holy things, dedicated to prayer. He used to advise others on the basis of his own ample experience, in everything to trust prayer more than one's own industry or effort. He was abundant in faith, patient in hope, eager in love, supreme in humility, and renowned for his piety. He was shrewd in his advice and a good businessman and never less idle than in times of leisure. He was pleasant when insulted and bashful when shown honor. He was gentle in his behavior, holy by his merits, and glorious by his miracles. In a word, he was amply endowed with wisdom and virtue and grace with both God and human beings.[15]

[14]*Sermo in anniversario obitus s. Bernardi*; PL 185:573–88.
[15]VP 3.1; PL 185:303b.

This list of twenty-three qualities is so conventional that it tells us nothing about what Bernard was like. It does, however, inform us that Geoffrey understood holy men as moderate, withdrawn, pious, and industrious. This is the side of Bernard to which he gives the emphasis, perhaps continuing the approach taken by William of Saint-Thierry. The more colorful, eccentric, and amusing aspects of Bernard's life and personality are necessarily muted. Instead he is presented as a sweet child, a modest boy, and a serious youth.[16] All the ingredients for an utterly boring life! The qualities of humanity and warmth which made Bernard so attractive seem to be less important. How is it possible for a man to be humble, to understand so well the interplay of sin and grace, and to insist so strongly on the need for conversion if he has not experienced what it is like to fall captive to the power of sin? Bernard's expertise in mapping the road of return can come only from having himself made the same journey. Bernard's status as a spiritual master means that Geoffrey's picture of bland, uncomplicated goodness must be fundamentally modified.

Notwithstanding this general picture of sweet piety, Geoffrey presents a Bernard who can be perceived as a tough and aggressive hardliner when it comes to matters of monastic policy or theological orthodoxy. Perhaps because his own conversion involved a clash of loyalties, Geoffrey seems to have felt constrained to present Bernard as even more vehement in his repudiation of Abelard and his supporters than other witnesses. If it is true that Geoffrey habitually presents Bernard as stern and uncompromising, then perhaps this severity is to be attributed to the author and not to his subject.

To a lesser degree, the same filtering out of personal priorities needs to be done with both William and Arnold. There is always a possibility that the qualities we praise in others may be selected on the basis of our private agenda rather than for their objective importance in the lives of those we are promoting.

INDEPENDENT CORROBORATION

Multiple attestation gives an *a priori* claim to credibility. Once the distinction is made between assertion of fact and interpretation, it becomes necessary to correlate what is stated about Bernard with evidence from other sources. Obviously this possibility exists mainly in relation

---

[16]*Sermo in anniversario* 7; PL 185:577d. The quality of seriousness, *gravitas*, is evoked repeatedly; for instance 578d, 579a, 579c.

to his public life; his personal and domestic life is known only through hearsay and rumor—often at several removes. Bernard was a high-profile abbot; he was involved in some of the important events of his time, and, as he moved around, he left a trail of legal documents in his wake.[17] His visits are recorded in chronicles and local histories, and those who had contact with him sometimes wrote of him to others. There is no shortage of relevant information; the problem lies in containing it within a single framework.

Sometimes a simple statement in the *Vita prima* can be expanded and given context by reference to other sources. It seems very unwise to attempt to interpret Bernard and his writings without a fairly comprehensive knowledge of the period in which he lived, of the details of the lifestyle followed in monasteries and outside, and, in general, of the ferment taking place in society and in the Church and particularly within the cistercian order. Too often the *Vita prima* is used as a text complete in itself, without substantial reliance on parallel channels of information.

With regard to Bernard's circle of acquaintances, some *networking* yields positive results. His contacts all knew one another—perhaps better than they knew Bernard. The *Vita prima* presents Bernard always as the center. It is possible that he may, in some cases, have been on the rim. His friendship with William of Champeaux, for instance, meant that a relatively obscure young man was given access to many of the luminaries of the day. It is even possible that it was through the bishop's mediation that Bernard became friends with William of Saint-Thierry. It may be from the same source that he learned to think ill of Abelard. The point is this: unless we begin to make connections between other characters in the *First Life* and to appreciate their autonomous existences, we may begin to attribute too much importance to Bernard, mistaking the tight focus of the *Vita prima* for the actual historical perspective.

The same caution needs to be exercised with regard to Bernard's letters. It is risky to make inferences about the nature of a relationship from a consideration of one side of a correspondence. Bernard's secretariat may have been efficient in keeping copies of his letters, but we do not always know whether they were received, how they were interpreted, or what response was given them.[18]

---

[17]See Anselme Dimier, 'Sur le pas de S. Bernard', Cîteaux 25 (1974) 223–48.

[18]For instance, fifty-six of Bernard's letters to Innocent II are preserved; there is no evidence that Innocent was assiduous in responding to these, perhaps importunate, interventions.

Herbert of Clairvaux's *De miraculis* redresses the balance somewhat.[19] Written twenty-five years after Bernard's death, it aims to bring together all sorts of wonderful stories which might confirm the faith of his monastic readers. Saint Bernard is often mentioned, and sometimes the stories about him are original and were later retold by Conrad in the *Exordium magnum*.[20] Yet Bernard is far from being the principal focus of attention. Most of the stories about Clairvaux and the other monasteries have no relationship with Bernard. Collectively they evoke a monastic world in which grace was operative; Bernard represented only a relatively small part of this totality. The extraordinary expansion of the cistercian order in the twelfth century owed much to Bernard and to Clairvaux, but it would be an error to presume that he was the only star in the firmament.

The patient collation of relevant facts is necessarily a cooperative venture which will take many years. The result will certainly not be a radically new image of the saint which will be immediately self-evident to all. It will be simply the slow accretion of facts and nuances to be submitted to the *judgment* of the prospective biographer. There will still be scope for conjecture and hypothesis, and different conclusions will be reached. But progressively, one hopes, these conclusions will be based more on real historical knowledge than on the misreading of a single source.

HISTORICAL ACTOR AND WRITER

The most important texts for the understanding of the *Vita prima* are the writings of the saint himself. If no contemporary life had been written it would have been interesting to see what sort of man emerges from the bernardine literary *corpus*. To what extent is our understanding of the writer dominated by what we have learned of him from the *Vita prima*? Geoffrey and his collaborators have succeeded in marketing their image of this extraordinary man. And his admirers in subsequent centuries have added their own nuances.

The *Vita prima* and the register of letters have the effect of concentrating our attention on Bernard as a man in contact with many important people and involved in some of the most significant events of his time.

---

[19]See M. Casey, 'Herbert of Clairvaux's "Book of Wonderful Happenings"', CSt 25 (1990) 37–64.

[20]See Bruno Griesser (ed.), *Exordium Magnum Cisterciense sive Narratio de Initio Cisterciensis Ordinis*, Series Scriptorum Sacri Ordinis Cisterciensis, 2 (Rome: Editiones Cistercienses, 1961) introduction, pp. 36–37.

The abbot of Clairvaux merits at least a passing reference in any historical treatment of the twelfth century. Because of this, Bernard is seen through the prism of his public life; his importance as a human being, as a monk, and as a writer is thereby appreciably diminished. It is not uncommon to see Bernard presented as a hardnosed, right-wing political manipulator, evidenced in his involvement in the condemnation of Abelard and others, in his preaching of the Second Crusade, and in his dealing with various princes, potentates, and prelates. To this blend is added some incidents from the hagiographical tradition and some pious nineteenth-century translations. The end product is not attractive, even though elements of it are certainly factual. What is lacking is the image of the man that comes from a close and sympathetic reading of what he wrote.

The negative impression created by approaching Bernard as a minor historical actor is incomprehensible to those who have learned to love him through direct contact with his writings. It seems as though there is question of two different men. The humane, sensitive, light-hearted man with his sights fixed on God has become a bigot. This is, perhaps, one reason why many persons can be avid readers of Bernard's writings without showing very much interest in the *Vita prima*. It probably also explains the lack of enthusiasm for a sound working edition of the *First Life*.

The *Vita prima* needs to be read through the prism of Bernard's writings and not vice-versa. There are texts which give us information which supports, complements, and extends that which we find in the *Vita prima*. These add some more details to the sum total of our factual knowledge. More important is the general picture that we form of Bernard's character and personality. He is not a cold writer who hides behind a rational exposition. He writes with passion and, in so doing, reveals himself. If Bernard really were a saint, we would expect to find an emerging consistency between his fundamental values and choices and the way that he actually lived. In such an hypothesis, such incidents as Bernard's preaching of the Second Crusade toward the end of his life need to be approached in terms of what inner values they express rather than as merely external events governed by external expediencies.

A good biography allows the subject to appear as he was. It ought not to be exploited as a means of presenting a partisan position on some issue. Inevitably, the closer one moves to reality, the more complex the character will appear. To arrive at such a point, one needs to deal not only in facts and probabilities, one also must address less tangible qualities which are not subject to measurement or verification and yet which exert a real, though hidden, influence on the outcome of events.

Intuited Totalities and Lateral Thinking

There is a real danger that the interpretation of the *Vita prima* will fall into the hands of minimalists whose work will consist in making us aware of the historical fragility of this contemporary witness. The end result may be a profound doubt that we can ever know anything at all about the life and character of the abbot of Clairvaux.

It is at this point that we must congratulate ourselves on having available such a wonderful contemporary witness to the life of Saint Bernard as the *Vita prima*. Not that we intend simply to repeat its assertions uncritically! We are going to take it very seriously, acting on the presupposition already mentioned that most of its assertions—unless it can be demonstrated otherwise—have a *fundamentum in re*. In the absence of contrary evidence, we must conclude that a desire to influence our perception of Bernard by directing our attention to some aspects at the expense of others need not amount to a serious deception. At least once we know what games are being played!

Perhaps we need to be more adventurous. Instead of approaching Bernard's life as a jigsaw puzzle to be completed piece by piece, it may be possible to work with totalities. In this case there would be question of supplementing detailed analysis with an educated intuition. One tries to bring to bear on each particular problem the whole weight of many years of bernardine research. It means having the courage to say: 'I think in this situation he would probably have been inclined to act in this way.' This is to use the methodology of the physical sciences, in which a working hypothesis is elaborated at the mid-point of an investigation, bringing together what is already known and filling in the gaps with guesswork. This is then put to the test to see if it works. If everything runs smoothly, then one has guessed correctly; there is no absolute need to know why or to be able to demonstrate the reasons behind the suggestions. The fact that the model works legitimates everything. Even if the result tests negatively, the process is not a complete loss. Knowledge has been increased by closing the file on one particular possibility.

Such a procedure is, of course, fraught with the danger of subjectivism, since history is not an experimental science. Yet it is not without its methods of verification. A working hypothesis can be tested in two ways. First, it must be seen to include and, in some sense, integrate relevant known data. Secondly, the educated intuition of one must be compared with the equally educated intuition of others. An enlightened process of dialogue can result only in refinement of the hypothesis and the emergence of some tentative consensus. The way to understanding in such matters is not the lineal progression of logical deduction, but a series of successive approximations, gradually purified of different subjective biases.

This calls for the exercise of lateral thinking. In practice, this means reinterpreting some of the data from the hagiographical tradition in ways which give priority to the Bernard revealed in his writings. Sometimes this is simply a matter of separating narration and interpretation, accepting the basic facts and offering a different perspective. Thus Bernard's ignorance of the details of his immediate environment, instead of being a pointer to a deep spirit of prayer, can be explained as the normal abstraction typical of an intuitive introvert.[21] This is a relatively simple example; other instances are more complex.

How seriously are we to take Berengar's picture of Bernard's youth?[22] Here is something quite different from what we find in the *Vita prima*! Are we to dismiss it as coming from a biased source who has elsewhere in the same work shown little concern for the accuracy of his accusations and who, moreover, later remarked that he was only joking.[23] Is it such a crime to entertain the idea that Bernard as a student was famous for his dirty limericks (if you will pardon the anachronism)? He was clever and competitive, as Berengar indicates, and he enjoyed using the sort of language that makes pious translators blush. Who else would have yoked in paronomasia *deificatio* and *defaecatio*?[24] Bernard seems to have been friendly with Burchard of Balerne, the author of *De barbis*, a totally frivolous treatise, seasoned with a soupçon of sexual jibes;[25] perhaps this was a fun-loving side to Bernard that William of Saint-Thierry

[21]See M. Casey, 'Bernard the Observer', in E. Rozanne Elder (ed.), *Goad and Nail*: *Studies in Medieval Cistercian History*, *X*, CS 84 (Kalamazoo, Michigan: Cistercian Publications, 1985) pp. 1–20.

[22]R. M. Thompson, 'The Satiricial Works of Berengar of Poitiers: An Edition with Introduction', *Mediaeval Studies* 42 (1980) 89–138. The relevant text from the *Apologia* is on p. 111.

[23]Thompson, p. 136. This is from a letter to the bishop of Mende, written before 1150: 'si quid in personam hominis Dei dixi, ioco legatur, non serio.'

[24]Dil 28; SBOp 3:143, 13–15. Bernard's faecal vocabulary is widely attested. The *Sententiae* are particularly rich in examples of less than polite usage.

[25]Burchardus de Bellevaux, *Apologia de barbis*, ed. E. Ph. Goldschmidt (Cambridge: Typis Academiae, 1935). Burchard entered Clairvaux during Bernard's abbacy and in 1136 became abbot of Balerne, the daughter-house of Aulps. In 1156, he assumed the abbacy of Belleval. To him Bernard addressed Ep 146, and he was the author of a note appended to the first books of the *Vita prima* after the death of William of Saint-Thierry. A letter of his addressed to Nicholas of Clairvaux is printed in PL 196:1605.

and Geoffrey did not appreciate. The point I am making is that, by thinking laterally about such possibilities, we are challenged to sharpen our perceptions of what sort of man Bernard was. Whether the hypothesis is accepted or rejected, the process of examining it is illuminating.

Let us take another example from Bernard's pre-monastic career. William treats of Bernard's chastity in his third chapter. He describes him as a very presentable young man zealous for chastity but adrift in a world of bad morals and stormy friendships. He drowns his lust in an icy pond and is thenceforth unmoved by the attentions of women getting into bed with him. All of this is described as taking place *before his conversion.*

Here are six hypotheses, each of them having some slight merit. 1) The incidents happened exactly as described. Bernard was from childhood a person of heroic virtue with a special love for chastity. 2) Such incidents are the commonplaces of hagiography; they give us no information about Bernard. They may throw some light on the fantasy life of the author. Questions could be asked about the sources of the story of the pond and that of the naked girl. The 'Thief!' story could have been common knowledge. 3) Bernard was undersexed; physically he was sickly; by disposition he was bookish. Excluded from the typical activities of his class, he may also have held back from their amorous opportunities. 4) William is correct in saying that he was notably bashful and diffident. Terrified by the overtures being made to him, he is rendered impotent, responding in the first case by denial and in the second by turning the whole business into a joke. 5) Bernard is nonresponsive because he has no sexual interest in women. This is not necessarily to say that he is actively homosexual, although it is reported that wives and mothers locked up their men when he came to town. 6) Perhaps the incidents narrated took place *after the conversion* and not before it. The reason women kept jumping into Bernard's bed is that there was a time when they knew they were welcome. This might explain why Bernard insists so much on conversion, why he excludes himself from the ranks of the virgins[26] (and others are careful

---

[26]Asspt 6.1; SBOp 5:260, 13–261, 1. In interpreting this passage one must avoid confusing a rhetorical first person with autobiography. It is possible that Bernard, knowing that he was known to his audience/readers, is humbly acknowledging that he is not a virgin. It is also possible that he is speaking *in persona audientis*, that he is using the first person as a means of giving expression to the thoughts of those to whom the words are addressed. We see such sympathetic inclusiveness in Conv 4; SBOp 4:75, 7. Instead of speaking at others, he includes himself in their plight. He begins with second

not to claim it for him[27]), and why he demonstrates a familiarity with the details of intimate behavior. In this hypothesis, the freezing pond would represent a typically extreme attempt to make a break with his former way of life.

In similar vein, questions can be asked about the entry of the thirty into the New Monastery. Not only what year it was, but also whether Bernard truly was the center of this group from the very beginning. Is it possible that the movement began simply as a corporate attempt to live a more christian life in the family residence at Châtillon?[28] Is Bernard's active leadership of the group as represented by the *Vita prima* another example of retrojection?

In such cases, we are, for the most part, confronted with the choice of following the data of the *First Life* or of leaving a blank. In a biography which aims to present a nuanced yet integrated picture of Bernard's life, neither extreme is acceptable. We need to go for the middle ground of possibility and probability, necessarily involving a certain amount of guesswork. And we must be able to live with the insecurity and lack of certainty which such an approach yields.

A biography of Bernard for our age must speak to our contemporaries. It cannot ignore their questions either by recycling the unexamined assertions of another culture or by retreating into the sterile void of critical doubt. The fact remains that we have an enormous amount of information about Bernard of Clairvaux—more than enough to construct a sound biography. And, among the resources to be exploited to this end, the *Vita prima* must be reckoned highly significant.

But we need a good text, we need to understand the nature of hagiography, and we need to appreciate the intentions of the collaborators, especially those of Geoffrey of Auxerre. Our reading of the *Vita prima* needs to be supplemented by a knowledge of its background and of parallel sources, especially Bernard's own writings. Finally, we who

person singular, goes on to third person singular, then to first person singular, then to first person plural, and back to third person singular. The whole creates an impression of sympathy and understanding and gives Bernard the opportunity of speaking directly without appearing judgemental.

[27]The usual word *integritas* is not found in VP 6–7; nor is *virginitas* used. It is true that the summary of the previous chapter begins, 'De integritate Bernardi pueri', but the word is not used in the chapter itself which, moreover, has nothing to do with chastity.

[28]VP 1.15; PL 185:235–36. For background, see Georges Duby, 'Youth in Aristocratic Society', in *The Chivalrous Society*, trans. Cynthia Poston (Berkeley: University of California Press) pp. 112–122: 'Youth in Aristocratic Society: Northwestern France in the Twelfth Century'.

would attempt to translate the *First Life* into a coherent biography need the courage to make intuitive leaps—as necessary and subject to the jugement of our peers.

ABSTRACTS

La tâche déjà intimidante consistant à rédiger une biographie de S. Bernard est encore compliquée par le manque de consensus quant au rôle que la *Vita prima* devrait jouer dans une telle entreprise. Six domaines méthodologiques sont traités: 1. la nécessité d'une édition critique de la *Vita prima*, 2. une évaluation de son genre littéraire, 3. le besoin qu'il y a d'apprécier exactement le rôle de Geoffroy d'Auxerre, 4. la recherche d'une corroboration par des sources indépendantes, 5. la complementarité de Bernard comme acteur historique et comme écrivain, et 6. la nécessité de suppositions calculées et l'acceptation de la probabilité là où il faut combler les lacunes des données historiques.

The daunting task of writing a Bernardine biography is further complicated by the lack of consensus about the role to be played in such an entreprise by the *Vita prima*. Six methodological areas are discussed: 1. the need for a critical edition of the *Vita prima*, 2. an appreciation of its literary *genre*, 3. the necessity of assessing accurately the role of Geoffrey of Auxerre, 4. the search for independent corroboration, 5. the complementarity of Bernard as historical actor and as writer, and 6. the necessity of calculated guesswork and the acceptance of probability in bridging the gaps in historical data.

Die entmutigende Aufgabe, eine Bernhard-Biographie zu schreiben, wird noch weiter dadurch erschwert, daß ein Konsens über die Rolle der Vita Prima in solch einem Unternehmen fehlt.
Es werden sechs methodische Gebiete diskutiert: 1. die Notwendigkeit einer kritischen Ausgabe der *Vita prima*, 2. eine Würdigung ihrer literarischen Gattung, 3. die Notwendigkeit, die Rolle Gottfrieds von Auxerre genauer zu bestimmen, 4. die Suche nach unabhängiger Bestätigung, 5. die Komplementarität Bernhards als historische Person und als Schriftsteller und 6. die Notwendigkeit berechneter Mutmaßung und die Akzeptanz der Wahrscheinlichkeit bei der Überbrückung der Lücken in den geschichtlichen Daten.

PART II
BERNARD'S THOUGHT

BERNARD AS CONTEMPLATIVE

John R. Sommerfeldt
The University of Dallas

UNDERSTANDING THE ROLE of contemplation in the spirituality of Bernard of Clairvaux presents many difficulties. Bernard's vocabulary of contemplation is complex. What Bernard means by contemplation is not always clear. And Bernard seems to give contradictory evidence on the question whether he was indeed a contemplative.

It is clear that, for Bernard, contemplation is an experience which transcends ordinary exposition. In describing this unique relationship between God and man, Bernard most often uses the metaphor of the Bridegroom and bride of the *Song of Songs*:

> What is this that she says: 'He is mine, and I am his' [Sg 2:16]? We do not know what she says because we do not know what she feels [Jn 16:18]. O holy soul, what is your beloved to you? What are you to him? What is this intimate relationship, this pledge given and received?...If you will, speak to us, to our understanding; tell us clearly what you feel [Jn 10:24]. How long will you keep us in expectation? Is your secret to be for you alone [Is 24:16]?[1]

The answer Bernard puts in the mouth of the bride is rich, but deliberately arational:

> It is thus: it is the feelings not the intellect which have spoken. And it is not for the intellect to grasp. What then is the reason for these words? There is none, except that the bride is transported with delight

[1]SC 67.3; SBOp 2:189–90; CF 40:4–6.

73

and enraptured by the long-awaited words of the Bridegroom. And when the words ceased she could neither keep silence nor yet express what she felt.[2]

Bernard then gives a reasoned explanation for the arational expressions of the bride:

The feelings have their own language, in which they disclose themselves even against their will. Fear has its trembling, grief its anguished groans, love its cries of delight. . . . Do they constitute a reasoned discourse, a deliberate utterance, a premeditated speech? Most certainly such expressions of feeling are not produced by the processes of the mind but by spontaneous impulses. So a strong and burning love, particularly the love of God, does not stop to consider the order, the grammar, the flow, or the number of the words it employs when it cannot contain itself, providing it senses that it suffers no loss thereby. Sometimes it needs no words, no expression at all, being content with aspirations alone. Thus it is that the bride, aflame with holy love, doubtless seeking to quench a little the fire of the love she endures, gives no thought to her words or the manner of her speech. But, impelled by love, she does not speak clearly but bursts out with whatever comes to her lips.[3]

There is much here that is instructive. Contemplation is an 'intimate relationship' involving 'delight' and 'rapture'. And the experience cannot be expressed in the language of reason alone.

What then is the nature of contemplation as Bernard understands it? It is above all an experience, the experience of a lover:

Happy the man who has attained the fourth degree of love; he no longer loves even himself except for God. 'O God, your justice is like the mountains of God' [Ps 35:7]. This love is a mountain, God's towering peak. Truly indeed, it is a fat, fertile mountain [Ps 67:16]. 'Who will climb the mountain of the Lord [Ps 23:3]?' 'Who will give me the wings of a dove, that I may fly away to find rest [Ps 54:7]?' This place is made peaceful, 'a dwelling place in Sion' [Ps 75:3]. 'Alas for me, my exile has been lengthened' [Ps 119:5]. When will flesh and blood [Mt 16:17], this vessel of clay [2 Co 4:7], this earthly dwelling [Ws 9:15], understand the fact? When will this sort of affection be felt that, inebriated with divine love, the mind may forget itself and

[2]SC 67.3; SBOp 2:190; CF 40:6.
[3]SC 67.3; SBOp 2:190; CF 40:6–7.

become in its own eyes a broken dish [Ps 30:13], hastening toward God and clinging to him, becoming one with him in spirit [1 Co 6:17], saying: 'My flesh and my heart have wasted away, O God of my heart, O God my share for all eternity' [Ps 72:26]. I would say that man is blessed and holy to whom it has been given to experience something like this, so rare in life, even if it be but once and for the space of a moment. To lose yourself, as if you no longer existed, to cease completely to be aware of yourself, to reduce yourself to nothing, is not a human sentiment but a divine experience [see Ph 2:7].[4]

In this experience not only the feelings are affected, but the intellect in understanding and the will in love. Contemplation may occur in this life, but it is an experience in which one transcends one's normal state and which taxes one's faculties to their utmost. The ' . . . contemplative gift [is that] by which a kind and beneficent Lord shows himself to the soul with as much clarity as bodily frailty can endure.'[5]

Because of the transcendent nature of the contemplative experience, it is incommunicable, ineffable. Bernard writes:

Do you suppose that, were I granted that experience, I could describe to you what is beyond description? . . . The tongue does not teach this, grace does. It is hidden from the wise and prudent, and revealed to children [Lk 10:21].[6]

The desire to communicate the incommunicable, to express the ineffable, requires Bernard to resort to poetic language. The image which Bernard employs again and again to evoke his understanding of the contemplative experience is sexual. The love between God and the human being culminates in an intimate and rapturous union. The delights of that union are expressed in silent song.[7] Sometimes Bernard's sexual imagery is violent. He speaks of a ' . . . spirit ravished out of itself [2 Co 5:13]. . . .'[8] Those thus ravished are the happiest of humans.[9] Whether Bernard's imagery is marital union or ravishment, the result of the contemplative experience is ecstasy: ' . . . The delights of contemplation lead on to that ecstatic

[4]Dil 10.27; SBOp 3:142; CF 13:119.
[5]SC 4.1; SBOp 1:19; CF 4:22.
[6]SC 85.14; SBOp 2:316; CF 40:210.
[7]SC 1.11; SBOp 1:7–8; CF 4:6–7.
[8]SC 41.3; SBOp 2:30; CF 7:206–207.
[9]Asc 2.6; SBOp 5:130; Luddy 2:239. See also SC 31.5 (SBOp 1:222; CF 7:128) and Hum 6.19 (SBOp 3:30–31; CF 13:46–47).

repose that is the fruit of the kiss of his mouth.'[10] Bernard associates the images of repose,[11] sleep,[12] and even death[13] with contemplative ecstasy.

Contemplation, however expressed, Bernard knows as a rare and brief experience: '. . . Contemplation holds the beholder suspended in astonishment and ecstasy, if only for a brief moment.'[14] Bernard bemoans this rarity and brevity: 'Alas, how rare the time and how short the stay!'[15] His dismay is the result of the intense joy contemplation imparts: 'But when does this happen, and for how long? It is sweet intercourse, but lasts only a short time and is experienced so rarely!'[16]

Bernard laments that the contemplative experience is rare. The question is whether the experience is so rare as to be non-existent—at least for Bernard himself.[17] The question may seem absurd, given the descriptions Bernard gives of contemplative experience—descriptions which seem to shout out that they are the product of his own intimate awareness of what he describes. Yet Bernard frequently denies that he has received the gift of contemplation.[18] In these cases, however, it is clear that Bernard is employing rhetorical humility.[19] Bernard is surely identifying with those in his audience who are taking the first steps on the path to perfection and who need his support and encouragement.[20] Bernard is ever aware of his role as teacher, a role which requires identification with those whom he would teach.[21] Bernard's motivation is clear. In denying or revealing his contemplative experience, he wishes to serve those who seek the same goal as he. Bernard was indeed a contemplative.

Contemplation is so important to Bernard's spirituality that it is important to avoid confusion about the subject. For Bernard, contemplation is not meditation, it does not entail visions or dreams, and it is not the Beatific Vision of the blessed in the life he firmly believed would come.

---

[10]SC 4.4; SBOp 1:20; CF 4:23.

[11]SC 52.6; SBOp 2:93; CF 31:54.

[12]SC 52.3; SBOp 2:92; CF 31:52.

[13]SC 85.13; SBOp 2:315–16; CF 40:209.

[14]Csi 5.14.32; SBOp 3:493; CF 37:178.

[15]SC 23.15; SBOp 1:148; CF 7:38.

[16]SC 85.13; SBOp 2:316; CF 40:205–210.

[17]For a discussion of this question, see Ingeborg Brauneck, *Bernhard von Clairvaux als Mystiker* (Hamburg: G. H. Nolte, 1935) pp. 29–31.

[18]See, for example, SC 8.1 (SBOp 1:36; CF 4:45) and Hum 9.24 (SBOp 3:35; CF 13:53); and SC 23.10 (SBOp 1:145; CF 7:35).

[19]See Hum 22.57 (SBOp 3:58; CF 13:82) and SC 3.1 (SBOp 1:14; CF 4:16).

[20]See SC 3.2 (SBOp 1:14; CF 4:16–17) and SC 69.1 (SBOp 2:202; CF 40:27). See too Jean Leclercq, *Saint Bernard mystique* (Paris: Desclée De Brouwer, 1948) p. 137.

[21]SC 22.3; SBOp 1:130; CF 7:15.

Bernard clearly differentiates meditation or consideration from contemplation:

First of all, consider what it is I call consideration. For I do not want it to be understood as entirely synonymous with contemplation. The latter concerns more what is certainly known, while consideration pertains more to the investigation of what is unknown. Consequently, contemplation may be defined as the mind's true and sure intuition, the apprehension of truth without doubt. Consideration, on the other hand, can be defined as thought searching for truth, the mind's searching to discern truth. Nevertheless, both terms are often used interchangeably.[22]

It is precisely the interchangeability of the terms which can lead to confusion. For meditation the prerequisite is '. . . an eye that is pure and simple' [Lk 11:34].[23] For contemplation, the prerequisite is not human activity, but the action of God: '. . . If at times she [the soul] is even rapt toward it [God's majesty] in ecstasy, this is the finger of God deigning to raise man up . . .' [Ex 8:19; Lk 11:20].[24]

Visions and dreams may be works of God, but they too are not what Bernard means by contemplation.[25] Bernard does not deny that God may communicate with humans through visions. But he does insist that contemplation is communication of a vastly different sort which takes place interiorly.[26] Contemplation, then, is an internal exprience of the soul who delights in ecstatic union with God.

Bernard sometimes uses the word contemplation to indicate yet another sort of ecstatic union with God. And this usage can also lead to confusion. In the Beatific Vision, Bernard believes, '. . . the only activity is repose, and contemplation and affection will be the only duty.'[27] The similarity of usage is based on Bernard's deep conviction that contemplation here is a foretaste in this life of the happiness of heaven.[28] Contemplation is the food of the perfect in this life; it is a foretaste of the banquet they will enjoy in the Beatific Vision.

[22]Csi 2.2.5; SBOp 3:414; CF 37:52.
[23]SC 62.4; SBOp 2:157; CF 31:154.
[24]SC 62.4; SBOp 2:158; CF 31:155.
[25]SC 2.2; SBOp 1:9; CF 4:9.
[26]SC 31.4 (SBOp 1:221; CF 7:127) and SC 31.6 (SBOp 1:223; CF 7:128–29).
[27]SC 72.2; SBOp 2:226; CF 40:64.
[28]Hum 2.4; SBOp 3:19; CF 13:32–33.

Bernard is confident that the earthly contemplative experience, so like that of the blessed in heaven, is indeed possible in this life.[29] Moreover, the happy soul who has been visited by the Bridegroom can eagerly anticipate a frequent return: ' . . . Anyone who has received this spiritual kiss from the mouth of Christ at least once, seeks again that intimate experience and eagerly awaits its frequent renewal.'[30] And the bride's anticipation is confident, for she knows that the Bridegroom loves her:

> It is in this confidence that she says he cares for her, and she for him. And she sees nothing but herself and him. How good you are, Lord, to the soul who seeks you [Lm 3:25]. You come to meet her, you embrace her, you acknowledge yourself as her Bridegroom—you who are the Lord, God blessed forever above all things [Rm 9:5].[31]

And this confidence is proper to all who seek God, all who travel the path to perfection:

> We find a contemplative Mary [the sister of Martha and Lazarus] in those who, cooperating with God's grace over a long period of time, have attained to a better and happier state. By now confident of forgiveness, they no longer brood anxiously on the sad memory of their sins, but day and night they meditate on the ways of God with insatiable delight [Ps 1:2]—even at times gazing with unveiled face [2 Co 3:18], in unspeakable joy, on the splendor of the Bridegroom, being transformed into his likeness from splendor to splendor by the Spirit of the Lord.[32]

The outwardly unheard song which the bride hears and sings in contemplative union with the Bridegroom requires a highly trained ear and voice:

> Novices, the immature, those but recently converted from a worldly life, do not normally sing this song or hear it sung. Only the mind disciplined by persevering effort, only the soul whose years, as it were, make her ripe for marriage—years measured not in time but in merits—is truly prepared for nuptial union with the divine partner. . . .[33]

---

[29]See, for example, SC 52.2 (SBOp 2:91; CF 31:50–51) and SC 74.5 (SBOp 2:242; CF 40:89–91).

[30]SC 3.1; SBOp 1:14; CF 4:16.

[31]SC 69.8; SBOp 2:207; CF 40:35. See also SC 8.9; SBOp 1:41–42; CF 4:52.

[32]SC 57.11; SBOp 2:126; CF 31:106. See also Div 8.1; SBOp 6/1:111.

[33]SC 1.12; SBOp 1:8; CF 4:7.

Only those whose intellect is ready for Truth and whose will is prepared for Love are the 'friends and lovers [to whom] God communicates his secrets.'[34] The Bridegroom's kiss of the mouth '. . . is the experience of only a few of the more perfect.'[35] Since, for Bernard, perfection is a process, not a state—at least in this life—the perfection Bernard describes is '. . . only a sort of imperfect perfection.'[36] Yet, one who has traveled the path to this perfection, who has turned toward the Lord and devoted oneself to the practice of virtue, should be open to the gift of contemplation.[37]

One is made capable of contemplation both by one's created nature and by one's properly oriented desire.[38] The soul who longs for union with her lover seduces him:

> So now, when she feels the opportunity is ripe, she announces that the bridal suite has been furnished. And, pointing to the bed with her finger, she invites the beloved to rest there, as I have said. Like the disciples on the way to Emmaus, she cannot restrain the ardor of her heart [Lk 24:13- 29]. She entices him to be the guest of her soul and compels him to spend the night with her. With Peter she says: 'Lord, it is good for us to be here' [Mt 17:4].[39]

Her desire for union is clearly the result of her overwhelming love:

> 'I cannot rest', she said, 'unless he kisses me with the kiss of his mouth [Sg 1:1]. I thank him for the kiss of the feet; I thank him too for the kiss of the hand. But, if he truly cares for me, let him kiss me with the kiss of his mouth. There is no question of ingratitude on my part; it is simply that I am in love. The favors I have received are far more than I deserve, but they are less than I desire. It is desire that drives me, not reason. Please do not accuse me of presumption if I yield to this impulse of love. My shame indeed rebukes me, but my love is stronger still. I am well aware that he is a king who loves justice [Ps 98:4]. But headlong love does not wait for judgment, is not chastened by advice, not shackled by shame nor subdued by reason. I ask; I crave; I implore. Let him kiss me with the kiss of his mouth.'[40]

[34]Div 29.1; SBOp 6/1:210.
[35]SC 4.1; SBOp 1:18; CF 4:21.
[36]QH 10.1; SBOp 4:443; CF 25:193.
[37]SC 3.5; SBOp 1:17; CF 4:19.
[38]SC 80.2; SBOp 2:277–78; CF 40:146.
[39]SC 46.1; SBOp 2:56; CF 7:241. See also SC 46.7; SBOp 2:60; CF 7:245–46.
[40]SC 9.2; SBOp 1:43; CF 4:54. See also SC 32.3; SBOp 1:227; CF 7:135.

The soul's overwhelming love for her beloved is a sign of the perfection which renders her ripe for nuptial union:

The soul which has attained this degree [of perfection] now ventures to think of marriage. Why should she not, when she sees that she is like him and therefore ready for marriage? His loftiness has no terrors for her because her likeness to him associates her with him. And her declaration of love is a betrothal. . . . When you see a soul leaving everything [Lk 5:11] and clinging to the Word with all her will and desire, living for the Word, ruling her life by the Word, conceiving by the Word what she will bring forth by him . . . you know that the soul is the spouse and the bride of the Word.[41]

While the perfection which readies the spouse to be ravished in contemplation is the result of the growth of the intellect in knowledge and of the will in love, the contemplative experience itself is pure gift. The soul may desire her lover and prepare the couch, but he must come into her bed as a free gift of love.[42] The gift the Bridegroom gives the soul with his kiss is no less than participation in the very life of the Trinity:

For her it is no mean or contemptible thing to be kissed by the kiss, for it is nothing less than the gift of the Holy Spirit. If, as is properly understood, the Father is he who kisses, the Son he who is kissed, then it cannot be wrong to see in the kiss the Holy Spirit. For he is the imperturbable peace of the Father and the Son, their unshakable bond, their undivided love, their indivisible unity.[43]

The bride who longs for her beloved seeks only his loving kiss and nothing else.[44] But in that kiss she receives much not requested.

She receives the gift of knowledge in contemplative union with her spouse.[45] And the knowledge she receives is on a truly cosmic scale. Not only are the nature of reality and the reality of nature known

[41]SC 85.12; SBOp 2:315; CF 40:208–209.
[42]Hum 8.22 (SBOp 3:33; CF 13:50–51); SC 52.5 (SBOp 2:93; CF 31:53–54); SC 8.6 (SBOp 1:39; CF 4:49); and SC 69.2 (SBOp 2:202; CF 40:28).
[43]SC 8.2; SBOp 1:37; CF 4:46.
[44]SC 7.2; SBOp 1:32; CF 4:39.
[45]See my 'The Epistemological Value of Mysticism in the Thought of Bernard of Clairvaux', in John R. Sommerfeldt (ed.), *Studies in Medieval Culture* [*I*] ([Kalamazoo, Michigan]: Western Michigan University, [1964]) pp. 48–58. See also my 'Bernard of Clairvaux: The Mystic and Society', in E. Rozanne Elder (ed.), *The Spirituality of Western Christendom*, CS 30 (Kalamazoo, Michigan: Cistercian Publications, Inc., 1976) pp. 72–84 and 194–96, esp. pp. 76–81.

in contemplation, the right ordering of things, justice, is open to the contemplative gaze.[46]

In the contemplative kiss, the bride receives not only knowledge of God, his creation, and its right order. She also receives wisdom, an appreciation of the proper moral order. As knowledge perfects the intellect, so does wisdom perfect the will in love.[47] This infusion of love is accompanied by awe, awe at the experience which will make the bride wise.[48] The soul blessed by the kiss of her beloved is not only filled with love, but that love is directed toward continuing perfection.[49]

Thus, in the ecstatic embrace of the Bridegroom, the bride's intellect is filled with knowledge and her will fulfilled in love:

> For the favor of the kiss bears with it a twofold gift: the light of knowledge and the fervor of devotion. Truly, the Spirit of wisdom and knowledge [Is 11:2], like the bee bearing its burden of wax and honey, is fully equipped both to kindle the light of knowledge and infuse the delicious nectar of grace. . . . So let the bride, about to receive the twofold grace of this most holy kiss, set her lips in readiness—her reason for the gift of knowledge, her will for that of wisdom—so that, overflowing with joy in the fullness of this kiss, she may be privileged to hear the words: 'Your lips are moist with grace, for God has blessed you forever' [Ps 44:3].[50]

The soul, perfected in humility and love, is united to God in contemplative marriage:

> See now this perfect soul. Her two powers, reason and will, are without spot or wrinkle. Her reason is instructed by the Word of Truth [2 Co 6:7], her will inflamed by Truth's Spirit [1 Jn 4:6]. She is sprinkled with the hyssop of humility [Ps 50:9]; she is fired with the flame of love. She is cleansed from any spot by humility, smoothed of wrinkle by love [Eph 5:27]. Her reason does not shrink from the truth; her will does not strive against reason. This blessed soul the Father binds to himself as his own glorious bride.[51]

[46]SC 23.11; SBOp 1:145–46; CF 7:35. See also OS 4.4 (SBOp 5:358; Luddy 3:377) and Par 2.4 (SBOp 6/2:270; CSt 18:197).
[47]SC 69.2; SBOp 2:203; CF 40:28.
[48]SC 23.12–14; SBOp 1:146–47; CF 7:36–37.
[49]SC 74.6; SBOp 2:243; CF 40:91–92.
[50]SC 8.6; SBOp 1:39–40; CF 4:49–50. See also SC 9.3; SBOp 1:43–44; CF 4:55.
[51]Hum 7.21; SBOp 3:32; CF 13:49.

But even the fulfillment of intellect and will does not exhaust the effects of contemplation. The soul's third faculty is also perfected in the contemplative union. The feelings too are purged of pain and filled with pleasure.[52] To pleasure God will add peace.[53] And to peace he will add joy.[54] The joy of the bedroom is an image on which Bernard builds to express the fullness of the bride in all of her faculties.[55]

The bride's soul is indeed full; her intellect, will, and feelings are perfected. The bride's body, which has never lost its likeness to its Creator, is in perfect harmony with her soul. It is she who is totally united with God.[56]

What can be added to this? Perhaps only the permanence of the Beatific Vision. But the very impermanence of the contemplative experience brings with it a question. What is the activity, function, role of the bride after she has left her nuptial bed and until she returns to it? The bride, overflowing with love for her Bridegroom, is called back from her bed by the 'violent' demands of brotherly love.[57] Like Paul, Bernard is compelled to share the fruits of contemplation with the world.[58]

The bride, fresh from her bed of union with God, is sent out to work in the vineyards of the Lord.[59] She who is filled with the fruits of contemplation—knowledge, wisdom, and joy—is sent to share her happiness with mankind.

Bernard saw himself as the bride. And he believed himself sent. These convictions had enormous consequences for the society of his time.

ABSTRACTS

Le vocabulaire de la contemplation chez Bernard est complexe, et ce qu'il entend par 'contemplation' n'est pas toujours clair. Il est cependant clair que, pour Bernard, la contemplation est une expérience qui transcende l'exposition ordinaire. Elle affecte l'intelligence, la volonté et les sentiments, en un mot l'âme toute entière.

[52]Gra 5.15; SBOp 3:177; CF 19:71.
[53]SC 8.7; SBOp 1:40; CF 4:51.
[54]SC 23.15; SBOp 1:148–49; CF 7:38–39.
[55]SC 23.16; SBOp 1:149–50; CF 7:40.
[56]SC 67.8; SBOp 2:193–94; CF 40:12.
[57]Dil 10.27; SBOp 3:142; CF 13:119–20.
[58]PP 1.2 (SBOp 5:189; Luddy 3:195) and SC 8.7 (SBOp 1:40; CF 4:50–51).
[59]SC 58.2; SBOp 2:128; CF 37:109.

La nature transcendante de l'expérience la rend ineffable; aussi Bernard doit-il recourir pour l'exprimer à un langage poétique, où l'imagerie primordiale est de nature sexuelle. La contemplation, dit-il, est une expérience rare et brève. Elle n'est ni méditation ni considération; elle n'implique ni visions ni songes; elle n'est pas la vision béatifique, dont elle est pourtant un avant-goût.

Bernard est confiant que l'expérience contemplative terrestre est possible dans cette vie et accessible à tous ceux qui s'avancent sur le chemin de la perfection. La contemplation est un don, mais l'âme qui aspire à l'union avec son bien-aimé doit préparer son intelligence à la Vérité et sa volonté à l'Amour.

Le don que l'Epoux fait à l'âme dans le baiser de la contemplation n'est rien moins que la participation à la vie même de la Trinité. L'entreinte de l'Epoux, celle de l'exstase, remplit l'intelligence de l'âme de connaissance et accomplit sa volonté dans l'amour. Les sentiments sont purifiés de toute douleur et remplis de plaisir, de paix et de joie.

L'épouse est rappelée de son lit nuptial par les 'violentes' exigences de l'amour fraternel; elle est envoyée pour travailler dans la vigne du Seigneur et partager son bonheur avec l'humanité. Bernard se voyait lui-même comme épouse, et il s'estimait envoyé. Ces convictions eurent d'immenses conséquences pour la société de son temps.

Bernard's vocabulary of contemplation is complex, and what he means by contemplation is not always clear. It is clear, however, that, for Bernard, contemplation is an experience which transcends ordinary exposition. In this experience, the intellect, will, and feelings—the whole soul—are affected.

The transcendent nature of the contemplative experience makes it ineffable, and thus its communication requires Bernard to resort to poetic language, within which the primary image is sexual. Contemplation, he says, is a rare and brief experience. It is not meditation or consideration; it does not involve visions or dreams; it is not the Beatific Vision of which it is, however, a foretaste.

Bernard is confident that the earthly contemplative experience is possible in this life and accessible to all who travel the path to perfection. Contemplation is a gift, but the soul who longs for union with her lover must prepare her intellect for Truth and her will for Love.

The gift the Bridegroom gives the soul in the kiss of contemplation is no less than participation in the very life of the Trinity. In the ecstatic embrace of the Bridegroom, the soul's intellect is filled with knowledge and the will fulfilled in love. The feelings are purged of pain and filled with pleasure, peace, and joy.

The bride is called back from her nuptial bed by the 'violent' demands of brotherly love; she is sent out to work in the vineyards of the Lord and share her happiness with mankind. Bernard saw himself as the bride, and he believed himself sent. These convictions had enormous consequences for the society of his time.

Bernhards Wortschatz hinsichtlich der Kontemplation ist komplex, und was er mit Kontemplation meint, ist nicht immer klar. Dennoch ist deutlich, daß Kontemplation für Bernhard eine Erfahrung ist, die die übliche Darstellung übersteigt. In dieser Erfahrung sind Intellekt, Wille und Gefühle—die ganze Seele—einbezogen.

Die transzendente Natur der kontemplativen Erfahrung macht sie unaussprechlich, und deshalb verlangt ihre Vermittlung von Bernhard, seine Zuflucht in einer dichterischen Sprache zu suchen, deren grundlegende Bildhaftigkeit aus dem Bereich des Geschlechtlichen genommen ist. Kontemplation, sagt er, ist eine seltene und kurze Erfahrung. Sie ist nicht Meditation oder Betrachtung; sie hat nichts zu tun mit Visionen oder Träumen; sie ist nicht die *visio beatifica*, aber ein Vorgeschmack darauf.

Bernhard vertraut darauf, daß die irdische kontemplative Erfahrung in diesem Leben möglich und allen zugänglich ist, die auf dem Weg zur Vollkommenheit unterwegs sind. Kontemplation ist ein Geschenk, aber die Seele, die sich nach der Vereinigung mit ihrem Liebhaber sehnt, muß ihren Intellekt für die Wahrheit und ihren Willen für die Liebe vorbereiten.

Das Geschenk, das der Bräutigam der Seele gibt im Kuß der Kontemplation, ist nichts weniger als das Teilhaber am wahrhaftigen Leben der Dreieinigkeit. In der ekstatischen Umarmung des Bräutigams ist der Intellekt der Seele angefüllt mit Erkenntnis und der Wille erfüllt mit Liebe. Die Gefühle werden geläutert von Schmerz und erfüllt mit Vergnügen, Frieden und Freude.

Die Braut wird von ihrem Hochzeitsbett zurückgerufen durch die 'gewalttätigen' Bitten brüderlicher Liebe. Sie wird ausgesandt, um in den Weinbergen des Herrn zu arbeiten und ihr Glück mit der Menschheit zu teilen. Bernhard sah sich selbst als die Braut, und er hielt sich selbst für gesandt. Diese Überzeugung hatte weitreichende Konsequenzen für die Gesellschaft seiner Zeit.

THE CONCEPT OF DEATH IN BERNARD'S *SERMONS ON THE SONG OF SONGS*

Burcht Pranger
Universiteit van Amsterdam

THERE IS A SENSE in which life in the benedictine/cistercian monastery can be seen as an anticipation of heaven. Cutting loose the ties with the world, the monk has left behind the realm of death, decay, and destruction and is on his way to perfection. And, even more significantly, the progress he makes is met or, indeed, preceded by the goal for which he is striving. For the norm of his conduct is set by the wholeness of angelic life rather than by the confused nature of the world. This state of affairs is reflected in the shape of the monastery. The *paradisus claustralis* is a *locus amoenus*, an idyllic place enclosed in itself, without beginning or end, and well protected from the outside world.[1]

However solid and material the shape of monastic life may be, questions might be raised as to its literary expression. What do we mean if we describe monastic life as a striving for perfection, as contemplation, as the establishment of spiritual/religious life, and the exorcising of death? Of course, a more or less traditional answer might point to the use of exegetical schemes, of the different spiritual *sensus* in which meaning(s) are added to the existing playground of language. However, this discovery of spiritual meaning never comes about in a formal or

---

[1]See Etienne Gilson, *The Mystical Theology of Saint Bernard*, trans. A.H.C. Downes, CS 120 (Kalamazoo: Cistercian Publications, 1990) chapter 4; and Jean-Baptiste Auberger, *L'Unanimité cistercienne primitive: Mythe ou Réalité?* (Achel: Administration de Cîteaux: Commentarii Cistercienses; Editions Sine Parvulos, 1986) pp. 87–133.

mechanical way. In Bernard's case, at least, it is the arrangement and the rearrangement of different sets of images which creates possibilities of meanings as yet unheard of, rather then the implementation of a strict and predictable procedure. The summit of manipulative skill is achieved if the reader or the listener is captivated by Bernard's stylistic adroitness to the extent of no longer noticing shifts of meaning. The fluency of the discourse is such as to present a natural unity which makes the reader forget about any possible distinction between the literal and the spiritual, the world and the monastery.

Yet the greater the suggestion of unity, the more interesting it seems to trace back the development of meaning and to discover elements of tension and incongruity which are at the source of the very literary success of Bernard's prose. In this paper I wish to make an inquiry of this kind by looking at the meaning of death in the *Sermons on the Song of Songs* 48–52 which, generally dealing with the relationship between the active and the contemplative, the 'affective' and the 'effective' life, offer the opportunity to put death into spiritual perspective. At the end of the paper I shall turn to sermon 26—the famous lament on Gerard's death—to check the degree to which death has maintained its literal self within the walls of the monastery.

In sermon 52,[2] Bernard attempts to describe the feelings of the bride sleeping the sleep of ecstatic death in the arms of the Bridegroom. The point being made in the sermon is that, according to the Canticle text under consideration, the bride should not be disturbed in this happy slumber: 'I charge you, daughters of Jerusalem, by the gazelles and the hinds of the fields, not to stir my beloved or rouse her until she pleases' (SC 2.7). Obviously, mystery is at hand here, and it is only the hard, textual factuality which counters natural feelings of disbelief at the earthly possibility of such a sweet state of mind. In one way or another, experience—Bernard does not say whose experience—must precede the production of such a beautiful text. The exceptional nature of this situation is further strengthened when Bernard puts it into celestial perspective. It is the pretaste of that which is to come: 'That in heaven it is like this, as I read on earth, I do not doubt, nor that the soul will experience for certain what this page suggests, except that here she cannot fully express what she will there be capable of grasping, but

[2]The English translation used is Bernard of Clairvaux, *On the Song of Songs*, *III*, trans. Kilian Walsh and Irene M. Edmonds, CF 31 (Kalamazoo, Michigan: Cistercian Publications, 1979).

cannot yet grasp.'[3] Underlying the suggestion of modesty in this passage
is a rather bold assumption. It is, after all, no mean achievement for a
literary text like the Canticle to have produced, in however preliminary
a fashion, a state of sweet slumber which is beyond the awakenings
of everyday life. Not surprisingly, it turns out to be difficult, if not
impossible, to find the categories by which this sleep is to be explained.
And even the more or less traditional biblical connotations of sleep,
such as the sleep of Lazarus or the sleep of sin, must be declared null
and void in this matter. It is only in paradoxical terms that the true
meaning of this sleep can be hinted at: 'For it is a genuine sleep that
yet does not stupefy the mind but transports it. And—I say it without
hesitation—it is death, for the apostle Paul in praising people still living
in the flesh spoke thus: "For you have died, and your life is hidden with
Christ in God" [Col 3:3].'[4]

This state of bliss is indeed to be called ecstatic, since in it the soul is
carried beyond the narrow bonds of normal life into a peculiar lightness of
being: 'O that I had the wings of a dove! I would fly away and be at rest.'[5]
Fly away into what? Obviously into the state of pure contemplation. But,
in view of its ecstatic nature, one might inquire into the recognizability
of its structure. Or is the power of death in the quotation from Saint
Paul, 'For you have died and your life is hidden with Christ in God,'
such as even to destroy the subtle paradox of the secret evocation of life
out of its very denial? If that is true, the contemplative might as well be
dead. As long as there is life, on the other hand, it seems hard to avoid
putting it in terms of activity, thus threatening its special mortal status.
As far as Bernard is concerned, he clearly uses the poetry of the Canticle
in phrasing this ecstatic state of mind whose 'sharpness of vision and
swiftness of motion' is compared with the gazelles and hinds in the field.
More realistically, in religious terms at least, it is the life of the angels
which is hinted at in this context:

> Men alone experience this. But, if I may say so, let me die the death
> of angels [another paradox since dying is not what angels normally
> do] that, transcending the memory of things present, I may cast off
> not only the desire for what is corporeal and inferior but even their
> images, that I may enjoy pure conversation with those who bear the
> likeness of purity. This kind of ecstasy, in my opinion, is alone or

[3]SC 52.2; SBOp 2:91; CF 31:51.
[4]SC 52.3; SBOp 2:92; CF 31:52.
[5]Ps 54:7, quoted in SC 52.4; SBOp 2:92; CF 31:52.

principally called contemplation. Not to be gripped during life by
material desires is a mark of human virtue, but to gaze without the
use of bodily likeness is the sign of angelic purity.[6]

In my view it makes little sense to concentrate exclusively on this ecstatic
and angelic state of mind, separating this angelic death from the life—or,
for that matter, death—preceding it. Not only would a life made up of
ecstatic highlights be impossible, but the very same highlights owe their
origin to material existence in the same way as a metaphor includes the
objects it is compared with, and the spiritual with the literal.

Now a familiar way to express this connection between different
mystical stages and their culmination in an *excessus mentis* is an itinerary,
a schematic survey of steps which are in themselves unambiguously clear.
Further, there is a fundamental gap between the linguistic outlook of
those stages and their final transformation into things as yet unheard of.
As far as Bernard is concerned, however—at least in and around sermon
52—a completely different procedure is followed. Angelic death—life
hidden with Christ in God—is preceded by a long series of allusions
to death and dying rather than by an itinerary consisting of positivistic
phrases borrowed from real life. From sermon 48 on, death is in the air,
only to culminate in sermon 52 in the simplicity—and the contemplative
void—of the angelic way of dying. This rhetorical organization of the
discourse is a technique often applied by Bernard. Starting with a casual
dropping of a word or idea like death, then developing that single word
or idea into thematic sets like life, death, shadow, existence, memory,
forgetting, he creates clusters which, apparently floating around without coherence, in the end turn out have to have directed the train of
thought all along.

Of what, then, does this particular cluster, with death at its center,
consist? First and foremost, it is of shadow:

'In his longed for shadow I am seated' [Sg 2:3]. The prophet says:
'A spirit before our face is Christ the Lord; in his shadow we live
among the pagans' [Lm 4:2; Septuagint]. In the shadow among the
pagans; in the light with the angels. . . . You see that faith is both life
and the shadow of life. On the other hand, a life spent amid pleasures,
since it is not by faith, is both death and the shadow of death. 'To set
the mind on the flesh is death' [1 Tm 5:6]. It is also the shadow of
death, of that death which torments into eternity. We too once sat in

6SC 52.5; SBOp 2:92–93; CF 31:53.

darkness and the shadow of death. . . . Now we live in the shadow of Christ, provided that we are alive and not dead.[7]

From whatever angle one looks at it, life is a shadow, either with death as its final destination or sustained by faith as a reflection of a brightness which is yet to come. So, life, in the latter sense of faith, is an anticipation of its own fullness of being which is hidden with Christ in God— anticipation also of the angelic way of dying which is experienced in contemplation. And, if there is any dissatisfaction to be felt in this process, it is due to the lack of progress caused by the interfering shadows of the other less sublime and more sinful form of death:

O Truth, home of the exile, end of exile. I see you, yet I am not allowed to enter, held fast by the flesh. . . . In tears I ask [Ph 3:18]. How long shall we smell and not taste, gazing toward the fatherland, and, not asking possession, sighing for it and saluting it from afar?[8]

The predicament of the pilgrim, being squeezed in between those two appearances of death, seems to be far from pleasant, as well as far from simple. The situation is further complicated if one realizes that anticipation of contemplative life cannot be taken literally. For it is hard to see how the 'likeness of purity' by its very nature can be anticipated at all without becoming self-contradictory. If there is any preliminary effect of angelic life to be detected in the present monastic order, it is in the form of a self-contained cluster rather than of analogy, a cluster which brings into effect the hidden power of angelic death. Apart from dealing with shadows, this death manifests itself—and that is the second characteristic of the cluster—as oblivion. This process of forgetting is concerned not only with the sinful things *quae retro sunt* but also with removing all obstacles which detract from pure contemplation.

Quae retro sunt obliviscens, ad ea quae ante sunt me extendo; 'forgetting what lies behind, I strain forward to what lies ahead' [Ph 3:13].[9] It is exactly at the meeting point of these two extremes that Bernard locates the practice of monastic life, structured according to the order of love (*ordinatio caritatis*). Out of the depth of exile one cries: 'O Wisdom, reaching mightily from end to end in establishing and controlling things sweetly by enriching the affections and setting them in order!'[10] The

---

[7]SC 48.6–7; SBOp 2:71; CF 31:17–18.
[8]SC 50.8; SBOp 2:83; CF 31:37.
[9]SC 49.7; SBOp 2:77; CF 31:28. See SC 48.7; SBOp 2:72; CF 31:19.
[10]SC 50.8; SBOp 2:83; CF 31:37.

very mentioning of order in the context of deathly void might sound
ironic, and ironic it is. Admittedly, the shape of this order is clear
enough. There is effective/actual and affective love, the love of Martha
and Mary, Leah and Rachel. And, although the former is indispensable
for 'making a living', the latter is preferable if one wishes to die the
death of contemplation.

The question, however, how that blessed state is to be achieved, reveals
a paradox which confronts the would-be contemplator. On the one hand,
there are the cursed necessities of every-day monastic life in which the
petty concerns and troubles of the community deter one from proper contemplative rest. On the other hand, those very same necessities stimulate
the desire for contemplative rest, with the opportunity heightened by
the almost ritualized impossibility of achieving it. Of course, it is much
sweeter to rest in the arms of Rachel and to be dead like an angel. Time
and again, however, Bernard, as soon as he embarks on describing the
delights of spiritual life, has his discourse interrupted by his indebtedness
to his fellow-monks:

> While the fruits of your progress grow in profusion about me, I
> patiently accept being torn away from the fruitful embraces of Rachel.
> The interruption of my leisure in order to prepare a sermon will
> not trouble me in the least when I shall see my seed germinating
> in you [Is 61:11] and an increase in the growth of the harvest of your
> righteousness [2 Co 9:10]. For love, which does not seek what is its
> own [1 Co 13:5], has long since easily convinced me not to prefer
> my own cherished desires to your gain. To pray, to read, to write, to
> meditate, or any other gains that may result from the study of spiritual
> things, these I consider no loss because of you [Ph 3:7].[11]

The affective form of love does not come after the effective; rather the
one is implied in the other.

How tempting it would be to consider those intertwined forms of love
a predecessor of friendly franciscan spirituality. In fact, however, there
is a much grimmer aspect to it, a personal reservation on the part of
Bernard in the face of his community and of himself, and that is death,
angelic or otherwise. Whatever order there is turns out to be intrinsically
infiltrated with a power which cuts it off from being anything more or,
for that matter, anything less than a moment in the theatre where shadows
play the part of fathomless existence personified. But who is acting?

[11]SC 51.3; SBOp 2:86; CF 31:43.

Is it a coincidence that Bernard, in an earlier stage of the *Sermons on the Song of Songs*, had reflected on the virtues—and vices—of the contemplative and active life, again in the context of death? In sermon 26—the famous lament on the death of his brother Gerard—Bernard's point of departure had been the exact opposite of angelic, spiritual death, the occasion being the blunt fact of Gerard's passing away.[12] Yet, in spite of the crude literalism underlying the outburst of grief, the cluster of death themes obtains equally here. In the absence of his brother, the realm of Bernard's existence is shadowy, more so than ever. And it is precisely the looseness of shadows—the inconsistency of their organization—which provides the opportunity for the introduction of bitter-sweet irony. It appears that the brothers have changed places after all; a change which has shaken the order of monastic existence to its very roots. Bernard, as a professional contemplator, is replaced by his brother, the humble laborer, schooled in the active and effective life; it is the world turned upside down. The quiet superiority of the monk—and abbot—who in his pursuit of freedom before God has himself been taken care of as an angelic prince, is now overtaken by the short-cut by which Gerard has achieved eternal bliss. Being dead like an angel, Gerard is out of reach for his beloved brother, whatever his contemplative qualities may be. There is a legitimate reason, then, for Bernard to cry out desperately to his brother not to forget him. All of a sudden, the monastery, which by definition is the supreme memorial of celestial order, proves to be nothing but a structureless, murky affair. For where death reigns, oblivion is never far off.

In a subtle process of forgetting and remembering, the activities of Gerard are brought back to mind. His was the life of the quintessential benedictine monk at work: in the buildings, on the fields, at the streams, in the gardens. 'He was most useful to me', so Bernard says, 'useful in little and great things, in private and in public matters, externally and internally. . . . Rightly I was completely dependent on him who was everything to me. . . . Rightly my spirit rested in him who created the opportunity for me to enjoy myself in the Lord, to preach more freely and to pray more safely.'[13] Once more, however, oblivion strikes back. The one and only person who gave life to the mechanics of monastic order of love, as evoked by the picture of the fields, the streams, the gardens, the laborers—and, somewhere inside all that, the meditating abbot—is

---

[12]SC 26; SBOp 1:169–81.
[13]SC 26.7; SBOp 1:175. Translation my own.

no more. Disappearing into heaven, he has taken with him the key to the structure of remembering which makes the benedictine monastery work. It now appears that, the world of external activities having broken down, the contemplative monk cannot survive for long. As a result, there is no other conclusion for Bernard to draw from this situation than that it is he and not his brother who is affected by death: 'The Lord has touched and shaken me, not him whom he has called to rest; it is me whom he has killed when he cut my brother off.'[14]

Somewhere behind the scene of active life, a drama has been going on. To pray, to read, to write, to mediate, Bernard (in sermon 52) will count as loss for his fellow-monks. At the end of that sermon, after having sweetly spoken of angelic death, he will complain again about being disturbed by monastic busy bees around him even during the rare moments of contemplation. And yet now he is death-struck as soon as his more active self, his brother, has been upgraded to the higher life. Who is this man, and wherein exactly lies his tragedy?

'For you are dead, your life is hidden with Christ in God.' Obviously it is not sufficient for the monastery to represent ordered love against the confusion of worldly activities. Life within its walls is hidden: a *vita abscondita*. Whatever external activities can be discerned are in one way or another attached to this secret source and must be judged accordingly. From that point of view, active life is no longer a prelude to contemplation. Rather it must be considered as part of a drama in which all can participate but which cannot bear the absence of a single one. And yet what Bernard seems to be constantly doing is creating missing links as if to destroy the completeness of his play. Consequently, the tragic element of this dramatic scene is to be found in the correspondence of the hidden life with the continued presence of death, whether literal or spiritual. In the same way as Bernard (in sermon 26) moves out of his own story by identifying himself with his dead brother, he withdraws in sermon 52 when it comes to identifying the person who is able to live a completely ordered love life: 'Give me a man who loves God before all things. . . . Give me such a man, I repeat, and I shall boldly proclaim him wise, because he can truthfully boast and say: "He set love in order in me." '[15] In both cases the author can be observed in a process of self-effacement in the direction of contemplative life. What is left of that self is by definition hypothetical and fictional. Theoretically

[14]SC 26.8; SBOp 1:176.
[15]SC 50.8; SBOp 2:83; CF 31:37.

speaking, contemplation as angelic death, as *puritatis similitudo*, brings realization of this hypothetical state within reach. For dramatic reasons of the utmost urgency, however, it seems more convenient for the time being to interpret this *vita abscondita* in terms of exile and shadows. Thus the effect of the angelic likeness of purity is guaranteed, in the same way as death is the meeting point of the literal and the spiritual, the active and the contemplative, memory and oblivion.

ABSTRACTS

Dans cet article je me propose d'examiner la conception que Bernard se fait de la mort, au sens tant littéral que spirituel. J'envisage d'abord le sens de la mort dans les sermons 48 à 52 sur le Cantique des Cantiques qui, du fait qu'ils traitent de façon générale de la relation entre vie active et contemplative, présentent l'occasion de placer la mort dans une perspective spirituelle. A la fin de l'article je me tournerai vers le sermon 26—la célèbre lamentation sur la mort de Gérard—afin de vérifier à quel degré la mort a gardé son sens littéral à l'intérieur des murs du monastère.

In this article I will examine Bernard's concept of death, both in its literal and in its spiritual meaning. First I look at the meaning of death in the *Sermons on the Song of Songs* 48–52 which, generally dealing with the relationship between the active and the contemplative life, offer the opportunity to put death in a spiritual perspective. At the end of the article I shall turn to sermon 26—the famous lament on Gerard's death—in order to check the degree to which death has maintained its literal meaning within the walls of the monastery.

In diesem Artikel möchte ich Bernhards Auffassung vom Tod sowohl in seiner wörtlichen als auch in seiner geistlichen Bedeutung untersuchen. Zuerst wende ich mich der Bedeutung des Todes in den Hoheliedpredigten 48–52 zu, die, indem sie allgemein von der Beziehung zwischen dem aktiven und dem kontemplativen Leben handeln, die Gelegenheit bieten, den Tod in eine geistliche Perspektive zu rücken. Am Ende des Artikels komme ich auf die 26. Predigt zurück—die berühmte Klage über Gerhards Tod—, um zu überprüfen, in welchem Grad Tod seine wörtliche Bedeutung in den Mauern des Klosters behalten hat.

THE RHETORICAL EPISTEMOLOGY
IN SAINT BERNARD'S *SUPER CANTICA*

Luke Anderson, O. Cist.
St Mary's Cistercian Priory

AFTER A CONGRATULATORY WORD to the teachers of his day, Saint Bernard would extract from them a word of tolerance:

> Far from disapproving of those whose purer minds enable them to grasp sublimer truths than I present, I congratulate them, but expect them to allow me to provide a simpler doctrine for simpler minds.[1]

Bernard speaks here of a contemporary situation: the 'sublimer truths' grasped by 'purer minds' are allusions to the rising schools of academic dialecticians; while the 'simpler doctrine' and 'simpler minds' suggest the modest claims of the traditional monastic schools and their concern for grammar, rhetoric, and primitive dialectics.[2]

In Bernard's distinction we hear an echo of Cicero's *divorce* theme in his *De oratore*. In this text, he speaks first of the oneness of wisdom: '...the stream of learning flowing from the common watershed of wisdom.' But almost immediately the watershed divides into two distinct rivers of doctrine (*sunt doctrinarum divortia*): philosophical waters and oratorical waters.[3] Here, then, we have two methods of discourse and

---

[1]SC 22.3; SBOp 1:130, 25–27; CF 7:15.
[2]SC 23.14; SBOp 1:147, 21–27; CF 7:37.
[3]Marcus Tullius Cicero, *De oratore* 3.19.73; Loeb 2:58. The Cicero citations are to the translations in the Loeb Classical Library.

two methods of attaining truth.[4] Bernard, like Cicero, united speech and thought : ' . . . *voluissent societatem dicendi et intelligendi'*.[5]

Bernard is heir to the classical roman rhetorical tradition that comes to the medieval world indirectly and in fragmentary form. A brief history can establish the link.

While Boetius is the basic source of medieval dialectical/logical theory, Fortunatianus in his *Artis rhetoricae libri III*, preserved the rhetorical Ciceronian *corpus* in abstracts and *compendia*. These teachings are simply repeated by Capella, and copied by Cassiodorus and Isidore of Seville. Alcuin made an unsuccessful attempt to return to pure Ciceronian theory, but did succeed in bringing an ethical coloring to rhetoric after the manner of Quintilian. Rabanus Maurus, the pragmatic disciple of Alcuin, in his *De clericorum institutione*, selected from Cicero on the 'useful'. And Albert of Cassino follows the same path.

From this tradition, Bernard derived three discernable Ciceronian contentions : (a) rhetoric is a genuine knowledge, essentially practical and persuasive, and is never merely ornament; (b) rhetoric's search for truth is valid and honest, if indeed limited; (c) rhetoric's conclusions, although most frequently probable, suffice to produce action.

In the seventy-fourth sermon *Super Cantica*, and by way of digression, we have a formal statement concerning Bernard's rhetorical epistemology. He proposes to 'enlighten' the mind of his audience, and to 'root our affection in God'. The 'incomprehensible' and 'invisible' will be manifested 'by means of figures'; and these images will be 'drawn from the likeness of things familiar to us'. What is 'precious' will be attained through the 'cheap'.[6]

Rhetoric and dialectics, as in the classical period, were in Bernard's day in somewhat ambivalent relations. These arts had moved from an initial friendship on to bitter enmity only to end in smug indifference. Paris contends with Chartres; and Orleans is over against Laon and Rheims. But these rifts are not to be interpreted in too simplistic a fashion. William of Champeaux, for example, taught the redoubtable

---

[4]We have distinguished dialectical from rhetorical epistemology because the definitions of knowledge, truth, and certitude in the former differ from those of the latter. Frequently, as in Bernard, both species of discourse are used in any given text. Hence, although the methods are not contradictory in any formal sense, they manifest significant differences.

[5]Cicero, *De oratore* 3.19.73; Loeb 2:58.

[6]SC 74.2; SBOp 2:240, 17–22; CF 40:86.

Abelard dialectics; then some years later Abelard returns to Paris to study rhetoric under the same Master whose dialectics he had already rejected.

CICERONIAN DOCTRINE AND BERNARD'S RHETORIC

Cicero did not wish to limit himself to any *one* philosophical system. But this free decision was tightly controlled by his conviction that rhetoric fostered authentic knowledge; produced a valid, if practical, truth; and offered a bonafide degree of certitude. Bernard's use of rhetoric is not merely stylistic; it is a vehicle of doctrinal discourse as it was for Cicero.

Philosophical skepticism appealed to Cicero as a doctrine which both recognized and respected *contingencies*. Knowledge was in this view useful; truth was judged to be practical; and our human certitudes probable. Cicero, therefore, in order to deal with the contingencies rejects the agnosticism of the extreme skeptics.[7] At the other extreme, Cicero accepts no dogmatic philosophy which claims to possess all truths.[8] But he grossly overstates his case when he agrees with the academic skeptics that he could argue persuasively on either side of a philosophical question in affirming or denying any practical truth. Bernard too is suspicious of the logicians' claims of certitude: '. . . beware of those who teach new doctrines, who are not logicians but heretics.'[9] The necessary conclusions of the logicians must necessarily be wrong if they conflict with the 'truth' of faith.

Cicero recalls the older masters at the ancient greek schools; they imparted doctrine in two distinct areas: first the *recte faciendi* and then the *bene discendi*. He concludes that the same master taught both arts: the precepts of ethics, *vivendi*, and the precepts of rhetoric, *dicendi*.[10] But Socrates' followers separated the masters and separated the disciplines, *neque disiuncti doctores et disciplinas*. Cicero will now repair the dichotomy by placing ethics and rhetoric together again under the guidance of philosophy.[11] To succeed at this task he needs the aid of some portion of doctrine from the dogmatic philosophers, as the *content* of his rhetoric.

Late republican Rome had its share of epicurian dogmatists; in his *De finibus*, Cicero records his dislike for them. Their opposites, the Stoic

---

[7]Cicero, *Academics* 2.25.113; Loeb 4:613.
[8]Cicero, *De oratore* 3.19.71; Loeb 2:55.
[9]SC 80.6; SBOp 2:281; CF 40:152.
[10]Cicero, *De oratore* 3.15.57; Loeb 2:46.
[11]Cicero, *De oratore* 3.19.73; Loeb 2:59.

dogmatists, and their theory of spartan morality, strongly attracted him. Stoic *indifference* to health, wealth, and good fortune and its frank zeal for *honestas*, defined as the panoply of virtues, impressed Cicero. But Stoic rigidity of mind and frigidity of heart he deemed repulsive.

Therefore, in his *De officiis*, we read of his conversion to 'middle' Stoicism. This renovated dogma took *decorum* rather than *honestas* as its central virtue; this teaching favored the bonding of private ethics and public political and social morality as the central good. Such a morality was highly esteemed by the roman aristocrat. Bernard's doctrine of the *vulnera Christi* goes far beyond *honestas* and *decorum*, transforming Stoicism into something specifically christian, but enshrining some of its tenets.[12]

Cicerio's teacher, Antiochus of Ascalon, a convert from the 'New' Academy', freely departed form the skeptical views of that school. He formed the 'Old Academy' and it reverted to the earlier peripatetics and to Aristotle. The 'moral good' in this theory included health, wealth, and good fortune. But its principal contribution was a vital concern with *reasoned freedom*: desiderative reason or intellectual desire render moral activity voluntary, nay more, free.[13] For Bernard, the innate movement toward God is only corroborated by 'free choice'. The God-capacity is at once necessary and free.[14]

Cicero is not a relativist, but he chooses philosophies in terms of his oratorical needs, i.e., information and persuasion': '. . . not which system of philosophy is the truest [for him Stoicism], but which is most akin to the orator [for him the Peripatetics].'[15] He admires the Stoics for their consistency and coherence and an undeviating pursuit of virtue. But *honestas* is a condition somewhat remote to ordinary peoples' lives: *decorum* is a more proximate condition. The Peripatetics, less stringently logical, less devoted to a theory of *total* perfection, yet reasonable champions of human freedom, address men more realistically: all men are somewhat unreasonable and somewhat enslaved. But such men can respond to the orator's call to virtue.[16] Bernard, mystic and idealist, is also a realistic ascetic.

[12]SC 61, 8; SBOp 2:153; CF 31:147.

[13]Aristotle, *Nicomachean Ethics* 6.2.1139b, 4–5; and 3.4.1111b, 29–30. Translated in *The Basic Works of Aristotle*, ed. Richard McKeon (New York: Random House, [1941]) pp. 1024 and 968.

[14]SC 27.8; SBOp 2:187–88; CF 7:81–82.

[15]Cicero, *De oratore* 3.14.64; Loeb 2:53.

[16]Cicero, *De finibus* 4.9.21–22; Loeb 4:262.

Cicero correctly estimated the damaging effect of the first attack on rhetoric in Plato's *Phaedrus*. In this text oratory is said to be *by its very nature* sophistical and *by intention* devious.[17] Then by a slight of hand it is redefined: true rhetoric *is not* built on rhetorical principles, but rather on dialectical ones. Hence the rhetor must give proper definitions and adequate divisions of things and arrange discourse not to meet audience needs or orator's intentions, but the inner logical structure of the subject under discussion.[18] When it fails to accomplish these tasks, rhetoric is reduced to a stylistic and ornamental function at the service of dialectic. Bernard reads the popular rise of twelfth-century dialecticians in the same threatening way. Cicero emphatically rejects rhetoric's *severance* from philosophy; and he denies the more subtle *subordination* of rhetoric to dialectics. For Cicero, Socrates is '. . . the source from which has sprung the undoubtedly absurd and unprofitable and reprehensible severance between tongue and brain, leading us to having one set of professors to teach us to think and another to teach us to speak.'[19] Cicero does not deny the *per se* superiority of philosophy over rhetoric, but given the needs of a general audience and the intentions of the orator, the philosopher needs the figures of thought and speech. And thus Cicero concludes that, because peripatetic language is more immediately intelligible than stoic, its doctrine is preferable because attainable.[20] This reminds us again that philosophy and rhetoric come from a 'common watershed.' Cicero is devoted to rhetoric and employs it to expound philosophy, 'this grander and more fruitful art.' But this philosophy in its finished form needs rhetoric, 'the power of treating the greatest problems with adequate fullness, and in an attractive style'.[21]

There are striking likenesses between Bernard's presuppositions and the Ciceronian tensions. Bernard does not view his rhetorical theologizing as radically either sophistical or devious; he rejects out of hand the dialectician's pretension that he *alone* has the only apt instrument for

[17]Plato, *Phaedrus* 261A; in *The Works of Plato*, ed. and trans. Irwin Edman (New York: Tudor Publishing Company, 1931) p. 300.

[18]'Until a man knows the truth of the several particulars of which he is writing or speaking, and is able to define them as they are, and having defined them again to divide them until they can not longer be divided, and until in like manner he is able to discern the nature of the soul, and discover the different modes of discourse. . . he will be unable to handle arguments according to the rule of art. . . either for the purpose of teaching or persuading. . . .' *Phaedo* 265D ff., and 277B-C; *Works*, p. 312.

[19]Cicero, *De oratore* 3.16.59–61; Loeb 2:47–49.

[20]Cicero, *De finibus* 5.27.80; Loeb 4:487.

[21]Cicero, *Tuscan Disputations* 1.3.6–4.7; Loeb 5:78.

theological exposition or expansion—a position that necessarily leads to the severance of wisdom and eloquence; and finally, he sees no reason why rhetoric should be subordinate to dialectics, since each art is governed by its own dynamics and issues in its proper epistemologies of knowledge, truth and certitude. But all these propositions need to be defended.

OUTLINE FOR THE INVESTIGATION

The epistemological problem neither formally monastic nor formally scholastic can nevertheless be carefully investigated in its twelfth-century context by a return to the methods proposed by Aristotle in his *Topics* and *Post Analytics*. In the *Topics*, it is suggested that the correct solution to any problem involves the investigation of conflicting doctrines and the ultimate resolution of these by way of refutation.[22] But in the *Post Analytics* we are told that the inquiry into 'opposing views' is only a partial mode of searching out solutions; one must move on to the 'investigation of reality' in itself.[23] On the solid experiential assumption that knowledge *exists*, we will now inquire as to *what* it is, following the lead in the *Analytics*.

Clearly, *knowing* is a human activity which must include in its definition man as *subject*, both as efficient cause and, in a measure, as final principle. But the definition must also include *another*, that is, some object of knowledge. Epistemology deals with this union of knower and known in a wide variety of ways. The dialectician and the rhetorician represent the union in ways proper to their concerns. Hence, *knowledge* may be seen as speculative or practical; *truth* is viewed as conformity to reality or conformity to right appetite; and *truth's conditions* as either certitude or probability.

WISDOM ROOTS OUR AFFECTION ON GOD

Bernard's epistemological conclusions expressly demand his predilection for *caritas*, *delectio*, and *amor*.[24] This is because ultimately, as he teaches, the *vision* of God is denied the earthling. But, more proximately,

---

[22]Aristotle, *Topics* 1.2.101a, 34–38; *Basic Works*, p. 189.

[23]Aquinas, *In Aristotelis libros Peri Hermeneias et Posteriorum Analyticorum Expositio*, ed. Raymundi M. Spiassi (Milan: Marietti Editori Ltd., 1955) L 1.11–12, lectio 20 and 21.

[24]SC 75.9; SBOp 2:252, 11–20; CF 40:105.

it is because, as Bernard says, *faith*, vision's inadequate substitute, is severely constrained by the conditions of all human noetics in its mode of appropriation, and hence it is that love runs on ahead of knowledge.[25] And for this reason, too, *will* is a specially excellent human ability: '. . .exellit in naturae donis *affectio haec amoris.*'[26] Cistercian anthropology shares the common teaching that the human soul relates itself to things other than itself in two distinct, but necessarily related ways: the soul knows, and the soul loves. Bernard offers us his succinct understanding of the distinction and the relations: 'Nec enim potes aut amare quae nescias, aut habere quae non amaveris.'[27] Love can not be without knowledge, but possession (*habere*) can not be had without love. Moreover, the two basic faculties, intellect and will, by their natures relate differently to the object, God. God *known* is present to the soul after the manner of the soul's existence, *secundum esse animae*, and by way of 'intention', *intentionaliter*. On the other hand, God *loved* is present to the soul according to God's mode of existence, *secundum esse proprium*; so that the soul *tends* toward God as he is in himself, *tendentionaliter*. Tendency *toward* is called *desiderium* by Bernard. It has an essential need of knowledge. But because knowledge shrivels and desiccates God's *proprium esse*, reducing it to the *esse animae*, it is inadequate. The bride's love in the form of *desiderium*, stirred up by knowledge's intentionality, follows fleetfooted toward the Bridegroom's *proprium esse*, and *tendentionaliter*.[28]

Bernard admits that he does not now understand exactly how intentionality will be cured of its intrinsic limitations when the bride comes to vision.[29] But he does understand with many pagan authors that lasting *fruitio* on this earth is not possible.[30] *Desiderium*, therefore, better expresses union than either understanding or fruition; and this is because *desiderium* respects the *proprium esse* of the Bridegroom, but fails to attain to *visio*. Any understanding of Bernard's epistemology must end in the frank recognition that love outstrips knowledge, and that

---

[25]SC 7.2; SBOp 1:32, 5–14; CF 4:39.

[26]SC 7.2; SBOp 1:31, 21–22; CF 4:39.

[27]SC 37.1; SBOp 2:9, 16–17; CF 7:181.

[28]'Talis conformitas maritat animam Verbo, cum cui videlicet similis est per naturam, similem nihilominus ipsi se exhibet per voluntatem, diligens sicut dilecta est. Ergo si perfecte diligit, nupsit. Quid hac conformitate iucundius.' SC 83.3; SBOp 2:299, 21–24; CF 40:182.

[29]SC 31.2; SBOp 1:200, 5–20; CF 7:125.

[30]Aristotle, *Metaphysics* 6.4.1027b, 10–17; *Basic Works*, p. 781.

doctrines of cognition, truth, certitude, and probability are tinged by the light that emanates from his teaching on *caritas*, *delectio*, and *amor*. It is also important to note here that in this matter Bernard is not expressing some merely personal preferences for will over intellect, but that he is rather yielding to the exigencies of the bride's psychic structure and the Bridegroom's transcendent nature.

Bernard's psychology of tendentionality is graphically described when he comments on the text: 'Have you seen him whom my soul loves [Sg 3:3]?'[31] The elicited love act is seen as *urging, consuming, vehement,* and *impetuous.* Hence it is an act *in motu* and *ad esse* with all the fire of *desiderium.*[32] There follows a series of statements calculated to register the abandoned extroversion of tendentionality: love confuses order, belies usefulness, ignores moderation, mocks what is fitting, what is reasonable, what is modest, what is prudent.[33] Finally, Bernard hypostatizes love: '. . . triumphas intemetipso et redigis in captivitatem.'[34]

The ordered, useful, and self-possessed intentionality strongly contrasts with the bride's act of love. Indeed, the fruit of cognition, the *verbum,* appears pale when matched with the fruit of love. 'Unde in epithalomio hoc non verba pensanda sunt, sed affectus.'[35] In this context, the act of love—necessarily conditioned by understanding—is not injected into the bride by way of form's intentionality. Rather it is the loved object, the Bridegroom himself, who evokes and elicits from the bride the act of love. *Verbum* is thus in opposition to *opus*! And Bernard gives us the reason: '. . . Because the sacred love which is the subject of the whole Canticle *cannot be described in the words of any language* [*non verbo sit aestimandus aut lingua*] but *is expressed in deed and in truth* [*sed opere et veritate*].'[36] The experience of love's extroversion is the *sine qua non* condition for any authentic appreciation of the Canticle. 'It is vain for anyone who does not love to listen to this song of love, or to read it, for a cold heart cannot catch fire from its eloquence.'[37] The bride's ecstasy, the displacement of herself by the headlong pursuit of the Bridegroom, makes her question especially poignant: 'Have you seen him whom my soul loves?'

[31]SC 79.1; SBOp 2:272; CF 40:137.
[32]SC 79.1; SBOp 2:272, 5–6; CF 40:137.
[33]SC 79.1; SBOp 2:272, 7–10; CF 40:137.
[34]SC 79.1; SBOp 2:272, 9–10; CF 40:137.
[35]SC 79.1; SBOp 2:272, 16–17; CF 40:137–38.
[36]SC 79.1; SBOp 2:272, 17–19; CF 40:138.
[37]SC 79.1; SBOp 2:272; CF 40:138.

TENDENTIONALITY-LOVE

The union of God and man is carefully described by Bernard: the two are understood to be not in substantial union, but in volitional union. Hence, intentionality is clearly excluded. Bernard sees the union *non substantiis confusos*, but rather as *voluntatibus consentaneous*.[38] Hence the *unio* involves two wills, a *communio voluntatum*, and two agreements, *consensus in caritate*.[39] Bernard then introduces the verb *adhaerere*, as a description of the bride's relation to the Bridegroom: 'Mihi autem adhaerere Deo bonum est [Ps 72:28].' Here the position of the will is not *to seek*, but *to have found* and *to adhere*. The permanence of the state is expressed by the terms *in Deo manens*. Then, in a rather unusual reversal, the bride is seen to *attract* the Bridegroom: 'Deum...in se traxit.'[40] Going a step beyond this, the depth of this volitional union, intimate and mutual, is spoken of in a strong verbal form drawn from Augustine, *inviscerati*.[41] This visceral union goes far beyond faith's intentional union, because now the object of charity's tendentiality, that is, God, is transformed into a subject with his own proper, but free, love tendency toward the bride. Hence, the Bridegroom's love, radically antecedent to the bride's love, is yet, after a manner of speaking, *consequent* on the bride's love.[42] Bernard is able to conclude: 'Porro cum iam etiam diligit qui ante diligebatur, et homo in Deo, et Deus in homine est.'[43] Something of the ardent nature of tendentiality, and the movement of the human will toward the object as it is 'in itself', is captured in Bernard's words: '...But headlong love does not wait for judgement, is not chastened by advice, nor shackled by shame, nor subdued by reason.'[44] All the passive verbal forms in this text obliquely point to cognitive intentionality and paint this *cognitio* as somewhat inhibiting. While love is seen to run headlong, *praeceps amor*, cognitive elements counsel caution, restraint, and patience. The nominative terms *iudicium*, *consilio*, and *rationi* are directly cognitive subject, *pudore* is indirectly such. When comparing their functions to that of extroverted, headlong love, they appear passive if not repressive:

[38]SC 71.10; SBOp 2:221, 10; CF 40:56.
[39]SC 71.10; SBOp 2:221, 10–11; CF 40:56.
[40]SC 71.10; SBOp 2:221, 13–14; CF 40:57.
[41]Augustine, *In sermone 24*; PL 38:162.
[42]SC 71.10; SBOp 2:221, 16–17; CF 40:57.
[43]SC 71.10; SBOp 2:221, 25–26; CF 40:57.
[44]SC 9.2; SBOp 1:43; CF 4:54.

praestolatur, temperatur, frenatur, and *subicitur*.[45] There is something almost irrational in the *praeceps amor*; yet it would be better seen as supra-rational. What Bernard intuits is that love goes beyond knowledge, moving forward from what is possessed cognitively and *in intention*, to an encounter with the thing 'in itself', and as it is 'in itself'. In another text, Bernard points out that, if indeed the love-relation is a special and conspicuous quality of bride and Bridegroom, then calling the human soul a bride is fitting. And so her love approaches her lover boldly and seeks an intimacy beyond cognition:

> About to ask a great favor from a great personage . . . there is no preamble, no attempt to conciliate favor. No, but with a spontaneous outburst [*repente prorumpens*] from the abundance of the heart, direct even to the point of boldness, she says: 'Let him kiss me with the kiss of his mouth.'[46]

The *repente prorumpens* coming *ex abundantia cordis* in a mood of *nude frontoseque satis* is the perfect expression of the vitality and sureness of an elicited act of the will.[47]

Bernard the rhetor, bent on the act of persuasion as he marshals his reasoned arguments and insights, has as his final aim the production in the audience of this elicited act of love for God. The concern he has for knowledge that is practical, for truth that is prudential, is not founded on a pragmatism that despairs of coming to truth. Rather it is that having espied, in faith, something of the reality of the Bridegroom and incapable of *visio*, in this present life, the will rushes forward with its pitiable knowledge to grasp at the *esse proprium* of a Bridegroom who escapes comprehension. If the bride can not now know fully, she can love fully. And that love assuages temporarily the pilgrim bride. 'Let him kiss me with the kiss of his mouth' are the words that best express the bride's need and desire to be received.

PRACTICAL KNOWLEDGE

As rhetor, Bernard views knowledge as practical, and he sees the intellect as the instrument of practicality. It is not that he is an enemy of speculation; it is, he says, not a primary concern of his. Commenting on the Bridegroom's words: 'Your neck is as jewels', he points out that the

---

[45]SC 9.2, SBOp 1:43, 13–15; CF 4:54.
[46]SC 7.2; SBOp 1:32; CF 4:39.
[47]SC 7.2; SBOp 1:32, 12–14; CF 4:39.

functions of the neck *are like* the functions of the intellect. For as the neck links head and body, so the intellect links the rational soul to the rational appetite. The rational soul *receives* its vital nourishment through the intellect, and, in turn, the intellect *communicates* this vital nourishment to the inward faculties of will and affection.[48] Yet the intellect is unable 'to penetrate to where light is total'.[49] For this reason the bride will receive 'ornaments [earrings] of gold studded with silver'. These earrings signify the gift of faith, which comes by hearing. This faith is the temporal substitute for the eternal vision; it brings to the human mind *true*, but *partial* light. The 'silver' studding signifies the written record of faith, the sacred Scriptures. Bernard sees them as rhetorical pages: a clear message and elegant discourse.[50] But this truth of faith is given that one may *do* the truth.[51]

Bernard, in five sermons, thirty-four through thirty-eight inclusive, expounds his doctrine of truly important objects of knowledge, and the destructive forms of ignorance of these objects. He freely concedes that all knowledge is good.[52] But he immediately explains that because of the '...brevity of time', you must '...hurry to work out your salvation'. It follows, then, that one must 'principally and primarily' know those general objects of knowledge on which '...our salvation is more intimately dependent'.[53]

The first necessary and foundational object of knowledge for Bernard is authentic self-knowledge. This immediately begets humility because it kills self-importance.[54] He then enumerates a number of volitional consequences which corroborate the presence of this knowledge and render it authentically practical.[55] But this knowledge is merely foundational, a mere beginning.

A second and higher necessary object of knowledge is the knowledge of God. Here, too, the concern is practical: 'what can God *do* for us?' He turns out to be a do-gooder, a bene-factor: 'God makes himself known to us for our own good.'[56] What specifically are we to know about God?

[48]SC 41.1; SBOp 2:28, 20–25; CF 7:204.
[49]SC 38.5; SBOp 2:17, 14–18; CF 7:190–91.
[50]SC 41.4; SBOp 2:31, 5–11; CF 7:207.
[51]SC 50.4; SBOp 2:80, 18–22; CF 31:33.
[52]SC 36.2; SBOp 2:4, 14; CF 7:174.
[53]SC 36.2; SBOp 2:5, 6–10; CF 7:175.
[54]SC 36.5; SBOp 2:6–7; CF 7:177–78.
[55]SC 37.2; SBOp 2:10, 2–11; CF 7:182.
[56]SC 36.6–8; SBOp 2:36–38; CF 7:179–80.

We are to know '. . . how good God is, how kind and gentle, how willing
to pardon'.[57]

Man's purposing in knowing is also practical: knowledge is not sought
for its own sake; when it is, it is vain curiosity. Knowledge is not to be
sought for material profit; when it is, it is avarice. The proper purpose of
knowledge is the prudent benefit of self and others.[58] Bernard's intention
in these texts is '. . . to offer some consoling doctrine to improve our
lives'.[59] Both the knowledge of self and of God deal with operables and
not simply with cognoscibles: knowledge is not merely for apprehension;
it is causative and intended to 'work'. When, for example, Bernard speaks
of a threefold love, of the flesh, of the reason and of wisdom, he says
of *reason's love* that 'it does good deeds', that it is 'practical', and that
it is '. . . vehemently aflame with . . . love'. Knowledge of self and of
God allows the intellect to *do* the truth.[60] At times, Bernard sets strong
contrasts between speculative and practical knowledge. In his opinion,
we may, for example, 'listen to Wisdom as a teacher in a lecture hall
delivering an all-embracing lecture'.[61]

But there is a place to find Wisdom other than the lecture hall, and in
that place Wisdom is received *inwardly* and moves beyond instruction to
action: '. . . hic et suscipimus' (and the wise man *acts*), and '. . . ibi
instruimur quidem' (and the wise man is *instructed*).[62] The term of
speculative knowledge is instruction. But in practical knowledge, on
condition of the mind's illumination, the will is led to decision and
action; Bernard states this briefly: '. . . sed hic afficimur'.[63] Bernard says
that *instruction* produces *doctos*; and this is an admitted perfection. But
affection, the elicited act of the will (*afficimur*), produces *sapientes* which
is also a perfection. To explain his teaching he gives us two examples.
As the sun does not always *warm* those whom it *enlightens*, so the
light *to see* does not always *warm* those whom it has enlightened; in a
word, the light *to see* does not unfailingly spur a man *to act*. Bernard,
the rhetor, preaches so that men may act! There is another example.
As knowing where wealth is to be found is not possession of that
wealth, so *possession* differs from *knowledge* (. . . nec notitia divitem

---

[57]SC 38.1; SBOp 2:14, 3–19; CF 7:187.
[58]SC 36.3; SBOp 2:5–6; CF 7:176.
[59]SC 39.1; SBOp 2:18–19; CF 7:192.
[60]SC 50.4; SBOp 2:80; CF 31:33.
[61]SC 23.14; SBOp 1:147; CF 7:37.
[62]SC 23.14; SBOp 1:147, 23; CF 7:37.
[63]SC 23.14; SBOp 1:147, 24; CF 7:37.

facit, sed possessionem').[64] Bernard preaches possession of truth, but actions on the heels of truth. In his conclusion, in this sermon, he relates seeing and doing to the known object, God: 'And so it is with God: to know him is one thing, to fear him is another; nor does knowledge make a man wise, but the fear that motivates him.'[65] Yet, however significant practical knowledge is, it is not the final word on the goal of human knowing. But, as rhetor, Bernard's goal is the communication of *cognitio practica*.[66]

In his opening sermon on the *Cantica*, Bernard expresses his rhetorician's concern with an enlightenment which leads to action. The sacred text of *Ecclesiastes* places the vanity of the world before the reader's eyes so that one may *recognize* it for what it is and then *have done with it*, the knowing is for doing. The *cognoscere* leads to the *contemnere*.[67]

A similar rhetorical axiom is applied to the reading of *Proverbs*: ' . . . Has not your life and your conduct been sufficiently amended and enlightened by the doctrine it inculcates?'[68] In Bernard, all the terms and their position in this text are redolent of the rhetor's purposes: *vita et mores vestri* suggest the direct interest in the personal welfare of the reader; the *inventur doctrinam* of *Proverbs* contains not mere admonitions, but also true doctrine; a set of truths is offered, but they are truths to live by. And this meaning is clarified when Bernard names the *effects* of these truths, *sufficienter emendati et informati sunt*; there is information *and* amendment of life.[69]

For Bernard, the study of these two books, and the fear of God and the observance of the commandments which naturally follow from the reading, are prerequisites for an unpresumptuous reading of the *Canticle of Canticles*. Rhetoric, as the art of discovery and the art of persuasion, labors to move the hearer or reader *to do the truth*. The integral rhetorical experience requires *apprehension and appreciation*. Bernard recognizes the *de facto* distinction that frequently separates knowing from doing, but he urges their *de jure* union when the knowledge is *practical*. He sees two possible contacts with the *Cantica*: 'Let those who are versed in the mystery revel in it. . . .'[70] The *experti recognoscant*,

[64]SC 23.14; SBOp 1:147, 27; CF 7:37.
[65]SC 23.14; SBOp 1:147–48; CF 7:37–38.
[66]SC 23.14; SBOp 1:148, 13–26; CF 7:38.
[67]SC 1.2; SBOp 1.3, 16; CF 4:1.
[68]SC 1.2; SBOp 1:3; CF 4:1.
[69]SC 1.2; SBOp 1:3, 18–19; CF 4:1.
[70]SC 1.11; SBOp 1:7; CF 4:6.

the first kind of reader, knows the doctrine of the book and contacts the truth it offers. But this reading is really inadequate. And so there is another kind of reader: 'Let all the others burn with desire. . . .'[71] The use of the term *inexperti* is a literary usage and must not deceive us. The distinction suggested is not between knowing and know-nothing. What is suggested is the distinction between speculative and practical knowing: the *experti know* and for them this suffices; but the *inexperti* are much nearer to the purpose of the *Canticle*'s message: they *inardescant desiderio*.[72] For the *inexperti*, knowing is a point of departure; the will must be fired with desire, and the experience to which Bernard refers here is the act of elicited desire, *non tam cognoscendi quam experiendi*.[73] Hence the *truth* about love is that *love* should be fostered by truth.

PRUDENTIAL TRUTH

For Bernard, practical knowledge must attain to practical truth. As a goal proper to rhetoric, this is verified only in *prudential* truth.[74] The genuinely practical is essentially *prudential*. This means that the rectified human will must, for the integrity of this act, vitally share in the execution of this truth-act. When the *rectifying forces* of justice, fortitude, and temperance make the will 'right', then, and only then, can the will *act* as 'constitutive' of the prudential reasoning process. It is then, too, that prudence, the first sign of the cardinal virtues, consorts with the rectified will and that the judgement of *conscience* and the judgement of *election* (*liberum arbitrium*) conspire to produce the perfect expression of practical truth; and the truth is then done![75]

There is another important text. Bernard is defining the reality of 'investigation'. He says that the *order* of investigation gives precedence to all that proves an aid to the spiritual life in us. When he speaks of

[71]SC 1.11; SBOp 1:7; CF 4:6.
[72]SC 1.11; SBOp 1:7, 29; CF 4:6.
[73]SC 1.11; SBOp 1:7, 30; CF 4:6.
[74]SC 49.6; SBOp 2:76; CF 31:26.
[75]'Ex intentione finis, voluntas applicat intellectum ad inquirendum de mediis ad finem, seu *ad consilium. Consilium* est syllogismus practicus cujus conclusio est judicium practicum (seu indifferens), non proponens unum medium, sed plura media. Consilio correspondet, ex parte voluntatis *consensus* qui est approbatio utilitatis mediorum. Vis consensus intellectus applicatur *ad ultimum judicium practicum* de uno medio determinato hic et nunc eligendo. Ex parte voluntatis sequitur *electio*. Electione facta, movetur intellectus *ad imperium* quo intimatur *executio mediorum electorum*: fac hoc.' Henrico Grenier, *Cursus Philosophiae* (Quebec: Edidit Le Seminaire de Quebec) 1:458–59.

the *application* of investigation, he explains that we must pursue more eagerly those things which better strengthen love. And finally, he insists that the *purpose* of investigation is to benefit self and neighbor.[76]

We can conclude then that *ad salutem*, and *ad amorem* and *ad aedificationem*, require of the investigator that his appetite be 'right', so that his practical prudential truth is attained in the very act by which he does the truth. Bernard's commentary on the *Cantica* as an investigation, therefore, can be seen as a pursuit of salvation, love, and edification. Titles of probable certitude, proper to rhetoric and primordial dialectics, must be carefully understood as we predicate this condition of truth to Bernard's teaching.

The conformity of intellect to reality, that is, extra-mental reality, ordinarily defines *truth*. But in dealing with *contingent operables*, the *agibilia*, no infallible conformity can be achieved because of the contingent matters with which one treats. Indeed the conformity proper to practical truth looks beyond the conformity required in speculative truth. Bernard, the rhetor, proposes to his audience goals which are clearly contingent operables; he persuades in order to move. The bride is for Bernard an *exemplar*, a *fac similiter*; she is concerned with the contingent operables.[77] The conformity here is to a 'rectified' will; and the truth here is 'directing'.[78] In short, there is a special conformity between the *judgement of the mind* and the *demands for a right appetite*, in the pursuance of a *particular end*. On the one hand, then, practical truth has as its basis a relationship of mind regulated by the thing known (the end to be pursued). The term truth here is used univocally for both speculative and practical truth. But truth is said to be practical in yet another, simultaneous but analogical sense: the mind is *regulated* by a right appetite because the right appetite permits the mind's act of judgement to function without inhibitions or obstacles. Hence we conclude that the *judgement of conscience* is real cognition, and that the *judgement of election* (*liberum arbitrium*) applies this cognition under the guidance of right appetite. The affections, that is, the concupiscible and irascible appetites and the will, the rational appetite, are, when rectified by the cardinal virtues, conditions of free election. And it is the rectified will which offers no impediment to the actions of the final practical judgement. Any failure in the judgement of election violates the unique

[76]SC 36.3; SBOp 2:6; CF 7:176.

[77]Aquinas, *Summa contra Gentiles*, ed. Apud Sedem Commissionis Leoninae (Rome: Desclée & C., Herder, 1934) 3.86.

[78]SC 83.3; SBOp 2:299, 21–24; CF 40:182.

kind of conformity of practical truth. Because, in the case of failure, the judgement of conscience is impeded either by bad will or disordered passions, if not a combination of both. Practical and prudential truth is, then, unfailingly righteous. This truth is manifested whenever the will, rectified by the cardinal and moral virtues, chooses in the judgement of election what the practical reason through the prudential judgement of conscience proposes and dictates. For Bernard, then, the regulating and normative function of the mind is safeguarded, and the directing and tendential nature of the rational appetite is preserved.[79]

The problem of certitude can now be seen in its integrity. The *probable* certitude of conscience becomes in the act of prudent free choice, *an imperative*, and hence, for the moment, in this particular act, a certain 'necessity' obtains: *I ought* to do this, and *I will* do this!

However, Bernard's rhetoric through *logos* and *ethos* can reach only as far as *synderecis* and the universal practical judgement.[80] It is left to his audience through its proper *pathos* to complete the judgement of conscience, move ahead to the judgement of election, and, finally, to act.[81] Practical knowledge, prudential truth, and probable certitude are the elements of Bernard's epistemology in the *Super Cantica*. But his message is 'heard' only by those of 'good will'.

Bernard understands that practical truth does not deal with the very deepest levels of truth: 'I leave deeper truths to those competent to comprehend them.'[82] He says this because he sees that prudence can be the subject of error. Since, by the very nature of its object, the singular operables, it deals with things that 'can be otherwise'. The margin of error, then, can not be excluded as a *real possibility*.[83]

Bernard firmly grasps the contingent nature of practical truth which frequently appears to contradict itself. Love informing prudence allows this virtue uninhibited freedom:

> But how often does dutiful response yield dutifully to the uproar of business. How often is a book laid aside in good conscience that we may sweat in manual labor. How often for the sake of administering worldly affairs we may rightly omit even the solemn celebration of

---

[79]'. . . O anima. . . Verbum familiariter percucteris consultesque de omni re, quantum intellectu capax, tantum audax desiderio?' SC 83.3; SBOp 2:299, 26–27. CF 40:182: '. . . with an intellectual grasp proportionate to the boldness of your desire.'

[80]SC 32.10; SBOp 1:232; CF 7:142.

[81]SC 58.12; SBOp 2:135; CF 31:119.

[82]SC 57.5; SBOp 2:120; CF 31:100.

[83]Aquinas, *Summa theologiae* 1–2.57.5 ad 3.

masses! A preposterous order; but necessity knows no law. Love in action devises its own order. . . .[84]

In this text, Bernard shrewdly repeats the doctrine of Aristotle in a mode calculated to stir the attention of his monks. In Aristotle we read:

What affirmation and negation are in thinking, pursuit and avoidance are in desire; so that, since moral virtue is a state of character concerned with choice, and choice is deliberate desire, therefore the reasoning must be true and the desire right, if the choice is to be good, and the latter must pursue just what the former asserts. Now this kind of intellect and this kind of truth is practical.[85]

The choice of pursuing 'worldly affairs' over the solemn 'celebration of masses' is made in terms of 'right desire' rendering the intellect 'true'. This is not to deny in fact that 'masses' are of higher value than 'worldly affairs'. But that is another question. To this question Aristotle also gives us an answer: ' . . . Of the intellect which is contemplative, not practical, not productive, the good and the bad state are truth and falsity respectively (for this is the work of everything intellectual). . . .'[86] If the simple 'truth' of the matter be considered, then *lectio divina* is certainly a higher activity than *labor manualis*. But Bernard can put the one aside for the sake of the other, because of a mandate from practical prudential truth: ' . . . While of the part which is practical and intellectual the good state is truth in agreement with right desire.'[87] For Bernard, practical truth is ultimately ordered to contemplative *visio*, and authentic virtue suggests the coming of this *visio*. 'The face that can focus on the brightness of God must of necessity be pleasing. Nor could it accomplish this unless it were itself bright and pure, transformed into the very image of the brightness it beholds. Otherwise it would recoil through sheer unlikeness.'[88] Virtue as a judgement of mind and as a response to the demands of right appetite is sometimes defined in terms of the union of bride and Bridegroom. Virtue can be seen as a 'sign' of the Bridegroom's *coming*: ' . . . praenuntia imminentis adventus Sponsi'. And virtue can also be seen as a 'sign' of the bride's *reception* of him: ' . . . et praeparatio quaedam ad digne suscipiendum supernum visitatorem. . . .'[89]

---

[84]SC 50.5; SBOp 2:81; CF 31:34.
[85]Aristotle, *Nicomachean Ethics* 6.2.1139a, 21–27; *Basic Works*, pp. 1023–24.
[86]Aristotle, *Nicomachean Ethics* 6.2.1139a, 27–29; *Basic Works*, p. 1024.
[87]Aristotle, *Nicomachean Ethics* 6.2.1139a, 30–31; *Basic Works*, p. 1024.
[88]SC 62.7; SBOp 2:160; CF 31:158–59.
[89]SC 57.5; SBOp 2:122, 18–19; CF 31:100.

Bernard makes a rather interesting distinction between the contemplative activity/repose *functions* of the bride, and the *object* of those functions, the Bridegroom. He defines the object as '. . . the majesty, the eternity, and the divinity of the king himself'.[90] Hence, even in the higher forms of prayer, there is some distance between subject and object.

This distance is dramatically extended whenever man's vineyard, his soul, is overgrown with thorns and covered with nettles, that is, vices. This new distance occurs '. . . by [man's] neglecting the endowments of nature and the gifts of grace which he has received in the cleansing waters of rebirth.'[91] And this failure introduces fresh distances; for man '. . . has reduced his very own first vineyard (which God, not man, had planted) to something that is no vineyard.'[92] As the vineyard has no life, so the soul has no life.

Another metaphor used for contemplation and virtue is the symbol of light: 'Martha is sister to Mary. And though she loses the light of contemplation, she does not permit herself to fall into the darkness of sin, or the idleness of sloth, but holds herself within the light of good works.'[93] In this text the 'a contemplationis lumine cadit' is replaced by the works of virtue, '. . . in luce bonae operationis'.[94]

Commenting on the text 'The vines in flower yield their sweet perfume (Sg 2:3)', Bernard speaks of the temporal goal of good works. The vines, he says, are human souls; the flowers represent good works; the sweet perfume is good repute; and the fruit of good works, the highest of works, martyrdom. Prudential practical truth can be built on exemplarity: 'To me, Lord Jesus, you are . . . both the mirror of endurance and the reward of the sufferer. . . . By the example of your virtue you train my hands for war; by your regal presence you crown my head with victory.'[95] Yet virtue and vice frequently are found together: 'Virtue stands in the midst of vices and therefore needs not only careful pruning but a trimming. . . . As the vices steal upon it from all sides and nibble at it, it will gradually wither unbeknownst to you, and suffocate when overgrown.'[96]

Bernard's doctrine of the 'little foxes' is especially pertinent to his teachings on practical intellect and right appetite. The foxes are said to

[90]SC 62.4; SBOp 2:157; CF 31:154.
[91]SC 63.2; SBOp 2:162; CF 31:163.
[92]SC 63.2; SBOp 2:162; CF 31:163.
[93]SC 51.2; SBOp 2:85; CF 31:41.
[94]SC 51.2; SBOp 2:85, 10–12; CF 31:41.
[95]SC 47.6; SBOp 2:65; CF 31:8.
[96]SC 58.10; SBOp 2:134; CF 31:117–18.

spoil the flowering vines; they represent the temptations which plague the virtuous man. Yet they are essential to the formation of a genuine interior life: '. . . All who wish to live a godly life in Christ must suffer persecution.'[97] These 'cunning little animals' are by no means little in malice. But they are called little to draw attention to the fact that they are subtle. And their subtlety ends in a damage done swiftly and secretly. The foxes are the crafty purveyors of vice. They may attack the will directly by offering an object as an apparent good as opposed to a real good: presenting certain subtle vices cloaked in the *likeness* of virtues. Bernard gives strong expression to this: 'videtur mihi congruentissime designare subtilissima quaedam vitia specie pallita virtutum.'[98]

The power of these temptations resides in false representation: 'quod virtutes virtutum quadam similitudine mentiuntur.' This mendacious quality of the foxes is an attack on the intellect: presenting as true what in fact is false. Bernard speaks of the sources of falsehood: temptations from within, 'cognitationes hominum vanae', and temptations from without, 'per angelos malso' who transform themselves into 'angelos lucis'.[99] Bernard reminds us that the heart and mind must be alert to this deceitful malice and lying perversity. Only the perfect and the experienced and those 'qui habeant illuminatos oculos cordis ad discretionem boni et mali', can effectively deal with the foxes. This discretion about good and evil is the work of the practical intellect which requires for its proper functioning the rectified appetite.

Bernard says that we can extend the allegory and see the *vines* as standing for the christian community and the *foxes* as heretics.[100] Church ministers must confront and confute error, and must convert the perverse from evil. The assent of the mind to the truth and the consent of the will to do good will alone capture the foxes:

> Let it not be supposed, however, that it is a small and unimportant thing for a man to vanquish a heretic and refute his heresies, making a clear and open distinction between shadows and realities and exposing the fallacies of false teaching by plain and irrefutable reasoning in such a way as to bring into captivity a depraved mind which had set itself against the knowledge revealed by God.[101]

[97]SC 64.1; SBOp 2:166; CF 31:169. See 2 Tm 3:12.
[98]SC 64.6; SBOp 2:169, 4–5; CF 31:173.
[99]SC 64.6; SBOp 2:169, 9–10; CF 31:173.
[100]SC 64.8; SBOp 2:170; CF 31:175.
[101]SC 64.9; SBOp 2:170–71; CF 31:176.

Virtue will always need our mind's vigilance and our will's diligence. The *veritas practica* and the *appetitus rectus* are a daily need, so that the *visio per fidem* may be a quotidian possibility. Bernard sums this up nicely:

> Therefore if the winter is past, the rain over and gone, if the flowers have appeared again in our land and the spring-like warmth of spiritual grace indicates the time for pruning, what is left for us but to bend our energies totally to this work, so holy and so necessary. . . . And let each one judge that he has progressed, not by finding nothing to correct, but by correcting what he does find.[102]

BERNARD'S EPISTEMOLOGY AND THE ACTS OF HIS MIND

Bernard perceives, judges, and argues in ways peculiar to the mode of rhetorical discourse. Abelard and, more especially, the more radical dialecticians of the day challenged the accuracy and indeed the pertinence of this kind of discourse as applied to theological exposition and investigation. Nevertheless, these intellectual acts taken in consort reveal knowledge as practical, truth as prudential, and certitude as probable, but sufficiently sure to promote action.

The battle joined over the falsely supposed opposition between *intellectio* and *ratio*, the two functions of the one intellect. Rhetoricians were said to read 'into' things, *intelligere*; while dialecticians were said to read 'out' of things, *ratiocinare*. The almost exclusive use of rational deductions in theological work, for example, tended to view principles as mere starting points for an advance to new frontiers of knowledge. On the other hand, a seeming unwillingness to advance knowledge through the use of *ratio* appeared to doom theological science to stale repetitiveness. And while the conviction that knowledge is *certain* only by way of *proof* had a solid aristotelian basis, the same philosophical source clearly affirmed that the structure and validity of any deductive conclusion depends necessarily on the structure and validity of the principles.[103]

Bernard as rhetor knows that the principles he perceives and recounts guide (*inducere*) the reasoning process, and that these *starting points* yield a higher, deeper, and prior knowledge than that which emerges from the labor of *ratio*.[104] When Bernard does use *ratio*, like other rhetoricians,

---

[102]SC 58.12; SBOp 2:135; CF 31:119.
[103]Aristotle, *Posterior Analytics* 1.2.72a, 25 and 27; *Basic Works*, p. 113.
[104]Aristotle, *Posterior Analytics* 1.2.72a, 30; *Basic Works*, p. 113.

he employs elements outside of mere *logos*, and adds *ethos* and *pathos* to his 'words' of persuasion.[105] To the dialectician *logos* is sufficient; the other elements are at best adventitious and at worst dishonest.

We need now to understand something of the three basic intellectual acts as manifested in Bernard's rhetoric, so that we can see how these condition his epistemology.

PERCEPTIONS

To begin with, Bernard's intellectual perceptions, drawn from sense experience, issue in fantasies concocted from the same sense experiences. These 'images' in the hands of the rhetor connect and enlarge—to a point of dramatic exaggeration—the ordinary sensory effects of sensible phenomena. The mind reflecting on these images is suddenly blinded with the flashing lightening created by a unique intellectual 'seeing of likenesses in relations'. This is an authentic reading 'into', a creative intuition.[106]

This rhetorical epistemology does not deny the abstracting motions usually associated with simple apprehension; nor does it deny that the *singular* and *particular* are thus known only indirectly. What it does stress, however, is that there is no genuine knowledge of these singulars and particulars without reflecting, without bending back on the phantasm, without an intellective revisiting of sense phenomena. It is only in the next century that Bernard's refined and instinctive perceptions will be well elaborated and ably defended.[107] But his mode of concrete and synthetic insight set over against abstract and quasi-analytic apprehension suggests a peculiar habit and exercise of perception.

Plato calls this faculty *dia-noia*, or the genius for immediate insight.[108] Cicero names it *ingenium*, and defines it as the ability to catch sight of relationships of similitude.[109] To clarify his point, Cicero says that the *discovery* of truth differs from the *defense* of truth. And this is because, as he says, the *ars demonstrandi* proper to *ratio* gives no indication as to *how* we are to find the truth, *quo modo inveniatur*, that is, *inventio* and *intelligere*. For the work of *ratio* is properly to defend the truth,

[105]Aristotle, *Rhetoric* 1.2.1356a, 1–21; *Basic Works*, pp. 1329–30.
[106]SC 9.5; SBOp 1:45–46; CF 4:57.
[107]Aquinas, *Summa theologiae* 1.86.1.
[108]Plato, *Phaedrus* 266A and 277B-C; *Works*, p. 312.
[109]Cicero, *De inventione* 1.30.49; Loeb 4:25.

to judge it, *quo modo indicetur*.[110] We conclude, then, that invention-knowledge is correctly named *archaic* since it indicates understanding's radical beginnings, the *per se* manifestive. Defense-knowledge is called *apodictic* because it searches out the 'reasons' for things and is always manifestive *per aliud*. The *ars inveniendi* is the natural habitat of rhetors like Bernard; while the *ars demonstrandi* is the accustomed haunt of dialecticians like Abelard.

Hugh of Saint Victor (1096–1141), a contemporary of Bernard and Abelard, stands over against the dialecticians at the other parisian schools. For him *all* human knowledge depends on *inventio* and expresses itself *universally* through the *use of analogies*. In his *Didascalion*, he tells us that the soul by grasping the 'similarity of things returns to itself', and that the similitudes are 'declared' (judged) only when the comparison of the sensory appearances is made with that which human realization demands.[111] Knowledge, then, is a 'going back to oneself', and always in terms of one's 'needs'.[112] The mind, says Hugh, finds the distinction of like and unlike within and because of itself: *in se* and *ex se*.[113]

Everywhere in his *Super Cantica*, Bernard so swiftly and surely declares the pythagorean tradition's *similia similibus conprehendere* that his intuitions and their figurative expressions are deceptively simple. Like Hugh's declared comparisons, Bernard's immediate inferences are given in analogous propositions. These are often overtly multiple categorical statements joined because of 'likeness'.

In his *De oratore*, Cicero allows no distinction between man as actual 'knower' and man as 'capable of speech'.[114] This is because fantasy reveals the human world to the knower in all its immediacy and hence only figurative speech can adequately translate this *known* immediacy. In Bernard, concept and word, thought and expression, knowing and speaking, are inextricably combined. And as with every rhetor, for Bernard the figurative word is the external form of the original, interior, and interpretative intellectual act of *ingenium*.

Figurative speech in simple perceptions and in immediate judgements is always for the rhetor imagistic, directive, effective, and allusive. Chief among these figures is metaphor, and in the case of our text we have

---

[110]Cicero, *De oratore* 2.38.157–58; Loeb 1:310–11.
[111]Hugh of St Victor, *The Didascalion of Hugh of St Victor*, trans. Jerome Taylor (New York, London: Columbia University Press, 1961) 742A, 5.
[112]Hugh, *Didascalion* 742A, 2.
[113]Hugh, *Didascalion* 742A, 9; 742B, 10.
[114]Cicero, *De oratore* 2.13.56; Loeb 1:238–39.

an extended metaphor or an allegory. In its root meaning, as Herodotus understood metaphor, it is literally 'to carry something from one place to another'. The watchmen of the bride's city become the 'apostles' and 'apostolic men'.[115]

For Bernard, God himself, in the Scriptures, offers us divine and spiritual truth in human and material guises. This mode of discourse, he says, answers to our needs as humans. Man naturally attains to intellectual things through sensible experience, and God respects the order that he himself has established. Nevertheless, God does not act out of any indigence, but rather from indulgence.[116] God surely understands that we are constituted rational not merely in virtue of the soul, but insofar as the soul inhabits a 'body'.[117]

Again, a metaphor raises up from the *sensed* particular to another *known* particular in virtue of the 'literal' representation of phenomena within the 'images'. Aristotle spoke of this as 'correct' transferral. We, through the uses of images and metaphors, both *perceived and spoken*, liberate ourselves from the welter of colliding sense experiences. *Ingenium* attains to higher and deeper insights, and these are spoken by metaphor, which both disguises and reveals realities *beyond* sense phenomena: 'Christ delights in the radiance and fragrance of virtues, and so he is said "to feed among the lilies". And so also he is fed at the house of Martha and Mary among the lilies of their devotion and virtues as radiant as they are fragrant.'[118] Thus, the metaphor allows us *to speak* the difference between what the senses experience and what human intuition creates.[119]

Yet metaphor surprises us: for there is a real cognitive space or distance between the *sign* and the *signified*. The subtle mental trick is to unearth what is common in each, and so express it, as to overcome the distance.[120] For when anything that can hardly be expressed in *proper* terms is expressed *metaphorically*, the meaning we desire to communicate is made clear precisely by the resemblance of the thing that we have expressed, by the *word* (metaphor) that does *not* belong, that is, the *alieno verbo*.[121]

---

[115]SC 77.3; SBOp 2:263; CF 40:123.

[116]SC 5.9; SBOp 1:25; CF 4:30.

[117]SC 5.1; SBOp 1:21; CF 4:25.

[118]SC 71.4; SBOp 2:216; CF 40:50–51.

[119]Cicero, *De oratore* 3.38.155–56; Loeb 2:122–23.

[120]Aristotle, *Poetics* 22.1459a, 5; *Rhetoric*, 2:24.1401b, 2; *Basic Works*, pp. 1479 and 1429.

[121]Cicero, *De oratore* 3.38.155; Loeb 2:123.

The distinction between simile and metaphor may also better help us to understand the hidden riches and accuracy of Bernard's *Super Cantica*. Similes are *expressed* and, to a degree, *external* comparisons; metaphors are *merely implied*. But they speak of something beyond simple likenesses, and move forward to express cautiously *a kind of identity*. This distinction opens the way to the larger question of analogy. The *Super Cantica* text includes not simply analogies of *attribution* based on casual relations, but analogies of *proper proportionality* rooted in *formal* similitudes as discovered by *ingenium*.[122]

In brief then, Bernard's phantasmic thinking and metaphoric expressions combine to corroborate Cicero's claim that the rhetor calls the authentically human world into existence. The metaphor manifests this because (1) it connects sensory appearances in order to assign them *unexpected meanings* and (2) because it connects these same sensory appearances to supply *answers to human needs*. For Bernard spousal love has an *unexpected meaning*: it images divine love; but it also supplies the *answer to our deepest human needs*: it answers the human need for divine union.

Simple perceptions issue in concepts or thought-objects, and are *expressed* in words or thought-terms. Frequently, Bernard's *ingenium* produces striking analogies that are not merely complex perceptions in concept/words, but are immediate inferences or judgements and their corollary propositions. Seeing relationships of likenesses, for all its immediacy, is, in fact, an intricate logical structuring. Yet the power of *ingenium* is to present the 'perception' as one.

Concerning the concept/word in isolation, it is evident that the descriptions *concrete* and *abstract* refer to an *understanding* of the *content* and *meaning* of the mind's object/word, what we technically call *comprehension*. On the other hand, the descriptions *singular* and *universal* refer to what is named extension, that is, the application to either one or many subjects. Bernard's comprehension most often appears as *concrete*, but his use of extension is both singular and universal.

Important for our understanding of inferences, or immediate judgements, is the derivative use of *concrete* and *abstract* in this context. The *subject* of a proposition is called concrete: the subject is seen as *something* to which one attaches *attributes*. (This is a strictly logical principle

---

[122]Aquinas, *De veritate* 2.11. 'Summarium: Analogia proportionalis *metaphorica*, i.e., in sensu improprio seu translatio seu figurato inest; Analogia proportionalis *proprie dicta*, i.e., in unoquoque subjecto intrinsece et proprie inest.'

since the some-thing in isolation, or in its extra-propositional state may be either concrete or abstract.) The *predicate* of a proposition, on the other hand, is seen as *abstract* because the *attribution* can either stand apart from the some-thing, or be applied to a variety of some-things. Hence, the true reading and exact understanding of words and their underlying concepts is to be found contextually in their logical, propositional usage, even when that use seems merely perceptional.[123] In rhetorical reading and understanding, a problem arises because the author's insight, which in the nature of things deals with contingents, seems to be arbitrary and hence of little value in the search for intelligibility. What rhetoric works with is a *suppositio* which is *accidental*; this means that the word that is accepted as a *subject of attribution* is, in fact, related to that attribution, that is, *predicate*, not by intrinsic relation, but by extrinsic and accidental relation. The genius of the rhetor 'discovers' the relationship of likeness and 'conveys' this to his audience.

Let us test these assertions against the bernardine texts. The Bridegroom's two breasts are, says Bernard, 'the two proofs of his native kindness'. He is *patient*, awaiting the 'sinner', and he is *merciful* 'welcoming' the penitent.[124] Thus the two divine attributes are seen as *like* the comforting support of the breasts. The insight starts from *support*: the support of God's patience and mercy, the support for sinner and penitent. While the rather concrete, *duo sponsi ubera*, are *de facto* removed from the abstract concepts of divine patience and mercy, yet there is a likeness.[125]

In another bernardine comparison, the bride is likened to the lily: radiant and fragrant. The bride must join good conscience to a good name, virtue to reputation; this is *her* radiance and fragrance. 'Therefore what proceeds from a pure heart and good conscience is virtue, white and shining; and, if it is followed by good reputation, it is *a lily, too*, for it has both *color* and *fragrance*.'[126] Moreover, the Bridegroom is to be attracted because of the bride's brilliance and scent.[127] For he dwells only with the virtuous and morally renowned. The Bridegroom is spoken of as 'hunc habitorem liliorum', so that, if the bride has lilies in her soul,

---

[123]'Suppositio dividitur: ex parte *significati*; secundum ordinem *ad copulam*; et ex parte *extensionis*.' See John of Saint Thomas, *Cursus philosophicus*, ed. Reiser, 1:31.
[124]SC 9.5; SBOp 1:45; CF 4:57.
[125]SC 9.5; SBOp 1:45, 12–14; CF 4:57.
[126]SC 71.1; SBOp 2:215; CF 40:48–49.
[127]SC 71.1; SBOp 2:214–15; CF 40:48.

he will dwell in her, 'habitantem in te'.[128] The immediate perception here seems to be that, as radiance and fragrance appear, so they attract; so, in like manner, virtue and good reputation attract and indwelling results. The concrete effect of lilies is so transformed that indwelling is effected. The space between *sign* and *signified* is thus bridged, but only because of Bernard's *ingenium*.

In another place, speaking of the breasts that are better than wine and smelling sweet of the best of ointments (Sg 1:1–2), Bernard declares the 'ointments worthy of the breast of the bride and capable of winning the Bridegroom's attention.'[129] He associates three moral qualities, or virtues, which, *like* fragrant unguents, render the bride attractive and the Bridegroom attracted. The first ointment (contrition) is pungent, causing pain; the second, devotion, mitigates and soothes pain; and the third (piety) heals the wound and rids the patient of illness, and hence kills the pain.[130] Here intuition relates the bride's aromatic ointments to virtue, and virtue's effects to the effects of ointment: *purgativum, temperativum,* and *sanativum*.[131] These perceived relations are ingenius.

Concerning the embrace of the Bridegroom, Bernard says: 'Happy the soul who reclines on the breast of Christ [Jn 13:25], and rests upon the arms of the Word. . . . The bride, as soon as she sensed the grace of his left hand, offered thanks without waiting for the teeming fullness of his right. . . . She did not go on to say that she was embraced at the same time by his right. She said rather it "will embrace me."'[132] The arms of the Bridegroom, the Word, express divine love and affection: the left hand, spontaneous and free love, the right, his agreeable response to the bride's gratitude which increases his love. Thus the concrete embrace tells of an unseen, divine love both gratuitous and rewarding. In this sermon Bernard defends his *ingenium*: 'We are taught by the authority of the Fathers and the usage of the Scriptures that it is lawful to appropriate suitable analogies from the things we know, and rather than coin new words, to borrow the familiar with which these analogies may be worthily and properly clothed.'[133] Lacking this choice, the conclusion is obvious: 'Alioquin ridicule ignota per ignota docere conaberis.'[134] In the text,

---

[128]SC 71.1; SBOp 2:214, 19–20; CF 40:48.
[129]SC 12.1; SBOp 1:60; CF 4:77.
[130]SC 10.4; SBOp 1:50; CF 4:63.
[131]SC 10.4; SBOp 1:50, 21–22; CF 4:63.
[132]SC 51.5–6; SBOp 2:87; CF 31:44.
[133]SC 51.7; SBOp 2:88; CF 31:46.
[134]SC 51.7; SBOp 2:88, 8–9; CF 31:45.

'See how he comes leaping upon the mountains, bounding over the hills [Sg 2:8]', Bernard sees a *likeness* to the Word's condescension in taking on himself our human nature. He has passed over the mountains and the hills, that is, he has passed over the higher and lower angelic natures to take up his abode and dwell in a house of clay, in a *lowly* human nature. Indeed, as a boy, he obeys Mary and Joseph; and as a youth he bows under the hand of the Baptist, each a sign of his condescension.[135] Earlier in the sermon, Bernard insists that the Church, the bride, beholds with joy her Bridegroom leaping and bounding, hastening to the redemption of this bride.[136] And he then explicitly warns against a *physical* interpretation of leaping and bounding: 'Verum non decet istiusmodi corporeas phantasias imaginari praestertim tractantes hoc Canticum spirituale.'[137]

Let us look at one final example. Bernard sees Paul's description of Christ's head in terms of Christ's divinity. Therefore, he thinks it not inappropriate for him to ascribe to Christ's feet his humanity. Of the feet he says: 'Let us call one of these feet mercy and the other judgement.'[138] Here the attributes pertain to the God-man! Christ was tempted that he might be merciful. He is the God who 'assumed the foot of mercy in the flesh to which he united himself.'[139] Since he knows temptation, he knows our need of mercy. As regards the foot of judgement/justice: 'Does not God-made-man plainly point out that this also belongs to the assumed humanity where he declares: "Because he is the Son of Man, the Father has appointed him supreme judge [Jn 5:27]."'[140] And Bernard concludes by seeking a relationship of likeness in another dimension: 'His certe pertansit et nunc, benefaciendo et sanando omnes oppressos a diabolo, sed spiritualiter, sed invisibiliter.'[141] The sacred humanity once physical, and visible to the world, continues its spiritual and invisible work, but spiritually and invisibly.

Let us now reduce our findings to their common denominator:

As the physical breasts of the Bridegroom support the bride, *so* do divine patience and mercy support the human soul.

[135]SC 53.8; SBOp 2:101; CF 31:66.
[136]SC 53.3, SBOp 2.97; CF 31:60.
[137]SC 53.3; SBOp 2:97, 27–28; CF 31:61.
[138]SC 6.6; SBOp 1:29; CF 4:35.
[139]SC 6.6; SBOp 1:29; CF 4:35.
[140]SC 6.6; SBOp 1:29; CF 4:36.
[141]SC 6.7; SBOp 1:29; CF 4:36.

As the lily is fragrant and radiant, *so* is virtue radiant, white, and shining, and good repute fragrant. *As* radiance and fragrance attract attention, *so* does the virtuous bride attract the attention of the Bridegroom and win his presence.

As ointments purify, soothe, and heal the body, *so* do the ointments of contrition, devotion, and piety, purify, soothe, and heal the soul.

As the two arms of the Bridegroom embrace the bride, *so* does God's unmerited and merited love enfold the soul.

As the Bridegroom's leaping and bounding over mountains and hills manifest his preference for the bride, *so* the Word's passing over higher and lower angelic natures manifests his preference for humanity.

As Christ's human feet tread on temptation and walk in justice, *so* does he continue to judge in mercy spiritually and invisibly.

In all of these instances the exigency of the *copula*, the demands of the joining and bonding element, although the *suppositio* and the attribute are distanced, is so strong that breasts, lilies, ointments, arms, leaping, and feet speak, through the rhetor's art, of spiritual realities as in *one* perception.

JUDGEMENTS

Ingenium's insights are not only perceptive; they are also immediately inferential. This is an important point because only in *judicare* does the knower declare truth, and the rhetor is concerned with truth. The pronouncement that two concepts agree or disagree with one another is the sole and basic expression of truth: the judge declares a thing to be true or false. But the *de facto* relationship between the subject and the predicate determines the quality of the pronounced or declared truth. A knowledge, therefore, of the modes in which dialecticians and rhetoricians cast these *connections* will clarify the epistemology of each species of discourse. Connections are said to be *necessary* in any fully logical pronouncement, while connections are said to be *contingent* in rhetorical statements. In rhetorical pronouncements, whether the inferences are immediate or mediate, the subject is *not contained* in the *comprehension* of the predicate; this constitutes its contingent nature. The subject and predicate are connected only by a *perceived similitude*. And this is not a subjective judgement, because the similitude is indeed present. As regards the words or terms, then, the juxtaposition seems arbitrary, but this speech is rendered *reasonable* by the *ingenium* which judges proportionate similitudes to be present.[142]

If the knower and speaker is called on to defend his *ingenium* and its metaphoric attire, he takes refuge in *experience*.[143] For the rhetorician, it is his experience which ultimately validates his insight; he communicates the experience by declaring his insight in metaphor; subject and predicate are in contingent relation. These are hard sayings for the dialectician. Connections, he insists, must be necessary; other connections are at best probable truth. But to this the rhetor replies: there are large areas of human life in which the establishment of necessary connections is not possible. And, in Bernard's case, his concern with mystical/ascetical doctrine places him in the area of 'contingent operables', an area where necessity cannot be established.

In its generic sense, the contingent is that which can be other than it is, or we may say that it is that which can be or not be.[144] The term can be applied to natural created causes, that is, non-human actions, and is spoken of by Aristotle as the *generabilia* and *corruptibilia*. The scientific community seeks out those 'conditions' which will assure us a *relative* amount of regularity, necessity, and predictability. But Bernard is concerned with what is changeable or perishable in human actions. His contingency refers to the vicissitudes of human attitudes, desires, and free actions. As in the case of natural created causes, here the rhetor aims at judgements of relative regularity, tentative necessity, and modest probability. And these goals are attainable only by 'contingent' connections. This is not, however, to deny that Bernard from time to time deals with propositions in which the comprehension of subject and predicates are related necessarily. In his famous critique of Gilbert de la Porée, Bernard makes a deft use of 'necessary' connections.[145] On other occasions, when inferences are not immediate, Bernard uses simple categorical statements.[146]

Bernard's judgements are sometimes made in extended metaphors, joined under the rubric of a common theme. So, for example, he imaginatively associates God's saving act with nutrition; the sinner provides the source of this nutrition: 'For I am a sinner; it is I who am the ashes

[142]SC 80.5; SBOp 2:280; CF 40:150.
[143]SC 24.7; SBOp 1:159; CF 7:47.
[144]Aquinas, *Summa theologiae* 1.86.3.
[145]SC 80.6–9; SBOp 2:281–83; CF 40:152–56.
[146]SC 20.4; SBOp 1:116–17; CF 4:150.

to be eaten by him [Gn 18:27].'[147] Then follows an ingeniously paired series: 'Mando cum arguor, glutior cum instituor, decorquor cum immutor, digeror cum transformor, unior cum conformor.'[148] Man's ashes are chewed, swallowed, digested, assimilated, and united with the ingestor. And corresponding to these divine nutritive functions, man's gradual salvific improvement emerges: man is reproved, taught, changed, transformed, and, finally, conformed. The subject, in passive verbal forms, *is united* to the predicates, also in passive verbal forms, contingently, and, at first blush, almost arbitrarily. God does not have nutritive processes, nor do nutritive processes terminate in moral improvement. But for Bernard, *just as* food, initially distinct from the one who eats, becomes through the nutritive processes *one* with the person nourished, *so too* man's ashes take on a 'higher' life in Christ feeding and fed, *unior cum conformor*. The concept of 'participation' explains the 'relationship of likenesses' between eating and salvation. What, at first, seems almost bizarre, through *ingenium* is made intelligible: the *stuff* of salvation is *sin*, the *term* of salvation *union*, the *efficient cause* of salvation *God, the bearer of sin*. And to the question of appropriateness Bernard says: 'Do not wonder at this, for he feeds on us and is fed by us that we may be the more closely bound to him.'[149] It may not be too far fetched to see in this series of judgements an incarnational theme: Christ's association with man includes his assimilation of man's ashes. The logically necessary union of subjects and predicates gives *clearer* understanding of a given proposition, but it cannot provide the *richness* and *width* of a contingent judgement.

ARGUMENTATION-RATIO

The combination of two truth-propositions by which the march of truth is assured is the fundamental ingredient of argumentation. When agreement or disagreement between the two propositions, by way of direct observation, logical analysis, or experience, is not possible, the mind is necessarily propelled into argumentation or *ratio*. Bernard is quite capable of *ratio*: he can, at times, make an effective use of demonstrative reasoning, but his preference is for the narrowly 'dialectic' reasoning of the rhetor, not to be confused with Abelard's dialectics. Bernard's

---

[147]SC 71.5; SBOp 2:217; CF 40:52.
[148]SC 71.5; SBOp 2:217, 14–15; CF 40:52.
[149]SC 71.5; SBOp 2:217; CF 40:52.

contemporary, John of Salisbury, explains the distinction. Demonstrative argument, he says, 'rejoices in necessity', and this necessity exacts from the mind 'necessary assent' because the truth proposed is independent of the audience.[150] The strictly or narrowly constructed dialectical argument leads to rhetoric's probable conclusions because it is dealing with contingent operables. This argumentation is defined by John as the 'ready instrument of moderate probability'.[151] Yet, as we have seen, Bernard's persuasions are ordered to something beyond intellectually probable conclusions. The persuasions move as nearly as possible to the judgement of election, and then onward to action. Bernard only repeats the augustinian doctrine: the rhetor is *to instruct* and *to move*. It is clear that in cases of *persuasive instruction*, 'to give one's assent implies nothing more than to confess that they [the established truths, but probable] are true.' But because instruction is for motion, the rhetor must '*sway the mind* in order to *subdue the will*.'[152] In this case, granted that all the conditions for a practical prudential judgement's *execution* are present, the *probable* conclusion leads to an *imperated* act, and with its special kind of urgency.

The principal and central instrument of rhetorical argumentation is the *enthymeme*; this is defined by Aristotle as the 'orator's demonstration'.[153] Cassiodorus describes it as ' . . . an imperfect syllogism . . . since, in order to gain credence, it employs an argument which disregards the law of syllogism.'[154] But because—as Aristotle points out—the *true* and the *approximately true* are apprehended by the *same* faculty, Bernard must have some radical understanding of the full nature of syllogisms to be able successfully so to condition them, and so defy their laws as to come to approximate truth and thus persuade.[155]

The first element in the construction of any *enthymeme* is the *inventio*, growing out of the *ingenium*, of a 'middle term', and a binding force to put premises together. So, for example, Bernard speaks of Christ as

[150]John of Salisbury, *The Metalogicon*, trans. Daniel D. McGarry (Berkeley, Los Angeles: University of California Press, 1955) 2.3.79.

[151]John of Salisbury, *Metalogicon* 2.3.79.

[152]Augustine, *De doctrina christiana* 4.13.29. English trans. in *The Nicene and Post Nicene Fathers*, ed. P. Shaff (New York: Charles Scribner's Sons, 1887) 2:583–84.

[153]Aristotle, *Rhetoric*, 1.1.1355a, 7; *Basic Works*, p. 1327.

[154]Cassiodorus (Senator), *Secular Letters* 2.11.12 and 14; in *An Introduction to Divine and Human Readings*, trans. Leslie Webber Jones (New York: W. W. Norton Company, Inc., 1946) pp. 156–57.

[155]Aristotle, *Rhetoric* 1.1.1355a, 10–15; *Basic Works*, p. 1327.

both Esau and Jacob; as Esau was black, so Christ is black; and, as Jacob is beautiful, so Christ is beautiful. Esau's hands are black; in his coverings we see our 'blackness'; mortality and death are our 'blackness'; our minds see the black; our senses tell us that Christ is black; but his blackness is exclusively so only to the foolish. Yet, like Esau, he is black, because he is associated with our 'fallen' race.[156]

Here Bernard's *ratio*, like its dialectical counterpart, needs a 'bonding' of propositions. Any doubtful comprehension (that is, inclusion) of subject and predicate in a *ratio*'s conclusion is only resolved by a comparison with *a third known idea*, the middle term. When subject and predicate are identified *with* and *in* this third term, they are pronounced identical to each other. In its logical formulation, then, this conclusion gives us the principle of identity.[157] When the third known idea is neither *with* nor *in* the subject and predicate, we have the logical principle of contradiction.[158] Identity and contradiction are not so cleanly cut in rhetoric's *ratio*: the perceptions are 'created', the judgements are contingently connected. Hence the 'bonding' of propositions takes on the color of the metaphoric and the contingent. At first, the inferences drawn from these sources appear somewhat arbitrary. But, on analysis, they manifest a subtle, consistent, and extended use of *ingenium*. And, while the kaleidoscope of singulars, particulars, and metaphors seem to obscure the 'truth', on careful study, these factors, which function as the *known*, are radically necessary as the only gateway to the *unknown*. The understanding of the full power of the *enthymeme* requires a study more prolonged than we offer here.[159]

Bernard's epistemology, deeply marked by his rhetoric discourse, defines knowledge as *practical*, truth as *prudential*, and certitude as *probable*, but *imperating*. Bernard's perceptions, judgements, and arguments are colored by his gift of *ingenium*. The linking of concepts and propositions is unfailingly contingent as Bernard addresses the mutable human situation. But the goal of his persuasion, by way of *logos*, *ethos*, and *pathos*, is never attained without the consent of his audience. Bernard labored diligently as a rhetor. He himself was practical, prudential, and was able to command. But his mind and heart were fixed on higher

---

[156]SC 28.2; SBOp 1:193–94; CF 7:89–90.

[157]Aristotle, *Posterior Analytics*, 1.9.10.11; 2.11.

[158]Aristotle, *On Interpretation*, 1.7.9.

[159]See Luke Anderson, 'Enthymeme and Dialectic: Cloister and Classroom', in E. Rozanne Elder (ed.), *From Cloister to Classroom: Monastic and Scholastic Approaches to Truth*, CS 90 (Kalamazoo, Michigan: Cistercian Publications Inc., 1986) pp. 239–74.

things: 'Surely when perfection is reached, nothing remains to be done. There remains only to enjoy it, not to bring it about; to experience it, not to strive for it; to live by it, not to carry it out laboriously.' But he can say it even more briefly: '. . . Ubi omnium negotium otium, soloque in intuitu et affectu res erit.'[160]

ABSTRACTS

Les épistémologies du XIIe siècle répètent les tensions de l'époque gréco-romaine. L'épistémologie de Bernard est colorée par des thèmes rhétoriques cicéroniens. Leur idéal commun est le mariage de l'*ars dicendi* et de l'*ars intelligendi*. Ils insistent tous deux que la rhétorique n'est pas subordonnée à la dialectique. Les notions chrétiennes de *caritas*, *dilectio* et *amor* influencent également les épistémologies bernardines. Pour Bernard l'union cognitive (intentionnalité) est absolument insuffisante si on la sépare de l'union affective (tendentionnalité). La structure psychique humaine de l'épouse doit être comprise en fonction de la transcendance divine de l'époux. Dans les *Sermones super Cantica* l'amour est en grande partie pratique, la vérité généralement prudentielle et les certitudes le plus souvent probables. Bernard préfère l'*intellectio* à la *ratio*. Dans ses perceptions, Bernard utilise l'*ingenium* et l'*ars inveniendi* de Ciceron; s'agissant du jugement, il recherche des connexions contingentes plutôt que nécessaires; avec 'ratio' il fait usage de la 'démonstration rhétorique', de l'enthymème et de l'épichirème. Sa pensée fantasmée est la racine de son langage figuratif.

Twelfth century epistemologies replay the tensions of the Greco-Roman eras. Bernard's epistemology is colored by Ciceronian rhetorical themes. Their common ideal: the marriage of *ars dicendi* and *ars intelligendi*. Both insist that rhetoric is not subordinate to dialectics. Christian notions of *caritas*, *dilectio* and *amor* also influence Bernard's epistemologies. For Bernard cognitive union (intentionality) is absolutely inadequate when separated from affective union (tendentionality). The bride's human psychic structure must be read in terms of the Bridegroom's divine transcendence. In the *Sermones super Cantica* knowledge is largely practical, truth usually prudential and certitudes most frequently probable. Bernard prefers *intellectio* to *ratio*. In his perceptions, he uses Cicero's *ingenium* and the *ars inveniendi*; in judgment he seeks

---

[160]SC 72.2; SBOp 2:226; CF 40:64.

contingent, not necessary connections; with 'ratio' he uses the 'rhetor's demonstration', enthymeme and epichireme. His phantasmic thinking is the root of his figurative speech.

Die Erkenntnistheorien des 12. Jahrhunderts wiederholen die Spannungen der griechisch-römischen Epochen. Bernhards Epistemologie ist gefärbt von ciceronisch en rhetorischen Themen. Ihr gemeinsames Ideal: Die Verbindung von *ars dicendi* und *ars intelligendi*. Beide bestehen darauf, daß Rhetorik nicht der Dialektik untergeordnet ist. Christliche Begriffe wie *caritas, dilectio* und *amor* beeinflussen die bernhardinische Epistemologie ebenfalls. Für Bernhard ist eine kognitive Einheit (Intentionalität, Absicht) völlig inadäquat, wenn sie von affektiver Einheit (Tendenzionalität) getrennt ist. Die menschlich en psychische Struktur der Braut muß gelesen werden in Begriffen der göttlichen Transzendenz des Bräutigams. In den Cantica ist Erkenntnis größtenteils praktisch; Wahrheit gewöhnlich klug und Gewißheit am häufigsten wahrscheinlich. Bernhard zieht *intellectio* der *ratio* vor. In seinen Erkenntnissen benutzt Bernhard Ciceros *ingenium* und die *ars inveniendi*; im Urteilen sucht er manchmal nicht notwendige Verbindungen; mit 'ratio' benutzt er die 'Demonstration eines Rhetors', Enthymeme und Epichireme. Sein phantasiereiches Denken ist die Wurzel seiner bilderreichen Sprache.

A TRADITION OF AESTHETICS IN SAINT BERNARD

Emero Stiegman
Saint Mary's University

THE STUDY OF AN ANCIENT AUTHOR should result in the uncovering of new areas of a tradition. Those who read Bernard of Clairvaux come upon an intriguing aesthetic power that is not accounted for as proper to the major themes of his spirituality, nor is it explained away as competent rhetoric. Viewing the architecture built under his administration, surveying the work of his scriptorium, and reflecting on his norms for effective chant leave us similarly bemused. Near the center of that pleasure taken in artistry which surprises us is an irrepressible theoretical question: is there perhaps an aesthetic principle, however unformulated, which guides this artist? For those, like myself, who cannot dismiss the question with a suspicion that cistercian art is the byproduct of monastic asceticism, the issue of theory remains. In the order of art and the beautiful, what were the assumptions and aspirations of the culture that formed Saint Bernard?

The point can be established that Bernard worked within a tradition of aesthetics screened from our view by later developments in the field. In christian spirituality there is no doubt: we can reach him only by breaking through the barricades of a later mode of theologizing. Just as that effort is judged highly profitable (because of the merit of the alternative mode), so will the pains taken to chart the intellectual landscape of art fixed in our author's psyche.

Our own range of vision can suffer constriction. The developments of our century conspire to challenge the narrow concept we have held of the western tradition. In spirituality, closer acquaintance with the Orient has led many to wish that Christianity were directed more toward vision, or enlightenment—until, happily for the dispossessed, the rich western stratum of contemplation is rediscovered.[1] In the domain of the beautiful, the wholesome scandal of modern art, with its frequently noted leanings to social morality and the transcendent, awakens us to the incompleteness of what we had received as our heritage. Paul Tillich lecturing at New York's Museum of Modern Art, speaking of 'ultimate reality' in his favorite pieces, was a generally welcomed reversion to a distant past.[2] Critics have at times felt that some of the twelfth century's art (romanesque sculpture, for example, and cistercian architecture) are of a twentieth-century spirit. A. Forest's comment on some elements of contemporary taste was that there exists in our times 'une véritable actualité de S. Bernard'.[3] Must we not suspect there was once a way of thinking about the beautiful which we have not altogether lost, but which our transient systems and ideological definitions of the tradition effectively exclude? It would be helpful to find a figure who exemplified that different way.

Today it seems natural to turn to Saint Bernard as such an example. In the past half century cistercian scholarship has reversed an unfortunate apprehension of the abbot's artistic mind. Erroneous readings of his *Apologia* and a failure to perceive the contemplative direction of his asceticism had formed obstacles to any linkage between what the generation admired in cistercian art and the writings of that towering figure presiding over its golden age.[4] Without such a connection, the difficulty of locating manuscript support for any specific *meaning* in cistercian art

[1]Northrop Frye, *The Great Code: The Bible and Literature* (Toronto: Academic Press Canada, 1982) p. 105, finds that, 'to many people today', the 'strongly moral and voluntaristic' nature of biblical religions compares unfavorably with the seeking of 'enlightenment' in oriental religions.

[2]Paul Tillich, 'Art and Ultimate Reality', *Cross Currents* 10 (1961) 1–14.

[3]A. Forest, 'S. Bernard et notre temps', in *Saint Bernard théologien: Actes du congrès de Dijon 15–19 Septembre 1953* (Rome: Curia generalis Sacri Ordinis Cisterciensis, 1953) p. 289.

[4]Saint Bernard's comments on monastic art, as known to historians generally, are contained in one of his earliest writings (c. 1125), *Apologia ad Guillelmum abbatem* (SBOp 3:61–108). See the translation of Michael Casey, with introduction by Jean Leclercq, in *The Works of Bernard of Clairvaux* 1, Treatises 1, CF 21 (Shannon: Irish University Press, 1970) pp. 3–69. The Latin text of St Bernard is from J. Leclercq, C.H. Talbot, and H.M. Rochais, *S. Bernardi Opera* [SBOp], (Rome: Editiones Cistercienses, 8 vols., 1957–1977). The *Apologia* has been studied comprehensively by Conrad Rudolph in *The 'Things of Greater Importance': Bernard of Clairvaux's Apologia and the Medieval Attitude toward Art* (Philadelphia: Univ. of Penn. Press, 1990). See also Rudolph's 'The Scholarship on Bernard of Clairvaux's *Apologia*', *Cîteaux: Commentarii cistercienses*, 40 (1989) 69–105.

was greatly aggravated. It is no accident that, in those years, the scholar who first demonstrated an unsuspected cohesiveness in Bernard's thought was also the one whose appreciation for the saint's artistic vigor was the clearest: Gilson, addressing himself in 1932 to historians, remarked of Bernard, 'One has to have a manuscript for a heart not to sense that he was an artist.'[5] A decade later, even while Ernst Curtius was perpetuating the tired stereotype of Bernard as 'anti-humanist', Edgar DeBruyne, with scholarly precision, demonstrated the aesthetic relevance of Bernard's religious thought.[6] Since that time, explorations of the abbot's literary artistry have been numerous, though the subject is far from exhausted. His powerful influence in the conception of cistercian architecture and in a cistercian style of manuscript production has been virtually established.[7]

To be exposed to Bernard's work is to want to know it more intimately. We cannot here study the artistry; limiting ourselves to the content of his language, we propose only to probe for elements of an underlying aesthetic, and to identify it in its tradition.

Aesthetics, in its formal sense, is a perilous bridge to the cistercian twelfth century, but it is finally so useful that its crossing should be attempted. As a systematic study aesthetics is a product of the Enlight-

---

[5]'Il faut avoir un manuscrit à la place du coeur pour ne pas sentir que c'était un artiste.' Etienne Gilson, *Les idées et les lettres* (Paris, 1932) p. 47, quoted in Jean Leclercq, 'Le Saint Bernard de Gilson: Une Théologie de la Vie Monastique', *Doctor communis* 38 (1985) 227. This may be a reminiscence by Gilson of a remark by Bernard himself, who had spoken of things to be possessed not *in codicibus* but *in cordibus* (SC 14.8; SBOp 1:81, 6).

[6]Ernst Robert Curtius, *European Literature and the Latin Middle Ages*, trans. Willard Trask (1948; New York, 1953), e.g. at 481. Edgar DeBruyne, *Études d'esthétique médiévale*, (Bruges: De Tempel, 3 vols., 1946), especially vol. 3:37–42.

[7]For Bernard's writing, see Christine Mohrmann, 'Observations sur la langue et le style de saint Bernard', in SBOp 2:ix-xxxiii. Of the many literary studies of Jean Leclercq, see 'Essais sur l'esthétique de S. Bernard', *Studi medievali* 9 (1968) 688–728; 'Problèmes littéraires', in *Recueil d'études sur saint Bernard et ses écrits* (Rome: Edizioni de Storia et Letteratura, 3 vols.) 3:13–212. For architecture, see Karl Heinz Esser, 'Les Fouilles à Himmerod et le plan bernardin', in *Mélanges Saint Bernard: XXIVe Congrès de l'Association bourguignonne des sociétés savantes, 8e Centenaire de la mort de Saint Bernard* (Dijon: Marilier, 1953) pp. 311–15. Marie-Anselme Dimier, 'Eglises cisterciennes sur plan bernardin et sur plan bénédictin', in *Mélanges René Crozet* (Poitiers, 2 vols., 1966) 2:697–704; 'Architecture et spiritualité cistercienne', *Revue du Moyen Age Latin* 3 (1947) 255–74. Regarding cistercian manuscript production, see Fr Jean-Baptiste Auberger, *L'unanimité cistercienne primitive: mythe ou réalité?*, Cîteaux: Studia et Documenta 3 (Achel: Administration de *Cîteaux, commentarii cistercienses*, 1986) 183–249. Among art miscellanies, see Meredith Parsons Lillich, ed. *Studies in Cistercian Art and Architecture* (Kalamazoo: Cistercian Publications, 3 vols., 1982, 1984, 1987).

enment, an age of rationalism and empiricism. Alexander Baumgarten (*Meditationes*, 1735), working within the cartesian tradition, wished to study poetry as knowledge: art, he determined, was about species and not individuals. John Locke's quest for truth, on the empiricist side, led him to conclude that metaphor was a 'perfect cheat'.[8] Match these ideas to Saint Bernard's reliance on experience, *cognitio sui*, and the expression of the deepest knowledge through images. Baumgarten coined the term *aesthetics*, from the Greek word for sensation (*aisthesis*). The study of beauty was now to mean the approach to the beautiful through the senses. The faculties are separated here for a clearer concept of their functions. Match this to the cistercian tradition, received from the Fathers, of *amor-intellectus* and the spiritual senses. The generation which envisioned that systematic approach to art and the beautiful which has governed all successive reflection founded its vision on postulates diametrically opposed to those accepted by Bernard and his models.

The Enlightenment, of course, did not pretend to initiate the human inquiry into the nature of art and beauty. But, looking back to an era that preceded the Enlightenment, from this side of the divide, will place us in the necessity of seeing through its lens. As we look through to that other time, we must continually transpose our assumptions into others. It would be dangerous to assume that because we have come to respect another *forma mentis*—that of the twelfth-century Cistercians, for example— we therefore possess it. Only with difficulty do we come sufficiently to hold suspect the inclination to believe that we are comfortable cultural comrades of the ancients we admire. Concerns of aesthetics, because they engage us at a level where self-examination is difficult, place us in special need of rehearsing this commonplace.

The caution should assist us in formulating appropriate questions for our subject. We will consider these: first (a complex of issues regarding the relation of beauty and art) what is the source of Bernard's idea of the beautiful? What did his era consider to be the objective of art? Was there an intellectual model according to which one explained the effectiveness of art? Secondly, what position does the concept of the beautiful occupy in Bernard's thought? What importance does it have?

[8]*Essay Concerning Human Understanding* (1690) 3.10.34. For this and other references to sources in the history of aesthetics in the classical and Enlightenment periods, I am indebted to Monroe C. Beardsley, *Aesthetics from Ancient Greece to the Present* (New York, 1965), and to Beardsley's 'History of Aesthetics' in *The Encyclopedia of Philosophy*, ed. Paul Edwards (New York: Collier Macmillan, 8 vols., 1967) 1:18–35.

PROPORTION AND LIGHT

Without formulating a theory, Saint Bernard manifests his notion of the objective of art. In his *Second Sermon for Christmas*, he speaks of God forming humankind from the clay of the earth and breathing into its face the spirit of life. 'What an artist!' he exclaims. *Qualis artifex, qualis unitor rerum, ad cuius nutum sic conglutinantur sibi limus terrae et spiritus vitae!*[9] Bernard is in awe of what he sees as the highest possible achievement of creativity, bringing unity to the most varied of elements, matter and spirit. Unity in variety as the essence of beauty defines that aesthetics of proportion which reigned in the ancient world and in the Middle Ages until the beginning of the thirteenth century, when an aesthetics of light replaced it. It is traceable to the *musica mundana* of the Pythagoreans, preserved in Plato.[10] A classic statement of it is found in Galen: 'Beauty does not consist in the elements, but in the harmonious proportion of the parts, . . . of all parts to all others.'[11] Beauty was transcendent, in the sense that every visible beauty was a proportionate participation in the good. When Augustine christianized this notion with the concept of a divine ordering of all things, he did not change it as aesthetics.[12] The principal mediator of this aesthetics to the Middle Ages was Boethius, who accentuated its mathematical character as found in Augustine's *De musica*.[13] The code words are

---

[9]Nat 2.1; SBOp 4:251, 16–252, 11. M. Kilian Hufgard, OSU, *Saint Bernard of Clairvaux: A Theory of Art Formulated from His Writings and Illustrated in Twelfth-Century Works of Art* (Lewiston, New York: Edwin Mellen Press, 1990) reflects upon this sermon—e.g., p. 57.

[10]'Beautiful things are made with care in the due proportion of part to part, by mathematical measurement' (*Timaeus* 87C-D; *Statesman* 284A). 'The qualities of measure [*metron*] and proportion [*symmetron*] invariably . . . constitute beauty and excellence' (*Philelbus* 64E; Hackworth translation). What the masters of Chartres studied in the *Timaeus* had always been the aesthetics of the West.

[11]Cited in Umberto Eco, *Art and Beauty in the Middle Ages*, trans. Hugh Bredin (1959; New Haven: Yale University Press, 1986) p. 29, n. 6.

[12]Augustine's thoughts on beauty are scattered through his works—especially in *De ordine, De vera religione*, and *De musica*. The dominant ideas are unity, number, equality, proportion, and order. The unity of a thing makes it possible to compare it to other things with respect to likeness (*De ordine* 2.15.42); and in this we discover proportion, measure, and number (*De musica* 6.14.44; 17, 56; *De libero arbitrio* 2.8.22). A 'divine illumination' renders judgment of beauty objectively valid (*De Trinitate* 9.6.10; *De libero arbitrio* 2.16.41).

[13]'Boethius provides the foundation-stone for what in the Middle Ages can be called aesthetics.' Hans Urs von Balthasar, *The Glory of the Lord: A Theological Aesthetics*, 4, *The Realm of Metaphysics in Antiquity* (1967; San Francisco: Ignatius Press, 7 vols., 1989) p. 325. Eco, pp. 30–31.

consonantia (an allusion to music and numbers), *congruentia, proportio, aequalitas.*

The language of Bernard and the Cistercians in this regard is linked to the Bible, where the same aesthetics obtains: all things are conceived as particular relationships to God. *Imago Dei* was a more meaningful concept than *animal rationale*. Wisdom 11:21 had provided the tradition with a text that made pythagorean ideas religiously intelligible: 'You have disposed all things in measure, number, and weight.' In the *Super Cantica* Bernard speaks of this measure in creation: the Word has truth, wisdom, and justice *ad aequalitatem* with the Father, while the soul has these *ad mensuram.*[14] This concept of measured, proportionate participation in the transcendent is one of those themes that caused the Fathers to suspect that Plato had plagiarized the Bible.

Despite the fact that we have a present-day version of this theme in our openness to saying that art works (particularly abstracts, or the abstract dimension of all art) are expressions of an ultimate reality, there is an essential part of the aesthetics of proportion that has been almost lost to us. We can identify this faded idea in a remark like the following from Saint Bernard's *De consideratione*: 'Observe the delightful and harmonious intermingling of the virtues [*concentum complexumque virtutum*] and how one depends on the other.' Here he invites us to contemplate 'the harmony of the four virtues,...their beautiful connectedness and coherence [*pulchram connexionem et cohaerentiam*]'.[15] If the beauty of virtue has a moralistic ring to the modern ear, it is because we have learned to perceive the intelligibly beautiful and the morally good as separate realities. The Scholastics accepted the aristotelian distinction between *praxis* and *poiesis* and discussed separately the *agibilia* and the *factibilia*.[16] Later generations would then find the relationship between morality and art problematic. To Saint Bernard and the culture that bred him, this relationship, at the level of theory, is not in doubt. What is properly proportioned, whether ontologically or morally, is one beauty. The *pulchrum* which is made and the *honestum*

[14]'Verbum est veritas, est sapientia, est iustitia: et haec imago. . . . Haec ad mensuram accepit, illa ad aequalitatem.' SC 80.2–3; SBOp 2:278, 1 and 23.

[15]'Ibi etiam advertere tibi est suavissimum quemdam concentum complexumque virtutum, atque alteram pendere ex altera. . . .' Csi 1.9; SBOp 3:404, 10–11. 'Intuere etenim nunc mecum etiam huius pulchram connexionem et cohaerentiam cum temperantia, et item ambarum cum duabus superioribus.' Csi 1.10; SBOp 3:405, 8–10.

[16]Curtius, p. 146.

which is done are not aesthetically different. The definitions of Plato, the Stoics, Plotinus, and the Fathers are clearly of the same aesthetics in this.[17] In the medieval conception of the microcosm, *homo quadratus* acted out his or her divinely proportioned being, an exemplar of the proportion between an action and its end.[18] Saint Bernard's maxim in the matter is his frequently quoted pauline exultation: *Gloria nostra haec est, testimonium conscientiae nostrae* (1 Co 1:12), a good translation of which, *secundum sensum*, is this: 'The only witness to our beauty is that of conscience' (or perhaps, stripped of classical elegance: 'Pretty is as pretty does').[19] We shall see, below, how *gloria* is the equivalent of *pulchritudo* or *decus*.

Here is the theoretical storm-center in the difference between our post-scholastic and Enlightenment approach to the beautiful and that of the old aesthetics of proportion. We are inclined to relegate talk of life-as-a-work-of-art—that is, of an aesthetics of action—to the area of figurative language. Umberto Eco, however, in an early treatise on medieval aesthetics, has rejected the notion that there is any latent primitive didacticism in the aesthetics of proportion. Thinkers in that culture did not separate the beautiful and the moral, 'not because of some defect in their critical sense, but because of the unity of their moral and aesthetic responses to things.'[20]

For Saint Bernard it is a matter of what he called whole knowledge, *integre cognoscere*.[21] He seeks, in the doing of the good, a *sapor boni*, an *amor virtutis*.[22] His comment on the distinction of the good into *honestum*, *utile*, and *delectabile*, is that where they existed truly they were one.[23] We read the *concordantia* of the aesthetic of proportion in

[17]Beardsley, 'History of Aesthetics', pp. 19–22.

[18]Eco, p. 36.

[19]P. Delhaye, 'La conscience morale dans la doctrine de S. Bernard', in *Saint Bernard théologien*, pp. 209–222, studies the importance of the pauline sentence in Bernard. *Gloria nostra* is not a boast but a rejoicing in the presence of God to which a good conscience is witness (p. 209).

[20]Eco, p. 16.

[21]'Si enim integre cognovissent, bonitatem qua pro eorum redemptione in carne nasci et mori voluit non ignorassent.' SC 8.5; SBOp 1:39, 3–5.

[22]'Et si quis sapientiam virtutis diffinierit, non mihi a vero deviare videtur. . . . Nec duxerim reprehendendum, si quis sapientiam saporem boni diffiniat.' SC 85.8; SBOp 2:312, 19–24.

[23]'Haec ubi vere sunt, unum sunt.' V Nat 5.7; SBOp 4:234, 10. Cited in Pacifique Delfgaauw, *Saint Bernard: Maître de l'amour divin* (Diss., Rome, 1952) p. 81, n. 43.

his reflection that 'The day must come when the work [creation] will conform to and agree with [*conformet et concordet*] its Maker.'[24] The aesthetic *concordantia* and the moral *conformitas* are one.

The aesthetics of proportion was essentially quantitative. There had always been a qualitative element in it, not really consistent with it but assisting as if extrinsically; this was an aesthetics of light. The contribution came from the immediacy of the experience of light. The simplicity of light had made it indispensable to the mystics of every age as a metaphor for God. But, in the early thirteenth century, when light wholly displaced proportion as the central aesthetic figure, a boundary in cultural history was crossed. DeBruyne traces a tradition through the cistercian commentaries on the Song of Songs: in relation to the newly exclusive aesthetics of light, which emphasized the intellectual as such, the cistercian sensibility was more broadly humanistic.[25]

The light aesthetic in the contemplative Bernard is strong (e.g., in SC 33.6, 45.9, 71.1), but not dominant. (In accord with biblical literature, which presents a God who 'speaks' but is never seen, he prefers metaphors of the ear to those of the eye.[26]) Writing of the divine Word or of the soul, he frequently employs such terms as *candidus, lucidus, spectabilis, rutilans, clarus*.[27]

The visual implications of radiance in the image of *gloria* are significant (e.g., 2 Co 3:18). If one looks for a category in the writings of the abbot of Clairvaux which simultaneously works within a light aesthetic while implying a proportionality of God's pre-eminent presence in the soul, then *gloria*, I suggest, is that category. In a deep sense, *gloria* is the beauty which can be predicated of God alone. (God can no more share God's glory with humans, says Bernard, than Pharoah could share

---

[24]'Quoniam tamen Scriptura loquitur, Deum omnia fecisse propter semetipsum, erit profecto ut factura sese quandoque conformet et concordet Auctori.' Dil 28; SBOp 3:143, 3–5.

[25]DeBruyne 3:37.

[26]For example, Bernard chooses precisely the text of the Song 1.14, 'Behold, how beautiful you are, my dearest!' (where he explains the bride's visible beauty), to express his preference for metaphors of hearing—SC 45.5; SBOp 2:52, 14ff. See Conrad Rudolph, '*The Things of Greater Importance*', 116 n.361: 'To Bernard sight is the principal sense'. The difference seems to lie in our present limitations as contrasted to our eternal destiny, and in bodily senses as against what the tradition called the spiritual senses. Frye, p.116, observes the predominance of metaphors of the ear in the Bible.

[27]Find these terms collected in SC 45.9; SBOp 2:55, 7ff.

his wife with Joseph.[28]) Bernard, then, is free to refer to the beauty of the soul and of creation as *gloria*, precisely because its meaning in christian tradition is so unambiguously analogical. 'Know what you are', he counsels, 'and that you are not that by your own strength, lest you fail to glory at all, or engage in vain glory.'[29] The glory we see in ourselves is not to be stolen; it is God's. On the other hand, we must not narrow the beauty of humanity by limiting it to what is of the creature, ignoring the essential dignity of the human being, which is the image of God.

Jean Leclercq points out how frequently Saint Bernard speaks of glory when one might have expected the term to be beauty.[30] Our point is simple: in his great fondness for *gloria* and all its related forms, Bernard reveals that he is treating his subject at an aesthetic level. This fact is opaque to those who read him as a pragmatic moralizer.

Even so rapid an overview of the history of medieval attitudes to the beautiful, from the point of view of Saint Bernard's work, can open us to accepting a few of the saint's dominant ideas as of interest to aesthetics. We must turn now to these ideas. Without suggesting that he can lay our problems to rest or that he lived in wholly admirable times, we may point out, from this side of the Enlightenment, the high degree of integration his culture achieved. The extent to which everything bernardine is a part of everything else is a challenge to our fragmented minds and suggests that an aesthetic approach may render him less elusive.

THE BEAUTIFUL IN BERNARD'S THOUGHT

It has been said that the abbot of Clairvaux speaks rarely of the beautiful.[31] Before narrowing our perspective to Bernard's text to ascertain whether this is so, we must concede that there is a certain development in the treatment of beauty through the Middle Ages. Hilduin in the ninth century (to pick an example) translated the biblical greek

[28]'Advertit homo Dei sapientia prudens, virum uxorem fortiter tamquam propriam zelare gloriam, sibique ipsi retinuisse servandam, non alii credidisse, et manum ad non concessum extendere non praesumpsit.' SC 13.4; SBOp 1:71, 3–6.

[29]'Utrumque ergo scias necesse est, et quid sis, et quod a teipso non sis, ne aut omnino videlicet non glorieris, aut inaniter glorieris.' Dil 4; SBOp 3:122, 8–9.

[30]'Essais sur l'esthétique de S. Bernard', p. 703. Christine Mohrmann, pp. xv-xvi, remarks that *gloria* (biblical *doxa*) is associated with a traditional synonym group for epiphanic terms, *apparere, declarare, apparitio, declaratio*. See also *claritas* at p. xv.

[31]Leclercq, 'Essais sur l'esthétique de S. Bernard', p. 694.

kalon (the beautiful) with *bonum*; in the twelfth century this became *pulchrum*.[32] Something had changed. At the height of the scholastic movement, Aquinas will not include beauty as one of the transcendentals (it is part of *bonum*), and his observations on beauty, which are admired to this day, are offered rather casually. Evidently we shall have to accept the thinkers of the era on their own terms, and Bernard among them.

When Dom Leclercq makes the observation that Bernard seems to have little to say about beauty, however, it is to concede that this is only superficially true and to correct the impression by a study of certain characteristics of the abbot's vocabulary.[33] (No one has so frequently and fruitfully returned to the subject of the aesthetic dimension of Bernard's work as Leclercq.)

Something of the feeling behind Bernard's aesthetic terminology is perceptible in his account of the first temptation in paradise (SC 82). First, the beauty compromised in sin is called glory: 'They changed their glory into the likeness of a calf who eats hay.'[34] Then, there are those words describing the sensuous attractiveness of the fruit in which Eve was deceived when 'her immortal soul of immortal glory was infected by the stain of mortality through her desire for mortal things':[35]

She saw that the tree was beautiful [*pulchrum*] to the eyes and pleasant to look upon and its fruit sweet to the taste. . . . O woman, this sweetness, this pleasantness, and this beauty are not yours. . . . What is truly yours is of a different kind. . . . What it [your soul] delights to possess, it fears to lose, and this fear is a color: while it colors your freedom it conceals it.[36]

The mistrust of what is 'beautiful to the eyes and pleasant to look upon' is clear. The 'color' of surfaces conceals inner truth.

This passage is representative of much in Bernard. It stands for the many ascetical texts which call us to self-knowledge and to a careful

---

[32]Eco, p. 21.

[33]Leclercq, 'Essais sur l'esthétique de S. Bernard', p. 694ff.

[34]'Mutaverunt gloriam suam in similitudinem vituli comedentis fenum.' SC 82.2; SBOp 2:293, 6–7.

[35]'Evam attende, quomodo eius anima immortalis immortalitatis suae gloriae fucum mortalitatis invexit, mortalia utique affectando.' SC 82.4; SBOp 2:294, 22–23.

[36]'Vidit, inquit, lignum, quod esset pulchrum oculis et aspectu delectabile, ac suave ad vescendum. Non est tua, o mulier, ista suavitas, ista delectatio, istaque pulchritudo. . . . Tua, quae vere tua est, aliunde et alia. . . . Enimvero quod delectat habere, id etiam perdere timet; et timor color est. Is libertatem, dum tingit, tegit. . . .' SC 82.4; SBOp 2:294, 25–295, 2.

weighing of reality, that we might come to 'know things for what they are' (SC 50.6). The theme figures so largely in Bernard's perception of the world that it can be taken to underlie an aesthetics of authenticity—a quest in which the danger of illusions is kept prominently in mind.[37] It in no way curtails his sensitivity to the transcendent beauty in which creation participates. To the contrary, it recalls us to the beauty commensurate with our own highest possibilities.

Nevertheless, if one becomes aware of an undefined discomfort with something in Saint Bernard's aesthetic attitude, this is likely the element to examine. For the abbot, the *regio dissimilitudinis* through which the soul moved was the earth itself; this is the consciousness from which his counsel to Eve in the garden proceeds. The degree of mistrust of all earthly beauty, whether of the senses or of the mind, is high. The determination to be undeterred and undistracted in the pursuit of that beauty which cannot be imaged or conceived is fierce. There is, of course, no doctrine which articulates degrees of mistrust. To explain preferences, Bernard appealed to experience, and his norm was simple: 'All things are allowed, but not all things are expedient' [see 1 Co 10:22].[38] He accounts for his life-choice of severe forms of abstinence with the heroically humble remark: '. . . because I am an unspiritual man.'[39] The mainstream of christian aesthetics in the West springs more from Saint Augustine's exuberantly expressed confidence in the fact that the world mirrored the divine than in the cautions of Bernard's reformed monasticism. And yet, few could have been as responsive to such a world as our 'unspiritual man'.

The desire to find a vocabulary of beauty in Saint Bernard seems to arise from the fact that it is the author himself who lifts his reader to the aesthetic register. We answer no meaningful question by counting how many times the word *pulchrum* occurs in Bernard's text. If we ask, instead, whether Bernard has an aesthetic approach to reality—if we ask for his evaluation of that which affords delight in its contemplation—

---

[37]I have spoken of this in 'Saint Bernard: The Aesthetics of Authenticity', in Meredith Parsons Lillich (ed.), *Studies in Cistercian Art and Architecture*, 2, CS 69:1–13. Self-knowledge, in Bernard's understanding of it, initiates the quest of the beautiful (p. 9).

[38]'Omnia licent, sed non omnia expediunt' [see 1 Co 10:22]. Apo 7; SBOp 3:87, 24. Here and in the following note, Saint Bernard explains his choice to become a Cistercian rather than a Cluniac.

[39]'Non quod scilicet Ordo sanctus et iustus non sit; sed quia ego carnalis eram, venumdatus sub peccato. . .' [see Rm 7:4]. Apo 7; SBOp 3:87, 24–25.

then we must answer that, for this author, everything in existence was seen in an *analogia pulchri, sub specie gloriae*, in the light of beauty. There is, in Bernard, a vocabulary of beauty, a family of synonyms and analogous terms; but a formalist quantifying of the phenomena will not yield as satisfying a result as will some determination of the character of his thought.

To this end, we might gather from the saint's works a vast augmentation of the evidence of that aesthetics of proportion we have discussed, along with his mystical use of an aesthetics of light. Certainly, while demonstrating his manner of conceptualizing religious experience, we would have to show its orientation to beauty. But, to abbreviate, let us move directly to what characterizes him very specifically—the aesthetic implications he sees in the traditional cistercian *amor-intellectus*—i.e., the insistence upon pronouncing love to be a true knowledge of God.

AMOR-INTELLECTUS IN SAINT BERNARD

We have spoken of the integration of the morally good and of the beautiful in the classical era and in the world of the Bible. In the patristic centuries this unity of object was matched by a unity of the subject. In the Platonism of the Fathers, *intelligentia* was not principally the domain of abstraction; it was equated with the spiritual.[40] Knowledge of spiritual being had to engage the entire person. Truth was an 'assimilation': one knew as one was, similar to similar. To provide a certain speculative apologetic at an important theological juncture, Bernard quoted the pythagorean maxim, *De ratione naturae similis similem quaerit.*[41] And, when he says that it is in virtue of the soul's likeness to God that it was *capax Dei*, he did not have to demonstrate that; it was a philosophical commonplace.[42] So, the very concept of intelligence approached that of love. One encounters the tradition well formed already in Origen as he reflects upon carnal knowledge in the Bible.[43] Once again we find something shared in the biblical and classical worlds—an integrated conception of the subject, this time—a conception logically prior to theology.

---

[40]Pacifique Delfgaauw, 'La lumière de la charité chez saint Bernard', Coll. 18 (1956) 44.

[41]SC 82.7; SBOp 2:297, 13–14.

[42] 'Harum rerum [iustitia, sapientia, veritas] nihil est anima, quoniam non est imago. Est tamen earumdem capax, appetensque: et inde fortassis ad imaginem.' SC 80.2; SBOp 2:278, 3–5.

[43]Delfgaauw, 'La lumière', p. 44, n. 11.

This is the tradition rediscovered by the early Cistercians in their quest for interiority.[44] It became the dominant trait of their spirituality.[45] It is the foundation of everything distinctive in the thought of Saint Bernard.[46]

Nevertheless, it is not a theme that Bernard isolated for systematic study. That was William of Saint-Thierry's contribution to the tradition, as David Bell has shown.[47] Saint Bernard twice quotes Gregory the Great's remark, *Amor ipse notitia est*; but these are passing references.[48] A common academic approach to the *amor-intellectus* theme leaves something to be desired: one studies it in William of Saint-Thierry, where it is clear, and then moves on to say that everything there applies *a fortiori* to Bernard, except that the saint is more affective. This perceptive critique is from Pacifique Delfgaauw, who also surveys expressions of the received wisdom about differences between William and Bernard and is discontent with the facile definition of Bernard as affective, not because nothing of it is true, but because what is easily and frequently clouded in this discrimination is the centrality of knowledge in Bernard.[49] It can be demonstrated that the abbot of Clairvaux orients the *amor-intellectus* theme to the light which love bestows.

This is meaningful to aesthetics, where, since its eighteenth-century inception as a discipline, there have always been lively discussions about the respective roles of the faculties. We have observed that Saint Bernard identifies beautiful action with beautiful being and associates all beauty with an ultimate cause and end; but we have yet to attend to his view of how the human being responds to beauty. His conception of *intellectus* will be significant in settling doubts about moralism in his thinking and in discovering the significance he gives to the ascertaining of beauty.

A useful approach to the notion and evaluation of *intellectus* in Bernard is to take notice of the scriptural text he employs most commonly to describe the fall of humanity. It is Psalm 48:13: *Cum in honore esset, non*

---

[44]Delfgaauw, 'La lumière', p. 45.

[45]Delfgaauw, 'La lumière', p. 47.

[46]Delfgaauw, 'La lumière', p. 47.

[47]David N. Bell, *The Image and Likeness: The Augustinian Spirituality of William of St Thierry*, CS 78 (Kalamazoo, Michigan: Cistercian Publications, 1984) pp. 217–49.

[48]Div 29.1 (SBOp 6/1:210, 11), Sent 3.127 (SBOp 6/2:249, 20). Notice also McGinn's remark concerning Saint Bernard's expression for freedom, *liberum arbitrium*: 'One great advantage of the term *liberum arbitrium* was its inclusion of the rational component in freedom.' Bernard McGinn, 'Introduction,' to *On Grace and Free Choice*, in The Works of Bernard of Clairvaux 7, Treatises III, CF 19 (Kalamazoo, Michigan: Cistercian Publications Inc., 1977) p. 8.

[49]Delfgaauw, 'La lumière', pp. 46–47.

intellexit—cited twenty-seven times.[50] If one overcomes the tendency to condescension regarding Bernard's exegetical methods, one asks why he accounts for sin as a case of not understanding—*non intellexit*. And the reward is the uncovering of another bernardine reversal of the process of ascent which we find in his first work, *De gradibus humilitatis et superbiae*, where the way down traces the way up. As we abridge the story, we must not lose sight of what is virtually its title, *non intellexit*; it is the story of the failure to know and of the consequent privation of knowledge.

The human being was created in the vision of God. Since Saint Bernard sees this as its state of normalcy as spirit, his fundamental exhortation is: *Vacate et videte quoniam ego sum Deus.*[51] Originally, human intelligence functioned without the mediation of the senses: *nec servili ad hoc indiget instrumento.*[52] Bernard's theology originates in a paradise situation to be regained.[53] God is purity, and only the pure can see God (see Mt 5:8). What might render the human being impure would be, not a flaw in its specifically seeing capacity, but a decision of the human spirit. We speak, then, of purity of heart.[54] Pure of heart in the beginning, humans possessed an intelligence—that is, a vision of God—like that of the angels.

From a collection of bernardine texts, we can reconstruct humanity's fall from *intelligentia*.[55] In the vision of heaven, it was the divine Word which nourished angels and humans alike (Tpl 12; SC 6.4; Adv 1.11). The Word was as well the teacher of the human being, who was open to God (Ann 1.6; see Jn 6:45). Humans knew other creatures through God, or starting in God. Bernard's nuptial mysticism, the relation of the soul to the Word, is grounded in this unity in spirit with God. Through the abasement of the Incarnation, the Word will pursue the soul by making

[50]Delfgaauw, 'La lumière', p. 53, n. 63, speaks of this as 'le texte classique' of the fall.

[51]Div 2.8; SBOp 6/1:85, 6–7.

[52]Div 2.8; SBOp 6/1:85, 9. Also: 'Deus innotescit mundis corde sine corpore.' SC 4.5; SBOp 1:20, 23. Cited in Delfgaauw, 'La lumière', p. 52. The vision of God is *purum et absque omni phantasia corporearum imaginum.* SC 41.4; SBOp 2:31, 3–4.

[53]Delfgaauw, 'La lumière', p. 52. Bernard makes his case frequently with Mt 5.8: 'Beati mundo corde quoniam ipsi Deum videbunt.'

[54]Bernard says: 'Cordis natura est puritas quia . . . cor humanum ad hoc factum est ut suum videat Creatorem.' Div 16.2; SBOp 6/2:145, 21–23.

[55]Delfgaauw, 'La lumière', pp. 53–55.

himself again knowable, beautiful, lovable, imitable.[56] The Bridegroom, then, in relation to the soul is never Jesus in the flesh but *Sponsus-Verbum, Sponsus-Spiritus, Sponsus-gloriae.*[57]

But, back to the narrative. Although the nourishment of the human spirit was the Word, says Bernard with the Psalmist (Ps 101:5), 'Man forgot to eat his bread, and his heart was sullied.'[58] 'While held in honor, he did not understand' (*Cum in honore esset, non intellexit*)—he did not receive the Word. Turning proudly from God in the disobedience of curiosity, the human distanced itself from its own heart. In *curiositas*, it curved itself toward the earth to seek the nourishment of the beast, and thus became a creature of earth (*terrestris*). The superior light of its spirit was extinguished: *cecidit a visione Dei.*[59] Human posterity would be born in sterility of spirit (*menti sterili*).[60] In the *interim* of its exile in the *regio dissimilitudinis*, the human being no longer has access to intelligence. The body is posed now as an obstacle between it and its Creator.[61] The *anima curva* is now too weak to look up.[62] *Ratio* functions instead of *intelligentia*: *Ratio discernit, intellectus capit.*[63] The permanent temptation will be to stop in reason, a knowing which is imprisoned within the self. What true knowledge attains beyond the self does not come from an *ob-iectum* outside the self; it is from a light proper to the heart. It brings about a union, a *commixio superni luminis et illuminatae mentis.*[64]

Incidentally, one cannot fail to notice in this story the mythological consistency, the imagistic coherence: the food of angels, for example, as against the forbidden fruit; the *intelligentia* displaced by *curiositas*

[56]I add 'beautiful' to the thought of Delfgaauw, 'La lumière', p. 53, in virtue of a text like SC 25.9; SBOp 1:168, 22: 'Quam formosum et in mea forma te agnosco, Domine Iesu.' Delfgaauw cites SC 6.3; SBOp 1:27, 14: 'Obtulit carnem sapientibus carnem per quam discerent sapere et spiritum.'

[57]Delfgaauw, 'La lumière', p. 53, offers, for *Verbum*, SC 56.1; SC 72.2; for *Spiritus*, SC 75.9; SC 53.4; for *Sponsus-gloriae*, Ep 126.6.

[58]The texts of Delfgaauw, 'La lumière', p. 53, are Nat 6.8; Miss 4.4; Div 2.8; Ann 2.4.

[59]Div 63; SBOp 6/1:296, 10–11.

[60]Csi 2.18; SBOp 3:426, 9.

[61]'. . . stante adhuc dumtaxat hoc ruinoso pariete corporis.' SC 57.8; SBOp 2:124, 15–16.

[62]'Istiusmodi ergo curvae animae non possunt diligere sponsum. . . .' SC 24.7; SBOp 1:159, 5.

[63]Miss 4.4; SBOp 4:50, 12. Delfgaauw, 'La lumière', p. 54, n. 71, notes that Bernard's vocabulary does not remain consistent here.

[64]SC 2.2; SBOp 1:9, 10–11.

directed to the tree of knowledge; the very physical *curva* attributed to
the soul which is nourished of the earth; and so on. The images bearing
each of the major bernardine motifs—they are gathered from the entire
opera—fit perfectly into one tableau.

This picture of the fall from paradise makes clear what the soul seeks
as she looks for her way back; it is *intellectus Dei*. One who misses
this orientation in Bernard's work, perhaps in a mistaken reading of his
affectivity, will fail to recognize the thought as a spirituality of vision—
as the word *contemplation* suggests. The aesthetic implications here need
not be labored.

Great aesthetic significance is found as well in Saint Bernard's *amor*,
though in this quick survey of *amor-intellectus* we can only point to
what that would be if it were developed. First, we would have to make
clear *amor*'s character as *eros*. Bernard wants to show how its *sapor*
grounds that *sapientia* which spills over into *intellectus*. Second, we
would enlarge upon *amor*'s bond to *intellectus* by studying the scriptural
texts to which the saint appeals for an interpretation of its meaning. The
principal one is 1 Cor 6:7: 'One who adheres to the Lord is one spirit
with Him' (*Qui adhaeret Domino*—which Bernard changes to *Deo*—*unus
spiritus est*).[65] He turns *adhaeret* into a sexual image, in a sentence where
unus spiritus est already denotes *intellectus*. The notion of love, under
the guise of desire, will carry with it the asceticism made necessary in
the fall, but this is almost incidental: the chief sense of love in Bernard is
joy, enjoyment, fruition (*frui*). It is the pleasure principle in the life of the
spirit. And, this function of love is unintelligible except as a dimension
of that assimilation and possession which is knowledge.

By inference we may say that in Saint Bernard love is always, ultimately, the love of beauty. The God whom he pursues is a God who,
in the *intellectus* of *amor*, the light of charity, is to be enjoyed—*quo
fruatur ad iucunditatem*. This is clear in his tract *On Loving God*, where
the fruition of love is represented as an intoxication of vision, an eternal
revelry.[66] It is most schematically stated in his last completed sermon
from the *Super Cantica* (SC 85.1), where one's progress to God is
represented in seven stages (we shall number them), and where each is
evaluated by its position in the continuum and each derives its meaning
from the consummation:

The soul seeks the Word, and (1) consents to receive correction, by

[65]Delfgaauw, 'La lumière', p. 67.
[66]'Comedite ante mortem, bibite post mortem, inebriamini post resurrectionem. Merito
iam carissimi, qui caritate inebriantur.' Dil 33; SBOp 3:147, 9–11.

which she (2) may be enlightened to recognize him, (3) strengthened to attain virtue, (4) moulded to wisdom, (5) conformed to his likeness, (6) made fruitful by him, and (7) enjoys him in bliss.[67]

'Enjoy him in bliss'? For a number of reasons, the abbot of Clairvaux is at times difficult to understand. One may inappropriately carry one's resistance to his political attitudes into the reading of his exposition of the christian mystery in its most interior reaches. One may see the institutional reformer and miss the witness to the life of the Spirit. One may fail to discern cultural gaps that divide us from him, such as the one made broadest in the Enlightenment, as we have here explained. One may be unprepared for the poetic sophistication of his imagistic Latin. But, no misunderstanding can be so radically falsifying as the one which construes him as a moralizer committing the monk to humanly unrewarding struggle and resigned to awaiting the enjoyment of God in the bliss that may follow death. His entire contemplative 'system'—for example, his encouragement to imageless prayer—contradicts this. The magnet of his consciousness is the beauty of God, now. He loves God because he experiences God as lovable.

In its richness, Bernard's concept of the light of charity is vastly more than that slim apophatic meaning (declaring the bankrupcy of the mind in divine things) which is, perhaps, frequently read into the cistercian *amor-intellectus*! The light that love sees is the beauty of God. The abbot's conviction is that we exist for beauty; God is approached by us appropriately and adequately only as the beautiful; our lives are fulfilled only in beauty. This orientation can be obscured when a reader confuses the seeking of pleasure in God—rightly held suspect—with the seeking of God, whose vision affords pleasure. As Bernard says: 'Quaerit anima *Verbum* . . . quo fruatur ad incunditatem' (SC 85.1). The augustinian view of beauty, which Aquinas would later reiterate (*id quod visum placet*), was held by Bernard in all its intellectuality: God was *enjoyed* in love because in love God was known—the *sight* of God gave pleasure. The affective Bernard, speaking for the enjoyment of love, is dependent on the intellectual Bernard, speaking for vision; or better, it is the knowledge of God which love affords that generates the joy in divine beauty which we recognize as Bernard's affectivity.

[67]'Quaerit anima Verbum, cui consentiat ad correptionem, quo illuminetur ad cognitionem, cui innitatur ad virtutem, quo reformetur ad sapientiam, cui conformetur ad decorem, cui maritetur ad fecunditatem, quo fruatur ad iucunditatem.' SC 85.1; SBOp 2:307, 14–17.

The man whose experience was of the depth we have been trying to suggest—sensitively attuned to a splendor at the heart of things, but nowhere less hidden than in himself, if he might only become himself—vibrantly responsive to a glory that loved him and called him out of himself—this man committed himself, in the buildings he envisioned and the chant he strove for and the sentences he wrote, to expressing that experience. The art works of Saint Bernard, which we have not considered, are attempts to represent, by the aesthetics of proportion, his encounter with God as longed for and enjoyed, the God in whom he rests. By definition this is God as beautiful.

That is why we read him now nine hundred years after his birth, and why we look for ways of saying to one another: 'Do not our hearts burn within us as he talks to us on the road and opens to us the Scriptures?'

ABSTRACTS

L'esthétique moderne découle des Lumières, époque dont les postulats sont à l'opposé de ceux de saint Bernard et de ses modèles. Son rationalisme est en contraste avec la connaissance de soi et l'*amor-intellectus*, son empirisme avec une esthétique des proportions commune à l'antiquité tardive et au moyen âge jusqu'à la première scolastique. Sa séparation des facultés et son refus d'inclure le moral dans le beau sont étrangers à l'univers de Bernard. Dans ses fréquentes références à la *gloria* (au sens néo-testamentaire), l'abbé unit l'esthétique des proportions à celle de la lumière. Dans un sens restreint, il se méfie plus qu'Augustin de la beauté sensuelle comme point de départ de la contemplation; mais son orientation vers Dieu concerne, bien plus qu'on ne l'a reconnu, la beauté ultime en tant que telle et la jouissance *présente* qu'on peut en avoir.

Modern aesthetics derives from the Enlightenment, an era with postulates opposite to those of Saint Bernard and his models. Its rationalism contrasts with self-knowledge and *amor-intellectus*, its empiricism with an aesthetics of proportion common to late antiquity and the Middle Ages up to High Scholasticism. Its separation of faculties and its exclusion of the moral from the beautiful are foreign to Bernard's universe. In his frequent reference to *gloria* (in a New Testament sense), the abbot combines the aesthetics of proportion and of light. He is, in a limited sense, more mistrusting of sensuous beauty as a starting point for contemplation than is Augustine; but his orientation to God regards ultimate beauty as such and the enjoyment of it now, much more than is generally conceded.

Moderne Ästhetik kommt von der Aufklärung her, einer Epoche mit Postulaten, die denjenigen des heiligen Bernhard und seinen Vorstellungen entgegengesetzt sind. Ihr Rationalismus steht im Kontrast zu Selbsterkenntnis und *amor-intellectus*, ihr Empirismus zu einer Ästhetik des Gleichmaßes, die der Spätantike und dem Mittelalter bis zur Hochscholastik gemeinsam war. Ihre Einteilung in Fakultäten und ihre Trennung von Moral und Schönheit sind Bernhards Denken fremd. Indem er sich häufig auf *gloria* (in einem neutestamentlichen Sinn) beruft, kombiniert der Abt die Ästhetik des Gleichmaßes und des Lichts. Er mißtraut in einem begrenzten Sinn der sinnlichen Schönheit als Ausgangspunkt für die Kontemplation mehr als Augustin es tut; aber in seiner Orientierung auf Gott hin bewertet er die letztendliche Schönheit und den Genuß daran im Jetzt und Hier viel mehr als es allgemein zugestanden wird.

VERBUM DEI ET VERBA BERNARDI: THE FUNCTION OF LANGUAGE IN BERNARD'S SECOND SERMON FOR PETER AND PAUL

Beverly Mayne Kienzle
Harvard University

BERNARD OF CLAIRVAUX perfected the beauty of his words in order to make them worthy of expressing the word of God. As abbot, Bernard felt the deep responsibility to communicate to his monks what the Holy Spirit made known to him, and that often necessitated fraternal correction; as sermon writer, he searched for words both beautiful and memorable that would fix themselves in the hearts of his audience. These concerns of abbot and writer are combined in the voice or *persona* of the preacher, the author of sermons who endeavors to convey the word of God with human words.

The opening passages of *Sermon Two for the Feast of Peter and Paul* are striking in the way they elucidate Bernard's careful use of rhetoric and the union of his message and method in the *persona* of the preacher. These passages will be analyzed in this essay and similar examples will be drawn from some other sermons, particularly those liturgical sermons from Rogation to Pentecost.[1] This analysis rests on certain conclusions about Bernard as a writer, and, before doing a close reading of the text, a few questions underlying those conclusions must be examined for the liturgical sermons: first, the place of these sermons in Bernard's

---

[1] *Sermons for the Summer Season: Liturgical Sermons from Rogationtide and Pentecost*, trans. Beverly Mayne Kienzle and James Jarzembowski, CF 53 (Kalamazoo: Cistercian Publications, 1991).

149

works; second, the manuscript tradition and Bernard's pattern of writing and revision; and third, the question of oral versus written form in the liturgical sermons.[2] The literary analysis that occupies the central part of this study is not intended to be exhaustive, but merely indicative of Bernard's careful attention to the beauty of his language.

First, what place do the liturgical sermons occupy in Bernard's works? In the *Vita prima*, Geoffrey of Auxerre described Bernard's works, writings, and preaching (*opus praedicationis*). He praised Bernard as a preacher who used language appropriately, addressing his audience on the level suitable for their background: learned for the learned and simple for the simple. When Bernard opened his mouth in the church, God filled him with the spirit of wisdom and understanding so that he could illumine hidden secrets. Along with these outstanding qualities of Bernard's preaching, Geoffrey included discretion, the ability to distinguish the time and place for encouragement or reproach (PL 185:306–308). Geoffrey's praises mirror the concerns of Bernard that we shall observe in *Sermon Two for Peter and Paul*: appropriate style, interpretation of God's message, and the fraternal correction enjoined on the abbot in the *Rule* of Benedict.

In discussing Bernard's works, Geoffrey of Auxerre counted the *Sermons on the Song of Songs*, the homilies on *Missus est*, and the *Sermon to the Knights Templar* among the books or writings, a clear indication of their composition as literary works.[3] The liturgical sermons are not mentioned among the writings but belong to the *opus praedicationis*.

From the manuscript tradition, what can we learn about Bernard's writing and revisions? From the work of Rochais and Leclercq, we know that the liturgical sermons as we have them, some 120 of them, also received careful attention as literary texts, and from Bernard's own hand. Study of the manuscript tradition has established four great series for the liturgical sermons: B (*Brevis*), M (*Major*), L (*Longior*), Pf (*Perfecta*). All the liturgical sermons are included in the Pf series manuscripts and

---

[2]For all of this background to my study, I am indebted to Jean Leclercq's work and to Emero Stiegman's study of genre for the *Sermons on the Song of Songs*: 'The Literary Genre of Bernard of Clairvaux's *Sermones super Cantica canticorum*', in John R. Sommerfeldt (ed.), *Simplicity and Ordinariness: Studies in Medieval Cistercian History*, *IV*, CS 61 (Kalamazoo, Michigan: Cistercian Publications, 1980) pp. 72–74.

[3]PL 185:320. See Jean Leclercq, 'Were the Sermons on the Song of Songs Delivered in Chapter?', in *On the Song of Songs II*, trans. Kilian Walsh, CF 7 (Kalamazoo, Michigan: Cistercian Publications, 1976) p. xiii.

consequently all were edited by Bernard himself during the last years of his life. *Sermon Two for Peter and Paul* is present in the B and Pf series.[4]

Jean Leclercq has demonstrated that during Bernard's process of revision or *emendatio* for the *Sermons on the Songs of Songs*, his attention was directed to stylistic improvements. He was preoccupied primarily with three aspects of his language: making his vocabulary more precise, modifying grammatical constructions to make his style strong and concise, and choosing words with greater euphony or musicality.[5]

Bernard's revisions to the liturgical sermons must have demonstrated the same concern with aesthetics. In *Sermon Four for the Ascension,* he uses the following image of the writer who endeavors to arrange words in a way that reveals divine mysteries:

> Just as a writer arranges everything for specific reasons, so the things that are from God are appointed; and especially those performed by his majesty present in the flesh.[6]

Hence we have sermons that have been revised and are works of literature. Are they still tied to oral form? Certainly the liturgical sermons more than others are rooted in cistercian daily life and are not completely removed from the style of their original setting. Emero Stiegman has pointed out that the *Sermons on the Song of Songs* deliberately imitate oral forms.[7] The liturgical sermons probably do likewise at times. Following Jean Leclercq's model for the *Sermons on the Song of Songs,*[8] it is possible to analyze the liturgical sermons according to various factors which may suggest actual delivery of certain sermons or passages within them: for example, length, use of second-person plural verb forms, and references to monastic life. Some sermons and some passages do appear closer to oral form than others, but it is difficult to draw

[4]See H. Rochais and J. Leclercq, 'La tradition des sermons liturgiques de S. Bernard', *Scriptorium* 15 (1961) 240–73.

[5]See 'The Making of a Masterpiece', trans. Kathleen Waters, in *On the Song of Songs IV*, CF 40 (Kalamazoo, Michigan: Cistercian Publications, 1980) pp. xvii-xx.

[6]'Sicut enim qui scribit, certis rationibus collocat universa, ita quae a Deo sunt, ordinata sunt, maximeque ea quae presens in carne est operata maiestas.' Asc 4.2; SBOp 5:139.

[7]Stiegman, 'The Literary Genre', pp. 72–74.

[8]See 'Were the Sermons', pp. viii-xxiv.

definitive conclusions.[9] One would expect that the written sermons of
a person who preached daily would generally reflect characteristics of
actual preaching.

The opening passage of *Sermon Two for Peter and Paul* does reflect
oral discourse in its consistent use of the second-person plural form
of address and its relevance to monastic life. The theme of fraternal
correction often appears elsewhere, however. Certainly Bernard must
have spoken about it often, and he doubtless revised his thoughts and
words on the topic many times. The voice or *persona* Bernard uses on
those occasions is generally that of the abbot. Here I have chosen to speak
of the *persona* of the preacher—at once abbot and writer—in order to
emphasize the strength of the writer's voice in this text.

The first three sections of *Sermon Two for Peter and Paul* are what
Bernard calls a digression. He reflects on his obligation to give fraternal
correction; like the vineyard-keeper he must apply manure to the fig
trees. After the opening passages Bernard returns to the feast itself, emphasizing that it commemorates the apostles' glorious deaths and urging
his brothers to follow the example of Peter and Paul in their lives, but
even more, to die as the two apostles died, having prepared themselves
with wisdom, understanding, and prudence. Thus the digression is closely
related to the eschatological message that follows.

These opening paragraphs clearly illustrate Bernard's concern for the
worth and beauty of language at a moment when he was worried about
the effectiveness of his message. Already in the sermon's second sentence
he expresses that worry: 'I do truly fear one thing: that words of salvation
heard so many times may begin to lose their value to us as words.' We
can imagine Bernard beginning another talk to his monks, concerned that
their minds were not totally fixed on what he had to say.

His next sentences are a literary tour-de-force by medieval standards.
The English translation reads as follows:

> A cheap and changeable thing indeed is a human word, of no space in
> time, no weight, no value, no solidity. It reverberates in the air (hence
> we say 'verb'), and, like a leaf caught by the wind, it floats, and there
> is no one who considers it.

The English only partially captures the highly figurative character of the
Latin. Beginning with the sentence where Bernard expresses the fear that
his message will be lost, it reads:

[9]These factors are examined in my introduction to *Sermons for the Summer Season*,
pp. 5–11.

Verum ego unum timeo, ne toties audita verba salutis vilescere nobis incipiant tamquam verba. Vilis siquidem et volatilis res verbum hominis, nullius morae, nullius ponderis, nullius pretii, nullius soliditatis. Aerem verberat, unde et verbum dicitur, et sicut folium quo vento rapitur, effluit, et non est qui consideret.[10]

The repeated alliteration with initial 'v' evokes the sounds of breezes: *verum, verba, vilescere, verba, Vilis, volatilis, verberat, verbum,* and *vento.*[11] The pronounced rhythm of the words *nullius morae, nullius ponderis, nullius pretii, nullius soliditatis* reflects the motion of the leaf blown about in the wind and away from the mind. The force of the two verbs, *rapitur* and *effluit,* conveys the escape of the leaf and the preacher's search to grasp for words of weight that will not drift out of his listeners' minds.

In contrast to the worthless human word, the word of God pertains to salvation and must not be allowed to slip away. Bernard issues a stern warning not to disregard the word of God on hearing it:

Let no one of you, brothers, so comprehend, rather let no one so reprehend the word of God. For I say to you: it would have been good for that man if he had not listened.[12]

He then returns to the leaf image, contrasting the word of God to the weightless leaf of the human word, and again he uses alliterative language:

God's words are the fruits of life, not the foliage; but if they are foliage, they are golden. Accordingly, let them not be slighted, not slide away, not slip by.

The Latin reads:

Fructus vitae sunt verba Dei, non folia; et si folia, sed aurea sunt. Proinde non parvipendantur, non pertranseant, non praetervolent.[13]

Garden imagery is pursued when Bernard introduces the parable of the barren fig tree (Lk 13:6–9). If still barren after applications of dung, it should be axed. Bernard explains the lesson drawn here, that God will have greater patience with people of the world than with monks who

[10]SBOp 5:191–92.

[11]The core of this series recalls Horace's 'Volat irrevocabile verbum'; Ep 1.28.71. See also Bernard's Pasc 2.9; SBOp 5:99, and note 2 below.

[12]'Nemo vestrum, fratres, sic accipiat, immo nemo sic despiciat verbum Dei. Dico enim vobis: Bonum illi fuisset, si non audisset homo ille.' SBOp 5:192.

[13]SBOp 5:192.

have had the benefit of the hoe of discipline and the dung of poverty and lowliness, and who have also been promised the rain of heavenly consolation. Therefore all the conditions for the tree's natural growth and their spiritual growth are met: the ground has been properly prepared, fertilizer applied, and the rains will come. Rain, according to Bernard, takes various forms: devoted prayer, pleasant repetition of the psalms, delightful meditation, the consolation of the Scriptures, and Bernard's very words. Bernard acknowledges the filthiness of dung, but states that it brings fruitfulness. An ugly heap of dung is carried into the field and a beautiful heap of sheaves is carried from it. Dung here represents the correction Bernard must give his monks. Hence Bernard's words are likened to heavenly consolation; they are human words, in appearance filthy, but capable of producing fruit.

Here Bernard's stylistic efforts are perhaps less elaborate, but still striking. The Latin reads:

Stercora plane vilia ad aspectum, sed ad fructum utilia. Non refugiat hanc foeditatem, qui fecunditatem desiderat: siquidem ex deformi stercorum acervo, qui portatur in agrum, formosus surget acervus manipulorum, qui reportabitur ex agro. Propterea non vilescat vobis vilitas pretiosa; sed pretiosius cunctis thesauris Aegypti, Christi improperium aestimate.[14]

We find alliteration with 'f' (*foeditate, fecunditate, formosus*) and 'v' (*vilescat, vobis, vilitas*) as well as internal rhyme (*vilia, utilia*) and parallelisms that reinforce the rhythm (*qui portatur, . . . qui reportabitur . . .*). The repetition of the 'or' sound laces together the first sentence: *stercora, deformi, stercorum, portatur, formosus, manipulorum, reportabitur*. All of this serves to make the passage stand out to a reader or a listener. The mere repetition of *stercus* in its various cases must have evoked strong images, both visual and olfactory.

After describing his lesson with imagery based on the daily work of the monastery, Bernard further brings the image to life, personalizing it and taking on the role of the vineyard keeper. As abbot, he is keeper of the garden, that is of the monastery and its trees, which are the monks. His position of responsibility requires him to dig about at times and apply manure. He speaks directly in the first person singular to explain that this is bothersome to him:

[14]SBOp 5:192.

Alas! I who have not cultivated nor kept my own vineyard am required, as long as I occupy this post, to dig around sometimes and to apply dung. This is a bothersome thing, indeed, but I dare not leave it undone, knowing as I do that an axe is much more harmful than a hoe, a fire than manure. Thus I have on occasion both to reprove and to chide. . . .[15]

Bernard continues, saying that he is aware that words of reproach are like dung. The one who utters them is less pleasant unless the words are excused by necessity. But the chiding of the just can bring about wholesome enrichment. One should receive it with mildness, respond to it gently and with gratitude, and willingly attempt to change. But while some are enriched by this manure of reproach, others perceive it as stones and persist in sinful ways.

Again Bernard's style is rhythmic and forceful:

. . . Nec ignoro fimum esse verbum increpatorium, verbum amarum, verbum improperii, et quod si non excuset necessitas, ipsum quoque minus deceat proferentem. Sed quid agimus, quod hoc fimo etsi aliquos impinguari, sed alios plane et lapidari, et indurari videmus?[16]

He reinforces the rhythm with the repetition of *verbum*, and he plays on the verb endings: *impinguari, lapidari, indurari*.

As Bernard finishes this reflection, he summarizes his purpose in delaying his address on Peter and Paul. What he has said instructs his brothers how carefully they ought to listen to whatever pertains to their salvation, even when they are being reproached, and receive it not as the human word but carefully, as they guard the word of God. The opposition between *verbum hominis* and *verbum Dei* forms the core of his digression. From the second sentence to the second-to-last, that pairing drives the thought and style of the passage. In the next-to-last sentence of this section, Bernard states:

These things I say, brothers, that you may know how mildly you ought to listen to whatever pertains to the salvation of souls, how devoutly you ought to receive it, and how carefully you ought to guard it, and

---

[15]'Heu! qui meam non colui nec custodivi, necesse habeo tamen, dum hunc occupo locum, et circumfodere nonnumquam, et apponere stercora. Molestum id quidem, sed dissimulare non audeo, sciens multo amplius securim nocituram quam sarculum, ignem quam fimum. Itaque et arguere, et increpare interdum necesse est. . . .' SBOp 5:193.
[16]SBOp 5:193.

'not as the word of humans, but truly as the word of God', whether it seems consoling, warning or even chiding.

The Latin reads:

> Haec idcirco dicta sunt, fratres, ut noveritis quam benigne audiendum sit, quam devote suscipiendum, quam sollicite conservandum quidquid ad animarum salutem pertinet, et non sicut verbum hominum, sed sicut vere est, verbum Dei, sive illud consolatorium, sive commonitorium, sive etiam increpatorium videatur.[17]

The sentence has a pronounced rhythm and balance accentuated by the three parallel constructions beginning with *quam*, their adverb and gerundive endings (*benigne, devote, sollicite*, and *audiendum, suscipiendum, conservandum*), then the three phrases introduced by *sive* and the adjective endings (*consolatorium, commonitorium, increpatorium*). Those adjective endings echo the ending of *verbum*, and its initial 'v' is echoed in *vere* and *videatur*, and within the words *noveritis* and *devote*.

Bernard ends this first portion of the sermon saying: 'I confess that I have digressed, nearly forgetting this feast, but not to your folly, I think, if these things you have heard adhere firmly to your mind.'[18]

Certainly Bernard's stylistic flourishes provide some adhesive for fixing his words in the memory. Along with the style, Bernard's admitted concern about the value of language distinguishes this passage in *Sermon Two for Peter and Paul* from similar passages with similar imagery where he speaks with the *persona* of the abbot reflecting on his responsibility for fraternal correction.[19] For example, in *Sermon Sixty-three on the Song of Songs*, he develops the vineyard and tree imagery with reference to a just person, and then compares young novices to trees in blossom and not yet bearing fruit.[20] *Sermon Forty-two on the Song* deals with fraternal correction. Bernard speaks of his obligation to reproach and says that he

---

[17]SBOp 5:194.

[18]'Excessi, fateor, ipsius propemodum festivitatis oblitus, sed, ut arbitror, non ad insipientiam vobis, si firmiter inhaeserint animo quae audistis.' SBOp 5:194.

[19]Bernard's ways of advising his monks in the sermons recall his styles of spiritual direction. See William O. Paulsell, 'Bernard of Clairvaux as a Spiritual Director', CSt 23 (1988) 223–31.

[20]*On the Song of Songs III*, trans. Kilian Walsh and Irene M. Edmonds, CF 31 (Kalamazoo, Michigan: Cistercian Publications, 1979) p. 166; SBOp 2:161–66. Paul Meyvaert points out this passage and other garden imagery used by Bernard in 'The Medieval Monastic Garden', in Elisabeth B. McDougall (ed.), *Medieval Gardens*, Dumbarton Oaks Colloquium on the History of Landscape Architecture, IX (Washington, D.C.: Dumbarton Oaks, 1986) p. 49.

fulfills the role of prophet and apostle, but considers himself unworthy of either.[21] In the liturgical sermons for Ascension and Pentecost, Bernard also justifies his duty to rebuke the members of his community. In *Sermon One for the Ascension*, he remarks that Christ rebuked the disciples just before his Ascension, when saddening them might have seemed inappropriate. Thus, if Bernard should reproach his audience, he would only be doing for them what Jesus did for his disciples.[22] Correction of the community is also a theme of *Sermon One for the Sixth Sunday After Pentecost*. Bernard relates to himself and his audience the order given the apostles in John 6:10 to make the people sit down. It perplexes Bernard, he says, to have to admonish people to sit down, but he must if they are to remain faithful to their monastic vocation.[23] The duty to rebuke when necessary is broadened to encompass the whole community in the *Sermon for the Feast of John the Baptist*. Bernard advises his audience that in certain matters they share this responsibility with him. Since to keep silent is to consent, they should not remain silent when they observe discipline being weakened in the order.[24] Fraternal correction is a theme of other liturgical sermons as well.[25]

---

[21]*On the Song of Songs II*, trans. Kilian Walsh, CF 7 (Kalamazoo: Cistercian Publications, 1983) pp. 210–229; SBOp 2:34–36.

[22]SBOp 5:123–24.

[23]SBOp 5:207.

[24]SBOp 5:182.

[25]Adv 3.5–7 deals with fraternal correction and the duty of monks towards their brothers and prelates; SBOp 4:178–81. In Sept 1.2, Bernard gives thanks that his monks are good listeners and states that he speaks to them often, even 'praeter consuetudinem ordinis nostri'; SBOp 4:346. QH 10 is also relevant. Bernard says that this time has been assigned to manual labor, not sermons, but that what God gives to him, he passes on to his brothers: 'Vereor deprehendi. Nempe horam hanc magnus ille et communis Abbas noster et vester non vacationi sermonum, sed operi manuum noscitur assignasse. . . . Et ego quidem non dubito, fratres, pluribus qui inter vos sunt abundantiorem spiritualium deliciarum suppetere copiam; sed quod vobis communico, non subripio mihi.' He explains that 'speaking' to them is his labor because of the illness that prevents him from doing manual labor: 'Verumtamen quod aliquoties vobis loquimur praeter consuetudinem Ordinis nostri, non nostra id agimus praesumptione, sed de voluntate venerabilium fratrum et coabbatum nostrorum . . . nec enim modo loquerer vobis, si possem laborare vobiscum'; SBOp 4:447. In Ben, Bernard reflects on being abbot; SBOp 5:2. In Pasc 2.9, he conveys thoughts about language used for reproaching, encouraging, and persuading and cautions against using words too lightly when they may harm the hearer: 'Videas multos, sincera licet intentione et benigno accedant animo, leviter dicere quod graviter audiatur.' Here Bernard directly cites Horace's 'Volat irrevocabile verbum'; SBOp 5:99–100. Finally, in OS 1, Bernard uses the image of spiritual food that he receives and distributes. ' . . . Non ego do vobis, sed Pater vester ipse est, qui dat vobis panem de caelo vivum . . .'; SBOp 5:329.

What sets apart *Sermon Two for Peter and Paul* is the combination of the theme of fraternal correction with the preacher and writer's expressed concern about language, that words of salvation are not heeded when so often heard, but that they must be guarded carefully, as the word of God and not as the human word. To grapple with this problem, Bernard as writer strives to make the worthless human word as beautiful as possible, to bridge the distance that separates the falling leaf that is the human word from the fruits or golden foliage that is God's word. By perfecting his language, the preacher seeks to ensure the nourishing power of his verbal fertilizer. Frequent alliteration, much of it echoing the 'v' of *verbum*, helps to tie the sermon together. Parallelisms, repetition of sounds, and plays on word endings mark the rhythm of his sentences. Contrary to the modern expectation that what is deeply felt will be simply expressed, Bernard's verbal acrobatics demonstrate the depth of his concern and emotion. Jean Leclercq has observed that Bernard's plays on words often serve as a psychic release, freeing a spiritual tension, and Christine Mohrmann stated that, as the level of Bernard's emotion increased, so did the movement and ornamentation of his style.[26] Bernard's intense love of the word of God drove him to perfect the beauty of his own words, to make the human word less volatile and to fix in his audience's memory the word of God conveyed by the words of Bernard.

ABSTRACT

Le deuxième sermon de Bernard pour la fête des saints Pierre et Paul met en lumière son désir de parfaire la langue du sermon afin d'imprimer ses paroles dans les coeurs des auditeurs et de communiquer ainsi de manière plus effecace à ses moines ce que l'Esprit Saint lui faisait connaître. Ce message avait souvent à voir avec la nécessité de la correction fraternelle. Les préoccupations de l'abbé et de l'écrivain s'unissent dans la *persona* du prédicateur qui s'efforce de transmettre la parole de Dieu par des paroles humaines.

Bernard's *Sermon Two for the Feast of Peter and Paul* elucidated his desire to perfect the sermon's language in order to fix his words in the

---

[26]Jean Leclercq, 'Essais sur l'esthétique de S. Bernard', *Studi Medievali* 9 (1968) 706; Christine Mohrmann, 'Observations sur la langue et le style de saint Bernard', SBOp 2:xxv.

hearts of the audience and thus to communicate more effectively to his monks what the Holy Spirit makes known to him. That message often dealt with the need for fraternal correction. The concerns of the abbot and the writer were combined in the *persona* of the preacher who strives to convey the word of God with human words.

Bernhards zweite Predigt zum Fest Peter und Paul zeigt sein Bestreben, die Sprache der Predigt zu vervollkommen, um seine Worte in den Herzen seiner Zuhörer zu festigen und umso wirksamer seinen Mönchen zu übermitteln, was ihm der Heilige Geist su erkennen gegeben hat. Diese Botschaft handelt oft von der Notwendigkeit brüderlicher Korrektur. Die Anliegen des Abtes und des Schreibers kamen zusammen in der Person des Predigers, der danach strebt, das Wort Gottes mit menschlichen Worten zu vermitteln.

THE USE OF PAUL BY SAINT BERNARD
AS ILLUSTRATED BY SAINT BERNARD'S
INTERPRETATION OF PHILIPPIANS 3:13

Denis Farkasfalvy, O. Cist.
Abbey of Our Lady of Dallas

THE USE OF PAULINE TEXTS in the writings of Saint Bernard is a difficult topic, especially because of its vast dimensions. Only a painstaking analysis of several thousand quotations could decide to what extent and in what way Bernard's theology and spirituality are 'pauline', as several authors have claimed.[1] For it is quite possible that his Paulinism does not go beyond the governing presence of a large yet limited number of 'favorite quotations', used with regular frequency and interpreted word by word, yet outside of their pauline context. If this is so, the main and central topics of Paul's letters would have only a moderate role in controlling or guiding Bernard's thought about God, man, Christ, and the spiritual life.

We cannot attempt to answer this large question in a small paper. Yet we may investigate it in a particularly interesting case: the use and interpretation of one of Bernard's favorite pauline texts, Philippians 3:13–14. What makes this study particularly interesting is the fact that Bernard—as he indicates in his second sermon for the feast of the Purification—is aware that his frequent use of this passage had been

---

[1]See G. Frischmuth, *Die paulinische Konzeption in der Frömmigkeit Bernhards von Clairvaux* (Gütersloh, 1933); or the conclusions in D. Farkasfalvy, 'Use and Interpretation of St John's Prologue in the Writings of St Bernard', ASOC 35 (1979) 205–226.

noticed by his audience. The passage is famous and is often quoted as a statement of Bernard's radical principle on spiritual progress:

> On the road of life, not to progress means to regress, for presently nothing can yet be in a permanent state. Furthermore, our progress consists in this (and *I remember having spoken of it quite frequently*) that we should never consider ourselves as having reached the goal as yet, but rather we must extend ourselves to what is ahead and try unceasingly to improve.[2]

The last few lines contain a free rendition of Philippians 3:13. Its frequent recurrence can be seen in Bernard's collected works: in his writings Philippians 3:13 is quoted twenty-five times, mostly in his sermons, particularly in those called *De diversis* which reflect his actual oral preaching better than many other texts. The lack of precision of the quotation is partly due to quotation from memory, but partly to the fact that the original text is somewhat awkward, even obscure, and therefore Bernard feels free to transform the pauline passage into a better balanced and, ultimately, bernardine latin sentence.

Some latin terms of the quotation obtain in Bernard's use a quasi-technical meaning, not found in pauline theology yet frequently recurring in Bernard's writings. In particular the verb *extendens*, which he either makes reflexive (*se extendens*) or passive (*extentus* or *extenta*), is applied to the spiritual person's soul with a special meaning. According to Bernard, the soul stretches itself out, 'grows', by its desires, when reaching out in inner acts of longing and yearning for the gifts of God. As a piece of dried and shriveled leather can be stretched out when permeated by oil, so the soul becomes pliable and increases its receptivity when it comes under the influence of Christ, the anointed one, or the Holy Spirit, the anointment descending from above.[3] This connotation of the expression *se extendere ad ea quae ante sunt* (to stretch out oneself toward those things that lie ahead) is certainly not pauline. But it fits well with both Bernard's favorite christological image of the *oleum effusum* (Ps 44:8) and his psychology of desire. Desiring great things from God makes the soul capable of receiving them; hence the importance of all prayers of petition as exercises of holy desires. In fact, he says, we cannot receive gifts that we do not ask for because the lack of praying would mean a lack of desire, a lack of appreciation for the gift and, thus, a lack of receptivity.

[2]Pur 2.3; SBOp 4:340.
[3]See Div 124.2; SBOp 6/1:403.

In Bernard's use of the pauline quotation, there is also a perception that the soul must possess a healthy restlessness; never should one be satisfied with the progress already obtained. This seems to be more genuinely pauline. It seems to expand on the original text's mood: the Christian should never pretend to have obtained the fullness of divine gifts, but must remain engaged in the 'running'—the reference is to some sort of an athletic contest aimed at obtaining a crown. We see Bernard explains this by combining Philippians 3:13 with another image derived from First Corinthians:

> Run, brothers, in such a way that you may reach the goal [see 1 Co 9:24: *sic currite ut comprehendatis*]. However, this can happen only if you do not think that you have already reached the goal but, forgetting about what is behind, you stretch out toward what lies ahead. . . .[4]

The 'forgetting what is behind' in our text is an expression that, through Bernard's use, gets substantially enriched, even transformed, by being inserted into the twelfth-century's anthropological thought on memory and oblivion. Bernard knows two kinds of forgetfulness: one that leads to sin and another that is part of one's conversion. The first is very well known: it is the *oblivio sui*, one's lack of reflexive self-knowledge which leads one to leave behind one's home—God's proximity—and to become a prodigal son in the *regio dissimilitudinis*. But there is another kind of forgetting: the one through which we leave behind the memory of our sins and, in fact, our entire past when we reach a certain radical inner detachment from our sinful past. In the sermon *De conversione ad clericos* there is an entire section speaking of how the memory must be cleansed, not by amnesia but by disowning our past evil deeds so much that we can look at them as if they had been committed by someone else. And Bernard says that, after conversion, the renewed person can become, indeed, 'another person'—so much so that this 'forgetting' actually takes place. One 'disowns' one's past sins of which one now begins to think as if they had been committed by someone else, not one's present self.[5]

Bernard enriches the end of Paul's text about 'reaching out to what lies ahead' by adding to it a variety of eschatological images: the palm of glory (*ad palmam gloriae*),[6] the palm of our heavenly calling (*ad*

---

[4]Ep 385.2; SBOp 8:352.
[5]Conv 28; SBOp 4:102–104.
[6]Ep 1.9; SBOp 7:8.

palmam supernae vocationis),[7] seeing the day of the Lord (*videre diem Domini*),[8] moving toward the spirit who is before our eyes, that is, in the future (*spiritus ante faciem id est in futuro*),[9] or simply 'eternity' and the 'promise' of heaven.[10] Similarly, the image of the past—all that we leave behind—is enriched by other biblical imagery to evoke monastic conversion: leaving home, even our people and our homeland, as Abraham did,[11] leaving all earthly things,[12] realizing that we do not have here an abiding city.[13]

Most noteworthy is, however, that in this pauline passage, Bernard finds an expression of his understanding of authentic spiritual existence as continued self-transcendence. This involves a constant attention to what one lacks rather than what one possesses;[14] it means a never ceasing urge to progress and to improve.[15] It also means being led by the Holy Spirit as a 'moderator'. Thus for him the meaning of Philippians 3:13 coincides with that of another pauline phrase: to walk in the Spirit (*in Spiritu ambulare*).[16] I find this vocabulary of self-transcendence quite significant: Bernard does not only speak about improving oneself, but of 'becoming always better than oneself' (*seipso semper melior effici studens*).[17] He also uses the word *transilire*, a biblical expression which, in this context, means 'jumping beyond' the self. This is a sudden and courageous change occurring under the influence of grace, so that one might become what one cannot be on one's own yet should strive to become: Christ-like, God-like, united to God by resemblance. The modern idea of self-transcendence is as well approximated by Bernard as one could expect in the following phrase: *quotidie se extendere ultra etiam mensuram suam* ('to extend oneself beyond one's own measure, one's own capability').[18] The *se extendere* here as elsewhere evokes

[7]Humb 2 (SBOp 5:442); Lab 1.2 (SBOp 5:218); Div 8.8 (SBOp 6/1:116).
[8]Lab 6; SBOp 5:226.
[9]SC 48.7; SBOp 2:72.
[10]Csi 5.32; SBOp 3:493. See Div 16.6; SBOp 6/1:148: 'ad aeterna bona se extendens'.
[11]Div 106; SBOp 6/1:106.
[12]III Sent 109; SBOp 6/2:185.
[13]Humb 2; SBOp 5:442.
[14]'. . . Plus attendis quae desunt tibi quam quae obtinuisse videris, oblitus quae retro sunt et extendens te in anteriora'. QH 3; SBOp 4:400.
[15]'. . . Semper extendamus in anteriora, conemur incessanter in melius'. Pur 2.3; SBOp 4:340.
[16]SC 21.4; SBOp 1:124.
[17]Ep 91.2; SBOp 7:240.
[18]Ep 443; SBOp 8:421.

Philippians 3:13. In the context the imagery describes one's daily effort to lift oneself above the earth, which means passing beyond the realm of bodily existence. The miracle of grace granting one a share in divine life is, indeed, represented here by the abbot of Clairvaux as an act in which some sort of a biblical 'Baron of Münchausen' grabs and pulls himself above the ground (*supra se quantum potest quotidie exaltare super terram*).[19] But, of course, Bernard does not intend such an absurdity; he simply states that for one to live according to the spiritual component of one's nature means a movement that leaves behind the bonds of bodily existence and that this truly happens when, under the influence of divine grace, one moves into a higher and better realm of existence.

My conclusion of this analysis of Philippians 3:13 in Bernard's works is threefold. 1) Bernard surrounds this pauline quotation with other quotations taken from Paul: running the race, to seek the things from above, to walk in the spirit, and other similar phrases are treated—and rightly so—as equivalent ideas. In these repeated references to general pauline theology, the quotation does not become diluted into anonymous 'biblical phraseology', but is carefully identified as the teaching of Saint Paul that can be shown to match Paul's personal life and experience. Bernard repeatedly points out that, in this quotation, Paul speaks about his own inner life which also serves as a concrete example for us to follow.[20] He frequently introduces the quotation as a call to follow the example of Paul, the Apostle!

2) The incorporation of Philippians 3:13 into the whole of Bernard's spiritual doctrine is made with the help of the patristic tradition. It is enough to refer to Saint Gregory the Great: his *Homilies on Ezechiel* Bernard explicitly quotes when explaining his understanding of spiritual progress as described in Philippians 3:13.[21] What is then specifically bernardine about the use of this quotation? My suspicion is that a couple of things are unique in Bernard's use of the pauline text. First, the understanding of conversion (one's breaking with the sinful past) in

---

[19]Ep 443; SBOp 8:421.

[20]The quotation is introduced with reference to Paul in at least eight passages: Lab 1.2; Ep 1.9; II Sent 109; Ep 15; De alt. et bass. cordis; Pre 44; Ep 91.2; SC 49.7.

[21]Pre 44 (SBOp 3:283–84) quoting *Hom. in Ez.* 1.3.18 (PL 76:814B). But the patristic roots go much deeper. Ph 3:13 is firmly established as a key text in the two greatest spiritual masters of greek patristics: Gregory of Nyssa and Origen. See R. E. Heine, *Perfection in the Virtuous Life: A Study in the Relationship Between Edification and Polemical Theology in Gregory of Nyssa's* De Vita Moysis (Philadelphia: Philadelphia Patristic Foundation Ltd., 1975) pp. 194–95, 241–46.

terms of 'forgetting' or 'loss of memory' seems to go a step beyond both Augustine[22] and Gregory the Great. Of course, these Fathers also speak of the memory of our sins, but they do not give a psychological explanation of how one forgets and leaves behind a past by becoming alienated from it and, in this way—literally—disowning it. Secondly, the bold description of self-transcendence as an understanding of *se extendere* seems to go beyond patristic antecedents and represent Saint Bernard's own rendition of the experience of spiritual progress within the context of the twelfth century's renewed interest in anthropology.

3) Furthermore, when Bernard appropriates this pauline verse fully into his own teaching, he attributes to its components—at least to the main expressions used in the sentence (*se extendens, oblivisci, anteriora, quae retro sunt*)—special meanings that refer to his own specific anthropology and system of spiritual doctrine. In doing so, Bernard not only couples the pauline sentence with references to his own personal spiritual experience,[23] but he also explains it in the context of his own structured understanding of man's inner life, based on concepts and insights that we must classify as belonging to the realm of a rather elaborate philosophical anthropology.[24]

ABSTRACTS

Cet essai examine le 'paulinisme' de la doctrine spirituelle de saint Bernard en se concentrant sur l'interprétation de Ph 3:3 qui, de l'aveu de

[22]On Saint Augustine's thought, I found very helpful the unpublished master's thesis of Sheila McGinn-Moorer, *St Augustine's Confessions: The Role of the Memoria in Participation*, submitted to the Braniff Graduate School of the University of Dallas.

[23]The references to experience are, of course, explicit at several places: 'reperisse mihi videor' (OS 2.2; SBOp 5:343); 'surgis desiderio...si demum ambulas' (Div 25.4; SBOp 6/1:190); 'attende cor tuum...cum Apostolo dicens' (Ep 1.9; SBOp 7:7); 'si attenditis, vestra vobis intus experientia respondet' (SC 41.4; SBOp 2:30); 'experiamur de verbo quod dixit [Ph 3:13]' (SC 48.7; SBOp 2:72).

[24]This last remark is important for counterbalancing certain characterizations of the so-called 'monastic theology' that deny its philosophical dimensions. This is endemic to the first definition of the 'théologie monastique' as much too rigidly distinguished from early scholasticism by Jean Leclercq in 'Saint Bernard et la théologie monastique,' in *Saint Bernard théologien*, ASOC 3–4 (1953) 7–23. Msgr. Zerbi's position on this point became more hardened at the Congress of Florence in 1974 in reply to my paper on Bernard's religious epistemology ('La conoscenza di Dio nel pensiero di San Bernardo,' in *Studi su San Bernardo di Chiaravalle* [Florence, 1975] pp. 201–214), pursued later in his introduction to Bernard's *De consideratione* in *Opere di San Bernardo* (ed. F. Gastaldelli) 1:738–40.

Bernard lui-même, est un verset souvent commenté dans ses sermons. Les vingt-cinq citations bernardines manifestent un riche héritage d'exégèse patristique; cette dernière, depuis Origène et Grégoire de Nysse, utilise abondamment ce verset à propos du progrès spirituel. Bernard le cite assez librement, transformant ainsi la formulation plutôt maladroite de la Vulgate en une phrase mieux balancée. Néanmoins, il s'attache de près aux mots-clef et donne un sens quasi technique à chaque expression, les référant à des termes importants de sa doctrine de la vie spirituelle. Ainsi une dose importante d'anthropologie augustinienne est liée à l'emploi de ce verset. La façon dont Bernard comprend l'expression 'se extendere' est assez particulière. Il met ce terme en rapport avec sa vue du progrès spirituel comme transcendance de soi sous l'influence de la grâce divine. Il semble que sa manière de comprendre la transcendance de soi dépasse les antécédents patristiques et représente les intuitions et l'expérience intérieure personnelles de Bernard.

This essay examines the 'Paulinism' of Saint Bernard's spiritual doctrine by focusing on the interpretation of Ph 3:13 which Bernard himself acknowledges to be a verse frequently commented upon in his sermons. The twenty-five occurrences of the quotation in bernardine texts show a rich heritage of patristic exegesis which itself, since Origen and Gregory of Nyssa, heavily uses this verse when speaking about spiritual progress. Bernard quotes the passage rather freely and thus transforms the somewhat awkward wording of the Vulgate into a better balanced sentence. Nevertheless he pays close attention to the key-words and attaches a quasi-technical meaning to each expression, by referring them to important terms of his doctrine on spiritual life. In this way a large amount of augustinian anthropology is connected with the use of this passage. Quite special is Saint Bernard's understanding of the expression 'se extendere'. He connects to this term his understanding of spiritual progress as self-transcendence performed under the influence of divine grace. It seems that his understanding of self-transcendence goes beyond patristic antecedents and represents Bernard's personal insights and inner experience.

Dieser Aufsatz untersucht den 'Paulinismus' der geistlichen Lehre des heiligen Bernhard, indem sie sich auf die Interpretation von Phil 3, 13 konzentriert, einen Vers, von dem Bernhard selbst bestätigt, dass er ihn in seinen Predigten oft kommentiert. Die 25 Vorkommen des

Zitats in bernhardinischen Texten zeigen ein reiches Erbe der patristischen Exegese, die seit Origenes und Gregor von Nyssa diesen Vers vor allem benutzt, wenn sie über den geistlichen Fortschritt spricht. Bernhard zitiert die Stelle ziemlich frei und überträgt somit den manchmal schwer verständlichen Wortlaut der Vulgata in einen ausgewogeneren Satz. Nichtsdestotrotz achtet er auf die Schlüsselwörter und fügt jedem Ausdruck eine quasi-technische Bedeutung bei, indem er sie auf wichtige Begriffe seiner Lehre und seines geistlichen Lebens zurückführt. Auf diese Weise ist eine grosse Menge der augustinischen Anthropologie mit dem Gebrauch dieser Passage verbunden. Ganz speziell ist Bernhards Verständnis des Ausdrucks 'se extendere'. Er verbindet mit diesem Ausdruck sein Verständnis des geistlichen Fortschritts als Selbsttranszendenz, durchgefürt unter dem Einfluss göttlicher Gnade. Es scheint, daß sein Verständnis von Selbsttranszendenz über patristische Vorläufer hinausgeht und Bernhards persönliche Einsichten und innere Erfahrung darstellt.

SAINT BERNARD AND THE *RULE* OF SAINT BENEDICT: AN INTRODUCTION

Francis Kline, ocso
Our Lady of Mepkin Abbey

THE *STATUS QUAESTIONIS*

THE FIRST CISTERCIANS have left us no formal commentary on the *Rule* which they held so dear. Many scholars have asked themselves why these benedictine reformers remained so relatively silent about the *Rule* they observed with such dedication. The closest the Cistercians came to an in-depth study of the *Rule* is, of course, Saint Bernard's treatise, *De gradibus humilitatis*, wherein the author takes us on a retro-tour of Saint Benedict's steps of humility, with all the fun that seeing things in reverse can bring. Saint Bernard, because he is the standard-bearer of cistercian spirituality, is the one to whom we shall look for an answer to the question: how did the Cistercians use the *Rule* of Saint Benedict? Our inquiry has a history, of course. So, before beginning my own contribution to the question, let me quickly review what others have said on the matter. Only then can the position taken in this paper be justified.

In its fiftieth anniversary year, Gilson's *The Mystical Theology of Saint Bernard*[1] has established itself as the starting point for all future commentary on the sources and theology of Saint Bernard. Whether we call Saint Bernard's theology 'mystical' or not, we cannot deny the fact

---

[1]Etienne Gilson, *The Mystical Theology of Saint Bernard*, trans. A.H.C. Downes (London, New York: Sheed and Ward [reprint 1955]). Also reprinted as CS 120 (Kalamazoo: Cistercian Publications, 1990).

169

that he constructed quite an edifice on top of something—something which was strong enough to sustain all that his mind could grasp. Gilson identifies that foundation as the *Rule*. Not only is the *Rule* a kind of presupposition to the spiritual thought of Saint Bernard, but it also acts as a catalyst in order to further monastic life into contemplative experience of the highest order. Some of the seminal ideas of Saint Bernard's theology—for example, the fact that *perfect love casts out fear*—come from, or at least are corroborated by, the *Rule* at its seventh chapter on humility.[2] The *Rule*, according to Gilson, is, therefore, a welter of ideas springing up into living thought for the Cistercians. It is far from being a lifeless code of usages. To find it in their writings, especially in the works of Saint Bernard of Clairvaux, we must use the bridge of ideas to cross to that place where it lies hidden within a speculative structure of the richest latin.

Whereas Gilson was mainly interested in a synthesis of ideas with regard to Saint Bernard, Jean Leclercq likes to view Bernard as part of the rich flow of tradition. His article, 'St. Bernard and the Rule of St. Benedict', in the collection of essays, *Rule and Life: An Interdisciplinary Symposium*,[3] considers with what literary and doctrinal means Saint Bernard uses the *Rule*. Saint Bernard apparently always has the *Rule* somewhere in his mind. More than a foundation or catalyst for other thoughts, the *Rule* is a major part of the saint's patterns of spirituality. In fact, after the Bible itself, the *Rule* stands as the most formative element in Saint Bernard's experience and teaching.

We get a better picture of what Leclercq is talking about when he states that Saint Bernard uses the *Rule* in the same way he uses the Scriptures. The *Rule* flows freely in and out of Saint Bernard's mind, simply because he meditated on it as a text of unimpeachable authority. The *Rule* became his own; its spiritual doctrine called forth from him a very creative response when he came to formulate monastic teaching.

Leclercq tells us that the *Rule* figures more prominently in Saint Bernard's monastic treatises and in the sermons *de diversis* and in the *Sententiae* than in the non-monastic treatises and the great liturgical sermons. Nevertheless, one must be ready to find the *Rule* anywhere in the works of Saint Bernard, since it played such a formative role in his own development.

[2]See Gilson, pp. 28–32: 'The Benedictine Ascesis'.
[3]Ed. M. Basil Pennington, CS 12 (Spencer, Massachusetts: Cistercian Publications, 1971) pp. 151–67.

Great teacher that he is, Leclercq points the way to new scholars who would take up this project. All the works of Saint Bernard must be combed through to find even the faintest allusion to the *Rule*. And then the mountain of data must be sifted and restructured to show the precise way in which the saint used the *Rule*. The résumé of Leclercq's article which I have given above already gives us a good idea of the main lines any possible future study will take. In fact, so complete is his analysis of his chosen texts that I wonder if Père Jean himself does not have in his personal index cards on Saint Bernard just about every allusion there is to the *Rule*. What a treasure house there must be in his cell at Clervaux!

Denis Farkasfalvy, the present abbot of Our Lady of Dallas Abbey, published in 1980 an article which moves the argument one step further.[4] Reasoning that Bernard's first and thus carefully considered treatise, *De gradibus humilitatis*, is based squarely on the *Rule*, and that his thoughts evolved very little once he started to publish in his maturity, we may have before us, in the *De gradibus*, an accurate indication of Saint Bernard's concept and use of the *Rule*. Since this treatise is his manifesto of monastic doctrine, Saint Bernard's use of the *Rule* here may give us important clues as to what to look for when we examine the rest of the corpus.

Saint Bernard's purpose in the *De gradibus* is to interpret for his contemporaries that quintessential part of the *Rule*, the twelve steps of humility in chapter seven. Bernard wants to appeal to his own experience and that of others. But how does one demonstrate the ascent to humility without compromising the very doctrine itself? The genius in Bernard listens very closely to his own experience and determines that one cannot show the way up, but one can tell what happens on the way down. He therefore reverses the steps and convinces his readers of the authenticity of his teaching.

Saint Bernard's move presupposes two fundamental steps which are indispensable for our investigation. First, by describing the twelve steps of pride, which are the exact reverse of the steps of humility, he shows how the *Rule* is indeed present in his own life. For he has wrestled with the text itself in order to bring himself in line with it, even though the often harsh, curt statements of chapter seven—perhaps the very heart of the desert tradition in the *Rule*—cut deeply into his twelfth-century sensibilities. Secondly, by struggling for a personal appropriation of the text, Bernard has seen fit to respond to it by appealing to a wide variety

---

[4]'St. Benedict's Spirituality and the Benedictine Rule in the Steps of Humility', ASOC 36 (1980) 248–62.

of sources in Scripture and Tradition. In other words, Bernard situates the *Rule* in a new theological context. As Farkasfalvy says:

> This context is much broader and wider than the one that Benedict has in mind, yet [Bernard's commentary] fits the words of the *Rule* so well that it lends them new riches and makes them appear as the description of the highest aim of human existence.[5]

Abbot Denis has demonstrated for us at least one of the major components of Saint Bernard's use of the *Rule*—the presentation to his contemporaries of his experience of it. Not only does Bernard make the text of the *Rule* relevant, he produces a remarkable synthesis of personal experience and monastic and theological tradition. The more faithful Saint Bernard was to the *Rule* and the wider tradition surrounding it, the more compelling did its message seem to his own time and situation. Saint Bernard's achievement is not a surprising, but rather a predictable conclusion, given the problem of infusing contemporary meaning into a centuries-old text. But what is eternally refreshing is the creativity which the polarities of his dilemma drew from him.

To Conclude the *Status Quaestionis*

Jean Leclercq has pointed the way, and it is easy to follow: one must look almost everywhere in Saint Bernard's writing, but principally in the monastic treatises and in the *Sermones de diversis*, for allusions to the *Rule*. How Saint Bernard struggled with the text of the *Rule* when writing his treatise *De gradibus* and what his purpose was in reformulating its teaching was the task of Farkasfalvy. From both of these writers we may forge a tool with which to continue our research.

Bernard at the Fountain of the Rule

Bernard is like a man drawing water from a well. On occasion he draws for his own sustenance, and therefore whatever he does is influenced in some way by the water. These are the ever present mild allusions to and the corroborative usages of the *Rule*. But, at other times, Bernard is drawing water for the specific purpose of giving others to drink of it. When it passes through his hand, it takes on some of his own personality, so that the thirsty reader tastes both the water and the

---

[5]Farkasfalvy, p. 251.

giver. All of the instances offered here fall into one or the other of these two categories. And, sometimes, we find both categories at work in the same allusion to the *Rule*. Nevertheless, the distinction proposed will be of help in appreciating Saint Bernard's use of the *Rule*.

I should like to return to the treatise *De gradibus*, not to its latter half, but rather to its opening paragraph. Saint Bernard blends his materials with such ease that we might fail to discern the considerable synthesis he has wrought using the image of the ladder of humility.

Saint Benedict makes no mention of Christ when he sets up his ladder. And though Christ is abundantly present as the very center of the *Rule*, there are places—and chapter seven is one of them—where twelfth-century monks who were forging a new christocentric spirituality, would be looking for something more. Saint Bernard proposes Christ as the goal to be reached at the top of the ladder. Using the johannine phrase, 'I am the way, the truth and the life' (Jn 14:6), Bernard shows how Christ is the *way* because he is the very form of meekness, and one can learn from him how to be humble in heart. And the *way* leads to Truth. But the *way* and the *goal* do not yet meet all our needs. We look for help on the way to the goal, and Christ gives that help by giving us his *life*. In an admirable formula, Saint Bernard illumines the inherently forward motion of his new Christ-ladder of humility: 'I am the way; I lead to truth. I am the truth; I promise life. I am the life, and life I give.'[6] The life which Jesus gives is a viaticum or refresher for those who languish on the way. Bernard's scheme is eminently geared to the problem of growth in monastic life! But he also seeks to make his thought generally applicable. The *way* of Christ is attractive to the erring and ignorant; while the *truth* of Christ reassures the doubting and incredulous. Not content with the *Rule*'s horizons of the first stages of conversion, Bernard, the contemplative, tempts the transcendent in us by describing the limitless speculation on Truth in Sion which is ours at the top of the ladder.

Throughout this intensely experiential and creative construction, Bernard never forgets his theme: Saint Benedict's ladder. In fact, the whole of the preamble to the steps of humility comes into play here when Bernard places Christ at the top of the ladder and has him gaze down on us to see if *any are wise and seek God*. The Christ who is at every moment (*omni hora*) seeking connection with us is the one whom Bernard preaches. This concept comes from *Rule* 7:13 and 7:27,

[6]Hum 1.1; SBOp 3:17.

as well as other places. Later on we shall see what a central position this benedictine theme occupies in the doctrine of Bernard.

Saint Bernard is intent on completing his picture of the most imminent Christ of the monastic way. Refreshment and rest are attractive to those who are laboring on the *way* of Christ. Jesus' words from Matthew 11:25–30 are interwoven throughout these few lines as a kind of binding and congealing element. Thus, the ladder of humility of the *Rule* becomes a christocentric doctrine of warm devotional character—a *vade mecum* for monks to live by. The evidence keeps suggesting a very simple fact. Bernard's aim is to make the doctrine of humility available and compelling to his monks. He seeks to sweeten, if he can, this most robust potion of christian monasticism.

Passing quickly to other bernardine works in which we might expect to find the *Rule*, we look briefly at the treatise *De praecepto et dispensatione*. At paragraph 16, Bernard sets forth quite completely his method of exegeting the *Rule*. He uses the standard triune formula:

> Obedience is 'good', according to our Father Saint Benedict, when one obeys out of fear of hell, or out of faithfulness to one's vows [RB 5:3]; it is better when one obeys out of love of God, substituting charity for necessity; and it is perfect, in my opinion, when the command is received in the spirit in which it is given. When the will of the subject is conformed to that of the superior, the subject, in carrying out his orders, will not be likely to confuse greater matters with lesser or lesser with greater, as often happens.[7]

Bernard is building on the *Rule* and, in so doing, developing his own doctrine. But it is not as if the foundation buried on the bottom and in the earth has no more to say about the shape of the structure above it. On the contrary, Saint Bernard remains faithful to the *Rule* and exhibits how his own doctrine only serves to highlight in more striking fashion the *Rule*'s teaching. A little later on in the same treatise, still speaking about the perfection of obedience, he says:

> I do not deny that the perfection of obedience is a difficult undertaking, but only for those who attempt it with the wrong dispositions. After all, it is a sign of an imperfect heart and a perverted will to examine cautiously the injunctions of our seniors, to hesitate at each command, to demand to know the reason for everything, to suspect

[7]Pre 7.16; SBOp 3:264. The translation is by Conrad Greenia, in *Bernard of Clairvaux, Treatises I*, CF 1 (Spencer, Massachusetts: Cistercian Publications, 1970) pp. 116–17.

the worst if this be denied us, never to obey willingly unless we are commanded something that suits us or which has been demonstrated to our satisfaction as necessary or useful. Obedience such as this is indeed a touchy affair and certainly a heavy burden as well, but this is not the obedience described in our *Rule*: 'Obedience without delay' [RB 5:1]. . . . It is no wonder that worldly souls are not only weighed down, but actually overwhelmed by this rashly assumed burden; for weak human nature simply cannot bear what is intended only for generous spirits [see Mt 26:41]. To such it is a light burden and a sweet yoke, because it is the burden and the yoke of Christ.[8]

With the return of the text of the *Rule*, 'obedience without delay', we see how Bernard's doctrine, no matter how creative, remains firmly and easily within the interpretive boundaries of the *Rule*. It is as though Bernard proclaimed the *Rule* to be an unending source of ideas and doctrine. Indeed, in calling the *Rule* a *turris evangelicae*,[9] he explains how this could be so. The *Rule* is quite simply a place where the Gospel can be found. With this advance in mind, we are encouraged to see how Bernard both drinks from the *Rule* and gives it forth as a foundation of his teaching on the Gospel and on the perfection of the spiritual life. This justifies us in looking beyond the obvious works having to do with strictly monastic and/or disciplinary doctrine.

One of the most remarkable examples that I have found of Saint Bernard's use of the *Rule* occurs, most surprisingly, in the *Sermons on the Song of Songs*. The work is sermon 10, and I limit myself to the first two sections. Bernard begins with a quotation from Romans 12:15: 'To rejoice with those who rejoice; to weep with those who weep.' This doctrine Bernard applies to a mother whose affections are conformed to her children, whether she be in joy or sorrow. The mother, as we know from the previous sermon, is the abbot himself. Bernard leaves little room for doubt that he is leaning heavily here on his own experience as abbot, though occasionally what he says may be applied to any spiritual leader— a bishop, for example. Scholars would point out to us that Bernard teaches the monastic life frequently from the point of view of his own experience as abbot. What he has learned from chapters 2 and 64 of the *Rule* (the chapters on the abbot), he sees as fit doctrine for all monks. Though Benedict's abbot is first of all a father, with none of the Middle

[8]Pre 10.23; SBOp 3:269–70; CF 1:122–23.
[9]Pre 10.23, 9; SBOp 3:270.

Ages' instinct for the feminine, Bernard's phrase in sermon 10.1 makes us think of the *Rule*: '... utrobique necesse est suis eam conformari visceribus'.[10] The clue is the word *conformari*. For Benedict has in 2:32: 'ita se omnibus conformet et aptet'. Saint Benedict seems to have divided his monks into two categories (or sometimes three), namely, the hard of heart or the more simple ones, and the capable disciples. This division is not the sorrowing and the joyful, as Saint Bernard describes them, but it is a two-fold division of his monks which Bernard seems to follow.

Bernard cautions those who are not able to give the appropriate milk to the joyful or the sorrowing:

> Should a person devoid of these affective qualities be confided with the direction of souls, or the work of preaching, he will do no good to others and great harm to himself.[11]

When the imprudent one assumes the direction of souls or the duty of preaching, he profits his disciples not at all, and he becomes an obstacle to himself. The direction of souls and the duty of preaching loosely reflect Saint Benedict's concern that the abbot encourage willing souls and exhort the wayward (see RB at 2:11, 23, 25, 27?). But there is little doubt that Bernard's '...ad regimen animarum...' depends on the *Rule*'s '...et arduam rem suscipit regere animas...' (2:31), or '...animas suscepit regendas' (2:34), or '...qui suscipit animas regendas' (2:37). Failure to live up to one's own preaching is castigated by Bernard in imitation of Saint Benedict: '...ne aliis praedicans ipse reprobus inveniatur' (2:13). Finally, Bernard's word *prodest* is probably an allusion to Benedict's *prodesse magis quam praesse* of chapter 64.

Saint Bernard continues with his description of the two breasts: the *congratulatio* of exhortation, and the *compassio* of consolation. The *congratulatio* is for those who are making good progress. Over them the abbot is glad, and he urges them on with encouraging words so that they might make further advances. The *compassio* is for those who are battered by temptation and, as a result, are disturbed, sad, and afraid. These require of the abbot words and gestures of solace and comfort. That we have here a transformation of Saint Benedict's discussion of the pastoral care of the abbot is clear enough. A closer comparison, however, is warranted if our tour is to be fruitful. Saint Benedict describes

---

[10]SC 10.1; SBOp 1:48–49.

[11]SC 10.1; SBOp 1:49. The translation is by Kilian Walsh, in *Song of Songs I*, CF 4 (Kalamazoo, Michigan: Cistercian Publications, Inc., reprint 1981) p. 61.

the two (or three) types of disciples in four places in chapter two. We have already seen (2:12) how the capable ones need only to hear the commandments proposed. The *duri corde* must see them put into practice by the abbot. Further on (at 2:23), Benedict advises the abbot to '. . . argue, obsecra, increpa. . . ' according to the situation at hand. He must vary with the circumstances, being now threatening, now stern, now paternal and loving. The undisciplined and rowdy (2:25) he must rebuke; the obedient and the meek, he is to encourage. But he must sternly correct the negligent and the contemptuous (see also 2:27 and 2:31). Clearly Saint Benedict's disciples are more drastically simple in how they differ from one another. Are the monks of Saint Benedict of a rougher and less cultured class, easily distinguishable as cooperative and unruly? Are their spiritual attainments less lofty than those of the Cistercians?

We shall probably never be able to answer this question with any degree of satisfaction, and it is not our task to attempt to do so here. Nevertheless, the same broad doctrine of Saint Benedict, namely, that the abbot should conform himself to the characters of his monks, is certainly at work in Saint Bernard's text. Saint Bernard transforms the father image into a feminine one. By his vocabulary he suggests that his relationship to his monks is expressed in terms, if not in actions, that are much warmer in affection than in the *Rule*. Close personal relationships also raise the possibility that the Cistercians may have been on a higher spiritual plane than the community that Saint Benedict knew. It may be, however, that the differences between them are no more than psychological in nature. Whatever the case, Saint Bernard has built his doctrine of abbatial care on the principles of Saint Benedict, not loosely, but strictly. Condensing the thought of the two sections under consideration, we see Saint Bernard using two central ideas of the *Rule* which he also quotes directly:

And you may see her unhesitatingly nourishing her little ones with the milk of these full breasts, from one the milk of *consolation*, from the other that of *encouragement, according to the need of each*.[12]

She becomes all things to all, mirrors in herself the emotions of all and so shows herself to be a mother to those who fail no less than to those who succeed.[13]

[12]SC 10.2; SBOp 1:49; CF 4:62. See RB at 34:1 (Ac 4:35); 55:20 (again Ac 4:35); and 64:14 ('. . . ut viderit cuique expedire sicut iam diximus').

[13]SC 10.2; SBOp 1:49; CF 4:62. See RB 2:32: '. . . et secundum uniuscuiusque qualitatem vel intellegentiam, *ita se omnibus conformet* et aptet ut non solum detrimenta gregis sibi commissi non patiatur.'

But the only way to discover this dependence is to sit long with the text of both authors and get beneath the diction and style to the normative thinking underneath.

Since we have penetrated to this level on our tour of the work, we must take note of another topic. In struggling with the text of the *Rule*, Saint Bernard seems to be asking the question: where does the abbot obtain the grace to minister so to his community? To put it in another form: what is the theology beneath the doctrine of pastoral care? The central and governing idea (question) is, after all, at the very heart of the *Sermons on the Song of Songs*. Saint Bernard formulates it in the most succinct fashion:

> As often as the spiritual mother receives the kiss, so often does she feel each kind [of pastoral care, for example, encouragement or consolation] flowing richly from heaven into her loving heart.[14]

Not only has Saint Bernard drawn into himself the very marrow of the *Rule*'s chapters 2 and 64, but he has also digested it and given it out again as a doctrine at once personalized and authoritative. One might even go so far as to say that the kiss of the Bridegroom is full of the flavor of the *Rule*. What Bernard receives from the *Rule*, transformed into divine teaching by the Word, he gives back to the Church in a form also given him by the Word. Contemplative experience is thus most eminently fruitful in the Church, and the very *disciplina* of monks becomes for them the very structure of contemplative theology.

We have examined specific *loci* where Saint Bernard spends time with this or that doctrine of the *Rule*. But if our line of thought is correct, we should also be able to identify in various works some pervasive doctrines from the *Rule* which Bernard has made his own and which serve to knit together his theology. First, we must look for consistent quotations or allusions in several sermons or works. We would do best here if we were also ready to see how Bernard may have assembled this doctrine from several places in the *Rule* and not just one place. The doctrinal block would probably also include some Scripture, in keeping with good patristic usage. Secondly, we need to see, as we have done above, what development Bernard makes of the *Rule*'s doctrine he has assembled. Because of the limited scope of this paper, I shall present only three of these doctrines in quick and cursory fashion. Yet they should be enough to point the way to a more elaborate investigation.

[14]SC 10.2; SBOp 1:49; CF 4:62 (adapted).

First, the doctrine of *omni hora*. Throughout the *Sermons on the Song of Songs*, but especially in sermons 9–32, there is a recurring theme of the intimate and ever-alert presence of God in the lives of monks. The *Rule* provides the material for this doctrine in the following places: the *ecce adsum* (Is 58:9, 65:24) which is so dear to those in conversion at the Prologue 18–19. God is ready at *every hour* to forgive the sinner (Prol 18). God calls to us *every day* (Prol 19). And we must know that God is aware of us at *every moment*, and that all our actions are seen by God and are everywhere and at every hour reported by angels (RB 7:10–14, 26–28). Consequently, we are to be vigilant at every hour over all our actions (7:28–30).

These are all significant and important *loci* for spiritual teaching. Bernard makes good use of them whether it be with regard to God's intimate presence to the bride (SC 9.4; SC 15.1) or to God's ready openness to a sinner (SC 9.5). At every hour the Holy Spirit waits to enlighten us (SC 17.2). At every instant, God stands ready to aid the poor one (SC 22.8), or to let the monk know what is acceptable (SC 22.8), just as, at all times, God protects the monk from carnal vices and from evil moments (SC 32.7). What was a fleeting pass at contemplative experience in the Prologue, or a stern warning about the constant vigilance we must keep in chapter 7, Bernard has turned into a spiritual teaching of compelling urgency and tenderness. Ultimately, we must call it the contemplative doctrine of continual prayer:

> How wonderful your love for me, my God, my love! How wonderful your love for me, everywhere mindful of me, everywhere eager for the welfare of one who is needy and poor, protecting him both from the arrogance of men and from the might of evil spirits. Both in heaven and on earth, O Lord, you accuse my accusers, you attack my attackers [Ps 34:1]; everywhere you bring help, always you are close to my right hand lest I be disturbed [Ps 15:8].[15]

The second doctrine is that of *vana gloria*. In the *Rule* it can be found at Prologue 5–7, where we read that we should never 'grieve God with our own evil actions [*de malis actibus nostris*], but rather let his good things [*de bonis suis*] work in us.' Those who experience God's help in this way know that it is not due to themselves but to God's initiative, and they cry out: 'Not to us, Lord, not to us give the glory, but to your name alone' (Prol 30 quoting Ps 113:9). Saint Benedict backs up his

[15]SC 17.7; SBOp 1:102; CF 4:131.

teaching by two passages from Saint Paul: 'By God's grace I am what I am [1 Co 15:10]', and 'He who boasts should make his boast in the Lord [2 Co 10:17]'.[16] Again, in the instruments of good works, Saint Benedict reminds us that 'if you notice something good in yourself, give credit to God, not to yourself, but be certain that the evil you commit is always your own and yours to acknowledge.'[17]

In Saint Bernard's mind, the pursuit of my own *gloria* or my own will is the worst of sins because it goes so contrary to humility. We need only think of his great difficulty with Abelard, who, in Bernard's opinion, was a *scrutator gloriae Dei*. God is only too willing to share his love and truth. But if, at such closeness, we choose to grasp at what cannot be ours, we plunge headlong into the worst kind of evil. This theme is frequent in Bernard's works. Of the first forty-one *Sermons on the Song of Songs* which I have studied closely, it appears in virtually every one. And just as frequently there is a strong verbal concordance with the key passages from the *Rule* which I have singled out above. It is not that this doctrine cannot be found in other patristic sources—indeed, it can with abundance. But it is so basic that Saint Bernard falls back on his primary sources of Scripture and the *Rule* to formulate it. *Vana gloria* is so fundamentally opposed to everything for which the *Rule* stands that Bernard evokes it freely when roused by its opposite. Let this text suffice:

> But where the error is dangerous, even fatal, there we are provided with a rule that is certain: not to attribute to ourselves what comes from God within us [RB 4.42, 43], thinking that the visit of the Word is no more than a thought of our own. The distance of good from evil is the distance between these two things; for just as evil cannot proceed from the Word, neither can good proceed from the heart unless it has been previously inspired by the Word, because a 'sound tree cannot bear evil fruit, nor can a bad tree bear good fruit [Mt 7:18]'.[18]

Finally, and very briefly, allow me to turn to perhaps the most monastic and compelling doctrine of them all—the *non quaerit quae sua sunt*; 'let the monk not seek his own' (1 Co 13:5). Only alluded to in the *Rule*, chapter 72, this small phrase from First Corinthians nevertheless sums up the whole of the good zeal of monks and perhaps of the *Rule* itself. Somewhat allied to the *conformet et aptet* doctrine of *Sermon 10 on the*

---

[16]RB prol, 32.
[17]RB 4:42–43.
[18]SC 32.7; SBOp 1:230; CF 7:139.

Song of Songs, which we examined above, it somehow crystallizes even more the essence of the monastic way. Chapter 72 of the *Rule*, especially when it quotes Romans 12:10 ('They should each try to be the first to show respect to the other'), captures the whole of it with help from First Corinthians 9:22 ('To the weak I became weak, that I might win the weak') and Second Corinthians 11:29 ('Who is weak, and I am not weak?'). Again, many of the *Sermons on the Song of Songs* carry this teaching. Sermon 23 shows it in its richness:

> Those who exercise authority for the welfare of others are comparatively few, and fewer still those whose power rests in humility. These both are achieved easily by the man of perfect discretion, the mother of the virtues [RB 64:19], the man who is drunk with the wine of charity even to contempt for his own good name, to forgetfulness of self and indifference to self-interest [1 Co 13:5; RB 72:5-7].[19]

Such a many textured passage as this, after we have studied to what extent Bernard has imbibed the *Rule*, demonstrates that his allusions to varied texts are deliberate and deep. It is marvelous how Bernard can balance such depth of meaning and the full resonance of words and still be clear and direct in his prose.

Both the taking in and the giving forth of the text of the *Rule* is what we have been privileged to see in this study. From the examination of single and obvious passages dependent on the *Rule*, we have passed to the growing synthesis of doctrines that hold from work to work, and, finally, to passages of great evocative power where the allusions are legion but still massively developed. That nothing is to be taken lightly or for granted when studying a bernardine text is the conclusion. A basis, the *Rule* surely is. A catalyst for development, it must be also. An authoritative text, too, we can safely call it. But perhaps the final word is that Saint Bernard acts as a disciple of the *Rule*, but a very mature one who can dialogue with the Master, and stretch and embellish and flex him as if he were a muscle in one's own body. Only sovereign freedom acts like this, and only a well-developed psychology. Utter faithfulness and devotion alone can earn such a freedom.

The lines of investigation given here are only an introduction to what would have to be an exhaustive study of every bernardine text in the light of the *Rule*. I only hope I have given some glimpse of the rewards that await such an undertaking.

[19]SC 23.8; SBOp 1:144; CF 7:32.

ABSTRACTS

L'article présente l'état de la question quant à l'influence de la RB dans les oeuvres de saint Bernard. Tant Gilson que Leclercq ont rédigé des chapitres ou des articles sur ce sujet. Farkasfalvy a étudié la deuxième partie du *De gradibus humilitatis*, qui est le commentaire de saint Bernard sur la Règle.

L'examen de plusieurs passages-clef des oeuvres de Bernard indique sa profonde familiarité avec la RB et l'exégèse qu'il en faisait à l'intention de son auditoire du XIIe siècle. Les premiers paragraphes du *De gradibus* et les paragraphes 16 et 23 du *De praecepto et dispensatione* servent à montrer respectivement la préoccupation christologique de Bernard à propos du chapitre 7 de la RB et son enseignement doctrinal sur l'obéissance à propos du chapitre 5. Mais la RB n'est pas absente des oeuvres plus spéculatives de Bernard elles-mêmes. Dans le dixième sermon sur le Cantique, nous trouvons un traitement étendu (et une transformation) de rôle de l'abbé sur la base des chapitres 2 et 64 de la RB. En fait, Bernard rassemble en grappes des doctrines-clef de la RB prises dans différents chapitres et les présente dans ses oeuvres comme autant d'îles flottantes dans sa mer. Un examen des sermons 1–41 sur le Cantique des Cantiques permet d'identifier au moins trois de ces blocs doctrinaux, mais il y en a davantage. Parmi eux: *omni hora*, tiré largement de RB 7:10–14, 26–30. Puis, *vana gloria*, de RB Prol 5–7, 30–32 et 4:42–43; et enfin, *non quaerit quae sua sunt*, un développement élaboré de RB 72:7 fondé sur 1 Co 13:5, 1 Co 9:22 et 2 Co 11:29.

The paper presents the *status quaestionis* of the influence of the RB in the works of Saint Bernard. Both Gilson and Leclercq have offered chapters or articles on this topic. Farkasfalvy has studied the latter half of *De gradibus humilitatis*, which is Bernard's commentary on the RB. An examination of several key passages in Bernard's writings indicates his profound familiarity with the RB and the way he exegeted it for his twelfth-century audience. The opening numbers of *De gradibus* and numbers 16 and 23 of *De praecepto et dispensatione* serve to show Bernard's christological concern over chapter seven of the RB and his doctrinal teaching on obedience at RB chapter five, respectively. But the RB is not absent even from the more speculative works of Bernard. In Sermon 10 on the Song of Songs, we have an extended treatment (and transformation) of the abbot's role based on chapters two and sixty-four of the RB. In fact, Bernard clusters together from various chapters, key doctrines of the RB and presents them in his works as so many floating islands in his sea. Scrutiny of Sermons 1–41 on the Song of Songs identifies at least three of these doctrinal blocks, but there are more. Among them: *omni hora*, taken largely from RB 7:10–14, 26–30. Next, *vana gloria*, from RB Prol 5–7, 30–32 and 4:42–43; and finally, *non quaerit quae sua sunt*, an elaborate development of RB 72:7, based on 1 Co 13:5, 1 Co 9:22 and 2 Co 11:29.

Das Papier bietet den *status quaestionis* des Einflusses der Benediktregel auf die Werke des heiligen Bernhard. Sowohl Gilson als auch Leclercq haben diesem Thema Kapitel oder Artikel gewidmet. Farkasfalvy hat die letzte Hälfte von *De gradibus humilitatis* untersucht, die Bernhards Kommentar zur Benediktregel darstellt.

Eine Überprüfung mehrerer Schlüsselpassagen in Bernhards Schriften zeigt seine genaue Kenntnis mit der Benediktregel und die Art, in der er sie für das Publikum des 12. Jahrhunderts auslegte. Die einführenden Abschnitte von *De gradibus* und die Paragraphen 16 und 23 von *De praecepto et dispensatione* dienen dazu, Bernhards christologisches Anliegen zu Kapitel 7 der Benediktregel und seine lehrmäßige Darlegung über den Gehorsam in Kapitel 5 der Regel zu zeigen. Aber die Benediktregel fehlt auch nicht in den mehr spekulativen Werken Bernhards. In der 10. Predigt zum Hohenlied haben wir eine ausgedehnte Abhandlung (und Übertragung) über die Rolle des Abtes, die auf den Kapiteln 2 und 64 der Benediktregel basiert. Bernhard stellt aus verschiedenen Kapiteln Schlüssellehren der Benediktregel zusammen und stellt sie in seinen Werken dar wie viele schwimmende Inseln in seiner See. Eine genaue Prüfung der Hoheliedpredigten 1–41 identifiziert mindestens drei dieser lehrmäßigen Blöcke, aber es gibt mehr. Darunter: *omni hora*, größtenteils aus Benediktregel Kap. 7:10–14; 26–30. Schliesslich *vana gloria* aus dem Prolog 5–7; 30–32 und Kap. 4:42–43; und zuletzt *non quaerit quae sua sunt*, eine sorgfältige Ausarbeitung von Kapitle 72:7 der Benediktregel, basierend auf 1 Kor 9:22 und 2 Kor 11:29.

PART III
Bernard and His Fellow Cistercians

A FURTHER STUDY OF THE *BREVIS COMMENTATIO*

Thomas X. Davis, OCSO
Abbey of New Clairvaux

ORIGINS OF THE *BREVIS COMMENTATIO*

IN HIS BIOGRAPHY OF BERNARD, William of Saint-Thierry describes the talks they had as they both lay sick at Clairvaux during that memorable spring visit.[1]

For while I was ill [at Clairvaux], the fact that he happened to be indisposed at the same time worked to my spiritual advantage. Both being ill together, we conversed all day long about spiritual matters, and about the remedial effect which the practice of the virtues has on souls weakened by sin. It was at this time that, whenever the state of my health permitted, he explained for me the *Canticle of Canticles*,

---

[1]Scholars date William's first visit to Clairvaux sometime between 1118 and 1120. 'That memorable spring visit' was one of the early visits William made after his first. See Jean en Marie Déchanet, *William of St Thierry: The Man and His Work*, trans. Richard Strachan, CS 10 (Spencer, Massachusetts: Cistercian Publications, 1972) p. 24ff. Also, Jacques Hourlier, 'Introduction' to *On Contemplating God; Prayer; Meditations*, trans. Sister Penelope, CSMV, CF 3 (Spencer, Massachusetts: Cistercian Publications, 1971) p. 8. See also, J. M. Déchanet, 'Introduction' to *Exposition on the Song of Songs*, trans. Columba Hart, OSB, CF 6 (Spencer, Massachusetts: Cistercian Publications, 1970) p. x; John D. Anderson, 'Introduction' to *The Enigma of Faith*, trans. John D. Anderson, CF 9 (Washington, D.C.: Cistercian Publications, 1974) p. 5; Stanislaus Ceglar, *William of St Thierry: The Chronology of His Life with a Study of His Treatise* On The Nature of Love, *His Authorship of the* Brevis Commentatio, *the* In Lacu, *and* The Reply to Cardinal Matthew (Diss. Catholic University of America; Ann Arbor, Michigan: University Microfilms, 1971) p. 40; Paul Verdeyen, SJ, *Guillelmi a Sancto Theodorico Opera Omnia*, I, *Expositio super Epistolam ad Romanos*, CC CM 86 (Turnhout: Brepols, 1989) p. xi.

enunciating the moral lessons only, and omitting the mystical interpretations associated with that part of Holy Scripture. This was as I
myself wished and as I had asked him to do. Each day, so that I should
not lose the benefit of his teaching, and helped by God's grace I wrote
down whatever I had heard from him about these matters, as far as I
could remember it. He explained everything to me in a kindly manner
and without any show of annoyance whatever, and imparted to me the
benefits of his understanding and the fruits of his experience. He tried
to pass on to me, who was unskilled and unlearned in these things,
something which can be learned only by experience; and, although
I was not yet able fully to grasp what I was being taught, yet it
permitted me to realize, better than ever before, how deficient I was
in my understanding of these great spiritual matters.[2]

These talks are accepted by some as the origin of the *Brevis commentatio*.[3] Whether this is true is not, there is no doubt that the friendship of
Bernard and William, the source of their mutual sharing and influence,
is certainly the matrix for the *Brevis commentatio*.[4] It is within this
traditionally accepted framework that I offer this present study.[5]

OUTLINE OF THE *BREVIS COMMENTATIO*[6]

The BC is composed of thirty-five numbered paragraphs (see fig. 1).[7]
The first five paragraphs speak of the three stages of the love of God:

[2]*Vita Bernardi prima* 12; PL 185:259BC. (I am indebted for this translation to Fr.
Flannan Hogan, OCSO.)

[3]Déchanet, *William of St Thierry: The Man and His Work*, p. 24ff., especially footnote
79 on p. 26; Louis Bouyer, *The Cistercian Heritage*, trans. Elizabeth A. Livingstone
(Westminster, Maryland: The Newman Press, 1958) pp. 78–79; G. R. Evans, *The Mind
of St Bernard of Clairvaux* (Oxford: Clarendon Press, [1983]) pp. 107–111.

[4]Ceglar, p. 350ff. Ceglar gives a good summary of the different positions regarding
the authorship of the *Brevis commentatio*.

[5]I wish to express a debt of gratitude to the scholars of previous studies on the *Brevis
commentatio*, for I see this present study as but a further development of their very
solid foundational work. See Jean Leclercq, *Etudes sur Saint Bernard et le texte de ses
écrits*, ASOC 9 (Rome: apud Curiam Generalem Sacri Ordinis Cisterciensis, 1953) pp.
105–124; Jacques Hourlier, 'Guillaume de Saint-Thierry et la "Brevis commentatio in
Cantica"', ASOC 12 (1956) 105–114; and Ceglar, pp. 350–79.

[6]Hereafter in this study, the *Brevis commentatio* will be referred to as BC.

[7]The latin edition of the BC that I have used is J. Mabillon's, found in his *Sancti
Bernardi Abbatis Claraevallensis Opera Omnia* 2/1, col. 555–92 (Paris: apud Gaume
Fratres, Biblopolas, 1839). This edition has the numbered paragraphs. Mabillon's edition
is also found in PL 184:407–456.

animal (*sensualis vel animalis*), rational (*rationalis*), and spiritual (*spiritualis*).[8] Paragraphs four to seven form a gentle movement that leads from these three stages of love into the actual commentary on the verses of the *Song of Songs*[9] itself. They present the nature of the kiss between the soul and God as a channel for such a movement. Paragraphs eight to thirty-four develop a commentary on Chapter 1:1 to Chapter 2:8 of the *Song of Songs*. This is a commentary on only the first of four canticles contained in the *Song of Songs*, a clarification made by William.[10] The concluding paragraph of the BC, no. 35, is a short but delightful parable[11] based upon the account of the woman who cried out to the Prophet Elisha that her husband, his servant, is dead.[12] This paragraph shows us a synthesis of the soul in the totality of its response to God.

LITERARY CATEGORIES IN THE BC

From my study of the BC, I should like to suggest that it contains four categories. These are: 1) a development of William's later well-known three stages of the love of God: animal, rational, spiritual; 2) the original writing of the BC, William being its author;[13] 3) the addition of direct quotations from the works of Saint Bernard; and 4) other additions, presumably by William, resulting from his own development of the concept of the *ratio fidei*.

THE DEVELOPMENT OF THE THREE STAGES OF LOVE

The three stages of love (being), as such, do not appear in the earlier works of William;[14] the same may be said of Bernard's earlier works. But, in the BC, there is a clear and defined treatment of these stages. If the earlier works do not contain these three stages, what, then, is their

---

[8]A concise definition of these stages of love is difficult to formulate, for they were in the process of being developed at the writing of this section of the BC. In the BC itself, there are several different descriptions of them, especially for the second stage.

[9]Unless otherwise qualified, the *Song of Songs* refers to the biblical book attributed to Solomon.

[10]Hourlier, p. 107.

[11]Leclercq, *Etudes*, p. 116.

[12]2 K 4:1.

[13]This is the position of Stanislaus Ceglar.

[14]Hourlier, p. 108. Works of William considered to have been written before 1135 are: *Contemplating God* (Contemp), *The Nature and Dignity of Love* (Nat am), *The Prayer of Dom William* (Orat), *Sacrament of the Altar* (Sacr altar), and parts of the *Meditations* (Med).

genesis? And what circumstances contributed to their development? I should like to propose one possible theory.

The early works of William assign the body no significant role in the spiritual life. In *The Nature and Dignity of Love*, the body returns to earth.[15] The body has no integral part in the various ascents by which the human soul mounts from its present fallen state to the vision of God.[16] As *Contemplating God* puts it: the body, that ass, must remain at the foot of the mountain while the intellectual faculties speed upward to see and to worship God.[17] These statements show a dichotomy between the body and the soul, with the body playing little, if any, significant part in the spiritual ascent to God.

Whether or not William rightly understood the eucharistic teaching of Rupert of Deutz,[18] Rupert's differentiation between animal life and spiritual life in the 'body of sacrifice' resulted in William's reformulation of the role of the body in his program of spiritual ascent. This questioning of Rupert's position produced in William's spirituality an anthropology more sound in terms of the relationships and roles between spirit, soul, and body. William defines animal life plainly as simply physical life, which he maintains is integral to the whole Christ in the mystery of the eucharistic presence. When he addresses animal life in terms of its quality of service, William accepts the implicit admission that the body, *along* with the soul, can serve the spirit.[19] That admission is important. It is the foundation principle which William will gradually develop

[15]Nat am 1; PL 180:367A: 'Quis enim corporis locus? Terra, inquit, es, in terram ibis.'

[16]E. Rozanne Elder, 'William of Saint Thierry: Rational and Affective Spirituality,' in E. Rozanne Elder (ed.), *The Spirituality of Western Christendom*, CS 30 (Kalamazoo, Michigan: Cistercian Publications, Inc., 1976) p. 85ff. The article develops the rational and affective dimension of William's spirituality, showing that in his earlier works reason's role as ancillary to love had no need to be a separate step (p. 90). Also in his earlier works very little role, if any, is given to the body in his ascent patterns.

[17]Contemp 1; PL 180:367A: 'Exspectate me hic, cum asino, corpore isto donec ego cum puero, ratio scilicet cum intelligentia usque illuc properantes. . . .'

[18]Jean Châtillon, 'William of Saint Thierry, Monasticism, and the Schools: Rupert of Deutz, Abelard, and William of Conches', in *William of St Thierry: Colloquium at the Abbey of St Thierry*, trans. Jerry Carfantan, CS 94 (Kalamazoo, Michigan: Cistercian Publications, [1987]) pp. 166–67.

[19]Sacr altar; PL 180:344B: 'Horum enim trium, spiritus, videlicet, animae, et corporis, cum duo ultima primo serviunt, vita est spiritualis; cum duo prima ultimo, vita est animalis.' This quotation is actually from the letter to Rupert, placed as an introduction to *The Sacrament of the Altar*. This eucharistic work of William is one of the earliest teachings to distinguish between substance and accident. See John H. Van Engen, *Rupert of Deutz* (Berkeley and Los Angeles, California: University of California Press, 1983) p. 173;

into the *status: homo animalis* (the body-person with its corresponding characteristics) as the first stage of love.[20]

Another important factor in the development of the stages of love is William's encounter with the dialectical theology of Peter Abelard. This caused him to reconsider the role of reason regarding faith, revelation, and love in the spiritual life.[21] William begins to see that reason is too powerful and too elemental a human faculty simply to be a subsidiary companion to love. He also begins to develop the idea of the use of reason and its faculty[22] in the ascent to God as a distinctive step, the mature dimension of the rational person (*status: homo rationalis*).

It was with this new awareness of the roles of the body and of reason, however vague and inarticulate it may still have been, that William went to meet with Bernard, in the spring of either 1139 or 1140, to discuss the issue of Peter Abelard.[23]

Like William, Bernard speaks in his early work of four degrees of love.[24] But in his *Diverse Sermon 29*[25] and *Sermon 20 on the Song of Songs*[26] Bernard clearly employs the imagery of the three stages of spiritual growth.[27] These descriptions of the love of the heart for the humanity/Incarnation of Christ (first stage), of the love that is prudent and

---

J. H. Van Engen, 'Rupert of Deutz and William of Saint-Thierry', *Revue Bénédictine* 93 (1983) 327–36.

[20]The genesis of the body-person as a consequence of orthodox eucharistic doctrine is important for a solid spirituality for this first stage of love. Catholic doctrine has maintained an important relationship between the Eucharist and that growth, which in William's terms of the body-person, is from carnal bonds and body domination to a freedom and autonomy that prepares the way for insight and understanding that is love itself. See Bouyer, p. 107ff, where he rightly makes this point. Finally, one example of William's evolution in the role of the body can be found in *The Enigma of Faith*, 21. Here he speaks of the purification of the sinful body, as the concupiscences of the flesh keep a person from seeing that which only the pure of heart can see. This is a quite different role than that found in Contemp 1.

[21]Elder, 'William', pp. 90–93.

[22]Elder, 'William', pp. 88–89: 'In his physiology, William made a distinction between *reason*, a part of the brain, and *rationality*, the ability to use reason. . . . Reason is one of the three faculties of the brain; rationality is one of three powers of the soul. . . . Despite his distinction in this one treatise [*On the Nature of the Body and Soul*] between reason and rationality, he usually spoke only of reason, by which he seems to have meant both the ability and the faculty.'

[23]Ceglar, pp. 172–87.

[24]Dil; SBOp 3:119–54. Ep 11; SBOp 7:52–60.

[25]SBOp 6/1:210–14.

[26]SBOp 1:114–21.

[27]M. Basil Pennington, 'Three Stages of Spiritual Growth According to St Bernard', *Studia Monastica* (1969) 315–26.

wise in its steady search into the mysteries of Christ (second stage), of a fearless, powerful, spiritual love (third stage), reveal a similarity between *Diverse Sermon 29, Sermon 20 on the Song of Songs*, and the BC. Such a similarity suggests that Bernard, having better developed his thought on these three stages of love, had a definite influence on William, who, in his turn, would eventually formulate his grasp of these three stages and develop them into the final form found in *The Golden Epistle*.[28]

The traditional dating of William's earlier works *Contemplating God* and *The Nature and Dignity of Love*, and Bernard's *Loving God*, are prior to 1130. Since these three stages are not mentioned in these earlier works,[29] it would appear that their development began around or after 1130. The significance of this dating implies that the sections of the BC dealing with these three stages of love (see figs. 1 and 2) were probably not composed prior to the completion of the earlier works on love, that is, prior to 1130. My opinion is that the teaching in these chapters of the BC received its final form as a result of the discussions between William and Bernard centered on the Abelard issue. The role of reason in the spiritual life was equally vital for William. This issue is basic to the development of William's second stage of love in which the *ratio fidei* figures so prominently. Once these discussions were over, William developed his *ratio fidei* and stages of love: animal, rational, spiritual. Bernard, on the other hand, content with the three stages of love which appear in his later writings and having no difficulty with the role of reason,[30] did not concern himself to develop further his understanding of these stages of love as an interrelated unit.

THE ORIGINAL WRITING OF THE BC; WILLIAM AS ITS AUTHOR

The first five paragraphs of the BC address the three stages of love. If we eliminate these references to the three stages, along with paragraph 6A, there remains Bernard's commentary on the kiss (fig. 1). The kiss is the theme in the first verse of the *Song of Songs*, and a commentary normally begins with this theme. The rest of the BC seems to flow quite naturally from this beginning, with topics running parallel to sermons 1

---

[28]*Epistola (aurea) ad frates de Monte Dei* (hereafter Ep frat).
[29]See n. 8 above.
[30]Elder, 'William', p. 86.

to 52 of Bernard's commentary on the *Song of Songs*. The BC is a sort of 'first draft' or framework for this later commentary by Bernard.[31] This commentary on the kiss is probably the beginning of the original notes made by William from Bernard's presentation. Later, as the teaching of the three stages of love began to take shape from their discussions, these first six chapters appear to have been added as an introduction to the BC.

THE ADDITION OF DIRECT QUOTATIONS
FROM THE WORKS OF SAINT BERNARD

Bernard has left us seven sermons *De diversis* on different verses of the *Song of Songs*.[32] One of these sermons, Div 90, is reproduced verbatim in BC paragraphs 9 to 11, save for the omission of a very small section. This insertion of *Sermon 90* appears to displace the short BC paragraph 12. Its proper place may have been after BC paragraph 8, because this paragraph comments on the verse: 'Your breasts are better than wine.'[33] *Sermon 90* comments on the verse: 'Fragrant with the best ointments'[34] (fig. 1).

There are also two *Sententiae* of Bernard that are reproduced. One, III Sent 73,[35] is put verbatim in BC paragraph 28. The other, III Sent 121,[36] is a direct quotation, but the passage is abbreviated, and is found in BC paragraph 31. The use of these *Sententiae* of Bernard illustrates the probability that the BC was originally a series of *sententiae*, that is, short summaries or brief statements, notes jotted down as quick outlines or comments.[37] Such an approach would have been a normal way of capturing Bernard's early thoughts on the *Song of Songs*. Moreover, a reading of the BC shows that paragraphs 4 to 17 are longer than paragraphs 18 to 34[38] (fig. 1). William, who most likely made the original notes, treasured them. They became the nucleus of the BC in

---

[31]Jean Leclercq, 'Introduction' to *On the Song of Songs II*, CF 7 (Kalamazoo, Michigan: Cistercian Publications, 1976) p. xxx.

[32]Leclercq, 'Introduction', p. xxv. These sermons are listed in Leclercq, *Etudes*, pp. 118–19.

[33]Sg 1:1.

[34]Sg 1:2.

[35]SBOp 6/2:111–12.

[36]SBOp 6/2:216.

[37]Jean Leclercq, *The Love of Learning and the Desire for God*, trans. Catharine Misrahi (New York: Fordham University Press, 1961) pp. 208–214.

[38]Hourlier, pp. 109–111.

its present form. It seems that William, over the years, may have fleshed out these original *sententiae* with his own ideas, using his own words and phrases.[39]

OTHER ADDITIONS, PRESUMABLY BY WILLIAM,
RESULTING FROM HIS OWN DEVELOPMENT OF
THE CONCEPT OF THE *RATIO FIDEI*

The first and third paragraphs of the BC have a rythmic movement between the three stages of love. For example: '. . . The first is delighted with the contemplation and sweetness of Christ's humanity, . . . the second has already a burning heart, yet its eyes are still restrained while Christ speaks to it, as it is still on the journey, and opens the Scriptures for it. The third now says . . . if we once knew Christ according to the flesh, we now no longer know him this way. . . .'[40] The two paragraphs are written entirely in this undulating style. They appear to form one unit.

BC paragraph 2, on the other hand, deals almost entirely with the second stage, the rational stage. It contains three elements proper to the *ratio fidei* developed by William. Its style is not a rhythmic movement[41] but a more straightforward prose. The first of these elements is a caution given to reason. In its penetration into the mysteries of faith, reason is not to be too bold and self-assertive. Reason '. . . sometimes directs its attention by the hand of devoted desire to the higher stage, only to take refuge quickly in itself. Like David, reason strikes its breast because it presumed to lift its hand against the Lord's anointed.'[42] The second element is the role of the *ratio fidei* which '. . . creates for itself its own type of reasons with which it returns from the hiddenness of the face of God to the lower stages which are in some way its companions.'[43] The third element is the lack of complication and of an intricate reasoning

---

[39]Ceglar (p. 350ff.) makes this point emphatically.

[40]BC 1: 'Primus adeo delectatur in contemplatione et dulcedine humanitatis Christi, . . . secundus cor jam habet ardens, sed oculi ejus adhuc tenentur, cum ei loquitur Christus, sed in via, et aperit ei Scripturas. Tertius . . . dicit: Et si novimus Christum secundum carnem, sed nunc jam non novimus. . . .'

[41]Hourlier, p. 107. Hourlier calls attention to this different literary style and says it is the style of William, whereas paragraphs 1 and 2 are in the style of Bernard.

[42]BC 2: 'Superiorem vero aliquando attentans manu pii desiderii, mox ad se refugit, et sicut David percutit cor suum, quia in christum Domini manum mittere praesumpsit.'

[43]BC 2: '. . . Sed tamen ipse nonnunquam sui generis sibi creat rationes, quibus de abscondito faciei Dei ad suos illos quodammodo socios inferiores regrediens.'

process in those people who, in simple faith, under the power of the Holy Spirit, search the deep things of God.[44]

Paragraph 2, because of these three elements, represents a more refined development of this rational stage in comparison to paragraphs 1 to 5. For, in these, the second stage is described in terms of dwelling in the soul (*anima*, and not *animus*, is the latin word), yet rational (*rationalis*) to the degree that this love is vivified by the mysteries of faith and the power of the sacraments. Nourishing and relishing insights into the Scriptures, and expressing itself in the practice of virtue, the mind remembers and reflects on what it has come to receive. One's rationality is captivated with awe at the mysteries of Christ's humanity. I believe the contrast between these paragraphs intimates that paragraph 2 was inserted between 1 and 3 at a date later than the addition of the section dealing with these three stages of love. Paragraph 2 may well represent one of the final touches given to the BC by William[45] (see figures 1 and 2).

Bernard distinguishes the kiss both as the Incarnation[46] and as each of three kisses[47] proper to each of the three stages of love. The third stage is the kiss of contemplation with which the bride is united to the Bridegroom through knowledge (*notitia*) and love (*amor*). Using this third kiss as a launching point, William continues on to give a compact presentation of his teaching on the spiritual person (*status spiritualis*).[48] 'By loving God, we are assimilated into God, and by being assimilated into God, we experience God by being what God is; and it is this experience of God which provides us here on earth with the most perfect knowledge we can have of God.'[49]

BC paragraph 6A, like William's commentary on the kiss, is actually a terse teaching on the Trinity. 'Person' is seen in terms of self-knowledge (*personae vel per se sonantes*). Love and knowledge (*amor ipse intellectus est*) are one and the same in God, but are divided into two when bestowed as a kiss on our will and reason. Associated with this kiss is the

---

[44]BC 2: 'Sunt autem rationes istae non ratiocinantium perplexionibus involutae...ut videatur dictum de eis: Spiritus omnia scrutatur etiam profunde Dei.'

[45]I am inclined to consider the second paragraph of the BC as a kind of *sententia* of William which preceded the writing of *The Mirror of Faith* and *The Enigma of Faith*.

[46]BC 7.

[47]BC 5.

[48]BC 6.

[49]David N. Bell, *The Image and Likeness: The Augustinian Spirituality of William of St Thierry*, CS 78 (Kalamazoo, Michigan: Cistercian Publications, 1984) p. 231. Chapter VI of this book is a clear and comprehensive presentation on 'love itself is understanding', *amor ipse intellectus est*.

place of participation and the role of incomprehensibility in our union with God.[50]

There are two observations germane to BC 6: the word used for knowledge is *notitia* rather than *intellectus*;[51] also, William speaks of the soul as being 'touched' by God; here he is not as bold as in *The Golden Epistle* where the soul is said to be midway in the embrace and kiss of Father and Son.[52] These two observations suggest that this presentation of love as understanding is more articulate in comparison with works of William earlier than the BC, but not as bold as in his final works.[53]

CONCLUSION

1) What we know as the BC was probably originally some form of *sententiae*, short hand notes to stir the memory. 2) The BC can be considered a composite work: the original source of thoughts and expressions being from Bernard, with William making his own unique contributions.[54] William may have begun this procedure of expressing his own concepts in the framework of Bernard's *sententiae* at the very first writing of the BC. Most likely, the first work on the BC was prior to 1130. 3) A small number of direct quotations from other works of Bernard were inserted into the BC in various redactions.[55] 4) William's notable contribution to the BC was his development of the three stages of love, and of the concept *ratio fidei* in particular. This teaching was most likely formulated immediately after 1139/1140 and before the completion

[50]Bell, p. 248. Here Bell shows that connatural knowledge (*amor ipse intellectus est*) is none other than self-knowledge, which is, in its turn, God-knowledge. Bell treats the role of incomprehensibility on p. 120ff. Also, for self-knowledge being God-knowledge, see E. Rozanne Elder, 'Introduction' to William of Saint Thierry, *The Mirror of Faith*, trans. Thomas X. Davis, CF 15 (Kalamazoo, Michigan: Cistercian Publications, Inc., 1979) pp. xx-xxi.

[51]Bell, pp. 231–32, especially n. 58. *Notitia* is, of course, the word used by Gregory the Great.

[52]Ep frat 16. Translation: William of St Thierry, *The Golden Epistle*, trans. Theodore Berkeley, CF 12 (Spencer, Massachusetts: Cistercian Publications, 1971) p. 96.

[53]Bell, p. 248, n. 106.

[54]Ceglar, p. 375.

[55]Since scholars see the BC as a work preceding Bernard's sermons on the *Song of Songs*, the insertion from other works is more likely than copying from the BC. This would certainly be the case if William did the writing and kept the notes himself. I have made a search for other direct quotations from Bernard that could possibly be in the BC, using the microfiche of the *Thesaurus Sancti Bernardi Claraevallensis* (Turnhout: Brepols, 1987). So far I have found only the direct quotations referred to in this study.

of his later works.[56] But here again, in this contribution, we have a mingling of both Bernard and William, accomplished possibly in the following manner. Bernard had composed the first twenty-four sermons of his commentary on the *Song of Songs* by the year 1136.[57] This means that Bernard had already developed his understanding of the three stages of love as found in *Sermon 20*: 'It seems to me, if no more suitable meaning for this triple distinction comes to mind, that the love of the heart relates to a certain warmth of affection [first stage], the love of the soul [*anima*] to energy or judgment of reason [*rationis*, the second stage], and the love of strength can refer to constancy and vigor of spirit [*animus*, the third stage].'[58]

Here we have a solid groundwork on which William could build. Undoubtedly William was acquainted with Bernard's version of these three stages.[59] He brought to them a refinement that was the result of his re-thinking his positions on the body and the use of reason. As this development unfolded, William inserted his own thoughts into the BC and proceeded to develop them until their final form emerged in *The Golden Epistle*. But here again, the same pattern is in evidence: Bernard supplies the original premise, and then William undertakes the theological and spiritual advancement of these original ideas until he reaches his own

[56]The works commonly accepted as after 1140 are: *The Nature of the Body and Soul* (Nat corp), *Mirror of Faith* (Spec fid), *Enigma of Faith* (Aenig), *Dispute Against Peter Abelard* (Adv Abl), *The Errors of William of Conche* (Er Guill), *Life of Bernard* (Vita Bern), and *The Golden Epistle* (Ep frat). The *Exposition on the Epistle to the Romans* (Exp Rm) and *Exposition on The Song of Songs* (Cant) were being completed around 1140. The introduction to Cant speaks explicitly about the three stages: animal, rational, and spiritual. The remainder of the work is more general in contrast to what is found in Ep frat. Does this suggest that this introduction was written after the main body of the work, and during 1139/1140, when William saw the full implication of these three stages?

[57]Michael Casey, *Athirst for God: Spiritual Desire in Bernard of Clairvaux's Sermons on the Song of Songs*, CS 77 (Kalamazoo: Cistercian Publications, 1988) p. 39, n. 2.

[58]'Mihi videtur, si alius competentior sensus in hac trina distinctione non occurrit, amor quidem cordis ad zelum quemdam pertinere affectiones, animae vero amor ad industriam seu iudicium rationis, virtutes autem dilectio ad animi posse referri constantiam vel vigorem.' SC 1.4; SBOp 1:116.

[59]The ancient, threefold view of the human person as spirit, soul, and body (πνεῦμα, ψυχή, σῶμα) can be found in Saint Paul (1 Th 5:23) and throughout the early patristic writings. This threefold division, as stages of love, does not seem to be prominent in the writings of Bernard prior to his sermons on the *Song of Songs* (in particular *Sermon 20*) and *Diversis 29*. Nor are these stages found in what I label the notes/*sententiae* or earlier parts of the BC. It is beyond the limits of this study to discern Bernard's initial or intermediate contact with and use of them. That discernment opens up the issue of Bernard's contact, knowledge, and use of the Greek Fathers, notably of Origen.

spiritual maturity. Bernard launches William on a spiritual path. William, in his fidelity to Bernard, composes the BC and uses this composition as a sort of 'launch pad' for his own spiritual growth and teaching.

In terms of the three stages of love, I think the BC represents an intermediary position between *Diverse Sermon 29* and *Sermon 20 on the Song of Songs*, on the one hand, and the final presentation that we have in *The Golden Epistle*, on the other. For, overall, the genre of the BC is in the category of Bernard's two works; at the same time, the genre expresses seminal thoughts that portend William's later development. In the BC, knowledge (*notitia/cognitio*) and love (*amor*) are one in God but distinct in us. They are given us through the kiss, the Holy Spirit. In *The Golden Epistle*, the spiritual state is participation, the kiss, the Holy Spirit, making us what God is, wherein we find love as understanding (*amor ipse intellectus est*).

A certain narrative relates how a good curé of the parish Church of Ville-sous-la Ferté, where the relics of Saint Bernard and Saint Malachy were kept, poured them together into one box (to save space?). All attempts to distinguish between them have so far proven unsuccessful.[60] The BC is something like this one box: it contains the ideas, thoughts, and expressions both of Bernard and of William. While some attempts to distinguish between them are successful, they nevertheless remain in a sort of harmony, in a 'oneness'—a symbol of presence to one another forever. Monastic friends could address one another in a sensual language taken directly from the *Song of Songs*. To a person reading the *Brevis commentatio* there comes a faint whisper: I will hold him and not let him go![61]

ABSTRACTS

Dans leurs recherches et leurs travaux, Dom J. Hourlier et Dom J. Leclercq ont posé un excellent et solide fondement à des recherches ultérieures sur la *Brevis Commentatio* (*BC*). La présente étude poursuit leurs efforts.

Cette étude envisage quatre catégories littéraires dans la *BC*:

    1) La *BC* représente un développement important et significatif des trois stades bien connus de l'amour de Dieu chez Guillaume:

---

[60]Ailbe J. Luddy, *Life and Teaching of St Bernard* (Dublin: M. H. Gill & Son, 1950) p. 681.

[61]Brian Patrick McGuire, *Friendship & Community: The Monastic Experience 350–1250*, CS 95 (Kalamazoo, Michigan: Cistercian Publications Inc., 1988) p. 291.

animal, rationnel, spirituel. La *BC* contient une évolution de ces trois stades: les trois stades dans la *BC* présentent un état plus avancé que dans le *Sermo 20 super Cantica canticorum* de Bernard, mais pas aussi développé que dans l'*Epistola ad fratres de Monte Dei* de Guillaume.

2) On peut voir dans la *BC* une oeuvre composite des deux abbés: la source originelle de sa pensée et de son expression fut Bernard, Guillaume apportant sa contribution propre et unique. La toute première rédaction de la *BC* se situe le plus probablement avant 1130.

3) Il y a un petit nombre de citations directes d'autres oeuvres de Bernard. Ces citations furent insérées dans la *BC* à diverses étapes de ses différentes rédactions.

4) Outre les contributions de Guillaume à la *BC*, surtout en termes de ses trois stades de l'amour, il y a son développement de la *ratio fidei*. L'enseignement fondamental sur la *ratio fidei* a été formulé en toute probabilité aussitôt après 1139/1140 et avant l'achèvement de ses oeuvres majeures. La *BC* contient cette doctrine fondamentale au paragraphe 2; ce paragraphe (ou chapitre) représente la dernière couche rédactionnelle de la *BC*.

Dom J. Hourlier and Dom J. Leclercq in their research and studies have given an excellent and solid foundation for further research concerning the *Brevis Commentatio* (hereafter referred to as *BC*). The present paper continues their efforts.

This paper considers four literary categories in the *BC*:

1) The *BC* represents an important and significant development of William's well-known three stages of the love of God: animal, rational, spiritual. The *BC* contains an evolution of these three stages: the three stages in the *BC* are more developed than in Bernard's *Sermo 20 super Cantica canticorum* but not as developed as in William's *Epistola ad fratres de Monte Dei*.

2) The *BC* can be considered a composite work of the two abbots: the original source of its thoughts and expressions come from Bernard, with William making his own unique contributions. The very first writing of the *BC* was most likely prior to 1130.

3) There are a small number of direct quotations from other works of Bernard. These quotations were inserted into the *BC* at various times during its different redactions.

4) In addition to William's contributions to the *BC*, especially in terms of his three stages of love, was his development of the *ratio fidei*. The basic teaching on the *ratio fidei* was most likely formulated immediately after 1139/1140 and before the completion of his later works. The *BC* contains this basic doctrine in Paragraph 2; this paragraph (or chapter) represents the last redaction of the *BC*.

In ihren Untersuchungen und Studien haben Dom J. Hourlier und Dom J. Leclercq eine ausgezeichnete und solide Grundlage für weitere Untersuchung des 'brevis commentatio' (abgek. BC) gegeben. Die vorliegende Arbeit setzt ihre Bemühungen fort. Dieser Artikel betrachtet 4 literarische Kategorien im BC:

1) BC repräsentiert eine wichtige und bezeichnende Entwicklung der wohlbekannten drei Stufen der Liebe Gottes bei Wilhelm: seelisch, rational, geistlich. BC enthält eine Entwicklung dieser drei Stufen: die drei Stufen im BC sind weiter fortgeschritten als in Bernhards SC 20, aber nicht so entwickelt wie in Wilhelms *Epistola ad fratres de Monte Dei*.

2) BC kann betrachtet werden als zusammengesetztes Werk der beiden Äbte: die ursprüngliche Quelle seiner Gedanken und Ausdrücke kommen von Bernhard, während Wilhelm seine eigenen, einzigartigen Beiträge macht. Die allererste Niederschrift des BC war wahrscheinlich früher als 1130.

3) Es gibt eine kleine Anzahl direkter Zitate anderer Werke Bernhards. Diese Zitate wurden im BC zu verschiedenen Zeiten eingefügt während der verschiedenen Überarbeitungen.

4) Zusätzlich zu Wilhelms Beiträgen zum BC, speziell in Ausdrücken seiner drei Stufen der Liebe, war seine Entwicklung der *ratio fidei*. Die grundlegende Lehre über die *ratio fidei* wurde sehr wahrscheinlich sofort nach 1139/1140 und vor der Vollendung seiner späteren Werke formuliert. Diese Grundlehre enthält BC in Paragraph 2; dieser Paragraph (oder Kapitel) zeigt die letzte Redaktion des BC.

Figure 1

OUTLINE OF THE *BREVIS COMMENTATIO*

Numbered Paragraphs (note 7)

3 stages animal/rational/spiritual	1	*
rational stage	2	last insertion to be made
3 stages, again	3	*
Let him kiss me & the 3 stages	4	* begin: longer reflection note 38
3 kisses as 3 stages	5	*
Trinitarian teaching	6A	a separate
other meanings of kiss	6B	insertion
Incarnation as kiss	7	
Your breasts are better than wine	8	
Fragrant with best ointments	9	begin Div 90
Fragrant with best ointments	10	
Fragrant with best ointments	11	end of Div 90
Your breasts are better than wine	12	
Your name as oil poured out	13	
Your name as oil poured out	14	
Draw me . . . we shall run	15	
Draw me . . . we shall run	16	
Draw me . . . we shall run	17	
The king led me. . . .	18	begin: shorter reflection note 38
The upright ones love you & I am black but beautiful	19	
Tents of Cedar	20	
Sons fought against me	21	
After the flocks	22	
Like Pharaoh's chariots	23	
Your cheeks are beautiful	24	
Pendants of gold	25	
King at his repose	26	
Cluster of grapes	27	
Behold you are beautiful	28	insertion III Sent 73
Behold you are beautiful and flowery bed	29	

Beams of our house	30	
I sat down under his shadow	31	insertion III
		Sent 121
King brought me into wine cellar	32	
King brought me into wine cellar	33	
Languish with love/two hands &		
daughters of Jer./Beloved's voice	34	
The woman who cried to Elisha	35	

*These sections, dealing with the three stages, are later additions. The original beginning of the commentary was somewhere around 6b.

Figure 2
A Chronological Hypothesis

'That memorable spring visit':	basic *sententiae* paragraphs 6b to 34
unknown dates, but later:	insertion of III Sent 73, paragraph 28
	insertion of III Sent 121, paragraph 31
	insertion of Div 90 paragraphs 9–11
	Trinitarian teaching paragraph 6A
around 1139/1140:	3 stages of love, paragraphs 1, 3, 4, 5
last addition:	rational stage, paragraph 2

THE FACE AND THE FEET OF GOD: THE HUMANITY OF CHRIST IN BERNARD OF CLAIRVAUX AND AELRED OF RIEVAULX

Marsha L. Dutton
Hanover College

T HE GREATEST OF THE LOSSES suffered by humankind in Adam's fall was banishment from the presence of God. Ever since that time, even in the new dispensation, God has dwelt apart from humans, hidden by a combination of distance and blinding glory from the eyes of ordinary men and women, until the last days, the end of time, the resurrection of the body, when, according to Aelred of Rievaulx, 'The Creator will be seen in himself. . . . The Father will be seen in the Son, the Son in the Father, the Holy Spirit in both. He will be seen not as a confused reflection in a mirror, but face to face. For he will be seen as he is.'[1]

Not everyone, of course, can stand to wait patiently for the sight of God's glory. The hunger for the sight of the face of God dominates and defines the spirituality of the cistercian fathers as they not only yearn for that vision in eternity but strive, urgently and importunately, for it here and now.[2] So the fathers cry out, over and over, in the words of

---

[1] Aelred, *De institutione inclusarum* [hereafter Inst incl] 33; CCCM 1:681; CF 2:101.

[2] Marsha L. Dutton, 'Eat, Drink, and Be Merry: The Eucharistic Spirituality of the Cistercian Fathers', and 'Intimacy and Imitation: The Humanity of Christ in Cistercian Spirituality', in John R. Sommerfeldt (ed.), *Erudition at God's Service*: *Studies in Medieval Cistercian History*, *11*, CS 98 ([Kalamazoo, Michigan]: Cistercian Publications Inc., 1987) pp. 1–69.

David: 'Your face I require, O Lord; your face I require' (Ps 26:8), and
the search is sometimes rewarded. As Bernard explains in sermon 87
De diversis:

Our soul, uplifted by a celestial desire, aspires, in the impatience of
love, to be introduced into the secret joys of the interior chamber, and
with a voice broken by sighs full of tenderness she sings in the fervor
of her heart: 'It is your face, Lord, that I desire.' And such is the
force of this desire that the Spouse makes himself present to her, him
whom she so loves, toward whom she so aspires, and for whom she
so sighs.[3]

Similarly Aelred urges the contemplative soul:

Strive with God as Jacob did, so that he may rejoice in being overcome. . . . Be insistent, welcome or unwelcome, and cry out: 'How
long will you turn your face away from me? How long shall I have to
cry out without your listening to me?' Give back to me, good Jesus,
the joy of your salvation, for my heart has said to you: 'I have sought
your face; your face, Lord, I will seek.'[4]

Desire for that face 'which angels love to look upon' (1 P 1:12),[5] the
face of him who is 'most comely of the sons of men, more resplendent
even than the sun and the stars in all their beauty' (Ps 44:3; Ws 7:29),[6]
lies at the center of the spirituality of both Bernard and Aelred. They
agree that it is invisible to human eyes, hidden by its own radiance from
humankind's postlapsarian myopia. And they agree, of course, that the
eternal vision of that face is assured through God's Incarnation. They
declare that what the old Adam lost the new Adam has restored, that the
separation once forged between God and humankind is in Jesus the God-
man overcome for eternity. Redemption is accomplished, the resurrection

[3]Div 87.1; SBOp 3:330.
[4]Inst incl 31; CCCM 1:666; CF 2:84.
[5]See Bernard's I Nov; SBOp 5:304, and Aelred's Inst incl 33; CCCM 1:681; CF
2:101. See also Chrysogonus Waddell, 'Notes About St Bernard and the Two Visions of
Isaiah: The First Sermon for the First Sunday in November', *Liturgy* 24 (1990) 77–121.
Waddell comments on this phrase that 'Bernard . . . quotes it some 24 times in his extant
writings' and that according to the greek text of Isaiah the angels 'long to gaze, not
on the face of Christ, but on the fulfillment of the promises now being accomplished
in ourselves' (p. 91). For additional discussions of the implications of these sermons
for Bernard's christology see Jean Leclercq, *Bernard of Clairvaux and the Cistercian
Spirit*, trans. Claire Lavoie, CS 16 (Kalamazoo: Cistercian Publications, 1976) p. 83, and
Alberich Altermatt, 'Christus pro nobis. Die Christologie Bernhards von Clairvaux in
dem "Sermones per annum"', ASOC 33 (1977) 3–176; pp. 141–143.
[6]Inst incl 14; CCCM 1:650; CF 2:63.

of the body is to come, and so the vision of the face of God is revealed for all eternity, *secula seculorum.*

So far Bernard and Aelred agree, and of course it is not merely that they agree but that Aelred relies on Bernard throughout. But on the effect of the Incarnation for humankind in this world, in this time, they differ. In what way the Incarnation enables humankind to know and love God here, in what way the man Jesus shows forth the Godhead, in what way humans may love God by loving God's Son made flesh—to what extent, in short, one may see the face of God through the kiss of the feet of God's Son—these are the areas of difference between these two great cistercian fathers. For while both profess their love for Jesus in his sacred humanity, they differ in their understanding of the way in which his love may lead humankind to God, and they disagree in their answers to the question of the relationship between the dusty feet of Jesus and the radiant face of God.

For Bernard the human Christ is both the beginning place and the first step toward the true love for and sight of God, but he is always distinct from that sight. Jesus may teach humans to love God and so woo them from the love of the flesh in which they find God, but if they are to love God, to see God's face, they must go beyond, coming to recognize that in Jesus God put off God's own beauty. For Aelred, however, love of Jesus is quite simply love of God, and devotion to him—the kiss of the feet—is not a first step toward the love for and sight of God but equivalent to the sight of God. In kissing Jesus' feet one knows God; in anointing Jesus' feet one sees God's face. Aelred, despite his reliance on Bernard throughout, teaches over and over, in work after work, that in Mary 'all the fullness of the divinity dwelled bodily',[7] that her son, Jesus, is to be adored as 'God in the man and the man in God',[8] and that in becoming man God became not less but more, adding human substance to divinity, in deference to human eyes covering his glorious because celestial nudity rather than stripping himself of his glory.

As Bernard's love for Jesus in his humanity results from and is evidence of human frailty, itself a result of the Fall, he reaches ever beyond it, longing to transcend love of God in flesh so as to arrive finally at the love of God in spirit. Bernard constantly reminds his readers that 'If we consider [God] in himself, his home is in inaccessible light' and

[7] Inst incl 29; CCCM 1:663; CF 2:80.
[8] Inst incl 31; CCCM 1:667; CF 2:85.

that 'he does not have these members—[a mouth, a hand, feet]—by his
nature, but they represent certain modes of our encounter with him.'[9]
So, as he urges his listeners to begin their penitential journey to God
with the kiss of Jesus' feet, he explains: 'If it seemed right to Saint Paul
to describe Christ's head in terms of the divinity, it should not seem
unreasonable to us to ascribe the feet to his humanity.'[10]

But Aelred enjoins his listeners and readers to love of the Incarnate
God, proclaiming that Jesus is God indeed and insisting that as surely as
Mary may embrace the feet of the infant in the manger, Mary Magdalene
may clasp the feet of the risen Lord, that in the feet before which the
paralytic was let down for healing 'kindness and power came to meet
one another.'[11]

BERNARD AND THE SACRED HUMANITY

Bernard's anxiety about devotion to Christ in his humanity and desire
to present that humanity as only a pale reflection of God in himself,
spirit unmarred by flesh, arise largely from his understanding of God's
decision to enter into flesh in order to win a recalcitrant humanity, deter-
minedly denying him the love he sought from his creatures. According
to this explanation, the Incarnation resulted from God's urgent desire
for the love of his creation. First seeking humanity's love through fear,
threatening eternal shadows, inextinguishable fire, God, finding that fear
did not win human love, at last resolved:

> 'Only one solution remains. In man there is not only fear and desire,
> but also love, and there is nothing more powerful than that to attract
> him.' God came therefore in flesh and showed himself so worthy of
> love that he made known that love than which there is no greater: he
> gave his life for us.[12]

But the love prompted in humankind by this appearance of God in
flesh is not the true love of spirit that God was seeking. Rather, it is, as
Bernard has already explained, a love of the heart:

> It is something like love of the flesh, because its affective urges begin
> in the heart. The soul has something more elevated; we may say thus

[9]SC 4.3; SBOp 1:19; CF 4:23.
[10]SC 6.2; SBOp 1:29; CF 4:35.
[11]Inst incl 31; CCCM 1:666; CF 2:84.
[12]Div 29.3; SBOp 6/1:211–12.

that it is the seat of wisdom, so it appears right to believe that it is reserved for loving God with discernment. . . . It is the memory of the Incarnation of Christ that raises it [this affective love of the heart] particularly, but it is also the memory of all the economy of salvation, which is accomplished in the flesh of Christ, and especially in the Passion. Realizing that mankind had become at root carnal, God manifested in the flesh a tenderness so great that it is necessary to be very hard of heart not to love him with affection entire and total.[13]

The love evoked by God's Incarnation, by Christ's Passion, is then a love born of human necessity and is thus second best. Bernard muses:

I think this is the principal reason that the invisible God willed to be seen in the flesh and to converse with man as man. He wanted to capture the affections of carnal men who were unable to love in any other way, by first drawing them to the salutary love of his own humanity, and then gradually to raise them to a spiritual love. . . . So it was only by his physical presence that their hearts were detached from carnal loves.[14]

Anxiety about this human love toward and elicited by the humanity of Christ shapes Bernard's treatment of the life of Christ. As Etienne Gilson has pointed out: 'This sensitive affection for Christ was always presented by St Bernard as love of a relatively inferior order.'[15] It is for the needs of spiritual beginners, whose eyes are insufficiently strong to see the glory of God, that the love of Christ in his humanity is necessary and explicitly available. But those beginners are, of course, most of humanity.

Chrysogonus Waddell has discussed Bernard's series of sermons on Isaiah's vision in the temple; he notes that in these sermons Bernard describes that vision of God in glory—'the Lord sitting on a throne high and lifted up'—as a sublime vision, reserved for 'the rare individual', while Isaiah's later vision, of the suffering servant 'without beauty and comeliness', is 'accessible to the generality of us.' Even Herod, that is, can see the humiliated Jesus and ridicule him: 'Those who mocked Jesus

---

[13]Div 29.2; SBOp 6/1:211.
[14]SC 20.6; SBOp 1:118; CF 2:152.
[15]*The Mystical Theology of Saint Bernard*, trans. A.H.C. Downes (London, New York: Sheed and Ward, 1940; reprint: CS 120; Kalamazoo: Cistercian Publications, 1990) p. 79.

on the cross could look on him so closely that they were able [to] count every bone of his body.'[16] While Waddell has argued persuasively that in both of Isaiah's visions the Lord who is seen is Christ, the Lord sitting high and lifted up as well as the Suffering Servant, Bernard continues in this sermon to explain that the Christ seen in the second of Isaiah's visions, the Christ who became man, was 'not only lower than the angels or on the same level as men, but as a leper, that is, not only in the flesh but in the likeness of sinful flesh.'[17]

Bernard does not intend here, of course, to denigrate Jesus' human body. Rather, the flesh taken on by Jesus was that corrupted by the Fall. And not only had the Fall corrupted the flesh in which Jesus clothed himself, but its damage to the human ability to see truth, to look upon God, made that clothing necessary. Before the Fall humankind was not dependent on the senses to see and love God, but could see God 'as he was'. The impurity brought about in the Fall, however, so clouded human eyesight that men and women became unable to see God in glory. Hence, as Bernard says in his third sermon on the Ascension, it became necessary if God was to be seen, known, and loved by humankind that he appear in a form human eyes could see:

> Inasmuch as the disciples were carnal, whereas God is a spirit, and spirit and flesh have little in common, he used the medium of a body to temper his brightness to their eyes, so that through the living veil of flesh they might see the Word in the flesh, the Sun of justice in a cloud, the Light of the world in an earthen vessel, the Candle in a lantern.[18]

Students of bernardine christology have long recognized Bernard's explanation of the Incarnation as made necessary by God's inaccessibility and unapproachability. The Word was made flesh, according to Bernard, to make God accessible to carnal humanity, to lead men and women through love of his flesh to love of his spirit. Dennis Farkasfalvy notes that in Bernard's writings love of Christ's flesh is the lowest step of charity, the weakness of Christ's flesh both hides the presence of the divine power and wisdom and serves as an instrument to express the divine.[19] Similarly Cuthbert Butler points out that despite

[16]Waddell, p. 95.
[17]I Nov; SBOp 5:305; Waddell 99.
[18]Asc 3.3; SBOp 5:132.
[19]Denis Farkasfalvy, 'St John's Prologue in the Writings of St Bernard', *ASOC* 35 (1979) 205–226.

Bernard's frequent 'stirring up a tender love of Our Lord's Humanity', that first sensible love 'progresses when it becomes rational love, and is perfected when it becomes spiritual love, in which the images of the Sacred Humanity no longer form part.'[20] Jean Leclercq says that Bernard

does not usually dwell on the circumstances of Jesus' earthly existence. . . He went immediately to the mysteries which these events contain and reveal. . . Bernard did not yield to sensory and imaginative piety: he accepted its legitimacy, but felt one must go beyond it. Like the Apostles on the day of the Ascension, Christians must live apart from the visible humanity of Jesus.[21]

Michael Casey best summarizes Bernard's essential teaching on the necessary rise through devotion to the Incarnate Christ to the divinity:

Conformity with Christ begins with sentiment, grows through imitation, and reaches its culmination in spiritualization—a progressive union with the Christ who has ascended to the place in which he was before. The soul is rising, with Christ, above the level of the earth in order to encounter him as the Word beyond all time, one in being with the Father. "The spiritual man must finally transcend the flesh and penetrate to the *Christus-Spiritus*." There is a clear distinction between the *amor spiritus* and the *carnis affectus*; only those who allow themselves to be made spiritual will experience a close union with the Word.[22]

Bernard further understands the Incarnation as prompted not only by God's wish to woo humankind to himself but by God's desire to know more of human experience. He explains in the *Steps of Humility*:

Our Savior. . . willed to suffer that he might know compassion. To learn mercy he shared our misery. . . . What in his divine nature he knows from all eternity he learned by experience in time. . . . I do not say that he became wiser by such experience, but he was seen as closer to men. And the frail sons of Adam. . . would have less hesitation about laying their weakness before him, who as God could

---

[20]*Western Mysticism* (London: Constable, 1922) p. 118.

[21]*Bernard of Clairvaux and the Cistercian Spirit*, pp. 81–83.

[22]*Athirst for God: Spiritual Desire in Bernard of Clairvaux's Sermons on the Song of Songs*, CS 77 (Kalamazoo: Cistercian Publications, 1988) pp. 204–205; quoting P. Delfgaauw, 'An Approach to St Bernard's Sermons on the Song of Songs', COCR 23 (1961) 148–161, p. 153.

heal them, as one close would heal them, and as one who had suffered the same would understand.[23]

So God reaches to win humankind's love not only through becoming visible and so known to humans, but by being like them, allowing them to love God in his likeness to them as they could not love God in distance and distinction from them. Unable to love the wholly other who is God, men and women may begin with God become one with them.

Futhermore, having learned to love Jesus and so begun to move toward the spiritual love of God, Christians are also, Bernard urges, to use Jesus' life as a moral pattern and so to free their bodies as well as their spirits from carnal ties. The Passion not only earns love but also models christian imitation. In a homily in praise of Mary, Bernard directs:

> Let us make every effort to be like this little child. Because he is meek and humble of heart, let us learn from him, lest he who is great, even God, should have been made a little man for nothing, lest he should have died to no purpose, and have been crucified in vain. Let us learn his humility, imitate his gentleness, embrace his love, share his sufferings, and be washed in his blood.[24]

Alberich Altermatt has noted in this context that 'Bei allen Geheimnissen des Lebens Jesu ist Bernhard bestrebt, Wort, Verhalten und Tat Christi als Beispiel, Belehrung, Modell und exemplarische Wirkursache hinzustellen.'[25] And Gilson has suggested that imitation of Christ as 'Man of Sorrows' is the 'place occupied in Cistercian mysticism by the meditation on the visible Humanity of Christ. . . . In this humiliated God we behold humility; in this Mercy we behold mercy; this "Passion by compassion" teaches us to have compassion.'[26]

Bernard's tenderness toward Jesus of Nazareth is well known, but whatever may have been the truth of it in his life, in his sermons and treatises it functions often as a moral force, a means to an end, whether to win humankind to God's love or to provide support in courage and virtue. It is 'God in himself' whom Bernard seeks to know and love, and he views the necessary steps on the journey to 'God in himself', even through God in flesh, as ultimately unsatisfying. So he, always looking ahead from God the Mediator to God the Logos, consistently

---

[23]Hum 3.6–7; SBOp 3:21–22; CF 13:35–37.
[24]Miss 3.14; SBOp 4:45; CF 18:44.
[25]Altermatt, pp. 148–149.
[26]Gilson, pp. 78–79.

transforms passages that begin in adoration of the human Christ into metaphorical or theological language. He speaks of the Spouse, God's Wisdom, and the Word much more often than of Jesus, even when recalling the events of Jesus' human life. So he writes in *Sermon 43 on the Song of Songs*:

> I made sure to gather for myself this little bunch of myrrh and place it between my breasts. It was culled from all the anxious hours and bitter experiences of my Lord; first from the privations of his infancy, then from the hardships he endured in preaching, the fatigues of his journeys, the long watches in prayer, . . . the insults, the spitting, the blows, the mockery, the scorn, the nails and similar torments that are multiplied in the Gospels, like trees in the forest, and all for the salvation of our race. . . . As long as I live I shall proclaim the memory of the abounding goodness contained in these events. . . . I have reaped the myrrh that [kings and prophets] had planted. This life-giving bunch has been reserved for me; . . . it shall be between my breasts.[27]

Shortly thereafter he urges his listeners also to place 'this delectable branch' between their breasts, also for their moral benefit rather than for increased love or knowledge of God:

> Be mindful that this is the Christ whom Simeon took up in his arms, whom Mary bore in her womb, fostered in her lap, and like a bride placed between her breasts. . . . And I can imagine how Mary's husband Joseph would often take him on his knees and smile as he played with him. . . . If you carry him as they did you will find that the sight of his afflictions will make your burdens lighter, helped as you will be by him who is the Church's Bridegroom, God blessed forever.[28]

Despite Bernard's tenderness for Jesus and explicitness that he is 'God blessed forever', he is firm in distinguishing between the man veiled in flesh and the Bridegroom sought and seen by the bride. The vision which the contemplative seeks is not to be found in Jesus in the manger or on the Cross. That vision Bernard always insists to be a spiritual event, divorced from the flesh of Jesus. So he writes:

> [Since the bride] acquired a keener power of spiritual understanding, she became pleasing to the Bridegroom, who always prefers to be seen

[27]SC 43.2; SBOp 2:42; CF 7:222.
[28]SC 43.3; SBOp 2:44; CF 7:223–24.

in a spiritual manner. . . . 'From now on', he says, 'contemplate me in the spirit, because Christ the Lord is a spirit before your face.' . . . I believe that in this vision images of his flesh, or of the cross, or any thing suggestive of physical frailty, were not imprinted on her imagination, since the prophet tells us that under these forms he possessed neither beauty nor majesty. But as she now contemplates him, she declares him both beautiful and majestic, making it clear that her present vision transcended all others. He speaks to her face to face as once he spoke to Moses, and she for her part sees God plainly, not through riddles and symbols.[29]

As Michael Casey has said, 'The soul transcends all that bespeaks limitation, even the humanity of Christ, *qua* limited, to become majesty of the divinity. Whatever foretaste the human being may receive of this heavenly vision, it remains vastly inferior to the complete experience, reserved to the future. . . . And at that time we shall be seen, even as we see, since we shall live "in the sight of God, not in the shadow", *in conspectu Dei, non in umbra*. . . . When the soul looks upon the face of God it lives.'[30]

So Bernard, often credited with originating twelfth-century devotion to the humanity of Christ, reveals himself as augustinian in his efforts to maintain a clear hierarchical distinction between God known in flesh, available to because necessary to spiritual beginners, and God known in spirit. He is always less drawn finally to the man Jesus, infant, boy, or crucified lord, than to the fruits of his flesh, faith, and salvation.[31]

AELRED ON THE SACRED HUMANITY

Aelred's treatment of the humanity of Christ contains the same elements as Bernard's, but with a distinctly different impact. Anna Maiorino Tuozzi is one of the few scholars to have noted both Aelred's grounding in and significant differences from Bernard. She notes that while for Bernard humankind is able to know something of the unknowable God through Jesus' flesh—as for example to know that 'Deus caritas est'—and is able through ascetic introspection, by knowledge of self, to advance some small way to knowledge of God, for Aelred alone is it

[29]SC 45.3–4; SBOp 2:52–53; CF 7:236–37.
[30]Casey, pp. 233–234.
[31]Dutton, 'Eat', p. 7.

possible to come to God through pure affectivity.[32] Louis Bouyer has also commented on the difference between Bernard and Aelred in this respect, saying that Aelred 'carefully avoided the equivocal term "carnal love"... he admitted that the "pious feeling" which "Our Saviour's flesh" inspires in us is the means by which we pass from [concupiscence to charity], provided this feeling is guided by faith... However, even this will be only a stage on his ascent to the love of God Himself in Christ'.[33]

Aelred, like Bernard, explains the Incarnation as emerging from God's desire for human love and as tempering God's glory to human eyes, and he writes of its allowing God to learn of human experience. Always he writes in tenderness for the God who is man. But Aelred betrays little desire to encourage Christ's lover to go beyond Jesus to the Godhead, little sense of the necessity to put away the carnal love of Christ for the love of Christ in spirit. Further, for Aelred the contemplative vision is always explicitly the face of Jesus, seen in this life as in glory.

Like Bernard, Aelred explains the Incarnation as due to human inability to know God's glory undisguised. He too explains its necessity in terms of humankind's corruption in the Fall, writing of the Logos of John 1 as

> ...the bread of angels, whose palate has not been dulled by tasting sour grapes. . . . Therefore they taste and see fully and perfectly that the Lord is sweet. But in order that man might eat the bread of angels, the bread of angels became man, taking on himself the husks of our poverty, the ashes of our mortality, the leaven of our infirmity. He who is great became a little child.[34]

In this passage Aelred, like Bernard, understands Jesus sacramentally, no longer the unleavened bread of the remote God of Exodus but the leavened bread of the new dispensation, offered forth to human palates in the Eucharist and known in the reception of that bread. In a sermon on the Nativity of Mary he makes the same point, suggesting a still greater transformation, both pauline and augustinian in its implications:[35]

---

[32]*La 'Conoscenza di Sé' nella Scuola Cisterciense* (Naples: Nella Sede dell'Istituto, 1976), 85, 98–99.

[33]*The Cistercian Heritage* (London: Mowbray, 1958) pp. 145–146.

[34]*De Jesu puero duodenni* 2.12; CCCM 1:259; CF 2:16.

[35]See 1 Co 3:1–2, 1 P 2:2–3; and Augustine, *Confessiones* 7.18.24; CC 27:108. See also Marsha L. Dutton, '"When I Was a Child": Spiritual Infancy and God's Maternity in Augustine's *Confessiones*', in Joseph C. Schnaubelt and Frederick Van Fleteren (edd.), *Collectanea Augustiniana* (New York: Peter Lang, 1990) pp. 113–40.

The Word of God, Son of God, Wisdom of God is bread and solid food. And therefore those who were strong, that is angels, ate of him alone. We who are weak were not able to taste this food, because it was solid; we who are on earth could not mount to this bread because it was in heaven. What then was to be done? This bread entered into the womb of the blessed Virgin and there was made milk. And what kind of milk? The kind that we are able to suck.[36]

For Aelred, in fact, the Eucharist itself gives rise to devotion to the Sacred Humanity. So in the *Mirror of Charity* he objects to music in church as much as anything because it distracts worshippers from their attention to the infant Christ known in the sacrifice of the altar, but that infant is as surely God as man:

Ordinary folk stand there awestruck, stupefied, marvelling at the din of bellows, the humming of chimes, and the harmony of pipes. . . . They do not fear the awesome majesty in whose presence they stand, nor do they honor that mystical crib before which they render cult, where Christ is mystically wrapped in swaddling clothes, where his most sacred blood is poured out in the chalice, where the heavens are opened and angels attend, where earthly things are joined to heavenly, and where human beings keep company with angels.[37]

While Aelred, then, allows the necessity of human weakness and spiritual beginners to require the bread of God and of angels to become milk for humankind, he is more concerned than Bernard to insist that in that transformation the Son of the Father is one with the Father and is himself always God. So in the remaining fragment of a sermon on the Nativity of Jesus he says again: 'Our Lord Jesus Christ, he is milk for us, he is solid food. He is solid food because God, milk because man; bread because the Son of God, milk because the Son of the Virgin. This milk Jerusalem administered to us when the company of angels announced his birth according to the flesh.'[38] In this sermon Aelred urges devotion to the infant lying in a manger and in his mother's bosom, and he directs his listeners to suck Jesus in the stable and imitate Jesus in his passion on the cross. It is the young and strong who are able, Aelred says, to know God made man.

---

[36]*Sermo* 23.9; CCCM 2a:186.
[37]*De speculo caritatis* [hereafter Spec] 2.23.67–68; CCCM 1:98; CF 17:211.
[38]*Sermo* 29.2; CCCM 2a:241.

Again like Bernard, Aelred adds that the old—presumably the spiritually advanced, though he says only *senes*—those who have lost the heat of the flesh, who are chilled from all bodily action and thought, may say with the apostle: 'And if we knew him according to the flesh now we know him no longer.' Aelred too, then, describes the human Jesus as milk for spiritual youths and indicates that one may know him more intimately as one advances in years and maturity.

But Aelred lacks Bernard's anxiety lest the young and strong fail to hasten beyond love of Jesus in the flesh to knowledge of Jesus in glory. In his lengthy meditation on the humanity of Christ in *On Reclusion*, Aelred not only urges the contemplative forward to touch and kiss, embrace and hold Jesus, God made man, but argues that she should resist her natural tendency to move on to something else, to advance in contemplative intimacy. So as she imaginatively approaches Jesus in her meditation on the Last Supper, he directs: 'Let love conquer modesty, friendly feeling shut out fear. . . . Why do you hurry to go out? Wait a little while.'[39] And at the end of the meditation on Christ's humanity he says again: 'Stay here for as long as you can, virgin. Let no sleep interrupt your delights, no outside disturbance hinder them.'[40]

Unlike Bernard, then, Aelred is insistent that the Word become flesh remains the Word, that in gazing on Jesus one sees God. So in a sermon on the Annunciation he writes of the Incarnation as God's covering the nakedness of his glory with a robe in order to temper to human eyes his inaccessible light, not stripping himself of glory but veiling it in new—human—beauty:

> In order then that [the sons of Adam] should not see the Son of God naked . . . it was necessary to make for him a long robe, which should so adhere to him that between the garment and the wearer there should be no difference in person, and that it should not be possible that the robe should be loved or worshipped or honored without its wearer being loved and worshipped or honored, but any honor or injury done to either one would flow back to the other. Therefore the Son of God entered into our mortality, bringing about so great a unity between himself and our human nature that, according to our catholic faith, he did not clothe himself with man but became man. 'The Word was made flesh and dwelt among us.' . . . This robe is long, because it touches

---

[39]Inst incl 31; CCCM 1:668; CF 2:86.
[40]Inst incl 31; CCCM 1:672; CF 2:92.

from end to end, on account of the divinity, and his flesh does not
see corruption. . . . Safely therefore, O Adam, safely gaze on the lord
your God in this robe. Safely adore in him so clothed the garment and
its wearer.[41]

In this sermon Aelred accents the indistinguishability between God as
the garment—Christ's humanity—and its wearer—Christ's divinity—by
moving briefly from the metaphor of the tunic and its wearer to simple
propositional insistence that all that Christ in his humanity does, Christ in
his divinity does as well: 'God sleeps, God thirsts, God saddens and dies;
man commands the winds, man walks the seas, man multiplies loaves,
man raises the dead: God in man, man in God.'[42]

Aelred is always clear that one may know and love Christ in his
divinity precisely through knowledge of his humanity, that finally the
two cannot be separated. So speaking of the Crucifixion he reflects:
'They crucify, but they do not know who it is they crucify. Had they
known, they would never have crucified the Lord of glory.'[43]

This insistence on the indistinguishability of God, Father and Son,
appears throughout Aelred's works, but most evidently in the late contemplative work *On Reclusion*. In this treatise Aelred directs the contemplative to the imaginative love of Jesus through meditation on the events
of his human life, often expressed in terms of embracing Jesus' feet
and gazing on his face. Aelred directs her in Jesus' baptism to 'search
out his secret depths. Thus at the River Jordan you may hear in the
voice the Father, in flesh the Son, and in the dove you will see the Holy
Spirit.'[44] When Aelred speaks of the woman taken in adultery, he asks
two questions that insist on one human and divine action there: 'Good
Jesus, when it is you who say "I will not condemn", who will condemn?
God justifies; who is it who will condemn?'[45] The paralytic, he says,
was let down before Jesus' feet, 'where graciousness and power came to
meet one another.'[46]

Even when concentrating, like Bernard in similar contexts, on the
moral value of approach to the sacred humanity, Aelred insists that the

---

[41]*Sermo in Annuntiatione Beate Marie de tribus tunicis Ioseph* [hereafter In Ann],
in C. H. Talbot (ed.), *Sermones Inediti Beati Aelredi Abbatis Rievallensis*, Scriptorum
S.O.C. 2 (Rome: Curiam Generalem SOC, 1952) pp. 86–87.

[42]In Ann; Talbot 87.

[43]Spec 3.5.15; CCCM 1:112; CF 17:231.

[44]Inst incl 31; CCCM 1:665; CF 2:83.

[45]Inst incl 31; CCCM 1:665; CF 2:83.

[46]Inst incl 31; CCCM 1:666; CF 2:84.

Son and the Father are one, that as one looks on Jesus with the eyes of the spirit one may indeed see the Father in the Son:

> Regarding the corruption that the great delight and pleasure of the flesh prompts, so one may easily repel or avoid it if towards the holy flesh in which our Savior clothed himself from love, he should rejoice with spiritual eyes to regard the Lord from majesty to his bending to the narrowness of the manger, to long for the virginal breasts, to be clasped in the mother's embrace, to be kissed by the happy lips of the trembling old one, that is, of holy Simeon.[47]

As in the manger so on the cross Jesus is wholly God, purposely remaining unrecognizable to those who fail to use the eyes of the spirit:

> Those eyes, which were the eyes of God, seeing and ruling over all things, he [Jesus] allowed to be darkened by evil men. . . . His head, the very sight of which made powers and principalities bow down in reverence, he bent low to be crowned by piercing thorns. . . . If they had known, they would never have put to death the Lord of glory. . . . His murderers believe him to be . . . a blasphemous upstart who claims to be equal to God in divinity. But our Lord has hidden his face from them so that they cannot recognize his divine majesty. . . . That we be not overcome by these pleasures [of the flesh], we must turn all our love for the flesh to the flesh of our blessed Lord.[48]

Aelred's concern here to explain human failure to recognize God in Jesus recalls twelfth-century explanations of the way in which the substance of the eucharistic feast, Christ's body and blood, lies hidden within the accidents of bread and wine. As theologians of the time explained human need for bread and wine by a natural *horror cruoris* and so implied Christ's graciousness in hiding his true substance in condescension to human need, so Aelred suggests here not that Jesus was not truly God, but that for the moment—for eternal human happiness—he sought not to be recognized.[49]

When Aelred, like Bernard before him, speaks of Christ as a bundle of myrrh, he transforms the image from one of moral and didactic significance into a token of intimate love; so in the meditation on the humanity of Christ in *On Reclusion*, Joseph of Arimathea 'embraces that sweet body and clasps it to his breast', saying, 'My beloved is a bundle

[47]Spec 3.5.13; CCCM 1:111; CF 17:230.
[48]Spec 3.5.14–16; CCCM 1:112; CF 17:231.
[49]Ambrose, *De sacramentis* 4.20; PL 16:443A.

of myrrh for me; he shall rest upon my breast.'[50] The pathos of such tenderness for the dead body of Jesus makes these words not theological, not moral, but rather words of human sorrow and passion.

Aelred's early *Mirror of Charity*, which he wrote while novice master at Rievaulx, probably at Bernard's direction, shares more closely than do later works Bernard's concern to distinguish between God known in himself and God tempered through flesh to humankind's perception, perhaps not only because he is a young monk writing his first book but because his audience in this work is, like Bernard's, a monastic community, made up of people for whom contemplation is only one part of the whole. In this work too, however, Aelred often urges the lover of God to meet him in Jesus, insisting on the identity of the two and the interchangeability of their relationship with those who love them. So he urges his reader: 'In sincere prayer hasten to the maternal breasts of Jesus, from them drawing for yourself an abundance of the milk of wonderful consolation. Then you will say with the apostle: "Blessed is God, who consoles us in all tribulation."' And 'As the sufferings of Christ abound in us, so also through Christ our consolation shall abound.'[51]

While Aelred's emphasis that love of Christ is love of God, that the kiss of Christ's feet is the sight of God's face, is most clear in his contemplative treatises, a certainty that the lover of God may come to God through love of Christ appears in all Aelred's spiritual works. At the same time, while he understands that the intimate knowledge of Christ in his divinity open to contemplatives is different from that available to non-contemplatives—that is always the privilege of the lover, after all—he also insists on the real knowledge available to the latter, to the one both content and able to know Christ in the flesh. So repeatedly he suggests different levels of intimacy with Christ, stages in the developing ability to know Jesus as God, and he offers his own experience as a model for that of the non-contemplative lover of God.[52] In the *Mirror of Charity* he cries out:

> Your knowledge is too excellent for me, O Lord, you are exalted far above my reach. Meanwhile I shall embrace you, Lord Jesus. I, small,

[50]Inst incl 31; CCCM 1:671; CF 2:91.
[51]Spec 1.2.59; CCCM 1:94; CF 17:204.
[52]Aelred frequently, as here, uses the augustinian confessional voice in his spiritual treatises, creating a persona that has frequently been mistakenly treated as identical to the author. Such passages may not be regarded as truly autobiographical, at least not reliably so; they do not provide sure biographical information about the abbot of Rievaulx.

shall embrace you small; I, weak, you weak; I, a man, you, a man. For even you, O Lord, were poor, riding on a donkey, on a colt, the foal of a donkey. So I shall therefore embrace you, O Lord. All my greatness is but small to you, all my strength is weak to you, all my wisdom is foolish to you. . . . I shall follow you, Lord, although not upon the mountains of spices, where your spouse found you, surely in the garden where your flesh, O Lord, was sown. There you leap; here you sleep.[53]

Similarly in *On Reclusion* he urges the contemplative midway on her journey to full knowledge of Christ in his conjoined humanity and divinity to seize all the knowledge and intimacy available to her from Christ even while she is less able, less advanced, than other contemplatives around her:

Exult now, virgin, draw near and do not delay to claim for yourself some portion of this sweetness. If you are not capable of greater things, leave John to inebriate himself with the wine of joy in the knowledge of the divinity, while you, running to the breasts of the humanity, press out milk by which you may be nourished.[54]

The spiritually mature may in contemplation, however, finally pierce behind the veil, enter Christ's sanctuary, and there see Christ as he is, God in man, God and man, eternal God. Over and over Aelred speaks of the joy of intimate knowledge of God granted to the contemplative by Christ and in Christ. So he writes:

The greater its devotion, the more securely does the soul purified by this twin love pass to the blissful embraces of the Lord's divinity, so that, inflamed with utmost desire, she goes beyond the veil of the flesh, and, entering into that sanctuary where Christ Jesus is spirit before its face, she is thoroughly absorbed by that ineffable light and unaccustomed sweetness. All that is bodily, all that is sensible, and all that is mutable are reduced to silence. The soul fixes her clear-sighted gaze on what is and is so always and is in itself: on the One. Being at leisure she sees that the Lord himself is God.[55]

---

[53]Spec 1.7.22; CCCM 1:21; CF 17:99.

[54]Inst incl 31; CCCM 1:668; CF 2:87. For a discussion of the contemplative's progress on the way to union with the crucified Christ in this work, see Marsha L. Dutton, 'Christ Our Mother: Aelred's Iconography for Contemplative Union', in E. Rozanne Elder (ed.), *Goad and Nail: Studies in Medieval Cistercian History*, *10*, CS 84 (Kalamazoo, Michigan: Cistercian Publications, 1985) pp. 21–45.

[55]Spec 3.6.17; CCCM 1:113; CF 17:232.

And in *On Reclusion* during the meditation on the crucified Christ he orders the contemplative now finally to act for herself to know both the humanity and divinity of Christ, to enter into Christ's flesh, and so to know God:

> Hasten, linger not; eat the honeycomb with your honey, drink your wine with your milk. The blood is changed into wine to inebriate you, the water into milk to nourish you. From the rock, streams have flowed for you, wounds have been made in his limbs, holes in the walls of his body, in which, like a dove, you may hide.[56]

For Aelred the contemplative's vision of Jesus the man is a vision of Jesus who is God, and as he is known now in meditation and in occasional contemplative vision he will be known in eternity. While the whole of the meditation on the humanity assumes the identity of the Son and the Father, occasionally Aelred makes that identity explicit. So in *On Reclusion*, outside the meditation on the life of Jesus, he speaks to the contemplative, saying: 'With how glad a face Christ hastens to meet the one who has renounced the world, with what delights he has fed the hungry one, what riches of his compassion he has revealed, what feelings he has aroused, with what a goblet of charity he has inebriated you.'[57]

The vision of Christ is confirmed in Aelred's description of the Judgment, when the blessed, united by the bond of charity, see that 'Jesus' face shines upon them, not terrible but lovable, not bitter but sweet, not frightening but beautiful.'[58] Then at last they may in seeing Jesus recognize that he is God, that the two are not two but one:

> The Creator...will be seen in himself.... That lovable face, so longed for, upon which the angels yearn to gaze, will be seen. Who can say anything of its beauty, its light, its sweetness? The Father will be seen in the Son, the Son in the Father, the Holy Spirit in both. He will be seen not as a confused reflection in a mirror, but face to face. For he will be seen as he is, fulfilling that promise which tells us: 'He who loves me will be loved by my Father, and I will love him and show myself to him.'[59]

[56]Inst incl 31; CCCM 1:671; CF 2:90–91.
[57]Inst incl 32; CCCM 1:676; CF 2:96.
[58]Inst incl 33; CCCM 1:679; CF 2:99.
[59]Inst incl 33; CCCM 1:681; CF 2:101.

So too in the *Mirror of Charity* he concludes that 'It is good to seek the company of the saints in this life, and even more to enjoy the presence of Christ in heaven for all eternity.'[60]

So Aelred argues in all orthodoxy that Jesus is indeed true God of true God. The failure to recognize him as such in this life has, he suggests, more to do with human failure to see than with any change, any instability, in God. It is not then necessary for Aelred to leave behind God known and loved in flesh, to put off the carnal love for Jesus in order to love God in spirit. It is only necessary to recognize that Jesus is in fact God and so to love him as God. The tunic, the veil of flesh assumed by God, only works to hide God, perhaps, from those who are not truly looking. Aelred essays throughout his spiritual works to strip away the tunic, to illuminate God within his sanctuary of flesh so that he may be seen through the veil, and so to open up humankind's spiritual eyes.

Bernard and Aelred are at one in their devotion to Jesus of Nazareth, the infant born of Mary, the child dandled on Joseph's knees, the friend of Mary, Martha, and Lazarus, and the man crucified under Pontius Pilate. Together they cry out: 'Your face, O Lord, I require!' Together with Paul they declare, in the words of Bernard: 'This is my philosophy . . . to know Jesus and him crucified. . . . I do not ask where he rests at noon, for I see him on the cross as my Savior.'[61] Together they see 'the Mediator of God and man hanging midway between heaven and earth, uniting the heights with the depths and joining the things of earth to the things of heaven.'[62] And together they urge adoration of 'the man in God and God in the man.'[63] They differ not in their devotion to God in his humanity but in their understanding of the appropriate human response to it.

Bernard sees God's recourse to the Incarnation as primarily a means to an end, to win humans to love him in spirit, and so concentrates on Jesus as a bridge, a mediator. In this he guides his audience toward the spiritual maturity that leaves Christ's flesh behind and reaches toward the spirit. Aelred, however, rejects any radical distinction between love in flesh and love in spirit. Arguing throughout his works that love in the flesh is love in the spirit, he explains to his readers and hearers that one need not leave behind the love of the Son to know and love the Father,

[60]Spec 3.24.56; CCCM 1:131; CF 17:259.
[61]SC 43.4; SBOp 2:38; CF 7:222–23.
[62]Inst incl 31; CCCM 1:670; CF 2:89.
[63]Inst incl 31; CCCM 1:667; CF 2:85.

but that as they are one, the one who loves the one knows and loves the other.

The apparent difference between Bernard's and Aelred's treatment of the Incarnation may well result more from the particular need of their audiences than from their christology. Bernard's teaching on the humanity of Jesus appears most often in sermons addressed to members of a monastic community, urging his listeners primarily not to contemplative knowledge of God through Christ but to love of God as he makes himself known in the daily life of the world, promising greater joy, greater intimacy, greater things to come.

Bernard writes not solely for the contemplative, but for the christian monk who wishes to love and follow Jesus here as man in order to see, know, and worship him as God in eternity. Thus his emphasis throughout his works is God's desire to know humans in order to show God's mercy to them, God's longing to show himself to humans in order to win their love, and Jesus as the manifestation of that love and the model of loving behavior. When he writes on the contemplative life, he emphasizes not Jesus the man, but the Bridegroom, God the lover of the soul. And when he writes of Jesus, he concentrates on the acts and effects of Jesus' earthly life, his modelling love and humility, his pain and death to redeem humankind.

Aelred, however, writes most frequently and most clearly on the sacred humanity of Christ in treatises with clear contemplative purpose, often indeed explicitly addressed to contemplatives. He writes to guide contemplatives to the face of God here and now. When he writes of Jesus, however, he usually seeks to guide the contemplative to the knowledge and intimate love of God in this life. Hence he urges his audience to understand that the Jesus they may come to love through meditation on his human life is himself the God they seek and that in loving Jesus they already know, see, and love God.

Where for Bernard finally the kiss of the feet of Jesus is merely the first step on the long human path toward the eternal vision of God's face, for Aelred the kiss of the feet of Jesus is the kiss of the feet of God, and the face before which one kneels is the face of the eternal Trinity, Father, Son, and Holy Spirit.

ABSTRACTS

Une comparaison de l'humanité sacrée du Christ dans les oeuvres de Bernard de Clairvaux et d'Aelred de Rievalux montre qu'en dépit de leur accord essentiel Aelred adopte une intelligence plus confortablement incarnationnelle de l'homme Jésus que Bernard. Tandis que Bernard exhorte les personnes ferventes à aimer Jésus mais à dépasser sa chair pour atteindre l'esprit qu'elle voile, Aelred insiste qu'en Jésus 'le terrestre est uni au céleste'.

Bernard présente plus souvent Jésus comme manifestation de l'amour de Dieu, modèle du comportement humain, et rédempteur de l'humanité que comme objet de dévotion. Dans ses oeuvres le baiser des pieds de Jésus entraîne à aller toujours plus avant jusqu'à aimer Dieu en esprit. Aelred, de son côté, encourage les personnes ferventes à s'attarder en méditations sur l'humanité sainte, affirmant qu'en baisant les pieds de Jésus on connaît Dieu et qu'en oignant les pieds de Jésus on voit la face de Dieu.

A comparison of the sacred humanity of Christ in the works of Bernard of Clairvaux and Aelred of Rievaulx shows that despite their essential agreement, Aelred espouses a more comfortably incarnational understanding of the man Jesus than does Bernard. While Bernard urges the devout to love Jesus but then go beyond his flesh to the spirit it veils, Aelred insists that in Jesus 'earthly things are joined to heavenly'.

Bernard more often presents Jesus as the manifestation of God's love, model of human behavior, and redeemer of humankind than as object of devotion. In his works the kiss of Jesus' feet draws one always onward to love God in spirit. Aelred, however, encourages the devout to linger in meditation on the sacred humanity, saying that in kissing Jesus' feet one knows God and in anointing Jesus' feet one sees God's face.

Ein Vergleich der heiligen Menschheit Christi in den Werken von Bernhard von Clairvaux und Aelred von Rievaulx zeigt, daß Aelred trotz der grundsätzlichen Übereinstimmung beider ein eher inkarnatorisches Verständnis des Menschen Jesus hat als dies bei Bernhard der Fall ist. Während Bernhard den Frommen auffordert, Jesus zu lieben, aber dann über das Fleisch hinaus zum Geist zu gehen, den es verdeckt, besteht Aelred darauf, daß in Jesus 'irdische Dinge mit himmlischen verbunden sind'.

Bernhard zeigt Jesus öfter als Offenbarung der Liebe Gottes, als Modell menschlichen Verhaltens und als Erlöser der Menschheit, als als Gegenstand der Hingabe. In seinen Werken zieht der Kuß der Füße Jesu einen immer dahin, Gott im Geist zu lieben. Aelred jedoch ermutigt den Frommen, in der Meditation der heiligen Menschheit Christi zu verweilen, indem er sagt: beim Kuß der Füße Jesu erkennt man Gott und beim Salben der Füße Jesu sieht man Gottes Angesicht.

SAINT BERNARD'S THREE STEPS OF TRUTH AND
SAINT AELRED OF RIEVAULX'S THREE LOVES

Elizabeth Connor, OCSO
Abbaye Notre-Dame du Bon Conseil

S AINT BERNARD'S TREATISE *On the Steps of Humility* and Saint Aelred of Rievaulx's *Mirror of Charity*, were the first important works of their respective authors.[1] Bernard was still a young abbot when he wrote *On the Steps of Humility*. A generation later, Aelred, with experience as novice master, undertook his treatise at Bernard's request.[2]

In 1142, Aelred, on his way to Rome to present to Pope Innocent II the opinion of his abbot concerning the succession to the archbishopric of York, stopped at Clairvaux. It is very probable that he met Bernard at that time. Whether he did or not, Bernard's influence on Aelred was so great that Aelred became known as the Bernard of the North.

These two treatises give us the fundamental features of the two Fathers' monastic teaching and their initial intuition concerning the cistercian community. Bernard and Aelred would develop, and re-develop,

---

[1]Bernard, Hum; SBOp 3:13–59. All quotations are from the English translation by M. Ambrose Conway, OCSO, in *The Works of Bernard of Clairvaux*, V; *Treatises II*, CF 13 (Washington, D.C.: Cistercian Publications, 1974) pp. 25–82. All references to the *Mirror of Charity* (hereafter Spec car) are to the CCCM 1 edition: *Aelredi Rievallensis Opera omnia*, 1, *Opera ascetica*, edd. A. Hoste and C. H. Talbot (Turnholt: Typographi Brepols Editores Pontifici, 1971). There is an English translation by Elizabeth Connor, CF 17 (Kalamazoo: Cistercian Publications, 1990).

[2]For the date of Hum, see the Introduction by Jean Leclercq in SBOp 3:3–4. For the date of the composition of Spec car, see Charles Dumont's Introduction in CF 17, pp. 55–58.

throughout their lives, these original intuitions which sparked the flame of their ardor for the cistercian life.

Though the works are very different, there are a number of points of convergence between what Bernard has to say about Truth in the first part of *On the Steps of Humility* and what Aelred tells us about the three loves, or sabbaths, in the *Mirror of Charity*. In this paper I shall explore these convergences.

In both works, within the framework of the 'three-degree' structure classic in medieval spirituality, the three types of fundamental human relationships, that is, with oneself, with others, and with God, are described. Both works give us a way of return to God, of union with God, a way to happiness. This is not surprising, because twelfth-century people and, *a fortiori*, twelfth-century monks were preoccupied with questions such as: who is man—who am I? How can I reach God? In other words, they were preoccupied with metaphysical questions and with anthropology, the meaning of human existence. Both works show the importance the Cistercians attributed to experience in the spiritual life, a person's own experience and at the same time what Christ experienced in his Incarnation, his experience of the human condition, so that in sharing it with us he might draw our love to himself.[3]

Both works also provide a theological and ascetic framework important for anyone desiring to grow spiritually, and especially for monks. Bernard's development of the three degrees of the perception of truth[4] and Aelred's of charity are centered on the twofold commandment of love of God and neighbor, with particular emphasis on the Lord's new commandment (see Jn 13:34). Quoting Saint Paul, Aelred writes:

'Be renewed in the spirit of your mind, and put on the new man who was created according to God' [Eph 4:23–24]. But how will this renewal come about except by the new precept of love, of which the Savior says: 'I give you a new commandment' [Jn 13:34]. . . .A summary of this one precept is presented to us in a very salutary way: divesting of the old man, renewal of his mind, and the reforming of the divine image.[5]

[3]Chapter 3 of Hum is a long meditation on the willed abasement of Christ so that he might save humankind.
[4]Hum 3.6: 'There are three degrees in the perception of truth.' CF 13:34.
[5]Spec car 1.8.24; CF 17:100.

Aelred, like Saint Augustine, sees the divine image in the human person as a reflection of the Trinity. The reforming of the image, therefore, implies the reforming of the three faculties which reflect the Father, Son, and Holy Spirit respectively: the memory, the capacity for eternity, so that a person might hold fast to God without forgetfulness; the understanding, so that one might recognize God without error; and the will or love (*caritas*), so that one might embrace God without self-centered desire for anything else.[6]

In the *Eleventh Sermon on the Song of Songs*, Saint Bernard also associates a Person of the Trinity with each of the three faculties of the soul:

'Put your hope in God. I shall praise him yet' [Ps 41:6], when error will have gone from the reason, pain from the will, and every trace of fear from the memory. Then will come that state for which we hope, with its admirable serenity, its fullness of delight, its endless security. The God who is truth is the source of the first of these gifts; the God who is love, of the second; the God who is all-powerful, of the third. And so it will come to pass that God will be all in all, for the reason will receive unquenchable light, the will imperturbable peace, the memory an unfailing fountain from which it will draw eternally.[7]

Bernard does not develop a doctrine of the image in his treatise on humility, even though such a doctrine is implicit. He would present his conception of the image later, in the last sermons on the *Song of Songs*.[8]

TRUTH AND CHARITY

The truth of which Bernard speaks in his treatise on humility is not ethical truth (telling the truth) or logical truth (speaking without error).[9]

---

[6]See Spec car 1.3.9; CF 17:92. See also Saint Augustine, *De trinitate* 14.8.11; 10.11.17; 11.1.1.

[7]Bernard, SC 11.6; SBOp 1:58. English translation is from *Song of Songs I*, trans. Kilian Walsh, OCSO, CF 4 (Kalamazoo, Michigan: Cistercian Publications, Inc., 1971) pp. 73–74.

[8]Saint Bernard develops his doctrine on the image of God especially in SC 80–85. English translation in *On the Song of Songs IV*, trans. Irene Edmonds, CF 40 (Kalamazoo, Michigan: Cistercian Publications, 1974) pp. 145–210.

[9]"The truth is reality. It is what *is*. . . . The procedure [in the treatise on humility], according to philosophical analysis, is: first: reflection—*se ante se*—returning to self; secondly, transfer from the individual to the universal; thirdly: intuitive knowledge, where

Just as God is *caritas* (1 Jn 4:16)—and this is the ever-present Reality for Aelred—so for Bernard Truth is a person. It is a God who is faithful, who does not deceive anyone or abandon us in our state of *miseria* and weakness. He is the God who is *veritas et misericordia* (Ps 84:11), who makes one free.[10] We might say that this Truth is three persons, because in the treatise Bernard sees a particular person of the Trinity particularly operative in each of the three degrees of perception of truth. Not that he denies the unity of the Trinity in all that it does, but he affirms that thus the operations can be more easily distinguished by our human understanding.[11] As we shall see, in the first step it is the Son, the Word, Christ, who gives example, teaches, and is the Master. In the second step it is the Holy Spirit, brother and friend, who gives love and consoles. And in the third step, it is the Father who embraces in glory.[12]

Aelred, on the other hand, stresses the unity of the three loves in God:

Every good work is founded on faith in the one sole God and progresses by the sevenfold gift of the Holy Spirit to reach him who is truly one, where all that we are is made one with him. And because there is no division in unity, let there be no outpouring of the mind in various directions, but let it be one in the One, with the One, through the One, around the One, sensing the One, savoring the One— and because always one, always resting, and therefore observing a perpetual sabbath.[13]

If Aelred uses the scriptural term 'sabbath' to signify the three loves, it is because humankind tends toward the Sabbath of Sabbaths: 'Love alone is his [God's] changeless and eternal rest, his eternal and changeless tranquillity, his eternal and changeless Sabbath.'[14] Once again, Aelred is following the line of thought of Saint Augustine, for whom the human person's end and final rest is to be attained in the peace of divine love.[15] This rest and peace are supremely dynamic:

the truth is grasped in itself.' Unpublished lecture, 'Saint Bernard's Steps of Humility', by Charles Dumont, OCSO, Gethsemani Abbey, 1974.

[10]See Jn 8:32. Also, SC 6.7; CF 4:36, and SC 67.10; CF 40:14.

[11]See Hum 7.20; CF 13:48. Also, SC 11.6; CF 4:74.

[12]Hum 7.20; CF 13:48.

[13]Spec car 3.1.1; CF 17:221.

[14]Spec car 1.19.56; CF 17:119.

[15]See endnote 1 to Spec car 3.1, in CF 17:302: 'Aelred built his doctrine of the degrees of charity on the three sabbaths prescribed in the book of Leviticus. . . . He follows as

His [God's] love is his very will and also his very goodness, and all this is nothing but his being. Indeed, for him this is to be always resting, that is, always existing, in his ever gracious love, in his ever peaceful will, and in his ever abounding goodness.[16]

But how is this God who is goodness and being to be sought? How is Truth to be sought? To reach it, says Bernard,

> There are three steps. We climb to the first by the toil of humility, to the second by a deep feeling of compassion, and to the third by the ecstasy of contemplation. On the first step we experience the severity of truth, on the second its tenderness, and on the third its purity.[17]

On this climb, humility is a good path (Ps 118:71): 'It seeks for truth; it wins love; it shares the fruits of wisdom. . . .When Christ came he brought grace; when truth is known it brings love [*caritas*].'[18] Truth, love, grace, wisdom—these are all one in the unity of God. Bernard associates each step of truth with one of the beatitudes: the meek, the merciful, and the pure of heart, respectively. And just as in the Beatitudes the merciful come before the pure of heart and the meek are spoken of before the merciful (Mt 5:5, 7, 8), so we should seek truth in ourself before seeking it in our neighbor (see Ga 6:1), and in our neighbor before seeking it in itself.[19]

Aelred has a like insight about the relationship among the three loves or sabbaths, but he expresses it somewhat differently. For him, love of self precedes love of neighbor, and love of neighbor precedes love of God. But he adds:

> Precedes it, I say, in sequence, not in excellence. . . .Of course, a certain part of this love [of God], even if not its fullness, necessarily precedes both love of self and of neighbor. . . .It seems to me that God is, so to speak, the soul of the other loves.[20]

---

well the account of the six days of creation given in Augustine's treatise *De Genesi ad litteram*, where no less than fourteen chapters of Book Four are devoted to God's rest. . . . Aelred grasped that in these chapters Augustine was expressing his theology on the human person's end and final rest in the peace of divine love.'

[16]Spec car 1.19.56; CF 17:119.
[17]Hum 6.19; CF 13:47.
[18]Hum 2.5; CF 13:34.
[19]Hum 4.14; CF 13:42, and Hum 3.6; CF 13:34.
[20]Spec car 3.2.4; CF 17:223–224. That love of God is the soul of love of self and neighbor is shown by Bernard in SC 50.7; CF 31:36, and in Dil 8.25; CF 13:117.

THE FIRST STEP: KNOWLEDGE AND LOVE OF SELF

To be meek and humble of heart, like Jesus, a person must know himself, exactly as he is, the real self, by an intuitive grasp coming from experience. This is an expression of the greek principle *gnothi seauton* which is found throughout christian spirituality. Once the beam has been cast from his own eye (Mt 7:5), he realizes that he is faced with a choice and aspires to something better.[21] Experiencing the limits of the human condition and the suffering resulting from these limits, and conscious of being a 'sinner' because of both original sin and personal guilt, he likewise grasps that he is unable to be happy by his own means, and turns to prayer. He must

> . . . set up in his heart a ladder of humility so that he can search into himself. When he has climbed its twelve rungs [an allusion to the *Rule of Saint Benedict*] he will then stand on the first step of truth.[22]

He realizes that he is merely a servant (Lk 17:10), but love of truth makes him hunger and thirst for justice (Mt 5:6).[23]

For Aelred, consciousness of this condition of *miseria* is more akin to disquietude, which has the taste of bread of bitterness.[24] Pride has led humankind away from God, not by footsteps but by attachments of the heart.[25] Aelred exhorts:

> Let us, who profess the cross of Christ, having taken up the key of God's Word, unlock the gates of our breast, and, penetrating as far as the division of soul and spirit, of joints and marrow [Heb 4:12], let us discern the thoughts and intentions of our heart.[26]

Then it will be possible to approach God by an attachment of spirit.[27]

In this passage, Aelred is concerned with the moral effort needed for return to God. In Book I of the *Mirror*, he had shown that all man has, is, or can do comes from God:

---

[21]Hum 5.18; CF 13:45. See also SC 3.4; CF 4:19: 'His hand must raise you up. How raise you? By giving you the grace to dare to aspire.'

[22]Hum 4.15; CF 13:43. See also SC 34.1 and SC 36.5. English translation by Kilian Walsh, OCSO, in *On the Song of Songs II*, CF 7 (Kalamazoo, Michigan: Cistercian Publications, 1983) pp. 160 and 177–78.

[23]Hum 5.18; CF 13:45–46.

[24]Spec car 1.1.2; CF 17:88. See Hum 2.4; CF 13:32.

[25]Spec car 1.8.24; CF 17:100.

[26]Spec car 2.1.3; CF 17:164.

[27]See Spec car 1.8.24; CF 17:100.

God [is the] supreme Being, supremely Good and Beautiful, and the Goodness of all things good. . . .So a creature is not happy of itself, but from the One who is supremely happy and therefore the Happiness of all the blessed.[28]

Unlocking one's heart, setting up a ladder in one's heart, means shouldering the Lord's yoke and learning from him who is meek and humble of heart (Mt 11:29). Though humility is bitter food, it is medicinal.[29] It is food while the soul grows wings in the nest of the Lord's discipline.[30]

The nest of discipline is the monastic rule. In the cloister a monk is forced to face the truth about himself. There is no escape to pretense or distractions. He begins to judge himself[31] and to experience the severity of the truth about himself.[32] Interiorly bowing his neck under the yoke of divine love, he does not yet fully realize that the Lord's yoke is easy and his burden light (Mt 11:30), because the new love infused into his soul is struggling with inveterate self-centeredness.[33]

Whereas Bernard stresses the beatitude of the meek in this first step, Aelred thinks more of being poor of heart, and cries out: 'Meanwhile [during our earthly pilgrimage] I shall embrace you, Lord Jesus. I, small, shall embrace you small; I, weak, you weak; I, a man, you, a man.'[34] Both beatitudes, practiced in imitation of Christ, are purifying and lead to the inner peace of the first sabbath described by Aelred:

> When a person withdraws. . . into the secret retreat of his mind and, once the gate is closed on the throng of noisy trifles around him, surveys his inward treasures, he finds. . . everything tranquil. . . like a well-ordered and peaceful family. He recognizes that whatever good there is in him is his [God's] gift. This is the solemnity of the seventh day. Six days must precede it, that is, the perfection of deeds. First we sweat at good works and then, at last, we pause in tranquillity of conscience.[35]

For Saint Bernard, too, knowledge of one's lowliness brings tranquillity, very sober tranquillity, which nevertheless leads to praise: 'When

[28]Spec car 1.3.8; CF 17:91.
[29]Hum 2.5; CF 13:33. See Spec car 1.31.88; CF 17:141: 'What is hope but food for the journey to support us in the miseries of this life?'
[30]Spec car 1.5.16; CF 17:95.
[31]Hum 7.21; CF 13:49.
[32]Hum 4.15; CF 13:43.
[33]Spec car 1.9.27; CF 17:101–102.
[34]Spec car 1.7.22; CF 17:98–99.
[35]Spec car 3.3.6; CF 17:225.

I had come to know Christ, to imitate his humility, I saw the truth and exalted it in me by my confession, but "I myself was humbled exceedingly" [Ps 115:10].'[36] He expresses the same sentiments in his *Thirty-sixth Sermon on the Song of Songs*:

> As long as I look at myself, my eye is filled with bitterness [Jb 17:2]. But if I look up and fix my eyes on the aid of divine mercy, this happy vision of God soon tempers the bitter vision of myself. . . .This vision of God is not a little thing. It reveals him to us as listening compassionately to our prayers, as truly kind and merciful. . . .By this kind of experience, God makes himself known to us for our good.[37]

THE SECOND STEP: THE YOKE WHICH UNITES

For Bernard, this second step is characterized by the beatitude of the merciful. Whereas in the first step Truth emerges in severity, here it appears as tenderness and compassion, the fruit of suffering (*compatior*):

> When in the light of Truth men know themselves. . .and are brought face to face with themselves,. . . .they fly from justice to mercy by the road Truth shows them. . . .They look beyond their own needs to the needs of their neighbors and from the things they themselves have suffered they learn compassion.[38]

When a person has experienced the suffering coming from his own weakness and limitations, he can see that everyone else is just like him and exclaim: *omnis homo mendax*; 'all men are false' (Ps 115:11). For Bernard, this is not a cry of pessimistic distrust of others. Here *mendax* has an almost metaphysical meaning: everyone is in a condition of precariousness; everyone is weak, finite, passing. No one can escape death; no one is stable. Bernard comments: '[The Psalmist] meant that every man is unreliable because too weak, helpless, and infirm to save either himself or others.'[39] As compassion for all humanity wells up in our heart, our gaze spontaneously turns to Jesus, who though infinite and eternal Mercy in the Godhead, willed to experience human misery:

> Our Savior has given us an example. He willed to suffer so that he might know compassion [Heb 2:17]; to learn mercy he shared

36Hum 4.15; CF 13:44.
37SC 36.6; CF 7:179.
38Hum 5.18; CF 13:45–46.
39Hum 5.16; CF 13:44.

our misery. It is written: 'He learned obedience from the things he suffered' [Heb 5:8], and he learned mercy in the same way. I do not mean that he did not know how to be merciful before; his mercy is from eternity to eternity [Ps 102:17]; but what in his divine nature he knows from all eternity, he learned by experience in time. . . .The work of his tender love had its beginning in his eternal mercy, its completion in the mercy shown in his humanity.[40]

Mercy disposes one to help, rather than judge others, and to react with gentleness rather than irritation when faced with their weakness and misery.[41] In Christ, human misery and divine mercy have met, so that it is *our* misery which we discover in Christ, but deified,[42] sacramentalized, and anointed by the virtue of the Word.[43] So also the ointment of loving-kindness has the power to heal.[44] This second step, taking place by the operation of the Holy Spirit, permits the merciful to grasp Truth in others and extend their own feelings to them, conforming themselves to them in love. In his commentary on the *Song of Songs*, Saint Bernard writes: 'As for your neighbor whom you are obliged to love as yourself, if you are to experience him as he is, you will actually experience him only as you do yourself; he is what you are.'[45]

Both Bernard and Aelred consider this step, where fraternal love is situated, as indispensable for growth in love of God in himself. Thus the cistercian community is a *schola caritatis*, a place where one learns to love God and others. The practice of love in community cleanses selfishness from the heart and frees it to love.

Aelred beautifully describes the transition from recognizing our own weakness to having compassion for others, at the same time showing how fraternal charity and purifying moral effort go hand in hand:

> If, from the quite secret chamber in which a person celebrates this first sabbath [of love of self], he directs himself to that inn of his breast where he usually rejoices with those who rejoice, weeps with those who weep [Rm 12:15], burns with those who are scandalized [2 Co

---

[40]Hum 3.6, 3.12; CF 13:35 and 40.

[41]See Hum 4.13; CF 13:41.

[42]See SC 6.3; CF 4:33: 'He became incarnate for the sake of carnal man, that he might induce him to relish the life of the Spirit. In the body and through the body he performed works of which not man but God was the author.'

[43]See SC 31.9; CF 7:132.

[44]SC 12.1; CF 4:77.

[45]SC 50.7. English translation by Kilian Walsh, OCSO, and Irene M. Edmonds in *On the Song Songs III*, CF 31 (Kalamazoo, Michigan: Cistercian Publications, 1979) p. 36.

11:29], and if he senses there that his soul is united with the souls of all his brothers by the cement of love, and that it is not vexed by any pricks of envy, set afire by any heat of indignation, wounded by darts of suspicion, or consumed by the gnawing of rapacious sadness, then he clasps all of them to the utterly tranquil bosom of his mind. There he embraces and cherishes them all with tender attachment and makes them one heart and one soul with himself. At the very pleasing taste of this sweetness, the whole tumult of self-centered desires soon falls silent and the din of evil habits quiets down. Within, there is absolute holiday from everything harmful, and in the sweetness of brotherly love an agreeable and joyful interlude.[46]

The yoke of the Lord does not oppress but unites; this yoke is love.[47] The monk comes to realize how good and pleasant it is for brothers to live together (Ps 132:1). This is the second sabbath. It is also the second step in the perception of truth.

THE THIRD STEP: TOWARD THE INVISIBLE

When, in zeal for justice and perseverance in works of mercy, fraternal love purifies the spiritual vision,[48] the slow climber, the pilgrim in search of a resting place, sees a light on the horizon. Truth's promise is close to being fulfilled: 'Blessed are the pure of heart, for they shall see God' [Mt 5:8]. This is the beatitude for the third step of perception of truth, where Truth is contemplated in its own nature. It is the beatitude of those who, by uprightness of intention, strive to please God alone and adhere to him.[49] Bernard writes:

With the foot of grace firmly planted on the ladder of humility, painfully dragging the foot of my own weakness behind me, I . . . safely mount upward, until, holding fast to the Truth, I attain the broad plain of charity.[50] . . . Already I see God, resting on the top of the ladder; already I have the joy of hearing the voice of Truth. He calls to me and I reply to him: 'Stretch out your right hand to the work of your hands' [Jb 14:15].[51]

[46]Spec car 3.4.7; CF 17:225–226.
[47]Spec car 1.27.78; CF 17:133.
[48]See Hum 6.19; CF 13:47.
[49]SC 7.7; CF 4:43.
[50]Hum 9.26; CF 13:55.
[51]Hum 9.24; CF 13:53.

Bernard is convinced that love is itself the rest which is promised to those who gain the top: 'To this, Saint Benedict says, the monk will quickly come when he has climbed all the steps of humility.'[52]

The soul has been led by the Holy Spirit from the school of humility, where Jesus has been her Master, to the storehouse of love.[53] Now she is led into the chamber of the King, where she is fed with the secrets of Truth. Such times of silence in heaven are short—'just one half-hour', says Bernard, alluding to the *Book of Revelation* (8:1)—but the soul will dwell on these secrets later, for she will still have to endure absence and trials and struggles, and will need the support of this remembrance.[54]

For Aelred, it is because the Word was made flesh and dwelt among us (Jn 1:14) that we are inclined toward the twofold love of self and neighbor. It is in consideration (meditation) of the flesh of our Savior, the Lord as a human being like us, that we can learn to love ourselves and our neighbor as we ought.[55] These two loves prepare the soul for the Sabbath of Sabbaths:

> Purified by this twin love [of self and neighbor], the soul passes to the blissful embrace of the Lord's divinity, so that, inflamed with utmost desire, she goes beyond the veil of the flesh and, entering the sanctuary where Christ Jesus is spirit before her face [Lm 4:20], she is thoroughly absorbed by that ineffable light and unaccustomed sweetness. . . .The soul fixes her clear-sighted gaze on what is and is so always and is in itself: on the One.[56]

The third love of Aelred involves 'leaving oneself completely and passing over into God'.[57] On the first sabbath the mind has savored the goodness of Jesus in his humanity; on the second, it has seen how perfect he is in love; on the Sabbath of Sabbaths it sees how sublime he is in his Godhead. The Sabbath of Sabbaths is also the inpouring of the fullness of the Spirit. This does not mean that the Spirit was not given at all before, but that he had not been given with such great fullness or such great perfection. He is given in the first and second sabbaths, but on the Sabbath of Sabbaths his fullness is poured out.[58]

---

[52]Hum 2.3; CF 13:32. See RB 7.67.
[53]Hum 7.21; CF 13:50.
[54]Hum 7.21; CF 13:50.
[55]Spec car 3.5.13; CF 17:230.
[56]Spec car 3.6.17; CF 17:232.
[57]See Spec car 1.1.2; CF 17:88.
[58]Spec car 3.6.18; CF 17:233.

For Bernard, contemplation signifies the perfection of a human being's nature; it signifies entry into the purity of Truth which sweeps one up to the sight of things invisible.[59] But love in its fullness will be reached only in heaven. All of Bernard's major treatises lead to the same vision: that contemplation is a foretaste of heavenly beatitude.[60] As Charles Dumont has written: 'The full experience is eschatological, and no grace of contemplation can ever be more than a foretaste comforting the monk in his quest and fanning the flame of his desire.'[61]

Aelred's vision is the same:

In experiencing a drop of your sweetness, may my soul have a foretaste of what to desire, what to long for, what to sigh for here on her pilgrimage. In her hunger let her have a foretaste, in her thirst let her drink. . . .[Those who hunger and thirst] will be filled when your glory appears [Ps 16:15].[62]

During this pilgrimage, on the laborious road which leads to beatitude, love is rest for the weary, an inn for the traveler, and full light at journey's end.[63] Christ, who invites all to come to him (Mt 11:28), is himself rest and light. For when he came, abasing himself, he brought grace; when Truth is known it brings Love.[64] Truth must not be separated from love, and it is only in truth that love finds its full flowering.[65]

When these two dwell in the soul, there is conformity of wills. Aelred writes:

The will of God is itself his love, which is nothing other than his Holy Spirit by whom love is poured out into our hearts [Rm 5:5]. It is an outpouring of divine love and a coordination of the human will with, or certainly a subordination of the human will to, the divine will. This happens when the Holy Spirit, who is the will and love of God, and who is God, penetrates and pours himself into the human will. Lifting it up from lower to higher things, he transforms it totally into his own mode and quality, so that, cleaving to the Spirit by the indissoluble glue of unity, it is made one spirit with him.[66]

[59]Hum 6.19; CF 13:47.
[60]Pacificus Delfgaauw, *Saint Bernard, Maître de l'amour divin* (Diss., Rome, 1952) p. 195.
[61]Charles Dumont, 'Experience in the Cistercian Discipline', in CSt 10 (1975) 137.
[62]Spec car 1.2.2; CF 17:88.
[63]Spec car 1.31.88; CF 17:141.
[64]Hum 2.5; CF 13:34.
[65]Delfgaauw, p. 195. See also SC 50.6; CF 31:35.
[66]Spec car 2.18.53; CF 17:200–201.

This is the melody which Bernard calls the very music of the heart, a harmony not of voices but of wills.[67]

ABSTRACTS

Dans leurs traités respectifs, les *Degrés de l'humilité* et le *Miroir de la Charité*, Saint Bernard de Clairvaux et Saint Aelred de Rievaulx déploient leurs intuitions initiales quant aux traits fondamentaux de leur vision monastique. La présente étude s'efforce de dégager les convergences des deux traités. Tous deux présentent un itinéraire spirituel où la quête de Dieu se situe dans la triple relation de l'existence humaine: à soi-même, à autrui et à Dieu. Chez Bernard, trois degrés d'amour sont liés aux béatitudes des doux, des miséricordieux et des coeurs purs. Chez Aelred, trois amours sont comparés à trois sabbats. Voici quelques-uns des principaux thèmes de cette voie spirituelle: l'abaissement du Christ, source de grâce, l'image de Dieu dans l'homme, le commandement nouveau, le passage de Jésus dans son humanité à Jésus dans sa divinité, le repos de Dieu, la contemplation comme avant-goût de la vie future. La vérité mène à l'amour; l'amour s'épanouit en vérité.

In their respective treatises, *On the Steps of Humility* and the *Mirror of Charity*, Saint Bernard of Clairvaux and Saint Aelred of Rievaulx unfold their initial intuitions on the fundamental features of their monastic vision. The present study endeavors to bring out the convergences between the two treatises. Both present a spiritual itinerary by which the search for God takes place in the threefold relationship of human existence: with self, others and God. For Bernard, three steps of truth are bound to the Beatitudes of the meek, the merciful and the pure of heart. For Aelred, three loves are likened to three sabbaths. Some of the principal themes on this spiritual way: Christ's grace-imparting abasement, the image of God in man, the New Commandment, passing from Jesus in his humanity to Jesus in his Godhead, God's rest, contemplation as a foretaste of the life to come. Truth brings love; love flowers in truth.

In ihren jeweiligen Abhandlungen *De gradibus humilitatis* und *Speculum caritatis* entfalten der heilige Bernhard von Clairvaux und der heilige Aelred von Rievaulx ihre anfänglichen Erkenntnisse über die grundlegenden Merkmale ihrer monastischen Vision. Die vorliegende Untersuchung

[67]SC 1.11; CF 4:6–7.

bemüht sich darum, die Konvergenzen zwischen den beiden Abhandlungen herauszuarbeiten. Beide bieten einen geistlichen Weg, auf dem
die Suche nach Gott einen Platz findet in den dreifachen Beziehungen der
menschlichen Existenz: mit sich selbst, mit anderen, mit Gott. Für Bernhard sind drei Schritte der Wahrheit verbunden mit den Seligpreisungen
der Sanftmütigen, der Barmherzigen und derer, die reinen Herzens sind.
Für Aelred sind drei Liebesarten drei Sabbathen gleichgesetzt. Einige
der Hauptthemen auf diesem geistlichen Weg: die Gnade verleihende
Erniedrigung Christi, das Bild Gottes im Menschen, das neue Gebot,
der Übergang von Jesus in seiner Menschheit zu Jesus in seiner Gott-
heit, Gottes Ruhe, Kontemplation als Vorgeschmack auf das kommende
Leben. Wahrheit bringt Liebe; Liebe blüht in der Wahrheit.

BERNARD OF CLAIRVAUX AND GILBERT OF HOYLAND ON THE *SONG OF SONGS* 3:1-4

M. Pamela Clinton, ocso
Mount Saint Mary's Abbey

IN THIS YEAR marking the nine-hundredth anniversary of the birth of Bernard of Clairvaux it is fitting that his life and works be the focus of congresses and the subject of papers. Bernard's influence swept across the Europe of his day and stretches to times and places of which he never dreamt. His most immediate influence was on twelfth-century Cistercians, most directly the monks of his monastery, and, through General Chapters and regular visitations on other abbots and monks. His writings and preaching extended his influence to most of the christian West.

Bernard of Clairvaux died before completing his commentary on the *Song of Songs*.[1] Having begun to comment on Song 3:1-4 in Sermon 75, he had returned to Song 3:1 in Sermon 80 and was continuing to comment on this passage in his last and incomplete sermon, SC 86. Gilbert of Hoyland, abbot of the cistercian monastery at Swineshead, England, continued the sermons on the *Song of Songs*, devoting his first thirteen sermons to the same scriptural text.[2] Being contemporaries and

---

[1]In the critical edition of J. Leclercq, C.H. Talbot, H.M. Rochais, *S. Bernardi Opera* (Rome: Editiones Cistercienses, 1957–1958) volumes 1–2. The english translation used in this paper is that of Irene Edmonds, *The Works of Bernard of Clairvaux, Vol. IV, On the Song of Songs* (Kalamazoo: Cistercian Publications, 1980). Bernard's sermons will be cited as SC followed by the number of the sermon and the paragraph number: e.g. SC 75.1.

[2]*Gilbert of Hoyland, Sermons on the Canticle of Canticles*, PL 184:1–165; trans. Lawrence Braceland, CF 14 (Kalamazoo: Cistercian Publications, 1978). Gilbert's sermons will be cited as S followed by sermon number and paragraph number.

sharing a common cistercian heritage, Bernard and Gilbert might be expected to expound similar spiritual doctrine when writing on the same scriptural pericope, and yet the differing *Sitz im Leben* of the two abbots might well have resulted in distinctive exegeses.

As point of reference it would be well to look at the text of Song 3:1–4:

1. In my bed by night I sought him whom my soul loves; I sought him, and found him not.

2. I will arise and go about the city; in the streets and the squares I will seek him whom my soul loves; I sought him and found him not.

3. The watchmen who keep the city found me: have you seen him, whom my soul loves?

4. When I had passed by them, I found him whom my soul loves: I held him; and I will not let him go, til I bring him into my mother's house, and into the chamber of her that bore me.[3]

As can be seen, the passage lends itself to an exposition of the benedictine/cistercian theme of seeking God.[4] And, recalling the integral role word association played in medieval exegesis,[5] we might guess that 'watchmen' would evoke comments on the role of abbots and/or ecclesiastical leaders. It is thus possible to test the expectations stated above by an examination of Bernard and Gilbert's use of the theme of 'seeking God', their comments on church leaders and leadership, and, because of their particular role as abbots, their specific monastic teaching contained in the sermons which comment on Song 3:1–4. This paper will focus on the theme 'seeking God'; a subsequent paper will examine their comments on leadership and their monastic teaching. The method is quite simple and yet can be revelatory. First texts are identified simply by their explicit mention of *quarere*/seeking God. Bernard's texts will be presented first, then Gilbert's. An analysis of the texts will follow.[6]

Bernard commences a discussion of Song 3:1 in sermon 75 and completes his comments on Song 3:4 in sermon 79. The search motif runs throughout these sermons. In sermons 80–82, he returns to Song

[3]Translated from the Vulgate by the author.
[4]See Michael Casey, OCSO, *Athirst for God: Spiritual Desire in Bernard of Clairvaux's Sermons on the Song of Songs* (Kalamazoo: Cistercian Publications, 1988) pp. 81–86.
[5]See P. Dumontier, *Saint Bernard et la Bible* ([Paris]: Desclée de Brouwer [1953]) pp. 107–115, 144.
[6]Space limitations allow for only an abbreviated presentation of texts.

3:1 and develops his doctrine of the image and likeness of the soul to the Word and here clearly states why the soul even dares to seek God. Sermon 83 gives the most lucid statement of the reason we seek: because God first sought us and so we can be confident in responding by seeking him. In Sermon 84, the search theme continues, and sermon 85 presents us with the outcome.

The texts dealing with seeking God in sermons 75–79 can be grouped according to several questions which they appear to answer:

> Who seeks God?
> How is God sought?
> When is he to be sought?
> Where is he to be sought?
> Who is sought?
> Why does the bride seek?
> What is the end of the search?

Who seeks? This question will be important in the comparison of Bernard and Gilbert. In sermon 80, Bernard says he is now going to discuss the moral meaning of Song 3:1, that he intends to 'consider the Word and the soul in the same way that we considered Christ and the Church.'[7] This would lead us to believe that in his previous sermons on Song 3:1 he had been commenting on the search by the Church for Christ, that is, that the bride in these earlier sermons was the Church and not the individual soul. We know that Bernard alternates between identifying the bride as the Church and as the soul.[8] For the moment, let us take Bernard at his word, that in sermons 75–79 it is the Church who seeks and that in sermons 80–86 it is the soul.

Gilbert's thirteen sermons that treat Song 3:1–4 fall into two distinct groups, the first group consisting of Sermons 1–8 and the second group of Sermons 9–13.[9] Within the spiritual pilgrimage, *circuitus*, the bride seeks and finds the beloved (SC 1–8). Sermons 9–13 treat of the half verse of Song 3:4 and as a group are really concluded by Sermon 14 which dwells on Song 3:5. These sermons discuss the more perfect union the bride has

---

[7]SC 80.1.

[8]Theresa Moritz, 'The Church as Bride in Bernard of Clairvaux's *Sermons on the Song of Songs*', in E. Rozanne Elder and John R. Sommerfeldt (edd.), *The Chimaera of His Age: Studies on Bernard of Clairvaux*, CS 63 (Kalamazoo: Cistercian Publications, Inc., 1980) pp. 3–11.

[9]See Lawrence Braceland SJ, Introduction to *Gilbert of Hoyland: On The Song of Songs*, CF 14: 29–30.

with the beloved when she has taken hold of him. This present study will be limited to the theme of seeking in Gilbert's first eight sermons.

We do not find in Gilbert's sermons a block analogous to Bernard's Sermons 75–79 which deal with the search of the Church for Christ. Rather, for the most part Gilbert is writing about the individual's search for Jesus. As he says, 'It is enchanting enough to seek you, good Jesus, but more enchanting to hold you. The former is a devout task, the latter is sheer joy.'[10] Why seek God? To experience him, to enjoy him.[11] And though the ultimate enjoyment is to be in sight, eternal vision, that enjoyment can be anticipated and to a certain extent experienced even now by seeking the beloved.[12]

We have so far simply presented a synopsis of texts from Bernard and Gilbert that illustrate the theme of seeking God in their sermons on Song 3:1–4. It is necessary now to examine those texts in light of the expectations proposed at the beginning of this paper.

A significant part of the common cistercian heritage shared by Bernard and Gilbert was derived from the practice of *lectio divina*. The texts they used for *lectio* were not only food for their own private prayer and spiritual growth, but were also sources for their teaching as abbots. Bernard and Gilbert had several sources for their thoughts and writings on seeking God. These included Scripture, the *Rule* of Saint Benedict, as well as patristic texts. Encountered in *lectio divina*, these sources would have been masticated, ruminated, and so much assimilated that when their sermons were composed what issued was the result of thorough digestion and assimilation and was therefore rightfully their own. As useful as it is to seek patristic antecedents, this discussion will be limited to reference to Scripture and the *Rule* of Saint Benedict.

There are four occurrences of *quaerere* (seek) in the *Rule* of Saint Benedict: Prol. 14–15; 2, 35–36; 27, 8–9; 58, 7. These texts are primary sources for the benedictine/cistercian emphasis on the theme of seeking God. Two texts are important to the present discussion, and two are relevant to the later consideration of monastic teaching and leadership. The four passages are:

Prol. 14–17: Seeking his workman in a multitude of people, the Lord calls out to him and lifts his voice again: 'Is there anyone

---

[10]S 1.2.

[11]See Pierre Miquel, 'Les caractères de L'expérience religieuse d'après Gilbert de Holland', Coll. 27 (1965) 150–159.

[12]S 2.4; S 4.8.

here who yearns for life and desires to see good days.' If you hear this and your answer is 'I do', God then directs these words to you: 'If you desire true and eternal life, keep your tongue free from vicious talk and your lips from all deceit; turn away from evil and do good; let peace be your quest and aim.'

2, 35–36: That he may not plead lack of resources as an excuse, he is to remember what is written: 'Seek first the kingdom of God and his justice, and all these things will be given you as well', and, again, 'Those who fear him lack nothing.'

27, 8–9: He is to imitate the loving example of the Good Shepherd who left the ninety-nine sheep in the mountains and went in search of the one sheep that had strayed. So great was his compassion for its weakness that he mercifully placed it on his sacred shoulders and so carried it back to the flock.

58, 7: The concern must be whether the novice truly seeks God and whether he shows eagerness for the work of God, for obedience, and for trials.[13]

The passage from chapter 58 is of particular interest to the present consideration. It is on the reception and formation of novice monks. After being received into the novitiate, the candidate's motives are carefully probed. The primary criterion by which his progress is judged is that he is truly seeking God. The sincerity of this seeking is ordinarily manifested in particular behaviors relative to the monastic way of life. All this is in response to God's call, God being the first to seek the monk (Prol. 14–15). The abbot is charged to seek first the kingdom of God (RB 2, 35–36), and, in imitation of Christ, to seek out the wayward, the ones who after the first fervor of the quest, have lapsed or been derailed form the journey (RB 27, 8–9).

These four texts from the *Rule* may serve as a lens through which to view Bernard's and Gilbert's writings on seeking God. Held within them is an outline of the teaching on the search for God such as we have seen in the writings of Bernard and Gilbert. A focus is obtained from the interacting relationships between God, monk, and his abbot,

[13]*RB 1980: The Rule of St Benedict*, ed. Timothy Fry, osb (Collegeville: Liturgical Press, 1980).

and by extension, between God, any individual, and the appropriate church leader.

$$\text{Monk} \longleftarrow \text{God} \longrightarrow \text{Abbot}$$

God first seeks the monk and seeks the abbot. The response of the monk and of the abbot is to seek God. The abbot has been charged to be a teacher, shepherd, physician, to be Christ in the life of the monk, helping him to return to the Father. This paper is concerned with part of the triad, the relationships of monk (or any person) in search of God. The texts from Bernard and Gilbert are an illustration of this. A subsequent paper will continue the discussion with an emphasis on Bernard's and Gilbert's teaching on the role of the watchmen, i.e. abbots and other church leaders.

If the primary criterion for judging a monk's vocation is whether he truly seeks God, then all that concerns the search for God is of utmost importance to him. He would want to know the answers to the questions posed in the bernardine texts. And if a monk were writing not only for monks, but for the greater christian community, all of whom share a common vocation, a call to nuptials with the Word (SC 83.1), then the author who took seriously his own search would want to share what had been learned on the quest. This is what Bernard and Gilbert did in the sermons in question.

Using the lens to focus on the texts, we ask: 'Who seeks God?' The one who seeks is the one who has first been sought (Prol. 14–17; Bernard, SC 84.5; Gilbert, Sermon 8.8). The initiative is always God's. Bernard and Gilbert are consistent with the judeo-christian tradition in this regard, and with the great spiritual teachers of many other traditions. Turning the lens slightly, we ask again: Who seeks God? First of all it is the Church, she who has been called by Christ and who now seeks him in glory. As the soul seeks because it has first been sought, so too the Church, who was first found by the watchmen, the apostles and apostolic men, and was chosen by God from all eternity to be Christ's bride, to be his people. The soul is not alone in the search, but is part of a community. The search is a response and not a self-initiated quest. In this the individual and the community are seen in their rightful stance before God—dependent on him for all, even the movement towards and the ability to seek him.

What is apparent when one carefully examines the texts is that Bernard

What is apparent when one carefully examines the texts is that Bernard is very much concerned about the Church and her search for God.[14] He developed this discussion in sermons 75–79, before considering the soul's search for God. This ecclesial stance is not directly related to the texts from the *Rule* of Saint Benedict, which are more concerned with individuals' search for God. However, the notion is not totally foreign. The early Cistercians thought of their monasteries as local churches in the sense that we call modern dioceses local churches. It is easy to extrapolate from this model and come to see the universal Church and its leaders in light of this local monastic church, and, vice versa, to apply the model of the universal Church as the bride of Christ to the local church.

Gilbert is much less explicitly ecclesial than Bernard. Whether this is out of deference to Bernard, whom he seldom repeats, or represents a more fundamental stance, we cannot adequately determine from the data presently at hand. It would be instructive in the future to examine all of Gilbert's writings and those of other english Cistercians as a group on this question. It is my suspicion that we would find some differences between the english and continental Cistercians of the twelfth century. What was the effect, for instance, of the isolation that was at times imposed on english abbots and bishops that prevented them from attending General Chapters or having access to Rome?

The most appropriate comparison of Bernard and Gilbert then is more adequately limited to Bernard's sermons 80–86 and Gilbert's sermons 1–8, in which they discuss the soul's search for God. The sermons are derived from their personal experience of God, including encounters with him in *lectio divina* within the milieu provided by the *Rule*. Bernard spent sermons 80–82 developing the doctrine of the soul's affinity to the Word: the soul is made in the image and likeness of the Word. Gilbert does not repeat this, but does make references to the doctrine, one that was common among monastic writers.[15] Nor does Gilbert comment at length on the soul having been first sought, though this reality underlies his presentation. An explicit mention is made in sermon 8.8.

How does the soul seek God? Bernard emphasizes seeking by desire and this desire is the fruit of love (SC 84.5).[16] Love/desire is the reason

---

[14]For a similar conclusion see the author's 'Ignorance or Innovation: Doxologies in the Sermons of Gilbert of Hoyland', Cîteaux 40 (1989), 479–484.

[15]Aelred Squire, *Asking the Fathers* (London: S.P.C.K., 1973) 15–16. Also David N. Bell, *The Image and Likeness: The Augustinian Spirituality of William of St Thierry*, CS 78 (Kalamazoo: Cistercian Publications, 1984) pp. 90, 107–108, 110.

[16]See Michael Casey, above, p. 190–191.

for the search and the praxis, the 'how-to' of the search. One must persevere in the search (SC 84.1). In sermon 86, Bernard introduces the idea of the bride seeking in modesty and in privacy.

Gilbert, who focused the lens and continued to illumine the *Song of Songs* after Bernard's death, says that the 'bride seeks her Beloved for the encounter and delight of love.'[17] She seeks to experience now and for all eternity. How does she seek? Above all through contemplation,[18] and to attain contemplation the soul requires leisure.[19] Gilbert makes frequent use of such monastic terms in describing the bride's search.[20] She must persevere in the quest and must not let difficulties impose detours but rather grow in humility and desire.

Where is the Beloved sought? Gilbert's universalist outlook appears in his answer to this question. While he uses monastic language and makes explicit reference to the members of the cistercian order and even of his own monastery, he says: 'In every way of life and in every order, she who is bride seeks traces of the one she chastely loves, so that from each of them she may draw a model for her actions and fuel for her love.'[21] And no means, strictness or dispensation, is to be preferred, for 'the Church accepts both and in both the bride seeks Christ.'[22] Practice of the virtues and contemplation are the ways to God.

In Bernard's incomplete sermon 86, he introduces the themes of leisure, deep silence or night, and begins discussing the meaning of the bed. It is these very themes that Gilbert elaborates on in his first sermons, not repeating what Bernard has written, but developing the ideas in his own style. He provides us with an instruction on the soul's search for God. In this sense, returning to the lens image, Gilbert has let the divine light pass through him and then become refracted on the individual soul and its search for God.

How was Scripture used by the two abbots? Here we see another difference between Bernard and Gilbert. Simply noting the scriptural citations and allusions at the end of each passage which speaks of *seeking* reveals that Bernard is lavish in his use of Scripture and Gilbert most

[17]S 2.6.
[18]S.1.4.
[19]S 1.2.
[20]See M. Jean Vuong-dinh-Lam, 'Le monastère: Foyer de vie spirituelle d'après Gilbert de Hoyland', Coll. 26 (1964) 5–21; 'Les observances monastiques: Instruments de vie spirituelle d'après Gilbert de Holland', Coll. 26 (1964) 169–99.
[21]S 5.4.
[22]S 5.5.

sparing. It comes as no surprise to see frequent use of johannine and pauline texts.[23] What should also be noted is that when writing of the Church's search for Christ, Bernard uses passages from Ephesians and Colossians, two epistles in which Paul or one of his disciples treats of the mystery that is the Church. If we are looking for an inspiration for Bernard's ecclesial sense, we might fittingly start with these two letters.

The expectations with which this study commenced have been realized. There is a similarity of spiritual doctrine expounded by Bernard and Gilbert in their sermons on Song 3:1–4. The monk's/soul's search for God is prompted by God first seeking the individual, who then responds. The search proceeds through faith, prayer, and good works. It is necessarily a long quest during which one must exercise perseverance. The end is none less than union with God to which all are called. Primary differences between the exegesis of Bernard and Gilbert are twofold: Bernard is both more ecclesial and makes greater use of scriptural texts than Gilbert.

As abbots, Bernard and Gilbert were men who sought God and who were charged with aiding others in their quest for union with God. We, with all who have benefited from their counsel through the ages, can say of them:

> But as they—I mean the watchmen—have received from the Spirit the desire to love, they know what the Spirit says, and as they understand the expressions of love, they are ready to reply in similar terms, that is, in loving zeal and works of mercy.[24]

ABSTRACTS

Bernard of Clairvaux est mort avant d'avoir achevé son commentaire sur le Cantique des Cantiques. Ayant commencé à commenter Ct 3, 1–4 dans le sermon 75, il poursuivait sur ce passage dans son dernier sermon inachevé, SC 86. Gilbert d'Hoyland, qui termina les sermons sur le Cantique des Cantiques, a consacré ses treize premiers sermons à ce même passage. Du fait qu'ils partagent un même héritage cistercien, on pourrait s'attendre à ce que Bernard et Gilbert exposent une doctrine spirituelle semblable lorsqu'ils traitent de la même péricope scripturaire, et cependant le *Sitz im Leben* différent des deux abbés pourrait avoir pour

---

[23]See Etienne Gilson, *The Mystical Theology of St Bernard*, (London: Sheed & Ward, 1940; reprint Kalamazoo: Cistercian Publications, 1990), especially pp. 20–25, 38.
[24]SC 79.1.

résultat des exégèses différentes. Ces hypothèses sont mises à l'épreuve au moyen d'un examen du contenu et du style des sermons 75–86 de Bernard et des sermons 1–13 de Gilbert sur le Cantique. Il s'avère instructif de se servir de passages pertinents de la Règle de saint Benoît comme d'une lentille pour examiner ces sermons.

Bernard of Clairvaux died before completing his commentary on the *Song of Songs*. Having begun to comment on *Song* 3:1–4 in Sermon 75, he was continuing on this passage in his last and incomplete sermon, SC 86. Gilbert of Hoyland, who completed the sermons on the *Song of Songs*, devoted his first thirteen sermons to this same passage. Sharing a common cistercian heritage, Bernard and Gilbert might be expected to expound similar doctrine when writing on the same scriptural pericope, and yet the differing *Sitz im Leben* of the two abbots might result in distinctive exegesis. These hypotheses are tested through an examination of the content and style of Bernard's SC 75–86 and Gilbert's S 1–13. Pertinent passages of the *Rule* of Saint Benedict are seen to be an instructive lens for examining the sermons.

Bernhard von Clairvaux starb, bevor er seinen Hohenliedkommentar beenden konnte. Nachdem er mit der Kommentierung von Hld 3, 1–4 in der 75. Predigt begonnen hatte, fuhr er mit dieser Stelle in seiner letzten und unvollendeten Predigt, SC 86, fort. Gilbert von Hoyland, der die Hoheliedpredigten vervollständigte, widmete seine ersten 13 Predigten derselben Passage. Da Bernhard und Gilbert ein gemeinsames zisterziensisches Erbe teilen, könnte man erwarten, dass sie eine ähnliche geistliche Lehre darlegen, wenn sie über dieselbe Schriftstelle schreiben, und doch könnte der unterschiedliche 'Sitz im Leben' der beiden Äbte in einer unterschiedlichen Auslegung münden. Diese Erwartungen werden in einer Untersuchung des Inhalts und des Stils von Bernhards SC 75–86 und Gilberts S 1–13 getestet. Zur Sache gehörige Passagen der Regel des heiligen Benedikt werden als instruktive Linse für die Untersuchung der Predigten benutzt.

CERTITUDO FIDEI: FAITH, REASON, AND AUTHORITY IN THE WRITINGS OF BALDWIN OF FORDE

David N. Bell
Memorial University of Newfoundland

WHEN WILLIAM OF SAINT-THIERRY alerted Bernard of Clairvaux to the danger of Abelard sometime between 1139 and 1141,[1] Baldwin of Exeter was still a young man.[2] And when Baldwin set pen to parchment to produce his *De commendatione fidei*, most probably around 1173,[3] Bernard had been dead for twenty years and

[1]See P. Zerbi, 'Guillaume de Saint-Thierry et son différend avec Abélard', in M. Bur (ed.), *Saint-Thierry, une abbaye du VIᵉ au XXᵉ siècle: Actes du Colloque international d'Histoire monastique Reims-Saint-Thierry, 11 au 14 octobre 1976* (Saint-Thierry, 1979) pp. 395–96 (English translation by J. Carfantan in CS 94 [1987] 181–82).

[2]Baldwin died in 1190, but the date of his birth is unknown. It can hardly have been much earlier than about 1110 and may have been closer to 1120. In his eleventh *Tractate* (TD XI 521B [39:68]), he refers to himself as an old man (*vetus homo*), but it is difficult to judge, in the context, how this comment should be assessed; see further ST II:116, n. 10.

[3]In the Preface to the CFi, Baldwin tells us that at one time, when he was returning from a General Chapter, he had occasion to visit Alexander, the tenth abbot of Cîteaux, at Dijon and there discuss with him certain 'secret matters'. It was at this time that the abbot asked Baldwin to write *quippiam de fide* for his edification, and Baldwin (who tells us that he had had such a project in mind for some time) was only too happy to accede to Alexander's request and have his permission to begin the work (see D. N. Bell, 'The Preface to the *De Commendatione Fidei* of B. of F.', Cîteaux 36 [1985] 156–57). Christopher Holdsworth, in his doctoral dissertation of 1959, suggested that the 'secret matters' might well have been concerned with the attempts of Pope Alexander III and the abbot of Cîteaux to 'negotiate peace between Henry II and his rebellious sons' and that the date must therefore have been 1173 (see C. J. Holdsworth, *Learning and Literature of English Cistercians 1167–1214, with Special Reference to John of Ford* [Diss., Cambridge University, 1959] pp. 360–61). If this were so, and the suggestion

Abelard for thirty. Yet the impact of the abelardian conflict, the problems encountered with such theologians as William of Conches and Gilbert de la Porrée, and the dangers inherent in aristotelian dialectics, had had an indelible effect, and the question as to just how far reason should extend and how it might be reconciled with the authority of faith was still a matter of deep concern.

To trace the long and complicated history of the concept of 'faith seeking understanding' from Augustine to Anselm, Abelard, and beyond is not our purpose here, but it might be wise at the outset to dispense with the foolish notion that either Augustine or the Cistercians were 'anti-intellectual'. To maintain this view is as absurd as condemning surgery because people get knifed in New York. Bernard of Clairvaux has no objection to knowledge, nor to the use of reason.[4] He certainly objects to its unwise application—what he refers to as 'shameful curiosity'[5]—but when he needs to use reason and dialectics, he can and does out-argue Abelard, and demonstrates clearly that within certain limits reason is as useful as it is necessary.[6] Indeed, a rejection of reason and its use would be nothing other than blasphemous, for since it was the rational soul that was created in the image of God, we have a duty as well as a responsibility to acknowledge our similarity to our Creator. 'I do not denigrate erudition in the arts', says Gilbert of Hoyland,

> . . .nor a good memory in liberal studies and a keen understanding [*intelligentia*], for in these consists the integrity of knowledge [*scien-*

is certainly very plausible, it would not be surprising if Baldwin, in the first flush of his enthusiasm, began work on the CFi almost immediately and completed a first draft within a year or two.

[4]One need only read SC 36 (SBOp 2:3–8) to have this made manifestly clear; but if further citations are necessary, one may refer to J. R. Sommerfeldt, 'Abelard and Bernard of Clairvaux', *Papers of the Michigan Academy of Science, Arts, and Letters* 46 (1961) 493–501; Sommerfeldt, 'Bernard of Clairvaux and Scholasticism', *Papers . . .* 48 (1963) 265–77; and Sommerfeldt, 'Epistemology, Education, and Social Theory in the Thought of Bernard of Clairvaux', in M. B. Pennington (ed.), *Saint Bernard of Clairvaux: Studies Commemorating the Eighth Centenary of His Canonization*, CS 28 (Kalamazoo, 1977) pp. 169–79.

[5]Bernard, SC 36.3; SBOp 2:5: *turpis curiositas*. Baldwin likewise condemns *curiosa inquisitio* (SA 679D [210]). But at the basis of their thought lies the augustinian condemnation, accepted by virtually everyone, of 'vain curiosity'. See, further, the delightful paper by Richard Newhauser, 'The Sin of Curiosity and the Cistercians,' in J. R. Sommerfeldt (ed.), *Erudition at God's Service: Studies in Medieval Cistercian History XI*, CS 98 (Kalamazoo, 1987) pp. 71–95.

[6]For examples of Bernard's use of logical argument, see Sommerfeldt, 'Abelard and Bernard of Clairvaux', pp. 498–500, 'Bernard of Clairvaux and Scholasticism', pp. 270–72, and 'Epistemology, Education, and Social Theory . . .', pp. 172–73.

tia]. An acquaintance [*notitia*] with the arts is a good thing provided one uses them legitimately: that is, as a sort of step or footprint where one does not stop and cling, but which one can use to rise to higher and holier things, to the more inward mysteries of wisdom [*sapientia*], to hidden and sweet retreats, and to the inaccessible light itself which God inhabits.[7]

On the other hand, a condemnation of the undisciplined application of reason beyond its appropriate bounds, when it 'treats audaciously of the Trinity and disputes irreverently about God',[8] could certainly be misunderstood, and the charges of obscurantism, of an insistence on blind faith, of an empty-headed and unquestioning assent to the teachings of the Church are nothing new. Walter Daniel, the biographer of Aelred of Rievaulx, certainly misunderstood Aelred's attitude toward worldly learning;[9] and if, indeed, we quote Aelred out of context, it is easy to see how such misapprehensions could arise. There are many, he says in the *Mirror of Charity*, who have given themselves up to empty philosophy (*inanis philosophia*), who in their reading and meditation combine Virgil with the Gospels, Horace with the Prophets, and Cicero with Paul. And to what does this lead? Nothing good at all![10] Yet later in the same text the same writer quotes Cicero on temperance and sobriety,[11] and it is, of course, Cicero who is the model for the treatise *On Spiritual Friendship*. But Aelred's Cicero is not a destructive Cicero, and if it comes to a clash between Cicero and Christ, it is the latter who will amend the teachings of the former, and not vice-versa. Aelred, writes Charles Dumont,

. . . applied to Cicero's *De amicitia* the same method which he admired

---

[7]Gilbert, Ep 2.2; PL 184:291C-D: 'Non quod ego artium eruditioni derogo, et liber-alium doctrinarum promptae memoriae, et perspicuae intelligentiae, in quibus scientiae consistit integritas. Bona enim artium notitia, sed si quis eis legitime utatur, id est tanquam gradu quodam et vestigio, non quo stetur et inhaereatur, sed quo utendum sit ad superiora quaedam et sanctiora et magis intima arcana sapientiae, in reconditos et suaves recessus, et in ipsam lucem inaccessibilem, quam inhabitat Deus.' Matthew of Rievaulx also sees the liberal arts as having a positive value for understanding the Scriptures; see C. J. Holdsworth, 'John of Ford and English Cistercian Writing 1167–1214', *Transactions of the Royal Historical Society*, Series V, 11 (1961) 134.

[8]In such words does Senatus of Worcester condemn Peter of Poitiers; see R. W. Hunt, 'English Learning in the Late Twelfth Century', *Transactions of the Royal Historical Society*, Series IV, 19 (1936) 29–30.

[9]See M. Powicke (ed./trans.), *Walter Daniel: The Life of Aelred of Rievaulx* (Oxford, 1978) pp. lxxxv-vii.

[10]See Aelred, *Speculum caritatis* [Spec car] 2.24.72; PL 195:573B-C; CCCM 1:100.

[11]See Spec car 3.31.75; PL 195:604D; CCCM 1:141. See further, C. Dumont, 'Aelred of Rievaulx's *Spiritual Friendship*', in J. R. Sommerfeldt (ed.), *Cistercian Ideals and Reality*, CS 60 (Kalamazoo, 1978) p. 188.

in the Fathers. What was lacking in Cicero was the *scientia salutaris*: the science of salvation, that is, of charity.[12]

Similarly, the fact that Baldwin of Forde disparages Plato and the Academics and the Stoics, and tells us that the wisdom which lies in their obscurities is far from the *via disciplinae* which God revealed to Jacob, is not a condemnation of reason *per se*.[13] It is a condemnation of reason unwisely applied to areas it has no business investigating. 'We see that there is a reason which attacks and a reason which defends', says William of Saint-Thierry:

> The former is animal and its tastes are carnal [*carnaliter sapiens*]; the latter is spiritual and judges all things spiritually. The former is undecided about things of which it has no experience; the latter submits all things to authority. Moreover, it can hardly bear it if, in any part of itself, it comes to doubt something which, by divine authority and unfeigned faith [1 Tm 1:5], should be given undoubting assent.[14]

Furthermore, we must not err in confining the application of reason solely to the facts of the faith. It is true that reasoned and rational attacks on heretical novelties[15] was of major importance in the twelfth and succeeding centuries—Gilbert of Hoyland calls the ecclesiastical doctors and those in authority 'the teeth of the church'[16]—and nowhere

---

[12]See Dumont, p. 189. Powicke, *Life of Aelred of Rievaulx*, p. lxxxvii, notes that when Aelred attacked those who combined Virgil with the Gospels and so on, then 'like St Bernard, he was attacking the moral dangers which beset the learned, not learning itself.'

[13]See CFi 590D–91B. But Baldwin has just quoted (anonymously) Ovid's *Fasti* I, 297–98 to make his point! See SA 681D (216), commenting on Ps 77:44: 'Omnis terrena sapientia Deo odibilis, de qua bibunt Aegyptii, id est amici hujus mundi qui sunt inimici Dei, aqua Aegypti est quae in sanguinem vertitur [see Ps 77:44].' See, further, D. N. Bell, 'B. of F. and the Sacrament of the Altar', in Sommerfeldt (ed.), *Erudition at God's Service*, p. 236, n. 15; and T. Renna, 'St Bernard and the Pagan Classics: An Historical View', in E. R. Elder and J. R. Sommerfeldt (edd.), *The Chimaera of His Age: Studies on Bernard of Clairvaux*, CS 63 (Kalamazoo, 1980) pp. 122–31. That the christian writers quoted the classics as often as they disparaged them has, of course, been recognized for a very long time; there are some amusing comments in F. S. Merryweather, *Bibliomania in the Middle Ages* (London, 1849) pp. 15, 154.

[14]William, *Speculum fidei* 32; PL 180:374C, SCh 301:96: 'Siquidem, et ratio videtur esse quae impugnat et ratio quae repugnat, illa animalis et carnaliter sapiens, haec autem spiritualis et spiritualiter diiudicans omnia [cf. 1 Co 2:15]; illa quasi de inexpertis haesitando, haec vero auctoritati omnia subdendo; insuper aegre ferendo, in aliqua sui parte aliquatenus sibi rem venire in dubium, cui ex autoritate divina, *et fide non ficta* [1 Tm 1:5], non dubium tribuit assensum.'

[15]The pejorative reference to heretical ideas as 'novelties' appears from the earliest times and derives from 1 Tm 6:20. See Baldwin, CFi 576C.

[16]See Gilbert, SC 23.6; PL 184:123C-D.

is this better exemplified than in the later domination of the universities by franciscan and dominican theologians and philosophers. But more important than that for the ordinary, practising, intelligent Christian was the application of reason to the path of virtue. Baldwin leaves us in no doubt on the matter:

> The penetrating insights of human genius and the human senses, together with the subtlety of our words, are a two-edged sword of the most subtle discernment, [a sword] which makes a division between the true and the false, the good and the bad, the honest and the dishonest, and all the other opposites which are subject to its shrewd and skilful investigations.[17]

Discretio, the mother of the virtues,[18] is a *rational* virtue; and if Baldwin stresses that it is the authority of the Church which should guide the faithful and not the individual opinions of the faithful themselves, that is only to be expected, given his place and his position.

God has revealed to us certain truths and a certain way of life, there is no doubt of that, but a naive and unquestioning acceptance of these revelations is far from ideal: it is incumbent on us to try to understand them.[19] And if we ourselves are unable to do this, the doctors of the church must do it for us. Baldwin is well aware that some people are not

---

[17]TD VI 454A (37:36): 'Praeterea acies humani ingenii et humani sensus, sermonisque subtilitas, tamquam gladius anceps [cf. Heb 4:12] subtilissime quasi per discretionem dividit inter verum et falsum, inter bonum et malum, honestum et inhonestum, ceteraque contraria, ingeniosae et artificiosae inquisitioni obnoxia. Hinc omnis mundana philosophia, humanaque sapientia manavit.' See further D. N. Bell, 'B. of F. and Twelfth-Century Theology', in E. R. Elder (ed.), *Noble Piety and Reformed Monasticism: Studies in Medieval Cistercian History VII*, CS 65 (Kalamazoo, 1981) p. 140. We may compare Bernard's discussion in SC 35.8; SBOp 1:254: since reason is the *praerogativa spiritualis* of the human species, a refusal to live by reason (*ratione*) renders us lower than the beasts (we see here, incidentally, an example of the influence of Stoicism on the monastic tradition; an influence which has been insufficiently emphasized). Gilbert of Hoyland, *Tractatus asceticus* 4.5; PL 184:269A, likewise says that one of the tasks of reason is *ambigua dijudicare*.

[18]See RB 64.18–19; SCh 182:652, and D. N. Bell, 'The Ascetic Spirituality of B. of F.', Cîteaux 31 (1980) 232, n. 49, referring to Bernard of Clairvaux and Richard of Saint-Victor.

[19]SA 667A (164): 'Nec licet nobis quasi per simplicitatem ignorare quid intellexerit, cum necesse nobis sit et id credere quod in his verbis intellexit, et id confiteri quod dixit. In hoc enim communis fidei articulo, et publicae confessionis testimonio, non sufficit simpliciter credere verum esse quod Christus his verbis dixit, quicquid in his intellexerit, non intellecto scilicet quid dixerit. Sed intelligentia et fides verborum tanto exactius a nobis requiritur, quanto calcatius et expressius quod credi oportet a Christo dicitur.' Augustine had already distinguished quite clearly between laudatory belief and foolish credulity; see *De util. cred.* 9.22; PL 42:80.

as intelligent as others. Like his colleagues and confrères he recognizes 'the simple' and acknowledges that, in their case, simple faith suffices for their salvation.[20] The *scientia mysticae significationis*, especially with regard to that most important of sacraments, the eucharist, is not for all. For the simple who, like the poor, are always with us, *pietas fidei* is counted as righteousness; but for those who teach and govern—for abbots and priests and bishops (like Baldwin)—a higher knowledge (*scientia*) is essential. It was, after all, Christ himself who showed the way: 'To you it has been given to know the secrets of the kingdom of God, but for others they are in parables' [Lk 8:10 (RSV)].[21]

The problem with reason, therefore, lies not in its use, but in its abuse, and Baldwin speaks for all when, in his sixth *Tractate*, he condemns reason for overstepping its limits:

[Reason], being ignorant of the limits to which it could go, has dared to attempt an examination of the things above it, things to which it could never attain if left to itself. It has busied itself with arduous and abstruse investigations into the nature of God, the origin of the world, the condition of the soul, and the quality of righteousness and blessedness, and [in so doing] has been able neither to find the way to truth nor to attain to the wisdom of God which is hidden in mystery [see 1 Co 2:7].[22]

[20]See my discussion, with numerous references, in 'B. of F. and the Sacrament of the Altar', pp. 218–19. The principle had been established by Augustine (see 'B. of F. and the Sacrament of the Altar', p. 236, n. 20), to say nothing of Jesus of Nazareth (see n. 21 below), and was a commonplace of patristic and medieval theology and spirituality.

[21]See the discussion in SA 712D–13B (346–48), ending: 'Non igitur oportet omnes, qui fidem habent, mystici eloquii prudentes esse, vel signorum aut sacramentorum profunda penetrare. Sed mysteriorum intelligentia illis magis est necessaria, quibus docendi et regendi dispensatio est credita. Hinc Dominus ad discipulos loquens ait: *Vobis datum est nosse mysterium regni Dei*; *ceteris autem in parabolis* [Lk 8:10].' See also SA 736D (440). Bernard opens his series of sermons on *Songs* with a statement of the same theme: 'Vobis, fratres, alia quam aliis in saeculo, aut certe aliter dicenda sunt' (SC 1.1; SBOp 1:3). Compare Augustine, *De ord.* 2.26; PL 32:1007: 'Itaque, quamquam bonorum auctoritas imperitae multitudini videatur esse salubrior, ratio vero aptior eruditis.'

[22]TD VI 454A-B (37: 36): 'Quae modum suae possibilitatis ignorans, supra se ausa est attentare, ad quae, in se relicta, nullatenus potuit pertingere. Nam se exercens circa arduas et profundas inquisitiones de natura Dei, de origine mundi, de statu animae, de justitiae et beatitudinis qualitate, viam veritatis non invenire et ad sapientiam Dei in mysterio absconditam [cf. 1 Cor 2:7] non valuit pervenire.' Similarly, if one esteems human reason so greatly that one is prepared to accept only those parts of the faith that seem to be in accord with it, this, too, will bar one from heaven. 'Oculus enim humanae rationis invisibilia Dei [cf. Rm 1:20] comprehendere non potest, nisi collyrio gratiae inungatur, veroque lumine illustretur, de quo scriptum est: *Praeceptum Domini lucidum illuminans oculos* [Ps 18:9]. *Si oculus tuus*, inquit Dominus, *scandalizat te*,

In other words, there are some things which we must take on trust, on authority, on faith, and there can be no doubt that, as a consequence of the abelardian controversy, a reassertion and reassessment of the authority of faith was universal among the monastic theologians of Baldwin's era. His own treatise *De commendatione fidei* is one of the longest and most complete investigations of the question.

As everyone knows, the problem with Abelard's definition of faith was his unfortunate use of the term *existimatio*, and whatever he himself meant by it is, in a sense, irrelevant.[23] For William of Saint-Thierry, what he meant was *aestimatio*, and *aestimatio* could be nothing other than fallible, human opinion.[24] William, therefore, wrote to Bernard to tell him of the danger, and Bernard accepted both his warning and his terminology.[25] Abelard, they said, is wrong on three counts: first, he defines faith as *aestimatio rerum non apparentium, nec sensibus corporis subjacentium*, 'an opinion with regard to things not seen nor subject to the bodily senses'; secondly, in so doing he is contradicting Augustine

---

erue eumet projice abs te [Mt 18:9]! Hoc de oculo humanae rationis non inconvenienter intelligitur, qui pietati fidei saepe scandalum est, sed, cum scandalizat, eruendus est. Melius est enim unum oculum sanae fidei habentem ingredi ad vitam, quam duos oculos habentem, alterum fidei, alterum rationis humanae, mitti in gehennam' (TD I 407C-D [35:46]; ST I:50). But let us note once again: the problem here is not reason, but reason acting improperly.

[23] I shall not even attempt here to enter into this complicated discussion. There are some useful notes in A. V. Murray, *Abelard and St Bernard: A Study in Twelfth Century Modernism* (Manchester, New York, 1967) pp. 77–78, but the question has many ramifications. Abelard's actual definition is to be found in his *Intro. ad theol./Theol. 'schol.'* 1.1; PL 178: 891C, CCCM XIII:318: '*Est* quippe *fides* existimatio *rerum non apparentium* [Heb 11:1], hoc est sensibus corporeis non subiacentium.' See also n. 24 immediately below.

[24] See William, *Adversus Abaelardum* [Adv Abl] 1; PL 180:249A: 'In primo limine theologiae suae fidem diffinivit aestimationem rerum non apparentium, nec sensibus corporis subjacentium, aestimans fortasse, vel communem fidem nostram aestimationem esse, vel licitum esse, in ea quodlibet cuilibet ad libitum aestimare. Beatus Augustinus: "Fides enim, ait, non conjectando vel opinando habetur in corde in quo est, ab eo cujus est, sed certa scientia acclamante conscientia" [see n. 26 below]. Absit enim ut hos fines habeat Christiana fides, aestimationes scilicet, sive opiniones academicorum sint aestimationes istae, quorum sententia est nihil credere, nihil scire, sed omnia aestimare.' But according to D. E. Luscombe, *The School of Peter Abelard* (Cambridge, 1970) p. 112, 'when Abelard used the term *aestimatio* in respect of faith in things unseen, he did not intend to minimize the certitude of faith but to define the nature of an act of knowledge which is not yet *experientia* and which does not attain to *cognitio*.' William, Bernard, and Baldwin, however, cannot be blamed for understanding *existimatio/aestimatio* as simple opinion.

[25] See William, Ep 326.3; PL 182:531A–33A (J. Leclercq, 'Les lettres de Guillaume de Saint-Thierry à Bernard', *Revue Bénédictine* 79 [1969] 376–78), to Geoffrey of Chartres (the papal legate) and Bernard; Bernard, Ep 327; SBOp 7:263 to William; Bernard, Ep

who says specifically that faith is not possessed in the heart by conjecture or opinion (*opinio*), but by the conscious awareness of certain knowledge (*sed certa scientia acclamante conscientia*); and, thirdly, he is also contradicting the apostle Paul, who says to Timothy: 'I *know* [*scio*] in whom I have believed, and I am certain [*certus sum*] [2 Tm 1:12].'[26]

Now Hugh of Saint-Victor, writing his great *De sacramentis* in about 1134, had already had problems with Abelard's terminology, for it is generally accepted that in his own definition of faith in Book I, Part X of that work—'Faith is the certainty [*certitudo*] of things absent, established beyond opinion [*opinio*] and short of knowledge [*scientia*]'[27]—he deliberately set out to improve on it. But for William and Bernard and Baldwin, this improvement is not enough: faith is not only *certitudo*, it is also true *scientia*. But to appreciate this idea and to comprehend it more fully we need to make a distinction between knowledge (*scientia*) and understanding (*intellectus*).

To know that $E=mc^2$ is one thing; to understand the mathematics behind it and appreciate the proof of the equation is another. To know that 2+2=4 is one thing; to have read the *Principia Mathematica* of Whitehead and Russell and to understand *why* 2+2=4 is, again, something quite different. There is much that we do and must take on trust. Understanding/*intellectus* implies a certain penetration into a concept, an experiential awareness of its truth. I may know and believe that people have hangovers, and I may be aware of the chemistry involved; but it is only when I have experienced one myself that I can truly say I understand it. Bernard, in distinguishing between opinion, faith, and *intellectus*, writes thus:

> Faith is a sort of voluntary and certain foretaste of truth not yet apparent; understanding [*intellectus*] is a certain and manifest knowledge

190 = Abael 4.9; SBOp 8:24–25 to Innocent II. Bernard himself never uses the term *existimatio* in any of his writings; the single occurrence in Ep 122 (SBOp 7:303) is in a letter *to* Bernard, not from him.

[26]William, Adv Abl 1; PL 180:249A-B; Bernard, Ep 190.4.9; SBOp 8:24–25. The quotation from Augustine is *De Trin.* 13.1.3; PL 42:1014, which actually reads: 'Non sic videtur fides in corde, in quo est, ab eo cujus est: sed eam tenet certissima scientia, clamatque conscientia.'

[27]Hugh, *De sac.* 1.10.2; PL 176:331B: 'Fides est certitudo rerum absentium supra opinionem et infra scientiam constituta.' Compare PL 176:330C: one can say 'fidem esse certitudinem quamdam animi de rebus absentibus, supra opinionem et infra scientiam constitutam'; PL 176:330D–31A: 'Patet etiam quare ipsam certitudinem quam fidem appellamus supra opinionem *vel aestimationem*, et infra scientiam dicimus esse constitutam.'

[*notitia*] of something unseen; opinion [*opinio*] is like holding as true something which you do not know to be false. So, as I said, faith contains nothing which is doubtful [*ambiguum*]; or, if it does, it is not faith but opinion. How, then, does it differ from understanding? Even though it is no more uncertain than understanding, it is still wrapped in a veil [*involucrum*] which understanding is not. Finally, what you have understood is not something about which you can inquire further; or, if it is, you have not understood it. We prefer to know nothing other than what we already know by faith. Our happiness will lack nothing when the things we already hold certain by faith will be equally unveiled [*nuda*].[28]

We must take note that Bernard insists that faith and understanding are not different in their degree of certainty. As Gilbert of Hoyland points out: 'It is not that there is a greater certainty in understanding [*intelligentia*] than in faith, but greater clarity [*serenitas*]',[29] and he continues:

Neither errs or is undecided. Where there is error or indecision, there is no understanding [*intelligentia*]; where there is indecision, there is no faith. But if faith seems capable of admitting error, it is neither the true nor the catholic faith, but an erroneous credulity. Faith, if I may put it thus, grasps and possesses the correct truth; understanding gazes upon [truth] unveiled and naked; reason attempts to unveil it.

---

[28]Bernard, Csi 5.3.6; SBOp 3:471: 'Possumus singula haec ita diffinire: fides est voluntaria quaedam et certa prelibatio necdum propalatae veritatis; intellectus est rei cuiuscumque invisibilis certa et manifesta notitia; opinio est quasi pro vero habere aliquid, quod falsum esse nescias. Ergo, ut dixi, fides ambiguum non habet, aut, si habet, fides non est, sed opinio. Quid igitur distat ab intellectu? Nempe quod, etsi non habet incertum non magis quam intellectus, habet tamen involucrum, quod non intellectus. Denique quod intellexisti, non est de eo quod ultra quaeras; aut, si est, non intellexisti. Nil autem malumus scire, quam quae fide iam scimus. Nil supererit ad beatitudinem, cum, quae iam certa sunt nobis, erunt aeque et nuda.' See further G. W. Burch (trans.), *The Steps of Humility by Bernard, Abbot of Clairvaux* (Notre Dame, 1963) pp. 31–33. For the idea of *intelligentia* (or *veritas*) *nuda*, compare Gilbert of Hoyland, SC 4.2 translated at n. 30 below, and Guerric of Igny, Epi 2.5 quoted in n. 35 below (and see, further, J. Morson, *Christ the Way: The Christology of Guerric of Igny*, CS 25 [Kalamazoo, 1978] pp. 137–41; but Morson failed to give Bernard proper credit for the idea). We might note here that any attempt at distinguishing clearly between 'knowledge' and 'understanding' in the cistercian writers is complicated by their inconsistent terminology: *notitia, scientia, cognitio, intellectus,* and *intelligentia* are used in different ways by different writers, and even within the same writer there is often a considerable degree of overlap.

[29]Gilbert, SC 4.2; PL 184:27A (see n. 30 below). *Serenitas* implies not only clarity, but 'serenity', calmness, tranquillity, and peace.

Reason, running between faith and understanding, raises itself up by the former, but governs itself by the latter.[30]

Reason, he says, tries to go beyond faith, but is supported by faith on the one hand and restrained by faith on the other.[31] With this, no Cistercian could or would disagree.

The quest for rational understanding, however, can not only be perilous, as we have seen; it can also be irrelevant. For a person dying of thirst in the desert, an intellectual understanding of the nature of water, its chemical properties, and its molecular structure, is utterly useless: it is the *experience* of water which is essential. Yet, on the other hand, an intellectual understanding of the chemical processes by which dew is formed may enable that person to manufacture water by heating and cooling stones, or an intellectual understanding of botany may enable that person to recognize those plants or cacti whose flesh can provide a modicum of drinkable liquid. In more theological terms, although it may be possible to prove rationally that God exists and although we may be able to discover rationally much about his nature and attributes— his wisdom, goodness, mercy, righteousness, indignation, wrath, and so on[32]—this understanding is essentially useless. As Chrysogonus Waddell pointed out a number of years ago:

A knowledge of God such as this is not what the monk is after. Rather than preoccupy ourselves with this type of rational, discursive knowledge about God, we have to enter with courage and conviction into a quite different universe. It is not an inaccessible God outside space and time, but the incarnate Word of God who is the proper object of our faith.[33]

And, although the writer was here speaking specifically of William of Saint-Thierry, the voice we hear is not just the voice of William, but of all monastic theologians of the twelfth century.

---

[30]Gilbert, SC 4.2: 'In intelligentia quam in fide non certitudo major inest, sed serenitas: neutra vel errat, vel haeret. Ubi vel error vel haesitatio est, intelligentia non est: ubi haesitatio est, fides non est. Et si fides admittere posse videtur errorem, non est vera nec catholica fides, sed erronea credulitas. Fides, ut sic dicam, veritatem rectam tenet et possidet; intelligentia revelatam et nudam contuetur; ratio conatur revelare. Ratio inter fidem intelligentiamque discurrens, ad illam se erigit, sed ista se regit.'

[31]See PL 184:27B.

[32]See SA 744D–45B (476).

[33]C. Waddell, 'Humility and the Sacraments of the Faith in William of Saint Thierry's *Speculum Fidei*', in Sommerfeldt (ed.), *Cistercian Ideals and Reality*, pp. 129–30. And for William, Bernard, and Baldwin, the incarnate Word of God is, of course, wholly present in the Sacrament of the Altar (see nn. 48–50 below).

I would suggest, then, that the question we posed earlier, 'How far can reason go?', should be rephrased to read: 'How far can reason go *usefully*?' To *prove* that Christ is present in the sacrament of the altar, assuming it could be done, is no different from proving that water is H_2O: fascinating, no doubt, but of little use to someone dying of thirst. This is not the *intellectus* the Cistercians were seeking. For them, the highest *intellectus* is an experiential *intellectus*, and at this stage of our progress *intellectus*, love, and wisdom are all the same thing.[34] Guerric puts the matter neatly: 'It is faith which smells; *experientia* which tastes and enjoys.'[35] But however true this may be, it is still no denial of the true nature and positive value of the God-given gift of human reason.

For Baldwin, like all the western Fathers he so greatly esteems, faith stands at the foot of the ladder of spiritual ascent,[36] but it is a faith which may be assisted by reason and the senses.[37] It is not essential that it be helped in this way, that is true (the simple do not need it), but it is certainly possible. Faith may even be assisted by doubt—*pia dubitatio*[38]—and it only profits from the attacks levied against it.[39] Yet however much we investigate the content of the faith by means of our

[34]See, generally, R. Javelet, 'Intelligence et amour chez les auteurs spirituels du XIIme siècle', *Revue d'ascétique et de mystique* 37 (1961) 273–90, 429–50. The principle is summarized in Gregory the Great's famous phrase: 'Amor ipse notitia est' (*In Evang.*, hom. 27.4; PL 76:1207), quoted accurately by Bernard in Div 29.1 (SBOp 6/1:210) and III Sent 127 (SBOp 6/2:249) [these *sententiae* are not to be found in PL]), and by Baldwin (TD XV 554C [40:53]; see my 'Ascetic Spirituality of B. of F.', p. 247), and with *notitia* amended to *intellectus* by William of Saint-Thierry, whose consummate discussion of the concept cannot be bettered (see, further, D. N. Bell, *The Image and Likeness: The Augustinian Spirituality of William of Saint Thierry*, CS 78 [Kalamazoo, 1984] chapter VI [pp. 217–49]).

[35]Guerric, Nat BVM 1.4; PL 185:202C, SCh 202:480: 'Fides siquidem est quae odoratur, experientia quae gustat et fruitur.' Compare also Epi 3.7; PL 185:58C, SCh 166:284. Faith, says Guerric elsewhere, 'nascitur supernorum praedicatione luminarium, roboratur visione quarumdam imaginum, *per speculum in aenigmate* [1 Co 13:12] Deum velut incarnatum nobis exhibentium. Consummabitur cum praesens et nuda videbitur veritas rerum, *facie ad faciem* [1 Co 13:12] contemplantibus quod vix tenuiter et raptim in aenigmate nunc attingitur; cum et ipsa fides transibit in cognitionem, spes in possessionem, desiderium in fruitionem' [Epi 2.5; PL 185:53B, SCh 166:262].

[36]See CFi 594A-C (faith is the beginning of our spiritual substance, the first of our spiritual gifts), 594D (faith is also the beginning of our knowledge of the substance of God), and 595D–97A (faith is the first of the eight stages of spiritual ascent; see my 'Ascetic Spirituality of B. of F.', pp. 247–48 for a more complete discussion).

[37]See CFi 583D translated at n. 59 below, and CFi 586A-B (the case of Doubting Thomas).

[38]See CFi 577C, 579D–80A, and 580C-D (the case of Peter walking on the water). See further Bell, 'B. of F. and Twelfth-Century Theology', p. 140, and Bell, 'B. of F. and the Sacrament of the Altar', p. 219.

[39]See CFi 611C–13B, 614B-C.

reason, it can only take us so far. At some stage in the process God must intervene and, by the communication of his grace, transform what is now believed into what is experienced. William of Saint-Thierry speaks at length of the necessity and nature of this illuminating grace;[40] Baldwin is less analytical, but no less insistent. How do the righteous ascend to true security of mind and certainty of faith? Not by gaining a doctoral degree or winning a fellowship, but by *excessus contemplationis*![41] Beginners, who accept and approve the principles of the faith on trust, certainly have a cognition (*cognitio*) of faith, but it cannot yet be called *scientia*. 'But in the advanced and in the perfect—those who believe most firmly and most certainly and who, *by the inspiration of more abundant grace*, understand (*intelligunt*) more fully the reasoning of faith'[42]—the cognition which comes from faith may indeed be called knowledge. But let us note: it is only by God's intervention that this transition takes place, and God's intervention can hardly be expected in those who are not prepared to accept his ground-rules.

Yet even the acceptance of the ground-rules is a gift of the grace of God.[43] Faith, says Baldwin, is given to some but not to others; it is given to some with signs (*signa*) and to some without; some receive the signs but not the faith, while some receive neither; some see and believe; some do not see and do not believe; some believe but do not see; and some see and do not believe![44] How can we explain all this? How can we understand it? We cannot, Baldwin replies: it is quite incomprehensible

[40]See especially O. Brooke, 'William of St Thierry's Doctrine of the Ascent to God by Faith, I and II', *Recherches de théologie ancienne et médiévale* 30 (1963) 181–204; 33 (1966) 282–318, conveniently reprinted in O. Brooke, *Studies in Monastic Theology*, CS 37 (Kalamazoo, 1980) pp. 134–207. For a briefer account, see the same writer's 'Faith and Mystical Experience in William of St Thierry', *Downside Review* (April 1964) 93–102, reprinted in the same *Studies*, pp. 123–33.

[41]See CFi 581C-D: 'Sed sciendum nobis est quod justi nunc per excessum contemplationis supra se levantur in quamdam mentis securitatem et fiduciae constantiam, unde cuncta mala praesentia, mortisque pericula, in Deo despicienda cognoscunt, et cognoscendo despiciunt. Nunc vero propriae infirmitati dimissi, sicut homines inter pericula metuunt, et metuendo propriam infirmitatem quanto humilius, tanto verius recognoscunt. Hinc de illis scriptum est: *Ascendunt usue ad coelos, et descendunt usque ad abyssos* [Ps 106:26]. *Ascendunt* per excessum contemplationis et securitatis in Deo; *descendunt* per excessum pavoris et pusillanimitatis in semetipsis.' See further Bell, 'Ascetic Spirituality of B. of F.', pp. 246–47.

[42]CFi 584A, translated at n. 59 below.

[43]See CFi 587A–88A, the chapters entitled 'Quod fides donum sit Dei' and 'Quod fides opus sit Dei'; CFi 606C: 'Ipsa autem fides non humanae possibilitatis, sed divinae virtutis et voluntatis opus, inter mirabilia opera Dei magnam facit admirationem.'

[44]See CFi 606C. Compare CFi 613C-D.

and wholly transcends all the human senses and human reason. It is a wonder, a marvel, a miracle, and it rouses in us nothing but profound *admiratio* for the inscrutable workings of God.[45]

Faith, then, the gift of God, sets the stage for that greater knowledge of God which is also his gift. But just what is that knowledge which the angels know *per speciem* and we *per fidem*? We know three things, says the abbot of Forde: first, we know that Christ is the coeternal Word and one with the Father; secondly, we know that he came to earth and became human; and, thirdly, we know that in the eucharist we eat his flesh. These are the three forms of faith: faith of unity, *fides unitatis* (of Father and Son); faith of union, *fides unionis* (of God and humanity); faith of communion, *fides communionis* (of Christ and us at and in the eucharist).[46] This is the content of our faith, says Baldwin, this is its *summa* (he uses the scholastic term in a monastic context): to know .Christ in the Father, Christ in the flesh, and Christ in the participation of the altar.[47] This is the whole mystery of faith, for, since it is by faith that Christ dwells in our hearts, this indwelling finds its fulfilment and consummation in the sacrament of the eucharist when, through faith, Christ enters within the faithful and feeds them from within.[48] The eucharist, therefore, that celebration of the unity of a Church which is founded on faith,[49] is the supreme test and manifestation of faith,[50] and, in stressing this theme so strongly, Baldwin brings the use of reason and understanding out of the classroom and the schools and establishes it firmly within the walls of the Church.

Furthermore, he also makes it lucidly clear that faith is not just a matter of intellectual assent, God-given or not: it is not just an intellectual phenomenon, but is inextricably linked to works. Faith and service to God

[45]For Baldwin's 'théologie admirative' (Leclercq's term), see his introduction to SA, pp. 47–51; Bell, 'B. of F. and Twelfth-Century Theology', p. 147, n. 65; and Bell, 'B. of F. and the Sacrament of the Altar', pp. 221–22. 'Per fidem ad Christum trahimur', says Baldwin, 'cum judicio sensus vel rationis reluctante, mens virtute verborum Dei aut signorum attonita, admiratione stupet. . . ' [CFi 587D]. Compare also CFi 586C, 606C, 607C, 613C.

[46]See SA 694C–95A (268).

[47]See SA 695B (270).

[48]See SA 695B (270). For a full discussion of the importance of the eucharist for Baldwin, see Bell, 'B. of F. and the Sacrament of the Altar', *passim*.

[49]CFi 595B: 'Fides autem fundamentum dicit, quod fundavit Deus et non homo, ideoque Dei dicitur. Hoc est fundamentum quod nemo mutare potest. Haec est petra super quam fundata est Ecclesia [cf. Mt 16:18].'

[50]See Bell, 'B. of F. and the Sacrament of the Altar', pp. 219–22.

go hand in hand,[51] and Baldwin has no dispute with Saint Paul when he observes that faith works *per caritatem* (Ga 5:6).[52] But 'works' and their effects can be complex matters, and deciding just what one should do and how one should act at a particular time and in a particular set of circumstances may require, as we saw earlier, the most careful application of the principles of reason and logic. That Baldwin, in his practical day-to-day administration as bishop and archbishop, not infrequently made a total hash of things is not to deny this principle.

For Baldwin, then, Abelard's apparent assertion that faith was no more than fallible human opinion was not just wrong, but unthinkably stupid. No-one can possibly be saved by an opinion. Faith, which is founded on divine authority, is true knowledge, true *scientia*; and, although Baldwin does not cite Abelard by name, he specifically contradicts his view of faith and does so in terms more accurate than those used by either William of Saint-Thierry or Bernard. Let us here translate his important discussion of the certainty of faith as it appears in the *De commendatione fidei* and glance at its teaching, its sources, and its implications.

Of the Certainty of Faith

Because it is through faith that we trust in God and believe in God, then, since God is Truth [see Jn 14:6], that faith should be founded on such certainty, such firmness of undoubting assent, that it can rightly be called knowledge [*scientia*]. It exceeds every experience of the senses and transcends every conjecture of human reason: it comprehends most truly and most certainly those things which cannot be explored with the senses nor in any way investigated with human reason. For since it puts its trust in God rather than in the bodily senses or human reasonings, the dignity of faith far exceeds all worldly wisdom: it sees that which cannot be seen, senses that which cannot be sensed, comprehends that which cannot be comprehended. Certain indeed is the comprehension of the unchangeable truth, strengthened most firmly by the authority of Truth itself.[53] Faith,

[51]See CFi 575D–76A: 'Qui credit et servit, fidem quam lingua confitetur, moribus profitetur. Qui credit et non servit, Deum quem verbis confitetur, factis negat [cf. Tt 1:16].' See, further, Bell, 'B. of F. and the Sacrament of the Altar', pp. 227–28.

[52]See, for example, CFi 576D–77A (the chapter entitled 'De fide quae per dilectionem operatur'), CFi 587C, and SA 763B (544).

[53]This is an idea common from Augustine to the Middle Ages (but its roots lie in Plato): the faith must be true because it has been revealed by the Supreme Truth itself. Similarly, it must be reasonable because it has been revealed by the Supreme

admittedly, can be helped to a certain extent by the senses or by reason, as we shall subsequently show, but where the senses or reason utterly fail, faith, pressing onwards unhindered, advances further than the senses or imagination or reason can attain by examination or arrive at by discovery.

The light of reason, by which the mind is naturally illuminated so that it can understand,[54] is surpassed, with an incomparable splendor of clarity, by the light of grace. By this the mind is illumined so that it might believe what it does not understand, until, by a certain order of grace, it understands what it now believes.[55] So, since the true cognition [*cognitio*] of things that can be comprehended is called knowledge [*scientia*] and is [knowledge], then that most true cognition of things that cannot be comprehended, [a cognition] granted to us by God's revelation, has, on account of its certainty and infallibility, much more of a right to be called knowledge: [a knowledge] which occupies a position not only above uncertain opinion, but above all human knowledge and above the judgment of reason. It is as though knowledge surpasses knowledge, though not [the knowledge] which, in a certain way, will be bestowed in the future.

This is the knowledge of salvation which illuminates and saves, [that knowledge] of which it is written: 'You shall go before the face of the Lord to prepare his ways: to give knowledge of salvation to his people for the remission of their sins' [Lk 1:76–77]. If, however, cognition by faith in beginners and those who are just progressing is so mediocre and insignificant that it does not yet deserve the name of knowledge, in the advanced and in the perfect—those who believe most firmly and most certainly and who, by the inspiration of more abundant grace, understand [*intelligunt*] more fully the reasoning of

Reason. Compare the passages from Augustine translated at nn. 79 and 80 below; and Baldwin, TD I 408A-B (35:48): 'Subnixa est ergo fides nostra veritate, principium et fundamentum habens ab ipso veraci Deo, cui dictum est: *Principium verborum tuorum veritas* [Ps 118:160]. Non enim fallit Deus, quia summa Veritas est; non fallitur, quia summa Sapientia est; non infirmatur, quia summa Virtus est.'

[54]Baldwin is here echoing medieval theories of vision. He does so again (in much more detail) elsewhere, and his exegesis is by no means easy to follow: for a full discussion see ST II: 139–40, nn. 5, 9.

[55]Compare Bernard, Csi 5.3.6, translated at n. 28 above; Brooke, 'Faith and Mystical Experience in William of St Thierry', *passim*. The idea was common from Augustine onward.

faith [*ratio fidei*][56]—cognition by faith should certainly be called knowledge: and this is the more true the more often we find in holy Scripture that things which are perceived by faith alone are referred to as being 'known' [*sciri*].

In the *Letter to the Romans*, when the apostle is commending the faith of Abraham, he says: 'In the promise of God, he did not waver by distrust, but was strengthened by faith, giving glory to God: knowing most fully [*plenissime sciens*] that whatever he has promised, he is also able to perform' [Rm 4:20–21]. Note that he does not say 'knowing' [*sciens*], but 'knowing most fully' [*plenissime sciens*], so that from a plenitude of knowledge he might commend to us more highly the certainty of faith. In the *Second Letter to Timothy*, the same [apostle says]: 'I know [*scio*] in whom I have believed and I am certain [*certus sum*], that he has the power to keep that which I have committed to him until that day' [2 Tm 1:12].[57] And the same [apostle] to the same [Timothy says]: 'Know [*scito*] this: that in the last days there shall

---

[56]*Ratio fidei* is not an easy term with which to deal. In Baldwin and most other medieval theologians it may be interpreted in three main ways, though beyond these individual writers have their own individual elaborations. First, we may translate the term as 'the reason/s for the faith': that is, a logical proof of the truth of the faith. This is something we shall examine in a moment (from n. 61 to n. 67), and we need say nothing more about it here. Secondly, we may translate the term as 'reasoning within the faith': that is, the use of logical, discursive reasoning within the confines of the faith as that faith is defined by the Scriptures and the Church. Bernard provides a useful definition of this sort of reasoning in SC 20.9; SBOp 1:120: '[Love] is rational when, in everything it thinks [*sentiri*] concerning Christ, the reasoning of faith [*ratio fidei*] is so firmly held that it deviates in no way whatever from the purity of the sense [*sensus*] of the Church by any [false] likeness of truth or any heretical or diabolical deceptions.' We must not venture beyond the bounds of *discretio*, he continues, by any superstition or levity or *spiritus quasi ferventioris vehementia* (by which he seems to mean an over-excess of enthusiasm deriving from an super-abundant pride in our own reason) (see SC 20.9). This second use of *ratio fidei* may be likened to a game of chess: the rules are strictly logical and one is restricted to the board, but within these regulations and confines, the possibilities of development are virtually endless. Thirdly, we may translate the term as 'reasoning from the faith', and this is rather more subtle. What happens here is that we first accept, on authority, the facts of the faith as true; then, after immersing ourselves in them for some time and examining them by a combination of logic and experience, we come to realize for ourselves that they *are* true; and finally, after realizing this, we find ourselves in possession of certain materials from which, by the further use of logic and intuition, we are able to derive further truths and experience higher realizations. It is like wine-tasting: one must begin by accepting, on authority, that a wine of one vintage is much better than that of another; by subsequent study, tasting, and experience one comes to realize for oneself that this is true; and, once one has realized this, one can proceed to judge other, unknown wines and assess their potential. Reason and logic are still involved here—x plus x is still 2x, and 2x is still greater than x—but it is a logic with a greater experiential and intuitional content than is the case with, say, chess playing. Computers

come dangerous times' [2 Tm 3:1]. He instructs us to 'know' [*scire*] what he earlier said should be 'believed' [*credendum*]. And blessed Job says: 'I know [*scio*] that my Redeemer lives, and in the last day I shall rise out of the earth' [Jb 19:25]. And Martha says to Jesus: 'I know [*scio*] that he will rise again in the resurrection on the last day' [Jn 11:24].

But when, in the *Letter to the Romans*, the apostle says: 'I judge [*existimo*] that the sufferings of this time may not be worthy to be compared with the glory to come that shall be revealed in us' [Rm 8:18], he is not referring to uncertain opinion [*opinio*] as if he says he himself judges [*existimare se*] that this will be the case, but to that consciousness of knowledge and certainty [*ad conscientiam scientie et certitudinis*][58] which is confirmed in the *Second Letter to the Corinthians*, where it says: 'We know [*scimus*] that if the earthly house of this habitation be dissolved, we have a building from God, a house not made with hands, eternal in heaven' [2 Co 5:1]. See how the apostle says that he both 'judges' [*existimare*] and 'knows' [*scire*] those things which actually pertain to our future condition so that we might not separate the judgment of faith [*existimatio fidei*] from the certainty of knowledge [*certitudo scientie*].[59]

We might draw the reader's attention to five points in this important discussion: (1) Baldwin agrees with William of Saint-Thierry and Bernard, and disagrees with Hugh of Saint-Victor, that faith can truly

---

can play chess; but although they may be able to analyse wines for their chemical content, they cannot judge them. If, however, one is not prepared at the beginning to accept certain things on trust, this sort of reasoning never becomes possible; and it follows, therefore, that reasoning *from* the faith and reasoning *within* the faith have a certain overlap. Augustine provides us with an example of this third sort of reasoning in the passage translated at n. 80 below, but in its highest form, 'reasoning from the faith' is transformed into a reasoning in and from love (see the admirable discussion in William of Saint-Thierry, *Aenigma fidei*; PL 180:414C-D; *Guillaume de Saint-Thierry, Deux traités sur la foi*, ed./trans. M. M. Davy [Paris, 1959] p. 128, no. 41 [CF 9:68–69 no. 37]).

[57]This is the text cited by William and Bernard in their attack on Abelard's definition of faith; see n. 26 above.

[58]This undoubtedly echoes the augustinian definition—*certa scientia, acclamante conscientia*—introduced by William and Bernard (see n. 26 above). But it is significant, as we shall see, that William does not actually mention Augustine by name.

[59]CFi 583B–84C. Since this discussion is so important, I have presented, as an Appendix to this study, a critical edition of the text based on the two surviving manuscripts of the CFi (London, B. L., Add. 11,593 [s. xii] fo. 7a-b and Oxford, Bod. Lib., Laud Misc. 91 [s. xiii] fos. 77b–78) and the PL text (which derives from a lost manuscript from Longpont).

be called *scientia*; (2) he states that this *scientia* occupies a place above uncertain opinion, above all human knowledge, and above the judgment of reason; (3) he is confident that this knowledge can reach its consummation only with the aid of grace; (4) he makes it clear that the Scriptures themselves testify to the fact that faith is *scientia* by their unequivocal use of the verb *scire* (Baldwin cites the same proof-text as William and Bernard, and then adds a number of others); and (5) he brings his whole argument to a close by demonstrating how this combination of scriptural authority and rational logic leads inevitably to the conclusion that the *existimatio fidei* cannot be separated from the certainty of knowledge. *Existimatio fidei*, writes Baldwin, not *aestimatio*, and thereby indicates his awareness of the word which Abelard actually used, and he prefers to cite that rather than the unauthorized variant offered by William and Bernard. But Baldwin contradicts the ideas of Abelard not by further scholasticism, not even (as do William and Bernard) by quoting Augustine, but by the authority of Job, Saint Paul, and the Gospels.

In other words, says Baldwin, Abelard is wrong, and the Scriptures prove that he is wrong. But let us now leave the authoritarian Baldwin and turn again to Baldwin of the schools, Baldwin the Rational, Baldwin the Disputant. What if someone argues like this (he asks in the *De commendatione fidei*): 'You tell me that all this is God's word, and if this is really so, I'll believe straightaway. So it's up to you to prove it!'[60] What do you do in such circumstances? Do you just tell them to believe it or else? To accept without question what the Church teaches? To enter the perilous domain of blind faith and enter heaven ignorant but saved? No, says Baldwin, you do not. You must render to such a person *ratio fidei*, the reasons for the faith,[61] and for about the last third of the *De commendatione fidei* he spends his time proving rationally that the Scriptures *are* inspired by God, and that God is no liar. Why does he do this? Because 'the defences [*munimenta*] of our faith reduce to the authority of holy Scripture: if this is true, the witnesses of the faith are true, the testimonies of the faith are true, and consequently the faith itself is true.'[62] He therefore proceeds to demonstrate rationally the truth

[60]See CFi 621B-C.

[61]*Ratio fidei* is here being used in the first of the three senses outlined in n. 56 above. See further Bell, 'B. of F. and the Sacrament of the Altar', pp. 218–19.

[62]CFi 621A: 'Unde constare debet quod munimenta fidei nostrae ad auctoritatem sacrae Scripturae reducuntur, quae si vera est, veri sunt testes fidei, vera sunt [et] testimonia fidei, et consequenter vera est ipsa fides.' See further Bell, 'B. of F. and Twelfth-Century Theology', p. 140.

of Scripture, and discusses at length appearances of God, allocutions, visions, signs, inspirations, revelations, and especially prophecies, showing again and again how events prophesied in the Old Testament find their resolution in the New, and how only God can predict the future without hesitation and without error.[63] Furthermore, he adds, look at the profound depths of agreement, of accord, of *concordia* that we have on this matter: the prophets and the apostles are in accord, since all that was predicted by the former has been fulfilled by the latter; the Old Testament and the New Testament are in accord, 'so that the reason for faith [*ratio fidei*] might appear more clearly';[64] and the 'orthodox Fathers'[65] are in accord with the apostles. How could there ever be such a *concordia*, save by the revelation of the Holy Spirit, the Spirit of Truth?[66] But if we come across thinkers and theologians whose writings are not in accord with Scripture and the scriptural traditions of the Church—writers such as Arius or Donatus (or, presumably, Abelard)—these we do not believe. 'The Church is not in the petty councils of the heretics, nor are Donatus and Arius and the other heresiarchs princes of the Church; we are built on the foundation of the apostles and the prophets, and Jesus Christ himself is the chief cornerstone [Eph 2:20].'[67]

This stress on Scripture and the teachings of the New Testament may be seen clearly in Baldwin's discussion of the certainty of faith presented above. There is not the least doubt that William and Bernard's account of Abelard's errors is in his mind, but he does not cite Bernard or William, nor even—as they do—Augustine. He cites 'the Apostle', Job, and the

---

[63]See CFi 621–40. In Oxford, Bod. Lib., Laud Misc. 91 fos. 98–99, we find a unique and lengthy passage, occurring neither in London, B. L., Add. 11,593 nor the PL text, which contrasts human efforts at foretelling the future with God's prophecies. It will be found in my forthcoming edition of the CFi.

[64]CFi 628A.

[65]For the term and the identity of the 'orthodox Fathers', see Bell, 'B. of F. and Twelfth-Century Theology', p. 141. The expression derives from the *Rule* of Saint Benedict (RB 9.8; SCh 182:512; see further the discussion in C. Waddell, 'Notes About St Bernard on the Two Visions of Isaiah: The First Sermon for the First Sunday in November', *Liturgy O.C.S.O.* 24 [1990] 82–84).

[66]See CFi 627B–28C (the chapters entitled 'De concordia testium et testimoniorum, et de collatione dictorum et factorum' and 'Quod tanta concordia testium non poterat procurari, nisi a Spiritu sancto' [following the reading of Oxford, Bod. Lib., Laud Misc. 91 fo. 100b]).

[67]CFi 619C: 'Non [est] ergo Ecclesia in conciliabulis haereticorum, nec principes Ecclesiae sunt Donatus et Arius, caeterique haeresiarchae, *sed superaedificati* sumus *super fundamentum apostolorum et prophetarum, ipso summo angulari lapide Christo Jesu* [Eph 2:20].' In roman comedy, the term *conciliabulum* was sometimes used to mean a brothel; one wonders what Baldwin, that well-read prelate, had in mind.

Gospels. And the same is true of all of Baldwin's work. Few are more familiar than he with the western tradition (his learning, though not his character, was universally respected[68]); few are more frugal in their citing of their sources.[69] In all his works, but especially in the long study *De sacramento altaris*, Baldwin prefers to go behind the Fathers to the Scriptures. If the Fathers agree with the Scriptures, all well and good; if they do not, then God and his Word, in the flesh and on the sacred page, must surely take precedence. And if Baldwin, basing his own exegesis firmly on the Scriptures, arrives at an explanation which seems to conflict with that of the divine Augustine, Baldwin will argue for his own case (although, he carefully adds, the root of the problem lies not in the fact that Augustine was wrong, but that he was using a different translation of the Bible).[70]

Both these approaches, in fact, could be dangerous, and any criticism of the Fathers, implicit or overt, had to be done with the greatest delicacy. In 1113–1115, Rupert of Deutz was attacked for preferring Scripture to the Fathers; and in 1116, at Liège, he was put on trial, in theory for his eucharistic views, but primarily for his presumption in impugning the authority of the bishop of Hippo.[71] He escaped condemnation, that is true, but only by the skin of his teeth. Yet what John van Engen says of Rupert can be applied equally to Baldwin:

> Even in its boldest expression, Rupert's principle should not be construed in some proto-Protestant sense. He presupposed the teaching authority of the Church and was immersed in the Fathers' exposition of Scripture; but he also held, together with most others prior to the late middle ages, that Scripture was the unique source of divine truth, and tradition therefore the Church's authoritative exposition thereof.[72]

By the time of Baldwin, of course, a great deal had happened. Between Rupert and Baldwin was Abelard; and, whatever the true intention of Abelard's *Sic et non*, it revealed all too clearly that the Fathers were far from unanimous on a whole multitude of issues. How could one

---

[68]See Bell, 'B. of F. and Twelfth-Century Theology', p. 137, and ST I:9–18 *passim*.

[69]See ST I:25–28. To the pagan writers listed there must now be added Seneca the Elder (*Controversiae* 3.9.3), again cited anonymously; see B. J. Samain, 'Deux traités inédits de B. de F.: Le *De Oboedientia* et le *De Sancta Cruce*', Cîteaux 39 (1988) 25.

[70]See SA 732C-D (424–26).

[71]See J. van Engen, *Rupert of Deutz* (Berkeley, Los Angeles, London, 1983) pp. 157, 164.

[72]Van Engen, pp. 157–58.

address this problem? Undoubtedly, in one of two ways: one could either show that, despite appearances and an occasional explicable lapse, the Fathers were actually remarkably consistent, or one could accept tacitly the more orthodox interpretations of the more orthodox Fathe. s and lay greater stress on the Truth-inspired truth of Holy Scriptur, William of Saint-Thierry prefers the former route. In his *De sacramento altaris*, written against the errors of Rupert of Deutz in the 1120s,[73] William bases his arguments firmly on the writings, liberally quoted, of Augustine, Jerome, and Ambrose. It is their voice that dominates, and in this work we see William as one of the first 'to use the method of patristic study and criticism which Peter Abelard advocates in his celebrated *Sic et non*.'[74] It is a case of diamond cut diamond. Baldwin's much longer *De sacramento altaris* is quite different. It is bound tightly— excruciatingly tightly—to the text of Scripture, and although he certainly cites the Fathers— Ambrose, pseudo-Dionysius, Hilary, Jerome, Origen, and especially Augustine[75]—his real question is not 'What do the Fathers say?' but 'What do the Scriptures mean?'[76] He can prove rationally, to his own satisfaction, that they were inspired, and therefore authoritative;

[73]Most scholars still date the main part of William's treatise to about 1128 and the introductory letter to a year or two earlier (see A. M. Piazzoni, *Guglielmo di Saint-Thierry: Il Declino dell'Ideale Monastico nel Secolo XII*, Istituto Storico Italiano per il Medio Evo, Studi Storici, fasc. 181–83 [Rome, 1988] pp. 41–42). John van Engen, however, suggests 1122–1123 for the treatise and 1112–1114 for the letter (see his 'Rupert of Deutz and William of Saint-Thierry', *Revue Bénédictine* 93 [1983] 327–36). Personally, I do not find van Engen's arguments wholly convincing, but this is obviously not the place for an extended discussion of the question.

[74]J. M. Déchanet, *William of St Thierry: The Man and His Work*, trans. R. Strachan, CS 10 (Spencer, 1972) pp. 34–35. But one cannot press this analogy too far. As Piazzoni points out (*Guglielmo di Saint-Thierry*, pp. 62–63), 'una differenza sostanziale però esiste fra il testo di Guglielmo e quello di Abelardo (oltre all'evidente diversità di mole e di argomenti): se Guglielmo ci offre un *Sic et non*, ce lo offre commentato e, in qualche modo, risolto in partenza. Il *Liber* [*de sacramento altaris*] altro non è infatti che un commento a tutti quei passi e le notazioni metodologiche sono finalizzate ad aiutare la comprensione di quelle e di eventuali altre fonti dello stesso genere. Questo tipo di introduzione ad una raccolta è però assolutamente diverso, proprio nella sua impostazione, da quella che Abelardo presupponeva per il suo *Sic et non*, dove proprio le antitesi, nient'affatto ritenute solo apparenti, avevano il fine dichiarato di suscitare la discussione ed affinare lo spirito critico.' See also Piazzoni, p. 59. William had not read the *Sic et non* (which probably dates from sometime between 1123 and 1126 [see Luscombe, *School of Peter Abelard*, p. 25]) when he wrote to Bernard to alert him to the abelardian danger; see Ep 326.4; PL 182:532D–33A; Leclercq, 'Les lettres. . .' (see n. 25 above), p. 378.

[75]See SA, pp. 584–86, 'Index des noms propres', and Bell, 'B. of F. and Twelfth-Century Theology', p. 141, nn. 69–75.

[76]See Baldwin's comments cited at n. 19 above.

having proved that, it behooves us to examine them with the greatest care and diligence and determine just what it is that God has revealed, what exactly he means in and by his revelation, and just what we are supposed to do about it.[77]

Baldwin's view of reason, faith, and authority is not therefore to be seen as a fear-filled reaction to the onrush of scholasticism and dialectic. It is not a terrified retreat into blind authority. It is, on the contrary, a reasoned restatement of a position which had been accepted from Augustine onward and with which no Cistercian of his century would have disagreed. That the post-abelardian monastic theologians had been affected by Abelard is, of course, obvious. It is not just in Baldwin or William of Saint-Thierry that we see 'a heightened emphasis on obedience to authority';[78] but neither William nor Bernard nor Baldwin ever thought it necessary or even conceivable that reason should be rejected. A restatement of values was as inevitable as it was essential, but the view of Baldwin and the Cistercians was fundamentally the view of Augustine who long ago had pointed out that we are guided in a twofold way, by authority and reason, and that the former precedes the latter. The medicine of the soul, he wrote, is divided into authority and reason:

> Authority demands faith and prepares us for reason. Reason leads to understanding [*intellectus*] and cognition [*cognitio*]. Nevertheless, reason does not entirely abandon authority when the question of who should be believed is being considered. And certainly the highest authority is that of Truth already known and evident.[79]

Again, he tells us that in order to learn it is necessary that we be guided in a two-fold way, by authority and reason:

> Thus it follows that, for all those wanting to learn the great and hidden goods, it is authority alone which opens the door. Whoever enters and,

[77]But, he adds, it is not our business to inquire into what God has *not* wished to reveal (see CFi 607A).

[78]E. R. Elder, 'William of Saint Thierry: Rational and Affective Spirituality', in E. R. Elder (ed.), *The Spirituality of Western Christendom*, CS 30 (Kalamazoo, 1976) p. 93. See further Elder's discussion in William of Saint-Thierry, *The Mirror of Faith*, trans. T. X. Davis, CF 15 (Kalamazoo, 1979) pp. xiii-xv, and the useful account in William of Saint-Thierry, *The Enigma of Faith*, trans. J. D. Anderson, CF 9 (Washington, 1974) pp. 9–16.

[79]Augustine, *De vera relig.* 24.45; PL 34:141: 'Auctoritas fidem flagitat, et rationi praeparat hominem. Ratio ad intellectum cognitionemque perducit. Quanquam neque auctoritatem ratio penitus deserit, cum consideratur cui sit credendum; et certe summa est ipsius jam cognitae atque perspicuae veritatis auctoritas.'

without any doubt, follows the precepts of the best sort of life, and, through them, has been made receptive [*docilis*], may then finally learn [first] how well endowed with reason are those things which he followed before [he saw their] reason; [secondly], what that reason itself is which, after [establishing himself] firmly and properly in the cradle of authority, he now follows and comprehends; and [thirdly], the nature of that understanding [*intellectus*] in which are all things— or rather, which *is* all things—and the nature of the source of all things which is beyond all things. To this cognition few attain in this life; and after this life none can go beyond it.[80]

That this was also the view of Abelard is, of course, one of the great ironies of intellectual history.

APPENDIX

De commendatione fidei xiii (PL 204:583B–584C)

L = London, B. L., Add. 11,593 fo. 7a-b.
O = Oxford, Bod. Lib., Laud Misc. 91 fos. 77b–78.
ed. = PL 204:583B–84C.

<CAPITVLVM XIII>

De fidei certitudine

    1. Quoniam per fidem in Deo fidimus et Deo credimus, cum Deus veritas sit [cf. Jn 14:6], tanta certitudine, tanta non dubie assensionis firmitate eadem fides debet esse subnixa, ut recte scientia dici possit. Omnem enim sensuum experientiam excedit, omnem coniecturam
5 humane rationis transcendit, uerissime et certissime comprehendens que nec sensu explorari, nec humana ratione ullatenus ualeant inuestigari. Cum enim Deo magis credendum sit, quam uel sensibus corporis uel humanis rationibus, omnem mundanam sapientiam fidei dignitas superexcellit, inuisibilia uidens, insensibilia sentiens,

---

[80]Augustine, *De ord.* 2.26; PL 32:1007: 'Evenit ut omnibus bona magna et occulta discere cupientibus, non aperiat nisi auctoritas januam. Quam quisque ingressus sine ulla dubitatione vitae optimae praecepta sectatur: per quae cum docilis factus fuerit, tum demum discet et quanta ratione praedita sint ea ipsa quae secutus est ante rationem; et quid sit ipsa ratio quam post auctoritatis cunabula firmus et idoneus jam sequitur atque comprehendit; et quid intellectus, in quo universa sunt, vel ipsa potius universa; et quid praeter universa universorum principium. Ad quam cognitionem in hac vita pervenire pauci, ultra quam vero etiam post hanc vitam nemo progredi potest.'

10   incomprehensibilia comprehendens.

2. Certa quippe comprehensio est incommutabilis ipsius ueritatis, ueritatis auctoritate firmissime roborata. Quamuis autem fides sensu uel ratione ex aliqua parte possit adiuuari, ut in sequentibus ostendetur, tamen ubi sensus uel ratio omnino deficit, fides inoffensa

15   ultra progrediens procedit, quam uel sensus uel imaginatio uel ratio inquisitione possit pertingere, uel inuentione peruenire.

3. Lumen quippe rationis, quo mens naturaliter illuminatur ut intelligat, incomparabili claritatis splendore superat lux gratie, qua mens illuminatur, ut non intellecta credat, donec quodam ordine

20   gratie, que nunc credit, intelligat. Quapropter cum rerum comprehensibilium uera cognitio scientia dicatur et sit, multo magis incomprehensibilium uerissima cognitio, Deo reuelante nobis indulta, pro sui certitudine et infallibilitate, scientia dici debet: non solum supra incertum opinionis, sed supra omnem humanam scientiam et supra

25   iudicium rationis collocanda, quasi scientia scientie preferenda, sed non ei que futuri temporis aliquomodo conferenda.

4. Hec est autem *scientia salutis* que illuminat et saluat, de qua scriptum est: *Preibis ante faciem Domini parare uias eius. Ad dandam scientiam salutis plebi eius in remissionem peccatorum eorum*

30   [Lk 1:76–77]. Si qua est autem cognitio per fidem in incipientibus uel proficientibus adeo mediocris et tenuis, ut nondum scientie nomine digna sit, in prouectis tamen et perfectis, qui firmissime et certissime credunt, et rationem fidei per inspirationem abundantioris gratie plenius intelligunt, cognitio per fidem tanto certius scientia

35   dicitur, quanto frequentius in sacra scriptura sciri referuntur, que sola fide percipiuntur.

5. Fidem Abrahe commendans, apostolus in epistola ad Romanos sic ait: *In promissione Dei non hesitauit diffidentia, sed confortatus est fide, dans gloriam Deo, plenissime sciens quia quecumque*

40   *promisit, potens est et facere* [Rm 4:20–21]. Attendite quod non dixit *sciens*, sed *plenissime sciens*, ut certitudinem fidei ex plenitudine scientie altius nobis commendaret. Idem in secunda epistola ad Timotheum: *Scio cui credidi et certus sum, quia potens est depositum meum seruare in illum diem* [2 Tm 1:12]. Idem ad eumdem: *Hoc*

45   *autem scito, quod in nouissimis diebus instabunt tempora periculosa* [2 Tm 3:1]. Scire monuit quod credendum predixit. Et beatus Iob ait: *Scio quod redemptor meus uiuit, et in nouissimo die de terra surrecturus sum* [Jb 19:25]. Et Martha dicit ad Iesum: *Scio quia resurget in resurrectione in nouissimo die* [Jn 11:24].

50   6. Quod autem apostolus in epistola ad Romanos dicit: *Existimo*
quod non sint condigne passiones huius temporis ad futuram gloriam
que reuelabitur in nobis [Rm 8:18], non ad incertum opinionis refer-
endum est, quamuis existimare se dicat, sed ad conscientiam scientie
et certitudinis, quod ex secunda epistola ad Corinthios comprobatur,
55   ubi sic dicit: *Scimus quoniam si terrestris domus nostra huius habi-*
tationis dissoluatur, quod edificationem ex Deo habemus, domum
non manufactam eternam in celis [2 Co 5:1]. Ecce apostolus, que
ad statum futuri temporis pertinent, et existimare se dicit et scire,
ut existimationem fidei a scientie certitudine non separemus.

APPARATUS

1 Deo fidimus] Deum confidimus **ed.** 12 ueritatis[2]] *om.* **O, ed.** 13–14
ostendetur] ostenditur **ed.** 14 tamen ubi sensus uel ratio omnino deficit]
om. **ed.** 15 ultra progrediens procedit] procedit ultra progrediens **O** 16
inquisitione possit] *inv.* **O** 16 inuentione] intentione **ed.** 26 que] qui **O**
26 temporis] est *add.* **O** 27 autem] *om.* **O** 28 Preibis] enim *add. cum*
Vulg. **ed.** 30 incipientibus] insipientibus **ed.** 31 tenuis] est *add.* **ed.** 32
nomine] *om.* **L** 33 rationem] ratione **ed.** 38 promissione] repromissione
etiam *cum Vulg.* **ed.** 42 secunda] *om.* **ed.** 45 scito] scio **O** 48 sum] sim
ed., s. O 48 dicit] dixit **ed.** 50 in epistola] *om.* **ed.** 51 sint] sunt **ed. O**
54 quod] que **ed.** 54 secunda] *om.* **ed.** 55 si] *om.* **L** 56 quod] *om.* **ed.**

Abbreviations

B. of/de F. = Baldwin of Ford (now Forde)/Baudouin de Ford

    CFi = *De commendatione fidei*, cited by column number of PL
       204. A critical edition of the CFi has been prepared by the
       present writer and will be published in due course in the
       series *Corpus Christianorum, Continuatio mediaevalis*.

    PC = *Pain de Cîteaux*.

    SA = *De sacramento altaris*, cited by column number of PL 204
       and (in parenthesis) by page number of J. Morson (ed.)/E.
       de Solms (trans.), *B. de F., Le sacrement de l'autel* (SCh
       93–94 [continuous pagination]; Paris, 1963).

    ST = *B. of F., Spiritual Tractates*, trans. D. N. Bell, CF 39 and
       41 (Kalamazoo, 2 vols., 1986).

    TD = *Tractatus diversi*, cited by column number of PL 204 and
       (in parenthesis) by PC volume and page number of R.
       Thomas (ed./trans.), *B. de F., Traités*, PC 35–40 (Chimay,

6 vols., 1973–1975). A critical edition of the TD has been prepared by the present writer and will be published in due course in the series *Corpus Christianorum, Continuatio mediaevalis*.

ABSTRACTS

L'article étudie le but du *De commendatione fidei* de Baudouin de Forde. Il commence par démontrer que chez les Cisterciens la raison n'a jamais été condamnée comme telle, mais seulement lorsqu'elle outrepassait les bornes qui lui étaient prescrites par la foi de l'Eglise. Baudoin a beaucoup à dire sur la nature de la foi et l'aide que peut lui apporter la raison, mais il ne tolère pas l'approche 'abélardienne' suivant laquelle la foi devient une simple opinion humaine. La foi est une véritable *scientia* fondée en Dieu et en sa parole, et Baudoin lui-même préfère citer la Bible plutôt que les Pères. Il ne faut pas voir dans le *De commendatione fidei* qu'une réaction à la scolastique; c'est 'une réitération raisonnée d'une position reçue depuis Augustin et avec laquelle aucun Cistercien de son siècle n'aurait été en désaccord'.

This article is a study of the purpose of the *De commendatione fidei* of Baldwin of Forde. It begins by demonstrating that among the Cistercians, reason was never condemned *per se*, but only when it overstepped its prescribed limits: the limits set by the faith of the Church. Baldwin has much to say on the nature of faith and how it may be assisted by reason, but he will not tolerate the 'Abelardian' approach, in which faith becomes no more than human opinion. Faith is true *scientia* which is founded in God and his word, and Baldwin himself prefers to cite the Bible rather than the Fathers. The *De commendatione fidei* is not to be seen simply as a reaction to scholasticism, but as 'a reasoned restatement of a position which had been accepted from Augustine onward and with which no Cistercian of his century would have disagreed'.

Dieser Artikel ist eine Untersuchung der Absicht der Schrift *De commendatione fidei* von Balduin von Ford. Sie beginnt, indem sie zeigt, dass bei den Zisterziensern die Vernunft nie *per se* verurteilt wurde, sondern nur, wenn sie ihre vorgeschriebenen Grenzen überschritt, nämlich die Grenzen, die durch den Glauben der Kirche gesetzt waren. Balduin hat viel zu sagen über die Natur des Glaubens und wie er durch die Vernunft unterstützt werden kann, aber er toleriert den 'abälardschen' Zugang nicht, bei dem Glaube nicht mehr ist als menschliche Meinung. Glaube ist wahre *scientia*, die gegründet ist in Gott und seinem Wort, und Balduin selbst zieht es vor, eher die Bibel als die Väter zu zitieren. *De commendatione fidei* darf nicht einfach als eine Reaktion auf die Scholastik gesehen werden, sondern als 'eine begründete Neuformulierung einer Position, die seit Augustin angenommen worden war und mit der kein Zisterzienser seines Jahrhunderts brechen wollte.'

'UNDER THE APPLE TREE': A COMPARATIVE EXEGESIS OF *SONG OF SONGS* 2:3 IN THE SERMONS BY BERNARD OF CLAIRVAUX AND JOHN OF FORD

Elizabeth Oxenham, OCSO
Holy Cross Abbey

ONE OF THE MOST ATTRACTIVE and persuasive features of the writings of the cistercian fathers, one that makes their message so credible, is that they wrote out of the fullness of their own experience. John of Ford, speaking of those who had commented on the Song before him, said that 'they hand down to us nothing that they have not first read in their own hearts, dictated from the mouth of Jesus, deeply incised with his finger, inscribed by the Spirit of the living God as if in ink.' And he continues: 'The unction of the Spirit first made these men its pupils, and then made them into teachers. It was in the marriage chamber that they learned to understand the marriage song, and only then did they become able to explain this sacred song to us.'[1] From our own personal *lectio* of the fathers, we can verify that this statement is true. Can we also assert that John himself is in the same class as these great men? Through his commentary on the Song of Songs does he reveal himself as an apt pupil in the school of the Holy Spirit, worthy

---

[1]SC 24.2; CF 39:135. The english translation of the sermons, by Wendy Mary Beckett, has the title, *Sermons on the Final Verses of the Song of Songs*, and has been published by Cistercian Publications, Kalamazoo, Michigan, in the Cistercian Fathers series in seven volumes, between 1977 and 1984. All the quotations are from this translation. The latin edition of the sermons, prepared by Edmund Mikkers and Hilary Costello, is published in the series CCCM 17 and 18, 1970. Latin title: Ioannis de Forda, *Super extremam partam cantici canticorum sermones cxx.*

to sit beside Bernard, Gilbert of Hoyland, William of Saint Thierry? Is he, then, qualified as they are to initiate us into the mysteries of this marriage song? I shall attempt to give some kind of answer to these questions by comparing the commentaries written by Bernard and John on a verse in the Song, verse 3 of chapter 2. Here the bride says of the Bridegroom: 'As an apple tree among the trees of the wood, so is my beloved among the sons. With great delight I sat in his shadow, and his fruit was sweet to my taste.' The method I have adopted is to compare and contrast the development each of our authors has made of the images in this verse, namely, the apple tree, its shadow, the fruit and its taste, and sitting under the apple tree.

THE APPLE TREE

Let us first see what Bernard has to say about the apple tree. What does he think about the bride comparing her Beloved to an apple tree among the trees of the wood? We find the answer in his forty-eighth sermon on the Song, where he devotes sections 3–8 to this verse. In Bernard's eyes this comparison appears quite inadequate and altogether unworthy of the majesty of the Spouse. But there must be a reason for it; the Bride was not acting irresponsibly and without forethought when she spoke in this way, and Bernard resolves to find it. In this quest he employs one of his favorite literary devices, the rhetorical question, which has the two-fold effect of embellishing his style and quickening the attention of the reader or listener. 'Why', he asks,

> when the finer and nobler trees were ignored, was the insignificance of this tree brought forward to eulogize the Bridegroom? Should he thus receive praise by measure who has not received the Spirit by measure? For to compare him with that tree seems to indicate that he who has no equal has a superior. What shall we say to this? I say the praise is little because it is praise for one who is little [*parva laus, quonium parvi laus*]. The proclamation made here is not, 'Great is the Lord and greatly to be praised', but 'Little is the Lord and greatly to be loved', the child, namely, who is born to us [*Non enim hoc loco praedicatur, Magnus Dominus et laudabilis nimis, sed parvulus Dominus et amabilis nimis*].[2]

---

[2]Bernard of Clairvaux, SC 48.3; SBOp 2:69; CF 31:14.

This passage is a good example of how well nigh impossible it is to capture the beauty of the rhythm and the precision of Bernard's latin prose in translation. It is also a moving testimony to the magnetic attraction the mystery of Christ's birth held for Bernard, an attraction enshrined in the story of his childhood, when falling asleep one Christmas Eve as he waited for the midnight vigil to begin, he saw in a dream the birth of the Son from the Virgin Mary.

John of Ford, in his commentary on the Song, deals with this same verse in his sermon 102. When he reflects on the words of the bride, likening her Spouse to an apple tree, he concedes that, taken at its face value, the comparison is inappropriate, 'likening the fairest of the sons of men to an apple tree, is, of course, insufficient praise', but then he goes on to add: 'Though insufficient, it is not unbecoming. For one size of garment is right for princely sons, when they are small, and another size when they are grown. Each individual person or age is given according to his own measure, so that their garments fit.'[3] Certainly a novel comparison, but rather clumsy, especially when put beside Bernard's lyric passage on the same theme. However, although their comparisons differ, their interpretation is the same, since both Bernard and John are agreed that when the bride compares the Spouse to an apple tree, she is praising his humility. Bernard also marvels at 'the wonderful way in which the Son both subjected himself as man to the angels and, remaining God, retained the angels as his subjects. 'Because the littleness of Jesus gives sweeter relish to the bride' she is happy 'to contemplate him as a man among men, not as God among the angels.'[4] The angelic world, both in the order of creation and the economy of salvation, is just as important to John as it is to Bernard, and he too points out that the Son chose to become man rather than an angel, quoting from the Letter to the Hebrews: 'He did not concern himself with angels, but with the sons of Abraham' [Heb 2:16].[5]

That the Son of God should choose to be born of a sinful race and clothe himself in the likeness of sinful flesh, captures John's attention, and, in a passage of great beauty, rich in biblical allusions, he develops this truth under the image of a thorn tree. He speaks first of himself as a thorn tree, good for the eternal fires, a tree growing under God's curse with sharp thorns, which the soil of our human condition has made to

---

[3]John, SC 102.1; CCMM 18:690; CF 47:16.
[4]Bernard, SC 48.4; SBOp 2:69; CF 31:15.
[5]John, SC 102.3; CCCM 18:691; CF 47:18.

grow for our father Adam. 'I am fruitful only in thorns', John laments, 'and I tend them for my own burning, hurting with the prick of evil words and example of anyone who comes near or touches me.'[6]

Man's situation, as typified by John, seemed desperate, without hope, then suddenly, without warning, *ex insperato*, 'the only Son of God came from his Father's bosom, and in an utterly new and unthinkable manner, stooped to be grafted on to my mortal thorn. He became for me a tree of life, not in the midst of paradise, but in the midst of the trees of the wood, thorn trees, humble trees like me.'[7]

This imagery of the thorn tree lends itself to a consideration of the Passion, which John now develops with sensitivity and imagination. God's decision to become man was not the result of lengthy deliberations, a meticulous weighing up of pros and cons; it was rather something he longed to do with his whole being, to put it in human terms. 'He yearned to become a thorn', John tells us, and 'he became a thorn, in that flesh suffers and dies, a thorn in that he was encircled by the sorrows of our sins and beset on all sides with thorny prickles, like a hedgehog.'[8]

Despite appearances to the contrary, we are not to infer from this lengthy meditation on the thorn tree that John has lost sight of the apple tree in the text on which he is commenting. Both he and Bernard are agreed that the apple tree is a fitting image of Christ's humility, and John only introduces this secondary image of the thorn tree to emphasize still further the 'divine humility' which prompted the Son of God to take on himself the full burden of our sinfulness.

THE SHADOW

Turning now to the theme of the shadow, we find that Bernard devotes two long sections to it, an indication of how important it was for him. Unfortunately, we cannot do justice to his teaching within the limits imposed by this paper. For Bernard, the shadow of Christ is both his flesh and our faith in him. Just as 'the flesh of her own Son overshadowed Mary, faith in the Lord overshadows me', and he continues, 'why should his flesh not overshadow me too, as I eat him in the sacrament?'[9] We remember here that the Eucharist is known as the sacrament of faith par

---

[6]John, SC 102.3; CCCM 18:691; CF 47:18.
[7]John, SC 102.3; CCCM 18:691; CF 47:18.
[8]John, SC 102.4; CCCM 18:692; CF 47:18–19.
[9]Bernard, SC 48.6; SBOp 2:71; CF 31:17.

excellence. Bernard has already spoken of the shadow of faith in sermon 31, linking it there too with the Eucharist: 'We therefore who walk by faith live in the shadow of Christ; we are fed with his flesh, as the source of our life. For Christ's flesh is real food.'[10]

In these two sermons, 31 and 48, Bernard quotes from Lamentations 4:20: 'The spirit before our face is Christ the Lord, in his shadow we live among the peoples.' In both instances he states that while we are walking by faith in this life we are living in the shadow among the nations, but when we see God face to face we will be in the light with the angels [*in umbra in gentibus, in luce cum angelis*].'[11] In sermon 48, the shadow is equated with Christ's flesh, the light with his spirit: 'He is flesh to those who remain in the flesh, but "a spirit before our face", that is, in the future, provided we forget what lies behind and strain forward to what lies ahead, where on arriving we may experience exactly what he said: "The flesh is of no avail; it is the spirit that gives life." '[12] We have here an interesting blending of two scriptural texts which meant much to Bernard: Lamentations 4:20, quoted at least sixteen times in his sermons, and Philippians 3:13, used some six times in his commentary on the Song. It is not surprising that these two texts recur so often in Bernard's sermons, since his whole drive was toward the future, toward heaven. Only there will the desire of his heart be fully satisfied, only there will he see face to face the God sought with such ardor in the darkness of faith.

While the prophet spoke of living in the shadow, the bride claims to sit in the shadow of her Beloved, that is, to be at ease, to rest in contemplation: 'It is as much more to rest in the shadow', Bernard asserts, 'than to live in it, as it is to live in it rather than merely to be in it.'[13] This is the bride's prerogative; this is her privileged abode. 'I am seated in his shadow', she says, not 'we are seated'. And there she tastes the sweet fruit of contemplation, *gustum contemplationis*. But the time will come when the shadows will flee away, and in the light of the eternal vision she will taste to the full, untiringly, without satiety, the delights of her Beloved.

For John, too, the shadow also signifies faith, though he does not go into the same detail as Bernard. In sermon 102 he simply states that

[10]Bernard, SC 31.10; SBOp 1:225; CF 7:132.
[11]Bernard, SC 48.6; SBOp 2:71; CF 31:17.
[12]Bernard, SC 48.7; SBOp 2:72; CF 31:19.
[13]Bernard, SC 48.8; SBOp 2:72; CF 31:19.

if an eye is qualified to see eternal brightness, then the shadow of faith makes it accustomed to its light little by little. This is what is meant by 'purifying their hearts by faith', until the time comes when those who have dwelt in the land of his shadow, this saving land, are received into the country of heavenly radiance.[14]

In one of his earlier sermons, sermon 38, John also has a long section on the shadow of the Bridegroom, in which he comments on the words of the bride: 'His throat is most sweet and he is wholly desirable' [Sg 5:16]. According to John, when the bride describes her Beloved as 'wholly desirable', she implies that even his shadow is desirable, and so she is confident that the shadow of the Spouse, that is, the shadow of the tree of life, will bring her healing, which is why she speaks of sitting under his shadow. If, as we read in the Acts of the Apostles (5:14–15), even the shadow of Peter brought healing to the sick, how much more powerful will the shadow of his Master be? For Peter's shadow

> was proclaiming with great clarity the strong light that illuminated him and so made him cast a shadow, as if the shadow itself were telling those who fled to it for refuge: 'Why do you fix your eyes on me, or on Peter? It is not we who do these things, it is the Light, which has shone on Peter, and so produced me, Peter's shadow.'[15]

Not only does the shadow represent healing for John, he also states in this same sermon 38 that it is symbolic of the protection, the cool, and the concealment with which the Spouse graciously overshadows the soul that loves him, hiding her within the secret of his face. Under his protection she is shielded from the glare of fleshly temptation and from the far more dangerous heat of spiritual sin. Bernard likewise makes mention of relief from the fever heat of vices which the shadow of the Bridegroom provides, but he does not make John's distinction between carnal and spiritual temptation.

THE FRUIT AND ITS TASTE

It is clear from these extracts how important the image of the shadow is to both our authors, and the variety of interpretations which could be given it. The image of the fruit and its taste does not seem to have struck quite such a responsive chord, though both have something to say on the

---

[14]John, SC 102.7; CCCM 18:694; CF 47:22–23.
[15]John, SC 38.7; CCCM 17:288; CF 43:112–13.

subject, John more so than Bernard. When Bernard speaks of Christ as the tree of life, he seems to imply that, from one point of view, the fruit of the tree is the Eucharist, because he immediately goes on to say that Christ alone is the living bread which comes down from heaven and gives life to the world. I have noted earlier how Bernard links the shadow with the flesh of Christ and with faith in him. There is then a kind of convergent movement towards the Eucharist in this sermon, since the fruit of the tree can also be equated with the bread of life. A good summary of his thought occurs at the end of section 7, where he states that we can be certain of living in his shadow when we eat the flesh of Christ, honor his mysteries, follow his footsteps, and keep faith.[16]

The actual tasting of the fruit signifies contemplation for Bernard in the passage from the very end of the sermon, already quoted, where he speaks of the bride's prerogative of sitting in the shadow of her Beloved and there tasting the sweet fruit of contemplation. No matter how close the bride is to the Bridegroom, while she is still in exile on this earth, the gift of contemplation is not a permanent state; it comes and goes as the Bridegroom decides. The taste she is given here below is meant to whet her appetite and to intensify her longing for the plenitude of heaven.[17]

Although John does not say in so many words that the tasting of the fruit signifies contemplation, he comes very near to it when he states that, if one sits beneath the Bridegroom's shade, the apples of interior joy (*poma delectationis internae*) 'either fall freely down or can easily be plucked even here below.' 'Christ is a lowly tree', he continues,

and one that is rich in fruit and will never disappoint the prayers of the humble. But 'to sit' means to wait humbly and expectantly under the tree, until the fruit you long for falls into your lap as you are sitting. This is your labor and work until the time when, clothed with strength from on high, you yourself may shake the tree of life with the strength of your prayer and cut some of this lovely fruit from its branches with the vigorous arm of your good works.[18]

There are several comments to be made about this delightful passage. In the first place, it is a very good example of John's style and approach. It has a freshness and immediacy about it, as though the image had suggested itself to John as a result of his own experience of sitting under

---

[16]Bernard, SC 48.7; SBOp 2:72; CF 31:19.
[17]Bernard, SC 48.8; SBOp 2:72; CF 31:19–20.
[18]John, SC 102.7; CCCM 18:694; CF 47:23.

an apple tree on a late summer afternoon, with the occasional apple plopping down on top of him. This impression is strengthened when he adds that one way of gathering fruit from the tree of life is to shake it. It is worth recalling that John came from the West Country, that little corner of England where Devon, Somerset, and Dorset touch each other, famous for its apples and cider, what we might call 'the apple basket of England'.

We also notice in this passage how John refers to the humility of Christ, typified by the lowly apple tree, rich in fruit, fruit which is given to the humble of heart in response to their prayer. Humility implies waiting for the Lord, but waiting with expectation for the desired fruit; that is why the bride is prompted to *sit* under the apple tree. Just as at the Ascension Christ told the apostles to remain in the city—literally to *sit* there—until they were clothed with power from on high, so the bride is told to sit and wait until she too is clothed with power. John often refers to the Holy Spirit, and it is evident that he was well aware of the presence and action of the Spirit in his own life and in the life of every Christian. So it is not surprising to find a veiled reference to the Spirit, especially as John goes on to say quite explicitly that the Holy Spirit is himself 'the lovely fruit of this tree'.[19]

This section 7 of sermon 102, with its homely imagery, together with the beautiful passage on the thorn tree, are of particular importance in helping us answer the question posed at the beginning of this paper: is John's commentary on the Song worthy to take its place beside those of Bernard, Gilbert, and William? Is John being fair to himself when in sermon 46 he describes his role at the marriage feast as that of a lowly servant, acting under that great cupbearer, Bernard, not serving beside him? On the contrary, I believe that there is ample evidence to suggest that John too had been admitted into the marriage chamber and there learned to understand the marriage song and so to comment on it with authority. To adapt his own words when speaking of those holy and learned men who had commented on the Song before him, we can truly say that John's fiery speech is evidence of the fire that burned in his heart. When he speaks of the love of the Spouse and the bride, it is not with stealthy dependence on the experience of others, but with the open-handed sharing of his own experience.[20] From a comparison of their commentaries on verse 3 of chapter 2 of the Song, we can confidently

[19]John, SC 102.8; CCCM 18:694; CF 47:23.
[20]See John, SC 24.2; CCCM 17:203; CF 39:136.

affirm that both Bernard and John were blessed with a real understanding of what they said, for to have loved means to have understood.[21]

ABSTRACTS

Bien que dans leurs sermons sur le Cantique des Cantiques Bernard de Clairvaux et Jean de Ford aient commenté des parties différentes de ce livre, ils ont tous deux disserté sur Ct 2, 3. Bernard traite de ce texte dans le sermon 48 de son commentaire, et Jean s'y réfère dans son sermon 38, tandis qu'il en donne un commentaire plus étendu dans le sermon 102. Ct 2, 3 est riche en images bibliques et se prête particulièrement à une exégèse monastique. Le présent article examine la manière dont les deux auteurs développent les images que contient ce verset, par exemple le pommier, l'ombre, le fruit et son goût, et le fait de s'asseoir sous le pommier. L'étude s'arrête aussi sur les autres textes scripturaires que chaque auteur utilise pour élaborer son thème tandis qu'il commente le verset. L'enquête permet d'apercevoir à quel point l'exégèse de Jean dépend de celle de Bernard ainsi que d'apprécier l'originalité du premier, évidente par exemple dans la manière imaginative dont il développe des images bibliques telles que le buisson d'épines et l'ombre. Si Jean ne peut égaler Bernard quant à la brillance de sa rhétorique ni à la profondeur de sa pensée, il se montre dans ses sermons digne disciple du maître, mieux, maître de vie spirituelle de son propre droit.

Although in their sermons on the Song of Songs Bernard of Clairvaux and John of Ford were commenting on different sections, there is one verse, Sg 2:3, which they both discuss. Bernard deals with this text in sermon 48 of his commentary, and John refers to it in his sermon 38, while in sermon 102 he has a more extended commentary. Sg 2:3 is rich in biblical imagery, and particularly suited to a monastic exegesis. This paper examines the way in which both authors develop the images found in this verse, for example, the apple tree, the shadow, the fruit and its taste, and sitting under the apple tree. Attention is also given to the other scriptural texts of which each of the writers makes use to elaborate his theme when commenting on this verse. As a result of this investigation we gain some understanding of the extent of John's dependence on Bernard for his exegesis, as well as his own originality, evident, for example, in his imaginative development of biblical imagery,

[21]John, SC 24.2; CCCM 17:203; CF 39:136.

such as the thorn tree and the shadow. John may not equal Bernard in the brilliance of his rhetoric or the depth of his thought, but in his sermons he shows himself to be a worthy disciple of the master, indeed a master of the spiritual life in his own right.

Obwohl Bernhard von Clairvaux und Johann von Ford in ihren Hoheliedpredigten unterschiedliche Abschnittte auslegen, gibt es einen Vers, Hld 2, 3, den sie beide diskutieren. Bernhard behandelt diesen Text in der 48. Predigt, Johann kommt darauf in seiner 38. Predigt zu sprechen und kommentiert ihn ausführlich in der 102. Predigt. Hld 2, 3 ist reich an biblischen Bildern und speziell geeignet für eine monastische Auslegung. Dieses Abhandlung untersucht die Art, in der beide Autoren die Bilder aus diesem Vers entfalten, z.B. den Apfelbaum, den Schatten, die Frucht und ihren Geschmack und das Sitzen unter dem Apfelbaum. Beachtung finden dabei auch die anderen Schrifttexte, die beide Schreiber benutzen, um ihr Thema auszuarbeiten, indem sie diesen Vers kommentieren. Als Ergebnis dieser Untersuchung gelangen wir zu einem Verständnis des Ausmaßes der Abhängigkeit Johanns von Bernhard bezüglich der Auslegung und ebenso seiner eigenen Originalität, die z.B. in seiner schöpferischen Entfaltung biblischer Bilder evident wird, beispielsweise des Dornenbaums und des Schattens. Johann kommt vielleicht nicht an Bernhards Brillianz in seiner Rhetorik oder an die Tiefe seines Denkens heran, aber in seinen Predigten zeigt er sich als einen würdigen Schüler seines Lehrers, in der Tat eines eigenständigen Lehrers des geistlichen Lebens.

PART IV
BERNARD AND HIS CONTEMPORARIES

THE ROLE OF BERNARD OF CLAIRVAUX IN THE UNION OF SAVIGNY WITH CÎTEAUX: A RECONSIDERATION

Francis R. Swietek
The University of Dallas

THE UNION OF THE CONGREGATION of Savigny with the Order of Cîteaux in 1147 was a major event in twelfth-century cistercian history. The absorption of so large and diverse a group, numbering more than thirty abbeys and independent priories in England, Ireland, Wales, Flanders, and France,[1] marked a substantial expansion of the Order; but the considerable success that the savigniac congregation had earlier enjoyed also gave to the event a special resonance, pointing to the coalescence around Cîteaux of what had originally been a remarkably variegated movement of monastic reform, involving numerous independent houses.[2] It has, moreover, been argued that the peculiar practices which Savigny was allowed to retain after the union—particularly in the realm of finance—had a negative impact on the order as a whole, proving

---

[1]The filiation of the congregation is treated by Victor De Buck, 'De BB. Gaufrido et Serlone, abbatibus, Guilelmo, novitio, et Adelina abbatissa, Saviniaci in Normannia', *Acta sanctorum*, Oct. 8 (Brussels, 1853) pp. 1019–41; Dionysius Sammarthani (ed.), *Gallia Christiana in provincias ecclesiasticas distributa*, corr. Paulus Piolin, 11 (2nd ed., Paris, 1874) cols. 552–55; Leopold Janauschek, *Originum Cisterciensium t. 1* (Vienna, 1877) p. 96; Léon Guilloreau, 'Les fondations anglaises de l'abbaye de Savigny', *Revue Mabillon* 5 (1909) 290–335; Jacqueline Buhot, 'L'abbaye normande de Savigny, chef d'ordre et fille de Cîteaux', *Le moyen âge* 46 (1936) 15–16; and Bennett D. Hill, 'The Beginnings of the First French Foundations of the Norman Abbey of Savigny', *The American Benedictine Review* 31 (1980) 130–52.

[2]A convenient recent survey of the movement and the changes within it is offered by Henrietta Leyser, *Hermits and the New Monasticism: A Study of Religious Communities in Western Europe, 1000–1150* (New York, 1984).

to be an important factor in the decline of its original idealism later in the twelfth century.[3]

Given these facts, it is not surprising that special attention has been devoted to the possible influence of Saint Bernard in effecting the union, particularly since Savigny became a daughter-house of Clairvaux. The received opinion on the issue is well summarized by Louis Lekai. It was Bernard, he wrote, 'who was largely responsible for the fusion with Savigny'.[4] Thus, the real question was not *whether* he was the force behind the union, but—in view of the deleterious effects it is supposed to have later had—*why* he so zealously promoted it. In his formulation Lekai was following the conclusion reached by Dom Claude Auvry, prior of Savigny from 1698 to 1712; his history of the abbey, published in the late nineteenth century, identified Bernard as 'le principal entremetteur de cette grande affaire'.[5]

This paper has a modest purpose. It seeks to investigate Bernard's involvement in the union with Savigny by assessing modern scholarly reconstructions of his role and examining the primary sources relating to it.

Two basic modern descriptions of Bernard's involvement have been proposed; each portrays him as a central figure, although in one his role is active and in the other it is passive. The former is the work of R.H.C. Davis, who has discussed the union in his biography of King Stephen of England, first published in 1967. In Davis' reconstruction, Bernard's attention was drawn to Savigny during his dispute with the king over the election of a new archbishop of York—a struggle which began in 1141 but would not be settled until 1150. This dispute caused Bernard to become 'convinced that Stephen was opposed to ecclesiastical reform and the rule of righteousness.' At the same time, the king's attitude toward Savigny changed. 'Savigny was [Stephen's] special charity', but after it fell, along with western Normandy, into the hands of his rival, Geoffrey of Anjou, 'opposition from Stephen' prevented the abbot of Savigny from exercising his proper authority over the english foundations of the congregation; 'in these circumstances it would have been natural for St. Bernard to offer . . . the protection of the Cistercian Order', and thus he

---

[3]This point is made by Buhot, pp. 249–64, and especially Bennett D. Hill, *English Cistercian Monasteries and Their Patrons in the Twelfth Century* (Urbana, 1968) pp. 80–115.

[4]Louis J. Lekai, *The Cistercians: Ideals and Reality* ([Kent, Ohio], 1977) p. 49.

[5]Claude Auvry, *Histoire de la congrégation de Savigny*, ed. A. Laveille, Société de l'histoire de Normandie 30 (Rouen, Paris, 3 vols., 1896–1899) 2:377.

'intervened in the internal affairs of another monastic order when he thought it was being disrupted by Stephen.'[6]

Clearly Davis views the involvement of Bernard in the union of 1147 as direct and active, and his reconstruction is ingenious, if somewhat unflattering to Bernard, who in effect utilizes Savigny as an instrument of retaliation against the king for the royal role in the York affair. On close investigation, however, it proves to be based on little more than speculation. It is certainly true, on the one hand, that Bernard became deeply—and emotionally—involved in the dispute over the York election, and that he considered Stephen culpable in the matter. But there is no evidence that Bernard related this conflict to Savigny. We possess several of his letters castigating his english opponents, including Stephen, for their failure to support the proper archiepiscopal candidate; but we have no document suggesting that he blamed Stephen for the insubordination that was exhibited by some of the english savigniac houses.[7] Moreover, Davis' contention that Stephen must have encouraged the increased independence of the english savigniac houses is overstated.[8] The difficulty could have derived simply from the weakness of the savigniac system of visitation and general chapters, which had been instituted as recently as 1132, and which had apparently not functioned very efficiently even before the struggle between Stephen and Geoffrey had separated Normandy from England. It was the tendency toward dispersion within the congregation which had induced the creation of the system (by Geoffrey, Savigny's second abbot) in the first place, and its failure under the pressure of civil strife does not require royal intervention to explain it.[9] In this connection it is interesting to note that Stephen himself issued

[6]R.H.C. Davis, *King Stephen, 1135–1154* (3d ed., London, New York, 1990) pp. 97–105, 114. The argument regarding Savigny itself is to be found at pp. 99–101, and one can see it reflected in such later works as Colin Platt, *The Abbeys and Priories of Medïeval England* (New York, 1984) pp. 40 and 53.

[7]The disputed York election and Bernard's role in the affair are treated by David Knowles, 'The Case of Saint William of York', *The Cambridge Historical Journal* 5 (1936) 162–214, and C. H. Talbot, 'New Documents in the Case of Saint William of York', *The Cambridge Historical Journal* 10 (1950) 1–15.

[8]Davis, p. 100, states simply: 'It seems clear . . . that if the abbot of Savigny could not exercise his authority over the English houses, it must have been because of opposition from Stephen.'

[9]The establishment of the system of general chapters and visitations is described in the *Vita Gaufridi* XIII-XIV, ed. E. P. Sauvage, 'Vitae BB. Vitalis et Gaufridi primi et secundi abbatum Saviniacensium', *Analecta Bollandiana* 1 (1882) 403–405. See also Auvry 2:198–208; Buhot, p. 17; and Hill, *English Cistercian Monasteries*, p. 92.

Davis attempts to strengthen his case by noting (pp. 100–101) that shortly before the union of 1147, a dispute had arisen between Savigny and Furness, the dominant

—according to one authority, around 1142, the very year in which Davis says that Stephen's attitude toward Savigny altered—a charter reaffirming his original grant of Furness, the chief (and most disruptive) english savigniac house, to Savigny.[10] Such an act would not suggest an attitude of royal displeasure with Savigny.[11]

Thus, Davis' attempt to connect Stephen to the independent tendencies of the english houses is strained, and his further attempt to link Bernard to the situation by reference to the disputed York election is not supported by any evidence.

---

savigniac house in England, over the filiation of the monastery of Byland in Yorkshire, and he suggests that, since Furness had been founded in 1127 by Stephen, who was then lord of Lancaster, he must have been behind the trouble; he cites as his source the charters found in William Dugdale (ed.), *Monasticon Anglicanum* (London, 1846) 5:569–570. But Davis is confused here. The question at issue in the case to which he refers was not the filiation of Byland but the foundation of the monastery of Jervaulx, which did not directly involve Furness. The filiation of Byland had in fact been settled much earlier at the savigniac general chapter of 1142, which had made the monastery a daughter-house of Savigny rather than Furness; see Philip of Byland, *Historia fundationis domus Bellelandae* in Dugdale 5:350.

[10]The charter is printed by Léopold Delisle, 'Documents Relative to the Abbey of Furness, Extracted from the Archives of the Abbey of Savigny', *Journal of the British Archaeological Association* 6 (1851) 420, and by H. A. Cronne and R.H.C. Davis (edd.), *Regesta Anglo-Normannorum 1066–1154*, 3, *Regesta regis Stephani ac Mathildis imperatricis ac Gaufridi et Henrici ducum Normannorum 1135–1154* (Oxford, 1968) p. 295 (no. 803). Cronne-Davis merely date the charter to 1138–1143, but J. H. Round (ed.), *Calendar of Documents Preserved in France Illustrative of the History of Great Britain and Ireland* (London, 1899) p. 291 (no. 804), suggests a date around 1142.

The dating of the charter is complicated by the presence of Richard de Courcy among its witnesses. As was noted in Francis R. Swietek and Terrence M. Deneen, 'Pope Lucius II and Savigny', ASOC 39 (1983) 7, a Richard de Courcy served as prior of Savigny under Abbot Geoffrey and eventually became abbot of Savigny in 1153; but Jacob Johannes van Moolenbroek, *Vitalis van Savigny (+1122): Bronnen en vroege Cultus* (Amsterdam, 1982) p. 436, n. 40, points out that this Richard is last attested as a witness in a document of September 1136. There was, however, another Richard of Courcy, a member of an english baronial family, who served in King Stephen's army and was captured with him at the battle of Lincoln in February 1141 (see Davis, p. 50); he was probably the witness mentioned in the charter. Richard of Courcy witnessed a number of Stephen's other charters: see Cronne-Davis, nos. 114, 413, 442, 624, 780, 981, and 985. The latest of these, a general confirmation in favor of Nostell Priory, is demonstrably from 1153–1154 (see Cronne-Davis, p. 230). Cronne-Davis determine the *terminus post quem non* of no. 803, along with that of another charter (Cronne-Davis, no. 981) which was witnessed by Richard, William of York, and Robert de Vere, simply on the basis that Stephen 'was hardly likely to re-confirm it [his grant of Furness] to Savigny after he had lost that part of Normandy in 1143' (p. 295). This argument is not conclusive.

[11]Davis also prints, pp. 166–68, three recently-discovered charters of Stephen on behalf of Coggeshall, a daughter-house of Savigny (nos. 207a, 207c, and 207d), dated between 1140 and 1154. These suggest that the king did not evince any general animosity toward the savigniac congregation in the period after 1142.

An alternate explanation of Bernard's involvement in the union has been offered by Jacqueline Buhot in her brief survey of Savigny's early history published in 1936.[12] While Davis' Bernard is the active manipulator of events, Buhot's is a magnetic figure who—perhaps unconsciously —draws the savigniac congregation into the cistercian order.

Buhot's characterization has its origin in an aside offered by Auvry. In describing the decision of Serlo of Vaubadon, the fourth abbot of Savigny, to surrender his congregation to Cîteaux, Auvry had mentioned the abbot's 'ardent desire' to retire to Clairvaux and live under Bernard's guidance.[13] He explained that, according to a savigniac tradition, Bernard had stopped at Savigny while in Brittany in 1144, and Serlo had developed a strong friendship with him at that time.[14]

Buhot expanded enthusiastically on Auvry's observation. The first cause which she mentioned to explain the union was the 'personality of Serlo', in particular his admiration for Bernard, 'which led him to emulate the Cistercian in both the conduct of his life and his literary work.' As evidence of this, she cited the extant writings of Serlo, which, she observed, constituted such 'servile imitations' of Bernard as to be little more than 'inept pastiches' drawn from his works.[15] It was largely because of his extraordinary admiration for Bernard, Buhot suggested, that Serlo determined to surrender his congregation to the cistercian order; and this conclusion is supported by the fact that Serlo did in fact retire to Clairvaux after resigning his abbacy.

Buhot's conclusions have proven remarkably popular. They have been cited approvingly by Bennett Hill,[16] and as recently as 1989 their influence was reflected in an article on Serlo in which it is said that he was 'fascinated by St Bernard'.[17]

In reality, however, supportive evidence for the Auvry-Buhot thesis is quite thin. First of all, the tradition concerning Bernard's visit to Savigny in 1144 is not confirmed by any independent source; indeed, we cannot even be certain that Bernard and Serlo met before 1147. Moreover, the evidence regarding Serlo's desire to resign his abbacy and retire to

[12]Buhot, pp. 178–80.
[13]Auvry 2:368–69.
[14]Auvry 2:345–46.
[15]Buhot, pp. 178–79.
[16]Hill, *English Cistercian Monasteries*, p. 101.
[17]Maur Standaert, 'Serlon de Savigny', *Dictionnaire de spiritualité, ascétique et mystique: Doctrine et histoire*, fascs. 92–94 (Paris, 1989) col. 661.

Clairvaux shows that he did not act on this inclination until the cistercian general chapter of 1152, a full five years after the union.[18]

What of the indications afforded by Serlo's writings? Here too Buhot's arguments are unconvincing. As long ago as 1922, André Wilmart, in a study of which Buhot was apparently unaware, demonstrated that the *tituli* in one manuscript copy of Serlo's extant sermons indicate that the collection represents works delivered only after his retirement to Clairvaux late in 1153.[19] Other sources confirm that Serlo regularly preached to the monks of Clairvaux in his last years.[20] As such, the homilies can hardly be said to offer any conclusive evidence about Serlo's literary activity of six or more years earlier.

In any event, Wilmart concluded that although Serlo might have used Bernard as a model for the general plan of his later works—something that might be expected of anyone writing for the monks of Clairvaux— his style differed considerably from Bernard's; and in the one sermon which he edited in full, Wilmart detected only one passage which showed even a slight dependence on a bernardine text.[21] Indeed, a close reading of Serlo's few works leads to the conclusion that his style shows a marked similarity not so much to that of Bernard as to that of Hugh of Saint Victor. Two of the pieces included in the collection prove to be excerpts from works by Hugh, and they resemble Serlo's writings closely in approach and argument.[22]

Thus, Buhot's portrayal of Bernard as the figure who, through his extraordinary influence on Serlo, unconsciously drew Savigny into union with the cistercian order proves to be as poorly supported as is Davis' vision of Bernard as an ecclesiastical politician, playing a sort of savigniac card in his ongoing struggle against King Stephen.

---

[18]The *Chronicon Savigniacense*, in Stephan Baluze (ed.), *Miscellanea novo ordine digesta*, corr. J.-D. Mansi (2nd ed., Lucca, 1761) 1:326–27; and the *Auctarium Savigniacense*, in Léopold Delisle (ed.), *Chronique de Robert de Torigny* (Rouen, 1878) 2:162.

[19]André Wilmart, 'Le recueil des discours de Serlon, abbé de Savigni', *Revue Mabillon* 12 (1922) 26–38.

[20]The *Liber sepulcrorum Claraevallis*, quoted by De Buck, p. 1012; and the *Monumenta sacrae Claraevallensis abbatiae* in PL 185:1559.

[21]Wilmart, pp. 35–36.

[22]The first of them (Wilmart, p. 35, no. 33) is an excerpt from Hugh's *Explanatio in canticum beatae Mariae* (PL 175:422C–23A). The second (Wilmart, p. 35, no. 34) is *Didascalicon* V.9; see C. H. Buttimer (ed.), *Hugonis de Sancto Victore Didascalicon De Studio Legendi: A Critical Text* (Washington, 1939) pp. 109–111. On these texts, see also Lawrence C. Braceland (ed.), *Serlo of Savigny and Serlo of Wilton: Seven Unpublished Works*, CF 48 (Kalamazoo, Michigan, 1988) p. xiv.

If the modern literature is ultimately unsatisfactory regarding Bernard's role in the events leading to the union, what of the contemporary evidence? It is fair to say that when the few primary sources are permitted to speak directly on the matter, Bernard's role becomes peripheral. It was simply dissension within the congregation, they indicate, which led to Abbot Serlo's action. Thus Robert of Torigny, in his *Tractatus de immutatione ordinis monachorum*, writes: 'Serlo, because the monasteries subject to him did not obey him according to his will, by the authority of Eugenius, the roman pontiff, subjected himself and all his monasteries to the cistercian order.'[23] The so-called *Chronicon Savigniacense* published by Baluze explains, in a passage clearly derived from Robert: 'This man [Serlo], because the monasteries subject to him had not obeyed him according to his wishes, gave himself to the cistercian order, indeed into the hands of blessed Bernard, who at that time was abbot of Clairvaux.'[24] And Peregrinus, abbot of the savigniac house of Fountains from 1188 to 1211, wrote, in the history of his house:

Since this man [Serlo] was just, and began little by little to understand that certain of his coabbots were attempting to free themselves from subjection to Savigny, and were coming to the general chapter more slowly and unenthusiastically than they had been accustomed to do, assisted by divine aid and counsel, and after the permission and authority of the pope had been requested, he turned over his monastery, along with all the others associated with it, to the cistercian order, and put them into the hand of Saint Bernard, abbot of Clairvaux, the authority of whose life and sanctity resounded everywhere.[25]

The role of Bernard in the episode was also noted by the savigniac writer who made the additions to a copy of Robert of Torigny's *Chronicle* which

[23]Robert of Torigny, *Tractatus de immutatione ordinis monachorum* 4, in PL 202:1312: 'Hic [Serlo] quia pro velle suo ei non obtemperabant monasteria sibi subdita, auctoritate Eugenii Romani pontificis, subdidit se, et omnia sua Cisterciensi ordini.'

[24]*Chronicon Savigniacense*, in Baluze, *Miscellanea* 1:326: 'Hic [Serlo] quia pro velle suo non obtemperaverant monasteria aibi subdita, Cisterciensi ordini se dedit, in manus videlicet beati Bernardi tunc temporis Abbatis Clarevallensis.'

[25]Peregrinus of Vendôme, *Historia monasterii beatae Mariae de Fontanis albis* IX, in André Salmon (ed.), *Recueil de chroniques de Touraine* (Tours, 1854) pp. 266–67: 'Hic [Serlo] igitur cum esset justus, et paulatim coepisset intelligere quod quidam coabbatum suorum de subjectione Savigniensi sua colla molirentur excutere, ac tardius et tepidius quam solebant ad capitulum venirent, divino fultus consilio et auxilio, impetrata licentia et auctoritate summi pontificis suum monasterium cum caeteris omnibus ad illud pertinentibus ordini Cisterciensi contradidit et subjecit in manu Sancti Bernardi abbatis Clarae Vallis.'

are today called (following Delisle) the *Auctarium Savigniacense*. In a passage based on Robert's *Tractatus*, he wrote: 'In this year [1147], lord Serlo, abbot of Savigny, gave himself to the cistercian order along with all the abbeys associated with him, and he did so into the hand of lord Bernard, abbot of Clairvaux, in the presence of Pope Eugenius and all the abbots of the cistercian chapter.'[26]

Clearly all of these sources identify the essential cause of Serlo's decision as the increasing independence of some of the houses nominally subordinate to him; and, as Davis noted, the houses most troublesome in this respect were located in England.[27] But there is no need to postulate a direct intervention by King Stephen, as Davis does, to explain this circumstance. The savigniac congregation had grown so rapidly that it outstripped the construction of a savigniac constitution; the second abbot of Savigny, Geoffrey, had tried to remedy the situation by instituting a system of general chapters and visitations by the abbot of Savigny to other houses of the congregation. But this innovation did not occur until at least 1132, and it is uncertain whether the visitations were intended to occur regularly.[28] The constitutional structure of Savigny was therefore of very recent institution, and seems never to have been fully or carefully implemented. The death of Abbot Geoffrey, its creator, in 1140 would have made it even less secure, and its effective use throughout the congregation would have been further undermined by the civil strife which rocked England and Normandy during Stephen's reign.

In such worsening circumstances, it is entirely plausible that the abbot of Savigny should have sought union with an existing order. The question is not so much why he would have chosen Cîteaux, but rather what his alternative might have been. Savigny, like Cîteaux, had been founded as part of the general movement of reform monasticism of the eleventh and twelfth centuries: their ideals and goals were similar. Moreover, the efforts of Abbot Geoffrey had resulted in a savigniac constitutional system

---

[26]*Auctarium Savigniacense*, in Delisle (ed.), *Chronique* 2:161: 'Hoc anno, donnus Serlo, abbas Savigneii, se dedit ordini Cisterciensi, cum omnibus abbatiis ad se pertinentibus, et hoc fecit in manu donni Bernardi, abbatis Claraevallensis, in presentia venerabilis papae Eugenii et omnium abbatum Cisterciensis capituli.'

[27]Davis, pp. 99–100.

[28]For the sources which discuss Geoffrey's constitutional innovations, see above, n. 9. Insofar as the general chapters were concerned, it is possible that abbots of relatively distant houses were granted permission not to attend all of them, or simply failed to do so, as was the case with the Cistercians: see Louis J. Lekai, 'Ideals and Reality in Early Cistercian Life and Legislation', in John R. Sommerfeldt (ed.), *Cistercian Ideals and Reality*, CS 60 (Kalamazoo, 1978) pp. 19–20.

which, in its basic structure, was very similar to that of the Cistercians. (Indeed, it is difficult to imagine that Geoffrey could have devised his system except by imitation of Cîteaux.) By 1147, moreover, the cistercian order had already assimilated a number of originally independent houses; the monastic reform movement, as Henrietta Leyser notes, had come 'to converge on Cîteaux'.[29] In 1147 alone, Savigny was but one of several houses heading independent groups of monasteries to seek union with the Cistercians, although her congregation was by far the largest of them.[30] Once the abbot of Savigny had elected to link his congregation with an established order, therefore, the cistercian was the obvious—indeed, virtually the only—choice. The direct intervention of Bernard would not have been necessary, although his general renown (rather than any special 'fascination' he held for Serlo) would certainly have been an underlying element.

But even if Bernard's personal involvement in the savigniac decision might not have been necessary, might it nonetheless have occurred? The evidence is not strong. There is, first, the tradition of his visit to Savigny in 1144.[31] But such a visit, even if it occurred, would not prove that the abbot of Clairvaux, three years later, took an active role in effecting the union. There appears to be a stronger indication of Bernard's involvement in Bouton's assertion that, prior to the cistercian general chapter of 1147, the abbot of Savigny conferred with Bernard at Clairvaux, and then accompanied him to Cîteaux for the meeting at which the union would be effected.[32] Such a meeting would certainly support the assertion that Bernard had a central role in arranging the fusion, but on inspection, the evidence for it evaporates. Bouton's source is Auvry, but Auvry dates the incident to 1148, not 1147.[33] Bouton, rightly noting that Auvry's chronology of the events surrounding the union is erratic, merely transposes the incident narrated by Auvry to the previous year. This procedure, however, is unsound for several reasons. First, Auvry's

[29]Leyser, pp. 34–35 and 113–17 (Appendix II).

[30]Lekai, *The Cistercians*, p. 36, notes that of the fifty-one houses admitted to the order in 1147, more than half were members of the organizations led by Savigny, Cadouin, and Obazine. Gilbert of Sempringham is also reported to have come to the general chapter in 1147 to request, unsuccessfully, the union of his houses with Cîteaux; see the account in *The Book of St Gilbert*, edd. Raymonde Foreville and Gillian Keir (Oxford, 1987) pp. 40–45.

[31]Auvry 2:345–46.

[32]Jean de la Croix Bouton, 'Negotia ordinis', in *Bernard de Clairvaux*, Commission d'histoire de l'ordre de Cîteaux 3 (Paris, 1953) p. 154.

[33]Auvry 2:377.

account has no evidenciary basis, and must be considered doubtful *per se*. But even if one accepts it as generally accurate, it is far more appropriate to retain Auvry's basic chronology and date it at 1148. That year would have marked the first time that the abbot of Savigny would have attended the cistercian general chapter as a member of the order, and a year earlier his house had been absorbed into it as a daughter-house of Clairvaux. It would have been natural, in these circumstances, for Serlo to have gone to Clairvaux in order to accompany Bernard, now abbot of Savigny's mother-house, to the chapter of 1148.[34]

Thus the evidence for Bernard's direct involvement in the decision of Savigny's abbot to surrender his congregation to Cîteaux becomes, on close inspection, extremely slight.

What, however, of Bernard's role at the general chapter itself? One of the few points of detail on which most of the primary sources—at least all those of savigniac origin—agree, is that there Serlo of Savigny placed his congregation 'into Bernard's hand', and indeed Savigny entered the cistercian order as a daughter-house of Clairvaux.[35] Does this not demonstrate Bernard's dominant role in the affair?

Hill specifically argues that it does. '[I]t is interesting to note', he writes, 'that the submission of the Congregation of Savigny to the Abbot of Clairvaux rather than to the Abbot of Cîteaux was certainly a violation of the Cistercian rules'; he suggests that the unusual procedure implies that 'it was undoubtedly the enormous prestige of St. Bernard which facilitated this merger.'[36] But was this the case? As Leyser notes, many of Clairvaux's early daughter-houses had originally been independent establishments, accepted into the order in a fashion similar to that used for Savigny in 1147.[37] The notion that the entrance of an established house into the order could be properly effected only by surrender to Cîteaux is not supported by the evidence, and the fact that Savigny became a daughter-house of Clairvaux does not prove that Bernard was the guiding force behind the union.

---

[34]Given the limitations on the size of the entourage which an abbot was permitted to bring to the general chapter, it might also have been convenient for Serlo to have stopped at Clairvaux on the way to Cîteaux in order to leave some of his attendants there.

[35]See above, nn. 24, 25, and 26.

[36]Hill, *English Cistercian Monasteries*, p. 105, n. 67.

[37]Leyser, pp. 113–18, lists Fontenay (accepted into the order in 1119), Reigny (1128), Cherlieu (1131), Alafoes (1132), Vauclair (1134), Fountains (1134/1135), Les Dunes (1138), and Grandselve (1145).

Moreover, perhaps it has been too easily assumed that it was Bernard who directed events at the general chapter of 1147. After all, Pope Eugenius III was present at the meeting, and although some sources stipulate that he did not preside there by reason of his apostolic authority,[38] his influence could hardly have been ignored. In this connection, the elaborate narrative of Auvry is of interest. As has been mentioned, he errs in his chronology, ignoring the chapter of 1147 and portraying the Council of Reims in 1148 as the real occasion for the union. But his account of that council, and of the cistercian general chapter following it, is nonetheless suggestive. According to Auvry, Serlo approached the pope at Reims to request his permission for the union. Eugenius assented, and later, at the cistercian general chapter, it was actually he who accepted the surrender of the savigniac congregation, placing it immediately into the hands of Saint Bernard.[39]

Now it must be admitted that Auvry continually highlights Bernard's involvement in this chain of events, noting that it was he who secured Serlo's first audience with the pope and, as we have already noted, that Serlo conferred with him prior to the general chapter;[40] but one searches in vain for any documentary support of these asides. Indeed, what is really striking about his narrative is how closely it approximates—the vagaries of locale apart—the contemporary account of the surrender of Obazine to Cîteaux at the same general chapter of 1147 where the savigniac union was effected. That account is as follows:

Stephen [of Obazine]. . . came to Cîteaux with some brothers and sought out the pope there, for he had for some time wanted to secure the affiliation of that sacred order and to submit everything over which he had control to its rule. . . .When the blessed man arrived at Cîteaux, he humbly approached the pope and informed him of his intention, earnestly requesting that through the pope's authority his desire might be effected. Then the pope summoned Rainard [le Bar, abbot of Cîteaux from 1134 to 1150] to come to him, and the father of all commended the holy man to him as a son to a father, and directed him to take the abbot into the general chapter and join him to his holy order. Rainard, gratefully accepting Stephen from the pope's

[38]Josephus-Maria Canivez (ed.), *Statuta capitulorum generalium ordinis Cisterciensis ab anno 1116 ad annum 1786* (Louvain, 1933) I:37–38.
[39]Auvry 2:371–72, 378.
[40]Auvry 2:372, 377.

hand, took him into the chapter. . . . .Without delay, after the pope's instructions had been declared and Stephen's requests made clear, and since Stephen was present humbly asking it, he was received into the order unanimously by all the abbots and was specifically attached to the house of Cîteaux.[41]

Compare this to Auvry's narrative, shorn of inessentials. Serlo of Savigny approaches Pope Eugenius at Reims and explains his desire to submit his congregation to the cistercian order. The pope responds by pledging his support, and indeed produces a bull effectively announcing the union. Later the same year, at the general chapter at Cîteaux, the savigniac abbot hands his congregation over to Eugenius, and he, in turn, places it in the hands of Bernard, who would henceforth be regarded as father-abbot and immediate superior to the abbot of Savigny. The union is then unanimously affirmed by the general chapter.[42]

The similarity of the two accounts is apparent, and it becomes even greater if one emends Auvry's chronological inexactitude simply by relocating both elements in the episode to a single point, namely, the chapter of 1147. In such a reconstruction, Abbot Serlo would have approached Eugenius, as Stephen is reported to have done; it would have been the pope, not Bernard, who was instrumental in deciding the matter; and it would have been the pontiff who, in effect, placed Savigny and her houses within the filiation of Clairvaux. This understanding of the papal role in the affair would explain why contemporary sources on the union emphasize that it was effected on Eugenius' authority—a fact that has not been much discussed by researchers.[43] It would also help to explain the pope's anxiousness to implement the merger: he issued

[41]*Vita Stephani* 2.11–12, in Michel Aubrun (ed.), *Vie de saint Étienne d'Obazine*, Publications de l'Institut d'Études du Massif Central 6 (Clermont-Ferrand, 1970) pp. 110–12: 'Stephanus. . . Cistercium cum quibusdam fratribus venit ibique predictum apostolicum reperit. Erat enim ex multo tempore cupiens sancti illius ordinis societatem adquirere et cuncta que ad se pertinebant ejus submittere ditioni. . . .[C]um ad Cistercium beatus iste venisset, memoratum papam humiliter adiit et quid animo gereret apostolicis auribus intimavit, subnixe deposcens ut suum desiderium ipsius auctoritate ad effectum perduceretur. Tunc ille domnum Rainardum ad se venire mandavit eique sanctum virum ut patri filium ipse pater omnium commendavit atque ut eum in conventu abbatum duceret et sancto ordini sociaret precepit. Quem ille gratanter de manu pape suscipiens, in capitulum introduxit. . . .Nec mora, prolatis domini pape mandatis ejusque petitionibus declaratis, ipso etiam in presenti humiliter postulante, ab universis concorditer abbatibus in societatem ordinis est receptus et domui cisterciensi specialiter assignatus.'

[42]Auvry 2:366–82.

[43]See above, nn. 23 and 25.

a series of bulls confirming it and seeking to impose it on recalcitrant houses of the savigniac congregation.[44]

The suggestions made in this paper can now be summarized. There is no tangible evidence for a central and direct role by Saint Bernard in the union of the savigniac congregation with the cistercian order. The general assumption of such a role, ultimately based on Auvry, is grounded on a savigniac tradition which has no strong evidenciary basis. Moreover, the modern attempts to explain that presumed role have been unpersuasive.

On the other hand, a plausible case can be made that Bernard's involvement in the union was peripheral, although his powerful leadership of the cistercian order created an atmosphere which made it possible. Since it is generally agreed that the union was a significant event in cistercian history, this conclusion might seem to call into question Bernard's influence over the order at mid-century. But since the assimilation of Savigny, with its acquisitive financial practices, has often been portrayed as a major cause of the increasing loss of idealism and commitment among the Cistercians in the later 1100s, such a diminution of Bernard's role in the union might actually, in the long run, enhance his reputation.

ABSTRACTS

Cette étude conteste l'opinion reçue selon laquelle Bernard de Clairvaux a contribué à la fusion de la congrégation de Savigny avec l'Ordre cistercien en 1147. Elle examine les sources de première main relatives à la fusion et les tentatives modernes faites pour expliquer la part qu'y a prise Bernard, et conclut qu'il n'y a pas de preuves concluantes du rôle de force directrice de l'union qu'on lui a souvent attribué. L'article suggère en outre que le pape Eugène III a pu jouer dans la fusion un rôle plus important qu'on ne l'a cru précédemment.

This study challenges the accepted view that Bernard of Clairvaux was instrumental in arranging the merger of the congregation of Savigny with the Cistercian Order in 1147. It examines the primary sources relating to the merger and modern attempts to explain Bernard's part in it, and concludes that there is no conclusive evidence that he was, as is often

---

[44]The four bulls of Eugenius III are discussed in detail by Francis R. Swietek and Terrence M. Deneen, 'The Episcopal Exemption of Savigny, 1112–1184', *Church History* 52 (1983) 290–92.

claimed, the guiding force behind the union. The paper further suggests that the role played by Pope Eugenius III in effecting the merger might have been greater than has previously been believed.

Diese Untersuchung zieht die allgemein anerkannte Meinung, daß Bernhard von Clairvaux als Werkzeug diente, als 1147 die Kongregation von Savigny mit dem Zisterzienserorden verbunden wurde, in Zweifel. Sie prüft die Primärquellen, die die Verbindung betreffen sowie moderne Versuche, Bernhards Rolle dabei zu erklären und zieht die Schlußfolgerung, daß es keinen schlüßigen Beweis gibt, daß er, wie oft behauptet wird, die treibende Kraft hinter der Union war. Weiter legt die Abhandlung nahe, daß die Rolle, die Papst Eugen III. in der Durchführung der Union spielte, größer gewesen sein könnte als früher angenommen wurde.

THE DEVELOPMENT OF CISTERCIAN ECONOMIC PRACTICE DURING THE LIFETIME OF BERNARD OF CLAIRVAUX: THE HISTORICAL PERSPECTIVE ON INNOCENT II'S 1132 PRIVILEGE

Constance H. Berman
The University of Iowa

CISTERCIAN CONTRIBUTIONS to the economic growth of the Middle Ages and the effect of the order's economic activities on its spirituality have been the subject of lively debate over the past half century. Recently, assumptions about the white monks' earliest history, their economic practices, and their leadership have been reassessed. In this paper, I should like to review the debate between monastic and economic historians, that between those relying on the order's statutes and those using its local administrative documents, and that about ideals and reality. I should then like to suggest a direction for further consideration of the order and its economic practices. Such study as I suggest would, I hope, have the ultimate effect of bringing closer together our still diverging notions of the early Cistercians. To demonstrate this approach, I shall consider in particular the relationship between the order's twelfth-century rhetorical stance with regard to isolation or solitude, and its tithe exemption. Such a consideration can cast considerable light on our understanding of the links between ideals and reality. It can also clarify the economic policies and practices of the order in the 1130s—a decade on which the *prima collectio* of 1134 casts more confusion than light, and a decade which marks mid-career for Bernard of Clairvaux.[1]

---

[1]We no longer assume that the twelfth-century order was a monolithic entity modeled totally on the practice at Clairvaux. There were both considerable divergence from the

Looking back at the literature on Cistercians from the past half century, we find monastic historians studying the writings of Bernard and other Cistercians as found in treatises, letters, and the order's statutes. Those historians have often concluded that Bernard and his followers disdained the rising cities and economic growth of their time. They have tended to assume that the order was *opposed* to economic growth because Cistercians espoused a return to 'primitive monasticism' in the 'deserts' of the twelfth century. Such historians have explained the order's economic success as the result of a series of unforeseen developments, totally unintended by its founders. In this view, its expansion and the development of its endowment were the unexpected rewards of its eremitical frugality and isolation. The products of this asceticism were savings to invest in land and enthusiastic patronage which generated economic privileges.[2] The latter included not only the tithe exemption given by Innocent II, but rights to travel to and from markets and sell goods free of tolls and taxes such as those given by the viscounts of Béziers or the archbishops of Narbonne to the monks of Silvanès,[3] and such gifts as those of an annual boat-load of salt at Bordeaux bestowed by the Angevin kings on

order's ideals among individual abbeys and considerable variation in economic practice from one abbey to the next. Moreover, cistercian economic practices evolved considerably during the first half of the twelfth century. Indeed, what may have been standard among a group of semi-eremitical houses in 1118 was different from the practice of even those same houses in 1132, and still different from that of houses founded or incorporated in 1145 or 1147. See Jean-Baptiste Auberger, *L'unanimité cistercienne primitive: Mythe ou réalité?* (Achel, [Belgium]: Administration de Cîteaux: Commentarii Cisterciensis, Editions Sine Parvolos VBVB, 1986).

[2]Louis J. Lekai, *The Cistercians: Ideal and Reality* ([Kent, Ohio]: The Kent State University Press [1977]), summarizes this thinking on pp. 282–333. See also the studies of Dom David Knowles; for example, *The Monastic Order in England* (Cambridge, England: at the University Press, 1950); or *Great Historical Enterprises: Problems in Monastic History* (London, Edinburgh: Thames and Hudson, 1963). See also Marcel Pacaut, *Les ordres monastiques et religieux au moyen âge* (Paris: Fernard Nathan, 1970); or George Zarnecki, *The Monastic Achievement* (New York: McGraw-Hill, 1972); or even such recent studies as Lester K. Little, *Religious Poverty and the Profit Motive in the Middle Ages* (Ithaca, New York: Cornell University Press, 1978). Such notions were frequently incorporated into general surveys such as that by Hugh Trevor-Roper, *The Rise of Christian Europe* (London: Thames & Hudson, 1963); or C. W. Hollister, *Medieval Europe: A Short History* (New York: John Wiley & Sons, 1968) (opinions considerably revised in later editions); or Robert S. Hoyt, *Europe in the Middle Ages* (2nd ed., New York, Chicago, Burlingame: Harcourt, Brace & World, Inc., [1966]).

[3]*Cartulaire de l'abbaye de Silvanès*, ed. P.-A. Verlaguet (Rodez: Carrère, 1910) no. 400 (1159) is the gift of such rights by the archbishop Berengar of Narbonne; similar gifts were made by the viscounts of Béziers (no. 483 [1180]).

the monks of Grandselve.[4] Donations of this kind were frequently made to the 'poor monks' of Cîteaux and its order, even after they were *not* so very poor, perhaps because those monks kept up the *appearance* of the poverty espoused by Bernard and his companions, whether in dress, in meals, or in architecture.[5]

Monastic historians have been particularly wedded to the ideals set forth in the 'primitive Cistercian documents', but so too were the earliest economic historians to consider the order. The latter saw in these documents evidence of a cistercian 'plan'. In particular, the *prima collectio* of 1134 and other early texts were interpreted by economic historians as something akin to a managerial program laid down in corporate law and universally applied by those holding the cistercian equivalent of a Master's degree in Business Administration.[6] Economic historians differed from monastic historians, however, in assuming that the economic consequences of the cistercian ideology had been anticipated by the order. They saw the Cistercians as early capitalists or entrepreneurs, and they ignored almost completely the religious aspects of the reform. In their view of the new order, and it is one stated explicitly in such studies as Jean Gimpel's *The Medieval Machine*, each cistercian plant would be identical to every other, and each should be expected to be equally successful because of the founders' careful planning.[7] Thus, Bernard and his colleagues had introduced a sort of twelfth-century assembly-line for mass production of extremely capable monastic economies; the

[4]Paris, Bibliothèque Nationale, Latin MS 11010 is an entire volume of concessions of salts and boats of salt going to and from Grandselve on the Garonne river to Bordeaux, including those by the Angevins.

[5]On general observances, see Louis J. Lekai, *The White Monks: A History of the Cistercian Order* (Okauchee, Wis.: Our Lady of Spring Bank, 1953) *passim*. Complaints that the poor monks had become rich are cited in Giles Constable, *Monastic Tithes from Their Origins to the Twelfth Century* (Cambridge: Cambridge University Press, 1964) pp. 270–306; and James S. Donnelly, *The Decline of the Medieval Cistercian Laybrotherhood* (New York: Fordham University Press, 1949) p. 47. The cistercian response is found in *Statuta capitulorum generalium ordinis cisterciensis ab anno 1116 ad annum 1786*, ed. J.-M. Canivez (Louvain, 1933) 1 (1180), no. 1.

[6]In particular, see Richard Roehl, 'Plan and Reality in a Medieval Monastic Economy: The Cistercians', *Studies in Medieval and Renaissance History* 9 (1972) 83–113, as well as the earlier work by Henri Pirenne, *Histoire de Belgique* (Brussels: Lamertin, 1929) 1:301ff; and James W. Thompson, *Economic and Social History of the Middle Ages (300–1300)* (New York: Ungar, 1959, reprint of the 1929 ed.) 1:611; and references in the following notes.

[7]Jean Gimpel, *The Medieval Machine: The Industrial Revolution of the Middle Ages* (New York: Penguin, 1976) esp. pp. 3–5.

spread of the order was consequently the result of extreme and very conscious rationalization!

The earliest economic historians described what they interpreted as clearance and reclamation efforts by the early Cistercians as deduced from the order's legislative documents. Those historians estimated the economic benefits which accrued to the monks from such clearance and reclamation at sites 'far from cities and castles' where new, previously uncultivated, and, presumably, extremely fertile soils would have produced bumper crops.[8] They calculated the economies of scale available to cistercian grange agriculture. They demonstrated the dependent-cost savings which the order accrued by replacing tenant-farmers with lay-brothers and seasonally hired laborers. Finally, the economic historians described how in the twelfth century the intensified animal husbandry practiced by the Cistercians coincided with rising urban demand for meat and animal products, thereby resulting in exceptional profits for the new monks.[9]

Generally, the difference between these two groups of historians was in whether they described the order's wealth and profits as 'un-hoped-for' as did the monastic scholars, or attributed this growth to 'rational planning' as the economists did. Both groups shared a tendency to see a precipitous decline from a 'Golden Age' of cistercian self-directed agriculture. That decline coincided with the mid thirteenth-century crisis in lay-brother recruitment which was attributed to a 'failure of religiosity'. Both groups, until recently, based their conclusions about the order's early economic practices almost exclusively on its legislative documents.[10]

[8]See Marc Bloch, *French Rural History: An Essay on its Basic Characteristics*, trans. from the 1931 French edition by Janet Sondheimer (Berkeley: University of California Press, 1970) pp. 14–15; and Georges Duby, *The Early Growth of the European Economy*, trans. Howard B. Clarke (Ithaca, New York: Cornell University Press, 1974) pp. 219–20. But, see also Duby, *Rural Economy and Country Life in the Medieval West*, trans. Cynthia Postan (Columbia, South Carolina: University of South Carolina Press, 1968) pp. 70–71.

[9]In addition to Roehl, cited above, note 6, see Duby, *Early Growth*, pp. 141–43; Robert H. Bautier, *The Economic Development of Medieval Europe*, trans. Heather Karolyi (London: Harcout, Brace and Jovanovich, 1971) pp. 117–18; and Constance H. Berman, *Medieval Agriculture, the Southern French Countryside, and the Early Cistercians: A Study of Forty-three Monasteries*, American Philosophical Society Transactions 76:5 (Philadelphia, Pennsylvania, 1986) pp. 96–97.

[10]For example, Coburn Graves, 'The Economic Activities of Cistercians in Medieval England (1128–1307)', ASOC 13 (1957) 3–60, says on p. 13: 'In this survey of practices, one major conclusion stands out. The economic ideal as set forth in the *Exordium Parvum* was a failure. Serfs and mills were owned and exploited, the advowson of churches was normal, and secular involvement in commerce was a widespread fact.'

However, starting in the early 1950s, new historians of the cistercian order moved away from consideration of these documents to that of the local charters of land acquisition which make up the surviving archives and cartularies of so many houses of white monks.[11] When the first studies of these new materials showed considerable divergence in practice from the 'ideals' of the order, that divergence was explained as local aberration, as the failure of individual cistercian abbots to live up to a norm.[12] As more and more local studies showed such discrepancy, however, their authors began to stress the difficulty of adapting the order's early plan to local circumstances, or explained that conditions were not always appropriate to implement the pioneering activities which it favored. Increasingly, the Cistercians were discussed in terms of plan and actuality, or ideal and reality. Indeed, Louis J. Lekai, in his magisterial compilation of the history of the order published in 1978, used *Ideal and Reality* as a subtitle.[13] My own work on Cistercians in southern France has similarly stressed this divergence of their practice from their so-called legislative ideals. Although I have argued that the white monks were not pioneers and that their contributions to the economic growth of the High Middle Ages were in the secondary movements of consolidation and reorganization, I have also tried to wrestle with the problem of explaining why Cistercians became wealthy—since the old models do not work. As a result, I have emphasized not just the economies of scale of grange agriculture, dependency cost savings when *conversi* and

Many such studies draw heavily on H. d'Arbois de Jubainville, *Etude sur l'état intérieur des abbayes cisterciennes, et principalement de Clairvaux, aux XIIe et XIIIe siècles* (Paris: Durand, 1858).

[11]Examples of such recent studies include Robert Fossier, 'L'essor économique de Clairvaux', in *Bernard de Clairvaux*, Commission d'histoire de l'Ordre de Cîteaux, 3 (Paris: Editions Alsatia, 1953) pp. 95–114; and, more recently, Fossier, 'Economie cistercienne dans les plaines du nord-ouest de l'Europe', in *L'Economie cistercienne: Géographie—Mutations du Moyen âge aux temps moderns*, Publications de la Commission d'histoire de Flaran 3 (Auch, 1983) pp. 53–74; R. A. Donkin, *The Cistercians: Studies in the Geography of Mediaeval England and Wales* (Toronto: Pontifical Institute of Mediaeval Studies, 1978); Charles Higounet, *Paysages et villages neufs du Moyen Age* (Bordeaux, 1975); as well as Berman, *Medieval Agriculture*.

[12]A 'classic' case is in the notice on 'Ardorel' by L. de Lacger, in *Dictionnaire d'histoire et de géographie ecclésiastique* 7 (1924) 1617–20.

[13]My adherence to this viewpoint owes much to Louis J. Lekai's paper, 'Ideals and Reality in Early Cistercian Life and Legislation', in John R. Sommerfeldt (ed.), *Cistercian Ideals and Reality*, CS 60 (Kalamazoo, Michigan: Cistercian Publications, 1978) pp. 4–29. Lekai suggested that statutes were not legislative codes which could be enforced, but rarely achieved ideals towards which the order nonetheless aimed. He cited evidence of early divergence from ideals from a number of twelfth-century cistercian sources.

monks worked in the fields, and the economic benefits of pastoralism in an expanding economy, but, rather, the high return on invested capital when agriculture is tithe-exempt and the importance of expanding urban markets for cistercian growth.[14]

Most recently, a new direction has been taken in the study of the early Cistercians with the publication of Auberger's thesis, *L'unanimité cistercienne: Mythe ou réalité*, which argues for a diversity of voices among the first leaders of the white monks.[15] This notion of diversity, of lack of unanimity within the budding order, provides explanations not only for the differences between practice at early Clairvaux and elsewhere, but for such enigmas as the role of women. It has, I believe, initiated a new understanding of the Cistercians and one which I have found extremely compelling, but it does not solve the problem of divergence between ideal and reality. Although obviously ideologies are not easily changed, one must wonder: why did not the white monks simply change their ideals to fit their practice? Further: if reality did not coincide with ideals, what kept the ideology from changing? Ultimately: what were the payoffs to the order of maintaining ideals or a rhetorical stance considerably different from actual practice? Finally: why, as historians of the order's first years, must we resort to this dichotomy of ideal and reality particularly with regard to the economic practice of the early Cistercians?

I believe that it is now possible to begin to understand the Order in a view which combines those of economic and monastic historians and which attempts to avoid the polar treatment of ideal and reality. This is so because, although this dichotomy is a convenient device for compartmentalizing our thoughts, there was never a total divorce between ideal and reality in early cistercian history. For, in a variety of ways, even though ideology did not mirror the actual practice of the order, there was still a connection between its ideology and its economic practices. Moreover, ideology tended to sustain or justify practice, although often in indirect, even convoluted ways. I suspect that this is true with regard to a number of issues, but I shall concentrate here on how the order's tithe exemption was implicitly sustained by claims in cistercian rhetoric that cistercian houses were founded in deserted areas: 'far from human habitation, from castles, or from cities'.

Such purported cistercian settlement in remote areas, *in locis horroris*

---

[14]Berman, *Medieval Agriculture, passim,* and, more recently, 'Les cisterciens et le courant économique du XIIe siècle', *Bernard de Clairvaux. Histoire, Mentalités, Spiritualité* (Paris: Cerf, 1992).

[15]Cited in note 1.

et vastae solitudinae, has been shown to be more rhetorical than real by recourse to the order's early charters. Yet, such claims about site in the earliest legislative and narrative documents continue to be found through at least the third quarter of the twelfth century, for instance in the *vitae* of local founders Stephen of Obazine or Pons de Léras.[16] This rhetoric was particularly important in maintaining cistercian contentions that the order should be tithe exempt in face of increasing external criticism of this exemption. Tithe exemption was very significant to the Cistercians' economic well-being, in particular because tithes were collected on the gross harvest still standing in the fields, before seed was taken out. If tithes or tenths of the harvest had had suddenly to be paid on the white monks' agriculture, this would have amounted to a tax of approximately thirty percent on net yields to the order, or a precipitous decline in real revenues in the twelfth and thirteenth centuries when low yield/seed ratios of about 3:1 or 4:1 yield/seed were the norm.[17] Moreover, the traditional tithe exemption extended to the monks' very profitable animal husbandry—a pursuit by which their earliest wealth had been gained and which was enormously profitable in a period of expanding demand.[18]

The tithe-exemption had been granted in February 1132 to Cîteaux and its entire filiation, and a week later to Clairvaux by Pope Innocent II. It reiterated local privileges bestowed on the monks by several burgundian bishops from as early as the 1120s,[19] and, as Constable has shown, seems to have been part of a general policy on the part of Innocent II to limit monastic payment of tithes.[20] However, it is also obvious that Bernard's support in face of the anacletian schism was very important to Innocent. Although the latter's successors confirmed the grants of tithe exemption to individual houses of the order, there was increasing complaint about this privilege. The General Chapter itself seems to

[16]*La Vie de Saint Etienne d'Obazine*, ed. Michel Aubrun (Clermont-Ferrand: Institut des études du Massif Central, 1970), and 'Chronique de Silvanès', in *Cartulaire de l'abbaye de Silvanès*, ed. P.-A. Verlaguet (Rodez: Carrère, 1910) no. 470, p. 386.

[17]On yields, see B. H. Slicher van Bath, *The Agrarian History of Western Europe*, *A.C. 500–1850*, trans. Olive Ordish (London: E. Arnold, 1963) table 2, pp. 328–29; and Duby, *Rural Economy*, pp. 99–101.

[18]Berman, *Medieval Agriculture*, p. 40.

[19]J.-B Mahn, *L'Ordre cistercienne et son gouvernement des origines au milieu du XIIIe siècle (1098–1265)* (2nd ed., Paris: E. de Boccard, Editeur, 1951) pp. 102–107; the reference to the bishop of Toulouse granting tithes to Cistercians at Grandselve is faulty, at the very least because at that time Grandselve was not yet cistercian; however, there is no reason to doubt references such as those for Pontigny in which bishops granted tithe exemption to the early monks.

[20]Constable, *Monastic Tithes*, pp. 237–44.

have encouraged local houses to try to alleviate this ill-feeling by the repurchase of rights to tithes to which their lands had previously been subject.[21] By the time of Hadrian IV, there were attempts to limit the confirmations of the cistercian privilege of exemption to *novalia* rather than to continue the original terms of the privilege. These were unsuccessful until 1215 when the Fourth Lateran Council would effectively limit tithe exemption on any new acquisitions by the order to those which were actually 'noval' lands.

It was at mid-century, after the death of Eugenius III and Bernard, that the Cistercians began to promote a self-image involving isolated sites and noval lands which had the effect of justifying its tithe-exempt status—a status which had not been questioned in the 1130s when the order was poor, but would be increasingly questioned in the 1170s and 1180s when it was rich. It is at this point that monastic chronicles appeared that described in very hagiographical terms, inspired by the lives of the desert fathers, the isolated sites of cistercian houses. These houses may well have appeared isolated to monastic authors of the 1160s, but they had been *made* isolated by the strenuous efforts of their founders to remove any outsiders from their lands; the Silvanès chronicle provides a good example.[22] These writings very conveniently upheld the order's exemption from tithes, and might be viewed as part of its efforts to maintain the original terms of that exemption.[23] Indeed, much of its rhetoric about isolated and deserted sites must be seen in this light.

When the original exemption was granted by Innocent II, there was no particular concern about noval lands, and the very terms of the privilege belie any interpretation that the popes believed they were granting rights to lands which had never paid tithes. It speaks of land cultivated by Cistercians themselves or under their management and says nothing about land clearance or reclamation or noval tithes:

> Statuimus ut de laboribus quos vos et totius vestre congregationis fratres propriis manibus et sumptibus colitis et de animalibus vestris, a vobis decimas expetere vel recipere nemo presumat.[24]

---

[21]*Statuta*, 1 (1180), no. 1.

[22]Cited above note 16.

[23]Discussion of events leading to the Fourth Lateran Council's changes on cistercian tithes can be found in Constable, *Monastic Tithes*, pp. 298–306; Donnelly, *Decline*, pp. 44–50; and Mahn, *L'Ordre cistercienne*, pp. 112–18.

[24]The grant was made first to Cîteaux on February 10, 1132, and then to Clairvaux on February 17–19, 1132; see *Chartes et documents concernant l'abbaye de Cîteaux 1098–1182*, ed. J.-M. Marilier (Rome: Editions cisterciennes, 1961) no. 90. This act also

With the exception of some of the tithe privileges of Hadrian IV, in which an attempt was made to substitute *sane novalium*, most such privileges granted to individual cistercian communities by popes after Innocent II continued this exemption, usually in clauses beginning *Sane laborum*.[25]

I would contend, then, that one way in which ideology and practice become completely interwoven was with regard to the order's tithe exemption, the question of noval lands, and the isolation of cistercian sites. Cistercians justified their tithe exemption to the rest of the world with rhetoric about empty lands and deserted places, on which it was to be concluded that no tithes had ever been assessed. It was Bernard of course, with his writing derived from the Old Testament and from the *Lives* of the Desert Fathers, who had provided the Order's later leaders with the rhetorical materials to argue that their lands had once been empty and deserted places. It had been Bernard, as well, who had been undoubtedly most instrumental in getting the tithe exemption for the Order's communities. What we cannot tell about Bernard is to what extent he had been involved in the drafting of the precise wording of the tithe exemption granted by Innocent II. We do know that, as Bernard became more involved in the affairs of Christendom, he left decisions about such mundane things as economic activities or site-changes to his subordinates at Clairvaux. So it is likely that he had also left the discussion of the drafting of the tithe exemption to someone else. In actuality, of course, cistercian land was not noval land, had not been won from the forest by pioneering monks, but the myth of the isolated site of the cistercian abbey was sufficient to legitimize the order's privileged status with regard to tithes. Thus ideology upheld an important economic privilege. This intertwining of ideal and reality was an important factor preventing any reformulation of goals or rewriting of ideals by the order's leaders.

The most important consideration with regard to the 1132 tithe exemption is its significance in our assessment of the cistercian agricultural practice of its time. In direct contradiction to what has been inferred by those historians following the erroneous assumption that the *prima*

---

mentions the lay brothers: 'Porro conversos vestros, qui monachi non sunt, post factum in vestris cenobiis professionem, nullus archiepiscoporum, episcoporum, vel abbatum sine vestra grata licentia suscipere aut susceptum retinere presumat.' See *Receuil des chartes de l'abbaye de Clairvaux*, ed. Jean Waquet (Troyes, 1950) fasc. 1, no. 4, for which no original exists and copies vary in date from 17 to 19 February.

[25]Constable, *Monastic Tithes*, pp. 279–82; Mahn, *L'Ordre cistercienne*, pp. 102–107 and ff.; and Donnelly, *Decline*, pp. 44–50.

collectio of 1134 reflected current practice, the text of the 1132 papal bull of tithe exemption to Cîteaux, *Habitantes in domo*, suggests that the chief characteristics of fully-developed cistercian economic practice (direct cultivation, pastoralism, and *conversi*) were already present by that date. There is no question about the year of the tithe exemption documents. We must therefore conclude that, by 1132, the order had successfully merged earlier eremitical practices of intensified animal husbandry with the direct management of granges using the labor of monks, *conversi*, and hired workers. Early cistercian leaders knew that it was not exemption for newly-cleared land that they needed, but exemption for their direct management and pastoralism. Indeed, the wording of the tithe exemption, which was issued by Innocent II to Cîteaux while he was at Cluny in 1132, may well have been discussed with the order's leaders. If this is so, then we can infer that, in the eyes of such early leaders of the order, it was not the purported clearance stressed by modern economic historians, but cistercian direct cultivation and manual labor which served to distinguish their economic practice from that of earlier monasticism. It had not been Bernard's genius which had engendered this particular economic practice which distinguished the Cistercians. Bernard tended to leave such details to others. Without Bernard's support of Innocent II, however, and without the tithe exemption that Innocent II gave to the Order, in part as a reward for Bernard's support, the specifically Cistercian economic practice which the Order developed during these years would have been in no way as successful as it indeed became. It is in this sense that the Order's early economic practice derived from Bernard's activities.

ABSTRACTS

Cette étude passe en revue le développement des représentations modernes de l'économie cistercienne primitive et indique comment une relecture de la bulle *Habitantes in domo* d'Innocent II (1132) pourrait clarifier nos conceptions quant à l'idée que les premiers dirigeants de l'Ordre se faisaient en 1132 des caractéristiques dominantes de leur pratique économique. Dès cette époque, les dirigeants cisterciens se rendaient compte qu'ils ne cultivaient pas des terres nouvellement défrichées et que l'exemption de dîmes pour leur agriculture et leur élevage en faire-valoir direct était leur principal besoin. La culture directe et le travail manuel des moines et des convers importaient plus que des activités pionnières dérivées d'images de la nature sauvage.

This study surveys the development of modern notions of the early Cistercian economy and suggests how a re-consideration of Innocent II's 1132 bull, *Habitantes in domo*, might clarify our ideas of what the order's early leaders thought in 1132 were the distinguishing characteristics of their economic practice. Already by that time, cistercian leaders realized that they were not cultivating all new lands and that exemption from tithes for their directly-managed agriculture and pastoralism was their chief need. Direct cultivation and manual labor by the monks and lay-brothers were more important than any pioneering activities derived from images of the wilderness.

Diese Studie untersucht die Entwicklung moderner Meinungen über die frühe Wirtschaft der Zisterzienser und regt an, wie eine neue Betrachtung der Bulle Innozenz II. von 1132 *Habitantes in domo* unsere Vorstellungen von dem, was die frühen Führer des Ordens 1132 für die auszeichnenden Charakteristika ihrer wirtschaftlichen Praxis hielten, klären könnten. Schon zu dieser Zeit war es Realität, daß die Zisterzienser nicht alle neues Land kultivierten und daß Exemption von Zehnten ihr dringendstes Anliegen für die direkt organisierte Landwirtschaft und Seelsorgetätigkeit war. Direkte Kultivierung und Feldarbeit durch die Mönche und Laienbrüder waren wichtiger als jegliche Pionieraktivitäten, die aus Bildern von der Wildnis abgeleitet wurden.

SAINT BERNARD IN HIS RELATIONS
WITH PETER THE VENERABLE

Adriaan H. Bredero
Vrije Universiteit Amsterdam

I N THE YEAR 1173, the French Maurist Dom Charles Clemencet published a survey of the life-stories and writings of Saint Bernard
of Clairvaux and of Peter the Venerable. In this book, intended to
supplement the volume of the *Histoire littéraire de la France* concerning
the authors of the twelfth century, the mutual relations between the two
abbots, who represented respectively the cistercian and the cluniac orders,
did not receive much explicit attention. Nevertheless, Dom Clemencet
mentions in his introduction (*Advertissement*) that the qualities of heart
and mind of those two holy men, the nobility of their feelings, corresponding with those of their birth, and their congruent views about the
good, produced an alliance between them which brought about in that
century a revival of the splendid example of christian friendship, during
the fourth century, between Saint Basil and Saint Gregory of Nazianzus.[1]
Probably inspired by this remark, several authors of the nineteenth
and twentieth centuries have exerted themselves to describe the spiritual friendship reputed to have existed between these two abbots.[2] An

---

[1] *Histoire littéraire de S. Bernard, abbé de Clairvaux, et de Pierre Vénérable, abbé de
Cluny*, V: 'Les qualités du coeur & de l'esprit, la noblesse des sentiments qui répondoit
à celle de leur naissance, la conformité de vues pour le bien, formerent entre eux une
liaison qui renouvella dans le XII siecle le bel exemple d'une amitié chrétienne, tel que
saint Basile & saint Grégoire de Nazianze l'ont donné autrefois dans le IV siecle.'
[2] Recently by J. Leclercq, *Pierre le Vénérable* (Abbaye Saint-Wandrille, 1946) pp. 67–
87. See M. D. Knowles, *Cistercians and Cluniacs: The Controversy between St. Bernard*

argument proving this supposition seems to be offered by the letters they wrote to each other. In these letters they repeatedly delivered high-pitched attestations of such mutual friendship. But this argument has been rejected more recently by some other scholars, who have put forward the opinion that the utterances of friendship the abbots inserted into their letters derive much more from the manner of corresponding in those days, especially current in monastic circles, than to the close relation between them. The repeated efforts to prove the existence of such a friendship has even been referred to as an improper problem of historiography.[3]

With this criticism I basically agree. This criticism also corresponds with the functions that letters often had at that time. Because privacy of correspondence did not exist, letters were not primarily intended to inform in detail the one to whom a letter was addressed about the question which was the reason for writing and sending the letter. This more particular information the recipient received as an oral message, given to him by the person who brought the letter. Sometimes the letter itself gave general information; sometimes it treated an edifying topic with verbal expressions derived from frequently recited scriptural texts and so belonging to the common spirituality of monks.[4]

Those letters, in which the authors more or less continued their daily prayers, often contained a pious eulogy as well, specially flattering the Lord's servant for whom the letter was intended. Therefore, epistolary criticism teaches us not to consider the letters of both abbots as giving transparent information about the relationship between them and not to expect a satisfying answer from their correspondence to the old question of their mutual understanding.

---

and *Peter the Venerable* (London, 1955); J.-B. Auniord, 'L'ami de saint Bernard: Quelques textes', Coll. 18 (1956) 88–98; A. H. Bredero, 'The Controversy between Peter the Venerable and Saint Bernard of Clairvaux', in G. Constable and J. Kritzeck (edd.), *Petrus Venerabilis 1156–1956: Studies and Texts Commemorating the Eighth Centenary of his Death* (= *Studia Anselmiana* 40) (Rome, 1956) pp. 53–71; A. Proulx Lang, 'The Friendship between Peter the Venerable and Bernard of Clairvaux', in *Bernard of Clairvaux: Studies Presented to Dom Jean Leclercq* (Washington, D.C., 1973) pp. 35–53; J.-P. Torrell and D. Bouthillier, *Pierre le Vénérable et sa vision du monde* (Louvain, 1986) pp. 92–101.

[3]A. M. Piazzoni, 'Un falso problema storiografico: Note a proposito della "amicizia" tra Pietro il Venerabile e Bernardo di Clairvaux', *Bulletino dell'Istituto Storico Italiano per il Medio Evo e Archivio Muratoriano* 89 (1980–1981) 443–87.

[4]G. Constable, *Letters and Letter-Collections*, Typologie des sources 17 (Turnhout, 1976) pp. 52–55. G. Constable (ed.), *The Letters of Peter the Venerable* [hereafter *Letters*] (Cambridge, Massachusetts, 1967) 2:23–28.

In any case, their relationship must have been a rather complex one. For it was strongly determined by the context of the formal and informal functions which each of the abbots had at that time and by the vested interests which were at stake in connection with those functions. There were, of course, moments in which their social and ecclesiastical interests agreed, but often too those interests were rather in contradiction.

Moreover, we cannot isolate their relations from the action of others, as, for example, of Matthew of Albano, when he functioned in France as a papal legate, or, later on, from the activity of Abelard, hunted by Bernard and protected by Peter the Venerable, and, in the end, from the activities of Nicholas of Clairvaux, a former benedictine monk of Montièramy, who became the most important secretary of Bernard and who was also a close friend of Peter. On the other hand, we may also bring into consideration that genuine efforts toward the virtue of christian love by both abbots obliged them to give a testimony of such feelings in their letters.

To this complexity pertains the fact, furthermore, that the social importance attributed to their respective abbatial functions underwent some change in course of time. The social respect that Peter the Venerable received at his election, in 1122, as abbot of Cluny, strongly surpassed, in the beginning, the prestige Bernard held as abbot of Clairvaux. But the social respect Bernard held later on because of his preaching, his miracles, and his many activities outside his abbey may in some way have exceeded that of Peter the Venerable. This development also may have influenced their relationship.

Moreover, when trying to characterize this relationship, we must be aware that undoubtedly its most important aspect was the way in which these abbots first established their relationship and the manner in which they then treated each other. This treatment was unfortunate in the sense that they each later felt themselves obliged to remain on guard against the other, because they were never quite sure about the sincerity of the religious courtesy with which they had been accustomed to write to the other. Their first contact, or, better, their first confrontation, took place when they did not yet have any personal acquaintance with each other. Their actions then brought both of them serious difficulties, and, for Saint Bernard, it even brought some scandal. So they had, in later years, to pay constant attention, each in a different way, to the lasting consequences of those earlier experiences of conflict.

The beginning of those difficulties came from an interference by Saint Bernard in internal cluniac affairs, when, in 1124, he wrote his open letter to his cousin, Robert of Châtillon, followed in 1125 by his *Apology*, addressed to William of Saint Thierry.[5] In opposition to current opinion, we note that those writings were not primarily intended to confront the cistercian and the cluniac orders with each other concerning their way of life. Bernard had in view, or, better said, he had accepted the task of supporting a monastic reform movement started within the cluniac order during the abbacy of Pontius, but suppressed after Pontius' forced abdication in 1122. This movement experienced a revival in 1124, when Pontius returned from his pilgrimage to Jerusalem and settled down in northern Italy.

As already stated, Saint Bernard did not primarily intend by this writing to compare the monastic way of life at Cluny and Cîteaux. Rather, he intended, on behalf of the supporters of the reform movement, to take a stand against the more traditional monastic customs that prevailed once more after the abdication of Abbot Pontius and of which the new abbot, Peter the Venerable, was then the official exponent.[6] Bernard intervened in this controversy at the instigation and the instruction of his friend William of Saint Thierry, the reform-minded abbot of a monastery that belonged to the cluniac circle. But the first attempt of Bernard to intervene, his open letter to Robert of Châtillon, did not exactly correspond to the expectations of William. So William requested the Abbot of Clairvaux to write his *Apology*, and, in this marvelous treatise, the intention of Saint Bernard to intervene became much more outspoken.[7]

Afterwards, because of the scandal that followed Pontius' return to the Abbey of Cluny in 1125, Bernard must have regretted this interference. For it appeared, at least to some degree, that Pontius' return, which led to disorder and so to a complete defeat of the reform movement, had been provoked by the writings of Bernard. The reactions that followed obliged Bernard, for political reasons as well, to reconsider his attitude toward Cluny. A first reaction came already in 1126, when Cardinal-deacon Peter, who was sent by the Pope to investigate what had exactly happened at Cluny, invited the Abbot of Clairvaux to a meeting. Bernard declined, and for this reason he had to inform the Cardinal by a letter about his writings. So he did, but concerning his polemical writings his answer was rather evasive.[8]

---

[5]Ep 1 (SBOp 7:1–11) and Apo (SBOp 3:81–108).
[6]A. H. Bredero, *Cluny et Cîteaux au douzième siècle* [hereafter *Cluny*] (Amsterdam, Maarssen, 1985) pp. 27–73.
[7]*Cluny*, p. 32.
[8]*Cluny*, p. 72, n. 147, and pp. 313–14. See Epp 17 and 18; SBOp 7:65–69.

A reaction more embarrassing for Bernard came from Peter the Venerable himself, when the latter wrote a long letter in 1127, addressed to the Abbot of Clairvaux.[9] This letter has often been considered a direct answer of Peter to the earlier polemical writings of Bernard.[10] But Peter's chief intention in this letter must have been to avoid any further effort within his own order to introduce reforms in the traditional way of monastic life prescribed by the cluniac customs. For this letter, although formally addressed to the abbot of Clairvaux, was also intended for the priors of all the cluniac houses.[11]

In this way Peter defended the traditional customs within his own monastic order by a disguised instruction, while he was giving the impression that he was reacting only to criticism the Cluniacs had received about their way of life from the Cistercians. It may also have been his intention to inform later generations regarding a controversy brought about wholly from the outside by a cistercian abbot and in no way related to the abdication of Abbot Pontius, who was simply an unworthy man as was proved by the scandal he provoked by his return to Cluny in 1125.

On the other hand, it is even questionable whether Peter considered quite realistic the prescriptions on the customs in this letter to the cluniac priors. For, five years later, he himself pleaded in a prudent way for some revision of those traditionally sacred customs, which led in 1146 to his reforming statutes.[12] This point merits emphasis here. For, in his later correspondence with Bernard, Peter twice explicitly treated the relations between Cluniacs and Cistercians, but obviously with intentions other than those in this first letter.

Moreover, we may suppose that Peter the Venerable wrote his first letter to Saint Bernard on the very advice of Matthew, the elderly prior of Saint-Martin des Champs, who had been the most stubborn opponent of Abbot Pontius in the order of Cluny.[13] Since 1125, Matthew had been cardinal bishop of Albano and had a great share in the condemnation of Abbot Pontius, which took place in 1126 at Rome. From 1125 on, Matthew worked for some years as the papal legate in France, and in

---

[9]Ep 28; *Letters* 1:52–101; 2:115–20 and 270–74.

[10]According to Charles Clemencet (above n. 1), this letter was, however, addressed to Bernard, not as an answer to his *Apology*, but to a lost writing of some other cistercian monks. *Histoire*, p. 441.

[11]*Letters* 2:206, note at Ep 161.

[12]*Statuta Petri Venerabilis Abbatis Cluniacensis (1146/7)*, ed. G. Constable, in *Corpus Consuetudinum Monasticarum* VI (Siegburg, 1975) pp. 19–116.

[13]*Cluny*, pp. 47–51, 83, and 92, n. 68.

those years he was still strongly interested in the repression of any effort to introduce a measure of reform into the traditional way of life prescribed within the cluniac milieu. Matthew had already acted in this way immediately after the election of Peter the Venerable in 1122.

At that moment, Matthew became the temporary grand prior at Cluny, charged with supervising the monastic restoration which Peter the Venerable, as newly-elected abbot, was to initiate. During that period, Matthew also visited Clairvaux, and, profiting from the absence of Bernard, he brought Robert of Châtillon, Bernard's cousin, with him to Cluny. In Matthew's opinion, Robert belonged at Cluny, because he was dedicated as a child to this abbey.[14] Later on, Matthew still vigorously defended the preservation of the traditional customs of Cluny. Therefore, we may conclude that the hand of the Cardinal of Albano can also be traced in the instruction Peter the Venerable gave to the cluniac priors, disguised as a reaction to the polemical writings of Saint Bernard.

On account of the prominent part Matthew played, as cardinal-legate, in the ecclesiastical affairs in France and because of the control he exercised at the same time on benedictine monasticism, we must examine his relationship with both abbots. On his relations with the Abbot of Cluny we are more or less informed by some letters of Peter the Venerable and by the *Life of Matthew* written by Peter after Matthew's death in 1135.[15] But, looking at the relations between Matthew and Bernard we must consider, after the earlier conflict in the cluniac order in which Matthew had a great share as the opponent of Abbot Pontius, the origins of the papal schism of 1130, which resulted from several serious controversies within the Roman curia.

This schism was not only a result of the opposition of some of the cardinals against the way Cardinal Haimeric had arranged the elections of Honorius II (1124) and Innocent II (1130),[16] but also of other irritations. This opposition may even have been fed, at least for some cardinals, by the forced abdication of Abbot Pontius in 1121 and by his condemnation in 1126. This supposition is not only based on the fact that the 'antipope' Anacletus had formerly been a cluniac monk, but also on the cluniac background of Giles, cardinal of Tusculum. The latter became a monk

[14]*Cluny*, p. 49.

[15]*Petri Cluniacensis Abbatis, De miraculis libri duo* 2:4–26, in D. Bouthillier (ed.) CCCM 83:103–148.

[16]See M. Stroll, *The Jewish Pope: Ideology and Politics in the Papal Schism of 1130* (Leiden, 1987) which also gives the most recent bibliography.

at Cluny during the abbacy of Pontius, and, during his Roman period, Giles still had close relations with Pontius.[17] Anacletus received strong support from Giles until the end, notwithstanding the efforts of Peter the Venerable to bring him to the side of Innocent II.[18]

It is not our purpose to discuss here the origins of this papal schism, but we must point out that, before its outbreak, Saint Bernard had already entered into relations with two prominent actors in this schism, cardinal-chancellor Haimeric and Matthew, cardinal bishop of Albano, on behalf of Innocent II. Both Haimeric and Matthew had previously played a prominent role in the proceedings against Abbot Pontius in 1126. With Haimeric, who became chancellor about 1125, Bernard was already acquainted, probably because both came from Burgundy. In any case, about 1127 and 1128, Bernard wrote him several letters and had dedicated his first treatise, *On the Necessity of Loving God*, to him.[19]

The relationship of Bernard with Cardinal Matthew was initiated by the latter. In 1128, he invited the abbot to participate in the Council of Troyes, presided over by the cardinal himself. In his answering letter, Bernard declined this invitation because of illness and because of his wish not to leave his monastery.[20] In spite of this, he did go to Troyes, and there he took an important share in the deliberations. Matthew had convened this council for the chief purpose of giving support to the young and still rather insignificant Order of the Poor Knights of Christ

[17]J. Schmale, *Studien zum Schisma des Jahres 1130* (Cologne, Graz, 1961) pp. 77–78. Giles entered Cluny in 1119, and, after the canonization of Abbot Hugh in 1120, followed Pope Calixtus II to Rome. He wrote there, on the request of Abbot Pontius, a *Life of Saint Hugh*. See A. H. Bredero, 'La canonisation de Saint Hugues et celle de ses devanciers', in *Le gouvernement d'Hughes de Semur à Cluny: Actes du Colloque scientifique international, Cluny, septembre 1988* (Cluny, 1990) pp. 149–71.

[18]Ep 66; *Letters* 1:195–97, and 2:141.

[19]In 1127–1128, Bernard wrote to Haimeric Epp 15, 20, 51, 52, and 53; SBOp 7:64, 70, 143, 144, and 145. About the date when Bernard wrote *De diligendo Deo*, there is no clear information. Leclercq (SBOp 3:111–12) indicates sometime between 1126, the year Haimeric became the chancellor of the Roman Church, and 1141, the year of his death. One of the first letters of Bernard to Haimeric, Ep 311 (SBOp 8:239–41), dates from 1124–1127. Bernard also wrote this letter on behalf of Hugh, the abbot of Pontigny, because of a gift they had received from the cardinal. At the end of his letter, Bernard spoke of 'the gifts by which you were the first kindly to solicit our friendship', and in his comment he also said: 'We consider it an unmistakable sign of your friendship that an important man like your Excellency, always engaged in great affairs, should have seen fit even to greet such insignificant persons as are we, not to mention your gifts.' The translation is from B. S. James, *The Letters of Saint Bernard of Clairvaux* (London, 1953) p. 447. So Haimeric was the one who sought Bernard's friendship.

[20]Ep 21; SBOp 7:71–72.

and the Temple of Solomon, founded in 1119 by Hugh of Payns. Bernard had made more direct acquaintance with the Order of the Templars about 1125, when Hugh, the count of Champagne, who had previously granted Bernard the site of Clairvaux, decided to make his entrance into this military order instead of becoming a monk at Clairvaux.[21] Before Matthew's invitation to Bernard to participate in the Council of Troyes, Peter the Venerable wrote his letter to the cluniac priors, but addressed to the Abbot of Clairvaux. By pretending that Bernard had criticized the cluniac way of life only from a cistercian point of view, the letter might have facilitated a reconciliation of Bernard with Cardinal Matthew in that it quieted the suspicion that Bernard had formerly been an ally of the condemned and excommunicated Abbot Pontius. This letter gave Bernard at least the opportunity to come into contact with Matthew.

Later on, this closer contact with Matthew undoubtedly obliged Bernard to stand somewhat apart from the further efforts of William of Saint Thierry to introduce a reform of the monastic customs in the milieu of Cluny, a reform directly inspired by the cistercian way of life of which Matthew was an outspoken opponent. Bernard distanced himself from this movement in 1132, by declining the invitation he had received to participate in the synod of benedictine abbots of the ecclesiastical province of Reims, at which they wished to introduce such a reform into their abbeys.[22]

At a much earlier moment, however, it must have been clear to Matthew that Bernard was disposed to refrain from any immediate intervention in the internal problems of the cluniac order. A telling indication of his altered attitude is demonstrated by the invitation Bernard received in 1130 to voice the decision of the Council of Étampes that the Church of France had chosen the side of Pope Innocent II. If Bernard had resumed the articulation of unfavorable views on the monastic traditions at Cluny, Cardinal Matthew, and also Cardinal-chancellor Haimeric, could not have consented to Bernard's role at Étampes. Moreover, Pope Innocent II, whom Bernard declared the legitimate pope at Étampes, showed a particular attachment to Peter the Venerable and to Cluny by staying there during a whole week directly after the meeting.[23]

So it is, after all, possible to conclude that, by the letter he addressed in 1127 to Saint Bernard, Peter the Venerable may have had some

---

[21]Ep 31; SBOp 7:85–86.
[22]Ep 91; SBOp 7:239–41. See *Cluny*, pp. 128–31.
[23]The pope then consecrated the new abbatial church at Cluny. See *Letters* 2:259.

intention to further a closer connection between them, as he did in 1132 by introducing a first adaptation of the cluniac customs to the actual situation with which the order was confronted.[24] Nevertheless, this first letter of the abbot of Cluny to Bernard brought with it also a rather embarrassing consequence. This was because of Peter's interpretation in it of the polemical writings of Bernard. Bernard's work was characterized as an attack against Cluny from the outside—an attack which brought into existence a long lasting resentment between the orders at the very time when the social importance of the Cistercians began to overshadow that of Cluny.

As we can see from the later correspondence between the two abbots, it was the envy resulting from a growing rivalry between the orders that primarily determined Bernard's increasingly reticent attitude and also influenced the relations between them. In his later correspondence, Peter persisted in discussing this mutual resentment. For, as he wrote to Bernard several times, he viewed these antagonistic feelings as condemnable for monks. Yet Bernard always avoided responding to Peter's lamentations on this subject.[25] Furthermore, one should note that, while Bernard's polemical writings about Cluny received some reactions from the benedictine side,[26] no written reply was given on this subject by any Cistercian, at least during Bernard's lifetime.

Only after Bernard's death did a german Cistercian dare to write a rather extensive and influential *Dialogus* between a Cistercian and a Cluniac.[27] In this onesided defense of the cistercian order, the author did not express merely his own antagonistic feelings against Cluny. Although this text did not receive much dissemination, it nevertheless reflected an opinion about the Cluniacs that was widely accepted in the cistercian order. For example, it gives a traditional version of the origins of Cîteaux as later told in the *Exordium magnum*, from which it becomes evident that, during the days of Saint Bernard, resentment had grown in the cistercian order against the Cluniacs.[28]

[24]M. Chibnall, *The Ecclesiastical History of Ordericus Vitalis*, XIII, 13 (Oxford, 1978) 6:424–27.

[25]*Cluny*, pp. 243–44.

[26]A. Wilmart, 'Une riposte de l'ancien monachisme au manifest de saint Bernard', *Revue Bénédictine* 46 (1934) 309–344. C. H. Talbot, 'The Date and the Author of the Riposte', in *Petrus Venerabilis*, pp. 72–80. See *Cluny*, p. 70, n. 134.

[27]R.B.C. Huygens, *Le moine Idung et ses deux ouvrages: 'Argumentum super quatuor questionibus' et 'Dialogus duorum monachorum'* (Spoleto, 1980) pp. 91–186.

[28]*Cluny*, pp. 244–47.

In the *Exordium magnum* we do not find the untrue account, given by the *Dialogus*, that the monastery of Molesme belonged to the order of Cluny. But it states explicitly that Molesme had been abandoned by the founders of Cîteaux primarily because of the decline in the observance of the *Rule* of Saint Benedict at Cluny.[29] As this story reflects an oral tradition, which until then had been passed down within the cistercian order, we may suppose that there were two basic reasons why no further polemic writings against Cluny circulated among Cistercians. First, Saint Bernard prevented the diffusion of such writings, and, secondly, these writings were superfluous because of the polemical writings of Bernard himself. The Cistercians could satisfy their developing resentment against the Cluniacs with those writings, the manuscripts of which must have been reproduced at the *scriptoria* of many cistercian abbeys.

Therefore, as stated above, if we wish to analyze the relations between Peter the Venerable and Saint Bernard, we cannot restrict our attention to the spiritual messages and the friendly compliments their later letters contain. We also must look more closely at the somewhat difficult contacts between them when they had to defend opposing interests. But any such effort is strongly hampered by our meager information on the personal encounters between the abbots. When their first encounter took place, we can only guess. In any case, their meetings went on until the Council of Pisa in 1135, where they worked together on the healing of the papal schism, and thus on a problem not tied to their own monastic affairs and interests.

According to some historical comments on the intense letter which Peter wrote to Bernard in 1137, they opened their minds to each other at Pisa, and their close friendship followed. The letter seems, at first reading, to affirm this interpretation, because Peter seems to have evoked in it the deep religious satisfaction he had received from meeting Bernard. Peter expressed his gratitude for this spiritual experience: 'How much reverence, how much love toward you my soul holds in its inmost depths he [God] knows whom in you I reverence and embrace.'[30] But, on the other hand, we must not overlook the fact that, in this letter, Peter did not mention any practical reason for sending this flattering compliment to Bernard, except, perhaps, to encourage him in healing the papal schism in Italy.

---

[29]*Exordium magnum cisterciense sive narratio de initio ordinis*, auctore Conrado de Eberbach, dist. I, cap. XI-XVI; ed. B. Griesser (Rome, 1961) pp. 63–71.
[30]Ep 65; *Letters* 1:194. For its date see 2:140–41.

Since Bernard did not answer this letter, Peter wrote him again. This time he sent him only a short note in which he mentioned his previous, and longer letter. This note was carried to Bernard by Archdeacon Gebuin, from whom Bernard could have received further oral information.[31] Considering the contents of the first letter, primarily in praise of Bernard, we may conclude that the messenger who carried Bernard this former letter also brought him a spoken message.

Bernard's answer to both letters did not contain any information concerning the matter about which they had exchanged oral messages. It merely gave an appraisal of the attention he had received from Peter during his stay in a foreign land and an acknowledgment of the consolation those letters had brought him. Furthermore, he spoke of his joy at the end of the schism which might follow the death of Anacletus.[32]

Because the letters exchanged did not contain any substantial information, we must consider them primarily as courtesies covering the acceptance of the oral messages exchanged at the same time. About these spoken messages, however, any direct information is lacking. Nevertheless, there are reasons to suppose that this apparently amicable correspondence veils an oral altercation, based on the somewhat opposing interests of their orders.

As far as this altercation can be reconstructed, it perpetuated a conflict, which was raised between the Cluniacs and the Cistercians after the privilege the latter had received in 1132 from Pope Innocent II. This privilege exempted the Cistercians from paying the tithes attached to any of their lands. Peter had already strongly protested this privilege in two letters sent to the pope and to Cardinal-chancellor Haimeric,[33] probably written between 1135 and 1137, and directly related to the conflict which had arisen between the orders concerning the wealthy and influential cluniac priory of Gigny and the new cistercian abbey of le Miroir, founded in 1131 by Cîteaux itself.[34]

Between 1132 and 1140, Peter the Venerable twice wrote a letter to the Chapter General of the Cistercians. As he did not receive any direct

[31]Ep 73, *Letters* 1:206. About Gebuin, see *Letters* 2:144–45.
[32]Ep 147; SBOp 7:350–51 (= Ep 74; *Letters* 1:207–208). According to Constable (*Letters* 2:147), this letter was written in 1138 between February and May, that is to say between the death of Anacletus II and the final submission of his supporters.
[33]Epp 33 and 34; *Letters* 1:107–113; 2:122–24.
[34]G. Constable, 'Cluniac Tithes and the Controversy between Gigny and Le Miroir', *Revue Bénédictine* 70 (1960) 591–624. Reprinted in G. Constable, *Cluniac Studies* (London, 1980).

answer to his first letter, he sent another the following year. There are serious arguments for accepting the date of these two letters as about 1137 and 1138, about the same time Peter twice wrote Bernard.[35] Because of Bernard's stay in Italy, he was not directly involved in this controversy. Nevertheless, at that moment he was already the most influential member of his order. Considering the strong words used in the letters of protest Peter directed to the Chapter General, it is hardly conceivable that he should not have simultaneously tried to find a solution to this conflict through the intervention of the abbot of Clairvaux.

Although Bernard's answers to Peter's letters were very friendly and polite, Peter's expectation of direct help in the conflict remained vain. The litigation between Gigny and le Miroir did not end, and even continued after Bernard's death.[36] So it is improbable that Bernard put pressure on the Cistercians to change their stance even after the flattering letter he received from the abbot of Cluny. The Cistercians' position was based on the papal privilege providing that none of their monasteries were obliged to pay tithes formerly attached to land of which they had become the owners. Therefore, if this controversy between the Cluniacs and the Cistercians formed the basis of the oral message that accompanied the epistolary exchange between the abbots, then it seems contestable to conclude from those courteous and friendly letters that they then already had become close friends.

On the other hand, the reason why Peter may have written Bernard in 1137 and 1138, namely, to find a solution to the mounting conflict on tithes, may explain why, beyond very flattering expressions, his first letter did not contain any precise message for the Abbot of Clairvaux. For the same reason Peter wrote a third letter to Bernard, which, however, has been lost. But Bernard's answer to this letter has been preserved. It shows that the oral messages accompanying the letters had a serious content. This answer makes clear, at least, that Peter and Bernard desired a personal exchange of ideas. For Bernard wrote in his answer: 'When and where shall we have a suitable opportunity and talk as you suggest?'[37]

This correspondence cannot be seen as a manifest and convincing witness of an already existing personal friendship between the abbots. We may also conclude this from a conflict between Bernard and Peter

---

[35]Epp 35 and 36; *Letters* 1:113–17, 124. The approximate dates of these letters are 1132/1140 and 1133/1140, but Constable (*Clunic Tithes*, 616–17) is inclined to date the beginning of this controversy to between 1135 and 1137.

[36]Constable, *Clunic Tithes*, 620–24.

[37]Ep 148; SBOp 7:352. James, *Letters*, p. 222, no. 153.

the Venerable in 1138, concerning the episcopal election in one of the most important dioceses of France—in Langres, a diocese to which Clairvaux itself belonged, together with other abbeys such as Molesme and Morimond. The newly-elected bishop, a cluniac monk, was not acceptable to Bernard because of what was told him about the candidate. So Bernard intervened in person by sending several letters to the pope, and by writing to the dean of the chapter of Langres and to the bishops and cardinals of the roman curia.[38]

In this letter Bernard blamed Peter the Venerable and the archbishop of Lyon for the election, and spoke of them '. . . as the gods of the earth. . . trusting in their own strength and boasting of their great possessions.'[39] In another letter addressed to Pope Innocent II, Bernard tempered his blame of Peter. In it, he made the archbishop of Lyon,. together with the bishops of Mâcon and Autun, responsible for the election, and of them he wrote they were 'all friends of Cluny'.[40] In this affair Bernard avoided asking Peter the Venerable for an explanation, and we do not know what answer the abbot of Cluny received to the explanatory letter which he sent Bernard, of his own accord, concerning his personal share in this matter.[41]

It is unlikely that Bernard sent any answer to this letter of Peter the Venerable; for, if he did so, his answer would certainly have been preserved together with the other five letters Bernard wrote on this matter. He wrote those letters to have the election annulled, notwithstanding that the candidate had already been invested by King Louis VII and ordained by the archbishop of Lyon. Bernard's main argument against the election, given in his first letter to Innocent II, was that the pope had decided that it should take place with the advice of religious men. In Bernard's opinion, this had not happened, since he had been promised by the archbishop of Lyon and the dean of the chapter of Langres that he would be consulted, and such consultation had not taken place.[42] Since the pope annulled the election, under Bernard's pressure, the chapter of Langres wished to

---

[38]Epp 164–69; SBOp 7:372–82.

[39]Ep 168; SBOp 7:380–81. James, *Letters*, pp. 255–56, no. 183. Bernard was quoting Psalms 46:10, 48:7, and 35:12.

[40]Ep 166; SBOp 7:377.

[41]Ep 29; *Letters* 1:101–104; 2:120–21. For Peter's account of this election, see G. Constable, 'The Disputed Election at Langres in 1138', *Traditio* 13 (1957) 126. Reprinted in Constable, *Cluniac Studies.*

[42]Ep 164. 1; SBOp 7:372. James, *Letters*, p. 250, no. 179: '. . . It was their intention to leave the matter entirely in my hands and [that they] take no step without first consulting me. And this they promised me.'

designate him as the new bishop. When Bernard refused to accept this nomination, the canons elected Geoffrey, the prior of Clairvaux—thus depriving Bernard of his second in command.[43]

In the letter which Peter the Venerable wrote to Bernard on this dispute, because the opportunity to discuss it in a personal encounter had been lacking, he strongly denied the truth of the negative rumors circulating about the cluniac candidate. He regretted that Bernard, rather than asking a friend to inform him about the candidate, had believed what was told him by declared enemies of Cluny. Peter also expressed his wish that Cistercians and Cluniacs would respect and trust each other as was becoming to monks. He related, further, his conviction that the cluniac candidate, if he actually had become bishop of Langres, would have, of course, loved Cistercians and other monks, because love brings advantage as the absence of love brings an eclipse.[44]

How much Bernard may have appreciated Peter's reproving exposition is difficult to say, because he did not answer the letter. But some months afterward, he sent a letter to Peter in which he gave him, 'however unwillingly and with hesitation', some necessary suggestions. Bernard wished that Peter would act with greater moderation than he had done concerning the benedictine abbey of Saint-Bertin.[45] The difficulty was that the monastery of Saint-Bertin had been incorporated into the cluniac order against the will of the monastic community and now was striving to regain its independence.[46] It is rather surprising that Bernard wrote about this cluniac conflict; he had learned not to enter into other internal problems of the clunic order. Could it be that Bernard, after the correction he had received from Peter about the election at Langres, wished in turn to correct some of the actions of the Abbot of Cluny?

The next confrontation between the abbots, about which we have some information, followed two years later, in 1140, after the condemnation of the theological teaching and writings of Peter Abelard by the Council of Sens, convened at the instigation of Saint Bernard. Because Master

---

[43]Constable, *Letters* 1:140–41. In a letter to King Louis of France (Ep 170; SBOp 7:383–85) Bernard wrote: 'What happened at Langres concerning my prior happened contrary to all my expectations and contrary to the intentions of the bishops and myself.' James, *Letters*, 257–58, no. 186.

[44]Ep 29; *Letters* 1:104: 'Diliget ergo si monachus fuerit Lingonensis episcopus Cistercienses et ceteros monachos, quia diligendo maius sibi lucrum, non diligendo sentiet detrimentum.'

[45]Ep 149; SBOp 7:353.

[46]*Cluny*, pp. 99–106.

Abelard had made an appeal to the roman curia during that council, the council fathers had to suspend Abelard's condemnation as a heretic. In the several letters which, following the Council of Sens, Bernard wrote to the pope, to Cardinal Haimeric, and to other persons of ecclesiastical importance in Rome, he urged a confirmation of the verdict.[47]

The progress of this affair was altered by a rather drastic interference of Peter the Venerable. When Abelard, on his way to Rome, arrived at Cluny, he was a sick and broken man. But there he received hospitality and also the protection of Peter, who even intervened for him at Rome in a letter to Innocent II. The abbot wrote before the Pope had sanctioned the condemnation by the Council of Sens.[48] In this letter, Peter supported, without restriction, the appeal of Abelard to the roman curia, from which one must attain justice. Peter also related how Abelard had suffered under the suspicion of being a heretic and that, with the help of the abbot of Cîteaux, a reconciliating encounter had already taken place between Bernard and Abelard.

This reconciliation implied that Abelard could no longer be considered as a heretic, for otherwise it could not have taken place. Furthermore, Peter asked permission that Abelard, because of his age, his bad health, and his piety, might take up a permanent residence at Cluny. Although the answer of the pope to his letter is missing, the last request at least must have been consented to by Rome. At Cluny, Peter obtained the opportunity to write his two last apologies and to die in peace.[49]

About the contacts that Peter the Venerable and Bernard must have had concerning this question, all direct documents are missing. Nevertheless, from the letter Peter wrote to Innocent II, it becomes clear that Peter must have been rather strongly opposed to Bernard's agitation against Abelard and must have criticized the abbot of Clairvaux because of his actions. Between the letter Peter wrote to Bernard about the election at Langres and his letter to the pope concerning Abelard there is some resemblance.

---

[47]For a survey of those letters, see L. N. d'Owler, 'Sur quelques Lettres de saint Bernard, avant ou aprês le concile de Sens?', in *Mélanges Saint Bernard: XXIVe Congrès de l'Association Bourguignonne des Sociétés Savantes (8e centenaire de la mort de saint Bernard)*, *Dijon, 1953* (Dijon, 1954) pp. 100–108. See A. H. Bredero, *Christendom and Christianity in the Middle Ages: The Relations Between Religion, Church and Society* (Grand Rapids, Michigan, Edinburgh, forthcoming) chapter 8.

[48]Ep 98; *Letters* 1:258–59; 2:164–65. See P. Zerbi, 'Remarques sur l'Epistola 98 de Pierre le Vénérable', in *Pierre Abélard—Pierre le Vénérable: Les courants philosophiques, littéraires, artistiques en occident au milieu du XIIe siècle (Abbaye de Cluny, 2 au 9 juillet, 1972)* (Paris) pp. 215–32, especially pp. 201–202.

[49]Bredero, *Christendom*, chapter 8.

In both cases, there is a prudent and diplomatic approach, which Peter used to redress some of the noxious consequences of Bernard's hasty actions, which were based on insufficient and partial information. Peter's approach was evidently not primarily intended to injure the dignity of the abbot of Clairvaux.

In 1143, there began a revival in the correspondence between the two abbots. Several of those letters, however, are not preserved. It seems that the initiative for this correspondence came from Bernard, who wrote some letters to which he did not at first receive an answer. In a letter, addressed to Peter at the end of 1143, he recalled the earlier letters he had written:

> It is not so long ago that I greeted you in a letter with all the respect that is your due; yet you answered without one word. And, not long since, I wrote to you again from Rome, but even then I did not get a reply. . . .If it is blameworthy not to have written for some reason or other, how can you be free of blame for having neglected, not to say disdained, to write in answer to my letters?[50]

Bernard's letter, however, is a reply to the answer he received from Peter to an earlier letter, which is also lost. From Bernard's reply, we may deduce that these lost letters brought a rapprochement, at least temporarily bridging the gap between the abbots—unless Bernard's reply was facetious and rhetorical. In any case, Peter must have been very pleased with this reply, in which Bernard wrote:

> I welcomed your letter with open hands. I have read it and re-read it greedily and gladly, and the more often I read it the better pleased I am. I must say I enjoy your fun. It is both pleasantly gay and seriously grave, so that your fun had nothing about it of frivolity, and your dignity loses nothing by your gaiety. You are able to keep your dignity so well in the midst of your fun that those words of the holy man might be applied to you: 'Even when I smiled they did not believe me.'[51]

The way Peter answered Bernard's flattering reply makes clear that, in his earlier answer of 1143, the abbot of Cluny had already sought to create a good opportunity to discuss with Bernard the rather hostile relationship that had developed between cistercian and cluniac monks. This development oppressed Peter the Venerable, for the letter that he

[50]Ep 228. 1; SBOp 8:98. James, *Letters*, p. 375, no. 305.
[51]Ep 228. 2; SBOp 8:99. James, *Letters*, p. 385.

sent to Bernard at the end of spring 1144 was much more a treatise on that relationship than a letter, not only because of its length but also because of its recipient.[52]

Peter began this letter-treatise by expressing his delight at Bernard's last letter, and he spoke abundantly about the satisfaction he received by joking in this way, which he called 'love'. The only reason why he wrote this letter was, as he said, his conviction that this love would always last. He did not even despair that love could have its place between the monks of both orders because of Bernard's assiduity in promoting it. For he had experienced that this love between him and Bernard could not be extinguished by any flux, even not by the impetuous waves of Langres. Then Peter began to speak of the misunderstandings and bad feelings between the members of the two orders.

From Peter's elaboration of this subject, one may assume that he intended his epistle not only for Bernard but also for the monks of the cluniac order.[53] Peter had also probably written it with the expectation that his treatise would circulate in cistercian houses. For he picked up once again all the sixteen points, about the discrepancies between Cluniacs and Cistercians, formerly discussed by him in his answer to the polemical writings with which Bernard had intervened twenty years before in the conflict that had then divided the cluniacs.

In that earlier answer, Peter had consciously ignored Bernard's intervention and had given the impression that the abbot of Clairvaux had only spoken of a rivalry between the orders and of a feeling of superiority the Cistercians had because of the greater austerity of their way of life. To this feeling he refused admittance, as he did later on in the first letter he wrote, about 1137, to the Chapter General of the cistercian order, in which he remarked that the existing discord between the orders could easily dispel all the virtues gained by an ascetic way of life.[54]

One of the notable differences between the letter Peter sent to Bernard in 1127 and that of 1144 was that they were not written for the same

---

[52]Ep 111; *Letters* 1:274–99.

[53]See, for example, *Letters* 1:280: 'Si enim tu o Cluniacensis Cisterciensem, aut tu Cisterciensis Cluniacensem in assumpto proposito errare cognosceres. . . .' See also, p. 293: 'Causa michi scribendi ut superius professus sum, teste conscientia, sola vere caritas fuit, ut quantum ad utrumque nostrum attinet, flatu collocutionis eam recalescere, et in mutui affectus solitas vel maiores flammas erumpere cogerem.' See also n. 55.

[54]Ep 35; *Letters* 1:114: 'Iecit inter nos pomum discordiae, ut recedente una et sola caritate, universa virtutum genera minore labore valeat effugare, et praeciso bonorum omnium capite, membra simul omnia cogantur interire.'

reasons. As already said, Peter's first letter, about the discord between Cluniacs and Cistercians concerning the observance of the *Rule* of Saint Benedict, was written when he wished to defuse the observance controversy within Cluny itself—a controversy in which Bernard had dared to intervene. To gloss over this internal controversy, Peter had then given much attention to the divergences between Cluniacs and Cistercians and had even blamed the white monks for some aspects of their way of life. At that moment, however, the competition between the orders was still a question of minor importance.

Twenty years later, these divergences had led to a real rift between Cluniacs and Cistercians, and Peter probably realized that this rift was partially a result of the polemical response to his first letter to Bernard. His second letter on the subject Peter wrote because of his awareness of this rift. Now he wrote Bernard with a quite different intention: to restore mutual love between the monks of the two orders and not, as in his first letter to Bernard, to accentuate differences between them. Now he emphasized that these differences were not matters of importance.[55]

This contrast informs us also of a certain development within Peter himself. His insights into the meaning of the traditional customs within the cluniac order must have changed radically. In 1122, after the forced abdication of his predecessor, and even more after the dramatic condemnation of Pontius, it became Peter's task to defend the traditions of his order, rather than supporting any effort within Cluny to reform some of those traditional customs. But, in 1144, Peter had quite other opinions about the value of the traditional customs of the cluniac order. We know that he started some reform of them in 1132, and he was still introducing new statutes, which have been considered an approach to the cistercian way of life.[56]

Another clear indication of Peter's continuing reform intentions is given, furthermore, by the circular letter which Peter sent, at some time after 1144, to the cluniac priors and subpriors. There he was rather critical of their way of life, gave stricter prescriptions about monastic

---

[55]It seems that those differences between many monks of the two orders had already been accepted as critical. Ep 111; *Letters* 1:281: 'Sed exigis adhuc ut quod dixi probem, et quomodo sub eadem regula vel eiusdem regulae professione, per diversos tramites tuto monachus incedere possit ostendam. Ad quod michi perfacilis patet responsio, et auctoritas iuncta rationi non deest, posse et te Cluniacensem tuo usu, et te Cisterciensem tuo more, et feliciter per *viam mandatorum dei* currere, et felicius ad finem cursui debitum pervenire.'

[56]Knowles, pp. 26–29.

food, and showed, at the same time, a willingness to accept reasonable departures from a literal observance of the *Rule* of Saint Benedict.[57] So it becomes clear that Peter wrote his second letter-treatise to Bernard about the distinctions between the orders with quite different intentions than those in his first letter. Now he addressed himself to Bernard in order to promote a reform of the cluniac order, which he must have experienced as a very laborious task.[58]

On the other hand, there are no indications that Bernard shared Peter's concerns about the controversies between the monks of the two orders. It may be that the letter-treatise of 1144 reminded Bernard too much of Peter's earlier letter-treatise, which Bernard had undoubtedly not appreciated. In any case, it is evident that Bernard did not wish to discuss this subject. No answer from Bernard to this letter is preserved, but it is revealing that Peter returned to the problem four years later in another letter to Bernard.[59] In that letter, he intended once more to promote better understanding between the monks of the two orders. He wished to mitigate the rather negative judgment by the Cluniacs about the Cistercians and so further the changes in cluniac monastic customs which he wished to introduce by his reforming statutes.

In these problems of Peter, however, Bernard refused to be really interested. As we shall see, there is no indication that Bernard answered this letter or that he gave attention to the friction between the monks of the orders about which Peter cared so much—at least not until the reviving conflict between the monasteries of Gigny and le Miroir obliged him to do so. In his relations with the Abbot of Cluny, Bernard was primarily concerned, at that time, to avoid any incident.

Thus, he wrote Peter the Venerable a short letter, probably in 1145, to inform him kindly and with religious courtesy about a monk from Cluny who had entered Clairvaux:

> Your son Galcher has now become ours, according to the words: 'All my things are yours and yours are mine' [Jn 17:10]. Let him not be loved any the less for his belonging to us both. But, if possible, let him

[57]Ep 161; *Letters* 1:388–94. Knowles, pp. 22–23.
[58]See the comment of Orderic Vitalis, *Ecclesiastical History*, XIII. 13 (translation Chibnall, p. 427): 'The austere master forgot the precept of Solomon, "Remove not the ancient landmarks which thy fathers have set" (Proverbs, 22, 28), and, rivalling the Cistercians and other seekers after novelties, insisted on his harsh proposals and was ashamed to withdraw immediatedly from his undertakings.' See Constable, 'The Monastic Policy of Peter the Venerable', pp. 119–38; reprinted in his *Cluniac Studies*.
[59]Ep 150, *Letters* 1:367–71.

be loved all the more, and be all the more esteemed by me because he belongs to you, and by you because he belongs to me.[60]

Likewise, to prevent accidental misunderstanding, Bernard involved Peter in the election of Henry of France, a brother of King Louis VII, as bishop of Beauvais in 1149. Before his entrance as a monk at Clairvaux, in 1146 or 1147, Henry had already held, for a period of twenty years, a variety of ecclesiastical positions[61]—a circumstance which, along with his royal descent, may have recommended him for the episcopal dignity. So there were no problems expected about this election. Nevertheless, Bernard sent Peter a letter asking him for his opinion about the matter.

Bernard's letter has not been preserved, but Peter's answer has been, as well as the letter he wrote Henry about the election.[62] In his answer, Peter showed some amazement that the abbot of Clairvaux had asked his support. For, in his opinion, Bernard had enough wisdom and fear of God to make his own decision in consenting to the election. However, it may be that Bernard wrote Peter to receive from him a letter recommending Henry's election.[63]

In later years, the relationship between the abbots was determined by two concerns of a rather different kind, which must be considered. We must give primary attention to the aforementioned conflict between the Cluniacs of Gigny and the Cistercians of le Miroir, which had existed since 1132, but which revived with great violence in 1151. This time both abbots were obliged to intervene directly and seek a conclusive solution because of the extreme actions the monks of Gigny were now applying to force those of le Miroir to pay the stubbornly refused tithes. Secondly, we must treat the strange role Nicholas of Clairvaux played in the direct relations between Bernard and Peter as the somewhat fraudulent secretary of the one abbot and the close friend of the other.

In 1151, Peter and Bernard met at Cluny to reconcile the monks of Gigny and le Miroir. But, since those of Gigny had destroyed several buildings of le Miroir during the winter of 1151–1152, Peter received a letter from Eugene III, in March 1152, after his return from Italy, in which Eugene ordered that, under pain of interdict and excommunication, the monks of Gigny must make restitution. The Pope also expected Peter's

[60]Ep 267; SBOp 8:176. James, *Letters*, p. 378, no. 307.
[61]See *Letters* 2:195–96.
[62]Epp 145 and 146; *Letters* 1:360–62.
[63]Torrell and Bouthillier, p. 99, with n. 64.

assistance so that this satisfaction would be made.[64] Bernard visited Peter once again at Cluny, together with representatives of both monasteries.

After this second meeting, he complained to Eugene III about the meeting which, although it had lasted four days, had accomplished nothing.[65] Because the monks of Gigny offered such a meager compensation for rebuilding what they had destroyed, Peter the Venerable, exasperated by his own monks, paid the sum fixed by Rome in settlement of the claims of le Miroir.[66] This sum, however, the cistercian monastery was obliged to repay when, in 1154, after the death of Saint Bernard and Eugene III, the successor of the latter, Pope Anastatius IV, made a quite different settlement of this longlasting conflict between the houses.[67] The disparity between the decision of Pope Eugene III, a cistercian monk, and the subsequent judgment of his successor in favor of the Cluniacs, gives the impression that, in the reconciliation which both abbots tried to work out, Peter was much more flexible than Bernard. Supported by the privilege of his order concerning monastic tithes, Peter obtained quite easily the better share in the settlement.

More or less comparable with Bernard's rather unbending attitude appears to be his reticent behavior toward Peter in the crisis over the monk Nicholas of Clairvaux, which once more complicated the relations between the abbots. About this affair, which arose as early as the autumn of 1149, the existing information is less scarce. Some correspondence between Peter and Bernard regarding this monk, and also some of Peter's letters to Nicholas and of Nicholas to him, have been preserved. But Nicholas' character is enigmatic, and the account he gave of himself is rather scanty. On the other hand, several scholars have agreed that this ambitious monk had the 'talent for integrating himself with influential patrons' and have recognized 'his pleasure in displaying and cultivating these friendships.'[68]

Before his entrance at Clairvaux, Nicholas had been a benedictine monk at Montièramey, thus wearing a black cowl, and he had served

---

[64]Ph. Jaffé, *Regesta Pontificum Romanorum*, no. 9563; PL 180:1517–18. Some days before Eugene III had communicated his decision to the archbishop of Lyon; Jaffé, no. 9562; PL 180:1518–20.

[65]Ep 283; SBOp 8:197–98.

[66]Constable, 'Cluniac Tithes', p. 620.

[67]*Bullaire de Cluny* (Lyon, 1680) p. 63.

[68]J. Benton, 'The Court of Champagne as a Literary Center', *Speculum* 36 (1961) 555. J. Benton, in *Dictionnaire de Spiritualité* (1982) 11: cols. 255–59. See G. Constable, 'Nicholas of Montièramy and Peter the Venerable', in *Letters* II, 316–30.

Bishop Hato of Troyes as chaplain. In this function, he had already sought contact with the Abbot of Cluny, who, in 1141, wrote him a letter with the opening words *Carissimo filio Nicholao*.[69] But these connections must have ended about that time. Soon, Bernard also came into contact with Nicholas, probably at the Council of Sens, and charged him afterwards as a messenger to carry letters from him, directed against Abelard, to Pope Innocent II and others in Rome.[70]

When Bishop Hato resigned from the diocese of Troyes and retired to Cluny, Nicholas moved from Montièramey to Clairvaux, where he rather soon became one of Bernard's secretaries and a sort of chancellor to his new abbot.[71] Along with his assistance with Bernard's correspondence, he also wrote letters to his own friends, in which he complained of the mass of business with which he was charged.[72] When Peter the Venerable visited Clairvaux in 1149, the former friendship was renewed.

The reason why Bernard wished to have Nicholas at Clairvaux is obvious. He had to organize a new crusade, and that meant much more than oral preaching. The abbot had to send circular letters all over Europe and also write diplomatic, more personal letters to several princes and prelates. With the execution of his task, then, he charged Nicholas, who had indeed great qualifications for these tasks. He was skilled as a literary writer and well acquainted with the organization of a chancellery. He also must have been delighted to enter into correspondence with so many persons of social importance. Moreover, because of the usual epistolary style of those days, Nicholas could cultivate more or less friendly relations with those people. So it must not have been a difficult decision for him to come to Clairvaux and to exchange his black cowl for a white one by becoming a cistercian monk.

The social relations Nicholas was able to cultivate probably flattered his vanity, which also is reflected by his imitation of Bernard's literary gifts in the letters and sermons Nicholas wrote on his own behalf. As the chancellor to Bernard, he also enjoyed great confidence. He was given much freedom in the dispatch of the correspondence of his abbot, who was too occupied to give much attention to the final text of most of

---

[69]Ep 87; *Letters* 1:227.

[70]Constable, *Letters* 2:319.

[71]P. Rassow, 'Die Kanzlei St Bernhards von Clairvaux', *Studien und Mitteilungen zur Geschichte des Benediktinerordens* 34 (1913) 82.

[72]Ep 1, *ad fratres Girardum et Henricum nuncupatoria*: PL 196:1593–94. The correspondence of Nicholas, as published in this volume, contains fifty-seven letters he sent to or accepted from well-known personalities.

his letters. This freedom, already allowed by Bernard to his secretaries, included some risk, as becomes evident from a letter Bernard wrote to Peter the Venerable in the summer of 1149. In this letter, he offered the abbot of Cluny his apologies for the bitter words which were used in one of his letters, because Bernard (and also Nicholas) had omitted to examine its final draft.[73]

Bernard became aware of this painful lack of care thanks to the good relations of his secretary-chancellor with Peter the Venerable, who must have informed Nicholas about it after he had received the letter. Nicholas, in his turn, alerted Bernard, who then sent Peter a short letter to apologize for this lack of attention to his correspondence. From the grandiloquent titles Bernard used in this letter, 'Most Reverend Father and Most Beloved Friend', we can understand that he was rather unhappy about this incident. Peter, from his side, mocked this grandiloquence somewhat and sent an answer five times as long as the letter of apology he had received.[74] So, notwithstanding its kindness, this answer may have intensified Bernard's embarrassment.

Peter probably tried to draw some profit from Bernard's embarrassment, for he wrote him another letter rather soon afterward, in which he returned once more to the difficult relations between cluniac and cistercian monks.[75] As mentioned above, five years before Peter had brought up this matter in a letter-treatise. But Bernard had then refused to discuss those problems with Peter. This time the abbot of Cluny raised the matter of these difficulties between the orders in an even more alarming way. Nevertheless, as we shall see, there are no indications that Bernard then changed his opinion. He refused to discuss this matter with Peter until he was obliged to give direct attention to the renewed conflict between Gigny and le Miroir. Because of this affair, Bernard had, as mentioned, visited Peter twice at Cluny.

In addition to this letter, Peter the Venerable sent another to Clairvaux, addressed to Nicholas. The abbot of Cluny praised him as a monk who did not change the color of his heart when he exchanged his black cowl for a white one. Peter's allusion to the white and black clothing of Cistercians and Cluniacs makes clear that both letters are closely connected. Moreover, Peter wrote Nicholas about the other letter,

---

[73]Ep 387; SBOp 8:355–56. James, *Letters*, pp. 378–79, no. 308.
[74]Ep 149; *Letters* 1:363–66; 2:198–99. See S. R. Maitland, *The Dark Ages*, ed. F. Stokes (London, 1889) pp. 440–42.
[75]See above, n. 59.

which he had addressed to Bernard, urging Nicholas to present it to his abbot:

> Read it to him carefully and studiously, and exhort him as much as you can so that what I have written with a view to love, may be brought to good effect.[76]

Because Bernard was not disposed to inform Peter whether he accepted or did not accept this new invitation to discuss the problems that existed between the orders, he dictated to Nicholas a short reply to Peter. In this letter, Bernard restricted himself to the excuse that he was not able to write according to his feelings because of the multitude of people who had assembled at Clairvaux and with whom he was obliged to deal. As soon as he had more time, he would dictate a letter which would more clearly express his feelings.[77] In a note added to this letter, Nicholas informed Peter that he intended to visit him rather soon. This visit must have been delayed several times, for, in a letter which Peter wrote to Nicholas in autumn of 1150, he mentions his wish that Nicholas should visit him at Cluny before Christmas.[78]

One reason why Peter wished to see Nicholas at Cluny might have been his expectation that Nicholas could become an intermediary between him and Bernard in preparing the discussion he desired. In the letter Peter sent to Bernard in 1150, together with his letter to Nicholas, he asked him to allow his secretary such a visit—with this argument:

> Since it [having messengers from you] very seldom happens, I desire that your holiness will, as soon as possible, visit one who loves you until the Christmas week, through your Nicholas, in whom it appears to me that your spirit in a great measure reposes, while mine does so altogether. I shall see you, holy brother, in him, and hear you by him. And some things which I wish to communicate privately to your wisdom, I shall send by him.[79]

In his answer to Peter, Bernard called this a 'little request'. At that time, so it seems, this request did not embarrass him because Nicholas

---

[76]Ep 151; *Letters* 1:371–72. Maitland, p. 443.

[77]Ep 389; SBOp 8:356–57. James, *Letters*, pp. 379–80, no. 309: 'In the meantime I am scribbling this short note, but when I have more leisure I will write a careful letter expressing my sentiments more clearly.'

[78]Ep 175; *Letters* 1:416–17; 2:216. In Ep 176 (*Letters* 1:417), one can see that Peter wrote to Nicholas at the same time.

[79]Ep 175; *Letters* 1:416–17; 2:216; translation: Maitland, p. 444.

then had no opportunity to visit Peter at Cluny. In any case, Bernard's answer to Peter was correct:

> Let me now reply to the little request with which you concluded your letter. He whom you order sent to you is not present with me, but with the bishop of Auxerre, and so ill that he could not, without great inconvenience, come either to me or to you.[80]

From the letter Nicholas himself wrote to Peter in spring 1151, it becomes clear that Bernard was not inclined to allow him to visit Cluny as long as there was no great necessity to do so. Nicholas tried to construct such a necessity by telling Peter that, when he asked Bernard once more to send him to Cluny, he should speak also about the important manuscripts Nicholas had acquired for Cluny.[81] Some earlier exchange of manuscripts had already taken place between Cluny and Clairvaux through the mediation of Nicholas.[82] About the actual exchange, he told Peter that the prior and the cellerar of Clairvaux were also involved in its preparation. Therefore, he proposed to him to send, in addition to a letter to Bernard, letters to the prior and the cellerar as well, which suggestion Peter followed.[83]

One derives more information than this correspondence contains about the efforts of Nicholas and Peter to meet each other at Cluny from the letter which Peter wrote at the same time to Bernard (March 1151). There it becomes most clear how much the fulfillment of that wish still meant to Peter. From this letter, one can also see that Bernard remained unwilling to concede to Peter's request. He had called his request 'little', but now he required Peter to indicate the reason why he wished Nicholas to visit Cluny—a requirement which evoked Peter's vexation:

> You want to know my reason. Is it not reason enough to see a person whom one loves? He is yours indeed, but he is very dear to me, and are you not pleased with me liking what belongs to you? Does it not please you that one, whom I believe more dear to you than many who belong to you, should be still more dear to me? And what greater proof of true friendship is there than to love what my friend loves?[84]

---

[80]Ep 265; SBOp 8:174–75. James, *Letters*, pp. 377–78, no. 306; translation here from Maitland, p. 445.

[81]Ep 179; *Letters* 1:420–22.

[82]Ep 153, from Nicholas to Peter, October 1149, and Ep 176, from Peter to Nicholas; *Letters* 1:373 and 417, autumn 1150.

[83]Epp 183 and 184, both from March 1151; *Letters* 1:427.

[84]Ep 181; *Letters* 1:423–24; translation: Maitland, p. 447.

Shortly before, in connection with the revival of conflict between the abbeys of Gigny and le Miroir, Bernard had visited Cluny and spoken with Peter. According to this letter, Bernard had, on that occasion, asked what the abbot of Cluny wished to do with Nicholas. In this letter, Peter confessed that he had not given the right answer then, having said that it was not a matter of great importance. Now he remarked that he had responded in this way because Bernard already had posed this question several times without listening to his answer. To this remark Peter added that Bernard could himself imagine the reasons for his request, because he was not demanding anything out of his barns, out of his cellar; nor had he asked gold or silver out of his treasure, if, indeed, Bernard had any:

> What then am I asking? That you should send me Nicholas—and not only now, but whenever I send for him. For I shall take care, as far as possible, not to ask anything that can be reasonably denied or which may in any way annoy you, not to say myself.[85]

Bernard's answer to this letter has not been preserved, and it is doubtful if one were ever written. It was probably not until Easter 1152 before Nicholas found a new opportunity to come to Cluny, at least if he did indeed receive Bernard's permission this time. It is supposed that Nicholas went to Cluny then and that, during his absence from Clairvaux, the forgeries which he had committed with Bernard's letters and seals were discovered.[86] The only actual information we have about these forgeries is a letter in which Bernard complained to Pope Eugene III about his secretary's deception. This letter must date from after May 1152.[87] At that time, Peter had returned from a journey to Italy which had lasted about five months. But from the letters Peter wrote afterwards, in May, to Bernard and Nicholas, we might conclude that the forgeries were then still undiscovered.

It is unknown how much the charges of Bernard against Nicholas were exaggerated or even unjust.[88] But their 'discovery' meant the end

---

[85]*Letters* 1:424; translation: Maitland, p. 448.

[86]Constable, *Letters* 2:327.

[87]Ep 298; SBOp 8:214. Constable, *Letters* 2:326–27. See also the comment of F. Gastaldelli in *San Bernardo Lettere*, parte seconda (Opere VI/2) (Milan, 1987) pp. 278–79.

[88]See Constable, *Letters* 2:327, n. 52. Because of Bernard's complaint, Nicholas was not prosecuted. He became once more a monk at Montièramy and continued to cultivate his relations with influental patrons.

of Nicholas' career at Clairvaux. As Bernard reported to the pope, Nicholas had left the monastery because of this. In later discussions about the meaning of these forgeries and the expulsion of Nicholas, no attention was given to what this event signified for Peter the Venerable. It surely brought an end to the friendship between him and Nicholas. In the last letter belonging to Peter's preserved letter collection, he addressed himself to Nicholas. It was written before Bernard had caused alarm about those forgeries, for Peter still gave Nicholas instructions about the meeting which was to take place at Dijon between the abbots and which was fixed for the third Sunday after Pentecost of that year (June 8, 1152).[89]

Nicholas' expulsion caused a deterioration, if not a rupture, in the relations between the abbots. The manner in which Bernard acted against his secretary was, in any case, effective in preventing the need for a response to Peter's proposals. Because of the close friendship between Peter and Nicholas, Bernard would otherwise have been obliged to enter increasingly into discussions about the improvement of the relations between the Cluniacs and the Cistercians. In the end, Bernard must have experienced this relationship between Peter and Nicholas as a threat, for Nicholas did not support Bernard in his resistance to Peter's requests and even obstructed Bernard's policy in this matter.

Nicholas' independent attitude could have brought Bernard to complain to the pope about the forgeries of his secretary. Another of Bernard's letters to the pope shows, in any case, that for some time he had been aware that forgeries had taken place.[90] On the other hand, Nicholas was the first to be suspected of those forgeries. For the literary activities of this secretary, who had a strong inclination to imitate Bernard's style (and of other authors as well) may already have led to serious objections and complaints about his plagiarism. Moreover, from his own letters to Peter, we know that Nicholas dealt in manuscripts, and those commercial activities were also part of the charges that Bernard brought against him.

So one may ask why Bernard delayed his decision to expel Nicholas from Clairvaux. Obviously, he waited until the friendship of Nicholas

[89]Ep 193; *Letters* 1:448–50.
[90]In Ep 284 (SBOp 8:198–99), Bernard wrote, in 1151 or 1152, to Pope Eugene III: 'I am in peril from false brethern [1 Co 11:26] and many forged letters under my forged seal have come into the hands of many men, and, it is said, what I fear more, that this falseness may even have reached you. I have therefore thrown away that old seal and am now using a new one, as you see, with both my image and my seal.' Constable, *Letters* 2:326. James, *Letters*, pp. 430–31, no. 354.

with Peter the Venerable became a too serious inconvenience. By the means which Bernard followed in settling this affair, he also solved the problem, more and more pressing, that he could no longer ignore or refuse Peter's persistent requests for a discussion about an improvement in the spiritual relations between the two monastic orders, a discussion which Peter saw as a means of reforming the cluniac way of life.

As long as Bernard could avoid entering into such discussions, he was careful to remain on good terms with Peter, whose role as abbot general of the cluniac order Bernard undoubtedly appreciated. For, when there were rumors that Peter, at his meeting with Eugene III at Segny in February 1152 during his italian journey, might ask the pope to relieve him from his charge, Bernard exerted himself to prevent this. About those rumors, which are likely true in that the new statutes Peter introduced met serious opposition within his order, we are informed by the letter Bernard wrote in 1151/1152 to Eugene.

In this letter, beginning with an almost panegyrical appraisal of Peter, Bernard asked the pope to show the abbot of Cluny great favor and to consent to anything for which he might ask in the name of Jesus. The reason why Bernard wrote this recommendation, which Peter did not need, is clearly indicated at the end of the letter:

> Let me explain why I say 'in the name of the Lord Jesus'. It is because I fear and suspect he may ask to be released from the rule of his monastery. And no one who knows him would consider this a petition made in the name of Jesus.[91]

It is clear that Peter himself was not the messenger who delivered this letter addressed to Pope Eugene III. Bernard sent Peter a letter in about November 1151, when Peter was preparing his departure for Italy. This letter is missing, but, from Peter's answer to it written in May 1152, we may suppose that Bernard had comforted and encouraged him to continue his abbatial function. In his answer to Bernard, Peter gave a honest judgment about the moderate way in which he had asserted his authority over his own monks.[92] In this frank account, Peter dared to touch on an affair which until then he always had avoided mentioning in his contacts with Bernard, namely, the consequences for his order when his predecessor Pontius had to abdicate and was condemned in Rome

---

[91]Ep 277; SBOp 8:189–90. James, *Letters*, p. 428, no. 349.
[92]Ep 192; *Letters* 1:443–48; 2:226–30.

after his return to Cluny. Peter admitted to Bernard that, even in that crisis, he had renounced coercion against the many he then lost.[93]

The confidences Peter shared in this letter about his monastic policy may indicate that he thought that the beginning of the discussions with Bernard on behalf of his own cluniac order could be expected rather soon. But those expectations came abruptly to an end as Bernard exposed the forgeries of Nicholas and expelled him from Clairvaux. Bernard's decision must have been extremely disappointing for Peter, and this disappointment may explain why there is no further trace of correspondence between Bernard and Peter. Of course, it may be that they exchanged letters which may have been lost. But, significant for the absence of further relations between the abbots is that, in the *Life of Bernard*, no mention of Peter the Venerable can be found.

In those years, Ernauld of Bonneval, a benedictine abbot himself, wrote the second book of this *Life*, of which a considerable part was composed before Bernard's death, with the purpose of obtaining the canonization of Bernard directly afterward.[94] If Peter had then been considered a close friend or having good relations with Bernard, the author would, undoubtedly, have spoken of Peter when he mentioned Bernard's presence at the Council of Pisa—all the more because Ernauld did record that Matthew of Albano was one of Bernard's companions on the journey the abbot had to make to Milan directly after the close of the Council.[95]

Moreover, after the death of Bernard, the mention of Peter's name in the *Life of Bernard* might have been considered at the roman curia as a suggestion that one could ask Peter's agreement with the request for canonization. On the other hand, however, to obtain Bernard's canonization, the authors were wise not to mention any person still alive who could be an unfavorable witness, at least in so far as that witness was respected by the ecclesiastical society of those days. Therefore, the absence of the

---

[93]*Letters* 1:446: 'Assuetus sum pati, assuetus et indulgere. Declarat hoc, quod tamen non superbe iactatio, de Pontiano scismate, in quod cum innumeri declinaverint, ac nefanda et in ordine monastico inaudita fecerint, nunquam gladium meum, nunquam mucronem, nunquam frameam experti sunt, vix unquam asperum ab ore meo verbum audierunt.'

[94]A. H. Bredero, *Études sur la 'Vita Prima' de Saint Bernard* (Rome, 1960). Bredero, 'Les Vies de saint Bernard', in *Actes du colloque international pour le IXe centeniare de la naissnce de saint Bernard, 1090–1990* (Lyon, forthcoming in 1991).

[95]*Vita prima s. Bernardi*, lib. II, cap. II. 8.

name of Peter in this *Life* indicates rather clearly the absence of good relations between the abbots after June 1152.

Let us now sum up the results of this analytical interpretation of the preserved letters exchanged between Peter the Venerable and Bernard.[96] After the abbot of Clairvaux had interfered, in 1124/1125, with his open letter to Robert of Châtillon and his *Apology* to William of Saint Thierry, in the internal schism at Cluny which followed at the forced abdication of Abbot Pontius of Melgueil, Peter the Venerable addressed a letter-treatise to Bernard about 1127. This was really intended for the priors and subpriors of the cluniac houses as an attempt to re-establish the observance of the prescribed monastic customs. By this address to Bernard, Peter pretended that the objections against those customs and the wishes to introduce a reform of those customs had not been urged from inside his own order but only by the Cistercians, thus from the outside, as if there had been within Cluny no sympathy for and adherence to the monastic reform movement of those days.

This letter, which made Bernard more or less a scapegoat, signified, on the other hand, that Bernard could no longer be suspected of sympathies for Abbot Pontius, who after his condemnation had died without being reconciled with the Church. Peter's presentation of Bernard's role offered Bernard the opportunity to enter into direct relation with Matthew of Albano, who was at that time the papal legate in France.

The direct consequence of this was that, in the growing antagonism which already divided the roman cardinals, Bernard could freely join the side of the Cardinal-chancellor Haimeric, with whom he already had relations of personal friendship. In this way, Bernard became accepted by the cluniac leaders, at the beginning of the schism of Anacletus, as representing the french Church in proclaiming its acceptance of Pope Innocent II as the legitimate candidate. The drawback of Peter's letter turned out to be that Peter and Bernard afterward felt obliged to remain on guard against the other.

---

[96]In this analysis, we leave out of consideration Epp 364 and 521 (SBOp 8:318–19 and 483–84), by which, in 1150, Bernard asked Peter the Venerable to be present at the meetings of Chartres and Laon held after the disaster of the Second Crusade. See the comments on this question by Gastaldelli, *Lettere* 2:182–85, 440–41, and 696–97. Furthermore, we have not dealt with a charter, published by G. Hüffer, *Der heilige Bernard von Clairvaux: Vorstudien* (Münster, 1886) p. 215. This charter, dictated by Peter and addressed to Bernard, concerns a grant of rights on landed property to Clairvaux by the canons of Longovado because of the mediation of Bernard in a conflict they had had with the prior of Arcu. This charter lacks any precision in dating, and there is also insufficient information about the houses involved.

About 1137, after they had met each other at the Council of Pisa, Peter wrote Bernard a very flattering letter which may have accompanied his spoken request for Bernard's support in the controversy about the tithes which the cistercian abbey of le Miroir refused to pay to the cluniac house, Gigny. Bernard did not respond to this proposal.

After Bernard's return to France and this first effort of Peter to enter into good relationship, Bernard rejected the abbot of Cluny in a rather blunt way by his opposition to the election of a cluniac candidate to the diocese of Langres. He managed to have the pope annul the nomination of this cluniac bishop because of rumors about his character, and, in the end, Bernard obtained the bishopric for his own prior. Against the method Bernard had used to annul the election, he later received a letter from Peter the Venerable, in which Bernard was reproached for having believed only the information given by some enemies of Cluny without taking pains to ask Peter's opinion.

It may be that Bernard reacted to Peter's criticism by sending him a letter about his difficulties with the monks of Saint-Bertin. The community of this monastery wished to withdraw itself from Cluny, because its incorporation within the cluniac order had been forced. In this letter, Bernard asked Peter to moderate his attitude toward those monks.

The next point of friction between the abbots, of which we are informed, regarded the aftermath of the condemnation of the doctrines of Abelard at the Council of Sens. With the help of the abbot of Cîteaux, Peter the Venerable succeeded in reconciling Bernard with Abelard, at least formally. As a consequence, the personal condemnation of Abelard as a heretic, urged by Bernard at the roman curia, did not follow.

When, about 1144/1145, Peter the Venerable prepared the introduction of his reform statutes for the cluniac houses, he needed some support from Bernard for the realization of this reform. He wished to enter into a discussion with Bernard which would lead to a better understanding between the two monastic orders, and therefore he began to exchange letters with Bernard, written with great courtesy and later understood as indicating their close friendship. Peter followed this correspondence with a new letter-treatise, addressed to Bernard, which also circulated in the cluniac houses.

Although Peter the Venerable aimed, at this time, to further good relations between the orders, Bernard ignored his proposal and did not enter into any discussion of the subject. It may be that he did so because of some unpleasant reminiscences of that other letter-treatise he had received. In any case, Peter's initiatives to gain Bernard's help in reforming the cluniac way of monastic life remained without result.

Peter's next attempt to obtain Bernard's support for his endeavors toward finding acceptance at Cluny for the introduction of his reform statutes seemed more promising when Nicholas of Montièramey entered Clairvaux and there became Bernard's most important secretary. Between Nicholas and Peter a mutual friendship developed. Peter hoped to find in Nicholas an intermediary in gaining Bernard's interest for his efforts to reform the cluniac order.

Because of this, Peter asked, and even urged, Bernard to allow his secretary to visit him at Cluny. But these proposals were ignored or diplomatically pushed aside. As, in the end, it seemed no longer possible for Bernard to refuse Peter's repeated requests, he forced Nicholas to leave Clairvaux because of the forgeries Nicholas had committed in his function as secretary. Bernard's action had less to do with Nicholas' behavior than with the threat which his friendship with Peter the Venerable might have for himself.

Nicholas' expulsion also signified the end of Peter's long enduring efforts, because of which he had written several very courteous letters to Bernard and in which he usually presented himself as being his friend. The abbot of Cluny was in need of Bernard's help in realizing his efforts to reform his own monastic order. Bernard, on his part, stubbornly ignored or pushed aside the appeal for help. When, in the end, the abbot of Clairvaux could no longer present some pretext for his refusal, he used as his ultimate denial the exposure of Nicholas' forgeries.

This exposure, however, also brought Bernard's relationship with Peter the Venerable to an end. It is at least worth noting that, as far as we know, he sent no letter or any other sign to Bernard during his last illness and that, in the *Life of Bernard*, Peter the Venerable did not receive any mention. So it seems that the courteous relationship that these abbots had usually maintained for so many years might have ended more than a year before August 20, 1153, that is to say, before the day on which the earthly existence of Bernard came to its end. This was caused by the consequences inherent in an earlier controversy with Peter, a controversy which had taken place before the abbots had really become acquainted with each other.

ABSTRACTS

Les témoignages d'amitié et les assurances de sentiments dévoués insérés par saint Bernard et Pierre le Vénérable dans les lettres qu'ils échangeaient ne reflètent pas le vrai caractère de leur relation. Celle-ci fut très complexe. Depuis l'intervention de Bernard, vers 1124/1125, dans une controverse interne à Cluny et l'habile réponse que Pierre lui adressa en 1127 environ, ils restèrent mutuellement sur leurs gardes. L'information que nous livre leur correspondance n'est pas fiable à moins de connaître le véritable contexte de la rédaction de chaque lettre. C'est la méfiance de Bernard qui mit en échec les efforts déployés par Pierre pour obtenir le soutien de l'abbé de Clairvaux en vue de la réforme du monachisme clunisien. Quand enfin Pierre rechercha son appui par l'intermédiaire de son secrétaire Nicolas de Clairvaux, Bernard expulsa ce dernier de son monastère (en 1152). Il semble que cet incident fut cause d'une rupture définitive entre les deux abbés.

The expressions of friendship and assurances of mutual devotion inserted by Saint Bernard and Peter the Venerable in their letters to one another do not reflect the true character of their relationship, which was a very complex one. Since Bernard's intervention in a controversy internal to Cluny around 1124/1125 and the adroit answer which Peter sent him *c*. 1127, they remained wary of one another. The information furnished by their correspondence is not reliable unless one knows the true context of each letter. It was Bernard's distrust which caused the failure of Peter's efforts to secure the backing of the abbot of Clairvaux in reforming cluniac monasticism. When Peter finally sought his support through his secretary Nicholas of Clairvaux, Bernard expelled the latter from his monastery (in 1152). This incident seems to have caused a final break between the two abbots.

Die Bezeugungen ihrer Freundschaft und die Versicherungen ihrer gegenseitigen Hochschätzung, die der heilige Bernhard und Petrus Venerabilis in ihre gegenseitige Korrespondenz eingestreut haben, spiegeln nicht die wahre Beschaffenheit ihrer Beziehung wieder. Diese war sehr komplex. Seit Bernhards Einmischung etwa 1124/1125 in eine interne Kontroverse in Cluny und der geschickten Antwort, die Peter ihm etwa 1127 darauf gab, standen sie einander distanziert gegenüber. Die Auskunft, die uns ihre Korrespondenz gibt, ist nicht verlässlich, wenn man die wahren Zusammenhänge nicht kennt, in denen die Briefe redigiert wurden. Gleichzeitig war das Mißtrauen Bernhards daran schuld, daß manche Versuche Peters, die Unterstützung des anderen zu erhalten, um das cluniazensische Mönchtum zu reformieren, fehlschlugen. Als Peter schließlich durch die Vermittlung von Bernhards Sekretär Nikolaus von Clairvaux Hilfe suchte, schloß Bernhard diesen 1152 aus seinem Kloster aus. Es scheint, daß durch dieses Ereignis die Beziehung der beiden Äbten für immer zerbrochen wurde.

BERNARDUS SCHOLASTICUS: THE CORRESPONDENCE OF BERNARD OF CLAIRVAUX AND HUGH OF SAINT VICTOR ON BAPTISM

Hugh Feiss, OSB
Mount Angel Abbey

BERNARD'S LETTER 77 is interesting for the light it casts on Bernard's relations with the canons regular of Saint Victor and even more so for what it shows of his relations both with theologians of his generation and with nascent scholasticism.[1] Hence, this paper will first summarize Bernard's connections with Saint Victor, then examine his letter to Hugh of Saint Victor on baptism and Hugh's use of that letter. And, finally, I shall indicate several conclusions on Bernard's relations with nascent scholasticism.

BERNARD AND THE CANONS REGULAR OF SAINT VICTOR

William of Champeaux founded Saint Victor in 1108; in 1113 he became bishop of Châlons. When he became worried about Bernard's health, he took an active hand in ordering Bernard's life;[2] when some recruits to Saint Victor wanted to join Clairvaux, he supported them.[3] At his death in 1121, William was buried at Clairvaux in the habit of the canons of Saint Victor.

---

[1]My thanks to Fr. Bruno Becker, OSB, for his careful proofreading.
[2]E. Vacandard, *Vie de Saint Bernard* (Paris: Gabalda, 1927) 1:68, 76–78.
[3]Henry-Bernard de Warren, 'Bernard et l'Ordre de Saint Victor', in *Bernard de Clairvaux*, Commission d'histoire de l'Ordre de Cîteaux 3 (Paris: Editions Alsatia, [1953]) pp. 310–311.

Etienne of Senlis, bishop of Paris from 1124, on several occasions found support from Saint Bernard and refuge at Clairvaux when his reforming activities elicited violent reactions from his opponents. Most notably, in August 1133, Etienne took refuge with Bernard after Thomas, the prior of Saint Victor and a member of Etienne's entourage, was murdered. Bernard took up his pen on behalf of the bishop and the murdered Thomas.[4] Years later Bernard asked the canons of Saint Geneviève to share a water supply with the canons of Saint Victor.[5] On another occasion he wrote Saint Victor, asking them to give hospitality to young Peter the Lombard.[6]

BERNARD'S LETTER 77 TO HUGH OF SAINT VICTOR

Around or slightly after 1125, Hugh of Saint Victor wrote to Saint Bernard asking his opinion on four questions.[7] We do not now have Hugh's letter, but we do have Bernard's answer, his Letter 77, sometimes called his treatise *De baptismo*.[8] Ludwig Ott has analyzed Bernard's letter thoroughly in his study of theological letter-writing in the twelfth century,[9] and we can still learn more from it.

Bernard says that his responses are brief, but he is sure that Hugh can fill them out with convincing arguments and pertinent authorities (*rationes certas et congruas auctoritates*).[10] Several times in his letter Bernard refers to reason and authority as his guides; he will avoid novelties and follow the doctrines and words of the Fathers.[11] He also mentions once that in his initial letter Hugh has already provided considerable argumentation on at least one question.[12]

Hugh's four questions, Bernard says, were raised by someone whose name Hugh did not mention. Bernard is rather glad about this because

---

[4]On this incident, see Jean Châtillon, *Théologie, spiritualité et métaphysique dans l'oeuvre oratoire d'Achard de Saint-Victor*, Etudes de Philosophie Médiévale, 58(Paris: Vrin, 1969) p. 68 and the literature cited there in note 55; also de Warren, pp. 314–322.

[5]de Warren, p. 325.

[6]Ep 410; SBOp 8:391.

[7]Damien van den Eynde, *Essai sur la succession et la date des écrits de Hugues de Saint-Victor* (Rome: Pont. Athen. Antonianum, 1960) pp. 132–37.

[8]Ep 77; SBOp 7:184–200.

[9]Ludwig Ott, *Untersuchungen zur theologischen Briefliteratur der Frühscholastik unter besonderer Berücksichtigung des Viktorinerkreises*, BGPTMA 34 (Münster: Aschendorff, 1937) pp. 495–548.

[10]Ep 77; SBOp 7:184, 11–12.

[11]Ep 77 (SBOp 7:184, 18–19); 77.2 (SBOp 7:186, 11–15); 77.6 (SBOp 7:189, 12–13); 77.18 (SBOp 7:198, 19–21); 77.19 (SBOp 7:198, 22).

[12]Ep 77.11; SBOp 7:192, 27–28.

this enables him to argue the issues without involving persons.[13] In fact, it seems quite clear that the person whose opinions Hugh is opposing in the first three questions is Abelard himself, or someone from his milieu. Abelard taught at the Paraclete at Quincey between 1122 and 1127, and from these years dates the *Sic et non*. In this work, question 106 bears the title 'That without baptism of water no one can be saved, and to the contrary.' This question 106 and some of those which follow[14] raise, but do not resolve, the issues which prompted Hugh's first question. Abelard begins by citing a great number of scriptural and patristic authorities urging the necessity of baptism for salvation. Then he cites some which allow an exception for 'those who though unbaptised, pour out their blood in the Catholic Church' (q. 106, p. 343, lines 46–48), before citing authorities regarding the fate of infants who were not baptized. Subsequent questions deal with the efficacy of circumcision in Old Testament times (q. 109) and the baptism of John (q. 114).

Hugh's second question, regarding the extent of faith before the time of Christ, recalls Abelard's discussion of the virtues of the gentiles in *Theologia christiana*, one version of which seems to have been written before 1125:[15]

Therefore, since the Lord announced the contents of the catholic faith to the Jews through the prophets and to the gentiles through their philosophers or seers, both Jews and gentiles are rendered inexcusable if, having these teachers in certain matters for the salvation of their souls, whose foundation is faith, they failed to listen to them. In fact, many of the gentiles, and some of the Jews, instructed again by the teachers of their people, accepted in faith the Holy Trinity, and so were joined together like two sides in the one body of the Church (1.136, ed. Buytaert, p. 131, lines 1843–1851).

Hugh's third question, regarding sins of ignorance, points to Abelard's much later *Ethics*:[16]

However, if one asks whether those persecutors of the martyrs or of Christ sinned in what they believed to be pleasing to God, of

---

[13]Ep 77 (SBOp 7:184, 113–116); Ep 77.1 (SBOp 7:185, 4).

[14]*Sic et non*, qq. 106–114, ed. Blanche B. Boyer and Richard McKeon (Chicago: University of Chicago Press, 1977) pp. 341–71.

[15]Petri Abaelardi, *Opera theologica*, II, ed. Eligius Buytaert, CCCM 12 (Turnhout: Brepols, 1969) 1.136 (pp.130–31); see also 2.112–15 (pp. 182–84). For the date of this work, see pp. 43–50. The translation is my own.

[16]Peter Abelard, *Ethics*, ed. and trans. D. W. Luscombe (Oxford: Clarendon, 1979) pp. xxxiv-xxxv, 55–67. Note the discussion on pages 62–63, footnote 1.

whether they could without sin have forsaken what they thought should definitely not be forsaken, assuredly, according to our earlier description of sin as contempt of God or consenting to what one believes should not be consented to, we cannot say that they have sinned in this, nor is anyone's ignorance a sin or even the unbelief without which no one can be saved. (Tr. Luscombe, 55–57).

Bernard will argue that in condemning to hell those contemporaries of Christ who did not know of his conversation with Nicodemus, the un-named theologian was asserting a sin of ignorance and thus contradicting his position on question three. However, Abelard goes on to make a distinction which seems to respond to this objection:

Moreover, just as what they did through ignorance or even ignorance itself is not said to be properly sin, that is, contempt of God, neither is unbelief, even though this necessarily blocks the entry to eternal life for adults now using reason. It is sufficient for damnation not to believe in the Gospel, to be ignorant of Christ, not to receive the sacraments of the Church, even though this occurs not so much through wickedness as through ignorance. (Tr. Luscombe, 63).

The fourth question is something quite different, a novel opinion broached by Bernard in one of his sermons in praise of the Blessed Virgin;[17] this opinion has bothered some people, and Hugh asks Bernard for a clarification.

Abelard had been the student and then the adversary of William of Champeaux.[18] He was certainly not unknown to Hugh.[19] Whether Bernard really did not know the identity of this unknown 'inventor of novelties'[20] whose opinions he was refuting is impossible to say. Nor do we know if Hugh knew of Abelard's teaching through rumor, through reports of Abelard's students, or through first-hand knowledge of Abelard's texts. In his response, Bernard does make use of patristic texts included in the *Sic et non*, and Hugh uses some of the same texts in his *De sacramentis*.[21]

---

[17]Miss 1.2; SBOp 4:15, 2.

[18]Jean Châtillon, 'Abélard et les écoles', in *Abélard et son temps* (Paris: Les Belles Lettres, 1981) pp. 138–46; reprinted with the same pagination in Jean Châtillon, *D'Isidore de Séville à saint Thomas d'Aquin* (London: Variorum, 1985).

[19]D. E. Luscombe, *The School of Peter Abelard* (Cambridge: Cambridge University Press, 1969) pp. 183–97.

[20]Ep 77.7 (SBOp 7:189, 14–15); 77.11 (SBOp 7:192, 29–193, 2); 77.16 (196, line 18).

[21]Bernard refers to six patristic *auctoritates* in his response to the first two questions: (1) Ambrose, *De obitu Valentiniani* 51, CSEL 73, p. 354; (2) Augustine, *De baptismo*

Bernard's responses to Hugh's first two questions clarify the relationship between baptism and salvation; they occupy all but five of the eighteen pages of the letter as it appears in the critical edition. I shall concentrate on these two questions because Hugh deals with the issues they raise in his comprehensive study of theology, the *De sacramentis*, which he seems to have written in the 1130s. As far as I have been able to ascertain, Hugh does not mention the other two questions in his works. To help highlight the procedures Bernard uses in his letter to Hugh, my translation of the letter is appended, in which a detailed outline is given in the headings.

Bernard's response to question one is long and elaborate. His refutation seems to take the form of four counter proposals, for each of which he provides arguments. First, in counter thesis 1A, he establishes that the thesis, no salvation without baptism, is inadmissible. This he argues on the basis of (1) what we know about God's benevolence (argument one), (2) the biblical teaching about faith (argument two), and (3) what reason tells us about the different kinds of divine commands (argument three). Having thus argued against the unnamed thinker's thesis, he proceeds in three steps (counter theses 1B, 1C, 1D) to establish an alternative thesis. The steps are arranged in chronological order: the first concerns the ancients before the era of baptism; the second, those living between the time of Jesus' private conversation with Nicodemus and the public proclamation of the obligation to be baptized; the third, those living since the baptismal requirement was promulgated.

So, Bernard's second counter thesis (1B) is that, in ancient times before the era of baptism, other remedies for original sin were available: circumcision for Abraham and his descendants, faith and sacrifices for the gentiles, the faith of their parents for children.

Bernard's third counter thesis (1C) is that the command to be baptized did not begin to bind at the time of Jesus' private conversation

---

contra Donatistas 4.29, ed. M. Petschenig, CSEL 51 (Vienna: Tempsky, 1908) p. 257, (3) Augustine, *Retractiones* 1.25, ed. Pius Knöll, CSEL 36 (Vienna: Tempsky, 1902) pp. 124–25; (4) Augustine, *Quaestiones in Heptateuchen* 3.84, ed. J. Fraipont, CCSL 33 (Turnhout: Brepols, 1958) pp. 227–28; (5) Gregory, *Hom. in Ezech.* 2.5.2, ed. M. Adriaen, CCSL 142 (Turnhout: Brepols, 1971) p. 276, 55–62; (6) Bede, *Hom.* 2.15, ed. D. Hurst, CCSL 122 (Turnhout: Brepols, 1955) p. 281, 38–46. Three of these Abelard had cited in *Sic et non* q. 106: (2) in n. 11 (p. 343, 59–344, 75; (3) in n. 14 (p. 345, 108–111); and (1) in n. 22 (p. 347, 173–83). Hugh cites (2) and (3) in *De sacramentis* 2.6.7 (PL 176:453D–54B), and (5) in his extended quotation from Bernard's letter (PL 176:337D). Bernard says that Hugh cited (6) in his initial letter asking for Bernard's opinions (Ep 77.15; SBOp 7:196, 5–13).

with Nicodemus, but only became operative when it was promulgated. Bernard pursues several lines of argument in support of this counter thesis: (1) it would be an insult to the old law if the command of circumcision were abrogated abruptly, before its replacement was effective; (2) there would be no saving remedy for the thousands of Christ's contemporaries who lived between the abrogation of circumcision and the promulgation of baptism: 'Was God sleeping then, and during it there was no one who could redeem and save?'[22] Therefore, baptism became obligatory, and the old law's remedies abrogated, not when Nicodemus spoke with Jesus (Jn 3:5), nor even when Christ commanded the apostles to go teach all nations (Mt 28:19), but when there could be no excuse for someone to be ignorant of that precept. Moreover, for infants and others without the use of reason the old sacraments remained valid until they were expressly forbidden.

Finally, in counter thesis four (1D), Bernard argues that even centuries after the time of the apostles there could be what theology later came to call baptism of desire. The situation is this: an adult has put off baptism, but now she wants to be baptized, but she dies before she can receive the sacrament. She has faith, hope, and charity, and it does not seem right that she be denied salvation just because she lacks an opportunity to be baptized with water, provided of course, that she does not despise the outward sacrament.

For this thesis, Bernard gives three arguments. First, he appeals to authority by quoting passages from Ambrose and Augustine, who support his thesis. Secondly, he argues from reason. (1) Mk 16:16a says: 'Whoever believes and is baptized will be saved', while the next half-verse (16b) says: 'Whoever does not believe will be condemned.' This leaves open the fate of those who believe but are not baptized. Everyone grants that one sub-group of this class—the martyrs—are saved. What saves them is not their suffering but their faith. (2) To deny that faith can save apart from actual reception of the sacrament is to make faith very weak. (3) God can know one's interior state of faith without the visible proof of martyrdom; so, if he rewards the unbaptized martyr's faith, he can do the same for the faith of the unbaptized non-martyr. (4) To save such people, rather than condemn them, is also more befitting a God who is love. (5) A person who does not receive the sacrament when he can shows that he is not truly and fully faithful. (6) Unbaptized

----

[22]Ep 77.5; SBOp 7:188, 18–19.

children cannot be saved without receiving baptism; if they are saved by receiving baptism, it is in virtue of the faith of others.

So much for Bernard's treatment of the first question. His response to the second, regarding the extent of faith before the time of Christ, is shorter. He says that there is not much he can add to the points which Hugh made in his letter. He proceeds then to add two arguments. The first is short and *ad hominem*: the person who advanced this thesis is simply curious for novelty; he wishes to be different. The second argument is much more complex. The thesis (P) that the just of the Old Testament knew as much about the events of Christ's redemption as Christians do implies that either (Q) the number of elect in the old dispensation was limited to a small number who received a comprehensive private revelation of the saving events to come, or that (R) a large number received such a revelation. Logically, then, for (P) to be true, either (Q) or (R) must be true. (Q) is untrue, because it is not compatible with God's generosity. What then of (R)? Bernard offers four arguments against (R). (1) If before the christian era the many knew all that christian believers know, then the gospel brings nothing new, which is contrary to the New Testament. (2) It also contradicts Jesus, who said there had not arisen a greater than John the Baptist. (3) Numerous other scriptural and patristic texts suggest that knowledge of the events of salvation was rare in the Old Testament, but became more widely shared after the coming of Christ. (4) An argument from analogy: just as today there are many Christians who know little about the life to come, although they believe in it and hope to attain it, so before Christ many hoped for God's redemption even though they did not know what form it would take.

HUGH OF SAINT VICTOR'S USE OF BERNARD'S LETTER 77

Such were Bernard's answers to Hugh's first two questions. The effort Bernard expended to answer Hugh was not in vain. Hugh incorporated many of Bernard's ideas and even many of his exact words into the *De sacramentis*.

Hugh's treatment of the various aspects of the first question occurs in two separate places in the *De sacramentis*, first in regard to the institution of sacraments in general (1.9.5), then in connection with the sacrament of baptism (2.6.4–5). In regard to the sacraments in general, Hugh states a basic principle: 'In relation to God, their author, the institution of the sacraments is something he arranged [and could have arranged differently]; in relation to the obedient human being, their institution is a matter of necessity.'[23] God can save human beings without the sacraments, but human beings who have contempt for the sacraments cannot be saved.

In support of his thesis, Hugh argues: (1) that people are saved without the sacraments is clear from the Bible; (2) that God can thus save people is clear from his power: 'Either deny that [God's] power [*virtus*] can be present where there is no sacrament, or, if you admit such power, deny the damnation.'[24]

There are two situations in which people are saved without the sacraments: (1) if they lived before God instituted the sacraments as obligatory, or (2) if they did not have the opportunity to receive a sacrament which they wished to receive. In either of these cases, those having the reality (*res*) of the sacrament—right faith and true charity—are not damned for not receiving the sacrament.

An example is baptism. If the water of baptism can save those who do not believe, faith can surely save those who do not have the opportunity to be baptized. Someone may ask: how then do you interpret John 3:5 ('Unless one be born again of water and the Holy Spirit, he will not enter the kingdom of heaven')? Hugh replies: How do you interpret John 11:25–26 ('Whoever believes in me . . . will not see death forever')?

In chapter 4 of his discussion of baptism in book 2, part 6 of the *De sacramentis*, Hugh asks: 'When was the sacrament of baptism instituted?' He cites four opinions: (1) at Christ's conversation with Nicodemus, (2) when Christ sent the apostles to baptize, (3) when John the Baptist began to baptize, (4) at Christ's death on the cross. Contrary to all of these, Hugh says it seems preferable to say that John the Baptist, Jesus, and his disciples first baptized to accustom people to the practice; then it was generally instituted when preachers were sent into the whole world to baptize. In developing this suggestion, Hugh distinguishes three eras (which is characteristic of his way of thinking both in its historical structure and in its use of a triad): (1) before baptism was instituted, only circumcision existed as a sacrament of redemption; (2) after baptism was instituted and promulgated, it alone brought salvation; (3) in between, both baptism and circumcision existed—circumcision so it could be reverently phased out, baptism so it could be gradually introduced. This period came to an end with Galatians 5:2 ('If you are circumcised, Christ profits you not at all').[25]

---

[23]*De sac.* 1.9.5 (PL 176:323C): 'Institutio sacramentorum quantum ad Deum auctorem dispensationis est, quantum vero ad hominem obedientem necessitatis.'

[24]*De sac.* 1.9.5 (PL 176:324D).

[25]Compare Bernard, Ep 77.6 (SBOp 7:189, 1), which may have this text in mind.

The next chapter (*De sac* 2.6.5) argues that a person began to be obligated to receive baptism at the moment when, after its institution, he was commanded to be baptized (for example, the apostles just before the ascension), or, before its institution, when he was counseled to receive the sacrament (for example, Nicodemus). All became obligated when they heard the apostles' preaching. Hugh, like Bernard,[26] thinks that Psalm 19[18]:5 means that there is no one who has not heard their preaching: 'their sound went to all the earth, their voices to the ends of the world.'

In *De sacramentis* 2.6.7, Hugh asks whether, since the time baptism was commanded, anyone has been saved other than through actual reception of the sacrament. He notes that some raise this question out of either curiosity or studiousness. In response, (1) he cites the authorities upholding a negative answer: for example, John 3:5 and Mark 16:16a ('Whoever believes in me and is baptized will be saved'). But he counters this with the statement that martyrs who die without baptism are surely saved, even if Scripture does not explicitly say so. Martyrs are touched by the power of the sacrament, so that they are willing to give their lives, a greater thing than to receive water. (2) Biblical texts like Matthew 10:32 and John 11:25–26 indicate that where there is faith there is salvation. Similarly, in Mark 16:16b, Jesus goes on to say: 'Whoever does not believe will be condemned.' (3) Even stronger evidence is provided by the authority of Augustine. (4) Hugh poses a dilemma: 'You must therefore either (S) confess true faith and confession of heart can take the place of baptism in necessity, or (T) you must show how true faith and unfeigned charity can exist without there being salvation as well. Unless, of course, (U) you wish to say no one can have true faith and true charity who is not going to have the visible sacrament of water. By what reason or authority you might prove this I do not know.'[27] For additional arguments, Hugh refers the reader to the *De sacramentis* 1.9.5, which was analyzed above.

The second question regarding the extent of faith needed for salvation in pre-christian times is treated in *De sacramentis* 1.10, Hugh's treatise on faith. In chapter 6 of this part, he raises the question whether faith grew. He manifests some hostility toward people who deny it. There are those, he says, whose form of piety makes them impious toward God, whose thoughts go beyond what is in the truth and so offend against the truth. Such are those who say that one is not a believer who (a) believes

[26]Ep 77.2; SBOp 7:186, 20–23.
[27]*De sac.* 2.6.7 (PL 176:454BC).

something differently than he should because he cannot understand it properly, or (b) does not believe everything because he is ignorant of how much is to be believed. Those who say this think that Christ's birth, suffering, resurrection, and ascension were known to all the just and faithful since the beginning of the world, just as these events, now past, are known to us. They cite a passage from [Pseudo-] Augustine[28] in support of their views.

Hugh says that, if this is so, then either in ancient times salvation was very rare or the number of the perfect was very great. Both alternatives are unacceptable. Here, without acknowledging it, Hugh proceeds to quote Bernard's letter for three pages word for word, thus making his own the elaborate dilemma Bernard formulates in his second argument against this thesis. Hugh also adds a few arguments of his own: (1) When the Lord personally taught his disciples about the mystery of his person, they could not understand it; are we to think that the just of the Old Testament did? (2) If the details about the redeemer were revealed to all the good, the wicked would have heard of them also. (3) If the details of the redeemer were revealed interiorly by the Spirit to all the just before Christ, they were better than those who came after and had to learn by external preaching. 'Therefore, consulting correct faith, we confess what is more conformable to salvation and nearer the truth: just as we recognize that knowledge of things which pertain to faith differs in the same age according to the capacity of different people, so in the succession of ages from the beginning faith grows in the faithful by certain increments.'[29] Faith is the same, but knowledge of the faith (*cognitio fidei*) differs and grows.

CONCLUSION: BERNARD AND NASCENT SCHOLASTICISM

First, around 1125, Hugh of Saint Victor, one of the premier theologians of his time, wrote asking Saint Bernard for his opinion on three propositions associated with the school of Abelard and his explanation of a statement in one of his own works. That Hugh wrote Bernard to ask his opinion on theological issues which were being discussed in the schools indicates that Hugh had considerable respect for Bernard's theological prowess. Hugh's respect for Bernard's theological acumen is even more evident in his use of Bernard's ideas and his tacit quotation

[28]Gennadius, *De ecclesiasticis dogmatibus* 74 (PL 58:997CD).
[29]*De sac.* 1.10.6 (PL 176:339B).

of a considerable portion of Bernard's letter in his *De sacramentis*.[30] Alternatively, one might surmise that what Hugh respected was not so much Bernard's thought as his ecclesiastical influence, but, if that were so, one would think that Hugh would have asked for something more than Bernard's opinions and would have quoted Bernard by name.

Secondly, although there seems to be a certain grudging tone in the introduction to Bernard's letter, thereafter he seems to take up the task with enough enthusiasm to reply at some length to Hugh's questions. He would hardly have done so if he had not held in esteem both Hugh and the scholastic enterprise in which masters like Hugh and Abelard were engaged.[31]

Thirdly, called on to address theological questions which had arisen in the schools, Bernard employs the techniques of nascent scholasticism with impressive skill. He invokes the authority of Scripture and the Fathers; he uses reason to solve apparent contradictions among authorities, to create dilemmas, to drive home arguments, and to rebut objections. Neither Bernard nor Hugh achieved the dispassionate, formal rhetoric of high scholasticism; neither is above a clever *ad hominem* argument. Bernard does not attempt to draw any immediate spiritual fruit from the opinions he supports. In this work he is content to argue for the truth with the considerable resources of logic and erudition at his disposal.

And so a great champion of monastic theology—meditative and contemplative, experiential, symbolic, transcendent, seeking to move the heart as well as the head, literary and warmly rhetorical, rooted in Scripture and liturgy—shows himself in this one work at least a skilled practitioner of the theology of the schools—logical, speculative, impersonal, and argumentative. That we can recognize this almost unique moment in Bernard's theological career we owe to Jean Leclercq, who has taught us to recognize the differences and the validity of these two kinds of theology.[32]

---

[30]Jean Châtillon, 'L'influence de S. Bernard sur la pensée scolastique au XIIe et au XIIIe siècle', in *Saint Bernard théologien. Actes du Congrès de Dijon (15–19 septembre 1953)*, ASOC 9 (1953) pp. 268–88. Reprinted with same pagination in Châtillon, *D'Isidore*. See also John R. Sommerfeldt, 'Bernard of Clairvaux and Scholasticism', *Papers of the Michigan Academy of Science, Art and Letters* 48 (1965) 265–277.

[31]It is possible that Bernard had someone research or write his reply, but, in the absence of any evidence for that, it seems proper to assume Bernard wrote Ep 77 himself.

[32]Jean Leclercq, *Love of Learning and the Desire for God* (New York: Fordham University Press, 1961) especially chapters 4, 5, 8, and 9, and 'The Renewal of Theology', in Robert L. Benson and Giles Constable (edd.), *Renaissance and Renewal in the Twelfth Century* (Cambridge, Massachusetts: Harvard University Press, 1982) pp. 68–87,

BERNARD OF CLAIRVAUX, LETTER 77
TO MASTER HUGH OF SAINT VICTOR

Preface

Excuses for delay and brevity

If I seem to you to be slow in writing back, know that I was also slow to receive that to which I am replying. For what you sent was not brought directly to me, but was first kept for a long time at Pontigny. Once I received it, I did not delay in answering. Moreover, I may have answered more briefly than your request envisaged, but certainly not more briefly than I was forced to by all I am doing. While I have been careful that you are not unaware of what I think on the matters you asked about, I have left it to you to fill out my ideas as your leisure and insight allow, if you think it necessary. I have no doubt that you have at hand conclusive arguments and relevant authorities with which you could easily do it.

The character of Bernard's response

1.1 You do not mention the name of the man whose ideas you ask me to refute. From what I say to you, rather than by a direct refutation (even though we think differently than he does), he will know what I think about the matters about which I am consulted. If what we think is the truth, it is the truth, not us, which contradicts him. But even if he is not so confounded that he agrees to the truth, the truth knows, and we ourselves know, with him. Nevertheless, 'it is not right for a servant of God to engage in lawsuits; he should rather be patient toward all' [2 Tm 2:24]. So we do not seek verbal battles; also in accord with the apostolic teaching we avoid novelties of expression. We adduce only the opinions and words of the Fathers and not our own; for we are not wiser than our fathers. However, let him who wishes be as full of his own thought as he wants to be [Rm 14:5], while we allow ourselves to be full of the ideas of the Scriptures. As the apostle says: 'Not that we are sufficient of ourselves to think anything by ourselves as though it came from us, but our sufficiency is from God' [2 Co 3:5].

[Question/Thesis I: From the time of Jesus' conversation with Nicodemus (Jn 3:5), no one can be saved without actually receiving baptism or being martyred.]

with the literature cited there; also P. Th. Camelot, 'Théologie monastique et théologie scolastique', RSPT 42 (1958) 240–53.

You write that someone—I do not know who, for you do not name him—asserts on the basis of this first statement of the Lord—'Unless one be born again of water and the Holy Spirit, he will not enter the kingdom of heaven' [Jn 3:5]—that no one can be saved without actually receiving the visible sacrament or, in its place, martyrdom. Even if it should happen that someone desired baptism with true faith and a contrite heart, but because of his intervening death was unable to receive what he desired, he would be damned.

[Counter thesis 1A: It is unduly harsh to condemn those who lived before Jesus' command was publicly promulgated.]

First of all, this seems unduly rigorous and harsh from the standpoint of temporal limits. It means that a word which was still hidden could cause harm openly, and the judge would punish before he gave a warning; it means that what the Savior said in darkness and whispers [Mt 10:27] may not yet save, because it has not yet been manifested, yet already it fills the world with people who are condemned.

[Argument 1: To condemn on the basis of an unpromulgated law does not befit a loving God.]

Could the word of salvation and the commandment of life not first restore life before inflicting death on those who were innocent and still unaware of their Lord's will? To speak with the pagan, ought God to have killed an ignorant and just people? Who would think that? Is it congruent for the author of life, who had come to root out death, to make use of death at the very beginning of his ways, to the disadvantage of a world which was still ignorant of the latest heavenly decree? It is utterly wicked to think that the giver of all things good would make such a bad beginning at his coming. I certainly would not agree to any statement attributing to Christ what more rightly should be feared from the Antichrist, who has prepared an arrow in his quiver in order to shoot the upright of heart in the dark.

[Argument 2: Faith requires hearing; hearing, preaching; preaching, a mission.]

1.2 In the meantime how many non-baptized die throughout the world, completely ignorant about what Jesus spoke about with Nicodemus secretly and at night. What then? The law is not yet promulgated, and already those who violate it are held liable? 'And how', he says, 'can they believe in him of whom they have never heard? And how will they hear without a preacher? And how will they preach unless they are sent'

[Rm 10:14–15]? The command has not yet been enjoined or promulgated, the preaching has not yet been heard, and according to the opinion of a lazy and wicked servant the Lord is so hard that he wishes to reap where he has not yet sown, and to gather where he has not scattered [Mt 25:24–26]? Absolutely not!

[Argument 3: This is a positive command, not a natural law, and hence it is known only through revelation.]

Listen instead to the truth of the matter. The one who is the sole master in heaven and on earth handed on in familiar and private conversation to one who was the master only in Israel what he would hand on; he taught him what he would teach, not what he would require from the absent or prescribe even for those who had not heard. It is certainly very unjust to require obedience where hearing had not preceded. This is not something that even without any promulgation the natural law would not allow to remain unknown, such as is, for example, the precept 'What you do not want to be done to you, do not to another' [Tb 4:16, cited in RB 61.14]? This is rather a positive prescription, not a natural precept. For what is there in nature or reason that teaches that no mortals can receive internal and eternal salvation if their bodies are not moistened outwardly with a visible element? The sacrament of God the Most High is to be received, not discussed; venerated, not judged. It arises from faith; it is not innate. It is sanctioned by tradition, not discovered by reason. Hearing must precede faith, as the Apostle says: 'Therefore, faith is from hearing' [Rm 10:17]. If something is totally unknowable if it is not heard, how can it be required even before it is heard? See how the Apostle avoids this and convicts the unbelievers on the basis of hearing alone. 'But I say', he says, 'have they not heard?' That is, they could have been excused, if they had not heard. 'Where there is no law, there is no transgression' [Rm 4:15]. Now, however, when the sound of the preachers has gone into the whole world and their words to the ends of the earth, lack of hearing can no longer be alleged, and so the contempt [of unbelievers] is inexcusable.

1.3 To be sure, many things which should be known are not known, either through neglect of knowledge, laziness in learning, or shame of asking. Ignorance of this sort has no excuse. But is this matter such that it can be learned when sought through human instruction? One man does not understand the thought of another, unless he makes it known; how much less can anyone investigate the divine counsel, except him to whom He wishes to reveal it [Mt 11:27]? Finally, listen to him: 'If I had not come', he says, 'and if I had not spoken to them, they would have no sin' [Jn 15:22]. He does not just say 'and if I had not spoken', but adds, 'to them'. By saying 'And if I had not spoken to them', he shows without doubt that they were not judged without excuse for contempt before the command came to their attention. For if he had spoken, but not to them, ignorance would excuse the fault of disobedience. 'Now, however', he says, because I have spoken to them, 'they have no excuse for their sin' [Jn 15:22]. Hence he also said: 'I have spoken openly to the world and I have said nothing in secret' [Jn 18:20]. Not that he did not teach his close associates many things in secret and privately, but because for the time being he counted this as nothing, and so he passed no judgment in penalty or reward for those things which he handed on in secret, until they would come forward and stand forth in the light. Finally he also said: 'What I say to you in the darkness, say in the light' [Mt 10:27], so that he could rightly ascribe to those who heard them either the merit of obedience or contempt, since now they had been disclosed in their midst. Again, 'Whoever hears you', he says, 'hears me, and whoever spurns you, spurns me' [Lk 10:16]. That is, my judgment discriminating between the obedient and those who are contemptuous depends not on my secret tradition, but on your public preaching.

[Counter thesis 1B: Until the command to be baptized was promulgated, there were other ways to be cleansed from original sin.]

1.4 But perhaps someone will say that those who have not heard may not be judged for contempt, but they may be damned on account of original sin, from which they could be cleansed only by the [sacramental] washing. But who does not know that other remedies besides baptism were available for original sin in ancient times? For Abraham and his seed, the sacrament of circumcision was divinely handed on for this purpose. Among the gentiles we believe there were found many believers: adults who expiated [original sin] by faith and sacrifices; for their children the faith of their parents was the sole, but sufficient remedy. This state of affairs lasted until the era of baptism, when one replacement left all the others obsolete.

[Counter thesis 1C: Therefore, the era of baptism did not begin with Christ's conversation with Nicodemus, but when the precept of baptism was publicly promulgated.]

1.5 So we inquire about when the era of baptism began. He says it began when it was first said: 'Unless someone is born again, etc.'

[Jn 3:5]. Hold it certain that this was said to Nicodemus, who was a friend of Jesus, but 'a hidden one on account of fear of the Jews' [Jn 19:38]; he asked for this secret conversation at night. Meanwhile, how many thousands of the circumcised—not to mention the gentiles—died, do you suppose, in the interval when what was then said of baptism in the darkness had not yet come to light? What, then? Do we say that all those were damned, because they were not baptized? It would truly be an insult to the older command of God, if, when the new one supervened in a still secret and not yet helpful manner, the former command were thought to have been emptied suddenly of significance, so that from that moment it could no longer be of help. And how much longer afterwards do you think it was before it had been publicly preached and shouted from the housetops [Mt 10:27]: 'If you are circumcised, did Christ not profit you' [Ga 5:2]? How then will that other statement stand: 'From the days of John the Baptist the kingdom of heaven suffers violence' [Mt 11:12], if precisely for that time he arranged for a violent exclusion from the kingdom, such as occurred neither before nor after that time? When the decree of the new sacrament had been promulgated, but still only secretly, I ask, what access to the kingdom lay open for those who died in the meantime, when the old command had already lapsed, because it was excluded by the new, and the new was not yet of use, because, as long as it was not known, it could not be accepted? O those would be the unhappiest of times, which alone of all the ages passed deprived of every saving remedy, since circumcision, which had been in force until then, no longer dared be of benefit, since baptism had stolen it away, and baptism could not offer relief, since it was still hidden. Perhaps God was sleeping then, and there was no one during that time who could redeem and save.

2.6 I think it is surely clear from all this that the damnation of the unbaptized, the disappointment of the circumcised, and the abrogation of sacrifices, which the old dispensation had observed against original sin, did not come into general effect already when it was said to Nicodemus in secret: 'Unless one is reborn of water and the Holy Spirit, he will not enter the kingdom of heaven' [Jn 3:5]. Nor did these occur when the apostles were openly enjoined: 'Go, teach all nations, baptizing them in the name of the Father, and of the Son, and of the Holy Spirit' [Mt 28:29]. Rather, the old observance began to be valid no longer, and the non-baptized began to be liable for the new precept, only from the time when there could be no excuse for him to be ignorant of that precept. One should think that, as long as they were not openly forbidden, the old sacraments continued to be valid for infants and those who did not yet have the use of reason, because it is believed they were harmed only by the contagion of sin and not by the breaking of a commandment. Is there more? That is for God, and not for me, to say.

[Counter thesis 1D: Even now there is hope for someone who desires to be baptized, but dies before being able to receive baptism.]

Any adult who after the general proclamation of the remedy of baptism still refuses to be baptized adds on his own account the sin of pride to the general and original stain. He thus bears a twofold cause of most just damnation if he should depart from the body in this state. But if he should come to his senses before he dies and wish and seek to be baptized, but is unable to obtain it because death intervenes, then where there is no lack of right faith, devout hope, sincere charity, may God be gracious to me, because I cannot completely despair of salvation for such a one solely on account of water, if it be lacking, and cannot believe that faith will be rendered empty, hope confounded, and charity lost, provided only that he is not contemptuous of the water, but as I said, merely kept from it by lack of opportunity. If anyone thinks otherwise, he should look at what persuades him to assert what he does. For my part, I declare I do not easily assent, if there is not a very strong argument leading to understanding or authority leading to faith.

[Argument 1: From authority.]

2.7 But I am very much astonished, if this new inventor of new assertions and assertor of inventions has been able to find in this matter arguments which escaped the notice of the holy fathers Ambrose and Augustine or an authority greater than their authority. In case he does not know it, both are of the same opinion as we declare ourselves to be. Certainly he should read the book of Ambrose, *On the Death of Valentinian*,[1] if he has not read it; if he has read it, let him recall it; let him not pretend, if he does recall, and he will observe that the Saint confidently assumed on the basis of faith alone the salvation of a non-baptized person who had died. Without hesitation he attributed to good will what was wanting in opportunity. Let him also read Augustine's *On the One Baptism*, book four,[2] and let him either acknowledge that

[1]*De obitu Valentiniani* 51; CSEL 73:354.
[2]*De baptismo contra Donatistes* 4.29; ed. M. Petschenig, CSEL 51 (Vienna: Tempsky, 1908) p. 257.

he was foolishly deceived or prove that he is impudently obstinate. He says: 'Suffering can sometimes take the place of baptism; it is said of the thief who was not baptized: "Today you will be with me in paradise" [Lk 23:43]; Cyprian gives this evidence no little weight.' And he adds: 'Thinking this over repeatedly, I find that not only suffering for the name of Christ can supply for the lack of baptism, but even faith and conversion of heart, if perchance it is not possible, because of the press of time, to be helped by the celebration of the mystery of baptism.' And later he says: 'The great profit which derives, even without the visible sacrament of baptism, from what the apostle mentions—"It is believed in the heart unto justice, and confessed orally unto salvation"— is manifested in that thief'. 'But then', he says, 'he is perfected invisibly, since it is not contempt of religion which excludes the mystery of baptism, but lack of time.' And indeed I am not unaware that he made a retraction regarding the evidence of the thief and confessed that it was less suitable to prove his opinion, because it is uncertain whether he was not baptized.[3] For the rest, he boldly maintained the opinion and confirmed it in many ways. Unless I am mistaken, you will find he did not retract it anywhere. Likewise in another place, when he had brought forward some whom Scripture reports were sanctified invisibly but not also visibly, he finally concluded:[4] 'From this it follows', he says, 'that that invisible sanctification was available and profitable for some without the visible sacraments which change according to different eras, so that there were different ones then than there are now.' And a little later: 'This does not mean at all', he says, 'that the visible sacrament is to be despised, for anyone who despises it cannot be invisibly sanctified.' Thus does he show clearly enough that the believer who converts to the Lord is deprived of the fruit of baptism, not if he cannot be baptized, but if he disdains to be baptized.

[Argument 2: From reason: it is the martyrs' faith which saves them.]

2.8 Believe me, it will be difficult to separate me from these two columns, by which I refer to Augustine and Ambrose. I confess that with them I am either right or wrong in believing that people can be saved by faith alone and the desire to receive the sacrament, even if untimely death or some other insuperable force keep them from fulfilling their

---

[3]*Retractions* 1.25; ed. Pius Knöll, CSEL 36 (Tempsky: Vienna, 1902) pp. 124–25.
[4]*Quaestiones in Heptateuchen* 3.84; ed. J. Fraipont, CCSL 33 (Turnhout: Brepols, 1958) pp. 227–28.

pious desire. Notice also that, when the Savior said 'Whoever believes and is baptized will be saved', he cautiously and alertly did not repeat the phrase 'who was not baptized', but only 'Whoever does not believe will be condemned' [Mk 16:16]. This intimated that for a time faith alone would suffice for salvation, and that without it, nothing would be sufficient. For this reason, even if it is granted that martyrdom can take the place of baptism, it is clearly not the penalty which does this, but faith itself. For without faith what is martyrdom, if not a penalty? It is faith's doing that martyrdom can without any doubt be considered the equivalent of baptism. Would not faith be very sickly and weak in itself, if what it can give to another, it cannot obtain by itself? To be sure, to pour out one's blood for Christ is an indubitable proof of great faith—but to men, not to God. But what if God, who needs to perform no experiments to test for what he wants, saw great faith in the heart of someone dying in peace, not put to the question by martyrdom, but suitable for martyrdom nevertheless? If he remembers that he has not yet received the sacrament and sorrowfully and repentantly asks for it with all his heart, but cannot receive it because his death comes too quickly, will God damn his faithful one? Will he damn, I ask, a person who is even prepared to die for him? Paul says: 'No one can say Jesus is Lord, except in the Holy Spirit' [1 Co 12:3]. Will we say that such a one, who at the moment of death not only invokes the Lord Jesus, but asks for the sacrament with his every longing, either does not speak in the Holy Spirit, so that the Apostle was mistaken, or is damned even though he has the Holy Spirit? He has the Savior dwelling in his heart by faith and in his mouth by confession; will he then be damned with the Savior? Certainly if martyrdom obtains its prerogative only by the merit of faith, so that it is safely and singularly accepted in place of baptism, I do not see why faith itself cannot with equal cause and without martyrdom be just as great in God's eyes, who knows of it without the proof of martyrdom. I would say it can be just as great as far as obtaining salvation goes, but it is not as great in regard to the accumulation of merit, in which martyrdom surely surpasses it. We read: 'Everyone who hates his brother is a murderer' [1 Jn 3:15]; and again, 'Whoever looks at a woman lustfully has already committed adultery with her in his heart' [Mt 5:28]. How could it be more evident that the wish is considered the equivalent of the deed, when necessity excludes the deed? That is, unless one thinks that the will of God, who is love, is to be found more efficacious in evil than in good, and the merciful and compassionate Lord is more ready to punish than to reward. Suppose someone who is at the point of death happens to remember that he is bound by a debt to another. If he lacks the means to pay it, he is still believed to obtain pardon solely by repentance and contrition of heart, and so he is not damned on account of it. In the same way, faith alone and turning the mind to God, without the spilling of blood or the pouring of water, doubtlessly bring salvation to one who has the will but not the way—because death intervenes—to be baptized. And just as in the former case no repentance remits sin if, when he can, he does not restore what he owes, so in the latter faith is of no avail, if, when he can, he does not receive the sacrament. He is shown not to have perfect faith, if he neglects to do so. True and full faith complies with all the commandments; this particular commandment is the foremost of them all. Rightly, then, anyone who refuses to obey will be thought of not as faithful, but as rebellious and disdainful. How can someone be faithful, if he holds a sacrament of God in contempt?

[Argument 2a: Faith in the case of children.]

2.9 It is true that because infants, on account of their age, cannot have this faith, that is, conversion of heart to God, then they cannot have salvation either, if they die without receiving baptism. Not even they, when they are baptized, totally lack faith, because without faith it is impossible for them to please God. They are saved through faith—not through their own, but through another's faith. It is worthy and pertains to God's goodness, that grace grants that the faith of others profits those to whom age denies their own faith. The justice of the Almighty does not think it proper to require a faith of their own of those whom it knows have no fault of their own. Indeed, they need another's faith, since they were not born without another's taint. To this extent children are not an exception to the general statement: 'Cleansing their hearts by faith' [Ac 15:9]. There is no doubt that a defilement contracted from others can and should be cleansed away by others' faith. These are the judgements of divine justice, in which holy David exulted: 'I was mindful', he says, 'of your judgements from of old, O Lord, and I was consoled' [Ps 118:52]. So much for these matters.

[Question/Thesis II: The just of former times had just as much fore-knowledge of the future saving events as we have of these same events which occurred in our past.]

3.10 Furthermore, you say that the person of whom you are speaking asserts that all the just of former times, however long they lived before the coming of Christ, had just as much foreknowledge of future events as we, who come afterwards, have knowledge of past events. Thus, no simple, just person was ignorant of anything among all those things which the gospel story now teaches us, for example, the incarnate Word, the virgin birth, the teaching of the Savior, his miracles, cross, death, burial, descent into hell, resurrection, and ascension into heaven. Thus, all of the just of those times knew openly and distinctly each and every thing, just as these were made known later in due time and are now known by us. So, there were no just, none who were saved, to whom all these matters were not clear and evident. This idea is simply false.

[Argument 1: *Ad hominem.*]

3.11 In your letter you seem to have advanced so many points to refute it that I think nothing needs to be added, and I can find hardly anything which can be added. As for the man who says these things—peace to him, I say briefly what I think—he seems to me more curious for novelty than studious for truth, and aggrieved that he must think about everything with others and say what he was not the only one or the first to say. So it happens that in thinking and speaking about these matters, he either does not know or pretends not to know entirely how to keep within the bounds of moderation.

[Argument 2: His position puts him on the horns of a dilemma. If (P) the just of the past knew as much about the events of salvation as Christians do, then he is saying either that (Q) God is too sparing, or that (R) God is too generous. (If P, then Q or R, but Not Q and Not R, therefore Not P).]

Behold even in this assertion of his, when he makes all equals in knowledge, those who hope for what is to come with those who read the past, he proclaims that God is either too sparing or too generous, and in neither case does he open the eye of discretion. On the one hand, he restricts the number of the elect in the earlier era to the few rare spiritual persons, people outstanding and illustrious for the special excellence of their sanctity whom the Scriptures testify existed then, and who by a singular gift of the Spirit could foresee with certainty the things which were going to happen. In this way he shortens God's reach too much, since he thinks no one at that time could be saved except those few paragons of perfection. Or, alternatively, if he does not deny that there was in those times a multitude of the saved besides these, he is asserting that a great, unprecedented largess of the divine gift was granted to the people of the old era, if he claims that all that multitude clearly foresaw

Hugh Feiss

all the things enumerated above regarding the mystery of our redemption. But it is clear that none of these matters was then clearly written or publicly preached; it follows we must affirm that all these were revealed to all through the Spirit, and thus that all of those who were just and saved before the coming of the Lord were spiritual, all were perfect, all were prophets. Thus, in ancient times either salvation was exceedingly rare or the number of the perfect was excessive. To think either one is true is to go outside the bounds of discretion.

[Of these 2 possibilities (R) is to be preferred to (Q). Therefore Not Q.]

3.12 But if it seems more tolerable and it is judged more worthy of God that he filled and endowed those centuries with a multitude of the perfect rather than be content with such a small number of those to be saved, then not a few were saved and all were filled with the prophetic spirit and already then penetrated the mysteries which were not yet revealed.

[Not R. Argument 1: If before the christian era, the many knew all we know, then the gospel brings nothing new.]

If, I say, this position is accepted, we bless God in his gifts, but we do not see what is reserved for the time of grace. Perhaps, according to this opinion, that [earlier age] should be called the time of grace, since in it so many and so great riches of the spirit flowed to the people of God that it seemed to be filled with incredible happiness, as Moses desired when he said: 'Who will grant that all may prophesy?' [Nb 11:29]. I ask, did the gospel bring anything like this? In vain did Paul glory in the first fruits of the Spirit, which he thought he had received with his fellow apostles, since nothing similar could be experienced in his days. Finally, he said: 'Are all then prophets?' [1 Co 12:29]. It is, I say, in vain that he glories in his gospel because he received it not from or through a human being but by a special prerogative through the revelation of Jesus Christ, since even before him it was revealed to the peoples through the Holy Spirit. But neither ought the apostle Peter have forced that prophecy to apply to his own time which says 'I will pour forth my Spirit upon your sons and daughters, and your sons and daughters will prophecy' [Jl 2:28], if a more abundant outpouring of the Spirit had preceded him by some centuries. Or the prophet, or rather God in the prophet—if he really foresaw those apostolic times when he said this—ought to have said 'my spirit I will withdraw' rather than 'I will pour out'. What, then? If we make all the just among the ancients equal in knowledge to the children of the gospel, is it not therefore necessary to confess them to be superior in grace? For, it was neither reading, as it is for us, nor preaching, but an anointing which taught them everything about everything.

[Not R. Argument 2: R falsifies Scripture.]

3.13 So be it. We would tolerate the injury to ourselves, and the apostles would tolerate an injury to themselves, so that the least of the just of ancient times is comparable to ourselves in knowledge and preferred in grace. But there is something which under no conditions can we properly tolerate, namely, that the Lord of glory be thought ever to have been able to deceive or to have wanted to deceive. He himself claimed that there had not arisen a greater among the children of women than John the Baptist. See if we are not forced to declare this teaching of Truth false, if we attribute as much to the ancients as we are able to vindicate for John. John suffers no injury if he is believed or said not to have known something, and, moreover, he will not deny it. But if what we deny to the herald of Truth, we give to another contrary to the proclamation of Truth, this is not only an injury, it is blasphemy, and clearly it contradicts not just John, but the Truth. What then? The friend of the Spouse hesitates and asks: 'Are you who is to come, or do we wait for another' [Jn 3:29; Mt 11:3]. And by our lying we confirm the certainty of all this to thousands of people.

[Not R. Argument 3: Additional scriptural and patristic evidence.]

3.14 That even the ancients themselves did not think this way about themselves we can establish briefly. Moses wrote that God spoke to him thus: 'I am the God of Abraham, and the God of Isaac, and the God of Jacob, and my name Adonai I have not disclosed to them' [Ex 6:3] as I have to you (tacitly understood). He shows therefore that he has received something more of the knowledge of God than his fathers before him did. David also boldly presumed on a gift of understanding made to him beyond what his teachers and elders had received, when he said: 'I have understood more than all my teachers, because your testimonies are my meditation' [Ps 118:99], and again: 'I have understood more than the elders' [Ps 118:100]. And also the prophet Daniel who says: 'Many will pass by and knowledge will be manifold' [Dn 12:4]; that is, he too promises broader knowledge of things to those who come later. If then, as Pope Saint Gregory says,[5] knowledge of the spiritual fathers grows

---

[5]See Gregory the Great, *Hom. in Ezek.* 2.5.2; ed. M. Adriaen, CCSL 142 (Turnhout: Brepols, 1971) p. 276, 55–62.

with the passage of time, and the closer they were to the coming of the Savior, the more fully they understood the mystery of salvation, there is no doubt that the manifestation of the very realities and the presence of the one manifesting them conferred much more on those who were present. Finally, they hear: 'Blessed are the eyes who see what you see' [Lk 10:23]. And again: 'I call you my friends, because I have made known to you whatever I have heard from my Father' [Jn 15:15]. He adds: 'Many kings and prophets wanted to see what you see, and they did not see, and to hear what you hear, and they did not hear' [Lk 10:24]. Why? So that they might see more clearly and more fully what they perceived only weakly and obscurely. What need was there to see the flesh outside and hear the words of the flesh, if they had already been perfectly instructed internally by the Spirit about everything? This is especially so, since the Lord says: 'The flesh is of no avail; it is the spirit which gives life' [Jn 6:64]. But if the prophets, and those who seemed most illustrious among that people, were not all able to recognize all things equally clearly, but some more, others less, as the Spirit endowed them, dividing to each as he wished, then without prejudice to his holiness and perfection, how much more could the simpler among the just be ignorant of the time, manner, and order of salvation without detriment to their salvation, even though they held most firmly with a certain hope and faith to the things which had been promised?

3.15 How many are there today among the christian people who do not know, or hardly know, how to think about the form and status of eternal life and the world to come, which they firmly believe in, hope for, and ardently desire. Similarly, many, before the advent of the Savior, held to God almighty and loved the one who graciously promised their salvation, believing him faithful in his promise, hoping that he was the most certain redeemer, and in this faith and expectation were saved, even though they did not know when, how, and in what order the promised salvation would come about. Finally, Bede clearly teaches that the future events concerning Christ were not all open to everyone, a testimony which you also included in your letter. He says:[6] 'The prophets and Moses knew and preached the same triumph of the Lord's cross before the apostles did, but the prophets preached it with many kinds of figures and veiled speech, whereas the apostles and their successors always preached openly once the light of the gospel had been openly disclosed. As a result, now every christian people must know and confess the faith, which then only a few

---

[6]*Hom.* 2.15; ed. D. Hurst, CCSL 122 (Turnhout: Brepols, 1955) 281, 38–46.

and more perfect persons knew, although the whole people of God then supported the mysteries of the same faith typologically in the ceremonies of the law.' There are many things which converge to confirm this, but the epistolary form cannot convey them all, and there is no need that it do so. For, as I said already, I think that even if I had not answered, the things which your letter contained on this matter could have been sufficient. But I have added this, lest I leave any of the things you asked me untouched.

[Question/Thesis III: There can be no sin of ignorance.]

4.16 Now, I think that we need not work too hard against the third assertion, both because it presents an exceedingly obvious falsehood and because he, the inventor of it, refutes it satisfactorily himself in his earlier opinion, and thus contradicts himself.

[Argument 1: He contradicts himself.]

When in regard to that night-time and privately whispered conversation of the Lord with Nicodemus he laid a trap of public damnation for all those throughout the world who did not know about it, judging that from that hour no one who was not baptized could be saved, did he not openly admit a sin of ignorance, and a damning sin at that? That is, unless he is so shameless that he thinks God condemns human beings who are without fault. It is to be feared that, if not even a brief response is made to the fool regarding his stupidity, he may think it wisdom and more securely spread the seed of stupidity in the ears of the foolish, and thus his stupidity will become measureless.

[Argument 2: Evidence from authority: Old Testament.]

This manifest falsehood may be refuted by a few, evident testimonies to the truth. He who asserts that one cannot sin through ignorance is never moved to prayer regarding his ignorance, but rather mocks the prophet who says in prayer: 'Do not remember the crimes of my youth and my ignorances' [Lv 5:17–18]. Perhaps he will also reprove God who requires satisfaction for a sin of ignorance. For he says to Moses in Leviticus: 'If a soul who has sinned through ignorance and done one of these things which are forbidden by the law of the Lord and is thus guilty of sin understands his iniquity, let him offer a spotless ram from the flocks to the priest, according to the measure and estimate of the sin' [Lv 7:17–18]. And again: 'Whoever prays on account of that which he did unwittingly will have it forgiven him, because through a mistake he offended against the Lord' [Lv 5:18–19].

[Argument 3: Evidence from authority: New Testament.]

4.17 If ignorance is never a sin, why does it say in the letter to the Hebrews that the high priest went alone once a year into the second tabernacle, not without blood, which he offered for his ignorance and that of his people [Heb 9:7]? If there is no sin of ignorance, did Saul then not sin by persecuting the church of God, since he was ignorant of what he did since he was still unbelieving? If so, he did well because he was a blasphemer, a persecutor, abusive, because he was 'breathing threats and murdering the disciples' [Ac 9:1] of Jesus. In this he 'was a jealous defender of the traditions of his fathers' [Ga 1:14]. He should not have said 'I have received mercy' [1 Tm 1:13], but 'I have received a reward'. For ignorance rendered him immune from sin, and, in addition, zeal judged him deserving of a reward. If ignorance never sins, I say, why do we bring a case against the killers of the apostles, when not only were they ignorant that it was evil to kill them, but moreover they thought that by doing it they were offering honor to God? And in vain did the Savior on the cross pray for those who crucified him, who, as he himself testified, did not know what they were doing and therefore were not sinning. Nor is it right to suspect that the Lord Jesus was lying when he asserted openly that they were ignorant of what they were doing, even if one might doubt the apostle who, because he was vying with his flesh, could as a human being be lying when he said: 'If they had known, they would never have crucified the Lord of glory' [Rm 11:14; 1 Co 2:8]. From these considerations is it not sufficiently apparent how extensive is the darkness which surrounds him who is ignorant that one can sin through ignorance? Anyway, that is enough for these matters.

[Question/Thesis IV: The plan of God was revealed to no one, not even to the angels, before it was announced to the Virgin.]

5.18 At the end, you imply, amicably to be sure, that some are disturbed by my opinion, which I stated when I was expounding the gospel, that the plan of God was revealed to no one before the Virgin, not even to the blessed angels.

[Argument 1: I stated this position only tentatively.]

First of all, then, since I think their uneasiness is not sufficiently justified, they can notice that I did not state this opinion firmly, but with a qualification, making it one part of a disjunction with the particle *vel*. I say: 'Or, therefore, it is said: "from God". . . .' So, if I indicated one cause which occurred to me why the evangelist added the words 'from God' to 'the angel Gabriel was sent',[7] I cautiously added another alternative with the disjunction, so that there was no need for me to defend a position and the reader was given the option of choosing which of the two he wished. Therefore, if one of them can stand, why am I reviled for the other, since I do not affirm either, but instead leave both of them to the judgment of the reader?

[Argument 2: It is not reprehensible to state this thesis not regarding the fact of the incarnation, but regarding its time, place, manner, and the identity of the virgin chosen.]

However, suppose I had stated the opinion that before then the holy angels had not known the plan of God, not indeed the plan of God sometime to bring salvation on the earth through the mystery of the Word incarnate—to know and foretell this was granted to many mortals—but what exact time, what place and manner, and especially what virgin God had chosen to fulfill his plan. My point is that even if I thought and wrote that this plan of God, not regarding the deed itself, but concerning time, place, manner, and person, was unknown even to the holy angels, I certainly do not see why that should seem incredible. But let each abound securely in his own opinion, where neither certain reason nor authority worthy of respect rules out what he thinks.

[Time.]

5.19 What reason or authority compels me to think that from of old even the very time was known to the angels? The Apostle says of it: 'After the fullness of time arrived, God sent his son, born of a woman, born under the law' [Ga 4:4]. Perhaps it would seem more credible that, just as they did not know the day of the future coming of the Lord, as he himself testified, so also they did not know the time of his earlier coming. Who knows whether in that spiritual way the Wisdom of God told the angels about his first coming the same thing we read he answered through the mouth of his assumed flesh to the apostles regarding his second coming: 'It is not given to you to know the times or moments which the Father has established in his power' [Ac 1:7].

[Place.]

Again, what necessity compels me to believe that the angels already knew the city of Nazareth before they saw the archangel sent to greet

[7]Miss 1.2; SBOp 4:15, 2.

the Virgin and announce the divine birth? To be sure, that Bethlehem was chosen beforehand for the nativity and Jerusalem for the passion was clearly foreknown and foretold by the prophets. However, there is, I think, some clear testimony in Scripture that the fact that Nazareth was similarly destined for the conception was not similarly foreseen by the prophets. For it is written: 'For he will be called a Nazarene' [Mt 2:23]. The evangelist, who takes this from the prophet, shows clearly that it is to be referred not so much to his conception as to his education, for he was taken back there from Egypt and raised there. Moreover, the Jews say to Nicodemus: 'Look and see that no prophet will arise from Galilee' [Jn 7:52]. They were speaking to someone who knew the law and was a teacher in Israel, one who was not likely to be ignorant of anything in it. Nevertheless, they insisted on the point with full confidence, showing that the Scripture did not speak of Christ coming from Galilee of which Nazareth is known to be a town. Besides, they surely had at hand the testimony of the prophet with which they unhesitatingly answered the king, who was asking about the place of his birth, that it was Bethlehem. Therefore, Christ was born in Bethlehem, he suffered in Jerusalem, and it is clear that the prophets predicted both openly. Similarly, he was born in Nazareth, a town in Galilee, but nothing seems to have occurred to Nicodemus which would justify him in teaching that either Galilee or Nazareth was at all connected with the coming of Christ.

5.20 So also Nathaniel, who was also learned in the law, responded with an astonished question to Philip who told him of Jesus, son of Joseph, from Nazareth: 'Can anything good be from Nazareth' [Jn 1:46]? He was very surprised that the Christ was announced to be from Nazareth, because he remembered no Scripture text to that effect. But if it is argued that he answered this not as a question but as an affirmation, since he remembered the previously mentioned testimony—'For he will be called a Nazarene'—he would not be stating that he realized that Jesus was conceived in Nazareth, since there could be many other reasons why the prophet had predicted that. Thus the divine plan for the place of the conception could have been hidden from the angels, just as it was from the prophets.

[Manner.]

5.21 Next, where, I ask, can I be taught that that incomprehensible manner of conception, about which the Virgin herself made anxious inquiry, was foreknown by the angels? It seems to me that it was not even known to him—I say this with all due respect to him—who made the announcement, as he himself says, if we take careful note of his words. For he answers: 'The Holy Spirit will come upon you' [Lk 1:35]. In this does he not openly refer to the teaching of the Holy Spirit, by whose anointing she may be taught in regard to everything of which he does not presume to have knowledge himself, and so she may learn by experience what she could not learn by hearing? Then, he adds: 'And the power of the most high will overshadow you' [Lk 1:35], there indicating more expressly the most secret manner of the incomprehensible mystery and ineffable sacrament, by which, as if in a cloud, with and in one, solitary virgin, the one sole Trinity was going to bring about the divine conception. The great John himself confesses himself ill-suited to investigate this mystery, when he acknowledges he is unworthy to loose the lace of his sandal.

[Person.]

Moreover, I ask where is it proven that this virgin was known to the angels by name and by face, known, that is, as the one whom God had chosen to be his mother, with the sole exception of the archangel to whom it was conveyed from the beginning to be kept and believed. Moreover, if the devil did not recognize her after the conception, and Joseph was mistaken about the conception, it can be believed that the holy angels were totally unaware that she was going to be the mother of God. For the reprobate spirits, though deprived of participation in spiritual grace, do not lack lively natural industry.

5.22 Do you see, with all respect for the faith and the truth of the Scriptures, in how many ways the angels could have been ignorant of the divine plan, especially that these truths to be revealed might be kept the prerogative of the Virgin Mother? First, there is the time; second, the place; third, the manner; fourth, the choice of a person who was a virgin. Give this answer to the brothers, who hold me reprehensible for having said in praise of the Virgin, that one may think that God arranged so that the plan of God was not revealed to any of the blessed angels, except the archangel Gabriel, before it was revealed to the Virgin. I specifically spoke of his plan, not regarding the deed, but the time of the deed, its place, its manner, and the choice of the person. Farewell.

ABSTRACTS

S. Bernard eut de nombreux contacts avec les chanoines réguliers de Saint-Victor. Une lettre d'Hugues de Saint-Victor qui ne nous a pas été conservée donna lieu à une longue réponse de S. Bernard. Hugues demandait à Bernard de traiter de quatre opinions, dont trois concernaient des théories du baptême associées à Pierre Abélard; la quatrième était une théorie de Bernard lui-même. La réponse de Bernard montre qu'il était passé maître dans les techniques de la scolastique naissante. L'analyse de l'argumentation de Bernard est suivie d'une traduction de sa lettre-traité, dont aucune version anglaise n'avait, semble-t-il, encore paru.

Saint Bernard had considerable contact with the canons regular of Saint Victor. A no longer extant query from Hugh of Saint Victor brought about a long response from Saint Bernard. Hugh asked Bernard to deal with four opinions, three of which were concerned with theories on baptism associated with Peter Abelard; the fourth was a theory of Bernard himself. Bernard's reply shows him to be a master of the techniques of nascent scholasticism. The analysis of Bernard's argumentation is followed by a translation of his letter-treatise, which does not seem to have appeared in english translation until now.

Der heilige Bernhard hatte beträchtlichen Kontakt mit den Regularkanonikern von St Viktor. Ein nicht mehr vorliegender Brief Hugos von St Viktor rief eine lange Antwort des heiligen Bernhard hervor. Hugo bat Bernhard, vier Ansichten zu behandeln, von denen drei sich mit den Theorien über die Taufe in Verbindung mit Peter Abälard befassten; die vierte war eine Theorie Bernhards selbst. Bernhards Antwort zeigt ihn als Meister der Techniken der beginnenden Scholastik. Auf die Analyse von Bernhards Argumentation folgt eine Übersetzung seiner Briefabhandlung, die bis heute nicht in englischer Übersetzung erschienen ist.

PART V
THE INFLUENCE OF SAINT BERNARD

THE CLAIRVAUX SAINT BERNARD OFFICE: IKON OF A SAINT

Chrysogonus Waddell, OCSO
Abbey of Gethsemani

W HETHER THEY LOVE HIM or hate him, medievalists owe a special debt of gratitude to Saint Bernard of Clairvaux, for few major figures of the twelfth century have provided the scholar with such a wealth of documentary material. Whether the scholar is interested in Bernard's problems of digestion or in his contribution to the theology of paedobaptism or in his pivotal role in the organization of the Second Crusade, there is no dearth of source material on which to draw, nor dearth of scholars who have actually drawn on that material.

For the biographer of Saint Bernard there is, however, one source which has been, it would seem, wholly overlooked. It would be unreasonably captious to suggest that biographical studies of the saint have in any way been flawed as a result of this neglect, for the neglected source to which I am referring was in no way meant to serve as a biography of the abbot-founder of Clairvaux. Still, the source in question has an importance all its own, in that it provides a theological portrait of Bernard, and a presentation of his life and mission as interpreted by the very community apart from which Bernard would not have been Bernard, even as, apart from Bernard, Clairvaux would not have been Clairvaux. I am referring to the proper office of Saint Bernard.

'Nowhere in twelfth-century Europe', writes Brian Patrick McGuire,[1] 'can we get closer to religious attitudes and group mentality than at

---

[1]The opening sentence of the author's article, 'A Lost Exemplum Collection Found: The *Liber Visionum et Miraculorum* Compiled Under Prior John of Clairvaux (1171–79)', in ASOC 39 (1983) 26–62.

Clairvaux after the death of Saint Bernard and the completion of the
Vita Prima in the 1160s.' Perhaps it would be also true to say that
nowhere in the extant *monumenta* of clairvallian spirituality are these
religious attitudes and this group mentality more cogently expressed than
in the proper Saint Bernard office composed at Clairvaux itself at a date
unknown, but prior to 1175.[2] Here we find the very community that had
been formed and animated by Bernard himself bearing witness to what
Bernard meant to Clairvaux, to the wider monastic milieu, and to the
Church at large. We obviously ought not to expect to glean from this
office new facts of a biographical nature. But possibly what this office
has to offer is, in its own way, even more important than yet another
twelfth-century *Vita Bernardi.*

Perhaps the best way of understanding the true nature of a proper office
is to think of it in terms of an ikon. Like an ikon, it makes accessible to the
believer the spiritual realities it represents and re-presents. It is more than
a teaching instrument, in that it not only speaks about the realities of faith
but opens the door to those realities. It is less a photograph or a monument
of a historical nature than a source of grace that brings together the divine
and human in a living synthesis. The chief difference between ikon and
liturgical office lies in the medium. Instead of paint and wood and metal,
we have word and music. The ikon belongs, too, to the order of space,
while the liturgical office belongs chiefly to the order of time. The ikon
has a permanency of being, while the liturgical office exists only in the
moment of its actual celebration. Finally, the ikon is generally envisaged
in its relationship to the individual believer, while the office is in the
first instance an ecclesial celebration involving a concrete community.
Obviously, a liturgical office can be studied from the standpoint of just its
texts or of just its music, or of the two in combination. It can be studied,
too, with a view to identifying its sources and to tracing its subsequent
influence, whether in art or literature or music and so on. But, for a truly

[2]Why the *ante quem* date 1175? This date is supplied by the anonymous *Chronicon
Clarevallense*, which assigns to 1174 the canonization of Saint Bernard, and further notes
that in the following year the General Chapter approved the 'chant' (= proper office)
of Saint Bernard, as well as that of the Blessed Trinity: PL 185:1248D: *Et sequenti
anno, in capitulo generali receperunt cantum beati Bernardi, et cantum de Trinitate.*
The Chronicle covers the years from 1147 to 1192. The corresponding General Chapter
statutes are edited by Canivez, *Statuta Capitulorum Generalium Ordinis Cisterciensis* 1
(Louvain, 1933) p. 82, on the basis of a single manuscript from 'Mantellana' (Spain). The
manuscript, now in the library of San Isidro de Duenas, is actually from the monastery
of Bujedo de Juarros (near Burgos). The same two statutes are also in the unedited
manuscript, Laon, Bibl. mun., ms 246, f. 93r.

holistic understanding of a given office, we must situate all the important material and formal considerations within their ikonic perspectives.

To the best of my knowledge only Bruno Griesser, OCist (+ 1965) has made this Saint Bernard office the object of an extended study, 'Das Officium des hl. Bernard im Cistercienser Brevier und seine geschichtliche Entwicklung'.[3] Valuable as it is, however, this careful study is severely limited in its scope. Father Bruno simply edited the various major constitutive elements of the 'official' Saint Bernard mass and office as found in cistercian manuscripts and printed liturgical books from the twelfth century to the present day. He further identified, as often as possible, the sources drawn on for the creation of these texts. Father Bruno achieved, and brilliantly achieved, exactly what he had set out to do. But an *exegesis* of those liturgical texts lay well outside the scope of his concern.

In the present study, my own interest bears chiefly and directly on an exegesis of the texts of this remarkable twelfth-century Saint Bernard office—or at least on an exegesis of *some* of those texts. For, truth to tell, this considerable body of material deserves to be studied at much greater length and depth. Given the limitations of space, the best I can do is to select a limited number of representative formulas for particular comment, leaving aside others which might lend themselves equally well to closer study. Also left aside is any consideration of the music, and this I very much regret. For Bernard, the function of music was to render the text more fruitful,[4] and the cistercian-composed musical setting of these texts does just that. But, here again, this is the stuff of which doctoral dissertations are made; and all that the present article can do is, by treating of just a few of the formulas in question, call attention to the need for a book-length study of all the texts and chants of the Saint Bernard office, and suggest that, for a proper understanding of the texts, we need a hermeneutical method adequate to the object of our research.

THE SAINT BERNARD ANNIVERSARY OFFICE AT CLAIRVAUX

The office we are about to study is not the very first office to be celebrated for Bernard at Clairvaux on an annual basis. A General Chapter statute datable to 1159 (and therefore to within six years of the saint's

---

[3]In *Cistercienser-Chronik* 60 (1953) 57–86. In the last century Charles Lalore edited the proper office, but without commentary, in his *Reliques des trois tombeaux saints de Clairvaux* (Troyes: Impr. Brunard, 1877) pp. viii–xviii.

[4]Ep 389.2; SBOp 8:378, 14–15: [*Cantus*] *sensum litterae non evacuet, sed fecundet*; 'The music should not void the meaning of the text, but render it fruitful.'

death, and during the abbacy of Blessed Fastred, 1157–1161) grants the 'Clarevallenses' permission to celebrate the anniversary of Bernard: 'Conceditur clareuallensibus anniuersarium domni bernardi celebrare ita tamen ut abbates antiphonas non incipiant.'[5] This statute is not patently clear in every respect. Are the 'Clarevallenses' the brethren of Clairvaux? Or are they all the brethren belonging to the entire filiation of Clairvaux? (The statute probably concerns the 'Claravallenses' in the restricted sense of the immediate community.) The reference to an 'anniversary' is to a requiem mass and office celebrated on the anniversary of the abbot's death. This concession goes considerably beyond what was generally allowed by way of suffrages on behalf of deceased local abbots at the time of Bernard's death in 1153. The earliest recoverable redaction of the order's customary does indeed provide for an anniversary mass and office for the deceased local abbot.[6] But, in the redaction of the customary adopted toward 1147, the anniversary of the local deceased abbot has been absorbed into a more general anniversary for all deceased abbots and bishops of the order (11 January).[7] This elimination of a yearly anniversary mass and office for the local deceased abbot is confirmed by a General Chapter statute of 1161, which states that the anniversary day of the lately deceased abbot is to be announced in chapter, but omits any reference to a corresponding mass and office: 'Abbatum nostrorum in capitulo anniuersarium pronuntiamus.'[8] And of the eight recoverable manuscripts with this statute, two of them add that some kind of prayer is to be prescribed on their behalf: *et pro eis*

---

[5]The statute is preserved in only one manuscript, Montpellier, Bibl. Universitaire, Ecole de Médicine ms H 322, f. 85r. Edited in Canivez, *Statuta* 1, p. 70, under year 1159/7; and in Waddell, *Statutes of the Cistercian General Chapter ca. 1119–1189: Edition of Sources* 1, Cistercian Liturgy Series 23 (Trappist, Kentucky: Gethsemani Abbey, 1990) p. 88.

[6]See Bruno Griesser, OCist (ed.), *Die 'Ecclesiastica Officia Cisterciensis Ordinis' des Cod. 1711 von Trient*, in ASOC 12 (1956) 216, where, in cap. LXXV (re-numbered as cap. LII by the editor), lines 2–3, the anniversary of the local abbot is included in the list of principal solemn anniversaries celebrated on a yearly basis.

[7]As in Ljubljana (Yugoslavia), University Library, ms 31, f. 50r; edited by Canisius Noschitzka, OCist, *Codex manuscriptus 31 Bibliothecae Universitatis Labacensis*, in ASOC 6 (1950) 66, where the revised text (cap. LII) reads in part: *...sed et in anniversario omnium defunctorum ordinis nostri episcoporum et abbatum, quod fit III. idus ianuarii. . . .*

[8]Montpellier, Bibl. Universitaire, Ecole de Médicine ms H 322, f. 85v. See Canivez, *Statuta* 1, p. 47 (1152/8), p. 58 (1154/29), p. 63 (1157/32), p. 72 (1161/3). The statute belongs only to the series for 1161 according to the chronology established for the edition by C. Waddell (above, note 5).

oratio iniungetur.[9] Nothing is said, however, about an anniversary mass, and still less about an anniversary office.

Accordingly, the General Chapter of 1159 granted the community of Clairvaux a particular anniversary celebration for 20 August. The fact that the statute of 1159 specifies that abbots 'do not begin the antiphons' of this office is an indication of the non-festal character of the anniversary. For this is technical jargon, and concerns the intonation of the antiphons for the *Benedictus* (Lauds) and the *Magnificat* (Vespers). These intonations were reserved to the abbot on the feasts of Christmas, Easter, and Pentecost, during the octaves of these three feasts, as well as on all twelve-lesson feasts.[10] Clearly, then, Bernard's anniversary office is not to be confused with a festal office. This is further confirmed by a passing remark made by Abbot Tromund (or Transmundus) of Chiaravalle (Milan) in his letter to Gerard, abbot of Clairvaux, at the time of Bernard's canonization. Tromund had been instrumental in expediting the complex affairs connected with the canonization process, and, in announcing Bernard's formal enrollment in the catalogue of saints, Tromund notes happily: *ut non necesse sit iam amplius cantare ei cantus lugubres,* 'now we shall not have to sing lugubrious chants for him any longer.'[11] Clearly, till then the brethren of Clairvaux had been chanting the 'lugubrious' chants from the mass and office for the dead rather than festal chants of a proper Saint Bernard office, such as could now be celebrated as of 20 August 1174.[12]

THE PROVISIONAL SAINT BERNARD OFFICE

The earliest reference to a proper Saint Bernard office occurs in a General Chapter statute dated by Canivez to 1175.[13] The text of the

---

[9]Laon, Bibl. municipale, ms 246, f. 103v; ed. Waddell, *Statutes* 1, p. 295, n. 228; Lisbon, Bibl. Nacional, ms Alcobaça CXL–185, ff. 176r-v; ed. Waddell, *Statutes* 1, p. 249, n. 65. Neither manuscript was used for the Canivez edition.

[10]The prescription is found in the earliest redaction of the usages (p. 270, lines 5–6 of the Griesser edition referred to above, note 6), and was retained in all subsequent revisions.

[11]PL 185:626C.

[12]The date of the canonization was 18 January 1174, when Alexander III expedited from Agnani four letters concerning the successful completion of the canonization process—letters to the Church of France, King Louis of France, the cistercian order at large, and Abbot Gerard of Cîteaux (PL 185:622–25; *Acta Sanctorum* Augusti IV:244–45).

[13]See above, note 2.

statute is basically the same in the two manuscripts which contain it: *De sancto bernardo proprium seruicium dicetur. cum duabus missis. et fratres laborabunt*;[14] and *De sancto bernardo proprium officium et due misse et fratres laborent*.[15] So Bernard enjoys, as of 1175, a proper office and a feast with both a matutinal mass and a major mass—though the lay brethren are to work as on other work days. But the feast of the saint had already been celebrated in August of 1174—with which mass and office chants? Further, given the cumbersome process involved in copying and distributing a freshly composed proper office, it may be presumed that, in a number of instances, another year or two would pass before the new material could be introduced into the office books of this or that monastery. Bruno Griesser, in his article on the successive versions of the Saint Bernard Office, lists four twelfth-century manuscripts in which the proper office is a thirteenth-century addition, and from this he infers a time-lag, here and there, between the composition of the proper office and its effective introduction into the local choir-books.[16] Griesser's suggestion that the *interim* office was taken from the Common of a Confessor Not a Bishop is all the more persuasive in that, as he points out, even after the effective promulgation of the proper office, elements of this common continued to be used in the proper office—hymns, collects, chapters, versicles.[17]

There is, however, one proper formulary dating from the period of Bernard's canonization, a formulary the significance of which has been overlooked. In his letter to Gerard of Clairvaux, Tromund of Chiaravalle ends by urging that the mass-formulary used by Pope Alexander III on the occasion of Bernard's canonization be retained for use within the order: *Consulimus ad hoc ut Missa, quam dominus Papa cecinit in solemnitate sancti hujus non mutetur*.[18] Since the corresponding mass-formulas were standard ones already in the cistercian liturgical books, this posed no problem, at least in general. The mass collects were a case apart. 'So we are sending you these collects', writes Tromund by

[14]Laon 246, f. 93r; in the Waddell edition, p. 271, n. 7.

[15]San Isidro, ms 1, f. 88r; in the Waddell edition, p. 298, n. 4.

[16]P. 61 of the article referred to above, note 3. The four manuscripts mentioned are Troyes 2044 (Clairvaux), Erlangen 120 (Heilsbronn), Heiligenkreuz 18, and Vatican Chigi C.V. 138 (Tre Fontane).

[17]*Ibid*. Griesser refers, in point of fact, to a 'Common of Abbots'. The reference should read, more correctly, to the Common of a Confessor Not a Bishop (which, however, did indeed contain a few alternative formulas suitable for abbots).

[18]PL 185:627A.

way of conclusion,[19] thus clearly indicating that the mass collect (which traditionally served also as the principal office collect), the prayer over the offerings, and the post-communion prayer were *not* in keeping with cistercian usage. Which was the formulary recommended by Tromund? On the strength of an extract from a Corbie manuscript of the *Vita prima Bernardi*,[20] Mabillon specified that the mass-prayers were those of the *Adesto supplicationibus nostris* formulary in the Common of Saints.[21] This may have been true in the seventeenth century, but it was not true in 1174. At that time the formulary in question was used exclusively for the mass of Saint Augustine as transmitted by manuscripts of the gelasian tradition.[22] Since the cistercian sacramentary was based on an exemplar representative of the 'gregorian' tradition,[23] this formulary used by the pope had to be supplied by Tromund. This is the same set of prayers reproduced in full in the collection of General Chapter statutes and *varia* from the last half of the twelfth century, in the manuscript from Vauclair, Laon 246, f. 93v:

Adesto supplicationibus nostris omnipotens deus. et quibus fiduciam sperande pietatis indulges. intercedente beato bernardo confessore tuo. consuetue misericordie tribue benignus effectum. Per.
Secretvm Sancti confessoris tui bernardi nobis domine quesumus. pia non desit oratio. que et munere nostra conciliet. et tuam nobis indulgentiam semper obtineat. Per.
Postcommunio Ut tua nobis domine sacrificia dent salutem. beatus confessor tuus bernardus. quesumus precator accedat. Per.

Ignoring Tromund's recommendation, the Cistercians assigned the newly canonized saint the common formulary used for Saint Benedict and other abbots, and stalwartly refused to go outside their 'gregorian tradition' for a suitable Saint Bernard formulary.[24] As for the formulary

---

[19]*Mittimus enim vobis easdem Collectas*; PL 185:627A.

[20]A thirteenth-century manuscript now at Paris, Bibl. Nationale, ms lat. 13780; references for the mass formulary are given on f. 135v.

[21]PL 185:625D. This information is repeated by Jean Leclercq, 'Epîtres d'Alexandre III sur les cisterciens', in *Revue bénédictine* 64 (1954) 75.

[22]See O. Bruylants, *Les oraisons du Missel Romain* 1 (Louvain: Abbaye du Mont César, 1952) p. 138, formulary 393.

[23]An edition of the twelfth-century cistercian sacramentary is planned for publication in the *Cistercian Liturgy Series*.

[24]In point of fact, the formulary for Saint Benedict and other abbots (*Intercessio...patrocinio assequamur, Sacris altaribus, Protegat...experiamur insignia*) was taken over by 'gregorian' mass-books from a formulary originally proper to the gelasian

used by Alexander III in the canonization mass, there is nothing demonstrably 'bernardine' as regards the content of these mass-prayers. But this should not cause us to overlook the obvious import of the pope's choice of mass-texts. By adopting for Bernard a formulary hitherto proper exclusively to Saint Augustine, Pope Alexander III is stating equivalently that Bernard is a new Augustine. This is a point of capital importance, and, once our attention is called to it, we realize how easy it would be to shape a study based on parallels between the lives and missions of the two saints, showing how Bernard was for the Church of the twelfth century what Augustine was for the Church of an earlier age.

THE PROPER SAINT BERNARD OFFICE OF 1175

This section begins with a transcription of the pertinent texts, together with the identification, where possible, of the sources of these texts. It concludes with an exegesis of a few of the characteristic texts.

Transcription

There is only one real problem in transcribing the text of the office on the basis of the many surviving early manuscripts—the problem of punctuation. This is determined to a considerable extent by the musical setting, but, since the interpretation of the musical punctuation is none too evident, let it be said from the outset that the divisions of the text here suggested by the grammatical punctuation and format call for further study. It can be said in general, however, that the indications furnished by our modern chant editions are in a few instances quite incorrect, and in other instances open to discussion.

The transcription of each integral text is followed by a rather slavishly literal english rendering provided for the non-latinist reader. In some instances texts indicated in the manuscripts only by their latin *incipit* have been translated in full. The transcription adopts modern punctuation, but conforms to the orthography of the scribe. Abbreviations and standard signs are extended. Except for the numbers used to indicate the sequence of antiphons and responsories, editorial additions are bracketed. In the manuscript used as the basis of the following transcription, the scribe has

---

tradition. In 1201, Innocent III, at the request of Cistercians in high authority, authored a set of new Saint Bernard mass-prayers (*Perfice quaesumus, Grata tibi . . . offerimus maiestati, Suum in nobis*), and this new formulary succeeded in replacing the older one. See PL 185:625B-D; 923C–24C.

added at the very end the texts of the chapter-texts (*capitula*) and office collects; and these indications have been retained for brief commentary. As already indicated, the transcription of the office texts presents, in general, few problems. Manuscripts are many, variants few; and it would serve no purpose in the present severely delimited study to base the text on twenty manuscripts when two manuscripts coeval with Bernard's canonization and of exceptional quality will do as well. For my present purpose I have selected:

VATICAN STATE, Biblioteca Apostolica, ms Chigi C.V. 138, ff.348r2–51r2; noted breviary from the abbey of SS. Vincenzo ed Anastasio (Tres Fontes ad Aquas Salvias, today Tre Fontane), Rome.[25] The above indicated folios are an insert to accommodate the Saint Bernard office added to a manuscript written soon after 1175 (the Holy Trinity office, authorized by the General Chapter of that year, is already in the manuscript, and in first hand).

MICHIGAN, Institute of Cistercian Studies Library (Western Michigan University, Kalamazoo), Obrecht ms 1, ff. 65r–69v; sanctoral-cycle antiphonary from the abbey of Morimondo (on Lake Como, Italy); here again the Saint Bernard office is in secondhand on a late twelfth-century addition to a manuscript written soon after 1175 (the Holy Trinity office is in first hand and in its proper place in the companion temporal-cycle antiphonary, Paris, Bibl. Nationale, ms nouv. acq. lat. 1410).

The transcription is based on the Vatican Chigi manuscript. If there are no variant readings indicated from the Obrecht manuscript, this is because there are none—apart, of course, from inconsequential differences in orthography.

Sources

Sources have been identified, where possible, in parentheses positioned after the english translations. The abbreviations to the *Vita sancti Malachiae* and to other writings concerning Saint Malachy and Saint

---

[25]For a more detailed description of the manuscript, see P. Salmon, *Les Manuscrits liturgiques de la Bibliothèque Vatican* I (Città del Vaticano, 1968) pp. 123–24, under n. 243; and C. Waddell, *The Twelfth-century Cistercian Hymnal*, I, *Introduction and Commentary*. Cistercian Liturgy Series 1 (Trappist, Kentucky: Gethsemani Abbey, 1984) pp. 83–84, where a number of corrections of Dom Salmon's description are made.

Victor are easily identifiable, as are the standard abbreviations of biblical books. Parentheses preceded and followed by an asterisk *( )* indicate that the source specified requires further discussion provided by the commentary.

For the antiphons and responsories, two kinds of literary sources are in clear evidence: (a) biblical texts, usually excerpted and adapted with considerable freedom; (b) texts (chiefly about Saint Malachy and Saint Victor) from Saint Bernard's own writings, excerpted and adapted with the same freedom characteristic of the biblical citations.

/ In natale sancti Bernardi ad uesperas   *f.* 348r1

R. Beatus bernardus.

Ad Magnificat ana Magnificauit sanctum suum dominus,
              et dedit illi scientiam sanctorum,
              ut consummarentur in bonum opera eius,
              et pax Dei super eum in eternum.

The Lord magnified his holy one,
and gave him knowledge of things holy [Ws 10:10c],
that his works might be consummated unto good,
and God's peace might be upon him unto eternity
[see Si 38:7d–8].

[Ad vigilias]

Inuitatorium In confessione laudis adoremus dominum
          * Qui stola glorie confessorem suum decorauit
          bernardum. *Ps.* Venite.

In the confession of praise let us worship the Lord,
* Who adorned his confessor Bernard with a robe of glory.

Ana 1 Vie uiri sancti uie pulchre,
      et omnes semite eius pacifice,
      quia lignum uite apprehendit. [Ps 1]

The ways of the holy man are ways of beauty,
and all his paths are peaceable
for he has laid hold of the Tree of Life.
[see Pr 3:17–18a]

Ana 2 Semitas iustitie uiasque sanctorum custodiens,
      uir beatus cursum uite in pace consummauit. [Ps 2]

Keeping the paths of justice,
and guarding the ways of the saints [Pr 2:8],
the blessed man consummated the course of life in peace.
[see 2 Tm 4:7]

Ana 3 Benedictio domini super caput iusti,
memoria eius in secula seculorum [Ps 4].

The blessing of the Lord is upon the head of the just [Pr 10:6];
the memory of him is from age unto age. [see Si 24:28]

Ana 4 Consurgens diluculo
quesiuit bona pater sanctus;
quasi florens lilium germinauit. [Ps 5]

Rising early,
[our] holy father sought after good things [Pr 11:27];
flourishing like the lily, he blossomed. [see Is 35:1b–2a]

Ana 5 / In testamentis pacis stetit semen illius,   *f.* 348r2
et usque in eternum permanet gloria eius. [Ps 8]

His seed has stood in the covenants of peace,
and his glory will remain for ever. [see Si 44:12]

Ana 6 Exaltauit dominus
in eternum cornu christi sui,
et dedit illi testamentum uite,
et sedem glorie sue.

The Lord exalted the horn of his anointed for ever,
and he gave him the covenant of life,
and the throne of his glory. [see Si 47:13]

V. Iustum deduxit.

V. The Lord led the just man through straight paths.
R. He showed him the kingdom of God. [see Ws 10:10a]

/ *R.* 1 Prima uirtus uiri sancti   *f.* 348vl
habitus corporis sui,
quod ita composite
et uno semper modo agebat,
* Vt nil appareret in eo
quod posset offendere intuentes.

V. Totum in eo disciplinatum,
totum insigne uirtutis,
perfectionis forma. * Vt nil.

The first virtue [to be noticed] in this holy man
was the harmony of his bearing;
always his manner was composed and uniform,
* So that nothing might appear in him
to give offence to those beholding him.
Everything about him was well-ordered,
everything bore the mark of virtue,
and was a model of perfection. * So that
[see V Mal 19.43; SBOp 3:348, 16, 17, 22–23]

R. 2 Uirtu-/te multa et scientia preditus,   *f.* 348r
sanctus dei proximabat dignitati sanctorum,
* Cum fructu operum proferens
celestis sapientie uerba.
V. A puericia requisiuit auctorem uite,
et animum dedit ad eloquia dei. * Cum.

R. Endowed with much virtue and knowledge,
the holy man of God drew nigh the dignity of the saints,
* bringing forth, along with the fruit of works,
words of heavenly wisdom.
V. From childhood he sought after the Author of life,
and gave his soul to the words of God. * Bringing
[source?].

/ *R.* 3 Opera sancti patris   *f.* 349rl
Uelut sol in conspectu dei,
* Et oculi eius
sine intermissione respiciebant
in uias eius.
V. Non sunt abscondita ab eo
testamenta dei. * Et oculi.

The works of [our] holy father
are as the sun in the sight of God;
* And his [God's] eyes were constantly
on his ways.
There were not hidden from him
God's covenants. * And his eyes
[Si 17:16–17a]

/ *R*. 4 In timore dei   *f*. 349r2
         patris sancti gloriatio,
      et in sensu eius
         cogitatus dei,
   * Et omnis narratio eius
         in preceptis altissimi.
   V. Pastor populi dei factus est
         in sapientia sermonis sacri.   * Et omnis.
      Gloria patri et filio
      et spiritui sancto.   * Et omnis.

   In the fear of God
      was the glory of [our] holy father,
   and in his mind
      was the thought of God,
* And all his discourse
      was on the commandments of the Most High.
   He became shepherd of the people of God
   for the wisdom of his sacred speech.   * And all
   [Si 9:22b–23, 24b]

In II° Nocturno

Ana 7 Quasi oliua pullulans,
         et cipressus in altitudine se tollens,
         sic uir beatus ad gloriam sanctitatis ascendit [Ps 14].

   As an olive tree budding forth,
   and a cypress rearing itself on high,
   thus did the blessed man ascend to the glory of holiness
   [Si 50:11].

Ana 8 Porrexit manum suam uir sanctus
            in libationem altaris,
         et de sanguine uue
            effudit ordorem diuinum excelso principi [Ps 20].

   The holy man stretched forth his hand
      to [perform] the libation of the altar,
   and from the blood of the grape
      he poured forth a divine fragrance to the most high Prince.
   [see Si 50:16–17].

/ *Ana* 9 Ampliauit gentem suam uir iustus,　　　　　　*f.* 349vl
　　　　　adeptus gloriam in conuersatione eius. [Ps 23].

The just man enlarged his nation,
having obtained glory by its manner of life.
[see Si 50:5]

Ana 10 Honorauit deum uir sanctus in operibus suis,
　　　　　et in oblectatione susceptus est ab eo. [Ps 63].

The holy man honored God in his deeds,
　and was received by him with delight.
[see Si 35:20a]

Ana 11 Extulit manus suas pater uenerabilis
　　　　　dare gloriam deo a labiis suis
　　　　　et in nomine ipsius gloriari. [Ps 64]

[Our] venerable father lifted up his hands
to give glory to God with his lips,
and to glory in his name.
[see Si 50:22]

Ana 12 Dedit dominus sancto suo iocunditatem cordis,
　　　　　fieri pacem in diebus suis in populo dei.

The Lord gave joyfulness of heart to his holy one,
that there might be peace in his days
　among the people of God. [see Si 50:25]

V. Amauit eum dominus.

　V. The Lord loved him and adorned him.
　R. And clothed him with a robe of glory. [see Si 45:9]

/ *R.* 5 O odoriferum lilium　　　　　　　　　　　*f.* 349v2
　　　　　spargens ubique uiuificum suauitatis odorem,
　　　　* Cuius apud nos memoria in benedictione est,
　　　　　apud superos presentia in honore.
　　　V. Fac canentes te tante plenitudinis
　　　　　participio non priuari.　　* Cuius

　O fragrant lily,
　diffusing everywhere
　　　the life-giving scent of your sweetness,
　* Among us your memory is in benediction,

whose presence is in honor among those above.
Grant that those who sing of you
may not be deprived of fellowship in such plenteousness.
[S Mal 8; SBOp 6/1:55, 7–10]

R. 6 Accepit / uir sanctus a domino potestatem in preceptis   *f*. 350rl
    testimonia ueritatis docere subditos,
  * Et in lege dei lucem dare populo.
 V. Addidit ei gloriam dominus
    hereditatem pacis possidere in eternum.   * Et.

The holy man received from the Lord
    power in his commandments
to teach his subjects the testimonies of truth,
* And to give light to the people in the law of God.
And he [God] added glory to him,
to possess the heritage of peace unto eternity.
[see Si 45:21 and 25]

R. 7 Lex ueritatis in ore patris sancti,
  * Et iniquitas non est / inuenta in labiis eius.   *f*. 350r2
 V. In pace et equitate ambulauit coram deo.   * Et

The law of truth was in his mouth.
* And iniquity was not found in his lips.
In peace and equity
he walked in God's presence.
[see Mal 2:6]

R. 8 Testamentum / eternum cum beato patre bernardo   *f*. 350vl
    constitutit dominus,
  * Et iustitiam ac iudicia sua
    ostendit illi.
 V. Magnalia honoris dei
    uidit oculus eius.   * Et
    Gloria patri et filio
    et spiritui sancto.   * Et

The Lord made an everlasting covenant
    with [our] blessed father Bernard,
* And he showed him his justice and judgments.
His eye saw the majesty of the glory of God.   * And he
[see Si 17:10–11]

Glory be to the Father and to the Son
and to the Holy Spirit,   * And he

Ad cantica ana Repleuit sanctum suum dominus
                    spiritu intelligentie,
                    et ipse fluenta doctrine ministrauit
                    populo Dei.

The Lord filled his holy one
    with the spirit of understanding,
and he ministered streams of doctrine
    for the people of God. [see Si 39:8]

V. Iustus ut palma.

    V. The just man will flourish like the palm tree.
    R. He shall grow up like the cedar of Libanus.

Euangelium Dixit simon petrus. *Omelia* Grandis fiducia.
Quere omnia in vnius confessoris non pontificis.

R. 9 O oliua fructifera
            in domo dei!
        O oleum letitie
            fouens beneficiis,
            choruscans miraculis!
    * Fac nos eius qua frueris
        lucis suauitatisque participes.
    V. Introisti in potentias domini,
        et iam potentior ad impetrandum.   * Fac nos

    O fruitful olive tree
        in the house of God!
    O oil of gladness,
        warming us with blessings,
        shining bright with miracles!
  * Make us sharers in the light and sweetness
    you now enjoy. [S Mal 8; SBOp 6/1 55, 5–6]
    You have entered into the powers of the Lord,
    and are now more powerful to intercede for us.   * Make us
    [see Ps 70:16a; Vict 2.1; SBOp 6/1:33, 14–15]

R. 10 Beatus bernardus quasi uas auri solidum
            ornatum omni lapide preci-/oso,   *f.* 350v2

fluenta gratie propinauit in populo,
* Et accepit stolam glorie
in consummationem uirtutis.
V. Factus est quasi ignis effulgens,
et quasi thus redolens in diebus estatis. * Et accepit.

The blessed Bernard, like a vessel of solid gold
adorned with every precious stone,
poured out streams of grace for the people;
* And he received the robe of glory
as the consummation of virtue.
He was like a brighly burning fire,
like sweet-smelling frankincense in the time of summer.
* And he [Si 50:10, 9, 8d]

R. 11 Habebat pater uenerabilis in sapientia doctrine
claritatem ad turbas;
* Et facies principum admirabantur eum.
V. In uultu potentium amabilis erat,
et memoriam sui reliquit posteris in benedictione.
* Et facies.

[Our] venerable father, for the wisdom of [his] doctrine,
had glory among the multitude,
* And the faces of princes wondered at him.
In the sight of the powerful he was lovable,
and he left behind him his memory in blessing
to them that came after. * And the faces
[see Ws 8:10, 11b, 13b]

R. 12 Dedit dominus confessionem
sancto et excelso
in uerbo glorie;
de omni corde laudauit dominum,
* Et dilexit deum qui fecit illum.
V. Dedit decus in celebratione operis sancti,
et ornauit tempora sua usque / in finem. * Et dilexit. *f.* 351rl
Gloria patri et filio
et spiritui sancto. * Et dilexit

The lord made confession
to the Holy One and the Most High
with words of glory.

He praised the Lord with his whole heart,
* And he loved God that made him.
He added beauty
   in the celebration of the holy work [of God],
and set in order his holy times even to the end.
* And he loved [see Si 47:9, 10a, 12a].
Glory be to the Father and to the Son
and to the Holy Spirit.   * And he loved.

In laudibus

Ana Domum tuam, domine, decet sanctitudo,
   in qua tante frequentatur memoria sanctitatis.

Holiness becomes your house, O Lord,
in which is celebrated the memory of so great a holiness
[S Mal 7; SBOp 6/1:54, 14–15; see Ps 92:5b].

R. br. Iustum deduxit dominus.

  R. br. The Lord led the just man   * Through right paths.
  V. And he showed him the kingdom of God.   * Through

V. Iustus germinauit.

  V. The just man blossomed like a lily.
  R. He will flourish for ever before the Lord.

Ad Benedictus ana Benedictus dominus deus patris nostri,
           qui eius doctrina et exemplo
             edificauit ecclesiam suam;
           eius felici assumptione
             supernam letificauit ciuitatem suam;
           eius sollemni recordatione
             presentem hodie consolatur familiam suam.

Blessed be the Lord God of our father,
who by his teaching and example
   built up his Church;
by his [Bernard's] happy entrance into heaven
   he [the Lord God] gladdened the city on high;
by [our] solemn memorial of him,
   he consoles today his family here present.
[see S Mal 7.6; SBOp 6/1:54, 7–10]

Ad primam

Ana Beatus bernardus
      ad infantia spiritum sortitus est bonum,
      per quem erat puer docilis
      et amabilis ualde.

From his infancy the blessed Bernard
      received a good soul, [see Ws 8:19b]
whereby he was a docile lad,
      and very lovable.
[V Mal 1.1; SBOp 3:310, 8–9]

Ad tertiam

Ana In disciplina morum profectuque uirtutum,
      super docentes se in breui enituit
            unctione magistra.

In the training of his character
      and his progress in virtue
he soon outshone his teachers,
      taught as he was by the anointing [from the Holy One]
[V Mal 1.1; SBOp 3:310, 19–20].

V. Iustum deduxit dominus.

   V. The Lord led the just man through right paths.
   R. And he showed him the kingdom of God. [see Ws 10:10a]

Ad sextam

Ana Crescente / etate,   *f.* 351r2
      crescebat simul sapientia et gratia
      apud deum et homines

As he grew older,
he grew at the same time in wisdom and grace
before God and men.
[V Mal 1.2; SBOp 3:311, 20–21]

V. Amauit eum dominus.

   V. The Lord loved him, and adorned him.
   R. And clothed him in a robe of glory. [see Ps 45–49b]

Ad nonam

Ana Hodie, posito corpore,
pater sanctus diues meritis penetrauit in sancta,
similis factus in gloria sanctorum.

On this day, having laid aside the body,
[our] holy father, rich in merit,
made his way into the holy places,
himself become like unto the saints in glory.
[Vict 2.2; SBOp 6/1:33, 16–17]

V. Iustus ut palma.

V. The just man will flourish like the palm tree.
R. He shall grow up like the cedar of Libanus. [Ps 91:13]

Ad uesperas super psalmos

Ana Uie uiri. *Ana* Semitas iusticie. *Ana* Benedictio domini. *Ana* Consurgens.

R. br. Amauit eum dominus.

R. br. The Lord loved him   * And adorned him.
V. He clothed him in a robe of glory.   * And adorned
[see Si 45:9b]

V. Iustus germinauit.

V. The just man blossomed like a lily.
R. He will flourish for ever before the Lord.
[see Ho 14:6]

Ad Magnificat ana Exultet in domino spiritus uiri sancti,
quod mole leuatus corporea
totus pergit in deum,
et adherens illi
unus fit cum eo spiritus in eternum.

Let the spirit of the holy man exult in the Lord,
for, freed now from the weight of the body,
he goes onward wholly unto God,
and, cleaving to him,
becomes with him a single spirit unto eternity.
[see S Mal 6; SBOp 6/1:54, 10–14]

+

Ad tertiam Capitulum Dilectus a deo. *Collecta* Intercessio.

He was beloved by God and men,
whose memory is in benediction;
he made him like the saints in glory. [Si 45:1–2b]
May the intercession of the blessed abbot Bernard,
we beseech you, O Lord,
commend us unto you;
so that what we cannot have through our own merits,
we may obtain through his patronage.

Ad sextam Capitulum Dedit dominus confessionem sancto suo,
et excelso in uerbo glorie.
de omni corde suo laudauit dominum,
et dilexit eum qui fecit illum.

The lord gave confession [of praise] to the Holy One,
and to the Most High in words of glory;
with his whole heart he praised the Lord,
and loved God that made him. [Si 47:9–10a]

Collecta Sit domine quesumus Beatus Bernardus abbas
nostre fragilitatis adiutor.
et pro nobis tibi supplicans
copiosius audiatur.

May the blessed abbot Bernard,
we beseech you, O Lord,
aid us in our frailty.
and be heard in every fuller measure
as he pleads on our behalf.

Ad nonam [*Capitulum*] Iustum deduxit dominus per uias rectas.
et ostendit illi regnum dei.
et dedit illi scientiam sanctorum.
et honestauit illum in laboribus.
et compleuit labores illius.

The Lord led the just man through straight ways,
and showed him the kingdom of God;
he gave him knowledge of things holy,

made him honorable in his labors,
and accomplished his labors. [Ws 10:10]

Collecta Excita domine in ecclesia tua
       spiritum cui beatus Bernardus abbas seruiuit.
       ut eodem nos replente
       studeamus amare quod amauit.
       et opere exercere quod docuit.
       Per dominum. eiusdem.

Stir up within your Church, O Lord,
the Spirit whom the blessed abbot Bernard obeyed;
so that, as we are filled with that same Spirit,
we may strive to love what he loved,
and to put into practice what he taught.
Through our Lord . . . in the unity of the same.

NOTES ON SELECTED TEXTS

A detailed commentary on all the texts of this office lies outside the scope of this article, and a selection of texts has to be made. Antiphons and responsories will provide most of this material. Traditionally, the more characteristic or more important antiphons are those assigned to the gospel-canticles of Vespers and Lauds (that is, the *Magnificat* and *Benedictus* antiphons) and the antiphon for the psalms of Lauds (and be it noted that the cistercian office-structure admits of only a single antiphon here). The present notes will, however, treat of a few other antiphons: antiphons for the Night Office and for the Little Hours. Solemn (or prolix) responsories of special import are generally those assigned to First Vespers, the first of the Night Office series, and the final responsory of each of the three nocturns of the Night Office. Finally, a few remarks will be made about the short readings or chapter (*capitula*) and collects, even though these, like the hymns and versicles, are here borrowed automatically from the Common of a Confessor Not a Bishop.

First Vespers

The formulas proper to Saint Bernard's office begin only with the chapter or short reading. For the most part, the cistercian festal offices followed the ancient usage according to which the psalms and corresponding antiphons of First Vespers were those of the weekday office. One of the features of the cistercian antiphonary revised under Saint Bernard's aegis, sometime a bit before 1147, was the introduction of proper First Vespers antiphons for several of the major feasts. In the case of his own proper office, however, the psalms were, as usual, those of the current weekday, but the antiphons were those of the Assumption office, since 20 August fell within the Assumption octave (August 15–22). Interestingly enough, these marian antiphons, based on the *Song of Songs*, had been introduced into the cistercian repertory by Bernard himself; and, though their occurrence here as the introduction to the Saint Bernard office is wholly fortuitous, it is nonetheless singularly appropriate that Bernard's office should begin with a series of texts which recur time and time again in his sermons on the *Song of Songs*: *Ecce tu pulchra* ('Behold, you are lovely...'), *Sicut lilium* ('Like a lily among thorns...'), *Favus distillans* ('Your lips are a dripping honeycomb...'), *Emissiones tuae* ('Your plants are a paradise of pomegranates...'). If the scribe of the Saint Bernard-insert in the Vatican Chigi manuscript omits mention of these antiphons, it is because they do not belong, strictly speaking, to the Saint Bernard office which begins only with the *capitulum*. But neither is there a reference to the *capitulum* here, since the scribe is concerned only with antiphonary chants. The incipit of the *capitulum* in question, Ecclesiasticus 45:1–2a, is in point of fact indicated at the end of the office, in an appendix with the *capitula* and collects of Terce, Sext, and None; and, in the cistercian office, as in the tradition at large, the Terce *capitulum* served also at Vespers I and II and at Lauds. But these *capitula* are merely common ones used for any confessor not a bishop; and, though it is appropriate to be told that Bernard was 'beloved by God and men', and that his 'memory is in benediction', and that he has become 'like the saints in glory', there is nothing the least bit distinctive about the applicability of this text to Bernard. Again, Ecclesiasticus 45:1 occurs fairly often in Bernard's writings (thirteen times), but without particular contextual significance.

All this means that the first really significant formula in this office is the solemn responsory—designated here at Vespers I only by incipit, *Beatus Bernardus*, since the same responsory is given in full later on as responsory ten of the Night Office. The fact that we here have a solemn responsory rather than a standard short responsory indicates that this feast is celebrated with two community masses as on a Sunday, rather than, as on a number of other twelve-lesson feasts, with only a single mass (and with work for the monks as on an ordinary workday). Inevitably, the responsory assigned to such a position at First Vespers is chosen for its thematic relevance and its solemnity. Generally it is a responsory taken from the first nocturn series (responsories 1–4), but here it is the tenth responsory that has been anticipated; and the reader is asked to refer to this text in the transcription. As there indicated, the text is a pastiche of fragments in non-consecutive order from Ecclesiasticus 50:10, 9, 8d.

Most of chapter 50 of Ecclesiasticus is a hymn in praise of the reformer Simon the high priest, 'who in his life propped up the house, and in his days fortified the temple' (v. 1), who 'took care of the nation, and delivered it from destruction' (v. 4), and who 'prevailed to enlarge the city, and obtained glory in his conversation with the people. . .' (v. 5). Evidently, the entire passage from which the responsory has been excerpted is contextually significant for our understanding of the choice of the fragments applied to Bernard. And it is almost always important, for an understanding of the liturgical use of such texts, to *replace them in their biblical context*. But it would not be enough simply to conclude that our responsory means to suggest that Bernard is a reformer and restorer of Church and kingdom in the line of Simon the high priest.

Neither is it enough to stop short with the splendid poetic description of Simon/Bernard, who, the responsory tells us, is 'like a vessel of solid gold, adorned with every precious stone', clothed in 'the robe of glory', and surrounding us with warmth and with the fragrance of frankincense as on a sultry summer day. Not that this effusive poetic description is to be ignored as unimportant, but it is meant to serve as a starting point rather than as a terminus. I recall, for instance, a splendid Saint Bernard sermon by our Father Louis (Thomas Merton), who began by speaking with enthusiasm about this image of Bernard as a golden vase, shimmering and giving off clouds of incense. But in the final analysis, Father Louis was stating only that, when our text says that Bernard was 'like a vessel of solid gold', this means that Bernard was 'like a vessel of solid gold'—an interesting observation, but one hardly adequate to explain the relevance of Ecclesiasticus 50:10 for Bernard of Clairvaux.

The significance of our responsory-text emerges only when we replace it, not merely in its biblical context (a hymn of praise of Simon, reformer of temple and monarchy), but in its *biblical context as exegeted by the mainstream tradition of biblical exegesis*. Far too little attention has been paid to the concrete manner in which monks studied and prayed over the Scriptures. Their initiation into the sacred text came less by way of the unadorned biblical text than by way of the *glossed* biblical text — that is to say, Bibles in which the biblical text, written in large script, was surrounded in the margins and between the lines by exegetical and grammatical notes that expounded the text in its various layers of meaning. The novice who set to work learning the psalms did so, not from the bare biblical text of the psalms, but from a psalter glossed with explanatory texts drawn chiefly from Augustine, Cassiodorus, and Jerome. It was not enough to memorize the line, 'Blessed is the man who hath not walked in the counsel of the ungodly.' One had to know, in memorizing this line, who that man is, who the ungodly are, what it means to be 'blessed', and what the significance of 'walking' is in this particular verse. The question was less one of merely memorizing the psalms, than of memorizing the psalms as exegeted by the mainstream ecclesial tradition represented by the glosses.

In the case of the glossed version of Ecclesiasticus, such as we find in the Clairvaux manuscripts now in the Municipal Library at Troyes (mss 274, 418, 491, 1380) and in the University Library at Montpellier (Ecole de Médicine ms 17), the glosses are drawn almost exclusively from Rhabanus Maurus' commentary on Ecclesiasticus, composed around 835–840. And, for most readers, it might be easier to refer to Rhabanus' integral text—the edition in PL 109:763–1126 is the most accessible one—than to the glosses as found in manuscripts such as the above.[26] For the verses Ecclesiasticus 50:10, 9, 8d, I myself have my eye not only on PL 109:1115–16 (Book 10 of Rhabanus' commentary) but on the corresponding glosses in Troyes 1380, f. 109r.

What then does it mean, when we sing that Bernard is 'like a vase of solid gold adorned with every precious gem'? *In auro splendor sapientiae*, writes Rhabanus, *in lapidibus quoque pretiosis virtutum decor exprimitur. Cum ergo virtutes sacrae fulgori sapientiae intermiscentur, vas animae haec habens pretiosissimum esse demonstratur.* 'In the gold is expressed the splendor of wisdom, and in the precious stones is also expressed the loveliness of the virtues. When therefore the virtues are intermingled with the sacred sheen of wisdom, the vase of the soul that has these things is shown to be most precious.' The gloss says the same, but more succinctly: 'LIKE A VASE [the soul] OF SOLID GOLD [full of wisdom] ADORNED WITH EVERY PRECIOUS STONE [with every kind of virtue].' So Bernard is being characterized as a man who dazzles us with the splendor of his wisdom and, commensurate with that wisdom and of a single piece with it, with the attractive loveliness of his multi-faceted virtues.

[26]Even the edition of the *glossa ordinaria* attributed (wrongly) to Walafrid Strabo in PL 113:1183–232 refers the reader in many instances to the integral text of Rhabanus' commentary in PL 109.

Line 3 of the responsory, *fluenta gratiae propinavit in populo*, is non-biblical but very bernardine. In his sermon on the Birth of Mary, Bernard speaks about streams of grace being communicated to the human race through that 'desirable aqueduct', Mary.[27] And he repeats the expression later in the same sermon when, touching on one of his favorite themes, he speaks of the *fluenta gratiae* which is like the Word who comes to us through Mary and then returns to the Father so that his life may stream forth again in greater abundance. So also are the 'streams of grace' which, through us, must return to their point of origin in order to well forth again even more fruitfully.[28] *Fluenta gratiae* occurs, too, in *Sermon 51 on the Song of Songs*, where Bernard warns us that ingratitude can dry up the streams of grace.[29] While in his fourth sermon for the Vigil of Christmas, he tells us that our hearts have to keep low and humble—like the divine Babe—if we are to receive the *fluenta gratiae*: they flow *downwards* from God, not upwards.[30] It is clear, however, that the author of our responsory-text means to suggest, by describing Bernard as a vase from which streams of grace pour out for the people at large, that Bernard's wisdom and virtue are not for himself alone, but are in function of his ecclesial mission: through Bernard the people receive the life-giving streams of God's grace.

Lines 4–5 of the responsory modify the latin biblical text slightly, with a consequent shift in meaning: *in accipiendo ipsum stolam gloriae, et vestiri eum in consummationem virtutis* becomes *Et accepit stolam gloriae in consummatione virtutis*. The Douai translation gets the meaning of the Vulgate text just right. Simon the high priest 'put on the robe of glory, and was clothed with the perfection of power' [Si 50:11b]. And the gloss comments on these two parallel actions: the robe of glory stands for the dignity of the order of preachers, and the act of being robed with the perfection of power stands for virtuous conduct and activity. But our own author has reworked the text so that there are no longer two parallel actions: Bernard receives the robe of glory as the reward or consummation of his virtue—with *virtus* being understood in the sense of *virtus*-virtue rather than *virtus*-power. This gives the body of the responsory its dynamic thrust: Bernard's wisdom and virtue exercised on behalf of the people come to full flower in his heavenly

[27]Nat BVM; SBOp 5:277, 18.
[28]Nat BVM; SBOp 5:283, 25.
[29]SBOp 2:87, 20.
[30]SBOp 4:226, 24.

glorification. It is in this sense that Bernard himself uses the expression *ad consummationem virtutum* in *Sermon 33 on the Song*, where the bride's present concerns and endeavors converge on the future consummation of all that has preceded.[31]

The verset, with its imagery of a brightly blazing fire and of the summertime fragrance of frankincense serves to round out the portrait of Bernard: 'He was like a brightly burning fire'—and the gloss explains why. Departing a bit from Rhabanus, the interlinear gloss tells us that the fire is the fire of charity that radiates light. And the marginal gloss adds: *ardentes in se, lucentes aliis*, 'afire within themselves, giving off light for others'. The image has been a commonplace ever since Origen, in his *Homily 13 on Exodus*, rang the changes on John 5:35: *Ille* [John the Baptist] *erat lucerna ardens et lucens*.[32] This word-combination is frequent with Bernard.[33] Thanks in part to his Saint John the Baptist sermon *De lucerna ardente et lucente*, which features this johannine description of the Baptist,[34] the burning-and-shining-lamp-theme has become so identified with Bernard as to enter into the compositions of his own proper collect in the Paul VI Missal: *Deus qui beatum Bernardum abbatem . . . in Ecclesia tua lucere simul et ardere fecisti. . . .* And if, in the Clairvaux gloss, the plural form rather than the singular is used—*ardentes . . . lucentes*—this may perhaps be under the influence of Bernard himself, who pluralizes it on more than one occasion.[35] As for the summertime frankincense in the latter half of the verset, the gloss summarizes Rhabanus perfectly: *THUS REDOLENS* [*pura oratio*] *IN DIEBUS AESTATIS* [*in claritate fidei*]; 'pure prayer' that gives off its fragrance 'in the clear light of faith'. In the cistercian monastic context, where the vocabulary of prayer depends so often not only on Pope Saint Gregory, but on Cassian as well, a term such as 'pure prayer' (used also in the *Rule* of Benedict 20:4) can rightly be exegeted in the light of the first and second conferences of Abba Isaac on pure and continual prayer in Cassian's ninth and tenth *Conferences*. If, then, we take the reference to the light of faith together with the parallel gloss about the fire of love, we find in this verset still further strokes that delineate the true

[31]SBOp 1:234, 9.
[32]See G. Bardy, 'Saint Bernard et Origène', in *Revue du Moyen Age Latin* 1 (1945) 420–21.
[33]See Fiches 908–909 of the Corpus Christianorum *Thesaurus Sancti Bernardi Clarae-vallensis* (Louvain: Brepols, 1987).
[34]SBOp 5:176–84.
[35]See above, note 33.

physiognomy of the saint. And if we take the verset in combination with the body of the responsory, we have before us a portrayal of Bernard of Clairvaux remarkable for its theological richness.

But let it be remembered that this responsory-text is not for the eye only, but for the ear as well. It is meant to be sung, and sung to a melody that repeatedly bounds upward in enthusiastic leaps that outline fourths and fifths, that crests melodically even as Bernard receives his robe of glory, and that suggests something of the splendor of the word *virtutis* by spinning out the first syllable in a twenty-nine-note melisma.

The scribe of the Vatican Chigi insert skipped references to the hymn (*Iesu corona celsior*) and the versicle with response (*Iustus germinabit*), since these formulas came from the Common and required no specific mention. This means that the only other specially composed formula in the First Vespers formulary is the *Magnificat* antiphon.

The opening line is a bit predictable with its *Magnificavit*-incipit that smacks of the first line of the *Magnificat*:

Magnificat anima mea Dominum

Magnificavit sanctum suum Dominus.

And this parallelism between 'My soul magnifies the Lord' and 'The Lord magnified his holy one' is not particularly subtle. This parody-technique is typical of the period, and we shall find further instances of it in the *Benedictus* antiphon and the *Magnificat* antiphon of Second Vespers. Bernard himself used it in his Saint Victor office: *Magna est virtus* (Magnificat, Vesp. I) and *O magnifice Victor* (Magnificat, Vesp. II),[36] as did the author of the Clairvaux Saint Malachy office: *Magna est super te* (Magnificat, Vesp. I), *Benedictus Dominus Deus Malachiae* (Benedictus, Lauds), *Exsultet in Domino spiritus Malachiae* (Magnificat, Vesp. II).[37] More important, then, are the lines that follow.

'He [the Lord] gave him [Bernard] knowledge of things holy' seems to be a matter of fact reference to Wisdom 10:10c. But this reference may perhaps have been made under the influence of the gloss that occurs just before the last two lines which represent a reworking of Ecclesiasticus 38:7d–8, and which define the meaning of the text. *Altissimus dedit homini scientiam in rebus a se mirabiliter creatis*, writes Rhabanus;

---

[36]SBOp 3:502, 18; 508, 16.

[37]Edited in C. Waddell, 'The Two Saint Malachy Offices from Clairvaux', in *Bernard of Clairvaux: Studies Presented To Dom Jean Leclercq*, CS 23 (Washington, D.C.: Cistercian Publications, 1973) pp. 143, 147, and 148.

'The Most High gave man knowledge of the things he had wondrously created.'[38] This leads almost directly into a remarkable commentary on Ecclesiasticus in praise of physicians and the medicinal arts. 'By these [physicians] he [God] shall cure and shall allay their pains', writes the Sage, 'and of these the apothecary shall make sweet confections, and shall make up ointments of health, and of his works there shall be no end. For the peace of God is over all the face of the earth' [Si 38:7–8]. These sweet confections and ointments of health are the medicinal food and drink of Holy Writ, Rhabanus tells us, and are also disciplinary actions inflicted with a view to our restoration to spiritual health. 'But when it says, "and of his [the physician's] works there shall be no end [*et non consummabuntur opera eius*]", this means that our true Physician [the Lord] never stops working cures daily in the Church through his ministers, until, at the last judgment, through his grace everything that is mortal will be swallowed up by Life, and then will take place what follows: "The peace of the Lord will be over all the face of the earth [*pax Domini super faciem terrae*]." '[39] Our cistercian author has rephrased the Sage who has just told us that the physician's work will *not* be finished until the last judgement. But to say that the work of the physician Bernard, through whom the true Physician performs his ministry of healing in the Church, is 'consummated unto good' comes to the same thing. And we can think of the splendid line from Bernard's *De diversis* 76: *Neque . . . consummari in bono possumus, donec gloria repleamur;*[40] 'neither can we be consummated in good until we are filled with glory.' As for the final line of the antiphon, *pax Dei super eum in aeternum*, this is clearly an editorial transmogrification of Ecclesiasticus 38:8, *Pax enim Dei super faciem terrae*. So, as in the case of the preceding solemn responsory, we have another chant that begins with Bernard's ecclesial ministry and ends in his consummation in glory.

The Night Office

The *invitatory antiphon*, unremarkable for its terminology, is both non-biblical and, it would seem, non-bernardine. Still, Geoffroy of Auxerre—Bernard's secretary and biographer, fourth abbot of Clairvaux (1161–1165), and indefatigable promoter of the saint's canonization process—

---

[38] PL 109:1031B.
[39] PL 109:1031C.
[40] SBOp 6/1:315, 8–9.

has left us a sermon based precisely on this invitatory antiphon.[41] Geoffroy speaks of *three* confessions rather than the traditional two (confession of sin, confession of praise). And Bernard's robe of glory is, he assures us, a *matron's* robe (since the nuptials of the Lamb have now been celebrated, and Bernard is no longer merely *sponsa*, but *uxor*). Geoffroy seems so confident in his exegesis that one wonders whether he might be the author of the entire office.

All thirteen antiphons of the three nocturns share these characteristics: (a) their sources are biblical; (b) they are drawn almost exclusively from the sapiential books; (c) the biblical texts are treated with considerable freedom. We are at a considerable remove from those offices in which the antiphons are based on a biography of a saint. Here the author prefers to interpret Bernard's life and mission with the help of the wisdom literature. We ourselves would doubtless, in piecing together a Saint Bernard office from biblical sources, prefer texts drawn from New Testament sources, texts redolent of the great bernardine themes: God is love; God loved us first. Instead we have texts taken from books which, for us moderns, lack theological depth: proverbs, axioms, homely sayings of sages—a kind of literature not immediately distinguishable from the court literature of co-eval egyptian scribes and sages. For the author of this office, however, the whole of Scripture makes sense only when read by the light of the risen Christ, and with reference to the whole of salvation history. For him, a distinction between 'Old' and 'New' Testaments is here without real relevance. Recourse to the splendid *Anchor Bible* commentaries would be distinctly unhelpful for our present purpose. So once again we turn to the glosses. Since we have to be selective in our choice of antiphons, we shall simply take the first antiphon in each of the three nocturns.

Antiphon 1, 'The ways of the holy man', is re-working of Proverbs 3:17–18a, which is a fragment of a hymn in praise of wisdom. Of the four Clairvaux glossed manuscripts of Proverbs I have at hand, three present the 'ordinary' gloss based chiefly on Bede the Venerable's commentary *In Proverbia*[42] (Troyes 474, 1378, 1380), while the fourth (Troyes 1481) escapes identification, even with the help of F. Stegmueller's comprehensive eleven-volume *Repertorium Biblicum Medii Aevi*. This last manuscript offers these interlinear glosses, ff. 4v–5r: UIE EIUS UIE

[41]Edited for the first time by Jean Leclercq, *Etudes sur saint Bernard et le texte de ses écrits*, in ASOC 9 (1953) 157–60.
[42]CC, *Series Latina* CXIX B, pp. 23–163; PL 91:937–1040.

PULCHRE (doctrina euangelica puri hominis modum. legem excedunt) ET OMNES SEMITE ILLIUS PACIFICE (omnia que in carne gessit. et que precepit ad pacem ducunt; homines deo et angelis et sibi ipsis pacificant). LIGNUM UITE EST HIS QUI APPREHENDERINT EAM (intellectu uel amore). According to this gloss, then, Bernard's ways are the gospel teaching, which exceed the measure of mere man and the law. Further, 'all the deeds he performed in the flesh lead to peace; they restore peace between men and God, men and angels, men and men.' Finally, the gospel teaching is the 'tree of life for those who lay hold of it through understanding and love.' And the marginal gloss about the 'tree of life' adds a specifically christological note: 'Like the tree of life in the midst of paradise, so also Christ in the midst of the Church gives life to all things; by the sacraments of his flesh and blood we receive even now the pledge of life; and in the future we shall be rendered blessed by the vision of his presence.'[43] All this is so parallel with the *glossa ordinaria* that, despite textual differences, there is here no point in transcribing the glosses common to the other three Clairvaux manuscripts, and the reader interested in verifying these texts can do so equivalently by referring to Bede's commentary on Proverbs 3:17–18a.[44] Here, however, the point is that it is the gloss which demonstrates the supreme applicability of Proverbs 3:17–18a to Bernard of Clairvaux.

With *Antiphon 7*—the first antiphon of the second nocturn—we are brought back to the same passage utilized earlier for the First Vespers responsory. (We may note that the same chapter 50 of Ecclesiasticus is the source most drawn on for this Night Office—for antiphons 7, 8, 9, 11, and 12; and for responsory 10, sung also at Vespers I). 'As an olive tree budding forth', the antiphon begins, and Rhabanus, followed by the glossator,[45] explains: 'In the olive tree we may rightly understand the light of faith and the love of mercy'—and here Rhabanus takes for granted that the reader is bright enough to recognize an implicit reference to the traditional symbolism of oil, used both for light (= faith) and for medicinal balm (= mercy). The antiphon continues: 'and [as] a cypress rearing itself on high', which Rhabanus and glossator take to mean 'the heights of perfection'; and, though there is no explicit reference in the

---

[43]*Sicut in medio paradisi lignum uite est, sicut in medio ecclesie christus uiuificat omnia: cuius et nunc sacramentis carnis et sanguinis pignus uite accipimus, et in futuro beatificabimur presenti aspectu.*
[44]CC, Latina XIXI B, p. 42, lines 147–58; PL 91:952.
[45]PL 109:1116A; Troyes 1380, f. 109r.

412 *Chrysogonus Waddell*

biblical verse to the fragrance given off by the cypress, this fragrance seems so characteristic of the cypress that Rhabanus and gloss add: 'and the most sweet fragrance of a good will, which the saints possess.'[46] So frequent are references to the olive and to cypress trees in Ecclesiasticus, and so rich their symbolism, that Rhabanus refers the reader to other relevant parallel texts to flesh out his present brief note on the verse. For our own purpose, however, it suffices to note that when the antiphon has 'the blessed man' Bernard ascending to the glory of holiness 'as an olive tree budding forth, and a cypress rearing itself on high', we are to understand that it is by the light of his faith and the healing balm of his mercy (the olive tree) and the perfection of his life and deeds that had their roots in the depths of his being, in his 'good will' (the cypress tree), that the blessed man Bernard attained at last to the glory which is the crown of true holiness.

Anthiphons 8 and *9* are not among the first antiphons of the three nocturns selected here for commentary, but their significance is such that they deserve at least a passing comment. *Antiphon 8* (Si 50:16–17) refers implicitly to the christological dimension of Bernard's sacerdotal ministry. 'The holy man stretched out his hand to the libation of the altar, and from the blood of the grape he poured forth a divine fragrance to the most high Prince', says *Antiphon 8*. And Rhabanus comments: 'The consummated oblation is performed before the most high Prince when the Body of Christ is offered on the sacred altar to God, the ruler of all; there too [on the holy altar] takes place the libation of the grape, when the Blood of the Redeemer is showed forth in the chalice. "Which is poured out at the foundation of the altar", that is to say, all this is done in commemoration of our Redeemer; for he is the foundation that supports the whole edifice of the Church—the fragrance of whose oblation is most sweet to the Most High King. . . .'[47] *Antiphon 9* is based on Ecclesiasticus 50:5, which refers to the high priest Simon's rebuilding of Jerusalem and to his relationship with the people: 'He prevailed to enlarge the city, and obtained glory in his conversation with the people. . . .' Notes Rhabanus: ' "He prevailed to enlarge the city" when through the grace of Christ the toil of preachers brought about the salvation of many. For the City of God is holy Church. . . .This [Church] the order of preachers therefore prevailed to enlarge when it increased it through preaching the word and through the sacrament of baptism in the number of believers.

[46]PL 109:1116A; Troyes 1380, f. 109r.
[47]PL 109:1117A.

Thanks to the conversion of whom [*De quorum conversione*] it [the order of preachers] is indeed glorified when it obtains its reward. And so there is added: "and obtained glory by the conversation with the people." '[48] Rhabanus' text offers yet another instance of the sempiternal confusion between *conversatio* and *conversio*, and the Clairvaux gloss here explicitly gives *in conversione gentis* as an alternative reading of *in conversatione gentis*.[49] Hence, Simon the high priest obtains glory either through his 'conversation with the people' (namely, the way in which he lived with them), or, in the alternative reading, through the 'conversion of the people'. In the adaptation of the text to Bernard, the ambiguity of meaning makes for an increase of its richness, seeing that 'The just man enlarged his nation' could be taken to refer either to Church at large or to cistercian order in particular or to both. As for the meaning of the line *adeptus gloriam in conversatione eius*, which corresponds to the Vulgate *adeptus gloriam in conversatione gentis*,[50] this can suggest either that the results of Bernard's ministry for christian life in general redound to his glory, or, alternatively, that the observance at Clairvaux and elsewhere in the order redounds to his glory—or, again, both. What is here important is that we translate correctly the *eius* of the last line: Bernard obtains glory, not because of *his* manner of life (which would be, in Latin, *in conversatione sua*), but by *its* (the nation's) manner of life (*in conversatione eius*). Mistranslated, the text makes sense, since Bernard did indeed cover himself with glory by the way he lived his life. But, correctly translated, the text renders an even richer meaning, given that it is our own concrete way of life (*conversatio*) that redounds to the glory of our father Bernard, who contributed so richly to this way of life. Bernard's glory is not unrelated, then, to our own quality of life.

The first half of chapter 39 of Ecclesiasticus, from which the antiphon *ad cantica* is drawn in part (Ecclesiasticus 39:8) is a hymn in praise of the scribe. 'For if it shall please the great Lord, he will fill him with the spirit of understanding', says Sirach (39:8), and continues: 'And he [the scribe] will pour forth the words of his wisdom as showers . . .' [v. 9a]. By way of commentary Rhabanus explains: 'The Lord gives his faithful preacher and the one who, diligent, seeks for heavenly wisdom, the Spirit

[48]PL 109:1114D–15A.

[49]Troyes 1380, f. 108v.

[50]The Douai version correctly translates *adeptus est gloriam in conversatione gentis* by 'and [he] obtained glory in his conversation with the people.' But the latin also can be taken to mean—as Rhabanus and the cistercian author of the antiphon took it to mean—'he obtained glory through the manner of life [or conversion] of the people.'

of understanding, so that he may know when and where and how he is to utter the divine words. And he himself [the Lord] directs the counsel of his good will and the discipline of his right conversation, and consoles and strengthens him by his inward inspiration, so that he may confidently preach the precepts of God's covenants amidst the adversity of the world.'[51] The author of the antiphon has excerpted from Ecclesiasticus 39:8 a single snippet, changed the tense, and adapted the half-verse to its present context: *Dominus . . . spiritu intelligentiae replebit illum* becomes *Replevit sanctum suum Dominus spiritu intelligentiae*. The second half of the antiphon is verbally independent of Sirach and Rhabanus, but paraphrases in terms that smack of Bernard himself the substance of Rhabanus' remarks about the infusion of the spirit of understanding in function of the ministry of preaching. *Fluenta doctrinae* is not a common expression; Bernard uses it twice in contextually significant lines: first, in *Sermon 2 on the Song of Songs*, where he prays: 'Let him, in his own person, kiss me with the kiss of his mouth, whose grace-giving presence and streams of wondrous doctrine [*admirandae fluenta doctrinae*] may become in me a fountain of living water, springing up unto eternal life.'[52] More significant is Bernard's second use of the expression in his sixth Ascension sermon, where he says that those who drink from the streams of heavenly doctrine that flow from the only-begotten must afterwards offer those very same streams to the people, for them to drink: 'Blessed are they to whom the only-begotten Son who is in the bosom of the Father declared and made known all things whatsoever he has heard from the Father, so that they drank from the most pure fountain of very Truth the streams of heavenly doctrine [*fluenta doctrinae caelestis*] which they were afterwards to pour out [*propinanda*], or rather, indeed, to *belch* forth [*eructanda*, see Psalm 44:1] for all the peoples.'[53] (It is possible that Bernard and the author of Bernard's office are here somewhat dependent on Saint Gregory, whose use of the term *fluenta* is frequent in combination with words such as *mandata, scientia, doctrina, praedicatio, veritas*.[54]) Let it be noted in passing that Bernard himself was responsible for the adoption of an office for Evangelists

---

[51]PL 109:1039BC.

[52]SBOp 2:9, 13–15.

[53]SBOp 5:156, 25–157, 2. Note the similiarity with the line from the First Vespers responsory: *FLUENTA gratiae PROPINAVIT in POPULO*.

[54]See Fiches 7236–37 of the Corpus Christianorum *Thesaurus Sancti Gregorii Magni* (Louvain: Brepols, 1986).

in the reformed cistercian antiphonary,[55] and the fourth antiphon of the second nocturn may have provided the background for the antiphon under discussion: *Spiritu intelligentiae replevit eos Dominus, et ipsi tamquam imbres miserunt eloquia sapientiae suae*—based from beginning to end on Ecclesiasticus 39:8b–9a. But this antiphon refers to the scribe's own wisdom, *sapientiae suae*; whereas the antiphon under discussion refers, in terms Bernard had made his own, to streams of doctrine the source of which is not in Bernard but in God.

Every one of the Night Office antiphons deserves detailed comment, but we now must pass to four of the responsories—the ones positioned in places of relative emphasis.

The *first responsory, Prima virtus,* may possibly have been used to open the responsory-series for a rather material (and, for us, quite specious) reason: a text with the incipit 'The first' belongs first. But however this may be, it is true that this text is, of all these responsory texts, apparently the most 'material' in that it seems to show us Bernard under the aspect of his mere physical appearance. But, if we consider what the text takes for granted, we realize that more than physical appearance is here of concern: if Bernard's appearance and physical mode of expression can be described in terms of harmony and perfect order, this is only because the outward expression is an extension and a manifestation of the inward truth. This is the closest this office gives us to a 'photograph' of the saint. We are not told, however, that he was of a trifle more than average height, that his hair was somewhat reddish streaked with grey, and that his frame was frail and emaciated. At this point the glossed Bible is of no help, since the responsory is not biblical. Nor is it patristic. Its source is, rather, Bernard himself, at least indirectly.

This responsory is one of several of these office texts traced by Bruno Griesser to Saint Bernard's *Vita Malachiae*.[56] Actually, the *Vita Malachiae* is only the indirect source—the direct source being the Clairvaux proper office for Saint Malachy composed at Clairvaux itself with a view to the first attempt at Malachy's canonization in 1162. This office survives in its original form only in a single manuscript (Douai,

---

[55]This office, found in a number of monastic manuscripts from the eleventh century and onwards, has yet to become the object of scholarly attention. My own tentative hypothesis, based on the provenance and dating of a number of manuscripts, is that the office originated in the St-Bénigne de Dijon milieu. Whatever its source, it was adopted by the Cistercians for the reformed antiphonary a bit before 1147, and survived there until the 'romanization' of the same breviary in the middle of the seventeenth century.

[56]See above, footnote 3.

Chrysogonus Waddell

Bibl. municipale, ms 372) from the benedictine abbey of Anchin. It was written towards 1165 by the abbey's most reputable scribe, Siger.[57] This remarkable compilation is made up of three volumes of Bernard's *opera* copied largely from Clairvaux sources. At the time the final version of Saint Bernard's own proper office was finalized around 1174, the earlier Saint Malachy office was quarried for suitable material. Since this Saint Malachy office had been composed chiefly from texts drawn from Bernard's own writings about Malachy—the *Vita* and two sermons[58]— it follows that, unbeknownst to Bernard, he himself, in writing about Malachy, was authoring in part his own liturgical office. Years later his biographer and former secretary, Geoffroy, who claims to have taken down the *Vita Malachiae* at Bernard's dictation, found this wholly congruous, since, in writing about Malachy, 'our most holy Father made known what his own holy life was like; in the blessed Malachy he gave expression to his own image, without realizing it.'[59]

In the present instance, the first responsory of the Saint Malachy office has been adopted as the first responsory of Saint Bernard's office, with one variation: the substitution of *viri sancti* for *Malachiae*. The lines excerpted from the *Vita Malachiae* 19.43 represent the essential of the passage as here given in part in the Meyer translation:

> In my opinion, the first and the greatest miracle that he presented was the man himself. I do not even mention the inner man. His life and way of life showed forth his beauty and courage and purity, and he carried himself outwardly in so modest and becoming a manner that there was nothing in him that could displease those who saw him. . . .Who ever saw him using either his hand or his foot to no purpose? Was there anything in his walk, his appearance, his bearing, or his countenance that was not edifying?. . .He kept himself under strict discipline, totally marked with virtue, the model of perfection. . . .[60]

Responsory 4 brings us yet another Wisdom-text, this one from early on in Ecclesiasticus (9:22b–23, 24b). The immediate context is provided

[57]Copious details in C. Waddell, 'The Two Saint Malachy Offices from Clairvaux', pp. 123–59.

[58]For the *Vita* see SBOp 3:297–378; for the two sermons, SBOp 5:417–23 and 6/1:50–55.

[59]See Geoffroy's Saint Bernard sermon edited by Jean Leclercq in ASOC 9 (1953) 160: *Suos uero sanctissimus pater noster commendauit mores, in beato Malachia suam expressit imaginem non aduertens.*

[60]Robert T. Meyer (trans.), *Bernard of Clairvaux: The Life and Death of Saint Malachy the Irishman,* CF 10 (Kalamazoo, Michigan: Cistercian Publications, 1978) p. 57.

by the half-verse omitted by the author of the responsory: 'Let just men be your table-guests.' The general content of chapter 9—cautions against loose women and dangerous conversations—hardly seems appropriate for the purposes of an author of a Saint Bernard office, and Bernard himself never once quotes even in part any of the twenty-five verses of this chapter.[61] But, as usual, it is Rhabanus and the glossator who provide the key for our understanding of the text as adapted to its use as a responsory. To quote Rhabanus in part:

> This meal pertains more to spiritual banquets than to bodily delicacies. Whoever, therefore, assiduously abides with just men in the meditation of the holy Scriptures and in the practice of the sacred virtues, and at all times praises the Lord with heart and lips, will be filled beyond all doubt with eternal satiety. 'Blessed', says he, 'is the one who eats bread in the kingdom of God', that is, the bread of life; whosoever eats it will never die, but will live and rejoice with the saints in the heavenly kingdom.[62]

So the monk chanting the responsory was presumed to know, thanks to the gloss and Rhabanus, that the fear of the Lord which was Bernard's boast, the thought of God which was ever in his mind, and his every word about the precepts of the Lord—all this was the fruit of Bernard's companionship with the just (Augustine? Ambrose? Gregory?) in their meditation on Holy Writ and in their lives of virtue. As for the responsory-verse, this has been adapted from verse 24: 'Works shall be praised for the hand of the artificers, and the prince of the people for the wisdom of his speech. . . .' The 'princes of the people', says the gloss, are the holy doctors of the Church; they are princes of the people 'because in the words of the doctors wisdom and eloquence shine resplendent.'[63] This exegesis was doubtless meant to perdure even in the adaptation of the text, where Bernard is styled 'shepherd' rather than 'prince'. Even without reference to the glossed text the entire responsory makes excellent sense. But the text becomes even more focussed and rings even more true when exegeted with the help of Rhabanus and the glossator.

Responsory 8 is based on yet another text from Ecclesiasticus never quoted by Bernard and, if we look at the context, not *a priori* likely

---

[61] Si 9:1 is referred to in the apparatus for the second sermon in the Easter Octave (SBOp 5:119, 25); but here 'Eccli' (Ecclesiasticus) is a misprint for 'Eccle' (Ecclesiastes).

[62] PL 109:824A.

[63] Troyes 1380, f. 42r; the gloss, as usual, is based on Rhabanus, PL 109:824B.

as a source for an appropriate responsory. The first part of chapter 17
describes the creation of man and God's favor toward the human race,
with special reference to Israel. Our own author has taken verses that refer
to mankind in general and made them apply to Bernard in particular.
Thus, the 'everlasting covenant' that God makes with Adam and Eve
is now an everlasting covenant between God and Bernard. What gives
our particular text its real significance, however, is the more general
context provided by Rhabanus' exegesis of the Sage's description of the
creation of Adam and Eve, and of the gifts with which God endowed
them: it reads almost like a summary sketch of Bernard's anthropology,
according to which man is constituted, in virtue of his creation, *capax
Dei*. Care must be taken, of course, not to give Rhabanus' use of terms
such as *lex naturalis* the more precise signification they would acquire
in the heyday of scholasticism. Rhabanus says in part, commenting on
verses 9–12:

> By 'law' and 'discipline' [v. 9] understand here either the natural
> law [that is, the law inscribed in our nature] which God gave every
> man, that through it he might be subject to his Creator and might
> keep watch within himself over the honorable deeds of good works
> [*bonorum operum honorificentiam*], so that he may at every moment
> live his life in this world with prudence and justice and modesty and
> temperance. Or else it means the written law which he [God] decreed
> to be written down in order to correct and to repair the earlier law
> which was now abolished. For both the natural law and the written
> law teach that we are to love God with all our heart, with all our soul,
> and with all our strength, and that we are to keep his commandments
> by our worship of God and our love of our neighbor.[64]

In this context, God makes an 'everlasting covenant' with Bernard
by making it an absolute imperative of Bernard's very nature that he
love, love, and love. Bernard's nature can be fulfilled only through love:
love of God, love of neighbor. To be means to love—and here Bernard
stands, of course, for every monk, for every Christian, for every human
being. So, having established an 'everlasting covenant' with Bernard,
God reveals to him his justice and judgments—terms left undefined by
Rhabanus and the glossator as being, perhaps, too obvious to require
comment. And the responsory-verset adds from verse 11a: 'His eye saw
the majesty of the glory of God.' So Bernard is one of those whose

[64]PL 109:876CD.

nature has been restored to the integrity human nature enjoyed before the fall; he exists and he acts in function of love alone; and therefore he was able to see and understand God's decrees and deeds ('justice and judgments') and was able even to behold something of God's glory ('the majesty of the glory of God').

It may rightly be objected that at some undetermined point eisegesis has here replaced exegesis. But this is inevitable when we are dealing with a literary genre in which truth is communicated more by way of suggestion than by way of bald statement.

Responsory 12 pieces together and adapts fragments from Ecclesiasticus 47:9–10 and 12. What is said by the Sage in praise of David is now sung in praise of Bernard, whose life and mission are here summed up in terms of praise and love. Perhaps we might also see in the verse, which refers in the first instance to David's role in the reform of what was to become the Temple liturgy, a discreet allusion to Bernard's role in the reform of the order's liturgy: 'He [Bernard] added beauty in the celebration of the holy work, and set in order its holy time. . . .' But in the present instance it seems less likely that the author of the responsory depended on the parallel glosses to enrich the meaning of the text, given that, for Rhabanus and the glossator, the anti-type of David is Christ himself rather than Everyman or any individual saint or group of saints. Still, sections of the gloss serve admirably to enrich our understanding of the biblical texts here applied to Bernard:

> Our David. . . crushed and extirpated the enemies of the Church. In keeping with the type which the historical David preferred in his own person, he arranges the ecclesiastical ministry in that house of God which is holy Church, and by his own decision he disposes and dispenses the offices of each individual for the praise of God; so that in every place where he [God] governs, the heavenly and terrestrial created being may at all times ever sing out in praise of him.[65]

Lauds

Only two Lauds formulas are proper to this office. The antiphon *Domum tuam*, based on Psalm 92:5b (*Domum tuam decet sanctitudo, Domine, in longitudinem dierum*), was excerpted as indicated from one of Saint Bernard's two Saint Malachy sermons. The immediate source, however, is the original Saint Malachy office, where the antiphon served in

---

[65]PL 109:1096C; Troyes 1380, f. 106v.

the same place as in Saint Bernard's office.[66] In passing from Malachy's office to Bernard's, however, the original incipit was altered, and the final phrase was lopped off:

Malachy Domum istam decet sanctitudo, in qua tantae
Bernard Domum tuam, Domine, decet sanctitudo, in qua tantae

M frequentatur memoria sanctitatis. Sancte Malachia, serva eam
B frequentatur memoria sanctitatis.

M in sanctitate et iustitia.
B

In the Saint Malachy version, the intensive *istam*—'Holiness becomes *this selfsame* house . . .'—is singularly appropriate for Clairvaux, the scene of Malachy's death, the site of his tomb, and the place where Malachy's office was composed and where his *cultus* first began and flourished. The Saint Bernard variant form is less localized: 'Holiness becomes your house, O Lord . . .'—that is, any church, any community where the memorial of the man of God, Bernard, is celebrated. Recourse to the standard gloss on the Psalm 92:5b is unhelpful here, particularly since Saint Augustine (who lies behind most of the standard psalter glosses) takes the 'house' here to refer to the whole universe at the End Time, when Christ returns in glory and the whole of heaven and earth becomes the house of the Lord.

Biblical glosses will do nothing, either, to enrich our understanding of the *Benedictus* antiphon. We may recognize in the *incipit* a parody of the *incipit* of the *Benedictus*: *Benedictus Dominus Deus Israel* (Luke 1:68a). And the phrase *supernam laetificavit civitatem suam* is surely meant to remind us of Psalm 45:5a: *Fluminis impetus laetificat civitatem Dei*. But the sense of the antiphon is contained within itself. It may be of interest, however, to trace the transformation of the text as it passes from Saint Bernard's sermon on Malachy into Malachy's proper office, and from there into Bernard's proper office:

Sermon Benedictus Dominus Deus Malachiae,
Off.M. Benedictus Dominus Deus Malachiae,
Off.B. Benedictus Dominus Deus patris nostri,

S qui tanti Pontificis ministerio visitavit plebem suam,
M qui eius pontificio visitavit plebem suam,
B

---

[66]See p. 147 of the study indicated above, footnote 57.

S
M eius exemplo aedificavit ecclesiam suam,
B qui eius doctrina et exemplo aedificavit ecclesiam suam;
S et nunc assumpto eo in sanctam civitatem,
M
B eius felici assumptione supernam laetificavit civitatem suam;
S tantae recordatione suavitatis
M eius sollemni recordatione
B eius sollemni recordatione

S nostram non desinit consolari captivitatem.
M presentem hodie consolatur familiam suam.
B presentem hodie consolatur familiam suam.

All the other Lauds texts and chants, while contributing to flesh out the portrait of the saint, are taken from the Common.

The Little Hours

The Little Hour antiphons from Prime through Sext are all taken from the same passage of the *Vita Malachiae*, and are all adapted from antiphons which first appeared in the Clairvaux Saint Malachy office.[67] There is a certain congruity about the positioning of these three antiphons which trace Bernard's growth in appropriate terms even as the day progresses from daybreak through high noon (Prime: *infantia*; Terce: *profectus*; Sext: *crescere*). But despite the theologically rich *unctione magistra* in the Terce antiphon, these antiphons are the least significant ones in the entire office. We are reminded of those characteristically medieval proper offices whose antiphons and responsories are culled from the corresponding *Vita* with only slight editorial intervention. Until now, Bernard's office had moved along on a much higher level of theological sophistication.

None marks the terminus of the cycle of growth here below: death comes, and Bernard's body is laid aside even as he himself makes his way into the depths of heaven. The text is, like the preceding ones, by Bernard, but this one is from his Saint Victor office written for the abbot and community of Montiéramey.[68] As in the case of the Malachy

---

[67]In the Saint Malachy office, these three antiphons are the first three of the Night Office series. See pp. 143–44 of the study indicated above, footnote 57.

[68]The entire office received its first critical edition in SBOp 3:497–508. The covering Ep 398 which accompanied the office and offers Bernard's own ideas about the nature of liturgical music is in SBOp 8:377–79. Of particular interest is Leclercq's article, 'Saint

antiphons adapted for use in Bernard's office, we can trace the evolution of the text as it passes from Sermon 2 *in Natale s. Victoris* into his office and thence into Bernard's office:

Sermo Hodie Victor, posito corpore,

Off V Hodie, posito corpore, Victor,

Off B Hodie, posito corpore, pater sanctus

S quo solo praepediri ab introitu gloriae videbatur,

V quo solo praepediri ab introitu gloriae videbatur,

B

S tanto alacrior, quanto expeditior,

V dives meritis, signis clarus, expeditius

B dives meritis

S penetravit in sancta, similis factus in gloria Sanctorum.

V penetravit in sancta, similis factus in gloria sanctorum.

B penetravit in sancta, similis factus in gloria sanctorum.

We can perhaps catch a faint echo of Hebrews 4:14 (*Habentes ergo pontificem magnum, qui penetravit caelos*) and 9:12 (*introivit semel in sancta*) in the incise *penetravit in sancta*, but the final line is clearly borrowed from Ecclesiasticus 45:2a, from a passage in praise of Moses. Here we are dealing simply with an appropriate snippet borrowed for the sake of its *prima facie* meaning, and without reference to its precise context. Indeed, it is just as likely that the immediate point of reference is the principal *capitulum* of the office, Ecclesiasticus 45:1–2a (assigned to Vespers I and II, Lauds, and Terce). Like the preceding three non-biblical antiphons, this one is more 'historical' in nature, and stands on its own without any significant biblical point of reference.

Second Vespers

As a rule, the Cistercians, in keeping with the widespread monastic practice, repeated at Second Vespers the first four antiphons of the Night Office, and this is what they have done here. Almost all the remaining formulas are taken from the Common. The sole exception is the climactic

Victor écrivain d'après l'Office de Saint Victor', first published in *Revue bénédictine* 74 (1964) 155–69, and then reproduced in *Recueil d'études sur saint Bernard et ses écrits* 2 (Rome: Edizioni di Storia e Letteratura, 1966) pp. 149–68. As suggested by the title, Leclercq chose to treat more directly of the literary form of the office than of its theological content.

Magnificat antiphon in which, as earlier, Saint Bernard is now describing the apotheosis of Saint Bernard. The original text comes, as was the case with several other of these antiphons, from his second Saint Malachy sermon. In passing into the Saint Malachy office, where it also served as the *Magnificat* antiphon for Second Vespers, the text was tightened up. And this process of tightening up was continued when the antiphon was further adapted for Malachy's panegyrist Bernard:

Mal Exultet in Domino spiritus Malachiae,
Ber Exultet in Domino spiritus viri sancti,

Mal quod mole levatus corporea,
Ber quod mole levatus corporea,

Mal nulla iam terrena materia praegravatur quominus tota alacritate
     omnem transiens creaturam,
Ber

Mal pergat totus in Deum, et adhaerens illi,
Ber totus pergat in Deum, et adhaerens illi,

Mal unus fit cum eo spiritus in aeternum.
Ber unus fit cum eo spiritus in aeternum.

The opening incise is based on the second line of the *Magnificat* itself (*et exultavit spiritus meus in Deo salutari meo*; Luke 1:47), but this is the least significant part of an antiphon which implicitly contains the whole of Bernard's mystical theology. The last obstacle to the consummation of Bernard's perfect union with God has been removed through death. All his life he has been clinging to God, adhering to him (an allusion to one of Bernard's favorite texts, Psalm 72:28), becoming more and more perfectly 'one spirit with him'. Few New Testament texts were more often quoted by Bernard than this 'one spirit' text (1 Corinthians 6:17)— some fifty citations, and usually in passages where this pauline formula is central to the point under discussion. It is a tribute to Etienne Gilson's mastery of Bernard's teaching that the final chapter of his classic study of the saint's mystical theology bears the title *Unitas Spiritus*, and that the content of this insightful chapter is, in effect, an exploration of the implications of Bernard's use of the formula *Qui autem adhaeret Dominio, unus spiritus est*. Indeed, the best possible exegesis of our *Magnificat* antiphon may be found in the final lines of Gilson's final chapter:

To understand [Bernard's mystical theology] as it truly is we should have to be able to seize in one unique and simple intuition the work of a God who creates man in order to associate him, by way of beatitude, with His own likeness, Who gives man back the lost likeness that he may give back the lost beatitude, and Who, while awaiting the day when the work shall be fully accomplished, gratuitously raises to like felicity souls whom the gift of charity has already made conformable to His nature—*Deus charitas est* —closely enough to enable them to taste even here below of the blessedness of His life. And then it is that there reigns between God and his creature made to His image, this perfect conformity, this UNITY OF SPIRIT, in which the human substance finds at last its full actuality; and in that creature the great work of creation is completed, for he becomes at last that very thing for which he was made—a translucid mirror in which God now sees nought but Himself, and in which the soul now sees nought but God: a created participation of His glory and of His beatitude.[69]

In brief, the Clairvaux office of Saint Bernard, in arriving at this final antiphon, presents Bernard himself as the supreme exemplar of his own mystical theology.

Addenda from the Vatican Chigi Manuscript

Added to the manuscript as though by way of an afterthought, the Little Hour *capitula* and collects (indicated for Terce only by their incipits) are taken wholly from the Common for a Confessor Not a Bishop. They are identical with the formulas used for Saint Benedict, but also for any other abbot with a festal office in the cistercian calendar. The principal collect has already been discussed above, in note 24. The other two collects are for Sext and None respectively, with the Sext collect being modelled on a collect from the gregorian formulary for Saint John the Divine (27 December),[70] the None collect on a Saint Lawrence collect (10 August) from the same tradition.[71]

GENERAL CONCLUSIONS

The texts of the chant-formulas derive, for the most part, from two chief sources: (A) Bernard himself, whether from his Office for Saint Victor, or from his several writings about Saint Malachy—though in the

---

[69]E. Gilson, *The Mystical Theology of Saint Bernard*, trans. A.H.C. Downes (London: Sheed and Ward, 1940) p. 150.

[70]Deshusses edition, formulary 11, no. 72, p. 109.

[71]Deshusses edition, formulary 142, no. 642, p. 258.

case of the latter, these texts had already been re-worked for incorporation into the original Clairvaux Saint Malachy office. These formulas are responsories 1, 5, and 9 of the Night Office, as well as all the proper antiphons from Lauds onwards.[72] (B) The majority of the antiphons and responsories from Vespers I through the Night Office are based on texts from the wisdom books, with a marked preference being given to Ecclesiasticus. The exceptions are the invitatory antiphon and responsories 2 (source?) and 7 (Malachias 2:6).

This concentration on wisdom literature as particularly suitable for singing of the life and deeds and teaching of Bernard is difficult to explain until we exegete these texts with the help of the corresponding biblical glosses. What then emerges is a portrait or, better, an ikon of the sage (mystic) Bernard, whose wisdom, rooted in the word/Word, is identified with Wisdom/Charity, and whose ministry as teacher and preacher extends to the whole Church catholic, to which he brings unity and peace. The limitations of this article preclude any consideration of all but a few of these incredibly rich biblical responsories and antiphons. But a study of all the remaining formulas only re-enforces and enriches this ikonic presentation of the saint, who serves to illustrate so perfectly what Gerhart Ladner understands by the notions of that 'greatness' and that 'order' which shaped medieval european civilization. In the final pages of his insightful survey of the achievements of his teacher Gerhart Burian Ladner, John Van Engen, director of the Notre Dame Medieval Institute, has this to say:

> Greatness and order must, in Ladner's view, take human expression, not the form of empire, institutions, or even ideas. And the form human greatness took in the Middle Ages differed from that it assumed in ancient empires and city-states. . . .In the Middle Ages, under the impact of Christian teaching, the central feature that made human beings 'great' was *holiness* . . .—or, in the language of another of his [Ladner's] themes, of regaining and re-forming the true image of man in keeping with the incarnate image of Christ. . . .This notion of holiness as the constituent part of human greatness fit as well into the overarching notion of order. For the controlling notion here was that of man as pilgrim, still a stranger to the perfect order of holiness in heaven and estranged as well, as a Christian pilgrim, from the

[72]This prescinds, of course, from the repetition of the Night Office antiphons at Vespers II.

evil disorder of the present world. . . .And the perfect order is not something entirely other-worldly, but the renewal in men and women of their complete image-likeness to God.[73]

But let Bernard himself have the final word, where he tells us in the peroration of his *Eighty-second Sermon on the Song of Songs*:

When. . . iniquity shall be taken away, which is the cause of our part in unlikeness, then will there be union of spirit, then will there be mutual vision, and mutual dilection. When that which is perfect is come, then that which is in part shall be done away. And then between God and the soul shall be nought but a mutual dilection chaste and consummated, a full mutual recognition, a manifest vision, a firm conjunction, a society undivided, and a perfect likeness. Then shall the soul know God even as she is known; then shall she love as she is loved; and over his bride shall rejoice the Bridegroom, knowing and known, loving and beloved. . . .[74]

ABSTRACTS

L'office propre de S. Bernard (1175) présente une interprétation théologique profonde de la vie et de la mission du saint—mais seulement à condition de comprendre le langage symbolique. Les textes sont empruntés principalement à Bernard lui-même (son office de S. Victor et ses écrits sur S. Malachie) et des livres sapientiaux de la Bible (principalement l'Ecclésiastique). Le sens de ces textes, dans le contexte de l'office de S. Bernard, n'apparaît clairement que lorsqu'on les comprend à la lumière de la Bible glosée, qui transmet la tradition exégétique générale. Lue à la lumière des gloses, la littérature sapientielle, comme le reste de l'Ancien Testament, célèbre le mystère du Christ. Appliqués à Bernard, ces textes révèlent un Bernard transformé par ce mystère, et qui le communique au monde dans et hors du cloître. Bernard est le modèle du sage (mystique), dont la sagesse, enracinée dans le verbe/Verbe, est identifiée à la Sagesse/Charité, et dont le ministère d'enseignement et de prédication s'étend à toute l'Eglise, à laquelle il apporte l'unité et la paix.

[73]John Van Engen, 'Images and Ideas: The Achievements of Gerhart Burian Ladner, with a Bibliography of His Published Works', in *Viator* 20 (1989) 106–107.
[74]SBOp 2:297, 25–298, 2.

The proper Office of Saint Bernard (1175) presents a profound theological interpretation of the life and mission of the saint—but only on condition that one understands the symbolic language. The chant-texts derive chiefly from Saint Bernard himself (his Saint Victor Office and his writings on Saint Malachy) and from the wisdom books of the Bible (chiefly Ecclesiasticus). The meaning of these texts, in the context of Saint Bernard's Office, becomes clear only when one understands them in the light of the glossed Bible, which transmits the exegetical tradition at large. When read in the light of the glosses, the wisdom literature, like the rest of the Old Testament, celebrates the Mystery of Christ. When applied to Bernard, these texts reveal a Bernard who has been transformed by that Mystery, and who communicates it to the world inside the cloister and outside. Bernard is the model of the sage (mystic), whose wisdom, rooted in the word/Word, is identified with Wisdom/Charity, and whose ministry as teacher and preacher extends to the whole Church, to which he brings unity and peace.

Das eigene Offizium des heiligen Bernhard (1175) weist eine tiefe theologische Interpretation des Lebens und der Sendung des heiligen auf—aber nur unter der Voraussetzung, daß man die symbolische Sprache versteht. Die Liedtexte stammen hauptsächlich von Bernhard selbst (asu seinem Offizium des heiligen Viktor und seinen Schriften über den heiligen Malachias) und aus den Weisheitsbüchern der Bibel (hauptsächlich Ecclesiasticus). Die Bedeutung dieser Texte im Kontext des Saint Bernhard-Offiziums wird nur deutlich, wenn man sie im Lichte der glossierten Bibel versteht, die die exegetische Tradition ausführlich überliefert. Wenn sie im Licht der Glossen gelesen wird, dann zelebriert die Weisheitsliteratur wie der Rest des Alten Testaments das Geheimnis Christi. Wenn sie auf Bernhard angewendet werden, offenbaren diese Texte einen Bernhard, der durch dieses Geheimnis umgewandelt worden ist, und der es der Welt im Kloster und ausserhalb übermittelt. Bernhard ist das Modell des Weisen (Mystikers), dessen Weisheit, die im Wort/WORT wurzelt, mit Weisheit/Liebe identifiziert wird, und dessen Amt als Lehrer und Prediger sich auf die ganze Kirche erstreckt, der er Einheit und Frieden bringt.

ALTER MOYSES: THE ROLE OF BERNARD OF CLAIRVAUX IN THE THOUGHT OF JOACHIM OF FIORE*

Bernard McGinn
University of Chicago

THE ONLY CONTEMPORARY AUTHOR mentioned by name in the writings of Joachim of Fiore is Bernard of Clairvaux. As the avatar of the monastic life in the twelfth century, the abbot of Clairvaux is also given a distinctive place in the Calabrian's apocalyptic theology of history. For over a decade Joachim himself was at least a would-be Cistercian as he strove to incorporate his small monastery of Corazzo into the order of Cîteaux. He gradually abandoned the white monks in the late 1180s as his search for the most perfect form of the monastic life led him to establish his own order on the wooded heights of the Sila plateau. Though this action led to his condemnation by the cistercian general chapter in 1192, as well as a vicious attack by Bernard's one-time secretary, Geoffrey of Auxerre, Joachim never lost his immense respect for the man he thought of as the greatest of monks after Benedict.

We may ask, however, just how important Bernard's influence was on Joachim. The abbot of Fiore was very much an autodidact. He had received no formal education in theology. After training as a notary and some years of wandering, he had entered Corazzo about the age of 35 (in 1171). In contrast to his scholastic and even many of his monastic contemporaries, his intellectual baggage was not extensive,

* I should like to thank Robert E. Lerner and E. Randolph Daniel for valuable suggestions concerning the first version of this paper, though they cannot be blamed for my stubbornness in adhering to controversial views and any possible errors.

429

consisting mostly of some Augustine and a smattering of patristic and early medieval authors.[1] The fundamental source for his obscure but powerful thought was in the Bible and in his own visionary experiences. Did Bernard of Clairvaux, then, exercise any really decisive influence on Joachim? Though I admit that the qualifier 'decisive' is capable of many interpretations, I shall argue that Bernard did have such an impact on Joachim. To do so I shall look first at Joachim's explicit references to the abbot of Clairvaux and then at some hitherto unnoticed support in Bernard for several crucial terms of Joachim's vocabulary.

References to Bernard occur in two contexts in Joachim's writings: first, in terms of his witness to correct trinitarian theology against those who would introduce a quaternity into God; and, secondly, with regard to Bernard's place in salvation history. In both cases the abbot of Clairvaux is no marginal figure, but one of significant weight.

In all three of the Calabrian's major writings Bernard is singled out as an opponent of trinitarian heresy. In book 1 of the *Psalterium decem chordarum* Joachim discusses the three major trinitarian errors (Sabellianism, Arianism, and Quaternianism), quoting Bernard's *De consideratione* in two places.[2] An important text on the Cistercians and Bernard in the *Liber de concordia* 4.2.2 mentions the abbot's opposition to heresy.[3] Finally, the *Expositio in Apocalypsim*, emphasizing how holy men have often had recourse to written refutations of heresy, specifically praises

> Blessed Bernard, the abbot of Clairvaux, who in our own time illuminated the Church in a special way by his life, miracles, and knowledge. He was commissioned by the pope who at that time ruled the Church [to write] against some heretics when long disputation had been of no avail.[4]

These are more than peripheral comments. For the abbot of Fiore, proper faith in the Trinity was both the central message of Scripture and the total meaning of history. His noted attack on Peter Lombard for introducing a

---

[1]For a handy survey of Joachim's patristic sources, see Delno C. West and Sandra Zimdars-Swartz, *Joachim of Fiore: A Study in Spiritual Perception and History* (Bloomington: Indiana University Press, 1983) chap. 3.

[2]*Psalterium decem chordarum* (Venice ed., 1527) ff. 232r, 234v. The first passage quotes Csi 5.8; the latter Csi 5.7 (SBOp 3:482, 10–11; and 479, 11–12).

[3]Abbot Joachim of Fiore, *Liber de Concordia Novi ac Veteris Testamenti*, ed. E. Randolph Daniel, Transactions of the American Philosophical Society, 73.8 (Philadelphia: American Philosophical Society, 1983) p. 417, 194 (hereafter referred to as Daniel with appropriate page and line numbers).

[4]*Expositio in Apocalypsim* (Venice ed., 1527) f. 87v.

fourth 'something' into the Trinity through his discussion of *deitas* has been a crucial factor in the abbot's reputation since the Fourth Lateran Council at which this attack was condemned.[5] While there can be no doubt that Joachim misunderstood the Lombard (as Bernard probably had misunderstood Gilbert of Poitiers, the object of his scorn in book 5 of the *De consideratione*), the Calabrian's protest was grounded in a fundamental conflict between styles of theology and different views about the action of the Trinity in history.

Joachim's theology of the Trinity was very much his own, not one derived from Bernard's explicit trinitarian discussions in the *De consideratione* and *Epistola 190*, the tract against Abelard. But Joachim found a valuable ally in Bernard, one who seems to have helped him see 'quaternianism' as the distinctive error of his own perilous time, the end of the second *status* of history. In the complex history of the relations between the monastic and the scholastic modes of theology—a story that contains both alliances and tensions—Bernard and Joachim stand out as major proponents of an attitude of suspicion and condemnation, at least in the matter of trinitarian theology.

Although Bernard had a definite influence on the Calabrian's view of the Trinity, Bernard's real importance for Joachim is based on the position the abbot of Clairvaux and the cistercian order occupy in Trinity's great plan for history. To understand this, it will be necessary to begin with a brief survey of the patterns of Joachim's theology of history.

As is well known, Joachim's theology of history is grounded in two aspects of the mystery of the Trinity which he saw symbolized in the first and last letters of the Greek alphabet—the Alpha pattern of threes, which illustrates how the three divine persons give rise to the three *status* that embrace the whole historical process, and the Omega pattern of twos, which shows how the Old Testament, ascribed to the Father, and the New Testament, ascribed to the Son, produce the 'spiritual understanding' (*intellectus* or *intelligentia spiritualis*) ascribed to the Holy Spirit. In Joachim's view these two underlying patterns are intimately related through a complex system of inner connections based both on the literal understanding of the historical parallels between the Old and the New Testaments (the *concordiae*) and the spiritual understanding of the deeper meaning of both Testaments.

[5]For a survey of Joachim's trinitarian theology, see B. McGinn, *The Calabrian Abbot* (New York: Macmillan, 1987) chap. 6, especially pp. 166–68 on the conflict with Peter Lombard.

Saint Bernard's place in history is evident in both patterns, but will be easier to illustrate on the basis of the Alpha pattern of the three *status* of Father, Son, and Holy Spirit. According to the abbot, the whole of history (*universitas temporum*) rolls on to its appointed end through 150 generations of three *status* structured according to the parallels or concords found in Scripture and church history.[6] This progression is complicated by Joachim's historical dynamism, which, invoking models of organic growth, has each *status* overlap with the preceding one through a period of germination. Thus, the first *status* ascribed to the Father, in which the married life of the laity predominates, counts its first period of twenty-one generations from Adam to Isaac and its second twenty-one generations from Jacob to King Amasias. The third period of twenty-one generations from King Ozias to Christ also constitutes the *germinatio* phase of the second *status*. The second *status*, ascribed to the Son, in which the clerical life rules, has forty-two more generations divided into two periods of twenty-one generations of thirty years each. The final twenty-one generations of the second *status* witness the period of the germination of the third *status* ascribed to the Holy Spirit, the age which will see the predominance of the monastic life.[7] The following diagram may help make this clear:

Diagram 1.[8]

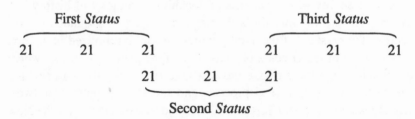

First *Status*   Third *Status*

21   21   21   21   21   21

21   21   21

Second *Status*

Bernard appears in a number of the concords illustrating the interlocking web of generations. We can begin with a passage in the *Liber de*

---

[6] The concordance between the 150 generations of history and the 150 Psalms is discussed at length in *Psalt.* II, ff. 243v–79r, especially 276v–77r.

[7] See *Calabrian Abbot*, pp. 187–89. This view implies a long duration to the third *status*, but Joachim is usually more cautious, claiming that it is impossible to tell its real length given the spiritual mode in which it will be realized.

[8] As this diagram (see *The Calabrian Abbot*, p. 189) makes clear, the total of generations is actually 147. *Psalt.* ff. 276vb–77ra notes the anomaly as a *magnum mysterium*, suggesting that one extra generation should be added for each Person of the Trinity in order to reach the required 150.

concordia, the work that contains Joachim's most important references to Bernard's role in sacred history. *Concordia* 2.1.14–17 contains a treatise on the generational computation of the *ordo monachorum* which provides the basic structure according to which Joachim understands Bernard's historical role. Since the order of monks expresses the mystery of the Holy Spirit, the person in the Trinity who proceeds from two (the Father and the Son), it must have a double origin, one in the time of the Father, or Old Testament, and a second in the time of the Son, or New Testament.[9] If the orders of married and clerics conform to the intervals of twenty-one generations, we can ask if the order of monks follows a similar logic.[10]

Joachim's answer is complex, and attention to the details is important. In the second period of twenty-one generations in the *status* of the Father there are actually two lines of succession, one according to *patres* from Jacob to Amasias, and one according to *principes* or *iudices* from Moses to Abias (*Conc.* 2.1.15). The first corresponds to the mystery of the Son and the second *status*, the other to the mystery of the Holy Spirit and the third *status* of the monastic life. In *Conc.* 2.1.16–17 Joachim shows how his computations prove that this second line illustrates the dual origin of the *ordo monachorum*, first from the prophet Eliseus in the sixteenth generation (that of Asa) in the Old Testament, and then from Benedict, who appeared at the end of the fifteenth and the beginning of the sixteenth generation of New Testament times. Chapter 16 puts it this way:

> According to what pertains to the mystery of the Holy Spirit, begin from Asa and the prophet Eliseus and proceed to Saint Benedict forty-two generations from Eliseus in order to make the beginning of the third *status* whose flowering is in these times, that is, from the time when the cistercian order proceeded from the order of Molesmes.[11]

In the next chapter he summarizes his method of concordances: 'And in all this the mystery of our faith is perfectly clear when by means of generations in mutual concord (as reason demands in a remarkable way)

---

[9]See *Conc.* 2.1.10 (Daniel, pp. 77–79). This is a constant theme of Joachim's teaching. For an overview of Joachim's thoughts on the significance of monasticism, see Edith Pasztor, 'Ideale del monachesimo ed età dello Spirito come realtà spirituale e forma d'utopia', in A. Crocco (ed.), *L'Età dello Spirito e la fine dei tempi in Gioacchino da Fiore e nel gioachimismo medievale: Atti del II Congresso internazionale di Studi Gioachimiti* (Fiore: Centro Internazionale di Studi Gioachimiti, 1986) pp. 57–124.

[10]*Conc.* 2.1.14 (Daniel, p. 84).

[11]*Conc.* 2.1.16 (Daniel, p. 87, 6–11).

both one order is shown to arise from another [that is, the order of clerics form the lay order] and another third order is shown to proceed from two [that is, the order of monks from both the preceding orders].'[12] In the manuscripts of the *Liber de concordia* these concordances are illustrated by a list of the generations of the second *status* that contain two rubrics, one marking the sixteenth generation with 'Benedictus' and 'secunda initiatio monachorum'; and another at the thirty-seventh generation reading 'Bernardus' and the 'ordo cisterciensium'.[13] Similar notations are found in the 'tree figures' that illustrate the *Liber de concordia*, as in Diagram 2.

Considerable work has been done on Joachim's view of the role of Benedict in salvation history.[14] Since the monastic 'spiritual men' (*viri spirituales*) were the agents of the ultimate meaning of history, their gradual revelation from the first beginnings with Elias and Eliseus in the Old Testament are of the utmost significance.[15] Although Joachim praises the early monks of the eastern church who were a part of this emerging tradition in the second *status*, it was not until monasticism moved West and was manifested in the career of Benedict that the third *status* began its real germination.[16] This is why the Calabrian considers Gregory the Great's life of Benedict found in Book 2 of his *Dialogi*, as well as Benedict's own *Regula monachorum*, as sacred texts, almost scriptural

---

[12]*Conc.* 2.1.17 (Daniel, p. 93, 7–11).

[13]*Conc.* 2.1.16 (Daniel, pp. 91–92). There is, it must be said, variation in the mss. concerning these rubrics. These notations, however, are similar to what appears in some of the mss. on the tree diagrams illustrating *Conc.* 2.1.25 (Daniel, pp. 110–11), on which see Daniel, pp. xxxi–xxxii.

[14]Especially Stephen Wessley, '"Bonum est Benedicto mutare locum": The Role of the "Life of Benedict" in Joachim of Fiore's Monastic Reform', *Revue Bénédictine* 90 (1980) 314–28.

[15]In *Conc.* 2.1.14–17, Eliseus alone marks the first initiation of the *ordo monachorum*. Elsewhere Joachim associates Elias as the predecessor of the eremetical life with Eliseus as founder of the coenobitical life; for example, *Conc.* 2.2.4 (Daniel, p. 152), and especially *Conc.* 4.1.16 (Daniel, p. 351). In this latter text the anomaly of placing Benedict in the eighteenth rather than at the end of the fifteenth and beginning of the sixteenth generations seems to be explained by the fact that Joachim is speaking of the time of the monk's *clarificatio* through Gregory's *Dialogi*. See *Conc.* 5.6, 5.13, and 5.15–16 (Venice ed., 1519, ff. 63r-v, 67ra, 67vb–68rb).

[16]On Benedict as marking the transition of monastic perfection from the Greeks to the Latins, see *Conc.* 5.70, f. 98r, and *Tractatus super quatuor evangelia*, ed. E. Buonaiuti, Fonti per la Storia d'Italia (Rome: Istituto Storico Italiano, 1930) pp. 183–84, 232. Joachim often mentions Benedict's role as initiating the third *status*; for example, *Conc.* 2.1.4, 2.1.5, 2.1.10, 2.1.21, 2.2.8, 4.2.1 (Daniel, pp. 67, 68, 77–79, 101, 179, 405–406); *Conc.* 5.21 and 5.73, ff. 70vb and 101ra-va; *Expositio*, f. 5rb; and *Tractatus*, p. 91.

Diagram 2.

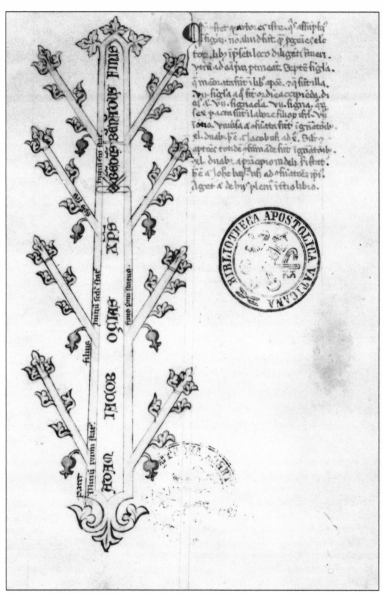

This diagram is based on the tree-figure found in Vat. Lat. ms. 4860, f. 289r, illustrated in Daniel, p. xxxiii. For general background on Joachim's trees, see Marjorie Reeves and Beatrice Hirsch-Reich, *The Figurae of Joachim of Fiore* (Oxford: At the Clarendon Press, 1972) pp. 24–38.

in their import. The treatise that he wrote on them about 1187, the *De vita sancti Benedicti et de officio divino secundum eius doctrinam*, amply demonstrates Benedict's role in history and tells us much about Joachim's view of the Cistercians and of his own monastic vocation, especially his search for solitude in service of ultimate monastic renewal.[17] Both this treatise and the *Liber de concordia* contain important concordances illustrating how the life of Bernard of Clairvaux relates to the imminent manifestation of the fullness of the third *status* of the Holy Spirit.

Bernard's significance, like Benedict's, is both personal and institutional, so we find two types of concords, those which concentrate on the importance of the cistercian order without mention of the abbot of Clairvaux, and those in which Bernard makes an explicit appearance. We shall combine both in the treatment that follows.

Joachim's attitude toward the Cistercians is not without ambivalence, for while he always sees the white monks as having a special place in the evolution of the *ordo monachorum* toward the fullness of the coming third *status*, he does not think of the Cistercians as the apogee of monasticism, but as a stage that would be left behind in the growing manifestation of the spiritual understanding.[18] The most common way by which the abbot of Fiore presents his view of the provisional status of the order is through the invocation of one of his most distinctive numerical symbols, the contrast between five and seven as forming the perfection of twelve. Throughout history, concords of fives indicating a preliminary stage of preparation for sevens marking the fulfillment to be achieved in the third *status* show the importance of this pattern.[19] In the first *status* we find the twelve tribes of Israel of which five received

---

[17]The *Vita* was edited by Cipriano Baraut, 'Un Tratado inedito de Joaquin de Fiore', *Analecta sacra Tarraconensia* 24 (1951) 10–86. Stephen Wessley is at work on a new critical edition. On the work as revelatory of Joachim's sense of his own monastic vocation as a new Benedict, see S. Wessley, ' "Bonum est Benedicto mutare locum" ', pp. 321–24, 327–28; and more recently, 'Female Imagery: A Clue to the Role of Joachim's Order of Fiore', in Julius Kirshner and Suzanne F. Wemple (edd.), *Women of the Medieval World: Essays in Honor of John H. Mundy* (Oxford: Blackwell, 1985) pp. 161–78.

[18]For Joachim's views of the cistercian order in general, see Sandra Zimdars-Swartz, 'Joachim of Fiore and the Cistercian Order: A Study of *De Vita Sancti Benedicti*,' in John R. Sommerfeldt (ed.), *Simplicity and Ordinariness: Studies in Medieval Cistercian History IV*, CS 61 (Kalamazoo, Michigan: Cistercian Publications, 1980) pp. 293–309; and Edith Pasztor, 'Gioacchino da Fiore, S. Bernardo ed il monachesimo cistercense', *Clio* 20 (1984) 549–61.

[19]For a summary, see *Expositio in Apocalypsim*, Liber introductorius, cap. 18, ff. 16vb–17vb. For discussions, see M. Reeves and B. Hirsch-Reich, *The Figurae*, pp. 13–19; and *The Calabrian Abbot*, p. 132.

their inheritance first and seven more completely thereafter. In the second *status* the five patriarchal churches connected with Peter, the type of the active life (Jerusalem, Antioch, Constantinople, Alexandria, and Rome), yielded to the seven churches of Asia Minor to whom John addressed the Apocalypse. In the twelfth century, the dawn of the third *status*, Joachim identifies the first five cistercian houses, Cîteaux and her first four daughters, as the harbingers of seven more perfect monastic houses or groups to come: 'These things pertain (as he who made all things in his Wisdom better knows) to the five cistercian monasteries whose fame is evident today and yesterday and in whom the third *status* itself seems to have begun, although its initiation preceded in the time of Saint Benedict and according to another way from Eliseus the prophet.'[20] In the *Vita* and in the *Concordia* he expresses caution about the identification of the latter seven,[21] but it is difficult not to think that they are represented by the seven oratories of the famous *figura* known as the *Dispositio novi ordinis pertinens ad tertium statum ad instar superne Hierusalem.*[22] We should also note that while the first two patterns of five and seven tribes and apostolic churches appear in the *figura* known as the 'Tree-Eagles' found in the *Liber figurarum*,[23] the five and seven monasteries do not, although they are found in the eagle figure of the *Psalterium.* (See Diagram 3.) In this rather complex figure the abbot's pattern of fives and sevens appears in two ways. First, inscriptions on the bird's body and tail feathers contrast the five patriarchs, apostles, and 'the five whom God knows' with seven patriarchs, apostles, and 'the seven whom God knows'. Then, inscriptions on and above the wings contrast the five spiritual senses of the right wing with the seven typical senses of the left. The third of these refers to 'quinque monasteria et septem futura'.

At the beginning of the *De vita s. Benedicti*, Joachim provides a *concordia* that sketches out the evolution of the *ordo monasticus* and

[20]*Conc.* 4.2.2 (Daniel, p. 415, 150–54; see pp. 413 and 419). For some other appearances of this theme, see *Conc.* 2.2.9 (Daniel, p. 184); *Psalt.* f. 267rb-vb; *Vita* # 7, 11 (ed. Baraut, pp. 21–22, 28).

[21]For expressions of caution, see *Vita* # 7 (p. 21, 35–36), and *Conc.* 4.2.2 (Daniel, p. 415, 155–60).

[22]On this figure, see *Il libro delle figure dell'abate Gioachino da Fiore*, edd. L. Tondelli, M. Reeves, and B. Hirsch-Reich (Turin: SEI, 1953), tavola 12; and the treatment in *The Figurae*, pp. 232–48. There is a translation and study of this figure in B. McGinn (ed.), *Apocalyptic Spirituality*, The Classics of Western Spirituality (New York: Paulist Press, 1979) pp. 142–48. There are a number of texts in the major works that cast further light on this *figura*, especially *Expositio*, f. 18r-v; and *Conc.* 5.23, ff. 71v–72r.

[23]The "Tree-Eagles" are tavola 5 and 6 in *Il libro delle figure*.

Diagram 3.

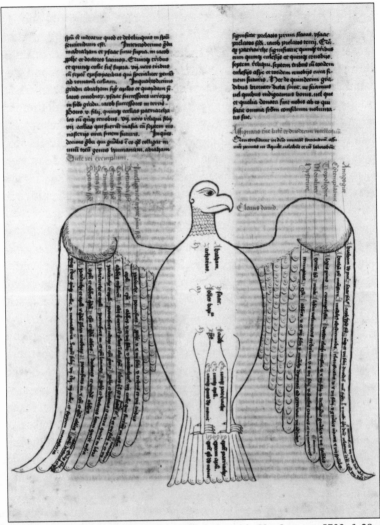

This diagram is adapted from the eagle which is found in Vat. Lat. ms. 5732, f. 28v. It is illustrated in Reeves and Hirsch-Reich, *The Figurae*, plate 6, and discussed on pp. 18–19 and 61–65. The version of the eagle found in the Venice ed. at f. 268r is defective.

place of the Cistercians. Abraham, signifying the order of the patriarchs, gives birth to Isaac, the order of the apostles. Isaac's two sons Jacob and Esau signify respectively the orders of the latin and the greek churches. The family of Jacob and Rachel, finally, is the highest of the latin orders, the monastic life, with Joseph as the order of monks begun by Saint Benedict. Joseph's imprisonment is the time of Cluny when monasticism is bound to carnal things, while the foundation of Cîteaux marks his release to spiritual liberty and exaltation in Egypt.[24] (This involved concordance of the patriarchs is close to another found in *Concordia* 5.49–51 which also mentions the Cistercians.[25])

Joachim's criticism of Cluny, which appears in a number of texts,[26] is also found in the *figura* known as the 'Tree with Side-Shoots'. (See Diagram 3.) In this diagram from the Oxford manuscript of the *Liber figurarum*, two flowering trees represent the theme of gradual election in the Old and the New Testaments. In the New Testament tree the trunk represents the line of promise, the side-shoots those who have been superseded—Gentiles over Jews, Latins over Greeks, monks over clerics, and, finally, Cistercians over Cluniacs. The Cistercians, however, do not attain the fullness of the third *status* signified by the flowering summit of the tree.[27]

It is clear that Joachim was not loath to criticize the Cistercians as well as the Cluniacs both in the *Vita* and in the *Liber de concordia*. The critique that tempers his praise of the white monks is often directed at current failings that underscore the provisional position of the order, especially concerning poverty;[28] but, as Sandra Zimdars-Swartz has shown, it is also directed to an underlying problem that Joachim found in cistercian monasticism, that is, the mixing of the active and

[24]*Vita* # 1 (ed. pp. 10–12) introduces the concord, which is resumed in various ways in the following sections. The Cluniacs are not mentioned explicitly as the time of imprisonment (p. 11, 25–35), but later references make it clear what Joachim had in mind.

[25]*Conc.* 5. 49–51, ff. 83vb–85va. Here Isaac represents the Jews while Laban is the clergy. The sons of Isaac are Esau (the greek monks) and Jacob (the latin *ordo monasticus*). The marriage of Jacob and Rachel remains sterile until the sixth year or age of the Church when it will bring forth Joseph, the *intellectus spiritualis* and *ecclesia contemplantium*. Jacob's six years of working for Laban and becoming rich (though Gn 29:18 says seven years) signifies the growing wealth of the cistercian order opposed by the clergy (f. 84ra). For another use of this theme, see *Expositio*, f. 19rv.

[26]For criticism of the Cluniacs, see *Vita* # 3 (p. 13, 1–8; p. 14, 12–16), # 4 (pp. 17–18), # 11 (p. 59, 1–29). See *Expositio*, f. 80v; *Conc.* 5.63, f. 94ra; *Tractatus* (ed. Buonaiuti, pp. 238–39).

[27]For a discussion of the figure, see *The Figurae of Joachim of Fiore*, pp. 174–83.

[28]For example, *Vita* # 3 (pp. 15, 22–16, 54), # 12 (p. 30, 55–60), *Conc.* 2.2.9 (Daniel, p. 184), and especially *Conc.* 4.2.2 (Daniel, pp. 419, 242–421, 297). Joachim also has a number of general attacks on the failings of contemporary monasticism which could apply to Cistercians and Cluniacs: for example, *Conc.* 4.1.39 (Daniel, pp. 393–94), and 5.41, f. 78vb; and *Expositio*, f. 202ra.

Diagram 4.

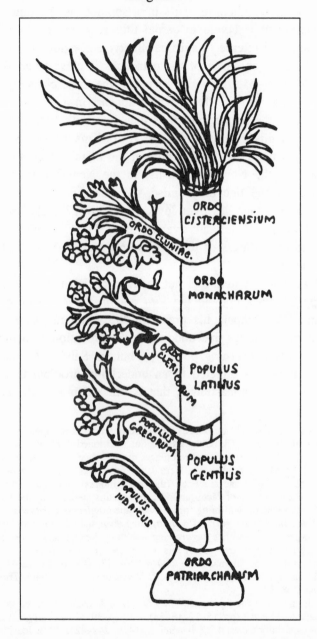

This diagram of the Tree with Side-Shoots figure is a simplified version of what appears in *Il libro delle figure*, tavola 23.

contemplative lives.[29] The Calabrian thought that this was an attempt to combine fire and water that could never succeed. This is why he finds a concordance for the Cistercians not in Benedict, who ascends the mountain of contemplation, but in his sister Scholastica, who remains at its foot.[30] The coming *viri spirituales*, the more perfect monks of the seven houses which would preside over the transition from the second to the third *status*, would have to be either contemplative or active. In the *Vita*, Joachim toys with the idea that they will first preach and then engage in contemplation,[31] but he also advances the solution, which becomes standard in his major works, that there must be two groups of *viri spirituales*, those whose essential task is pure contemplation on the mountain and those who convey the spiritual message of the former through preaching at the time of the persecution of the Antichrist.[32]

It appears to have been the example of Bernard, the model contemplative and preacher, which led Joachim to toy with the first pattern:

> . . . And so the Holy Spirit, . . . drawing near the cistercian order, came to fulfill the promises of the Father and the Son. He made her womb swell by giving himself to the minds of her sons, among whom Bernard held the first place. . . . Others will succeed them on whom he seems to descend visibly and in an almost corporeal form like a dove. They must preach for three-and-a-half years while the eleventh horn [the Antichrist] reigns and thus be led to suffering that they may reach glory.[33]

The way in which Joachim locates the abbot of Clairvaux within the scheme of history, especially the concords that he finds for him, indicates that he thinks that Bernard combined the tasks of man of prayer and preacher in a special way. Twice Joachim refers to Bernard as an 'alter Moyses', who ascends the mountain of contemplation and then brings God's message down to the people.

---

[29]S. Zimdars-Swartz, 'Joachim of Fiore and the Cistercian Order', pp. 299–303. See, especially, *Vita* # 15 (pp. 36, 19–37, 66).

[30]For the concordance with Scholastica, see *Vita* # 13–15 (especially pp. 31, 8–33, 68, and 38, 67–92); and *Expositio*, f. 20ra.

[31]*Vita* # 45 (p. 85, 13–30).

[32]On the two orders of 'spiritual men', see *The Calabrian Abbot*, pp. 112–13, 152–54, etc.

[33]*Vita* # 45 (p. 85, 18–26). On the role of Moses as one who ascends the mountain and then descends to lead the people, see *Vita* # 15 (p. 38, 86–92).

In the *De vita s. Benedicti* 7, after a discussion of various examples of five and seven forming twelve, Joachim argues that Benedict's miraculous discovery of a source of water on the mountain so that the monks would not have to descend into the valley (*Dialogi* 2.5) '... was a sign of the future gift which Almighty God was to bestow on the order of Benedict, that the outstanding doctor who would be like another Moses, his son in the people of Israel, would be born in his order. We see this fully fulfilled in Saint Bernard, the abbot of Clairvaux.'[34]

Bernard's identity as another Moses is expanded on in *Concordia* 4.2.2, Joachim's most important text on Bernard and the Cistercians.[35] Beginning from a treatment of the three orders and their respective generations, the Calabrian advances a series of concords designed to illustrate the role of cistercian monasticism in the transition to the third *status*. Just as Moses led his people out of Egypt into the desert but was not destined to lead them into the promised land, and as it was not the original twelve apostles but Paul and his ministers who went forth into the desert of the Gentiles, so too, in the twenty-third generation after Benedict, Robert left Molesmes to found Cîteaux (p. 415, 160–65). The New Monastery remained sterile until the arrival of Bernard who was 'another Levi' in the sense that he too was the third son that his mother, like Lia, gave to God (p. 416, 172–82). In the spiritual multiplication of the family of Cîteaux, however, Bernard 'was made also like another Moses, who led not so much his sons as his brothers and brothers' sons out of Egypt because the Lord made him great before Pharaoh and his servants when they saw the signs and wonders that he did' (p. 417, 189–92). In company with the 'alter Aaron', that is, Pope Eugenius III, he summoned a great multitude to leave Egypt through his preaching of the Second Crusade, though this multitude, like Moses's followers, perished in the desert because of their sins.[36] Bernard is the Moses who leads the people of God out of this world, the failing second *status*, but others shall lead them into monastic perfection.

Another extended treatment of Bernard provides us with a different concord. *Concordia* 5.62–64 puts a rather optimistic face on the

---

[34]*Vita* # 7 (p. 22, 44–48).

[35]*Conc.* 4.2.2 (Daniel, pp. 408–422).

[36]Here (pp. 417, 205–419, 241) Joachim cites a passage from Bernard's *De consideratione* 2.1–2 (SBOp 3:411–12) in which the abbot defends himself and also refers to Moses as his predecessor. On this text, see E. Pasztor, 'Ideal del monachesimo', pp. 92–96.

unseemly story of David, Uriah, and Bathsheeba.[37] Joachim understands Bathsheeba as the beauty of benedictine monasticism which the roman pontiffs, symbolized by David, bring within the safety of Rome during the time of the barbarian invasions (f. 93ra). But both David and Uriah involve the contemplative Bathsheeba in the conceiving of children, that is, in taking on pastoral duties. David correctly judges Uriah guilty of death for this (f. 93v–94r), and, although Joachim is always loath to criticize Rome, he thinks that the illegitimate mixture of action and contemplation in the monastic life allowed by the papacy is a mistake. Hence the prophet Nathan, who upbraids David for his sins of adultery and murder, is none other than Bernard, who criticized the ills of the papacy so effectively in his *De consideratione* (ff. 94vb–95rb).

To summarize the abbot of Fiore's view of the cistercian order and of Bernard of Clairvaux in his trinitarian scheme of history is not difficult. Since history centers on the gradual revelation of the spiritual understanding of Scripture and this understanding is at the root of the contemplative life lived by monks, the initiation of the Cistercians, but far more, their maturation in the supreme *vir spiritualis* of the age, Bernard of Clairvaux, is the greatest positive contemporary sign of the imminence of the third *status*. (Joachim usually concentrates on the negative signs.) Bernard's place in history was in no way accidental; it conformed fully to the concordances on which Joachim based his theology. If Joachim had not had a Bernard, he would have had to invent him.

While it was certainly Bernard's life which was the center of Joachim's thoughts about the abbot of Clairvaux, I should like to return in closing to the role that Bernard's writings may have had on those of the Calabrian. Joachim had read Bernard's *De consideratione*, as his citations make clear. Direct evidence of acquaintance with other works of the abbot of Clairvaux is lacking. However, it has not been noticed that Joachim interprets the opening verse of the *Song of Songs* ('Osculetur me osculo oris sui') according to the bernardine pattern of three kisses—the kiss of the feet, the hands, and the mouth—although he fits the kisses into his own theology of history.[38] The three kisses are not found in any of the

---

[37]*Conc.* 5. 62–64, ff. 92vb–95rb.

[38]*Psalt.*, f. 241v. Joachim uses the three kisses (citing Sg 1:1) to indicate the actions distinctive of the three orders (laity kiss the feet of Christ through action with fear; clerics kiss the hands through their learning; monks kiss the mouth in contemplation and psalmody), while Bernard uses them in SC 3–8 (SBOp 1:14–42) to indicate the various stages in the believer's spiritual progress. However, none of the other commentators on the *Song of Songs* who might have been known to Joachim (for example, Origen,

standard interpreters of the *Song* except for Bernard, thus suggesting that the Calabrian may have been familiar with Bernard's *Sermones super Cantica*.

If Joachim knew the *Sermones super Cantica*, it is possible that Bernard's masterpiece also made a contribution to Joachim's transmutation of two of the key terms of monastic theology that are central to the Calabrian's theology of history: *intelligentia spiritualis*, that is, the spiritual understanding of the Scriptures, and *viri spirituales*, the perfect spiritual men who constitute the acme of the monastic life. Admittedly, these terms are generic ones, and the abbot of Fiore never cites Bernard as his source when using them. Joachim could have found them in the major authors of the monastic tradition, especially Augustine, Cassian, and Gregory the Great. Nevertheless, Bernard, especially in his *Sermones super Cantica*, uses them frequently, and often in ways not far from Joachim, despite the difference in their respective theologies of history.[39] Though positive proof cannot be given, a brief survey of the evidence is suggestive of a possible link between Bernard and Joachim.

The term *viri spirituales* was central to Joachim's thought. The abbot of Fiore uses it most often to describe the coming monastic order of the third *status*, but he also says that there have been *viri spirituales*, such as Bernard, throughout the history of monasticism.[40] Henri de Lubac was the first to note that Augustine had used this term to describe those who had perfect knowledge of Scripture in opposition to the doctors wise only in the things of the world.[41] The ultimate origin, of course, is in Paul, who in 1 Corinthians 2:14–15 contrasts the 'animalis homo' (*psychikos de anthropos*) with the 'spiritalis' (*pneumatikos*), who judges all things and is judged by no one (see 1 Co 3:1, Ga 6:1).

Augustine used the term in a number of places,[42] and Cassian employed it to contrast monastics with those living in the world ('. . . tam

Ambrose, Gregory the Great, Bede, Alcuin, Haimo) make use of the three-kiss formula to interpret Sg 1:1.

[39]On Bernard's historical and eschatological thought, see B. McGinn, 'St Bernard and Eschatology', in *Bernard of Clairvaux: Studies Presented to Dom Jean Leclercq*, CS 23 (Washington, D.C.: Cistercian Publications, 1973) pp. 161–85.

[40]*Conc.* 5. 49, f. 84rb, interprets the peeled rods by which Jacob assured the fecundity of the flocks as the 'spiritual men established by the Holy Spirit to be examples' in the monasteries of the West.

[41]Henri de Lubac, *La posterité spirituelle de Joachim de Flore*, I, *De Joachim à Schelling* (Paris: P. Lethielleux, 1978) p. 48, n. 6. I have been unable to trace the reference provided by de Lubac to one of Augustine's writings against Julian of Eclanum.

[42]For example, Augustine, *De diversis quaestionibus 83*, q. 67.5 (PL 40:68), and *Conf.* 13.18.22 (PL 32:854) where it is used in the general sense of contemplatives. In *Tractatus*

apud spiritales viros quam apud saeculi homines').[43] Without engaging in
a full history of all the uses of *viri spirituales* in early medieval authors,
it is interesting to note that Bernard of Clairvaux used it at least a dozen
times, seven of which occur in the *Sermones super Cantica*. A number
of these passages are close to what we find in Joachim.

In *Super Cantica* 14.6, in speaking of his own coldness of love at the
beginning of his conversion, Bernard tells how the word or even the sight
of a 'spiritualis perfectusque vir' could warm his heart. This is not unlike
Joachim's description of how the sight of contemporary monastic *viri
spirituales* inspires others in *Liber de concordia* 5.41.[44] *Super Cantica*
44.1 affirms that the 'populus gentium' will never learn to overcome
temptation until 'they hand themselves over to the *viri spirituales* to be
instructed, those who, illumined by the Spirit of Wisdom and taught by
their own experience, can truly say, "We are not ignorant of the devil's
wiles and thoughts." '[45] This is reminiscent (or at least suggestive) of
the missionary and preaching activity that Joachim assigned to the *viri
spirituales* in the imminent crisis of the transition of ages. Preaching on
Pentecost, the feast of that Spirit whom Joachim saw as the empowerment
of the coming spiritual men, Bernard praises '. . . the spiritual men
[*spirituales viri*], using the world as if they do not use it, but seeking
God in the simplicity of their heart'.[46] Thus, Bernard's 'spiritual men'
perform many of the same functions as do Joachim's, though admittedly
not in the same apocalyptic framework of history.

Another possible bond between Bernard and Joachim seems to appear
when we look of the term *intellectus*, or *intelligentia spiritualis*, the
Calabrian's favored description of the deeper understanding of Scripture
which is the goal of the entire historical process.[47] Once again, this is

---

in Joannem 36.6 (PL 35:1666) the *viri spirituales* are closer to Joachim's use in being
those who have understood something of Christ's divinity from the Scriptures and who
are called to defend the faithful against heretics. In *Enarratio in Ps*. 73.19 (PL 36:940)
the *spirituales* are compared to the sun, the *carnales* to the moon.

[43]The passage cited is found in Cassian, *Conferences* 9.6, ed. E. Pichéry, SCh 54
(Paris: Editions du Cerf) p. 46. For other uses see *Conferences* 12.16 and 21.10.

[44]SC 14.6; SBOp 1:80, 1–8. See SC 29.6 (SBOp 1:207, 4–7) referring to the *spirituales*.

[45]SC 44.1; SBOp 2:103, 28–29, and 164, 7. See SC 13.3, 54.2, and 63.5 (SBOp
1:70, 14; 2:103, 28–29, and 164, 7). SC 27.12 (SBOp 1:190, 24–25) speaks of 'homines
spirituales'.

[46]Pent 3.4; SBOp 5:173, 16–18. For other appearances in Bernard, see Apo 12.28,
and Gra 5.13 (SBOp 3:106, 9; and 175, 21), as well as QH 7.10 and Palm 2.1 (SBOp
4:419, 27; and 5:46, 14).

[47]See *The Calabrian Abbot*, chap. 4.

a term with a long history in the latin tradition. Cassian's *Conlationes* 14.8, a *locus classicus* for the four senses of Scripture, uses *intelligentia spiritualis* to refer to the higher spiritual understanding.[48] The term also appears in other patristic authors, particularly Augustine and Gregory the Great.[49] However, Bernard seems to have revived its use in the twelfth century as a description of the profound understanding of Scripture which leads the soul to true freedom. It is found at least nine times in his writings, four times in the *Sermones super Cantica*. Preaching on the Epiphany, the abbot of Clairvaux exhorts his readers: 'Let us depart from the sense of the flesh to the understanding of the mind, from the servitude of carnal concupiscence to the freedom of the spiritual understanding'— words that might well have come right out of Joachim.[50] The notion of the 'libertas spiritualis intelligentiae' appears in Bernard's writings primarily in relation to the understanding of Scripture,[51] but the abbot also links it to contemplation, as did Joachim. A telling passage occurs in *Super Cantica* 85.13:

> Note that there are two kinds of giving birth in spiritual marriage and that different but not opposed progeny come from this. Holy mothers either bear souls by preaching or spiritual understandings [*intelligentias . . . spirituales*] by meditating. In this latter kind there is a surpassing and departure [*exceditur et seceditur*] from the corporeal senses, so that the soul that experiences the Word does not experience itself.[52]

Of course, other twelfth-century authors also make use of the term *intelligentia spiritualis* for the deeper understanding of Scripture.[53] Joachim,

[48]For this famous text, see *Conferences* 14.8 (ed. Pichéry) 2:189–90. Cassian also uses the term *intellectus spiritualis* in his *Institutiones* 3.4.1 and 7.16.

[49]For example, Augustine, *En. in Ps.* 33.1.7 (PL 35:305); Gregory the Great, *Hom. in Ezek.* 2.7.5 and 13 (PL 76:1015B and 1021B).

[50]Bernard, Epi 2.2; SBOp 4:302, 2–3.

[51]For example, Div 50.2 (SBOp 6:271, 11–12) for another stress on the liberty theme. For appearances of *intelligentia/intellectus spiritualis* in relation to the action of the Holy Spirit bringing deeper understanding of Scripture, see especially SC 45.5, 52.1, 56.1 (SBOp 2:52, 14–22; 90, 18–20; 114, 18–20). The term is also found elsewhere in Bernard's writings, for example, QH 7.11 (SBOp 4:420, 16); Asc 6.14 (SBOp 5:159, 3–4); and III Sent 119 (SBOp 6/2:217, 22).

[52]SC 85.13; SBOp 2:315, 26–316, 1. See Div 123.2; SBOp 6/1:402, 2). Bernard taught that contemplative experience involves both a *latitudo mentis* and *infusio luminis* which leads to a knowledge of Scripture and understanding of mysteries both for the recipient's own delight and for the use of others. See SC 57.8; SBOp 2:124.

[53]The *intellectus spiritualis* appears in other cistercian authors, for example, William

however, seems to have had a relatively selective library at his disposal, especially of recent authors. If he knew Bernard's *sermones* (something that seems quite plausible), his apocalyptic adaptation of the terms *viri spirituales* and *intelligentia spiritualis* may well have been aided by their frequent use in the abbot of Clairvaux's greatest work. This appears to be as much as can be said without further research into the long history of these crucial terms.

The life of Bernard of Clairvaux, and at least to some extent his writings, were important influences on Joachim's theology of history. Our knowledge of the Calabrian's biography shows that his commitment to the cistercian mode of life as the highest form of monasticism antedates the revelations he received at Casamari in 1183–1184 which were the foundation for his own theological agenda. From the perspective of Joachim's biography, there can be no doubt that Cistercianism, especially the Cistercianism of Bernard, whose reputation had been confirmed by his canonization in 1171, was the original context which molded the Calabrian's thought.

Though Joachim owed much to Bernard and the Cistercians, by the late 1180s he already had come to view the white monks as an interim stage in the progress of the *ordo monasticus* toward its true goal. Under the guidance of the Holy Spirit the coming *viri spirituales* would surpass all previous stages of monasticism, even the Cistercians. There is some evidence from the *De vita s. Benedicti* that Joachim may have viewed his departure from Corazzo and eventual removal to Fiore by 1189 as the initiation of the new order that would oversee the transition to the third *status*.[54] It is also interesting to note that the Calabrian may have taken a cue from his hero, Bernard, in identifying himself, if only for a time, with a 'new Moses' who would lead God's people out of a doomed Egypt into the desert of suffering to await entry into the promised land of the third *status*.[55] But these quasi-messianic passages must be balanced against the extreme reticence of the major works to identify the coming

of Saint Thierry, *Expositio super Cantica Canticorum* 67 (ed. Davy, pp. 94–96), but apparently on a more restricted basis.

[54]See, for example, *Vita* # 31 (ed. Baraut, p. 65, 1–8) on the foundation of the *tertius ordo* about 1190; and the articles of S. Wessley on this text.

[55]Some texts even seem to suggest that Joachim initially saw his own movement up the mountain in terms of Moses's ascent (see Reeves and Hirsch-Reich, *The Figurae*, pp. 32–33). It is possible that the Calabrian had an oral teaching that influenced the views of his early followers. See Stephen Wessley, 'Additional Clues to a Role for Joachim's Order of Fiore,' in *L'Età dello Spirito*, pp. 281–300.

viri spirituales with any existing institution, even the abbot's own order. In the last decade of the twelfth century Joachim may have come to realize that his own form of monasticism was as transitional as that of Bernard in the mysterious progression toward true spiritual freedom.

ABSTRACTS

Bernard de Clairvaux fut sans nul doute le Cistercien le plus influent du XIIe siècle, et il est de plus en plus évident que Joachim de Flore fut vers la même époque l'*ex*-Cistercien le plus marquant. Ces deux moines influencèrent profondément l'histoire ultérieure de l'Occident. Le présent article étudie la manière dont Joachim voyait le role de Bernard et de l'Ordre Cistercien dans l'histoire du salut. Pour Joachim, Bernard était signe de l'imminence d'une ère monastique, nouvelle et plus parfaite, de l'histoire mondiale. Ceci ressort avec évidence du rôle tant direct qu'indirect que joue l'abbé de Clairvaux dans la théologie de l'histoire originale qui est celle de Joachim.

There can be no question but that Bernard of Clairvaux was the most influential Cistercian of the twelfth century, and it is increasingly evident that Joachim of Fiore was the most important *sometime* Cistercian of the same era. Both monks exerted a profound influence on later Western history. This article investigates how Joachim saw the role of Bernard and of the Cistercian Order in the process of salvation history. For Joachim, Bernard was a sign of the imminence of a new and more perfect monastic era in world history. This is evident both from the direct and the indirect role that the abbot of Clairvaux played in Joachim's original theology of history.

Es kann keine Frage sein, dass Bernhard von Clairvaux der einfluß-reichste Zisterzienser des 12. Jh. war. Und es wird mehr und mehr deutlich, daß Joachim von Fiore der wichtigste *ehemalige* Zisterzienser derselben Epoche war. Beide Mönche übten einen tiefreichenden Einfluß auf die spätere westeuropäische Geschichte aus. Dieser Artikel unter-sucht, wie Joachim die Rolle Bernhards und des Zisterzienserordens im Prozeß der Heilsgeschichte sah. Für Joachim war Bernhard ein Zeichen für das Bevorstehen einer neuen und vollkommeneren monastischen Ära in der Weltgeschichte. Dies ist sowohl durch die direkte als auch die indirekte Rolle offensichtlich, die der Abt von Clairvaux in Joachims eigenständiger Theologie der Geschichte spielt.

THOMAS AQUINAS ON
BERNARD AND THE LIFE OF CONTEMPLATION

Mark D. Jordan
University of Notre Dame

EMBLEMS

MEDIEVAL HAGIOGRAPHERS share certain stories about Saint Thomas's death at the cistercian monastery of Fossa Nova. They agree, for example, that Thomas protested when the monks began to carry wood from nearby groves in order to heat his sickroom.[1] The hagiographers also record together that he broke forth with passionate expressions of faith on receiving the *viaticum*.[2] Again, the lives of the saint join in telling how the monks besought Thomas to leave them a memorial of his learning. He did it, the hagiographers concur, by dictating a brief exposition of the *Song of Songs*.[3] Such a testament would not only have recorded Thomas's fraternal love for the Cistercians at Fossa Nova, it would have marked his reconciliation with the great traditions of monastic teaching. The mendicant doctor nursed by a cistercian community, giving his final doctrine in imitation of Bernard's authoritative commentary—that is an emblem of reconciliation no hagiographer could resist. None did.

Unfortunately, the exposition supposedly dictated at Fossa Nova has never been securely identified in even a single copy. Its complete

---

[1]As in *Fontes vitae S. Thomae Aquinatis: Notis historicis et criticis illustrati*, ed. D. Prümmer (Toulouse, 1919-) pp. 47 (Calo sect. 27), 131 (Tocco cap. 57), 204 (Gui cap. 38).
[2]*Fontes vitae*, pp. 48 (Calo sect. 28), 132 (Tocco cap. 58), 204–205 (Gui cap. 39).
[3]*Fontes vitae*, pp. 47–48 (Calo sect. 27), 131 (Tocco cap. 57), 204 (Gui cap. 38).

disappearance would be extraordinary given the importance that the cistercian community is said to have attached to every bit of Thomas's remains. So it seems unlikely that the exposition ever existed. With it goes one attractive emblem of Thomas's indebtedness to Bernard's authorship. We must also set aside the sermon on Saint Bernard frequently attributed to Thomas. It seems not to be his.[4] Indeed, and generally, the emblems used to capture the relation of Thomas to Bernard are ornamental fakes. This is unfortunate, because the alternative to finding emblems is the difficult and diffuse business of aligning massive bodies of text. In place of the satisfying story or the encapsulating sermon, we have hundreds of textual affinities connecting—or failing to connect—Thomas's writings to Bernard's.

In this essay I should like to consider but three types of textual relations. For each, I shall describe briefly what I take the evidence of relation to be, and then I shall suggest how the evidence affects the asking of questions about Thomas's reception of Bernard. The first sort of textual relation appears as the *auctoritas*, the second as doctrinal comparison, the third as rhetorical motivation.

AUTHORITIES

The most basic textual relation in Thomas's writings is the citation or quotation of an authoritative precedent, an *auctoritas*. So the surest way to begin asking about Thomas's relations to any one of his predecessors is by tracing his use of authorities drawn from that predecessor. Since the main *auctoritates* were excerpted and applied to fixed topics long before Thomas's writing, his selection of authorities is most often inherited along with the canon of academic topics.

Among the citations that Thomas inherits are a number of texts from Bernard. These texts entered academic theology in the decades preceding Thomas's maturity.[5] Thus, while Bernard appears in Peter Lombard's

---

[4]The sermon '*Aurum, et multitudo gemmarum....* Possunt haec verba exponi...', has long been printed among the works of Thomas. See, for example, *Opera omnia* (Venice: Simon Occhi, 1758) 26:137. This sermon is excluded from the best recent lists of Thomas's authentic homilies. See L.-J. Bataillon, 'Les Sermons attribués à Saint Thomas: Questions d'authenticité', in Albert Zimmermann (ed.), *Thomas von Aquin: Werk und Wirkung im Licht neuerer Forschungen*, Miscellanea Mediaevalia 19 (Berlin, New York: W. de Gruyter, 1988) pp. 325–41.

[5]The best summary remains Jean Châtillon, 'L'influence de S. Bernard sur la pensée scholastique au XIIe et au XIIIe siècle', in *Saint Bernard Theologien*, ASOC 9 (1953) 268–88. For the fate of a particular treatise, see V. Faust, 'Bernhards "Liber de gratia

Sentences only anonymously,[6] he is very quickly received as an explicit authority by parisian commentators on the *Sentences*. In the *Glossa* of Alexander of Hales, for example, Bernard is cited on a variety of points in all four books. His *De gratia et libero arbitrio* is used as one of the mainstays of Alexander's discussion of free choice.[7]

In his early writings, Thomas takes up the bernardine *auctoritates* very much as a typical parisian master of theology. Thus there are about sixty citations to Bernard in Thomas's *Sentences*-commentary, and they cluster around predictable topics. By contrast, Bonaventure's commentary makes untypically heavy use of Bernard—-130 citations, most heavily concentrated in the third Book.[8] What is not typical in Thomas is that his citations in the *Sentences*-commentary make up almost half of all the explicit citations of Bernard in his corpus.[9] The *Summa*, as we have it, contains a scant fifteen citations to Bernard. Indeed, there is a marked decline in the use of Bernard throughout all of Thomas's later works.[10] Yet the mere numbers are mute. What matters is not how many citations, but of what kind and how deployed. We need to distinguish before asserting the importance of the decreasing use of Bernard.

The commonest citations to Bernard support maxims that Thomas can apply to various cases. One favorite maxim is that charity knows no limits.[11] Another holds that not to make progress toward God is to retreat from him.[12] Thomas's use of such maxims reveals little about his

---

et libero arbitrio": Bedeutung, Quellen und Einfluss', *Analecta Monastica* 6 = SAn 50 (1962) 35–52.

[6]See *Sententiae* 2.25.8.1–5, 9; 2.27.3.2: 'quidam non inerudite tradunt'; 3.3.1.2: 'ut quibusdam placet'; 4.12.3.2: 'licet quidam asserant'.

[7]See Alexander of Hales, *Glossa in quatuor libros sententiarum Petri Lombardi* (Quarachi: Coll. S. Bonaventura, 1951–1975) 2.25.10, 2.25.16, 2.25.20, 2.25.23, 2.25.28, 2.26.8, 2.26.17, 2.26.20, and so on.

[8]See Jacques-Guy Bougerol, 'Saint Bonaventure et Saint Bernard', *Antonianum* 46 (1971) 3–79, at pp. 6–30.

[9]By far the most exact list of them is that by Clemens Vansteenkiste in *Rassegna di letteratura tomistica* 10 (1978) 35–47. It replaces such partial surveys as those of Basil Hänsler in *Cistercienser-Chronik* 17–18 (1905–1906) and 36 (1924).

[10]Part of the decrease is due to Thomas's mature practice of pruning citations with an eye to pedagogical efficiency. Thus there is general decrease in the number and range of authorities from the *Sentences*-commentary to the *Summa*.

[11]The Latin contains an untranslatable pun: 'modus caritatis est non habere modum'. See the borrowings of this maxim from Bernard at *Super Sent.* 1.3.2.3, 3.27.3.3 sc 1, and 3.33.1.1.4.1; *QD De ver.* 21.6 arg 12; *Summa theol.* 1.27.6 sc; *QD De virt.* 9 arg 3; *QD De carit.* 2 arg 13.

[12]See *Super Sent.* 3.29.8.2.1, and *Super ad Hebr.* 6.1; compare *Summa theol.* 1.24.6 arg 3.

relation to a particular predecessor, whether that predecessor is Bernard or Aristotle. The maxims are almost entirely cut off from their original meanings; they function as rhetorical topics, as principles for invention rather than as formulations of judgment or argument.

For Thomas's doctrinal relation of bernardine authorities, a more promising site of exploration would be passages on free choice. We have seen that authorities from Bernard were attached most densely to distinctions in the *Sentences* that considered this power. So it is with Thomas. Bernard's definition of free choice as a *habitus* is quoted prominently in one objection of distinction 24. Thomas replies that Bernard employs the term *habitus* loosely, not technically.[13] In distinction 25, Bernard is invoked on behalf of a threefold liberty—of choice, of counsel, and of complaisance. Thomas likes the division and takes it up with his own explanation, but he does so on the margin of a more fundamental division of kinds of freedom.[14] And Bernard figures even less in later works. Only the first text from Bernard is preserved in the preliminary consideration of free choice within the *prima pars* of the *Summa*. More tellingly, there is no reference to Bernard whatever in the elaborate unfolding of the acts of the will that makes up Questions 6–17 of the *prima secundae*.

If Thomas withdraws more and more from Bernard's formulations on free choice, he frankly opposes formulations on other topics. So, for example, he corrects or qualifies Bernard's analysis of the sinfulness of Peter's denial of Christ.[15] More often, and more importantly, Thomas dissents from Bernard's analogy of the sacraments to merely symbolic acts.[16] In the second case, the bernardine *auctoritas* serves Thomas as a foil for clarifying his own doctrine of sacramental causality.

Further texts could be considered, but they would not much alter the first impression left by a survey of Thomas's explicit citations. The impression would remain that Thomas inherited some bernardine authorities, used them in typical ways early on, then gradually relinquished most of them. It would seem to follow that 'Thomas did not take Bernard too seriously as a theological source'.[17]

[13]*Super Sent.* 2.24.1.1 ad 1: 'Bernardus large utitur nomine habitus pro habitudine quadam' (Mandonnet-Moos 2:591).

[14]*Super Sent.* 2.25.1.5 ad 6.

[15]*QD De carit.* 5 arg 2, 13 arg 2, and *Quodl.* 9.14 arg 2. Compare *Super ev. Matt.* 26.74 and *QD De correptione frat.* 1 arg 11.

[16]*Super Sent.* 4.1.1.4.1 arg 1; *QD De ver.* 27.4 arg 1; *Quodl.* 12.14; *Summa theol.* 3.62.1.

[17]M. Basil Pennington, 'The Influence of Bernard of Clairvaux on Thomas Aquinas', *Studia Monastica* 16 (1974) 281–92, at p. 287.

I wish to suggest that the impression and its apparent entailment depend on anachronistic categories. It is not at all clear that Thomas counted Bernard 'a source' or that he read him as the unifying author of an organic corpus of works. In the passages I have mentioned, Bernard is the author only of authorities, of discrete formulations that come down to Thomas through the academic traditions. It is hard to know how much of Bernard he read straight through—as it is hard to know which whole texts of Augustine he read, or of Anselm, or of Avicenna. Only where we have the evidence of a commentary *ad litteram* or of a *lectio* within a curriculum can we be sure of the continuity of Thomas's reading. It is a mistake, then, to move from a summary of the complex fate of disjointed bernardine authorities in Thomas to a generalization about Thomas's judgment on Bernard as source or Bernard as author. It is not even clear that Thomas conceives of theological authorities with such personifications.

Hence the gradual disappearance of bernardine authorities from Thomas's writings does not mean that Bernard is being rejected as source or as author. It may be that Thomas has embarked on a new arrangement of topics and so has shifted the selection of authorities. It may be that Thomas is presenting certain technical languages for his readers to learn, and so excludes the more distant or difficult language of Bernard. Whatever the full account of the diminishing use of bernardine authorities would be, it would not yield an embracing judgment on the relations of Thomas to Bernard. It follows, then, that a survey of explicit or implicit citations does not get at the issue. We need another way of asking about Thomas's reception of Bernard.

DOCTRINES

The complexity of textual relations at the level of *auctoritates* has led many readers to try for comparisons at the level of doctrines or positions. Thus they are led to contrast, say, Bernard and Thomas on charity in contemplation.[18] Given the differences between the two bodies of writing in terminology, authorities, topics, permitted arguments, and genre, such comparisons must either practice strong misreading or else confess their failure to find any unequivocal basis on which to compare.

---

[18]For a recent and particularly egregious example of the attempted comparison of doctrines, see Enrico Piscione, 'Bernardo di Chiaravalle e Tommaso d'Aquino di fronte al problema dell'amore: Due posizioni antitetiche o complementari?', *Sapienza* 32 (1986) 405–414.

The better readers are soon enough led to see that 'it would be vain to search for an intellectual common denominator' under Bernard and Thomas,[19] or that 'their respective visions of the nature of theology and the resources which it should invoke were diverse'.[20]

I too think that comparisons of particular doctrines between authors as differently situated as Thomas and Bernard are bound to fail. It is misleading enough to pretend to extract a free-standing doctrine or thesis from either one of the bodies of text. To speak of 'Thomas's doctrine of contemplation' is to suppress all the complexities and nuances in his pedagogical unfolding of what he thinks. How much more peculiar it is to extract two doctrines and then compare them—as if there were some neutral language in which to reformulate and then adjudicate the disembodied thoughts latent in the two sets of text. But I also think that doctrinal comparisons between Thomas and Bernard on such central topics as contemplation are liable to a very particular misunderstanding. It is a misunderstanding about the sharpness of contrasts in moral language.

Let me illustrate this misunderstanding from Thomas's language about contemplative and active lives. It seems that we are always being led to read the contrast of lives as if it were already clear what he means by them. Some readers take 'contemplative' to mean monastic and 'active' to mean mendicant. Thomas's challenge is then thought to be that of justifying dominican life in the face of the monasteries. But the language of contemplative and active is much more complicated than that. It is complicated in its origins and especially in its applications.

The origins are complicated because Thomas's contrast between contemplative and active explicitly combines several different contrasts. It combines, for example, Aristotle's distinguishing between the virtues of philosophy and those of the city with patristic exegesis of the figures of Mary and Martha. Thus, at one point in the *Summa*, Thomas deliberately transforms Aristotle's eight arguments for the superiority of contemplation into their scriptural and patristic amplifications.[21] Still, diversity of

[19]André Hayen, *S. Thomas d'Aquin et la vie de l'Eglise*, Essais philosophiques 6 (Louvain: Publications universitaires; Paris: Desclée de Brouwer, 1952) p. 7. Hayen goes on to say: 'Et pourtant, saint Bernard aide singulièrement comprendre saint Thomas,... comme participant au même courant de vie de la pensée chrétienne' (p. 7). It is difficult to know what this means.

[20]Bernard McGinn, 'Introduction' to Bernard of Clairvaux, *On Grace and Free Will*, The Works of Bernard of Clairvaux, VII, Treatises III, CF 19 (Kalamazoo: Cistercian Publications, 1977) p. 45. McGinn's larger point is to give some sense to assertions of contintuity.

[21]*Summa theol.* 2–2.182.1.

meanings does not preclude analogical ordering, and one of Thomas's chief tasks in his discussions of contemplation is just to describe the central meanings that ground the analogy. 'Contemplation' means strictly the loving and delighted intellection of God, while 'action' means engagement with others, the outward practice of the moral virtues under the direction of prudence.[22] But the direction of the analogy is to show that the distinction between contemplation and action taken strictly does not entail their segregation. For Thomas, 'contemplation' and 'action' name two ways of sorting out ends, one of which is subordinated to another.

The subordination suggests why the contrast between active and contemplative is even more interestingly complicated when applied to actual human lives. Thomas insists wherever possible that action is properly a disposition to contemplation.[23] He does this most obviously when he argues, for example, that the virtues acquired in active life are prerequisites for contemplation, or that the active life must precede the contemplative in the order of generation.[24] But Thomas also insists on the interdependence of active and contemplative when he presents the most complete Christian as the one who can be both active and contemplative. This is the way of life he attributes to prelates and to preachers.

In doing so, Thomas does not mean to contrast mendicants and monks. On Thomas's account, Bernard would be very much a teacher and so very much engaged in the active life. One can see this already in the article that asks whether teaching belongs to the active or the contemplative.[25] Thomas argues that the inward act of teaching may be either contemplative or active, but the outward expression of teaching must always be active. Hence, the fact of Bernard's treatises and sermons, the very fact of his preaching, means that he is engaged in the active life. But it also requires that he be a contemplative, since one cannot teach without contemplation.

So much is clear in Thomas's description of teaching in the section of the *Summa* on the freely-given grace, those extraordinary graces bestowed on some so that they might help others back to God.[26] The authoritative text on these gifts is from Paul to the Corinthians.[27] Thomas

---

[22] I here summarize, very baldly, the dialectical inquiry of *Summa theol.* 2–2.180–81.

[23] See, for example, the contrast 'essentialiter...dispositive' in *Summa theol.* 2–2.180.2 sol, or the conclusion, 'Quamvis etiam dici possit quod vita activa dispositio sit ad vitam contemplativam', in 181.1 ad 3.

[24] Respectively, *Summa theol.* 2–2.182.3–4.

[25] *Summa theo.* 2–2.181.3.

[26] *Summa theo.* 1–2.111.4.

[27] 1 Co 12:8–10.

defends the pauline enumeration of graces as a fitting description of all
the ways in which one person may try to teach another about divine
things. He discovers in Paul a threefold description of the graced teacher,
who must have the 'fullness of divine apprehension', the ability to
confirm what is said, and the capacity for offering it plainly to his
listeners. With the freely-given graces, the confirmation is miraculous,
and the communication is by special gifts of speech. But the teacher's
own understanding depends equally on God. The teacher must first have
faith, which is certainty about things not seen. He next needs wisdom,
which is an apprehension of divine things. He then requires science,
which is a knowledge about human things so that they can be made
to show forth their divine causes. Yet the sum of teaching, the highest
attainment of faith, wisdom, science, of confirming miracles and angelic
eloquence, is nothing more than to be an occasion for the inward stirring
of God. Man teaches and persuades outwardly, Thomas says, but the
inner teaching 'is of God alone'. Now this description of the teacher
seems to me not only one that Thomas would apply to Bernard, but a
description of christian teaching that Bernard himself might recognize
and applaud.

There you have my illustration of the difficulties for any simply
doctrinal comparison between Thomas and Bernard. It is not only that
authors produce texts of great complexity. It is also that when they
talk about things that matter most to them—that is, about the living of
christian lives—they tend to combine rather than segregate, to embrace
rather than to divide. The overlapping of ends in human lives combines
with the transformation of every end in grace to make christian moral
discourse particularly resistant to analysis by dichotomy.

RHETORICAL MOTIVES

If we cannot compare Bernard and Thomas at the level of authorities
or at the level of separate doctrines, are we left without the means for
any comparison? Let me conclude by suggesting one means, at the level
of what I call rhetorical motives. This comparison would ask of each
text: what effect does it want to have on its readers? How does it intend
to move them? More specifically, and more importantly in view of the
purposes of our two authors, the question becomes: into what way of life
will the text call its best readers?

We are accustomed to thinking of Bernard as a master of persuasive
rhetoric. We do not think that of Thomas, but that is because we do not

read him well enough. Thomas's *Summa* shares many rhetorical motives with Bernard's most powerful pieces of rhetoric. Let me suggest how this might be so.

The last large portion of the second section of the *Summa*'s second Part considers what Thomas calls virtues that pertain to certain individuals.[28] It is by no means an appendix. Thomas has already said that the only useful moral discourses are concrete moral discourses. Here he will talk about the concrete integration of virtues into virtuous ways of life. The concretizing virtues are divided into three kinds: those pertaining to graces freely given, those pertaining to ways of life, and those pertaining to offices and states in life. The first division considers prophecy and gifts of speech, including teaching. The second division compares the active and contemplative lives, in ways that we have seen. The third division considers the states of perfection, which are the episcopacy and the religious life.

Notice the order. It might seem appropriate to place the extraordinary gifts of prophecy at the very end—a culminating description of human nature elevated beyond intself into the rapturous anticipation of the life to come. Thomas chooses to end instead with the comparison of lives and the description of the states of perfection. That is because these are not so much comparisons or descriptions as exhortations. He is here exhorting the reader to take up a way of life that will lead to beatitude.

Consider the Questions on offices and states. The first Question defines a state of life as a permanent undertaking that reconstitutes the person by reconfiguring obligations and liberties.[29] Differences of state in the Church are aligned with the grade of charity—that is, with the sprititual division into beginners, the practiced, and the completed.[30] The states of perfection are undertakings to obligations that teach the perfection of christian life, which is charity.[31] Charity is the universal precept for all Christians—the evangelical counsels of poverty, chastity, and obedience only instruments for attaining it.[32] Of course, not everyone who undertakes to use the instruments does use them—and some use them who do not publicly undertake to do so.[33] Then, too, the outward states of perfection are but reflections of the inward liberties and obligations to

[28]*Summa theol.* 2–2.171.prol.
[29]*Summa theol.* 2–2.183.1.
[30]*Summa theol.* 2–2.183.4.
[31]*Summa theol.* 2–2.184.1.
[32]*Summa theol.* 2–2.184.3.
[33]*Summa theol.* 2–2.184.4.

charity judged by God. And yet the public undertakings are powerful helps in human moral education—and the religious life offers itself as just that education in the best human life.[34]

The state of religion is a certain learning or exercise for coming to human completion.[35] It is like medical therapy or like a school, two potent analogies in Thomas, as in Bernard.[36] The three counsels are justified by reference to the needs of education in a charity that will lead one to God. So too the variety of religious rules: they represent the variety of ways to learn charity.[37] But Thomas is not describing religious life as an education; he is proposing religious life as a response to the reader's desire for contemplative beatitude. Do you want to learn how to enact the coherent human life described in the *Summa*'s second Part? Take up a way of life that is a school for charity. The religious life provides truly what the philosophical life anciently promised.

The very last Question of the second Part begins by arguing that one need not be proficient in the precepts before undertaking to practice the counsels. Grace can supply what is lacking. So too the benefit of the doubt ought always be given to any obligation to try religious life— whether because of a vow or an oblation, even against parental wishes or when one is a priest. The determination here is not special pleading; it is no unprincipled defense of dominican prerogatives. Thomas argues for a trial of the religious life because he considers it the privileged regime of moral formation, the state in which one is most likely to be taught how to attain God.

So the last two Articles place the choice of religious life squarely before the reader. Persuading someone to enter the religious life is not illicit, Thomas insists. Indeed, it is a great good.[38] The claims of religious life are so strong, Thomas adds, that it is not wrong to enter religious life *without* extensive counseling and protracted deliberation.[39] Because religion is something certainly from God, because it offers so sure a way to learn charity, Thomas urges all due haste.

At the center of the *Summa*, then, Thomas undertakes a kind of persuasion very familiar to readers of Bernard. Indeed, it is a genre of persuasion that Bernard did much to shape. Moreover, Thomas inherits

---

[34]*Summa theol.* 2–2.186.1.
[35]*Summa theol.* 2–2.186.2.
[36]*Summa theol.* 2–2.186.2 ad 1.
[37]*Summa theol.* 2–2.188.1.
[38]*Summa theol.* 2–2.189.9.
[39]*Summa theol.* 2–2.189.10.

the genre along many lines, not a few of which are directly indebted to cistercian spiritual pedagogy. Thomas's persuasion is not identically Bernard's persuasion, of course. It is spoken in a different kind of voice, proposes more diverse means, envisages an alternate form of community. Still, the comparison of persuasions offers surer footing than either of the other comparisons. The reader who asks after Thomas's rhetorical motives in constructing the account of contemplation that ends with a call to religious life will meet Bernard much sooner than the reader who hunts authorities or attempts to extract commensurable doctrines. If we wish to begin asking what Bernard and Thomas might say to each other, we should do so by asking how and to what they wish to persuade us.

ABSTRACTS

S. Thomas d'Aquin se réfère assez souvent à S. Bernard en tant qu'*auctoritas*, mais l'analyse de ces citations ne permet pas d'apprécier avec exactitude sa réception de la pensée de l'abbé de Clairvaux. De même, la comparaison de leurs positions doctrinales sur des points particuliers s'avère décevante faute d'un dénominateur commun suffisant entre leurs systèmes théologiques. Reste une troisième voie, consistant à comparer des motifs rhétoriques: quelle impression tel texte cherche-t-il à produire chez ses lecteurs, à quel genre de vie appelle-t-il les meilleurs d'entre eux? Au coeur même de la *Somme théologique*, S. Thomas insère une exhortation pressante à embrasser la vie religieuse. Les lecteurs de Bernard connaissent bien ce thème; il est entré dans la tradition spirituelle dont Thomas est l'héritier en partie grâce à son influence. C'est en se demandant comment et de quoi ils veulent nous persuader que nous pourrons commencer à entrevoir ce que Bernard et Thomas ont pu se dire.

St Thomas Aquinas refers quite often to Saint Bernard as an *auctoritas*, but analyzing these quotations does not allow us to evaluate his reception of Bernard's thought correctly. Comparing their doctrinal positions on particular points likewise proves disappointing for lack of a sufficient common denominator between their theological systems. A third means remains, i.e. comparison between rhetorical motives: what impression does a text seek to make on its readers, and to what way of life does it call the best of them? At the very heart of the *Summa theologiae*, Thomas has inserted a pressing exhortation to embrace religious life. Bernard's readers are familiar with this theme; it entered the spiritual tradition which Thomas inherited partly due to his influence. If we are to begin to glimpse what Bernard and Thomas might say to each other, we must ask how and to what they wish to persuade us.

Der heilige Thomas von Aquin bezieht sich ziemlich oft auf den heiligen Bernhard als *auctoritas*, aber die Analyse dieser Zitate erlaubt es nicht, seine Rezeption der Gedanken des Abtes von Clairvaux genau zu bestimmen. Ebenso erweist sich der Vergleich ihrer lehrmäßigen Positionen über spezielle Punkte als enttäuschend mangels eines ausreichenden gemeinsamen Nenners zwischen ihren theologischen Systemen. Bleibt ein dritter Weg, der darin besteht, rhetorische Motive zu vergleichen: Welchen Eindruck will so ein Text bei seinen Lesern hervorrufen? Zu welcher Lebensweise ruft er die besten unter ihnen auf? Ins Zentrum seiner *Summa theologiae* stellt der heilige Thomas eine drängende Mahnung zum Ordensleben. Bernhards Leser kennen dieses Thema gut: Es ist in die geistliche Tradition, deren Erbe Thomas ist, teilweise durch seinen Einfluß eingedrungen. Nur indem wir ahnen wie und wovon sie uns überzeugen wollen, können wir zu ahnen beginnen, was Bernhard und Thomas sich zu sagen gehabt hätten.

SINE PROPRIO: ON LIBERTY AND CHRIST, A JUXTAPOSITION OF BERNARD OF CLAIRVAUX AND JOHN DUNS SCOTUS

William A. Frank
The University of Dallas

AS MY POINT OF DEPARTURE, let me recall Thomas Merton's claim to the effect that John Duns Scotus (d. 1308) and Bernard of Clairvaux (d. 1153) can be situated along collateral lines of development growing out of a common source in Anselm of Canterbury (d. 1109).[1] Apparently Merton had the idea that there was a coherent unity of vision in the diverse intellectual strains represented by the cistercian, victorine, and franciscan traditions.[2] Such a suggestion, coming from a contemporary master of the spiritual life, gives substance to the suspicion that there is some bernardine influence to be found in Scotus. Indeed, it was with some expectation of finding a significant line of influence that I undertook John Sommerfeldt's gracious invitation to investigate the relation of Bernard of Clairvaux and John

---

[1]See *Thomas Merton on Saint Bernard*, CS 9 (Kalamazoo, Michigan: Cistercian Publications, 1980) p. 166, n. 18. This book contains notes from which Merton lectured novices at the abbey of Gethsemani, inducting them into the spiritual foundations of their monastic life.

[2]Anecdotal though the account is, let me report the remark of the well-known Scotus scholar, Allan B. Wolter, who taught for years at the Franciscan Institute at St Bonaventure University, that he had heard Merton had devised a course of studies to imbue students with the common spirit stretching from Anselm, including Bernard, up through Scotus. Though I have never encountered any verification of this 'hearsay', it does no doubt reflect a broad truth Merton held about the lines of spiritual influence that obtained in the Middle Ages. Indeed, the 'hard fact' behind the remark may be no more than the opinion reflected in the note cited in n. 1.

Duns Scotus in view of the nonacentenary celebration of Bernard's birth held at the Twenty-fifth International Congress on Medieval Studies in Kalamazoo, Michigan.

In what follows I shall consider the relation of Bernard and Scotus in two different ways. First, I shall make the simple point that there is very little evidence that Scotus was directly influenced by any substantial consideration of bernardine texts or doctrines. Following this negative assessment, however, I shall then try to justify somewhat Merton's intuition of an intellectual spirit common to these two medieval teachers. To carry out this second task I have isolated doctrines of each thinker on the topics of freedom and the love of God, christocentrism, and the ontology of the human person.

In the process of aligning these two quite differently shaped theologies, I have found it helpful to articulate somewhat speculatively, I must admit, the foundations of a scotistic spirituality. In the longer, second part of this paper, therefore, I have asked the questions: if Scotus had developed a theology of the spiritual life or what Gilson has called a mystical theology, what would its foundations be? And how would these compare with the foundations of Bernard's mystical theology? Our answer to the questions enable us to see the kindred spirit of our two masters, each of whom had special insights into the life of christian liberty and the love of God.

I

Inspection of Duns Scotus's *opera omnia* shows very few and then only minor instances where Scotus cites Bernard's texts or teachings. It appears therefore that Bernard was quite a minor partner in Scotus's theological dialectic. All of Scotus's extant works, which are exclusively dialectical or demonstrative inquiries, are developed in some variant form of the scholastic *quaestio* (with the arguable exception of his *De primo principio*). In addition to the near omnipresence of Aristotle and Augustine, one can find significant encounters of Scotus with figures such as Anselm, Richard of Saint Victor, Thomas Aquinas, Bonaventure, Godfrey of Fontaine, and Henry of Ghent, to mention only the more important sources. The absence of a more significant bernardine influence is surprising on several counts.

First of all, some of Scotus's direct sources seemed to have known Bernard well and engaged certain of his doctrines directly in their texts. One might especially point to Bonaventure and, to a lesser extent, to

Thomas Aquinas. Secondly, since Anselm of Canterbury profoundly influenced Scotus (a topic that has yet to be given the attention it deserves) it would not be surprising, one might think, to find Scotus turning to Bernard as to a kindred soul, presuming here, of course, that Anselm shares significant common ground with Bernard. Thirdly, because of some important doctrinal filiations, one might expect Scotus to draw on Bernard's authority. In this regard, one might think of Scotus's insistence on the primacy of freedom or of his idea that theology is a practical science or of his radical christocentric view of creation. One expects and, indeed, finds some, although minor, engagement of Bernard in his marian doctrine. Finally, Peter Lombard, in developing Book 2, distinction 25 of his *Sentences*, devoted to the topic of freedom of choice, draws heavily on Bernard's doctrine of freedom. In their own commentaries on this distinction, both Bonaventure and Aquinas directly engage Bernard's teachings. Yet we find no mention of Bernard or of his doctrine of freedom in Scotus's commentary on 2.25. Freedom, of course, is a central scotist theme, and in commenting on 2.25 Scotus poses for himself a question of great philosophical significance: whether an act of the will is caused in the will by an object moving the will, or by the will moving itself? Here Scotus formulates his position on the autonomy and primacy of the will as an active power. It was a topic that exercised him a good deal, as is evident from the obvious development his teaching underwent.[3] In light of the obviously great care he gave to this question,

---

[3]We possess three distinct versions of Scotus's commentary on 2.25. The sequence of development seems to be the following. (1) What is published in the Wadding-Vivès edition (vol. 13, pp. 196–227) is Scotus's earliest opinion. With some ambivalence, Scotus holds that nothing other than the will is the total cause of the will's volitions. In fact, Scotus is here more particularly intent on denying that the object or the phantasm is the total cause of a volition. Whether the will is the total cause is not said, though many commentators with some justification tend to so interpret Scotus. This version, his earliest, is Scotus's Paris lecture which was revised later in his Oxford commentary on the *Sentences*. (2) What is published in Alnwick's *Additiones Magnae* (see C. Balic, *Les commentaires de Jean Duns Scot sur les quatres livres des Sentences* [Louvain: Bureaux de la Revue, 1927] pp. 264–301) is a collection of materials from various sources. The first part excerpts from the Paris lectures, the second part excerpts from the Oxford lectures in which Scotus argues that the object is not simply a *sine qua non* condition, and the third part returns to the Paris lectures. (3) What is published as the *Second Additions* is now considered to be a faithful edition of the later Oxford lecture (see Balic's 'Une question inédite de J. Duns Scot sur la volonté', RTAM 3 [1931] 191–206). The best study of this question is Bernardine M. Bonansea, 'Duns Scotus' Voluntarism', in J. K. Ryan and B. M. Bonansea (edd.), *John Duns Scotus, 1265–1965: Studies in Philosophy and the History of Philosophy* (Washington, D.C.: The Catholic University Press, 1965) 3:83–121.

464   *William A. Frank*

and given the patent bernardine presence in both Lombard's *Sentences* and the commentaries of Bonaventure and Aquinas, two of Scotus's more proximate dialectical partners, the absence of bernardine sources in Scotus's commentary is a significant one. In view of these reasons, one might find it surprising that Scotus does not take on Bernard as a more significant dialectical partner, though the surprise probably says more about our own contemporary ignorance about the working 'hermeneutics' of the medieval schoolmen.

Nevertheless a survey of the *opera omnia* does show some few modest references to Bernard. Let me mention five. (1) In *Lectura* 1, dist. 17 (*Utrum caritas qua diligimus deum et proximum sit spiritus sanctus*), contra 2, Scotus cites approvingly Bernard's *De diligendo Deo* (12.35)[4] to the effect that the charity which is of the substance of God is distinct from the quality by which we love our neighbor. One should note, however, that this reference to Bernard is absent in Scotus's *Ordinatio* revision and amplification of the same question. (2) In *Ord.* 3, d. 3, q. 1, in his list of initial objections Scotus lists Bernard twice, testifying to the effect that the Virgin Mary was not conceived immaculately. Probably Scotus had in mind *Sermo 2 in assumptionis beatae Mariae virginis* and *Epistola 174*.[5] (3) In *Ord.* 3.6.1, Scotus cites Bernard in his first initial argument.[6] The question at issue is whether in Christ the *esse* of the Word is different from the created *esse*. The bernardine text cited is Book 5 of *De consideratione* (9.20). (4) In *Ord.* 4.1.4, in the first argument *contra*, Scotus cites Bernard's authority holding that the sacraments are only signs and not causes.[7] The bernardine referent is from the *Sermon on the Last Supper* in which the signs of investiture for the canon, abbot, and bishop are identified respectively as the book, the staff, and the ring. (5) In *Ord.* 4.22.2, in the second initial argument, Scotus cites, on Bernard's authority, the principle that what is instituted for the sake of charity ought not to militate against charity.[8] The principle is used as major in an argument concluding that the seal of the confessional can be broken in the interests of the common good, a position that Scotus subsequently rejects. The bernardine source is Book 4 of *On Precept and Dispensation*.

[4]*Opera omnia* (Vatican City: Typis Polyglottis Vaticanis, 1966) 17:186.
[5]See Allan Wolter, *John Duns Scotus: Four Questions on Mary* (Santa Barbara, California: Old Mission, 1988) esp. pp. 3, 17–18, 37, and 51.
[6]*Opera omnia* (Paris: Apud Ludovicum Vivès, 1891–1895; reprint of the Wadding 1639 edition of the *opera omnia*) 14:305, 311–12.
[7]Wadding-Vivès, 16:14.
[8]Wadding-Vivès, 18:730.

I have presented, then, five specific references to Bernard's work in Scotus's *opera omnia*. Each of them belongs to the initial arguments of their respective *quaestiones*. None of them figures prominently in the more elaborate development of the question. Another, more careful reading of the *corpus* may uncover several additional such bernardine references, but it is unlikely they would alter the evidence that there is little direct influence of bernardine sources in Scotus's work. Similarly, one might expect the publication of the critical edition of Scotus's work, as it gets to the last three books of the *Sentences* commentary, to give us a more complete picture of Scotus's sources, but, again, I should be surprised if it altered significantly our present evaluation.

Before going on to the doctrinal comparison of Part II, it is interesting to note in passing that the seventeenth-century scotists, who were the scholiasts and commentators for the Wadding edition of Scotus's *opera*, seemed to have had quite a broad and appreciative grasp of Bernard's thought and works. They considered Bernard one of the more profound of the 'ancient theologians', and tried at every opportunity to show the consistency of Scotus's doctrine with Bernard's. One sees this particularly in the Franciscan Antonius Hiqueo, but also in his confreres Franciscus Lychetti and Joannis Ponci.

II

If we are to judge only in the light of lines of direct influence evident in the authorial sources, we would have to say Scotus does not partake of the bernardine intellectual spirit. But the antecedent criterion need not be accepted as necessary. It may not be that Scotus was tutored directly or indirectly by the works of Bernard. The two men may not even espouse principles, images, or distinctions which can be lifted adequately from the rich network of their thought and then commensurated in order to be judged the same or even similar. Still there may be legitimacy to Merton's hunch of a common intellectual spirit in these two medieval masters. But we shall have to look for commonality in the larger shape of their thought.

As we proceed with our inquiry, looking to the larger shape of their thought, let me give this task some definition by appealing to a principle in Ralph Waldo Emerson's 1838 'Divinity School Address'. The job of a true preacher, he says, is *to convert life to truth*. He goes on to explain that the preacher—to which we might add: and the theologian—passes

life through the fires of thought.[9] We are thereby led to imagine truth
as the thought-tested conversion of life into the spiritual and intellectual
artifacts that make up a tradition. With such a conceit, then, we perhaps
can find a way to interpret what Merton intuited in both Bernard and
Duns Scotus. In spite of the fact that each man's writing carries the
distinctive character of its own proper *logos*, each independently testifies
to a kindred approach to the spiritual life. If one is entitled to claim a
personal encounter through the teachings of another, then Thomas Merton
may well have seen in Scotus and Bernard spiritual characters with a deep
commonality. It now becomes our purpose to discern the main lines of
this commonality.

ON BERNARD

According to Bernard, one finds, at the end of the spiritual life, ecstatic
union with the divine Beloved. The end, of course, is an achievement
of the soul's freedom, a power one can employ to unfold or mature the
inner nature of the human person conceived as an image and likeness of
God. The bernardine spiritual ascent from out of one's sinful *proprium*,
as is well known, begins with self-knowledge, moves through love of
neighbor, and ends in the love of God.[10]

What is to be emphasized is that the human person is fundamentally a
free agent whose very self is perfected in its outgoing regard for others.
The final union of man and God, however, as Gilson insists, entails no
annihilation of the human lover's personality or individuality.[11] Hence,
at both the beginning and the end of one's spiritual career there is a true
self, an inviolable center of subjectivity, whose nature it is, nevertheless,
to-be-for-others.[12] Personal being, then, is ordered to communal being, a
doctrine which perfectly coheres with Bernard's central understanding of
man as an image of God who is the most perfect unity of three persons.[13]
Yet, in addition to understanding personal being as being-for-others, one

---

[9]Ralph Waldo Emerson, *The Best of Ralph Waldo Emerson* (Roslyn, New York: Walter
J. Black, Inc., 1969) p. 38.

[10]My account of Bernard is heavily indebted to Etienne Gilson's *The Mystical Theology of Saint Bernard*, trans. A.H.C. Downes (London, New York: Sheed and Ward,
[1940]; reprinted CS 120, Kalamazoo, Michigan: Cistercian Publications, 1990).

[11]Gilson, pp. 121–22.

[12]See, for example, Hum 3.6, 4.15–16, 5.18; SBOp 3:20–21, 27–29, 29–30. See also
Dil, especially 2.6, 8.23–25, 9.26; SBOp 3:123–24, 125–26, 126.

[13]Csi 5.8.18; SBOp 3:482–83.

must see that human being is also a career; it is the life-long effort of extending oneself toward others, and ultimately toward the one who is the 'form' of all.[14] And Bernard stands forth as the master guide to christian folk seeking their Best Beloved in a fallen world. His genius in large part consists in his cultivation of the principles and practices of the ascetic life and in his charismatic ability to draw others into the life of conversion.[15]

The life of conversion, which for Bernard uniquely combines the active and contemplative modes, amounts to a reformation of the self, or better, its restoration to its original being as an image and likeness of God. The entire project of reformation is one made necessary by the unhappy disfigurement of God's original creation through Adam's fall.[16] Existentially, then, postlapsis men and women find themselves with both an ineradicable power of free choice and a disorderly will. Because of original sin, freedom is caught initially in the swirl of one's *proprium*. By one's *proprium*, one's 'proper will', one defines oneself, summons one's self up in opposition to all others. Formed in *proprium*, one is an ultimate solitude, a law unto oneself. The self of *proprium* is a false self, perversely imitating the divine self-sufficiency. We might conceive of it as the dross of evil, cloying to the true self; it is thus a 'disfiguring mask',[17] requiring a life-long process of purification, the final effect of which is to rectify the 'proper will', now bent resolutely upon itself, so as to align it with the will of God.[18] The bernardine ascetic life thus begins when the self first resists the centripetal forces of its own *proprium*; it ends when it finally loves God as God loves himself and loves both self and others as God loves them. Human beatitude consists in the union of consent, in the communion of the human and divine wills.[19]

Let me now isolate three elements central to Bernard's spiritual doctrine as sketched above. *Liberty.* For Bernard, free choice lies at the

---

[14]Gra 10.33; SBOp 3:42.

[15]As Raymond DiLorenzo reads the *Divine Comedy*, Dante has conceived his masterpiece with a critical, architectonic role being played by Bernard precisely in his role as a guide to the use of *freedom*. Indeed it is Bernard's 'theology of liberty of choice' which is 'recreated [by Dante] as the pattern informing the movement of the traveler from the dark wood to the uncreated light that is Dante's God' (DiLorenzo, 'Dante's Saint Bernard and the Theology of Liberty in the *Commedia*', paper read at Kalamazoo and published in this volume).

[16]See Merton, pp. 107–108.

[17]Gilson, p. 128.

[18]Gilson, p. 126.

[19]Gilson, p. 126.

ineffaceable substrate of the human person. Indeed, it constitutes the basis of human dignity.[20] Present and operative even in the midst of deepest sin, freedom of choice, which can be neither taken away nor coerced, is a necessary condition of personal being.[21] But we must think of it as more than a necessary condition; rather it is like a seed whose flower will unfold, under proper cultivation, as the ecstatic but pure love of God.[22] Finally one must note that the human person's ontological being as an image of God manifests itself in freedom of choice. In virtue of its basic freedom, the self possesses the power of self-disposal,[23] and it is precisely that power which is so evident in God's loving acts of incarnation and redemption.

Christocentrism. In his *Sermons on the Song of Songs*, Bernard's Best Beloved is Christ, who as Word 'is the image of man reconciled with the Father.'[24] Indeed, 'Bernard's spirituality is centered on the Incarnation.'[25] 'By means of the Incarnation, the Word assumed and sanctified not only man's nature, but his destiny—to return to God and be glorified with Him.'[26] Christ thus becomes the mediator, the model, and means of any human person being taken up into the life of God. Spiritual progress is no less than being always more perfectly 'assimilated by Christ' and thus thereby recovering 'the image and likeness of the Father' which is the destiny and the final dignity of human existence.[27]

Ecstatic personalism. For want of a happier term, let me call 'ecstatic personalism' that distinctive ontology, evident in our summary account, according to which the human person only becomes itself by bestowing itself to another.[28] We refer here to the notion Bernard has of the self's

[20]Dil 2.2; SBOp 3:121.
[21]Gra 9.30; SBOp 3:187.
[22]Gilson, p. 142.
[23]Gra 2.4–5; SBOp 3:168–70.
[24]Jean Leclercq, *Bernard of Clairvaux and the Cistercian Spirit*, trans. Claire Lavoie, CS 16 (Kalamazoo, Michigan: Cistercian Publications, 1976) p. 81. On Bernard's christology, see also Jean-Marie Déchanet, 'La christologie de S. Bernard', ASOC 9 (1953) 78ff.; Marsha L. Dutton, 'Intimacy and Imitation: The Humanity of Christ in Cistercian Spirituality', in John R. Sommerfeldt (ed.), *Erudition at God's Service: Studies in Medieval Cistercian History, XI*, CS 98 (Kalamazoo: Cistercian Publications, 1987) pp. 33–69; and A. Van den Bosch, O.C.R., 'The Christology of St Bernard: A Review of Recent Works', Cîteaux 8 (1957) 245–51.
[25]Leclercq, p. 84.
[26]Leclercq, p. 80.
[27]Leclercq, p. 81.
[28]Emero Stiegman probes the innate power to move from self to other in bernardine spiritual growth; see his 'Humanism in Bernard of Clairvaux: Beyond Literary Culture',

very being, which, without self-repression or self-annihilation, consists in its being-for-others. The essential nature of the human person follows the paradoxical law that perfect self-possession lies in perfect self-bestowal. Bernard has a keen sense of this paradoxical structure of the human person. He finds human being ordered to and perfectly exemplified in the love of the incarnate Word. It is interesting to note how Bernard's doctrines of liberty and the ecstatic nature of the person cohere in the redemptive action of Christ. Christ then provides the model for the nature of the ordinary person, for as both lover of God and God's own beloved, each person possesses an innate liberty which is both source and subject of one's eternal life.

When we presently turn to a collateral development of scotistic themes, we shall look for an analogous convergence of liberty and Christ in an understanding of the human person. Because in his life Bernard acted as the guide, the spiritual master, for so many of his generation, it is relatively easy to imagine him regarding fellow pilgrims as images of God and beloveds of Christ, reaching out to help each of his companions to open himself to the visit of the Word, one's divine lover.[29] As we turn to Scotus, however, the task makes greater demands on the imagination, for Scotus was a pure academician of the High Middle Ages—and a short-lived one, at that. Because history has left us nothing more than the refined doctrines of his thought, one needs the intuitive genius of an Emerson or a Thomas Merton to experience in them the shape of personal experience.

On Duns Scotus

Although Duns Scotus considers theology a practical science, which is to say, he thinks of it as knowledge of divinity ordered to the right love of God,[30] he does not descend to the particulars of spiritual formation. He gives us no ascetic teaching. There is in his works nothing that resembles

in E. Rozanne Elder and John R. Sommerfeldt (edd.), *The Chimaera of His Age: Studies on Bernard of Clairvaux*, CS 63 (Kalamazoo, Michigan: Cistercian Publications, Inc., 1980) pp. 23–38.

[29]SC 84; SBOp 2:303–307.

[30]See his Prologue to the *Ordinatio*; Vat. ed., 1:237. See P. Aegidius Magrini, O.F.M., *Ioannis Duns Scoti Doctrina De Scientifica Theologiae Natura* (Rome: Pontificium Athenaeum Antonianum, 1952); and Donald E. Daniels, 'Theology as a Science in Duns Scotus', in Venant Cauchy (ed.), *Philosophy and Culture* (Montreal: Editions Montmorency, 1988) pp. 837–40.

a mystical theology.[31] Notwithstanding this absence, however, there are teachings in Scotus's philosophy and theology that promise to provide the foundations for a kind of union with God that might be adequate for a mystical theology. Such foundations would have to portray the nature of the human person in such a way that its possibilities for desiring and striving to overcome the gap between the finite lover and infinite Beloved could become a matter of practical personal practice.

One way of speaking about the dignity of human being would be that of showing what man is capable of and how he is situated in the hierarchy of being. Bernard of Clairvaux does this when he says that 'man's dignity is his free will'.[32] In virtue of his free will man is distinguished from the beasts, and he is capable of attaining his destiny in the love of God. Duns Scotus has a comparable doctrine of freedom which we shall subsequently spell out.

A second way of representing the dignity of a being is to show how this entity is beloved and by whom. More worthy would be that individual who is beloved more perfectly by the more perfect lover. Accordingly, in the case of Bernard, it is the realization that Christ visits one in the bridal bed that more perfectly conveys the superior dignity of ordinary human souls than the knowledge of one's free will. Man's dignity is thus expressed in the fact that the human person can prepare himself to be the bride of Christ. In Duns Scotus's latter account of the dignity of man, Christ also plays a central role, but in comparison with Bernard, the franciscan master gives us a less particular and intimate portrayal, though I think it has its own comparable appeal and speculative daring. Let us begin with a brief account of Scotus's christology and then turn to his voluntarism.

Christocentrism. In a quite literal and radical way, Scotus's Christ is the cosmic Christ of *Colossians*, 'the first-born of all creation' (Col 1:15). This is elaborated as follows. In its first logical moment, God's creating act of will orders Christ's human nature to glory.[33] In fact this volition has two aspects to it. First, God wills that there be an individual of human

---

[31]For a sustained consideration of Scotus's spirituality, see Charles Balic's article 'Duns Scot' in *Dictionnaire de spiritualité* (Paris: Beauchesne, 1957) 3:1801–818.

[32]Dil 2.2; SBOp 3:121.

[33]*Ordinatio* [hereafter Ord.] 3, dist. 7, q. 3. The relevant texts on Scotus's christocentrism are collected in Allan Wolter's 'John Duns Scotus on the Primacy and Personality of Christ' in Damian McElrath (ed.), *Franciscan Christology: Selected Texts, Translations, and Introductory Essays* (St Bonaventure, New York: Franciscan Institute, 1980) pp. 144–67; hereafter: FC.

nature as a co-lover of the Godhead and as a partaker in his glory, and then he wills that this nature be united with the divine Word. Therefore, when the faith tells us that God created in order to glorify himself, Scotus takes this to mean that God willed Christ in his human nature, and all subsequent finite entity, all history, issues from this first divine volition. The rest of the created order, its angels, its non-divine men and women, its brutes, plants, and inanimate things—the whole cosmos—is ordered to Christ from the beginning of creation. In this scheme of things, Christ is thus not only first in creation in the order of eminence, but he is also first in a quasi-temporal sense as the object originally willed by God in his creative act.[34]

If we reflect on the implications of Scotus's christological doctrine for an understanding of human nature, a nature shared by ordinary folks such as, let us say, Francis and Clare, then two things stand out. It becomes clear, first of all, that human nature was created in God's original intent, if you will, in order to be assumed by the divine Word. And, secondly, human nature, the individual entity of which is finalized in personhood, was destined to be a co-lover of God. This latter point deserves an elaborative comment or two.

Referring to God's primal creative act, Scotus says God 'first loves himself ordinately and consequently not . . . in an envious or jealous manner.'[35] The basic idea is that love carries within it, as it were, the non-necessitating inevitability of willing co-lovers for one's beloved. Following this 'law of love'—which, incidentally, Scotus seems to have learned from Richard of Saint Victor—God's generosity flows beyond the sufficiency of the Trinity, and he thus contingently wills finite co-lovers.[36] Accordingly, the careers of ordinary persons such as Clare and Francis, making their way to the perfect love of God, have a foundation in the life of Christ who is the perfect creaturely co-lover willed by God in his first creative act and who is the eminent 'form' of all creation. When we observe then that the love of God is Francis's destiny and we understand this as the inner logic of his personal experience, this understanding is subject to a deeper interpretation in the light of Scotus's christocentrism, for we come to see Francis's life as an imitation of Christ. Yet Scotus has now given this pious *imitatio Christi* an ontological depth. For as a person of human nature, Francis appropriates a

---

[34]Ord. 3 (suppl.), d. 32; FC 154–57.
[35]Ord. 3 (suppl.), d. 32; FC 156–57.
[36]See, especially, Richard of Saint Victor's *On the Trinity* 3:2, 11, 15.

complete human nature meant from the beginning to be assumed by the
divine Word who, in turn, in the hypostatic union was meant to be a
co-lover of God.

Freedom and the love of God. Up to this point the major idea has been
that man's dignity rests on the fact that he, in his nature, has been chosen
from the beginning as first among creatures; his greatness consists in the
extraordinary way that he, through union with Christ, is *beloved* of God.
We might say that this cosmic privilege is not without its corresponding
personal obligation. Indeed, as we say, human nature was created out of
God's boundless generosity in accordance with the 'law' that the true
lover seeks co-lovers for his beloved. Accordingly, it is man's destiny
to be a *lover* of God. And for Scotus, *free will* especially names the
power by which men and women make themselves lovers of God, and,
in the process, bring others into the life of loving God. Let me now give
a precis of Scotus's teaching on the free will, bringing out the special
sense in which it empowers the self to be for others.

All acts of human love are, for Scotus, radically contingent acts, pro
ceeding from the active power of the will, a power which in its every
action is always open to its opposite.[37] Innately present to the will is its
inclination to the just good. Hence, when it acts, it is always possible
for the will to love honest goods out of a sheer regard for their intrinsic
worthiness.[38] The infinite goodness appears as the highest of such honest
goods, and so can be loved out of perfect freedom. Indeed, not only can
God be so loved, but that he is to be so loved is a first principle of the
moral law.[39] Free will is a power never lost to any man; nor is its *affectio
justitiae* ever lost.[40] The will's always available effective power can be
intensified by God's gift of charity, and through the work of charity the

---

[37]See, especially, *Quaestiones in Metaphysicam* 9, q. 15, in *Duns Scotus on the Will
and Morality*, ed. and trans. Allan B. Wolter (Washington, D.C.: The Catholic University
Press, 1986) pp. 145–72; hereafter WM. B. M. Bonansea in his *Man and His Approach
to God in John Duns Scotus* (Lantham, Maryland: University Press of America, 1983)
pp. 11–52, gives a dependable synthetic account of Scotus's anthropology. For solid
discussion of Scotus's doctrine of the will, see A. Wolter's studies 'Duns Scotus on the
Will as a Rational Potency', and 'Native Freedom of the Will as a Key to the Ethics
of Scotus' in his *The Philosophical Theology of John Duns Scotus*, ed. Marilyn McCord
Adams (Ithaca, New York: Cornell University Press, 1990). Also see W. Frank, "Duns
Scotus' Concept of Willing Freely: What Divine Freedom Beyond Choice Teaches Us',
Franciscan Studies 20 (1982) 68–89.
[38]See the texts collected in WM 179–206, and Wolter's 'Native Freedom of the Will'.
[39]WM 276–87, 424–57.
[40]WM 442–43; Wolter, 'Native Freedom of the Will'.

will's acts can be meritorious,[41] but the essential fact remains that the human will has always within it the effective power for a selfless love of God.[42]

In accordance with the victorine law of love mentioned earlier, one's selfless love of God perfects itself in the love of neighbor and even in the love of self. Since jealousy has no place in Scotus's notion of the free or just love of God, the lover, recognizing the universal lovability of God, wills that others also love God.[43] What this means, however, is that in willing others to love God for God's own sake, one wills a great and just good for one's neighbor.

The same analysis of love of neighbor proceeding from the love of God applies, *mutatis mutandis*, to the case of self-love. In other words, my prior love of God for his own sake is perfected in loving myself as one whose love is pleasing to God. Accordingly, I love myself because I am a lover of God, which self-love is an act of justice or charity.[44] The reason for willing that one's self and neighbor love God is that this love is pleasing to God. God is the infinite Beloved, and the perfect lover wills that others love the Best Beloved.[45]

Ontology of the person. Previously I spoke of the significance of the ordinary person's appropriation of its human nature. We envisioned, as an example, Francis or Clare's appropriation of a rational nature intended from the first moment of creation to be taken up by the divine Word and thereby glorify the Godhead. From an ontological point of view, it would seem not too wild a metaphor to think of Francis or Clare in

[41]WM 442–43, and *Quodlibet* q. 17, in *John Duns Scotus, God and Creatures: The Quodlibetal Questions*, trans. Felix Alluntis and Allan B. Wolter (Princeton, New Jersey: Princeton University Press, 1975) pp. 388–98.

[42]WM 434–35.

[43]WM 448–51.

[44]WM 454–57.

[45]What Scotus teaches about the ordering of our love of self and neighbor to the prior love of God for his own sake parallels Bernard's third and fourth degrees of love (Dil 8.23–10.29, 15.39; SBOp 3:138–44, 152–53). Also common to the two masters is the idea that one's superior love of God is the fruition of an innate freedom essential to the human person. For Bernard the beatifying love of God seems to be the inevitable unfolding of the dynamic of basic free choice. This dynamic of freedom and the love of God is most perspicuously developed by Bernard in his treatise *On Grace and Free Choice*. Beneath the particulars of his discussion of freedom and grace is a profound meditation on the question: *who am I*? When Paul says '*I* ran the good race'—the very race Bernard and his confreres are currently engaged in—Bernard wants to know: what is the nature of this 'I'? Here we see the convergence of freedom and the love of God in a profound, self-conscious christian psychology in which man appears as both lover and beloved of the divine Father.

their personal being as an imitation of Christ. The appropriateness of this image is tightened as one realizes with Scotus that the heart of the human nature appropriated in personal being is most fully expressed in a selfless love of God and neighbor. Indeed, according to the primal creative intent of human nature, being human *is* being Christ-like. There is another doctrine of Scotus's that perhaps enhances yet more the possibility for Francis and Clare to unite themselves with Christ. Let us briefly turn to Scotus' subtle doctrine of the *negative* nature of non-divine persons. Our intent in this investigation will be to suggest the possibility for a kind of union with God adequate to the ideals of a mystical theology. We can focus the issue to be discussed by asking: what is the most intimate sort of union with Christ to which Francis might aspire?

The salient characteristic of personhood is that it 'contracts' a rational nature into an unrepeatable and incommunicable entity; personhood names the *ultimata solitudo* of free, rational beings such as Francis and Clare, Michael and Lucifer, Christ, and the trinitarian Father, Son, and Holy Spirit. We might say that personhood finalizes the entity of persons such as Francis, giving them their complete ontological weight, as it were.

For reasons we need not pursue here, Scotus accepts Richard of Saint Victor's definition of the person as 'the incommunicable existence of an intellectual nature'.[46] This means that a personal entity is not the sort of thing that can be shared the way, for instance, a single nature is shared by two individuals, nor is it the sort of thing that has its existence by participating in the existence of another, the way, for instance, the soul 'communicates' with the body. Scotus saw in this victorine notion of personhood a particular challenge to one who would want to claim the full humanity of Christ. For if an individual of human nature is complete only insofar as it has been 'personalized', then it would seem that either the divine Word assumed an incomplete human nature (for it would have been made complete only in the 'personalization' of the hypostatic union), or in the hypostatic union the divine Word displaced a finite human person, taking over its nature. Above all Scotus insisted on the completeness of Christ's human nature,[47] and so he was forced to tackle the second alternative, explaining how in the hypostatic union

---

[46]See Scotus, Ord. 1, d. 23, nn. 15–16 (Vatican ed., 5:355–57); FC 166–69; and Richard of Saint Victor, *On the Trinity* 4.22. FC collects the relevant texts for Scotus's treatment of personhood.

[47]Wolfhart Pannenberg, among contemporary theologians, is especially keen in his appreciation of Scotus's achievement on this count. See, for instance, his *Jesus—God and Man*, trans. Wilkens and Priebe (Philadelphia: Westminster, 1974) p. 296.

there were not two persons to be accounted for. In dealing with this problem he was led to develop his theory of the *negative* nature of non-divine personhood.

As Scotus's theory unfolds, we come to understand that an individual of human nature needs the addition of no additional entity for it to be a person. Yet it is possible for such an individual to be assumed by an extrinsic person, as is evident in the case of Christ's human nature. With Christ we have an individual of human nature which is *communicated.* Yet it would seem that such an individual could not have been a person then, for persons are essentially incommunicable entities. What Scotus then realized is that, because an individual human nature could, without doing any violence to its nature, depend on some extrinsic person, it therefore does not suffice to say one has an individual human nature in order to say one is a person. One must add further that this individual is *not actually* assumed by an extrinsic person, and yet further stipulate that it is *not disposed by nature* for any such assumption. In this light, Scotus says:

> The formal reason our nature is invested with a created personality is not something positive, for we find no positive entity in addition to singularity that makes the singular nature incommunicable. All that is added to singularity is the negation of dependence or being communicated. . . . [48]

On the face of it, to define person negatively seems odd or unnecessarily convoluted. The reason, however, is that Scotus takes the fact of the hypostatic union to mean that a created nature always enjoys the possibility of being dependent on (communicated with) the divine person. As Scotus puts it: 'A created nature . . . though it may subsist in itself has nothing intrinsic that would make it impossible for it to depend [on a divine person].'[49] The implication is that 'only a divine person has a complete proper personality',[50] for every created nature lacks the impossibility of its so depending on a divine person.

Scotus, then, teaches that a complete human nature has the sheer ontological possibility to be assumed by the divine Word:

> . . . Everything is simply in obediential potency to depend on a divine person. . . . In fact every positive entity in such a nature [that is, one

[48]*Quodlibet* q. 19; FC 171.
[49]*Quodlibet* q. 19; FC 175.
[50]*Quodlibet* q. 19; FC 175.

able to be a person] is in obediential potency to depend on a divine person. . . . [51]

In other words, there would not be something incoherent or self-contradictory about the proposal of a human nature personalized by a divine person. What is *not* being said is that the human nature is somehow naturally imperfect insofar as it has not been assumed. Although an ontological possibility, being assumed by the divine Word is not the fulfillment of some potentiality of a nature; it is not the satisfaction of some inclination toward its perfecting form.

Let us bring this consideration of the ontology of personhood to a close by posing two concrete questions: how is it that an ordinary person such as Francis is a person? And what implications does it hold for Francis's efforts to become as much like Christ as possible? To the first question, Scotus would reply: (1) Francis is an individual of rational nature; (2) he has no inclination to be assumed by a divine person, that is, there is no naturally perfective form he lacks which would give him greater ontological autonomy or independent existence; (3) he enjoys the obediential potency to being assumed by a divine person; and (4) he has not actually been assumed by a divine person.

Before answering the second question, let us recall that the human nature Francis now appropriates was ordered in the first moments of creation toward the hypostatic union. We further recall that Francis has his free will within his complete effective control and is thereby capable of selflessly loving God above all and for his own sake. Now in light of the revealed truth of the primacy of Christ, as interpreted in Scotus's radical doctrine of christocentrism, Francis understands the fundamentally contingent nature of his own personhood. Although he enjoys his life, the full flowering of his personality, in the recognition of his self-identity and separation from all others,[52] would it be so absurd for Francis to will that his life be taken up by the divine Word?

Francis of Assisi, Duns Scotus's spiritual father, once explained to his friars minor that 'he lives most justly who lives without anything of his own' (*sine proprio*).[53] Read in the light of Scotus's thought, 'to live most justly' would mean to live most freely, loving God above

---

[51]*Quodlibet* q. 19; FC 170–73.
[52]See Wolter's commentary in FC 144.
[53]*The Admonitions* 11, in *Francis and Clare: The Complete Works*, trans. Regis J. Armstrong and Ignatius C. Brady, The Classics of Western Spirituality (New York: Paulist Press, 1982) p. 31; see also the translators' helpful n. 9.

all. And 'to have nothing of one's own', if taken most literally as was Francis's custom, could well mean to yield what is most properly one's own, one's personhood, one's self rendered as an independence from all others, including God. The height of evangelical poverty would then be to live in the total dedication of one's life to the love and glorification of God.[54] But this would be to be Christ-like in a most literal fashion. In the most perfect dedication Francis would allow himself to be appropriated by the divine Word.

In some such fashion, then, I would propose that Scotus provides the foundations for a mystical theology. At the heart are his doctrines of liberty and Christ. Both cohere, or so I have tried to suggest, in a theory of the human person. The human person is such that it can give up what is its ownmost, the very root of its independent existence, in the interest of the perfect love of God, a love most perfectly manifest in the love of the Son for the Father.

Through freedom and Christ, one moves from *proprium* to the love of God. This much, and it would seem a great deal, Bernard of Clairvaux and Duns Scotus hold in common. Perhaps it was the intuition of some such common spiritual ground that was behind the admiration Thomas Merton had for these otherwise so very different masters of the cistercian and franciscan traditions.

Abstracts

L'article démontre d'abord que Duns Scot ne comptait pas Bernard parmi ses *auctoritates* à un degré significatif. Il ressort du témoignage des textes qu'il fait un usage remarquablement minimal des textes et des doctrines bernardines. La deuxième partie de l'étude, qui est la plus importante, entreprend de comparer des doctrines analogues de chacun de ces penseurs. Les sujets développés sont : (1) liberté et amour de Dieu, (2) christocentrisme, et (3) ontologie de la personne humaine. Aux yeux de Scot, la personne humaine est telle qu'elle peut renoncer à ce qui lui appartient le plus en propre, la racine même de son existence indépendante, dans l'intérêt d'un parfait amour de Dieu, amour manifesté de la façon la plus parfaite dans l'amour du Fils pour le Père. Ce mouvement spirituel scotiste supporte la comparaison—que ne peut

---

[54]Pannenberg, in his discussion of Scotus's doctrine of the person (p. 296), distinguishes two ways for a created personality to become a person: (1) 'in dedication to God', or (2) 'in rendering one's self independent from God'.

manquer d'être passionante—avec l'ascension bernardine qui partant du *proprium* entaché par le péché et passant par la liberté et le Christ, aboutit enfui à l'amour de Dieu.

The article first demonstrates that Duns Scotus did not hold Bernard as one of his *auctoritates* to any significant extent. The textual evidence shows remarkably minimal use by Scotus of bernardine texts or doctrines. The second, major section of the study then undertakes a comparison of analogous doctrines from each thinker. The topics developed are: (1) freedom and the love of God, (2) christocentrism, and (3) the ontology of the human person. In Scotus' view, the human person is such that he can give up what is his ownmost, the very root of his independent existence, in the interest of perfect love of God, a love most perfectly manifest in the love of the Son for the Father. This scotistic spiritual movement bears interesting comparison with the better known bernardine spiritual ascent from sinful *proprium*, through freedom and Christ, to the love of God.

Der Artikel zeigt zunächst, dass Duns Scotus Bernhard nicht in einem bedeutenden Ausmaß für eine seiner *auctoritates* hielt. Der Textbefund zeigt einen bemerkenswert geringen Gebrauch bernhardinischer Texte oder Lehren bei Scotus. Der zweite, größere Teil der Studie unternimmt den Vergleich von analogen Lehren beider Denker. Die dabei ausgearbeiteten Themen sind: (1) Freiheit und die Liebe Gottes, (2) Christozentrismus, und (3) die Ontologie der menschlichen Person. Für Scotus finden wir, dass die menschliche Person derartig gestaltet ist, dass sie ihr eigenstes aufgeben kann, die Wurzel ihrer unabhängigen Existenz, im Interesse der vollkommenen Liebe Gottes, einer Liebe, die am vollkommensten offenbart ist in der Liebe des Sohnes zum Vater. Diese scotistische geistliche Bewegung steht in einem interessanten Vergleich zu dem besser bekannten bernhardinischen geistlichen Aufstieg von sündigen *proprium* über die Freiheit und Christus zur Liebe Gottes.

FROM BERNARD TO BRIDGET:
CISTERCIAN CONTRIBUTION TO A UNIQUE SCANDINAVIAN MONASTIC BODY

James France
Oxford, England

LTHOUGH THEY WERE SEPARATED by two centuries and came from opposite ends of Christendom, Saint Bernard and Saint Birgitta of Vadstena (or Bridget as she is commonly known in English) had a great deal in common. They are linked by the process of devotional development with its concentration on the person of Christ, and especially the passion, which is associated with Bernard and culminated with the mystical literature of the fourteenth century, of which Bridget was among the chief exponents. The Cistercians in large measure provided the bridge between them.

The linkage is of special interest, for Bridget's 'double' monasteries of nuns and monks remained influential centers of devotional life and of learning until the Reformation, and were unique in two ways: they not only belonged to the first religious order to be founded by a woman, but were also the only ones of scandinavian origin.

In examining the similarity between Bernard and Bridget, a number of facets spring to mind. First, they shared a privileged background. Bernard's father, Tescelin, was a great landowner and lord of Fontaines, Bridget's father owned extensive estates in northern Sweden, and was a knight and royal councillor.[1] Their ancestry on their mother's side was

---

[1]For Bernard's family, see J. Richard, 'Le milieu familial', in *Bernard de Clairvaux* (Commission d'Histoire de l'Ordre de Cîteaux, 3 (Paris 1953) pp. 3–15, and E. Vacandard,

even more exalted: Bernard's mother was descended from the dukes of Burgundy, Bridget was related to the swedish royal house.[2]

Second, such was their magnetism that large numbers joined them, among them many members of their own families, in Bernard's case his father, four brothers, an uncle, and two cousins; his sister became a nun at Jully.[3] Bridget's daughter, Catherine, who was herself canonized, became the first abbess of the mother-house at Vadstena, and another daughter became a cistercian nun.[4]

Third, although they were both intellectual giants, they shared a distrust of what was taught in the schools. Theirs was an instinctive rather than a trained appreciation of the liberal arts. To Aelred of Rievaulx's confession that he had come 'not from the schools, but from the kitchen', Bernard retorted that the 'knowledge that comes from the school of the Holy Spirit rather than the schools of rhetoric will savor all the sweeter to me'.[5] Like Bernard, Aelred 'despised the vain pursuit of eloquence',[6] recognizing the moral dangers which beset those who followed it. This would have become even more apparent by the fourteenth century. The intervening period had been one of continual controversy, and the mystical and ascetical body of literature, such as Bridget's, followed as a reaction to the excessive intellectualism of the schools. Bridget's words echo those of Bernard: true wisdom does not consist of 'the merit of the learned, deeply skilled in science and fine arts, but in the heart and in a truly christian life', and 'true wisdom, then, consists of works, not in great talents which the world admires'.[7] As a woman, Bridget was of course precluded from an education in the schools. Her down-to-earth practicality rested on the country pursuits of her youth, and on observing the administrative work connected with the duties of royal officials.

Vie de St Bernard (Paris, 1927), 1:1–10. The main authority for Bridget's life is *Vita sanctae Birgittae*, in *Scriptores Rerum Svecicarum Medii Aevi*, ed. C. M. Annerstadt, 3:185–206.

[2]She has mistakenly been called 'princess of Sweden' in the title of an abridged english edition of *The Revelations of St Bridget* (London, 1873), and she is referred to as Queen Birgitta in D. Knowles, *The Religious Orders in England* (Cambridge, 1957) 2:175.

[3]Vacandard (note 1), vol. 1: 65 and 86–87, and R. Fossier, 'L'installation et les premières années de Clairvaux', in *Bernard de Clairvaux* (note 1) p. 92.

[4]*Diplomatarium Suecanum*, 5:3558.

[5]*Epistola* (Ep) 523; SBOp 8:487; trans. Bruno Scott James, *The Letters of St Bernard of Clairvaux* (London, 1953) pp. 246–47.

[6]Walter Daniel, *The Life of Ailred of Rievaulx*, ed. and trans. F. M. Powicke (London, 1950) p. 27.

[7]*Revelations*, (note 2), p. 72 and 73.

Fourth, both Bernard and Bridget make extensive use of images drawn from the natural world around them. Many of Bridget's stories are based on detailed observations from everyday life, used to convey a spiritual message, for example, the all-embracing nature of divine grace:

> The hen which sits upon eggs to hatch her chickens is the image of the divine beneficence. This bird only gives warmth to those that are under her breast. When the chickens are nearly hatched, they try to break the shell of the egg with their beaks; then the mother takes all pains to obtain for them more warmth to hasten their coming out. God refuses his grace to none.[8]

This quotation compares with Bernard's mention of the hen gathering her chicks under her wings,[9] one of many allusions to the natural world around him, yet these were largely borrowed from the Scriptures. He was so detached from the external world that he was said not to notice many things around him,[10] and he used images from nature primarily to impart his message and not out of reverence for it or as a tribute to its wonders. Bridget revealed a more positive attitude to her natural environment and her approach was altogether more convincing as it was based on her own observation.

BERNARD AND BRIDGET: WATCHDOGS OF GOD'S HOUSEHOLD

As we have seen, a number of factors contributed to the affinity between Bernard and Bridget. Of these, their magnetism gives us a clue to the most important shared aspect of their character. Bernard's biographer alluded to it in the story of the dream which his mother had while she was expecting him. Terrified at the thought of bearing a puppy, she was reassured when told that he would

> become the guardian of God's household. He will bark on its behalf at the great enemies of the faith. He will become a great preacher, and, like a good dog, the healing grace of his tongue will cure many of many illnesses.[11]

---

[8]*Revelations*, p. 110.

[9]M. Casey, 'Bernard the Observer', in E. Rozanne Elder (ed.), *Goad and Nail: Studies in Medieval Cistercian History, 10*, CS 84 (Kalamazoo, Michigan, 1985) p. 17, n. 67.

[10]*Vita prima* 1.4.20; PL 185:238–39.

[11]*Vita prima* 1.1.2; PL 185:227–28: 'Ne timeas, bene res agitur, optimi catuli mater eris, qui domus Dei custos futurus, magnos pro ea contra inimicos fidei editurus est

This perfectly outlines the impact of Bernard on his world, and could with almost equal accuracy refer to Bridget two centuries later.

They shared a number of attributes: strength of character, compassion, asceticism, leadership qualities, energy, courage, single-mindedness, self-assurance, even the obstinacy that springs from strong convictions. They were imbued with an overwhelming desire to right the wrongs around them, and in 'barking at the enemies of the faith' they pursued a course in which their involvement with the world was at odds with their life dedicated to contemplation.

Bernard and Bridget: Noisy Importunate Frogs

Bernard's preoccupation with the affairs of the Church is well known, and the inconsistency between these activities and his monastic profession has formed the subject of a number of studies.[12] Although partly conducted from the cloister with the use of his pen, he also travelled endlessly to settle schism, combat heresy, preach crusade, engage in theological controversy, and resolve conflicts. The paradox was noted by his contemporaries, but no one was more aware of the dilemma than Bernard himself. He made frequent references to the pain of leaving the cloister, and likened himself to an 'unfledged nestling'[13] exposed to winds and tempests, and also to a triple-headed monster, having kept the habit of a monk but abandoned the life.[14] In another letter he pleaded to be relieved from non-monastic duties:

> May it please you to bid the noisy and importunate frogs to keep their holes and remain contented with their ponds.[15]

He justified his involvement as in obedience to a higher authority,[16] the overriding consideration being the welfare of the Church which he put

latratus. Erit enim egregius praedicator, et tanquam bonus canis, gratia linguae medicinalis in multis multos morbos curaturus est animarum'.

[12] The conflict between Bernard's monastic vocation and his involvement in the world has most recently been explored in J. R. Sommerfeldt, 'The Chimaera Revisited', Cîteaux 39 (1988) 5–13.

[13] Ep 12; SBOp 7:62; James, p. 49: ' . . . implumis avicula paene omni tempore nidulo exsulans, vento exposita et turbini, turbatus sum et motus sum sicut ebrius, et omnis conscientia mea devorata est'.

[14] Ep 250; SBOp 8:147; James, p. 402: 'Ego enim quaedam chimaera mei seculi, nec clericum gero nec laicum. Nam monachi iamdudum exui conversationem, non habitum'.

[15] Ep 48; SBOp 7:139; James, p. 81: 'Indicatur, si placet, clamosis et importunis ranis de cavernis non egredi, sed suis contentas esse paludibus'.

[16] Ep 48; SBOp 7:139; James, p. 81.

before the observance of his monastic duties. Perhaps the dominance of his personality was such that he was simply unable to contain himself within his monastery, and his emergence as a public figure may be partly explained by the assertion of a modern authority that 'in his soul was a continual temptation to power'.[17] This possibility invites another comparison with Bridget. A leading swedish historian says of her:

> She sought to exchange an active existence for one of contemplation, although a passive life was ruled out by her enormous vitality and masterful nature.[18]

Like Bernard, Bridget involved herself in numerous activities which were at odds with her vocation. She gained for herself a place on center stage in a way no other Scandinavian had ever done before or perhaps even since. Unlike Bernard, however, she spent a lifetime planning her foundation, drawing up the rule and seeking its ratification, and never experienced monastic life herself, the first head of her monastery at Vadstena being her daughter, Catherine. She saw no inconsistency in her involvement in the world. Her motivation was quite straightforward: the resolution of the ills of Christendom—the end of the Hundred Years' War and the pope's Babylonian Captivity in Avignon—were a precondition for the successful outcome of her plans, which depended on the right conditions in Sweden and on papal approval. Her war against widespread corruption in Rome brings to mind Bernard's letter in which he asks to be absolved from his ecclesiastical duties but concludes, with a final sting, that

> I do not think that because I am hidden away and keeping silent the troubles of the Church will cease so long as the roman curia continues to pass judgements to the prejudice of the absent in order to please those who are at hand.[19]

Although often studied as reformers of the Church and society, both Bernard and Bridget were, paradoxically, least successful in this respect.[20] One need only mention the length to which Bernard went to

---

[17]This view is advanced by Jean Leclercq and quoted by Sommerfeldt, p. 10.

[18]I. Andersson, *A History of Sweden*, trans. C. Hannay (London, 1962) p. 56.

[19]Ep 48; SBOp 7:140; James, p. 81: 'Non tamen idcirco, etiam me latente et tacente, cessare puto murmur ecclesiarum, si non cesset Romana curia pro voluntate assistentium facere praeiudicium in absentes'.

[20]A number of examples of works which emphasize Bernard's role as a leader of Christendom are given in Sommerfeldt, p. 6. Similarly, the overall picture which emerges from the whole chapter devoted to Bridget in Andersson, pp. 54–62, is of a national hero

promote what was an unmitigated disaster, the Second Crusade, and Bridget's failure to achieve peace or secure the return of the pope to Rome. Their lasting legacy lay not so much in their 'barking' or in their 'croaking', but in the sphere of their spiritual teaching.

BRIDGET GATHERING CISTERCIAN FLOWERS

Bridget's contact with the Cistercians was strong and had a profound influence on her. As a young married woman she lived near Alvastra, the first cistercian abbey in Scandinavia, founded in 1143 as a direct result of the intervention of Bernard himself. According to the *Exordium Magnum*,

> the venerable father was also anxious to reap some fruit among the people of the North, and he sent a convent of brothers to those regions at the request of a pious lady, the queen of Sweden.[21]

The environment with which the Cistercians were confronted upon their arrival in Sweden was quite the most uncongenial that they had so far encountered. The foreign monks from warmer climes undertook the long and difficult journey 'from the end of the world' to settle among 'uncultivated and wild men'.[22] Having reached their destination, they found themselves among an 'extremely remote people hidden in the last clime of northern winter'.[23] Christianity had not yet spread to all regions of the sparsely populated country, and the organization of the Church was as yet rudimentary. There was no previous monastic tradition, and, in the words of the *Exordium Magnum*, the people 'had only heard of the word monk, but had not previously set eyes on a monk'.[24] The monks settled close to the eastern shore of one of the great swedish

who 'felt the need of a wider arena for her prophecies and her calling—one is tempted to call it her spiritual ambition' (p. 58). More is made of the influence of her powerful personality on 'the view which later generations were to take of the history of this period' (p. 62) than of her contribution to late medieval spirituality.

[21]*Exordium Magnum Cisterciense* [EM], ed. B. Griesser, Series Scriptorum S. Ordinis Cisterciensis II, p. 258: 'Volens autem isdem venerabilis pater in populis aquilonarium partium sicut et in ceteris gentibus aliquem fructum habere petente religiosa femina, regina Sueciae, conventum fratrum ad partes illas direxit'.

[22]*Vita prima* 4.25; PL 185:335: 'a finibus terrae'. EM 259: 'hominibus rudibus et indomitis'.

[23]EM 259: 'licet remottissimas et in ultimo climate aquilonaris brumae abstrusas nationes non sine quodam horrore spiritus adire possent. . . .'

[24]EM 260: '. . . qui monachi quidem nomen audierant, sed monachum antea non viderant.'

lakes, Lake Vännern, in the vicinity of the royal residence. Powerful patronage insured the success of the enterprise. Alvastra was to become the most influential abbey in Sweden, the mother of three daughter-houses: Varnhem, Julita, and Gudsberga.[25]

We know from Bridget's writings that the level of observance at Alvastra was still very high two centuries later, a remarkable fact bearing in mind the extent to which monastic discipline had been shaken throughout Europe in what was an age ravaged by war, schism, and famine. No other evidence from Scandinavia points to a state of spiritual health comparable to that found at Alvastra. In view of the vagaries of the age, this was indeed quite exceptional.

Bridget and her husband had been frequent visitors to Alvastra from their estate nearby, and when they undertook a pilgrimage to the shrine of Saint James at Compostella they chose the cistercian monk, Svenung, who was later to become abbot at Alvastra's daughter-house, Varnhem, to accompany them as their confessor.[26] Bridget's closest connection with Alvastra, however, was through her friendship with the sub-prior, Peter Olafson, who later became prior and was one of her confessors for the rest of her life.[27] After her husband's death, Bridget went to live near the abbey, and she remained there for five years until her departure for Rome in 1349. According to her *Revelations*, Peter Olafson was ordered by Christ to translate these into Latin, with which she was not herself familiar at that time. For this he was to receive the reward, 'not of silver or of gold, but of treasure which will not grow old and perish'.[28] He had at first been reluctant to undertake the task of writing down the account of her visions,

---

[25]For Alvastra, see E. Ortved, *Cistercieordenen og dens Klostre i Norden* (Copenhagen, 2 vols., 1927–1933) 2:53–141.

[26]*Acta et Processus Canonizacionis Beate Birgitte*, ed. I. Collijn; Samlingar utgivna av Svenska Fornskriftsälskapet, Andre Serien, Latinska Skriftar Band 1 (Uppsala, 1924–1931) p. 503: '. . . quod audivit a quodam monacho nomine Svenungo, qui postea fuit abbas Warnensis ordinis Cisterciensis Scarensis diocesis, quod predictus monachus sequebatur predictam dominam Brigidam ad sanctum Jacobum peregrinando, qui infirmatus graviter in via, raptus fuit extra se et tunc vidit dominam Brigidam quasi septem coronis coronatam'.

[27]There is a good résumé in Swedish of the known facts about Prior Peter Olafson in *Svenska Män och Kvinnor* (Stockholm, 1949) 6:103.

[28]*Den Heliga Birgittas Revelationes Extravagantes*, ed. L. Hollman (Uppsala, 1956) p. 163: 'Audi igitur tu, frater Petre, illa, et scribe in lingua latina omnia verba, que ipsa tibi ex parte mea dixit, et dabo tibi pro qualibet littera non aurum vel argentum sed thesaurum, qui non veterascet'.

since he was a very simple man, and because of his humility wanted on no account to put his hand to writing, thinking himself unsuitable for so great a task because of his own ignorance.

It took a miracle for him to change his mind, for he

> was compelled by Christ through fear of death, and was almost dead himself, until he consented. When his consent had been given, he was suddenly cured.[29]

A vivid picture of cistercian life in fourteenth-century Sweden, of Prior Olafson and a number of his fellow-Cistercians emerges from the evidence that was collected by the official investigation of Bridget's claims to canonization. There was Svenung, who was cured on the pilgrimage to Santiago, and Abbot Styrbjörn of Julita, who was saved from shipwreck.[30] Another story relates how Bridget cured the monk Nicholas, who had recorded some of her revelations, from chronic attacks of hunger. On Christmas night he had been unable to endure his hunger until the first mass. He had asked Bridget to pray for him, and in his sleep he

> saw a woman touching his lips and tongue saying, 'Behold, you are healed—arise'. On waking, he never afterwards felt the uncontrollable hunger. The witness who reported this, and the brother, made a note of the time at which he had been liberated, and, after making enquiries about this, they discovered conclusively that at that time the Lady Bridget had been praying on behalf of the monk.[31]

However, most telling of the vigor of spiritual life at Alvastra were the accounts of the holy lives of a number of the lay brothers there, stories which are reminiscent of those found in the *Exordium Magnum* and other works of cistercian *exempla*. They are of particular interest as

[29]Collijn, p. 90: '... tunc idem prior, cum esset homo simplicissimus, et propter humilitatem nulla racione volens manum mittere ad scribendum, reputans se propter ignoranciam suam ad tantam opus minus ydoneum, coactus fuit metu mortis a Christo et fere mortuus, donec consensit, et consensu facto subito curatus est et non in successu temporis vel intervallo'.

[30]For the miraculous cure of Svenung, see note 26; Abbot Styrbjörn's rescue from a storm at sea is in Collijn, p. 110.

[31]Collijn, p. 535: '... vidit mulierem tangentem labia sua et linguam et dicentem: "Ecce sanus es, surge". Qui evigilans numquam sensit famem inordinatam postea, et tunc iste testis loquens et frater ille notaverunt illam horam, qua liberatus est, et post inquisicionem de hoc factam pro certo invenerunt, quod illa hora domina Brigida pro illo monacho oraverat'.

they provide evidence that there were still lay brothers at Alvastra in the middle of the fourteenth century, by which time their numbers had been greatly reduced everywhere else to the point that they had virtually disappeared.[32] These references to lay brothers in Bridget's writings are the last recorded in Scandinavia.

One of these stories tells of the lay brother, Gerekin, who in forty years never went outside the territory of Alvastra, and who was described as a man of great sanctity. While at prayer, he had visions of angelic choirs, and at the elevation at mass he is said to have seen the figure of Christ as a child in the priest's hands. Mary is said to have performed his tasks in the bakery, thus allowing him more time at prayer. Bridget prophesied that Gerekin would die before a great disaster (the Black Death) befell the house. When the time for him to die had come, he saw three golden letters before him, P, O, and T, and he called three of his fellow lay brothers with these initials to join him. Shortly afterward he died, and within a week all three had followed him in a holy death.[33] Gerekin had been disturbed at the prospect of Bridget, a woman, coming to live at Alvastra. The irregularity of a woman residing at a monastery was something with which he was familiar. He therefore asked: 'Why does that lady reside here in a monastery of monks, introducing a new custom against our rule?' The reassurance came from God who allowed her

> to dwell for the present near a monastery, not so as to abolish the rule, nor to introduce a new custom, but rather so that my marvelous work may be demonstrated in a holy place. For thus David in a time of need ate consecrated bread, which nonetheless in a time of justice is forbidden by some people.[34]

Another story tells of Bridget's cure of a lay brother, Asgot, who had been ill for over three years. Directed by Christ, Bridget urged him to confess a grievous sin about which he had previously remained silent. At first he claimed that he had not kept anything back, but Bridget pressed him, and he dissolved in tears, saying:

---

[32]For the breaches of discipline caused by lay brothers and an analysis of their gradual falling off, see J. S. Donnelly, *The Decline of the Medieval Cistercian Laybrotherhood*, Fordham University Studies, History Series 3 (New York, 1949).

[33]Hollman, p. 177; Ortved 2:97.

[34]Collijn, p. 82: '. . . sic ego Deus omnium, qui sum super omnes regulas, permitto tibi residere ad tempus presens prope monasterium, non ut dissolvam regulam nec ut consuetudinem novam adducam, sed magis ut opus meum mirabile in sancto loco ostendatur. Sic enim David tempore necessitatis comedit panes sanctificatos, quod tamen tempore iusticie ab aliquibus prohibitum est'.

'I have a certain secret which I have never dared to tell. Whenever I have made my confession, my tongue has always been as though bound, and too much shame has suffused me, lest I should reveal my sins. Because of this, whenever I confessed I found for myself a new ending to my words, saying "I render myself guilty of everything of which I spoke to you, Father, and of other things which I have been told", believing that by this ending I sent away all my sins. But now, if it pleases God, I would like to speak freely to the whole world.' When a confessor had been called, in tears he freely uncovered all his sins.[35]

This story bears an unmistakable resemblance to one in the *Exordium Magnum* of a lay brother who had come to Clairvaux from Denmark and to whom a whole chapter is devoted: 'Concerning the lay brother, who, by the grace of God and the prayer of our venerable Abbot Henry escaped the sentence of damnation.'[36] As a young man in Denmark he had been guilty of fornication and had fathered a child, but he had kept this secret and first confessed to it on his deathbed at Clairvaux. The abbot heard of his plight and granted him absolution, as a result of which he exclaimed: 'I believe, Lord, that even if I were placed in the deepest hell, your power would by your mercy free me from there.'

Through Bridget's writings we gain a clear picture of the vitality of the spiritual life at Alvastra in the fourteenth century. This was generally uncharacteristic of the period and probably unequalled in any other scandinavian abbey at this time. Although the number of monks in an abbey is not of itself an infallible guide to the level of observance, it may nevertheless be a valuable indicator when corroborated with other evidence, such as we have from Alvastra. The ability to recruit and support large numbers, as well as providing the necessary manpower to fulfill all essential monastic tasks, also makes it the more likely for a high standard of excellence to be sustained. The population at Alvastra is known to have been high during Bridget's lifetime. Through her we

---

[35]Collijn, p. 522: '. . . nam quoddam occultum habeo, quod prodere numquam audebam, quia quociens penitui, quasi semper lingua mea erat ligata et nimis eciam pudor invasit me, ne aperirem peccata mea. Ideo quociens confessionem feci, inveni mihi novam conclusionem verborum meorum dicens: "Reddo me culpabilem de omnibus, que dixi vobis, pater, et de aliis, que non dixi, credens per hanc conclusionem omnia peccata mea dimitti, sed nunc, si placeret Deo, libenter dicerem toto mundo". Vocato igitur confessore plene cum lacrimis omnia peccata sua detexit'.

[36]EM 138–40: 'De converso, qui per gratiam Dei et orationem venerabilis abbatis Henrici damnationis sentenciam evasit'.

have the only reliable data from Scandinavia. Thirty-one named monks from Alvastra are said to have perished as a result of the Black Death, and, if the other monks whose names are known are added, there were at least forty-one monks before the plague, a considerable figure for this period.[37] The evidence is confirmed much later by King Gustav Vasa who would refer to the figure of four to six monks in 1529 as a justification for his appropriation of the abbey and which he would contrast with the forty to fifty monks who were said to have been there in former times.[38]

Of greatest importance in Bridget's relationship with the Cistercians, as we mentioned earlier, was her lifelong friendship with Prior Peter Olafson of Alvastra. It was while at Alvastra that Bridget formulated the idea of founding a religious order which, although primarily for women, would also have a subsidiary male component. The outcome was the basic bridgettine document *Regula sancti Salvatoris*, which is included in the various latin editions of her *Revelations* and which is her greatest work. According to Bridget herself, it was conceived in a short time, dictated to her by Christ in a revelation, and written down a few days later by 'a religious man, a friend of God', namely Prior Olafson.[39] He was also responsible for the supplement to this, the so-called *Constitutiones* or *Additiones Petri prioris*, as well as being the co-author of Bridget's *Life*, written shortly after her death. He was probably responsible for the appeal from the cistercian abbots of Alvastra, Nydala, Varnhem, and Julita, together with the swedish bishops, to Pope Urban V for her canonization,[40] and he took an active part in the preparatory proceedings in Rome. When these were broken off in 1380, he returned to Sweden, bringing with him a large collection of bridgettine texts which he handed over to the monastery at Vadstena. His own contribution to its formation was considerable. He was not only better acquainted with conditions in his native Sweden than Bridget, who had been absent for many years, but his input during her lifetime had been such that he inevitably continued to take an active part after Bridget's death. He naturally became involved in the problems that arose as a result of the growth of Bridget's order and with which the Cistercians themselves had often had to grapple. When daughter houses were contemplated, they would either have to be

---

[37]Ortved 2:97.
[38]Ortved 2:40.
[39]*Sancta Birgitta Opera Minora*, ed. S. Eklund (Lund, 2 vols., 1972–1975) 1:213: 'vir religiosus, amicus Dei'.
[40]*Scriptores Rerum Svecicarum* 3.2.220.

dependent on Vadstena, following the example of Cîteaux, which would entail independence from their local bishop and the granting of exempt status, or they could become independent from their mother-house and subject to episcopal jurisdiction. The matter was not finally resolved in Prior Olafson's lifetime and it led to the exemption struggle at Vadstena in 1399 and 1403.[41]

The part which Prior Olafson played in the formulation of the bridgettine constitution and in its implementation naturally prompts us to investigate the extent to which knowledge and experience of cistercian custom and practice influenced the make-up of the bridgettine monastic body.

The first obvious similarity that the new order shared with the Cistercians was a deep devotion to Mary. All cistercian houses were dedicated to her, and the practice was followed by a large number of bridgettine monasteries which adopted marian names, for example, Maribo (Mary's home), Mariager (Mary's acre), and Mariendal (Mary's vale). It was based on the command of Christ, by whom the *Rule* was said to have been dictated, and in whose words, 'The Holy Virgin was, after my ascension, head and queen of my apostles and disciples'.[42] Bridget's fervent devotion to the person of Christ found its expression through a particularly fervent marian cult. The object was revealed in the words Mary used when she appeared to Bridget: 'I am the Queen of Heaven. You desire to know how to honor me. Know, then, that to sing the praises of my Son is to sing mine.'[43]

According to the bridgettine *Rule*, the monasteries were to consist of sixty nuns, thirteen priests, four deacons, and eight lay brothers, a total of eighty-five, corresponding to the number of Christ's apostles and disciples.[44] The first chapter states that the order was founded for women, and the first eleven chapters deal with the sisters exclusively.[45] The brothers were thus secondary, as indicated by the reference to the *monasterium monialium* and the *curia fratrum*, the former of which was clearly the more important of the two. Although of lesser importance and subject to the jurisdiction of the abbess, the monks nevertheless served

[41]T. Nyberg, *Birgittinische Klostergründungen des Mittelalters* (Lund, 1965) p. 32.
[42]H. Cnattingius, *Studies in the Order of St. Bridget of Sweden* (Stockholm, 1963) p. 19.
[43]*Revelations*, p. 12.
[44]H. Johansson and J. Gallen, 'Birgittinorden', in *Kulturhistorisk Leksikon for Nordisk Middelalder* (Copenhagen, 22 vols., 1956–1972) 1:565.
[45]Cnattingius, p. 16.

a vital function in that they enabled the nuns to pursue their religious duties uninterrupted. The presence of priests was, of course, essential for the celebration of mass and to hear the nuns' confessions. However, over and above the *cura monialium*, male members of the order were also responsible for the administration of the monastic estates, for collecting rents, as well as performing a number of menial tasks and manual labor unsuited to women and from which the nuns were consequently freed. It seems that the usefulness of such a small group of monks and lay brothers had gradually been appreciated and adopted by the Cistercians.[46] Prior Olafson would have been acquainted with a number of cistercian nunneries, two of which were under the rule of his abbot, Vreta in Östergötland not far from Alvastra, and Sko in Uppland.[47] Step by step the Cistercians had made provision for supplying the nunneries under their jurisdiction with their chaplains and confessors, with lay brothers to carry out the heavy work and with officials, lay or clerical, usually called procurators, to perform administrative and legal duties. These together made up the male household which developed alongside most cistercian nunneries.[48] A development of this kind is known to have taken place at one of the swedish nunneries subject to Alvastra, Sko. The terms of a burial grant in 1291 provided for the appointment of a perpetual vicar who was to celebrate a number of masses, as well as reciting psalms and litanies, and who was to be supported in the same way 'as the other priests who serve the monastery'—evidence that a male colony was attached to the nunnery with the purpose of assisting the nuns.[49] This group lived together in community, and, although they were subject to the father-abbot and not to the abbess of the house they served, they were in other respects analogous to the bridgettine *curiae fratrum* and were probably the model Prior Olafson followed when advising Bridget in the formulation of her *Rule*. The cistercian experience had shown that the support offered by the male element, priests, *conversi*, and lay, provided the best conditions for nuns to fulfill their vocations in what was to be a strictly enclosed contemplative community.

[46]The cistercian influence on the bridgettine constitution is examined in Nyberg, pp. 11–24.

[47]Ortved 2:483–519 and 431–71.

[48]Nyberg, pp. 16–18. J.-M. Canivez (ed.), *Statuta Capitulorum Generalium Ordinis cisterciensis ab anno 1116 ad annum 1786* [Statuta], Bibliothèque de la Revue d'histoire ecclésiastique 9–14 B (Louvain, 8 vols., 1933–1941) 2:92 and 76 (1231:6, 7 and 1229:7) and 3:49 (1267:10).

[49]*Diplomatarium Suecanum* 2:1049.

Further evidence of cistercian influence may be seen in the strictness of Bridget's demands for purity and lack of ostentation in the architecture and decoration of her churches, as well as to the importance she attached to uniformity of practice. The special needs of the Bridgettines in catering for both nuns and monks in their churches, and for their total separation, were at variance with those of the Cistercians, and, as a result, the plans of their churches and monastic buildings were of course totally dissimilar. Nevertheless, the spirit in which they were conceived was the same: they shared a simplicity in design, clean lines, and an absence of elaborate and colorful ornamentation. As an example, and following cistercian practice, the bridgettine *Rule* prohibited the use of colored glass in the windows of their churches.[50]

Uniformity and simplicity were also the hallmark of cistercian chant.[51] Bernard was charged with the revision of the original Metz antiphoner, and under his guidance a new one was produced. His view was that the words of the liturgy

> should shine with truth, tell of righteousness, incite to humility, and inculcate justice;

and the melody

> should be grave and not flippant or uncouth. It should be sweet but not frivolous; it should both enchant the ears and move the heart. . . .Not a little spiritual profit is lost when minds are distracted from the sense of the words by the frivolity of the melody, when more is conveyed by the modulations of the voice than by the variations of the meaning.[52]

This passage indicates the distinction Bernard made between the music that was suitable for monks as opposed to that for lay people, and his concern for the manner of performance is further expressed in his condemnation of 'grating and slack voices', which typified the practices

---

[50]V. Lorenzen, *De Danske Brigittinerklostres Bygningshistorie*, De Danske Klostres Bygningshistorie 4 (Copenhagen, 1922) p. 68.

[51]For cistercian chant, see L. J. Lekai, *The Cistercians: Ideals and Reality* ([Kent, Ohio, 1977]) pp. 251–52; and A. A. King, *Liturgies of the Religious Orders* (London, 1955) pp. 93–96.

[52]Ep 398; SBOp 8:378; James, p. 502: 'Porro sensa indubitata resplendeant veritate, sonent iusticiam, humilitatem suadeant, doceant aequitatem. . . . Cantus ipse, si fuerit, plenus sit gravitate: nec lasciviam resonet, nec rusticitatem. Sic suavis, ut non sit levis: sic mulceat aures, ut moveat corda. . . . Non est levis iactura gratiae spiritualis, levitate cantus abduci a sensuum utilitate, et plus sinuandis intendere vocibus quam insinuandis rebus'.

of Cluny in contrast to the *gravitas* of the Cistercians.[53] This mode of singing was also denounced in similar terms by the General Chapter, which prohibited 'shrilly singing in the feminine way or with "false voices" as if imitating the lewdness of an actor.'[54] The cistercian preoccupation with the correct method of chant was still being adhered to in the fourteenth century. A statute from 1302 speaks of 'novelties and conspicuous curiosities', and the General Chapter of 1320 condemned 'absurd novelties' such as the syncopation of notes (*sincopationibus notarum*) and hocketing (*hoquetis*) and required that the chant which had been handed down by Saint Bernard should be maintained. Both abbots and abbesses were ordered to enforce this.[55]

The style of performance adopted by Bridget for her nuns was based on the ideals of Bernard, and the closeness with which it adhered to the cistercian model has been traced to the influence of Prior Olafson.[56] The chanting of her nuns was to be 'not slack, not grating, and not disjointed, but decorous and deep and even, and above all humble'.[57] These words bear a remarkable resemblance to those of Bernard. The 'grating' or 'false' voice originally referred to falsetto singing in imitation of the female voice and was shunned by the Cistercians. When applied to nuns it naturally had to take on another meaning, that of singing with a thin and perhaps nasal quality.[58] A later bridgettine text re-defined the required chant as 'restrained, deep, plain, not with a grating voice, not with discant, but with all humility and devotion both by the sisters as well as the brothers'.[59] The *cum discantu* refers to what the Bridgettines considered the excesses of the fashionable polyphonic singing equivalent to the 'absurd novelties' which had threatened the purity of the cistercian chant and the part-singing with which the cistercian General Chapter of 1217 had already had to deal.[60]

---

[53]SC 47; SBOp 2:66: 'non fractis et remissis vocibus muliebre quiddam balba de nare sonantes. . . .'

[54]Statuta 1:30 (1134:73): 'viros decet virili voce cantare, et non more femineo tinnulis, vel ut vulgo dicitur falsis vocibus veluti histrionicam imitari lasciviam'.

[55]Statuta 3:306–307 (1302:4): 'novitates et notabiles curiositates'; 349 (1320:9).

[56]I. Milveden, 'Sjungen Ödmjukhet', in A. Lindblom (ed.), *Vadstena Klosters Öden* (Vadstena, 1973) pp. 145–51.

[57]Milveden, p. 145: 'non sit remissus, non fractus, non dissolutus, sed honestus et gravis et uniformis et per omnia humilis'.

[58]Milveden, pp. 148–49.

[59]Milveden, p. 147: 'modestus, gravis, simplex, non fractis vocibus, non cum discantu, sed omni humilitate et devocione plenus tam per Sorores quam per Fratres'.

[60]Statuta 1:472 (1217:31). The forbidden polyphony is described as being *more saecularium*.

The similarities between the cistercian and bridgettine regulations on liturgical chant may be clearly discerned and are indicative of a deeper kinship between the two monastic bodies. The emphasis on humility, the abhorrence of showy mannerisms, the opposition to elaborate modernisms, all point to the thread which runs from Bernard and his Cistercians to Alvastra in Sweden, and from Peter Olafson to Bridget and her order, and beyond them, and was only terminated at the Reformation. The large collection of cistercian manuscripts at Vadstena—the most comprehensive in Sweden—is evidence of the link.[61] It consists mainly of the works of Bernard, but other authors such as Alan of Lille are also represented. Cistercian influence lived on, and, in the sixteenth century, some of Bernard's writings were translated into Swedish at Vadstena.[62] This bond between Bernard and Bridget, based on the qualities which unite them, is summarized in the words about Bridget, addressed by Christ to the lay brother who was worried at the prospect of Bridget coming to live at Alvastra, in the shade of the Omberg hills:

Do not be amazed; this is a friend of God who has come here to gather flowers beneath the mountain, of which all may receive the saving odors, even beyond the sea and to the ends of the earth.[63]

The seeds from which these cistercian flowers sprang may be said to have been sown by Saint Bernard.

ABSTRACTS

Bien que très éloignés l'un de l'autre dans le temps (deux siècles) et et dans l'espace (aussi loin que la Bourgogne l'est de la Scandenavie), saint Bernard et sainte Brigitte de Vadstena avaient beaucoup en commun: milieux d'origine privilégiés, méfiance envers l'enseignement des écoles, magnétisme exceptionnel, et fortes personnalités qui ont trouvé à s'exprimer en intervenant dans les grandes causes politiques de l'époque. Les contacts de Brigitte avec les Cisterciens d'Alvastra, et surtout avec son confesseur et biographe, le prieur Peter Olafson, eurent une influence profonde sur elle et sur la règle de son Ordre qu'elle lui dicta. La fonction

---

[61]For a list of cistercian manuscripts in Sweden, the majority from Vadstena, see J. Leclercq, 'Textes et Manuscrits Cisterciens en Suède', ASOC 6 (1950) 125–130.

[62]*Helige Bernhards Skrifter i Svensk Öfversättning från Medeltiden* 15, ed. H. Wieselgren (Stockholm, 1866).

[63]Collijn, p. 82: 'Noli mirari, hec est amica Dei et ad hoc venit, ut sub monte isto flores colligat, de quibus omnes eciam ultra mare et fines mundi recipient medicinam'.

toute ministérielle attribuée aux moines dans le nouvel ordre—ils étaient là en effet pour permettre aux moniales de s'adonner à leur devoirs religieux—ressemble fort au role secondaire des religieux auprès des moniales cisterciennes. Un culte marial fervent, une absence d'ostentation dans l'architecture, et l'uniformité et la simplicité du chant sont d'autres signes d'une influence cistercienne.

Although separated by two centuries and from opposite ends of Christendom, Saint Bernard and Saint Birgitta (or Bridget) of Vadstena had a great deal in common: a privileged background, a distrust of what was taught in the schools, an exceptional magnetism, and a strength of personality which found its expression in their intervention in the most important political causes of the day. Bridget's contact with the Cistercians at Alvastra, and especially with her confessor and biographer, Prior Peter Olafson, had a profound influence on her and on the Rule for her Order which she dictated to him. The role of her monks—to enable the nuns to pursue their religious duties—was modelled on the male element which had evolved at cistercian nunneries to fulfill the same function. A fervent marian cult, lack of ostentation in architecture, and uniformity and simplicity in the chant are further evidence of cistercian influence.

Der heilige Bernhard und die heilige Brigitta von Vadsten sind zwar geographisch und chronologisch weit von einander entfernt, aber sie weisen doch sehr viel an Gemeinsamkeiten: eine privilegierte Herkunft, ein Misstrauen gegenüber der Schullehre, eine aussergewöhnliche Anziehungskraft und eine starke Ausprägung der Persönlichkeit, die ihren Ausdruck darin fand, dass beide in die wichtigsten politischen Angelegenheiten der damaligen Zeit eingriffen. Birgittas Kontakt mit den Zisterziensern in Alvastra und besonders mit ihrem Beichtvater und Biographen, dem Prior Peter Olafson, hatte einen starken Einfluß auf sie und auf die Regel ihres Ordens, die sie ihm diktierte. Die Rolle ihrer Mönche—nämlich, den Nonnen die Möglichkeit zu geben, ihren religiösen Pflichten nachzukommen—fand ihr Modell in dem männlichen Element, das sich in den zisterziensischen Frauenklöstern zu demselben Zweck entwickelt hatte. Ein glühender Marienkult, das Fehlen bildlicher Darstellungen und Ausschmückungen in ihrer Architektur, Einförmigkeit und Einfachheit im Gesang sind weitere offensichtliche Anzeichen für den zisterziensischen Einfluss.

DANTE'S SAINT BERNARD AND THE
THEOLOGY OF LIBERTY IN THE *COMMEDIA*

Raymond D. DiLorenzo
The University of Dallas

I N THE *COMMEDIA* Dante recreates a pattern of experience and thought present within the theology of Saint Bernard of Clairvaux—namely, a process of christian liberation which Bernard developed in his works *De gratia et libero arbitrio* and *De diligendo deo*. I have said Dante recreates it. To 'recreate' means, on the one hand, to reproduce recognizably the thought of another. On the other hand, it does not mean that Dante necessarily quotes Saint Bernard. To reproduce the thought of another creatively may well mean to go beyond quotation in the ordinary sense of the term. After all, Dante is a poet and presumably exercises when he pleases the license of poets; but he is also a learned poet, a medieval scholar of sorts.

In the *Commedia* Dante's philology, his manner of treating the *auctores* on whom he draws, depends on his mode of historical consciousness. This means that Dante treats his *auctores* according to his own sense of history as a revelation of divine providence. If there was a medieval model for Dante's philology, it may well have been something like Martianus Capella's allegorical maiden Philologia, who represents the erudition found in books. In order to be wed to the god Mercury, who is Jove's messenger, the maiden must expel the bookish learning within her and have it reorganized into the liberal arts and the disciplines. Only then may she be uplifted to the realm of the gods.[1] Dante's

---

[1] In Martianus Capella's *De nuptiis philologiae et mercurii*, ed. W. Adolphus Dick (Leipzig, 1925), the virgin Philologia vomits up her learning as books of many languages:

reproduction of the thought of Bernard undergoes a similar recreative uplifting according to the philosophical and theological dynamics within the *Commedia*.

Bernard's unexpected appearance as Beatrice's replacement near the end of *Paradiso* is Dante's own scholarly index to a deeply informing bernardine pattern within the narrative and thematic progression of the poem from its very beginning. Saint Bernard, I suggest, is a climactic figure in the whole sequence of figures and experiences which are, to the traveler Dante, media of revelation sent from the mysterious abyss of the eternal counsel. The poetic context of Bernard's appearance is crucial. If it is rightly read here, his role in the poem cannot be restricted to his brief business after his appearance—to showing Dante the blessed in the white rose, then explaining the presence of the little ones who died before having the power of true choice, and finally to making his famous intercessory prayer to the Virgin Mother.[2] Important as these

---

'tunc uero illa nausea ac uomitis elaborata in omnigenum copias conuertitur litterarum. cernere erat, qui libri quantaque uolumina, quot linguarum. opera ex ore uirginis difflue-bant' (2.136, 9–12). Then, several maidens, some called arts, others disciplines, gather up the books for their own use (2.138, 1–6). Dante's medieval scholarship, his philology, has yet to be fully explored according to the uplifting and transformative dynamics, both philosophical and theological, of the *Commedia*. In this regard, my argument in this study may be said to posit Bernard as the *auctor* who has the highest and most authoritative status among those from whose books Dante drew in making the *Commedia*.

To my knowledge no previous study of Dante's Bernard has claimed that his theology of liberty provides the pattern for the *experience* of Dante the traveler all through the poem. For modern historical philology encounters a great difficulty in dealing with Dante's own 'philology'. Raoul Manselli points out, in the *Enciclopedia dantesca* 1 (1970) 604–605, that Dante never names Bernard outside of *Paradiso* 31–33 and never seems to quote him even tacitly. The sole reference to Bernard—to his *De consideratione*—occurs in the *Epistle to Can Grande* (13:28), but his rather vague reference hardly proves that Dante knows Bernard's writings: '...La citazione assai vaga non attesta daverro una conoscenze dell' opera di Bernardo' (1.605). Thus arises the problem of why Dante chose Bernard as his last guide. Perhaps Dante's philology moves along lines undetectable by modern empirical conceptions of evidence, reference by name or by quotations of text. Dante's 'quotation' of Bernard's works may proceed along lines definable only by the manner of textual reception and transformation within the *Commedia*. To raise this possibility is not to invite adventurous interpretations which have little rigor or which respond to some historically alien problematic of a modern interpreter. Interpretation must find its procedural rigor and direction from what Dante recognizably does in the *Commedia*; the primary datum will be the poetical figure of Bernard within the context of the poem.

[2]An inadequate reading of Bernard's appearance has obstructed seeing him as a figure significant for the experience of Dante the traveler *before* he meets Bernard. Modern literary interpretation, which generally has followed the medieval tradition of personification allegory, focuses on Bernard's role *after* his appearance. That is, Bernard

matters are for understanding Dante's Saint Bernard, they remain but the tip of the iceberg. What lies below the surface, massively present within the *Commedia* before Bernard's appearance, is a bernardine theology of liberty recreated by Dante.

In the pages that follow, the argument should be understood as initiatory, for it is meant only to sketch the bernardine pattern of the liberation dramatized within the *Commedia*. Let us first attend to Dante's presentation of the transition from Beatrice to Bernard in *Paradiso*. Thereafter I will try to highlight the essential points of unanimity between Dante and Saint Bernard: first, that both theologically conceive of liberty of choice as the gift of God constituting the distinctive creaturely excellence of man and, second, that both envisage the process of liberation as achieved through grace-given counsel that promotes greater loving accord with God.

FROM BEATRICE TO BERNARD

Saint Bernard appears for the first time in *Paradiso* XXXI. The moment of transition from Beatrice to Bernard provides the author with an occasion to characterize his experience of the entire journey. In the

is a figure representing contemplation or mystical theology, and, one must admit, Dante's own words indicate the validity of this allegorical view of Bernard, who, says Dante, in contemplating, tasted the peace of beatitude while he was in this world (Par 31.110–11). The inadequacy of such allegorical interpretation has been pointed out by Peter Dronke in his *Dante and Medieval Latin Traditions* (Cambridge: Cambridge University Press, 1986) pp. 1–8. Nevertheless, allegorical interpretation for many remains very persuasive, even when its deficiencies are fully recognized. For example, in his *Dante and Philosophy*, trans. David Moore (1949; rpt. New York: Harper and Row, 1963), Etienne Gilson argues that Dante always chooses the most authoritative figure for any order of life or thought. Thus, the problem of why Dante chose Bernard is readily solved: his fame as a contemplative was enough to make him authoritative to Dante as a guide to the vision of God.

Modern historical scholars have also tried to make Dante's choice of Bernard plausible by examining what Pietro Vigo called 'the affinities' between Dante and Bernard: see 'L'ultima guida di Dante e le affinità di due anime grande', *Annali dei Regi Instituti tecnico e nautico di Livorno* 4 (1903). I have not been able to consult Vigo's study, but Edmund G. Gardner, in his *Dante and the Mystics* (1913; rpt. New York: Octogon Books, 1968), has doubtless pointed out the basic ways Bernard would have appealed to Dante: as a reformer of ecclesiastical discipline, who severely rebuked the vices of monks and prelates, as a mystic, and as a devoted servant of Mary (see pp. 111–43). However, the masterwork of such inquiry remains Alexandre Masseron's *Dante et Saint Bernard* (Paris: Albin Michel, 1953). Needless to say, there are other studies, too numerous to mention here, that are devoted to one or more of what Vigo called 'affinities'. None I know of has argued that Bernard's theology of liberty is a key to Dante's own poetical theology in the *Commedia*.

Empyrean, the traveler beholds the saintly host in the semblance of a white rose. Angels, like bees, dip into and fly out of it. Speaking as narrator, Dante remarks that, if barbarians were once struck at the sight of Rome, 'I, who to the divine from the human, to the eternal from time had come, and from Florence to a people just and sane, with what amazement must I have been full!' (Par 31.37–40).[3] He compares himself to a pilgrim who has just reached the temple of his vow, who looks about already hoping to report later what he is seeing now, that is, the whole general form of Paradise. Just at the moment when he is about to ask Beatrice some questions, he discovers not her but an old man: 'I thought to see Beatrice, and I saw an elder, clad like the folk in glory. His eyes and checks were suffused with benign gladness, his mien kindly such as befits a tender father' (Par 31.59–64). Dante asks where Beatrice is, and the old man responds in these words: 'To terminate your desire Beatrice urged me from my place; and, if you look up to the circle which is third from the highest tier, you will see her again, in the throne her merits have allotted to her' (Par 31.65–70). Like a pilgrim, Dante has come from the human to the divine, from time to eternity, and from the people of Florence to the just and sane people in the white rose. These phrases characterize Dante's journey in general, but they do not tell us precisely what this journey has meant to him in making it.

The next passage, however, does tell us, and it contains a formula of great moment. Addressing his farewell to the lady who did so much to help him, he says:

> O lady, in whom my hope is strong, and who for my salvation did endure to leave in Hell your footprints, of all those things which I have seen I acknowledge the grace and the virtue to be from your power and your excellence. It is you who have drawn me from bondage into liberty by all those paths, by all those means by which you had the power to do so. (Par 31.79–87)

Tu m'hai di servo tratto a libertate: this sentence formulates exactly what the experience of the journey has been for Dante. Beatrice has drawn him from servitude to liberty. What servitude? The reference of his words is unmistakable. It is the servitude of his entrapment in the dark wood, the *selva oscura* (Inf 1.2) where Dante found himself at the beginning of the

---

[3]Text and english translation of the *Commedia* herein quoted are from *The Divine Comedy*, trans., commentary, Charles S. Singleton, Bollingen Series 80 (Princeton, New Jersey: Princeton University Press, 6 vols., 1970–1975).

Commedia. From that place Dante found it impossible to escape by his own power. Three beasts blocked his way. Only Beatrice's intervention saved him. She it was who descended into Hell in order to send Virgil to lead him out of the wood. This is surely the servitude to which Dante is referring.

But what does he mean by liberty? Clearly he means liberty from the *selva obscura*, but not this alone. His entire journey has been for him a movement to liberty. In its positive sense, liberty is the result of his having traveled 'by all those paths, by all those means' which Beatrice and, through her, Virgil have employed to lead Dante to the place where he now stands beside Bernard. Thus we are led to conceive liberation as the experiential core of the entire *Commedia*. This point is not lost on Charles Singleton, whose scholarship has instructed all who study Dante. After glossing Dante's phrase *di servo a libertate* with a text from Thomas Aquinas, as is his wont, Singleton makes in passing an observation indicating unmistakably that he is aware of the comprehensive significance of Dante's words: 'In this light the whole *Divine Comedy* might be said to have as its central theme the attainment of liberty, which is complete subjection to God's will.'[4] Singleton is quite right, but the *auctor* for understanding liberty as the central theme of the poem is not Thomas Aquinas. Nor is Beatrice alone to be credited with the grace and virtue by which Dante has been guided to the liberty he now enjoys. The key to understanding that liberty and its source is the figure standing beside the traveler—Saint Bernard, medieval master of a theology of liberty.[5] He is the one to whom Beatrice yields, taking her place far off from Dante in the rose of the blessed. Let us note that Bernard's appearance is a surprise to Dante, for he was given no indication previously that Beatrice would not conduct him to the very end of his passage from servitude to liberty.

But the unexpected appearance of Bernard is much less surprising to us when we reflect on the habits of the pilgrim Dante and the experience

[4]*Paradiso*, commentary, p. 523. Singleton quotes Saint Thomas, in *Summa theol.* II-II, q. 183, a. 4, resp.

[5]Etienne Gilson was the first scholar to note that Bernard's mystical theology was, unlike William of Saint Thierry's, 'based on a doctrine of freedom', itself traceable back to Saint Paul's Epistle to the Romans, which guides Bernard's thought in *De gratia et libero arbitrio*. See *The Mystical Theology of Saint Bernard*, trans. A.H.C. Downes (New York: Sheed and Ward, 1940) p. 220, n. 23, and p. 237, n. 125. Gilson's second chapter 'Regio Dissimiltudinis' is a good account of the centrality of liberty in Bernard's theology.

of the journey itself. Dante has often been inclined to rivet his attention on Beatrice in too fixed a fashion. 'Troppo fiso!' cry three ladies who accompany Beatrice when she appears to the pilgrim Dante in Eden atop the mountain of purgation (Purg 32.9). Later, in the sphere of Jupiter, Beatrice must urge Dante to turn away from her: 'Turn and listen', she says, 'For not only in my eyes is Paradise' (Par 18.20–21). Even in his words of farewell to Beatrice, Dante has forgotten that it was not she who initially came to his aid in the dark wood. Virgil had told him of two other ladies, Lucia, and 'a gracious lady' of heaven (Inf 2.94), undoubtedly the Virgin, who in fact was the one who first pitied Dante in the dark wood. We can appreciate Dante's attachment to Beatrice, but it is an attachment that needs to be loosened. To praise Beatrice as the one whose power and excellence has drawn him from servitude to liberty is to praise her too lavishly. Beatrice must distance herself from Dante. She must take her seat far away from him and, to his surprise, send him another.

The transition from Beatrice to Bernard is not merely the substitution of one guide for another. The poetic context of his appearance suggests that Bernard comes as a figure having a teleological meaning within the process of liberation the *Commedia* recounts, beginning with the compassion of the Virgin. It is not hard, accordingly, to see that Dante's relation to Beatrice is itself a semblance of Bernard's relation to the Holy Virgin and, through her, to her divine son, the sight of whom within the Trinity ends the *Commedia*. It thus appears that the liberty to which the traveler Dante is being drawn finds its consummation in Christ and is attained by a process of being made to see him in all the various ways he is shown to Dante. Saint Bernard is one of these ways. Not merely the allegorical figure of mystical contemplation made possible by grace coming through the Virgin, Bernard is the surprising embodiment of the whole way of liberty at whose penultimate point Dante finds himself when Beatrice distances herself from him by taking her lofty position in the rose: ' . . . She, so distant as she seemed, smiled and looked on me', says Dante, 'then turned again to the eternal fountain' (Par 31.91–93).

The point bears repeating: Dante must be made to turn away from Beatrice. She is not the term of the traveler's desire—his love. Like all else in the *Commedia*, Beatrice possesses her own reality, and to that the traveler has no trouble relating. In fact, it is all too easy for him. But Beatrice is also a revelatory semblance, a sort of sign whose significance, when exhausted, must yield to another and greater likeness of the supreme and final image (Christ). Seeing in this fashion is not very easy for Dante the traveler. Beatrice gives way to Bernard. 'In order that you may consummate your journey perfectly . . . ', he says to Dante, 'Fly with your eyes throughout this garden; for gazing on it will better prepare your sight to mount through the divine ray. And the Queen of Heaven, for whom I am all afire with love, will grant us every grace, since I am her faithful Bernard' (Par 31.92–102). In himself Bernard so possesses a 'living charity' that Dante feels as one who from Croatia looks upon 'our Veronica' (*la Veronica nostra*; Par 31.104) and who then says to himself, while feeling the hunger of true vision, 'My Lord Jesus Christ, true God, was then your semblence [*la sembianza vostra*] like to this?' (Par 31.107–108). Bernard, like Beatrice, is a semblance of Christ, but he is not Christ, and he shows Dante other semblances in the white rose, especially the Virgin who has 'the face which most resembles Christ [*la faccia che a Cristo/ più si somiglia*]' (Par 32.85–87). Bernard's great prayer to the Virgin soon follows these words. Then come Dante's final visions. His vision of Christ brings the *Commedia* to its end.

The swiss theologian Hans Urs von Balthasar has remarked that Dante must be interpreted from the summit of his work, the *Commedia*.[6] The movement to the summit within the *Commedia* is a process of encountering and moving through semblances, basically a christological process. Thus, the process by which Christ liberates the traveler Dante through the media of his revelatory semblances becomes clear: a gradual enlightenment of the understanding so that all may be seen as media revealing Christ and, by this seeing, accompanying its clarification, a gradual ordination of love until it is perfectly conformed to the love moving the sun and the other stars.[7] The transition from Beatrice to

---

[6]Hans Urs von Balthasar, *The Glory of the Lord: A Theological Aesthetics*, trans. Andrew Louth *et al.*, 3, *Studies in Theological Style, Lay Styles* (San Francisco: Ignatius Press, 1986) p. 34: 'Dante must be interpreted from the summit of his work. The *Comedy* remains the key to the *Canzoniere* and the *Convivio*, which means that the Beatrice of the *Comedy* is the key to the earlier writings. The *Vita Nuova* is symbolic and melancholy, the *Convivio* is philosophizing and fragmentary, but the *Comedy* achieves a completeness of expression that raises the two previous works above themselves, liberates them and leads them to their true realization. At every stage of his life Dante strove for integration'. I can only add to these remarks that, at the summit of the *Commedia*, beyond Beatrice, stands Bernard, who, I suggest, is even more important than Beatrice; for he provides the way Beatrice herself must be comprehended.

[7]There is a fundamental congruity between Dante's experience in moving through semblances toward God and Saint Bernard's teaching. Despite Dante's undoubted debt to aristotelian epistemology, which is sometimes, if incorrectly, attributed also to Bernard, both medieval authors stress the necessity of sensible signs and symbols in knowing God, not by abstract concepts, but by an interiorization of personal experience to find

Bernard is a decisive moment in the internal, self-interpreting action of the *Commedia*. If the liberty to which Dante feels he has arrived when Beatrice departs means, in a somewhat negative sense, the liberty from entrapment in the *selva oscura*, in a positive sense liberty means the acquisition of the ability to judge semblances and to love according to their manifestation of that Christ who subsists as second person of the Trinity. And when we look back from this summit over the journey to other texts concerning liberty, we will find that the locus in the traveler Dante of the experience of liberty is precisely where and how Saint Bernard conceived it. The experiential locus of liberty in the *Commedia* is the rational choice of the will in loving.

BERNARD'S THEOLOGY OF LIBERTY

An adequate treatment of Dante's recreation of Bernard's theology of liberty will not be possible in this short paper. Two basic points can, however, be established. First, Dante exalts the will's liberty of choice exactly as Bernard did—as the divine gift that is the source of human dignity and nobility. This unanimity cannot be overstressed. Dante and Bernard conceive the creaturely excellence of human nature identically. Secondly, Dante, locating the will's liberty of choice in the same ana- lytical framework as had Bernard—*between* sense and appetite—sees, again as Bernard did, volitional liberation from sin as a process of grace-given counsel, making possible loving accord with God's will. The best and briefest way to highlight the significance of these two key points is to state that, if true, they suggest a demotion to secondary status within the *Commedia* of what are usually given primacy by the scholarly commentators—aristotelian and thomistic modes of thought wherein the intellect, speculative and practical, plays the dominant role;

therein the spiritual realities which sensible data signify. The words of Denis Farkasfalvy deserve to be quoted here, for they apply to what in the *Commedia* is often obscured by Dante's Aristotelianism: '. . . Secondo Bernardo i sensi non forniscono materia per formare concetti astratti. Essi constituiscono il punto di partenza dell' interiorizazione attraverso le quale il conoscente riflette a se stesso sforzandosi di trovare nella propria esperienza individuale le realtà spirituale conrete che i dati sensibili significano. Cioè il contenuto, o oggetto della conscenza, rimane sempre realtà concreta e specifica; il modo di significare dei segni sensibili è quello simbolico, appartiene all' ordine di causalità esemplare. . . .'

See 'La conoscenza di Dio nel pensiero di San Bernardo', in *Studi su S. Bernardo di Chiaravalle nell' ottavo centenario della canonizzazione: Convengno internationale, Certosa di Firenze, 1974* (Rome: Editiones Cistercienses, 1974) p. 211.

in their place is now elevated to primacy in the *Commedia* the rational component of the amorous will—namely, choice and its liberation by encounter with often paradoxical media of divine revelation. Dante is certainly interested in the truth, but it is the truth which makes us free. Of this liberation Dante has made Saint Bernard the exemplary figure. In other words, between Dante's enchantment with Lady Philosophy, who is ardently praised in his *Convivio*, and the writing of the *Commedia*, Dante seems to have moved to a theological view of poetry or a poetical theology centered on liberty of choice (*liberum arbitrium*). Though often couched in scholastic modes of thought, after the fashion of many of those teachers who abide in Paradise's solar sphere, Dante's presentation of his baffling experience with revealed exemplars of divine judgment in the afterlife recreates key elements in the bernardine theology of liberty.

In a well-known passage from his treatise *De diligendo Deo*, Bernard discusses the benedictions or goods of God by which human beings live: first, those of bread, sun, and air, which are necessities for the body; and, second, certain nobler goods found in the soul, human dignity (*dignitas*), knowledge (*scientia*), and virtue (*virtus*). What Bernard means by these words must be precisely understood, for they expose the religious dynamic and ambience of his mode of thought. He provides not an ontological analysis of human nature such as we may find in aristotelian philosophical science or in scholastic theological science; rather he speaks of the components of a primal, experiential awareness that may be best described as the motives of natural religion, thus immediately available not only to Christians but to pagans also, disposing all to the love of God. 'I call dignity in man', says Bernard, 'free choice' (*dignitatem in homine liberum dico arbitrium*).[8] In this liberty of choice consists human preeminence and rulership over the beasts of the earth. Human knowledge (*scientia*), we should note, is not composed of the liberal arts and the philosophical sciences. It is rather a recognition that one's dignity does not come from oneself (*non a se*).[9] Human beings, in other words, have a dignity that is not of their own making. Human virtue (*virtus*) is not for Bernard the kinds of excellence, moral and intellectual, which classical thinkers made familiar in the Middle Ages. Rather, virtue is that power by which a human being right away and without tardiness

[8]Dil 2.2; SBOp 3:121, 15–16.
[9]Dil 2.2; SBOp 3:121, 17–18: '. . . Scientiam vero, qua eamdem in se dignitatem agnoscat, non a se tamen. . . .'

seeks the one from whom he is and to whom, when found, he tightly adheres.[10] What evidently dominates Bernard's thinking in formulating this three-fold concept of human dignity is the pauline idea of being gifted. Bernard quotes the Apostle: 'What do you have that you have not received? But if you have received, why do you glory as if you did not receive?' [1 Co 4:7].

This sense of human dignity—the will's liberty of choice—as having been received from the gift-giver is the stimulus of natural religion. Thus, Bernard insists that God is to be loved above all else, even by pagans, and if they do not, they are, as Saint Paul says, inexcusable:

> Hence God deserves to be loved for his own sake even by the infidel who, although he is ignorant of Christ, yet knows himself. . . .For an innate justice, not unknown to reason, cries interiorly to him that he ought to love with his whole being the one to whom he owes all that he is. Yet is it difficult, impossible for a man, by his own power of free will [*suis . . . liberive arbitrii viribus*], once he has received all things from God, to turn wholly to the will of God and not rather to his own will and keep these gifts for himself as his own, as it is written: 'All seek what is their own' [Ph 2:21] and further: '. . . Man's feelings and thoughts are inclined to evil' [Gn 8:21].[11]

The entire problematic of Saint Bernard's theology of liberty is intimated in this passage. By an innate justice known to reason, even an infidel can recognize the gift of his dignity and the obligation to love the giver of the gift. But he cannot wholly turn to God 'by his own power of free will'. He attributes to himself what he has received from another. Ignorance, Bernard goes on to explain, afflicts knowledge and leads to bestialization or vaingloriousness.[12] Even worse is the presumptuous arrogance of pride

---

[10]Dil 2.2; SBOp 3:121, 18–19: '. . . porro virtutem, subinde ipsum a quo est, et inquirat non segniter, et teneat fortiter, cum invenerit.'

[11]See Dil 2.6; SBOp 3:124, 2–11. English translation taken from Bernard of Clairvaux, *Treatises II*, trans. Robert Wolton, CF 13 (Washington, D.C.: Cistercian Publications, 1974; rpt. 1980) p. 98.

[12]Ignorance (*ignorantia*) afflicts knowledge (*scientia*) in two ways. The first is bestialization, by thinking too little of ourselves: 'Fit igitur sese non agnoscendo egregia rationis munere creatura, irrationabilium gregibus incipiat aggregari . . .' (Dil 2.4; SBOp 3:122, 13–14). The second effect is vainglory, by thinking too much of ourselves: 'Itaque valde cavenda haec ignorantia, qua de nobis minus forte sentimus; sed non minus, immo et plus illa, qua plus nobis tribuimus, quod fit si bonum quodcumque in nobis esse, et a nobis, decepti putemus' (Dil 2.4; SBOp 3:122, 17–20). Bernard's concept of humility is here all but formally defined.

that afflicts virtue: it makes us like demons that knowingly usurp the benefactor's glory.[13] In short, it is sin and its effects that work against that innate sense of justice known to reason and that make it impossible for the will by liberty of choice to turn wholly to God. The need for liberation is clear.

In Saint Bernard's writings, the key doctrinal articulation of the experienced need for liberation, apparent to Christian and pagan alike, occurs in the work *De gratia et libero arbitrio*. From it emerges a vision of the spiritual life as a process of volitional liberation that in its general outlines is reconstituted in Dante's *Commedia* in the experience of the traveler.

For Bernard there are three liberties to consider in the spiritual life: first, a liberty of nature (or liberty from necessity); second, a liberty of grace (otherwise called liberty from sin or liberty of counsel); and, third, a liberty of glory (otherwise called liberty from misery or the liberty of accord [*libertas complaciti*]). He writes:

> There are, then, these three forms of liberty, as they have occurred to us: liberty from sin, from sorrow, and from necessity. The last belongs to our natural condition; to the first we are restored by grace; and the second is reserved for us in our homeland. . . .The. . . liberty [from necessity] therefore, might be termed liberty of nature, the second of grace, the third of life or glory. For in the first place, we were created with liberty of will [*in liberam voluntatem*] or voluntary liberty [*voluntariam libertatem*], a creature noble [*nobilis*] in God's eyes. Secondly, we are reformed in innocence a new creature in Christ. And thirdly, we are raised up to glory, a perfect creature in the Spirit.[14]

It is very clear that Bernard structures the whole of christian life by the clipped formulas designating these three liberties, all of them given to the human creature by God: the first by God's creation, providing him with his nobility of nature—what Bernard called his dignity in *De diligendo deo*; the second liberty, by the grace of redemption, liberating him from sin by reformation of his innocence; and the third liberty, by the grace of glory, granting him perfection of loving accord in the heavenly homeland. In this general structure of liberties, all of which pertain to the will, Bernard locates what he calls liberty of choice (*liberum arbitrium*).

---

[13] '. . . Per istam [arrogantia] et demonibus sociemur. Est quippe superbia et delictum maximum, uti datis tamquam innatis, et in acceptis beneficis gloriam usurpare benefici.' Dil 2.4; SBOp 3:123, 1–2.

[14] Gra 3.7; SBOp 3:171. English translation by Daniel O'Donovan in *Treatises III*, CF 19 (Kalamazoo, Michigan: Cistercian Publications Inc., 1977) pp. 62–63.

To explain more precisely the manner of its liberation, he explains its location and reformulates liberty from sin as liberty of counsel (*consilium*) and liberty from sorrow as liberty of accord (*complacitum*).

In general Bernard situates *liberum arbitrium* in the will and between sense (*sensus*) and appetite (*appetitus*). This same location, we will shortly see, Dante also provides for it. So located, Bernard tries to explain how *liberum arbitrium*, now restyled as voluntary consent, is itself a locus where will (*voluntas*) and reason (*ratio*) interact. For Bernard, will is a rational movement (*motus rationalis*), and it presides, like a judge, over both sense and appetite. Reason, we must note, is not will, but, wherever will turns, it always has reason as its 'attendant' (*comes*) and, in a way, its 'handmaiden' (*pedissequa*).[15] Reason's role in will is *arbitrium*, judgment, and counsel, *consilium*.[16] Because choice is rooted in will, it enjoys liberty. Bernard insists that such liberty is a matter of natural endowment by creation. Judgment is never lost, even after sin. The damned as well as the blessed retain their natural judgment. Yet reason's role in will is indeed affected by sin—is, in fact, enslaved to sin. Here we perceive the reoccurrence of the bernardine problematic of liberty noted earlier. One ministry of reason in will— *arbitrium* or judgment—is ever capable of knowing good from evil. What it loses through sin, original and personal, is styled by Bernard its liberty of counsel, that ability to accept the reasoning, either given by another in counsel or produced by reason itself, that leads or persuades the will to choose and to do what is good.[17] In losing its liberty of

---

[15]For the location of *liberum arbitrium* between *sensus* and *appetitus*, see Gra 2.3, which also contains Bernard's definition of will: 'Porro voluntas est motus rationalis, et sensui praesidens, et appetitui. Habet sane, quocumque se volverit, rationem semper comitem et quoddamodo pedissequam . . .' (SBOp 3:168, 1–3).

[16]Reason always ministers to will by judgment and counsel, but the will remains free to choose against reason's judgment and counsel: '. . . Non quod semper ex ratione, sed absque ratione moveatur [voluntas], ita ut multa faciat per ipsam [ratio] contra ipsam, hoc est per eius quasi ministerium, contra ejus consilium sive iudicium' (Gra 2.3; SBOp 3:168, 3–6). Thus, for Bernard, the ministerial roles of reason do not necessitate the consent of the will or liberty of judgment.

[17]Thus, of the two ministries performed by reason for will, it is *consilium*, not judgment, that sin destroys. On this crucial point, see the introduction of Bernard McGinn to the english translation cited in n. 14 above. McGinn (p. 22) writes: 'Original sin does not take away judgment, the ability to distinguish between right and wrong; counsel, on the other hand, that which determines " . . . the licit as more suitable and . . . the illicit as harmful" (4:11), is denied to fallen man. Neither of these intellectual acts can determine the will, for even the man who possesses grace and *liberum consilium* remains free to sin, but it is the lack of free counsel that is the cause of man's present sinfulness.'

counsel, the will also loses its liberty of accord, as he says in the following passage:

> Now, however, since we discern many things by means of the judgment as either to be done or omitted, which we nevertheless choose to reject through counsel in a manner quite at variance with the rectitude of our judgment; and since, again, we do not freely embrace as pleasing all that we observe with counsel as being right and suitable, but impatiently endure it, rather, as something hard and burdensome; it is evident that we possess neither liberty of counsel nor liberty of accord.[18]

In this way does experience always testify to the need and volitional problematic of liberty, which Bernard often expresses as the loss of the likeness of man to God. The problematic of human life is not so much a rational conundrum as it is a volitional servitude, at best fully recognized as self-inflicted but remaining beyond human power to escape. Having lost the liberties of counsel and accord (or of grace and glory), man still retains his liberty of nature, that liberty of judgment by which he can rightly judge his situation though he cannot liberate himself from it. Such judgment is rooted in the inviolable and indestructible liberty of the will itself, the very image of God in human nature.

BERNARDINE LIBERATION IN DANTE

When Saint Bernard examined himself and humankind in general, he saw, as Saint Paul did, that all are enslaved, captives of sin needing a liberation only possible through grace. The general pattern of that liberation coheres well with the general dramatic action of the *Commedia*. At the beginning of the poem, Dante presents himself as lost in a dark wood and as *knowing* that he is lost. In other words he has not lost, in bernardine terms, the liberty of judgment that is his by nature, for he can know his condition as evil. Even Dante's damned recognize their evil.[19] But the Dante who is in the dark wood cannot escape by his own power. Aid is necessary, aid that comes from three heavenly ladies and Virgil, the first of Dante's guides. Are not his guides the

---

[18]Gra 4.12; SBOp 3:179; CF 19:67.

[19]See, as examples, Francesca's admission of her and Paulo's 'mal perverso' (Inf 5.93). Ciacco openly admits his gluttony (Inf 6.53), Alessio Interminei his maliciously fraudulent flattery (Inf 18.125–26), Pope Nicholas III his simony (Inf 19.73–75), and Vanni Fucci his thievery (Inf 24.137).

embodiments of the grace that restores the judgment of Dante to liberty of counsel—that is, to liberty from sin—through their counsel? Virgil is explicitly called by Dante 'my wise counsel' (*mio consiglio saggio*; Purg 13.75). To Beatrice's words, as 'to her counsels' (*a' suoi consigli*; Par 23.76), Dante shows himself ever ready to turn in paradise. The entire instructive dimension of the *Commedia* seems to have no other purpose for the traveler than to provide counsel, thus allowing his will to develop correctly in love. Let us remember that to Cato, that extraordinary lover of liberty, Virgil represents Dante's journey as one in which Dante 'goes seeking liberty' (*libertà va cercando*; Purg 1.73). Later in the journey up the mountain of purgation, the discourses of Marco Lombardo and Virgil concentrate the search for liberty in liberty of choice, *libero arbitrio*. At the top of the mountain, just outside the Garden of Eden, Virgil declares to Dante: 'Free, upright and whole is your will' (*libero, dritto, e sano é tuo arbitrio*; Purg 27.140). 'It would be wrong', says Virgil, 'not to act according to its pleasure [*a suo senno*]' (Purg 27.141). Do we not hear in these remarks the echoes of bernardine liberty from sin (or *libertas a peccata*) and the liberty of accord (*libertas complaciti*)?

More striking than the general congruence of Bernard's theology of liberty with the dramatic action of the poem as a liberation of the will is the significant fact that Dante conceives of liberty of will precisely as Bernard does, as the source of human nobility and the greatest gift of God to man as a creature. This means that Dante shares with Bernard the same vision of human nature. Both stress, not intellect or reason, but liberty of will as the distinctive creaturely excellence of humanity. In the treatise *De monarchia*, Dante calls the will's liberty of choice (*liberum arbitrium*), which is the source of all human liberty, 'the greatest gift given by God to human nature' (*maximum donum humanae naturae a Deo collatum*; *De mon* 1.12).[20] This liberty of choice is located by Dante—just as it is by Bernard—between sensory apprehension (*apprehensio*) and appetite (*appetitus*). In judging, the will is free (*liberum*) when it is not held captive (*captivum*) by prevenient appetite that distorts choice.[21]

Another expression of the singular excellence of liberty of the will is made in the first sphere of Paradiso. Addressing the importance of the monastic vow, Dante's Beatrice says:

---

[20]*Le opere di Dante Alighieri*, ed. E. Moore, rev. Paget Toybee (4th ed., Oxford: Oxford University Press, 1924).

[21]*De monarchia* 1.12: ' . . . Si vero ab appetitu, quoqunque modo praeveniente, iudicium moveatur, liberum esse non potest, quia non a se, sed ab alio captivum trahitur.'

The greatest gift [*Lo maggior don*] which God in his bounty bestowed in creating, and the most conformed to his goodness and that which he most prizes, was the freedom of the will [*de la voluntà la libertate*], with which the creatures that have intelligence, they all and they alone, were and are endowed. (Par 5.19–24)

This paradisal teaching places on a higher and more authoritative level what in *Purgatorio* Marco Lombardo and Virgil said about liberty of will and liberty of choice within it. Marco's famous discourse has as its basic point that 'liberty of will' (*libero voler*) means freedom 'from necessity' (*di necessitate*), even that of the stars. Marco's point is exactly that of Bernard, who claims, as we have seen, that the human being enjoys an inalienable liberty of will which he in one formula called *libertas a necessitate*. Marco adds that 'liberty of choice' (*libero arbitrio*) would be destroyed if the stars did in fact move the will by necessity, but, even granted that the stars do initiate the movements of the will, Marco claims that 'a light is given to you to know good and evil' (Purg 16.75). The commentators I have consulted call this light the illumination of reason that enables the will to judge whether any impulse it undergoes is good or bad.[22] Virgil's discourse in the next two cantos makes clear that some appetites affecting will are innate and some arise by choice. Still more important is his claim that 'there is innate in you the faculty that counsels [*consiglia*]' and that ought to hold the threshold of 'assent' (*l'assenso*; Purg 18.62). This 'noble virtue' (*nobile virtù*), Virgil observes, Beatrice understands as 'liberty of choice' (*libero arbitrio*; Purg 18.74).

Whatever Dante may owe to Aristotle or to Saint Thomas in formulating these concepts, they are nevertheless perfectly congruent with those of Saint Bernard. The main thing to note, however, is that, unlike Aristotle and Saint Thomas, but very much like Bernard, Dante sees *libero arbitrio* as the source of nobility, and as God's greatest gift in creating human nature. Beatrice is explicit about this point, as I have already noted. And when Beatrice places her previous remarks about God's greatest gift to man in the context of sin, the bernardine resonances of her words seem unmistakable. Sin, says Beatrice in *Paradiso*, is what makes the soul unlike God and turns it from its dignity:

Sin alone is that which disfranchises [the soul] and makes it unlike [*dissimile*] the Supreme Good, so that it is little illuminated by its

---

[22]C. Singleton, *Purgatorio* commentary, p. 353, speaks of it as 'the light of rational discernment', which, by a quotation from Thomas Aquinas (*Summa theol.* I-II, q. 19, a. 4, resp.), is said to be derived from God.

light; and to its dignity [*sua dignità*] it never returns unless, where fault has emptied, it fills up with just penalties against evil delight [*mal diletar*]. (Par 7.79–84)

Disenfranchising the soul—that is, causing the soul to lose its liberty— and making it unlike the Supreme Good by turning it from its dignity: these are bernardine notions. What does Beatrice mean by the soul's *dignità*? It is the soul's liberty by creation, that which makes the soul most like God and most pleases him:

That which rains down from [God] immediately is wholly free [*libero è tutto*]. . . .It [the soul as free] is the most conformed to [the divine goodness] and pleases it most; for the Holy Ardor, which irradiates everything, is most living in what is most like itself [*nella più somigiliante è più vivace*]. (Par 7.70–75)

To disentangle from the tightly interwoven texture of Dante's imagery and concepts that pattern which, I have argued, is bernardine is surely difficult. But it is possible if one conceives of the inquiry in accordance with Dante's presentation of his experience as a traveler in the *Commedia*. That experience is identified as a journey from servitude to liberty, and Saint Bernard is the figure who best represents this in the poem. Let us hang on to this fact: it is Bernard and no other—not Aristotle, not Saint Thomas, not Boethius, not Augustine, not Joachim, not any other of Dante's undoubted *auctores*—who is Beatrice's replacement as Dante's last guide. Even if Dante did not write the famous epistle to Can Grande as a few scholars resolutely maintain, it nevertheless contains a truth that clarifies the complexity of Dante's poetical theology. All within the poem has a clear orientation to liberty: 'The subject of the whole work taken allegorically is man insofar as he, by meriting or demeriting through liberty of choice [*per arbitrii libertatem*], is subject to rewarding or punishing justice . . . ' (Ep 13.25).[23] Whatever else Dante as a learned poet may have drawn from Saint Bernard of Clairvaux— and I do think there are other things—the essential thing is, I hope, now clear: a theology of liberty of choice recreated as the pattern informing the movement of the traveler from the dark wood to the uncreated light that is Dante's God.[24]

---

[23]'Si vero accipiatum opus allegorice, subiectum est homo prout merendo et demerendo per arbitrii libertatem iustitie premiandi et puniendi obnoxius est.' Ed. E. Pistelli (1921), as reprinted in *Enciclopedia dantesca* 5 (1978) p. 814.

[24]I wish to thank John R. Sommerfeldt and Denis Farkasfalvy, OCist, for their bibliographical help to me when I began this study. A fuller study of Dante's Saint Bernard, part of a book on medieval poetic theology, is now in preparation.

ABSTRACTS

La thèse de la présente étude est que dans la *Commedia* Dante crée un schema narratif d'expérience et de pensée religieuses, appelé ici sa théologie de la liberté, qui reproduit en fait le processus essentiel de la libération chrétienne développé par saint Bernard de Clairvaux dans ses ouvrages, *De gratia et libero arbitrio* et *De diligendo Deo*. L'apparition inattendue et surprenante de saint Bernard à la place de Béatrice vers la fin du *Paradiso* est c'est du moins ma suggestion la citation érudite que fait Dante lui-même de la plus haute autorité théologique invoquée par son poème. Aussi, pour quiconque veut comprendre la théologie de la *Commedia*, le saint Bernard de Dante est une figure douée d'une signification décisivé et englobante qui ne se limite pas seulement à la brève intervention de Bernard après son apparition dans le *Paradiso* mais s'étend à la totalité du poème qui précède son apparition.

Dans cet article, je ne tenterai que d'esquisser le schéma bernardin de la libération, schéma qui informe le coeur narratif et thématique de la *Commedia*. Dans un premier temps, je me pencherai sur la transition de Béatrice à Bernard qui s'effectue dans *Paradiso* XXXI. Selon moi, la signification de la figure allégorique qu'est Bernard ne se réduit pas à une contemplation mystique de Dieu médiatisée par la Vierge Marie, mais au contaire renvoie à toute une théologie de la libération intérieure, libération vécue par le voyageur Dante au cours de son pélerinage dans l'au-delà. Dans un deuxième moment, je m'attarderai aux passages montrant les points de ressemblance indubitables entre le poète et l'abbé cistercien. L'un et l'autre considèrent le libre arbitre comme le don de Dieu, qui fonde l'excellence distinctive de l'homme dans l'ordre de la création. L'un et l'autre voient dans la libération un processus, réalisé sous l'impulsion de la gràce, qui rend possible et promeut un accord d'amour avec Dieu.

The thesis of this study is that in the *Commedia* Dante creates a narrative pattern of religious experience and thought, called here his theology of liberty, that in fact reproduces the essential process of christian liberation developed by Saint Bernard of Clairvaux in his works *De gratia et libero arbitrio* and *De diligendo Deo*. The unexpected, surprising appearance of Saint Bernard as Beatrice's replacement near the end of *Paradiso* is, I suggest, Dante's own scholarly citation of the highest theological authority of his poem. Accordingly, for anyone who would understand the theology of the *Commedia*, Dante's Saint Bernard is a figure having decisive and comprehensive significance extending not

514   *Raymond D. DiLorenzo*

just to Bernard's brief business after his appearance in *Paradiso* but to the entire poem before he appears.

In these pages, the argument should be understood as initiatory, for it is meant only as a sketch of the bernardine pattern informing the liberation that is the narrative and thematic core of the *Commedia*. First, there is an analysis of Dante's presentation of the transition from Beatrice to Bernard in *Paradiso* XXXI. Here it is argued that Bernard is not merely the allegorical figure for mystical contemplation made possible by grace coming through the Virgin Mother; he is the surprising figure for the theology of the whole journey of liberation previously experienced by the traveler Dante. Second in the order of argument is an analysis of texts indicating the essential points of unanimity between Dante and Saint Bernard. Both authors theologically conceive liberty of choice as the gift from God that constitutes the distinctive creative excellence of man. Both authors envision liberation as a process achieved through grace-given divine counsel that promotes and makes possible loving accord with God.

Die These dieser Abhandlung ist, daß Dante in der *Commedia* ein erzählerisches Muster von religiöser Erfahrung und Denkungsweise einsetzt—hier seine Theologie der Freiheit genannt—die in der Tat den wesentlichen Vorgang der christlichen Befreiung widerspiegelt, der von dem heiligen Bernhard von Clairvaux in seinen Werken *De gratia et libero arbitrio* und *De diligendo deo* entwickelt worden war. Das unerwartete und überaschende Erscheinen des heiligen Bernhard anstelle von Beatrice kurz vor dem Ende des *Paradiso* ist, meiner Ansicht nach, Dantes gelehrte Art, die höchste theologische Autorität seines Gedichts zu zitieren. Daher ist für denjenigen, der die Theologie der *Commedia* versteht, Dantes heiliger Bernhard eine Figur, die entscheidende und umfassende Bedeutung besitzt, die weit über Bernhards kurzen Auftritt nach seinem Erscheinen im *Paradiso* hinausreicht und sich auf das ganze Gedicht vor seinem Auftritt erstreckt.

Die Argumentation in diesen Seiten sollte als Einführung zu verstehen sein, da es sich nur um eine Skizze der bernadinischen Lehre handelt, die der Befreiung als erzählerisch-thematischem Kern der *Commedia* zugrunde liegt. Zum ersten wird eine Untersuchung von Dantes Darstellung des Übergangsprozesses von Beatrice zu Bernhard in *Paradiso* XXXI angestellt. Hier wird die These aufgestellt, daß Bernhard mehr ist als nur die allegorische Figur mystischer Kontemplation, die möglich geworden ist durch die Gnade ausgehend von der Mutter-Jungfrau; vielmehr ist er die überraschende Figur für die Theologie der gesamten Befreiungsreise, die zuvor von dem Reisenden Dante erlebt worden war. Als zweiter Punkt der Argumentation wird eine Untersuchung angestellt, die die wesentlichen Punkte der Übereinstimmung zwischen Dante und dem heiligen Bernhard herausstreicht. Beide Autoren verstehen im theologischen Sinn die Freiheit der Wahl als ein Geschenk von Gott, auf dem die besondere schöpferische Auszeichnung der Menschheit beruht. Beide Autoren sehen auch die Befreiung als einen Prozeß, der ermöglicht wird durch gnadegegebenen göttlichen Rat, der den liebenden Einklang mit Gott fördert und ermöglicht.

DIVUS BERNHARDUS: SAINT BERNARD
AS SPIRITUAL AND THEOLOGICAL MENTOR
OF THE REFORMER MARTIN LUTHER

Franz Posset
Beaver Dam, Wisconsin

WHAT COULD CLAIRVAUX, the 'clear valley' in France, have to do with Wittenberg, the 'white hill' in Saxony? What does a german austin friar of the sixteenth century have to do with a french cistercian abbot of the twelfth century? What could Luther, the 'archheretic', have to do with the saint whose nine-hundredth birthday we celebrate? My answer is formulated in the ecumenical theological thesis that Luther is *Bernardus redivivus*. Saint Bernard is the spiritual and theological mentor of Luther, the friar, the ex-friar, the younger and the elder reformer. 'By remote control', so to speak, Saint Bernard guides Luther's thoughts across the centuries. Saint Bernard is quoted or mentioned more than five hundred times in the critical edition of Luther's works;[1] Saint Bernard's famous foe, Peter Abelard, is not mentioned at all. Although Luther generally liked the german mystics (such as the anonymous Frankfurter and John Tauler), he did not seem to care for Meister Eckhart, who is not mentioned by name anywhere in his works.[2]

---

[1] *D. Martin Luthers Werke: Kritische Gesamtausgabe* (Weimar 1883-), cited hereafter as WA. It is impossible to analyze here all the references listed in the index, WA 63. The abbreviation LW stands for *Luther's Works*, American Edition (Philadelphia: Fortress Press; and St Louis: Concordia, 1955-).

[2] The index volume, WA 63, does not indicate any reference to Eckhart or Abelard. As is generally known, Luther was so impressed by the so-called Frankfurter's manuscript which he found that he edited it under the Title of *Theologia Germanica*.

Luther very much preferred our older monastic theologian from Clairvaux. Yet it is not so much Bernard's mysticism as his biblical theology which attracted him and is thus alive in his spirituality, theology,
and preaching. Luther had been nurtured by the monastic theology of
divus Bernhardus, as he called him, and he preferred him to any of the
scholastic theologians.[3] Rejecting the scholastics as 'sow theologians',
and their exponent, Thomas Aquinas, as an 'arch-heretic' who tells lies,[4]
Luther by-passed them and returned to the older monastic theology
represented by his dear 'divine Bernard'. In particular, Luther returned
to Bernard's sermons on the history of salvation as celebrated during the
liturgical year, starting from the feast of the Annunciation and moving
through the sermons on Advent, Christmas, and the Circumcision, up to
the lenten sermons and the meditations on the passion of the Lord in
certain sermons on the Song of Songs. With these sermons Bernard became a permanent spiritual companion to Luther with his Christ-centered
reformation theology. In other words, Luther's reformation theology had
its *Sitz im Leben* in the monastic, Christ-centered piety of the Middle
Ages as it was shaped decisively by Saint Bernard. In addition, Luther
drew on Bernard's *On Consideration* for his initial criticism of the non-
pastoral aspects of the contemporary papacy.[5]

[3]See Franz Posset, 'Monastic Influence on Luther', *Monastic Studies* 18 (1988) 136–
63. Reinhard Schwarz, 'Luther's Inalienable Inheritance of Monastic Theology' (trans.
Franz Posset), *The American Benedictine Review* 39 (1988) 430–50. Peter Manns, 'Zum
Gespräch zwischen M. Luther und der katholischen Theologie: Begegnung zwischen
patristisch-monastischer und reformatorischer Theologie an der Scholastik vorbei', in
Thesaurus Lutheri (Helsinki, 1987) pp. 63–154. Luther and Erasmus both called the
abbot of Clairvaux *divus Bernardus*. See *Diuus Bernardus in libris quibus titulum fecit
De consideratione . . .*, Erasmus' letter to Jodocus Jonas of May 10, 1521, Allen edition
4:487 (no. 1202). See Luther in *Operationes in Psalmos* (1519–1521): '. . . Video D.
Bernhardum hac arte praestitisse et omnem suae eruditionis copiam hinc hausisse'; WA
5:47, 13–14. See WA 2:15, 18 (*Acta Augustana*, 1518).
[4]'S. Thome fabulis' (WA Briefe 1:214, 23); 'ertzketzer' (WA 12:625, 7). 'O Sawthe-
ologen!' (WA 56:274, 14).
[5]See Franz Posset, 'Recommendations by Martin Luther of St Bernard's *On Consideration*', CSt 25 (1990) 25–36. See Posset, ' "Bernardus Redivivus": The *Wirkungs-
geschichte* of a Medieval Sermon in the Reformation of the Sixteenth Century', CSt 22
(1987) 239–49. Posset, 'St Bernard's Influence on Two Reformers: John von Staupitz
and Martin Luther', CSt 25 (1990) 175–87. Posset, 'The Elder Luther on Bernard: Part
I', *The American Benedictine Revue* 42 (1991) 22–52. Posset, 'Bernard of Clairvaux as
Luther's Source: Reading Bernard with Luther's "Spectacles" ', *Concordia Theological
Quarterly* 54 (1990) 281–304. See also Martin Elze, 'Das Verständnis der Passion Jesu
im ausgehenden Mittelalter und bei Luther', in Heinz Liebing and Klaus Scholder (edd.),
Geist und Geschichte der Reformation: Festgabe Hanns Rückert zum 65. Geburtstag
(Berlin: Walter de Gruyter & Co., 1966) pp. 127–51. Erich Kleineidam, 'Ursprung und

BERNARD'S PRINCIPLE OF GRACE ALONE AND FAITH ALONE

The passage which made a decisive impact on Luther occurs in the introduction to Bernard's lengthy *First Sermon on the Annunciation*:

First of all, we ought to believe that we cannot have forgiveness of our sins other than through God's indulgence; secondly, that we are powerless to do any good work whatever except by his grace; thirdly, that by no works of ours can we merit eternal life, unless it is given to us freely as well. . . . Undoubtedly, that which has been done can never be undone; yet if God wills not to impute it, it shall be as if it had not been. The prophet [Ps 31:2] had this in mind when he exclaimed: 'Blessed is the man to whom the Lord imputes not sin.'[6]

Bernard preaches here the exclusivess of grace. He also concludes that all our merits are God's gift: *merita omnia Dei sunt dona*.[7] He furthermore advises: 'But add to this that you also believe that through him your sins are forgiven. This is the testimony which the Holy Spirit brings in your heart, saying "your sins are forgiven you", for thus the Apostle concluded that a man is freely justified by faith.'[8] Bernard teaches again that one must believe that our merits are God-given.[9] He grounds his theological position in Psalm 31 and in pauline and johannine theology when he explains the remission of sins by grace and faith alone. Bernard relies primarily on these two biblical theologians whom Luther will call later on the 'high commanders' (*duces*) of his theology.[10]

Bernard's sermons were available to friar Martin through the monastic libraries, but we do not know any *marginalia* by Luther on Bernard's works. We possess Luther's notes on Peter Lombard and on Augustine, for example,[11] but we do not know at what exact time Luther was

Gegenstand der Theologie bei Bernhard von Clairvaux und Martin Luther', in Wilhelm Ernst *et al.* (edd.), *Dienst der Vermittlung: Festschrift zum 25-jährigen Bestehen des philosophisch-theologischen Studiums im Priesterseminar Erfurt* (Leipzig: St Benno-Verlag, 1977) pp. 221–47. Theo Bell, *Bernhardus Dixit: Bernard van Clairvaux in Martin Luthers werken* (Delft: Eburon, 1989).

[6] Ann 1.1; SBOp 5:13, 10–13.
[7] Ann 1.2; SBOp 5:14, 11–18.
[8] Ann 1.3; SBOp 5:14, 22–15, 2.
[9] Ann 1.3; SBOp 5:15, 2–6.
[10] WA 18:757, 9–10. LW 33:241.
[11] See WA 9:5–27 (on Augustine); WA 9:29–94 (on Peter Lombard). For further details, including Luther's notes on Bernard in his copy of *Opuscula Anselmi*, see Bell, pp. 38–74. The Erfurt library had Bernard's *Sermones de tempore et de sanctis, Sermones super Cantica canticorum*, and *De consideratione*. See Jun Matsuura, 'Restbestände aus

reading Bernard's first homily for the feast of the Annunciation. We do, however, find Luther quoting this homily several times over the years. Luther definitely was familiar with Bernard's sermons during his first lectures on the Psalms, given between 1513 and 1515.[12] That there was an earlier point of contact, concerning specifically the message of Bernard's *First Sermon on the Annunciation*, we know from Luther's dear friend and colleague, Philip Melanchthon. In his preface to the second volume of Luther's works (Wittenberg, 1546), Melanchthon explicitly mentions Luther's first awareness of Bernard's sermon on the Annunciation. There is no reason to question the validity of Melanchthon's reminiscence. In it he preserves the biographical hint that an unknown senior friar of the 'Augustinian College of Erfurt' had taught Luther really to believe in the forgiveness of sins as prayed in the Creed: 'I believe in the forgiveness of sins.' The consternated young Luther was strengthened by this senior friar who made him aware of Bernard's *dictum* in the *First Sermon on the Annunciation*, which Melanchthon quotes:

> But add to this that you also believe that through him *your* sins are forgiven. This is the testimony that the Holy Spirit brings in your heart, saying 'your sins are forgiven you', for thus the Apostle states that a man is freely justified by faith.[13]

Having been introduced to these weighty insights from the *First Sermon on the Annunciation* at such an early date, Luther from then on remembered the essential content of this sermon, especially the reference to Psalm 31, concerning God's non-imputation of sin. When, in 1513, Luther arrived at the exposition of that crucial Psalm verse 31:1, he remembered that Bernard had used it in one of his sermons. But, at that moment, Luther did not remember the exact locus. He related, however, the essential content of Bernard's sermon without identifying it in his lecture:

der Bibliothek des Erfurter Augustinerklosters zu Luthers Zeit und bisher unbekannte eigenhändige Notizen Luthers', in Gerhard Hammer and Karl-Heinz zur Mühlen (edd.), *Lutheriana: Zum 500. Geburtstag Martin Luthers von den Mitarbeitern der Weimarer Ausgabe im Auftrag der Kommission zur Herausgabe der Werke Martin Luthers*, Archiv WA 5:315–32.

[12]See Wilhelm Maurer, 'Cisterciensische Reform und reformatorischer Glaube', *Cistercienser Chronik* 84 (1977) 6.

[13]*Praefatio Melanthonis* [sic] in *'Tomum secundum omnium operum Reverendi Domini Martini Lutheri, Doctori Theologiae'* (Wittenberg, 1546), *Corpus Reformatorum* 6:159. Emphasis in the original. See note 8 above. The issue whether Melanchthon's preface should be taken as pure legend or historical fact remains open to debate.

The beginning of the Psalm teaches two things: first, that all are in sin and no one is blessed; secondly, that no one is capable of meriting the forgiveness of sin, but it is the Lord alone who forgives freely by not imputing. However, the whole world has disregarded these two teachings and has therefore fought against the apostles preaching them and has rejected Christ who has removed these two, as Bernard meditates on it beautifully in a certain sermon. Hence he says: 'Blessed are they whose iniquities are forgiven', and then: 'Blessed is he to whom the Lord does not impute sin' [Psalm 31:2]. . . . And there are none who have no iniquities, but there are only some whose iniquities are forgiven, etc. And this is what the title of the Psalm has in mind when it is called the 'erudition of David'. For by the understanding through faith we are taught, and not by feeling or reason.[14]

Here Luther quotes Bernard in a positive, complimentary way by referring to his 'beautiful' meditation 'in a certain sermon', thus definitely stating his congeniality with Bernard's preaching on this subject. In his subsequent, 1516, lectures on the Letter to the Romans, Luther made his indebtedness to Bernard's first sermon even more explicit in commenting on Romans 8:16: 'For the person who trusts with strong faith and hope to be a son of God, is indeed a son of God, what no one can be without the Spirit. Thus [says] blessed Bernard in sermon one on the Annunciation.' In his *scholium* on Romans 8:16, Luther presents Bernard's sermon in a lengthy, almost literal quotation:[15]

Bernard	*Luther*
	Quod testimonium istud sit ipsa fiducia cordis in Deum, preclarissime ostendit B. Bernardus, plenus eodem spiritu, sermone de annunciatione,
Porro hoc testimonium in tribus	1. dicens: 'Hoc testimonium in tribus

[14]WA 3:175, 33–38 (emphasis added). LW 10:147. The american edition of Luther's works does not indicate any editorial source reference at this point.

[15]Quotation marks in Luther's text are corrected, while spelling and capitalization remains as in WA 56:369, 28–370, 23. Ann 1.1–3; SBOp 5:13, 9–15, 5. See also Luther in his gloss: *Vnde B. Bernardus ser. 1 de annunciatione Dominica*; WA 56:79, 15–17. See Posset, 'Berhardus Redivivus', pp. 242–44, especially note 26. See also Bell, pp. 84–86.

consistere credo.
Necesse est enim primo
omnium credere, quod
remissionem peccatorum
habere non possis nisi
per indulgentiam Dei;
deinde, quod nihil prorsus
habere queas operis boni,
nisi et hoc dederit ipse;

postremo, quod vitam
aeternam nullis potes
operibus promereri, nisi
gratis tibi detur et illa. . . .
Verum haec, quae nunc
diximus non omnino
sufficiunt,
sed magis
initium quoddam et velut
fundamentum fidei sunt
habenda.
Ideoque si crederis
peccata tua non posse
deleri nisi ab eo cui soli
peccasti, et in quem
benefacis.
Sed adde adhuc:
ut et hoc credas,

quia per ipsum tibi
peccata donantur.
Hoc est testimonium quod
perhibet in corde nostro
Spiritus Sanctus, dicens:
DIMISSA SUNT TIBI PECCATA
TUA.
Sic enim arbitratur

---

consistere puto.
Necesse est enim primo
omnium credere, quod
remissionem peccatorum
habere non possis nisi
per indulgentiam Dei.
Deinde, quod nihil
prorsus habere queas
boni operis, nisi et
hoc dederit ipse.
Postremo, quod eternam
vitam nullis potes
operibus promereri, nisi
gratis detur et illa.
Verum hec,
non omnino
sufficunt,
Sed magis initium
quoddam et velut
fundamentum fidei
habenda sunt.
Ideo si crederis peccata
tua non deleri nisi ab
eo,
peccatum non cadit, bene
facis; sed adde adhuc

ut et hoc credas,'
non quod possis tu, Sed
necesse est, ut spiritus
faciat te hoc credere,
'quia per ipsum peccata
tibi donantur.
Hoc est testimonium, quod
perhibet in corde nostro
spiritus sanctus dicens:
Dimissa sunt tibi peccata
tua.
Sic enim arbitratur

Apostolus iustificari hominem gratis per fidem.	Apostolus hominem Iustificari per fidem' (assertive de te ipso etiam, non tantum de electis credere, Quod Christus pro peccatis tuis mortuus sit et satisfecit).
Ita de meritis quoque si credis non posse haberi nisi per ipsum, non sufficit, donec tibi perhibeat testimonium Spiritus veritatis, quod ea habes per illum. Sic et de vita aeterna	'Ita de meritis quoque, si credis non posse haberi nisi per ipsum, Non sufficit, donec testimonium perhibeat spiritus veritatis, quia habes ea per ipsum'. . . . 'Sic et de vita eterna' non satis est credere, Quod ipse eam gratis donet, Sed 'testimonium
habeas necesse est testimonium Spiritus, quod ad eam divino sis munere perventurus.	spiritus habeas necesse est, quod ad eam divino munere sis perventurus.'

Several more times during the subsequent decade Luther would make this same reference to Bernard's sermon, particularly in his lectures on Hebrews in 1517, and in his lectures on the First Letter of John in 1527.[16] We see that Luther's gradual reformation discovery of salvation by faith was decisively influenced by Bernard's *First Sermon on the Annunciation*. In this theological question Luther is *Bernardus redivivus* as he takes up Bernard's theological concerns. After having experienced Bernard's great help in his early consternations and again in his professional task of expounding the Sacred Scriptures, Luther continued to use the bernardine meditations throughout his entire career, especially Bernard's Advent and Christmas sermons, to which we turn our attention now.

[16]*Scholion* on Hebrews 5:1 (1517); WA 57/3:169, 10–23. Against Cajetan in 1518 (*Acta Augustana*); WA 2:15, 36–16, 3. On 1 John 4:10 (1527); WA 20:746, 13–18. For details, see Posset, 'Bernardus Redivivus', pp. 242–49. Luther may have had Bernard's sermon in mind also in 1519 when lecturing on Galatians 1:4–5; WA 2:458, 10–26. See Manns, pp. 144–45.

BERNARD'S CONCEPT OF THE TRIPLE ADVENT
OF CHRIST AND LUTHER'S USE OF IT

During his first Psalm lectures, when Luther arrived at Psalm 101:1 ('When will you come to me?'), he found help for his exposition in Bernard, specifically in his 'distinction'[17] of the 'three advents of Christ'. Accordingly, Luther answered the Psalm's question by declaring that at any time the advent of Christ may occur in the soul. Here Luther followed Bernard's concept of the spiritual advent of Christ in the soul. Luther complimented Bernard for presenting Christ's advent in the soul 'in a beautiful way'. Then Luther described the triple appearance of Christ's face by adopting the bernardine concept of the 'triple advent'. He wrote:

> First, in his first advent when he was incarnated as the Son of God who is the face of the Father. . . . Secondly, in the spiritual advent without which the first is good for nothing. And so one has to recognize his face through faith in which all good things are. . . . Thirdly, in the second and last advent when his face will be fully visible.[18]

By the time Luther was lecturing on Psalm 106, he explicitly referred to the conclusion of Bernard's third Advent sermon, in which Bernard had spoken of the soul accusing itself before God. In declaring that when we judge ourselves, we are not judged by God, Luther uses latin wording close to Bernard's original. Luther cites Bernard where he 'expresses this verse with other words in this way: "O happy soul which before the eyes of God always judges and accuses itself." '[19] Yet another facet of Bernard's Advent sermons caught Luther's repeated attention. It is

---

[17]WA 4:134, 6–7. Walther Köhler, an eminent expert on Bernard and Luther, has opined that Luther had Bernard's sermon 69 or 84 in mind; *Luther und die Kirchengeschichte* (Erlangen, 1900) p. 306. But his Advent sermons fit much better with Luther's interpretation. See Adv 3.5–7 (SBOp 4:177–81); Adv 7.2 (SBOp 4:196, 9–14). Therefore, one must assume that Luther had those Advent sermons in mind, and not those on the Song. This is not too far fetched because, elsewhere in these lectures, Luther refers to the Advent sermons; thus we know that he read them. See below on Psalm 106. The theme of the Word coming to the soul permeates Bernard's entire series of sermons on the Song, but in it no specific concept of the triple advent is found.

[18]WA 4:147, 10–20.

[19]'Diligit enim animam, quae in conspectu eius et sine intermissione considerat, et sine dissimulatione diiudicat semetipsam. Idque iudicium non nisi propter nos a nobis exigit, quia si nosmetipsos iudicaverimus, non utique iudicabimur.' Adv 3.7; SBOp 4:181, 4–7. Luther: 'Unde b. Bernardus sermone de adventu istum versum aliis verbis sic exprimit: O felix anima que in conspectu Dei seipsam semper iudicat et accusat. Si enim nos ipsos iudicaremus, non utique a Deo iudicaremur.' WA 4:198, 19–21.

Bernard's speculation on the incarnation—and not in-angel-ation—of Christ. However, while Bernard's *third* Advent sermon was influential during Luther's first course on the Psalms, Bernard's *first* Advent sermon, on the topic of Lucifer's envy, began to leave a traceable mark only a decade later.[20]

BERNARD'S SPECULATION ON LUCIFER'S ENVY AND LUTHER'S USE OF IT

God had hidden from the devil his decision that his Son would become man while remaining God. The devil was envious and wished to be like the divine Son. This bernardine speculation was first processed by Luther in mid-career in a sermon of the year 1526.[21] Apparently, the abbot's thoughts in this regard were so interesting to the reformer that he also integrated this particular speculation into his Christmas sermons in the 1530s. On Christmas 1533, Luther referred to Bernard's speculation, as we know from Georg Rörer, the secretary who wrote the name *Bernardus* in the margin of his notes to Luther's sermon in order to explain further the line in that sermon: 'There were Fathers who gave some thought to this matter.'[22] Two years later, again on Christmas (1535), Luther gave his afternoon sermon on Luke 2:10–13. There he spoke again of his theological mentor's speculation:

> Saint Bernard is a wonderful man [*mirabile vir*]; he believes that the devil in paradise has noticed that God will become man. . . . They [the angels] do not mind at all and they are happy that God is not called an angelic God [*Engelischer Gott*] and that God does not become an angel. . . .[23]

And Luther will speak again of this idea in September 1537, in his exposition of John 1:14, and for the last time in his final exegetical project, his commentary on Genesis, on which he worked for about a decade, starting June 1535 and published between 1544 and 1554.[24]

[20]Adv 1.2; SBOp 4:162, 8–25.
[21]WA 20:334, 8–335, 1 (1526).
[22]WA 37:235, 10–22; here 10, with footnote 6 (1533).
[23]WA 41:486, 13–28 (1535).
[24]See Franz Posset, 'The Elder Luther on Bernard: Part II: Last Exegetical Work', *The American Benedictine Review* 42 (1991) 179–201.

BERNARD'S CONCEPT OF THE TRIPLE MIRACLE
AND LUTHER'S USE OF IT

Still another bernardine teaching about the incarnation mystery also inspired Luther's preaching: Bernard's marveling about the 'miracle' of the Virgin Mary's faith in connection with the incarnation. Bernard had preached about it extensively in his third sermon for Christmas Eve. His sermon focuses on the mystery of the omnipotent divine majesty which performed 'three works, three mixtures when assuming our flesh'. They are 'so wonderfully unique and uniquely wonderful' that they were not done again: 'Indeed, conjunct to each other are God and man, mother and virgin, faith and the human heart.'[25]

In Luther's Christmas sermon of 1520, we find him using Bernard's reflections on the faith of the Virgin. His text was from Luke 2:14, that the Savior is born to people of good will. One must feel this birth in the heart, Luther said. To consider this birth the right way, one must do it in faith alone. At this point Luther introduced Bernard:

Saint Bernard says that in this birth three great and remarkable signs occurred. The first is that God and man became one by the unification of the divine and human nature. The second is that she who gave birth remained a virgin and nursed. The third is that in this even the human heart and faith in such matters could come together and became one. I tell you, the first sign is easy to believe and moves only a few people. The second is easier yet to believe. The third is easiest of the three. Herein lies the real miracle, namely that the Virgin Mary believed that this will happen 'in her'. This is so great that we cannot marvel enough about it.[26]

Luther continued by preaching that, if Christ's birth is to become of any use to us and move our hearts, we must follow Mary's example, and the birth must occur in our hearts as well. Everyone must act as if the child were born to him alone. And anyone who does not accept the Christ child in this way, loses this birth.[27]

Bernard's meditation on the three wonders surfaces again in another sermon of Luther (collected by John Poliander between 1519 and 1521):

[25]V Nat 3.7; SBOp 4:216, 27–217, 1.
[26]'Sanctus Bernhardus sagt, das in diser gepurt drey grosse und merckliche wunderzeichen gescheen sindt. . . .' WA 7:188, 18–189, 7.
[27]See WA 7:189, 7–30.

Bernard reminds us of the three miracles: 1. That God and man became one person. 2. That the Virgin gives birth. 3. That the human heart and the word of the faith can come together and be united. This heart in which faith and the word are united must be reborn daily and renewed.[28]

For the feast of the Annunciation in 1525, Luther again made use of Bernard's sermon on the threefold miracle, adding that such belief is possible only by the work of the Holy Spirit.[29] The idea emerged again in the Summer Postil for Pentecost Monday,[30] and yet again in the sermon for the feast of the Visitation of Mary (July 2, 1533).[31] Late in his career, when working on Genesis 28:14–15, Luther reiterated Bernard's admiration of Mary's faith, a faith which is as miraculous as the incarnation of the Word:

Concerning the faith of the Virgin Mary, Saint Bernard says that, when it was announced to her by the angel that she would be the mother of Christ, the strength of faith of the Virgin who could believe the words of the angel was no less a miracle than the incarnation of the Word itself.[32]

This resembles Luther's comment to Cardinal Cajetan, in 1518, that Mary's exemplary faith is admired by '*divus Bernhardus* and the universal Church.'[33] Elsewhere in his commentary on Genesis, an older Luther reflected on Bernard's incarnation theology in words which may serve as the summary of Luther as *Bernardus redivivus* with regard to his incarnation theology: 'St Bernard really loved Christ's incarnation.'[34]

BERNARD'S REASONING ABOUT THE CIRCUMCISION AND LUTHER'S USE OF IT

In his sermons on the Feast of the Circumcision of the Lord, Bernard had meditated on the meaning of the circumcision, saying that Christ is

---

[28]WA 9:498, 23–26. See also WA 9:517, 14–28. A reference to Augustine follows, and again mention of Bernard; see WA 9:518, 4–8.
[29]WA 17/1:150, 23–26 (March 25, 1525).
[30]See WA 21:489, 31 (Summer Postil, 1544).
[31]WA 37:96, 25–35 (July 2, 1533).
[32]WA 43:590, 16–19. LW 5:234.
[33]See WA 2:15, 18 (*Acta Augustana*).
[34]WA 43:581, 11–12.

made a 'sinner' for us; that 'he has the form of a sinner'.[35] In his sermon of 1 January 1517, 'On the Circumcision and the Righteousness of Faith', Luther took up this meditation with explicit reference to Bernard who 'gives the moral reason for Christ's circumcision', that Christ wished to be made a sinner for us, which, of course, he was not.[36]

BERNARD'S *FASCICULUS MYRRHAE* AND LUTHER'S USE OF IT

Another contributing factor to Luther's maturing reformation theology was Bernard's *Forty-third Sermon on the Song of Songs*, which was known throughout the Middle Ages as the *fasciculus myrrhae*. Song 1:12 is the basis of Bernard's famous sermon, which begins as follows:

'A little bundle of myrrh that lies between my breasts is my beloved to me' [Sg 1:12]. . . . You too, if you are wise, will imitate the prudence of the bride, and never permit even for an hour that this precious bunch of myrrh should be removed from your bosom. Preserve without fail the memory of all those bitter things he endured for you. Persevere in meditating on him, and you in turn will be able to say: 'My beloved is to me a little bunch of myrrh that lies between my breasts.' . . . The life-giving bunch has been reserved for me; no one will take it away from me [Jn 16:22]; it shall lie between my breasts. I have said that wisdom is to be found in meditating on these truths. For me they are the source of perfect righteousness, of the fullness of knowledge [Is 33:6], of the most efficacious graces, of abundant merits. . . . For anyone traveling on God's royal road, they provide safe guidance amid the joys and sorrows of this life, warding off impending evils on every side. These win me the favor of him who is the world's judge, revealing him, despite his awesome powers, as one who is gentle and humble. Though beyond the reaches of princes and filling kings with fear [Ps 75:13], he is yet not one who not only forgives but even offers himself as an example to follow. . . . This is my philosophy, one more refined and interior, to know Jesus and him crucified [1 Co 2:2]. I do not ask, as the bride did, where he takes his rest at noon [Sg 1:6], because my joy is to hold him fast where he lies between my breasts. I

[35]Circ 3.3–4; SBOp 4:283, 19–284, 16. Circ 2.4; SBOp 4:280, 13. Circ 1 (SBOp 4:273–76) is probably closest to Luther's sermon of 1517.
[36]WA 1:120, 7–8.

do not ask where he rests at noon, for I see him on the cross as my Savior. . . .[37]

Luther spoke of this sermon in his first course on the Psalms, during his exposition of Psalm 84, which dealt with the desire for the Lord's place. He explicitly stated that 'blessed Bernard' had discussed this matter of the Lord's dwelling place in *de fasciculo myrrhe*: '. . . According to Saint Bernard, the soul does not find rest except in the wounds of Christ.'[38] Apparently, verse 84:4, which Luther was expounding and which mentions the sparrow finding a home and the swallow a nest for her young, triggered the remembrance of Bernard's *fasciculus* and yet another association, that is, a text from Bernard's sermon 61, on the wounds of Christ, which are like nests and resting places for the troubled soul. The 'fascicle' itself (sermon 43) does not contain this specific reference to the nest and resting place. Bernard's 'fascicle' centers in the statement, drawn from First Corinthians 2:2: 'This is my philosophy, one more refined and interior, to know Jesus and him crucified', a line repeated in his sermons 45 and 62 on the Song.[39] This same pauline reference to the crucified Christ surfaced later in Luther's Psalm lecture,[40] that is, long before Luther explicitly dealt with a pauline text in a subsequent academic course.

It was the augustinian superior, John von Staupitz, who had directed Luther toward affective Christ-centered meditation. As Luther himself testified: 'My good Staupitz said, "one must keep one's eyes fixed on that man who is called Christ". It was Staupitz who started this teaching.'[41] In a later table talk, Luther connected Staupitz's advice directly to Bernard: 'It is Bernard's saying: One must build nests in the wounds of Christ. . . .'[42]

CONCLUSION

As we have seen, it was an unknown senior friar of the 'Augustinian College of Erfurt' who led Luther to Bernard's *First Sermon on the*

---

[37]SC 43.1–4; SBOp 2:41, 1–43, 25.

[38]WA 3:640, 40–43 (gloss). WA 3:645, 31–646, 20 (scholium). LW 11:140–41.

[39]SC 43.4; SBOp 2:43, 21–22. See SC 45.3; SBOp 2:51, 19–20. See also SC 62.6; SBOp 2:159, 12.

[40]WA 4:153, 27–29 (on Psalm 101/102).

[41]WA TR 1:245, 9–12 (no. 526). LW 54:97.

[42]WA TR 5:395, 1–2 (no. 5898). See Luther on Romans: WA 56:400, 1. On the connections of Bernard, Staupitz, and Luther, see Bell, pp. 236–44.

Annunciation. Then it was Johann von Staupitz, a superior in his order, who guided Luther to his Christ-centered spirituality. Apparently, the german Augustinians were appropriating and handing on Bernard's spirituality. These friars thus made history with their influence on Luther's spirituality and theology. Through them Bernard became Luther's spiritual and theological mentor. Let it be noted, however, that it was not Bernard the preacher of the crusade, but the theologian of the cross and the incarnation, who came alive in Luther's thought world. Bernard remained a theological and spiritual mentor for Luther throughout his career as a preacher and teacher. This fact is mirrored in the reformer's numerous praises uttered during and long after the famous reformation year of 1517. These I shall list in chronological order.

In 1517, while expounding on Hebrews 4:12, Luther referred to a spiritually pregnant passage from Bernard's fifth book *On Consideration*: 'On this matter Saint Bernard speaks beautifully and extensively.'[43] Luther, in his reformation treatise on the monastic vows (1521), complimented his great spiritual mentor by saying: 'No one could better teach the Word of God than the monks, as Saint Bernard and others did.'[44] 'I esteem Saint Bernard higher than any monk or priest on earth. I have not heard nor read anything comparable' (1525).[45] 'I myself have paid attention to no holier monk than Bernard, I place him over Gregory, Benedict. . . .' (1527).[46] And in contrast to any overdrawn marian devotion, Luther, when working on Psalm 130:4, emphasized that Bernard had a specifically Christ-centered spirituality; Luther, therefore, praised him as a 'beautiful teacher, who ascribes everything to Christ' (1532–1533).[47] Luther exclaimed that there is 'no friendlier word on earth' than Bernard's phrase about Christ being 'bone from my bones and flesh from my flesh' (1537).[48] 'He is the only one worthy of the name *Pater Bernhardus* and of being studied diligently' (1538).[49] 'I often use the example of Saint Bernard' (1538), Luther said, by which he meant the

---

[43]WA 57/3:162, 9–12 (scholion). LW 29:165.

[44]WA 8:648, 25–27.

[45]WA 16:400, 20–21 (sermon on Exodus 19; September 10, 1525).

[46]WA 20:746, 12–19. See Franz Posset, *Luther's Catholic Christology According to His Johannine Lectures of 1527* (Milwaukee: Northwestern Publishing House, 1988) pp. 119–20.

[47]WA 40/3:354, 3–5 and 16–24.

[48]WA 45:304, 1–3 (stenogram), lines 9–14 (print); referring to Bernard's SC 2.6; SBOp 1:12, 1–2.

[49]WA 47:109, 18–23. LW 22:388.

Bernard story in *The Golden Legend*.[50] 'With his sermons Bernard excels all the other teachers, and even Augustine himself.'[51] 'Bernard is golden when he teaches and preaches. . . . Bernard is above all the teachers in the Church. . . .'[52] The elderly Luther angrily refuted any criticism of not having studied the authorities of the Church and their theology: 'I have read more than they think; I have worked through all the books. They dare to think that I had not read the Fathers' (1539).[53] One of the most revealing statements in Luther's theological self-analysis was uttered in 1539, six years before he died:

To be sure, I did teach, and still teach, that sinners shall be stirred to repentance through the preaching or the contemplation of the passion of Christ, so that they might see the enormity of God's wrath over sin, and learn that there is no other remedy for this than the death of God's Son. This doctrine is not mine, but Saint Bernard's. What, Saint Bernard? It is the preaching of all of Christianity, of all the prophets and apostles.[54]

Toward the end of his life, in 1545, the reformer summarized his praises of the abbot of Clairvaux: 'I prefer Bernard over all the others. He had the best knowledge of *religio,* as his writings show.'[55]

ABSTRACTS

Bernard est pour Luther un conseiller spirituel et théologique, par 'télécommande' en quelque sorte. Comme les humanistes de son temps, Luther le nomme *divus Bernhardus*. Il le préfère aux scolastiques. Il utilise surtout les sermons de Bernard pour les fêtes de l'année liturgique. Le premier sermon de Bernard pour l'Annonciation à Marie est d'une importance particulière: il contient la principe théologique de la *sola gratia*. Si l'on en croit Melanchthon, le jeune Luther aurait connu ce sermon à Erfurt. C'est bien à ce texte que Luther renvoie dans sa première leçon sur les Psaumes, et il le cite abondamment dans sa leçon sur l'Epître aux Romains. L'idée bernardine de la triple venue du Christ

---

[50]WA 47:585, 19–20. On Luther's use of the Bernard story from *The Golden Legend*, see Posset, 'St Bernard's Influence', p. 183.
[51]WA TR 3:295, 6–9 (no. 3370 b).
[52]WA TR 1:272, 4–8 (no. 584). See WA TR 5:154, 6 (no. 5439 a).
[53]WA 50:519, 27–31.
[54]WA 50:471, 1–6 (Against the Antinomians).
[55]WA 42:453, 41–454, 1.

et du triple miracle de l'Incarnation, ses réflexions sur la circoncision du Christ ont laissé dans l'oeuvre de Luther des traces visibles, de même que le *fasciculus myrrhae* (Sermon 43 sur le Cantique) largement connu au Moyen Age a été d'une importance décisive pour la dévotion de Luther à la Passion. Vers la fin de sa vie, Luther jugeait ainsi Bernard: 'Il a la meilleure connaissance de la *religio*, comme le montrent ses écrits'.

Bernard is a spiritual and theological advisor for Luther, so to speak, by remote control. Like the humanists of his time, Luther calls him *divus Bernhardus*. He prefers him to the scholastics. He uses especially Bernard's sermons for the feasts of the liturgical year. Bernard's first sermon for the Annunciation is especially important: it contains the theological principle of *sola gratia*. If we are to believe Melanchthon, the young Luther became acquainted with this sermon at Erfurt. It is to this text that Luther refers in his first lecture on the Psalms, and he quotes it abundantly in his lecture on Romans. The bernardine idea of Christ's triple coming and of the triple miracle of the Incarnation, Bernard's reflections on Christ's circumcision, left visible traces in Luther's works, just as the *fasciculus myrrhae* (Sermon 43 on the Song of Songs), widely known in the Middle Ages, was of decisive importance in Luther's devotion to the Passion. Towards the end of his life, Luther judged Bernard as follows: 'He had the best knowledge of *religio*, as his writings show'.

Bernhard ist Luthers geistlicher und theologischer Berater—sozusagen via 'Fernsteuerung'. Luther nennt ihn *divus Bernhardus*, wie die Humanisten seiner Zeit. Er zieht ihn den Scholastikern vor. Insbesondere macht er von Bernhards Predigten zu den Festen des Kirchenjahrs Gebrauch. Von besonderer Bedeutung ist Bernhards erste Predigt zum Fest Mariae Verkündigung, in der das theologische Prinzip der *sola gratia* zu finden ist. Will man Melanchthon glauben, hat der junger Luther diese Predigt bereits in Erfurt kennengelernt. Luther weist wohl auf diese Predigt in seiner ersten Psalmenvorlesung hin und zitiert sie am ausführlichsten in seiner Römerbriefvorlesung. Bernhards Vorstellung vom dreifachen Kommen Christi und vom dreifachen Wunder anläßlich der Menschwerdung sowie seine Ausführungen über die Beschneidung Christi haben nachweislich ihre Spuren in Luthers Werk hinterlassen, ebenso wie der im Mittelalter weit bekannte 'Fasciculus Myrrhae' (Predigt 43 über das Hohelied), welcher wohl von entscheidender Bedeutung für Luthers Passionsfrömmigkeit war. Gegen Ende seines Lebens urteilte Luther über Bernhard: 'Er hat die beste Kenntnis über "religio" wie seine Schriften zeigen'.

BERNARD OF CLAIRVAUX:
A FORERUNNER OF JOHN CALVIN?

A.N.S. Lane
London Bible College

BERNARD OF CLAIRVAUX has been appreciated and appropriated by Christians of many different traditions in the centuries since his death. One of his admirers was the sixteenth-century reformer John Calvin.[1] Calvin's works contain numerous references to four medieval writers.[2] Two of these, Peter Lombard and Gratian, he cited because their works were standard textbooks of the time. Two others, Gregory the Great and Bernard, he cited because of his appreciation of them. Of these, it is Bernard whom Calvin most appreciated.

Calvin regarded Bernard as an exponent of patristic teaching, born out of due time. He would have concurred with Mabillon's description of him as 'the last of the fathers, but by no means inferior to the first'.[3] Calvin appealed to Bernard as a witness to the preservation of true (augustinian) teaching during the Middle Ages.

Calvin cites Bernard forty-one times between 1539 and 1559, that is, for most of his literary career, but Bernard does not appear in his earliest works. By 1536, Calvin had acquired an impressive mastery of the fathers, but it seems that this did not yet extend to Bernard.

---

[1]Much of this essay is taken from the author's 1982 Oxford B.D. thesis, *Calvin's Use of Bernard of Clairvaux*, which is being prepared for publication. Fuller documentation will be found there.

[2]See R. J. Mooi, *Het Kerk- en Dogmahistorisch Element in de Werken van Johannes Calvijn* (Wageningen, 1965) pp. 297–338.

[3]PL 182:26.

533

His knowledge of Bernard and his attitude towards him can be seen by examining when and how he refers to him. In the first edition of his *Institutio*, which appeared in 1536, there is no mention of Bernard. The first mention comes in the second edition of the *Institutio*, which appeared in 1539. Here Bernard is three times briefly cited. It is clear from these citations that Calvin still has little knowledge of Bernard: one of them misrepresents Bernard;[4] another comes in a list of definitions of free will which is also found in a number of earlier writers.[5] Clearly Calvin has borrowed the list from someone else and need not have read Bernard himself. Again, in 1539, in his *Response to Sadolet*, Calvin refers briefly to Bernard's protests against clerical corruption.[6] Only a superficial knowledge of Bernard is necessary to be aware of this, and at this stage Calvin shows no evidence of a deep knowledge of Bernard.

The second stage of Calvin's awareness of Bernard begins with the publication in 1543 of the third edition of his *Institutio*. Here there are eight citations in which Calvin quotes at length from four of Bernard's sermons and from his work *On Consideration*.[7] It is clear that Calvin is by now familiar with Bernard. Bernard is cited extensively and approvingly to support the points being argued by Calvin. Calvin also cites Bernard more briefly in six other works written between 1543 and 1547, mostly drawing from the material which had already appeared in the *Institutio*.

All the bernardine material cited between 1543 and 1547 probably derives from Calvin's reading of Bernard during his years at Strasbourg, between 1538 and 1541. When Calvin returned to Geneva in 1541, he had to sell most of his books. He seems to have left behind the copy of Bernard which he had read at Strasbourg, either because it was not his own or because he had sold it. There are no more citations of Bernard after 1547 until 1554, shortly after the publication of Bernard's complete works at Basel in 1552. There is good evidence for believing that Calvin owned and used this edition.[8]

The third stage of Calvin's use of Bernard extends from 1552 to the final edition of the *Institutio*, which appeared in 1559. During this period Calvin again quotes Bernard extensively and approvingly. As in

---

[4]*Inst.* 2.2.6.

[5]*Inst.* 2.2.4. For the earlier use of these definitions, see A.N.S. Lane, 'Calvin's Sources of St Bernard', *Archiv für Reformationsgeschichte* 67 (1976) 275f. The third citation is from *Inst.* 2.3.5.

[6]P. Barth (ed.), *Johannis Calvini Opera Selecta*, 1 (Munich, 1926) p. 476.

[7]*Inst.* 3.2.25, 3.12.3, 3.13.4, 3.15.2, 4.5.12, 4.7.18 and 22, 4.11.11.

[8]Lane, 'Calvin's Sources', pp. 258f., 264f., 278.

the second stage, Calvin quotes Bernard for support in his anti-roman polemics. But in this third stage a new element appears. Calvin also quotes Bernard on occasions simply because he has expressed something well, in an elegant style. Calvin's humanist training instilled in him a lifelong concern for good style, for expressing the truth clearly and persuasively. In this concern he finds an ally in Bernard.

Calvin shows a broad knowledge of Bernard, quoting from most of his major works. He cites Bernard for support on a variety of topics. These include the bondage of the will, the role of grace, the place of merit, justification by faith, assurance of salvation, predestination, the state of the departed, clerical corruption, and the role of the papacy.

Of all the topics on which Calvin quotes Bernard, justification by faith is perhaps the most interesting, for a number of reasons. In the first place, the doctrine of justification was one of the main points of controversy in the sixteenth century. Many would see it as the crucial point of difference between protestant and catholic. And yet the difference turns out to be less acute than at first appears. A number of the Roman Catholic humanist disciples of Erasmus were sympathetic to the protestant doctrine of justification and wished to see it incorporated into the framework of catholic doctrine. They wanted the Roman Catholic Church to embrace the doctrine, but were not willing to accept the division of the Church which followed from the Protestant Reformation. Some of them, including leading cardinals such as Pole and Contarini, came extremely close to the protestant doctrine of justification.[9] But their view was rejected by the Council of Trent in 1547. At least this was the perception until, in 1957, Hans Küng, in his famous doctoral thesis, argued that Trent is compatible with the protestant doctrine as expounded by Karl Barth.[10] By no means all scholars are convinced by Küng's case,[11] but the important point is that it has met with widespread acceptance within the Roman Catholic Church, and there is a feeling that the protestant doctrine of justification is an important biblical insight rather than a wicked heresy. It is in this setting that various catholic-protestant dialogues on this topic have taken place in the 1980s, in particular the Catholic-Lutheran dialogue and the less satisfactory Catholic-Anglican dialogue

[9]There is debate concerning this point, but this is not the place to enter it.

[10]H. Küng, *Justification: The Doctrine of Karl Barth and a Catholic Reflection* (London, New York, 1964).

[11]For example, A. E. McGrath, 'Justification: Barth, Trent and Küng', *Scottish Journal of Theology* 34 (1981) 517–29.

of ARCIC II.[12] The ARCIC document has been criticized both by an-
glican evangelicals and by Rome, so it is clear that there remains more
work to be done.

Justification is also of interest for another reason. Unlike most of the
other points at issue in the Reformation, the doctrine of justification was
largely undeveloped at the beginning of the sixteenth century. Part of
the confusion surrounding this doctrine arose from the fact that there
was no clearly defined catholic position, which is why leading Catholics
could embrace the protestant doctrine. The specific issues debated had
not received much attention prior to the Reformation. The reformers were
aware of this in their study of the early fathers. Calvin's *Institutio* contains thousands of citations of the early fathers, but these become much
thinner when one turns to the eight chapters on justification by faith. It
is here that Calvin makes one of his rare admissions that Augustine is
not on his side: 'Augustine's view, or at any rate his manner of stating
it, we must not entirely accept.'[13]

In the light of this, there has been debate over the centuries concerning the 'forerunners of the Reformation'. Were there pre-Reformation
figures who held to a protestant doctrine of justification? In earlier,
less historically acute centuries there were protestant theologians who
confidently affirmed that there were. One, for instance, modestly claimed
in 1867 that the protestant doctrine 'was held and taught by some of the
greatest writers in every successive age.'[14] No historically qualified writer
would make any such claim today. The leading evangelical exponent of
the doctrine, Alister McGrath, who has written a masterly two-volume
history of the doctrine, has argued that there are *no* precursors of the
reformation doctrine.[15] But he reaches this conclusion from a study of
the medieval *theologians* and neglects spiritual writers like Bernard. It
is significant that Bernard is, together with Augustine and Ambrose, one
of the writers to whom Calvin appeals for support in this doctrine.

---

[12]H. G. Anderson, T. A. Murphy, and J. A. Burgess (edd.), *Justification by Faith*:
Lutherans and Catholics in Dialogue VII (Minneapolis, 1985); *Salvation and the Church*:
An Agreed Statement by the Second Anglican-Roman Catholic International Commission
ARCIC II (London, 1987).

[13]*Inst.* 3.11.15. Quotations from the *Institutio* are taken from J. T. McNeill and F. L.
Battles (edd.), *Calvin: Institutes of the Christian Religion* (Philadelphia, 1960).

[14]J. Buchanan, *The Doctrine of Justification* (London, 1961) p. 110f.

[15]A. E. McGrath, *Iustitia Dei: A History of the Christian Doctrine of Justification*
(Cambridge, 2 vols., 1986); McGrath, 'Forerunners of the Reformation?: A Critical
Examination of the Evidence for Precursors of the Reformation Doctrines of Jutification',
Harvard Theological Review 75 (1982) 219–42.

What were the points at issue in the controversy over justification? The popular picture of justification by faith versus justification by works is a grotesque caricature. As is well known, the reformers used the words justification and faith in the pauline sense, which differed from that found in the catholic tradition. This caused considerable misunderstanding and has also led some to the false conclusion that the differences were *purely* semantic.

McGrath correctly states that the following three points of protestant doctrine (each of which is clearly found in Calvin) go to the heart of the controversy.[16] First, justification is understood in a 'forensic' or legal sense, as referring to our status before God rather than our state. To be justified means to be reckoned by God as righteous, to be acquitted and declared righteous rather than to be transformed and made righteous.[17] Secondly, and following from this, justification thus understood is deliberately and systematically differentiated from sanctification. Justification refers to our status before God. Sanctification refers to our actual state, to our regeneration and moral transformation.[18] But one misunderstanding needs to be removed. The reformers differentiated between justification and sanctification and saw them as distinct and not to be confused, but they did not *separate* them. They are not the same thing, but they always go together. Calvin likened this to the heat and light of the sun. They are not identical, but they always come together.[19] Thirdly, we are justified or reckoned righteous not because of anything in ourselves but because of the 'alien' or external righteousness of Christ reckoned or imputed to us. This is appropriated by faith alone, not on the basis of our good works.[20]

To these three points we may add a fourth. Another distinctive of the protestant doctrine, which follows from the others, is the assurance of salvation, the conviction that my sins are forgiven, that I am a child of God. This is part of the very definition of saving faith according to Calvin.[21] And yet, according to the Council of Trent, 'no one can know with the certainty of faith, which cannot be subject to error, that he has obtained the grace of God.'[22]

---

[16]McGrath, 'Forerunners', p. 223; *Iustitia Dei* 1:182.
[17]For Calvin, see *Inst.* 3.11.1f.
[18]For Calvin, see *Inst.* 3.3.1, 3.11.1 and 5f.
[19]*Inst.* 3.11.6; see 3.16.1.
[20]For Calvin, see *Inst.* 3.11.13–23.
[21]*Inst.* 3.2.7.
[22]*Decree on Justification*, 9, in J. Leith, *Creeds of the Churches* (2nd ed., Atlanta, 1973) p. 414. See ch. 12, can. 13–16.

Are these distinctive features of protestant doctrine to be found before the time of the reformation? Alister McGrath argues that they are not. His case is broadly correct, but suffers from its neglect of spiritual writers such as Bernard. An examination of Bernard's teaching reveals not that it was consistently protestant, but that it contains elements which prefigure all of the above points. This shows that, while the explicit statement of the protestant doctrine of justification *was* a novelty in the sixteenth century, the elements that made it up were not without precedent.

First, the forensic understanding of 'justify' as meaning to acquit or reckon righteous rather than to make righteous. Augustine considered the former meaning and rejected it in favor of the latter.[23] For this reason, medieval theologians understood 'justify' to mean 'make righteous'. Bernard uses it in this augustinian sense, but occasionally he appears also to understand it in the forensic, pauline sense: 'Therefore wherever there is reconciliation, there is remission of sins. And what is this except justification?'[24] And again: 'If he accuses me, I shall not accuse him back, but rather justify him.'[25]

Secondly, the distinction between justification and sanctification. It is true that Bernard does not make a consistent distinction between them. But does this mean that there is *no* distinction between them in his thought? This does not follow. It can be said that anyone who believes in the forgiveness of sins thereby makes a distinction between justification and sanctification, at least implicitly. If my sins are forgiven, it means that there is a difference between what I am (guilty) and how God views me (forgiven). The protestant distinction between justification and sanctification is simply the formal development of this implicit distinction. But Bernard also goes beyond a merely implicit distinction. In one of his Dedication sermons he contrasts at length our true state with God's estimate of us.[26] This is in effect a differentiation between sanctification and justification.

Thirdly, on what basis are we reckoned righteous? There are some passages in Bernard which support the protestant understanding. First, Bernard warns against relying on one's own merit. In his treatise *On*

---

[23]*On the Spirit and the Letter* 26.45; see McGrath, *Iustitia Dei* 1:30f.
[24]Abael 8.20; SBOp 8:34. Translations of Bernard are my own except where indicated.
[25]SC 83.4; SBOp 2:301.
[26]Ded 5.2–8; SBOp 5:389–95. See R. Thomas 'Le Sermon V de saint Bernard pour la Dédicace', Coll. 50 (1988) 239, where it is argued that ultimately the sermon has a single theme, 'faire pénétrer profondément la conviction que nous ne sommes rien, vraiment rien du tout, rien que misère, et que, dans le même temps, nous sommes grands, par pure faveur divine.'

Grace and Free Choice, he argues that God rewards our merits. The merit for which reward is promised is the merit of cooperation, of freely consenting to grace. Not that we can boast of our merit as if it were our own achievement. Our merits are God's gifts; they are the fruit of God's grace. Like Augustine, Bernard holds to a doctrine of merit while ultimately referring all to the sole operation of grace. This teaching is reiterated in Bernard's sermons, but with the addition of a new element. In the sermons we are told not just that our merits are God's gifts but also that we are not to rely on these merits. Bernard repeatedly cites the parable of the pharisee and the publican[27] and also Luke 17:10.[28] 'Human merits are not such that on account of them eternal life is owed to us *ex iure*, or that God would do us an injury if he did not bestow it.'[29] As our merit is insufficient, we should put our trust in God's mercy, in the passion of Christ.[30] If, as the Jews, we approach him on the basis of justice, on the basis of our own righteousness, he will deal with us on the basis of justice and give us our just condemnation. If, on the other hand, we approach him on the basis of mercy, conscious of our sin and need of mercy, he will accept us in his mercy.[31] To trust in our own merits rather than in God is dangerous and leads to ruin.[32] The sermons go beyond, not against, the teaching of the treatise in warning against trust in merit and pointing to another ground of confidence independent of human merit: the mercy of God.

In addition to warning against reliance on our own merits, Bernard twice states that justification is by faith alone:

Wherefore, let whoever feels remorse for his sins and hungers and thirsts after righteousness believe in you who justify the ungodly and, being justified by faith alone, he shall have peace with God.[33]

He who will not have believed will be condemned, [Mark] says, doubtless implying that faith alone sometimes suffices for salvation, and that without faith nothing suffices.[34]

---

[27]Thirteen times, with fourteen further allusions.
[28]Seventeen times, with four further allusions.
[29]Ann 1.2 (SBOp 5:14); see SC 85.14 (SBOp 2:316).
[30]SC 14.1 (SBOp 1:75f.); SC 22.8 and 11 (SBOp 1:133–35 and 137); SC 43.1–4 (SBOp 2:41–43); SC 50.2 (SBOp 2:79); SC 60.4f. (SBOp 2:143–45); SC 67.11 (SBOp 2:195); SC 68.6f. (SBOp 2:200f.); SC 73.4 (SBOp 2:235f.); *et al.*
[31]SC 14.1; SBOp 1:75f.
[32]QH 1.1 and 3; SBOp 4:385–88.
[33]SC 22.8; SBOp 1:134.
[34]Bapt 2.8; SBOp 7:190.

But what did Bernard mean by this? Cardinal Bellarmine was right to argue from the context that Bernard meant a 'living faith which is joined together with love'.[35] But the reformers never imagined that saving faith could exist *without* love—they merely insisted that love was not the *ground* of justification. 'It is therefore faith alone which justifies, and yet the faith which justifies is not alone', as Calvin put it.[36] It should however be noted that, while Bernard can talk of justification by faith alone, he can also talk of justification by love[37] or humility[38] or confession of sins.[39] His teaching on this point is not consistent.

Bernard comes closest to Calvin's doctrine of justification not when he actually uses the word but when he speaks of imputation. He repeatedly refers to the non-imputation of sins. But this was a commonplace of the medieval tradition. More significant is his teaching about the imputation of reckoning to us of Christ's righteousness: 'Shall Adam's sin be imputed to me and Christ's righteousness not belong to me?'[40] There is no true righteousness save from Christ's mercy.[41] Our righteousness is inadequate, but his passion is our refuge and remedy.[42] Christ's righteousness suffices for me as well as for him.[43] This comes most fully in Bernard's response to Abelard:

> What could man, the slave of sin, fast bound by the devil, do of himself to recover the righteousness which he had once lost? Therefore another's righteousness was ascribed to him who lacked his own. . . .If one died for all, then all have died, so that, just as one bore the sins of all, the satisfaction of one is imputed to all. . . .Why should I not have someone else's righteousness since I have someone else's guilt? It was someone else who made me a sinner, it is someone else who justifies me from sin: the one through his seed, the other through his blood. Shall there be sin in the seed of a sinner and not righteousness in the blood of Christ?[44]

[35]R. Bellarmine, *De justificatione* 1.25.
[36]*Canons and Decrees of the Council of Trent, with the Antidote*, in H. Beveridge (ed.), *John Calvin, Tracts*, 3 (Edinburgh, 1851) p. 152. See *Inst.* 3.16.1.
[37]Ep 107.4f; SBOp 7:270f.
[38]SC 34.3; SBOp 1:247.
[39]SC 16.12 (SBOp 1:96); SC 22.9 (SBOp 1:135f.); SC 56.7 (SBOp 2:118f.).
[40]Tpl 11.23; SBOp 3:233.
[41]SC 22.11; SBOp 1:137.
[42]SC 22.8; SBOp 1:134f.
[43]SC 61.5; SBOp 2:151.
[44]Abael 6.15f; SBOp 8:29f.

Bernard's teaching here is closely related to his view of the cross: 'Death has been put to flight in the death of Christ, and Christ's righteousness is imputed to us.'[45] His passion is our ultimate refuge, so if we lack merits we can always rest on the sufferings of Christ.[46] The satisfaction of one is imputed to all, as that one bore the sins of all.[47] Christ's passion brings us forgiveness of sins, righteousness, and justification.[48]

Finally, an interesting incident is noted in the first *Life* of Bernard. Bernard was at death's door, and the devil was accusing him of his sins. Bernard's reported reply is significant:

> I admit that I am myself neither worthy nor able to obtain the kingdom of heaven by my own merits. But my Lord has obtained it by a double right: by inheritance from the Father and by the merit of his passion. Being content with the former, he gives the latter right to me. I claim it for myself on the basis of his gift and so will not be put to confusion.[49]

This last quotation illustrates the important point that here is not just a theoretical doctrinal question. At issue is our attitude to our own righteousness, our continuing need for the mercy of God right up to the Last Judgement, and the proper object of our trust. This probably explains why precedent for the protestant doctrine is to be found in a spiritual writer like Bernard rather than in the scholastic theologians.

It is noteworthy that Bernard's support for the first point of protestant doctrine (the forensic definition of justification) is minimal, his support for the second point (the distinction between justification and sanctification) is slight, while his support for the third point (the imputation to us of Christ's righteousness) is substantial. What should one make of this? In many ways the first two points are more a matter of terminology and definition while the third goes to the heart of the matter. Clarity on the first two is necessary in order to express the third in a fully clear and consistent manner. Bernard's lack of clarity on the first two coheres well with the way in which he can hold to the substance of the third, but alongside other views which appear to be incompatible with it.

If the first two points provide the conceptual framework for the clear formulation of the third, then the fourth point (assurance of salvation) can

---

[45]Tpl 11.22; SBOp 3:232.
[46]SC 22.8 (SBOp 1:134f.); SC 43.1–3 (SBOp 2:41–43).
[47]Abael 6.15; SBOp 8:29f.
[48]SC 2.8 (SBOp 1:13); SC 71.11 (SBOp 2:222); IV HM 4 (SBOp 5:58); Abael 7.17, 8.20 (SBOp 8:32 and 34).
[49]*Vita prima* 1.12.57.

be said to follow from it. This is true for Calvin, whose very definition of saving faith includes assurance of salvation:

> Now we shall possess a right definition of faith if we call it a firm and certain knowledge of God's benevolence toward us, founded on the truth of the freely given promise in Christ, both revealed to our minds and sealed upon our hearts through the Holy Spirit.[50]

For Calvin, saving faith includes confidence or assurance of future salvation. Since faith reposes in Christ alone, there is no room for uncertainty. Since the promise of the gospel includes *final* salvation, this confidence extends to the future. Calvin cites Bernard for support on this matter. With how much justice? Bernard speaks of the possibility of knowing that we are sons of God.[51] Sometimes he goes even further and speaks of this assurance as not merely possible but even essential. When we confess our sins we must do so not doubting that they are pardoned.[52] We must not merely believe that God can forgive our sins, we must also believe that he does pardon them. If we are to attain eternal life, we need the testimony of the Holy Spirit that we will attain to it.[53]

Despite this teaching, Bernard elsewhere states that we can have no certainty. Signs of our election are given to us, but these lead us to rejoice in hope rather than in security.[54] There can be signs and testimonies of predestination, but no certainty.[55] Bernard's concept of assurance is limited by the fact that no one can know whether or not he will persevere to the end. But his teaching even here is a little confusing. He can speak of assurance of *final* salvation.[56] But this is in hope, not yet a certainty.[57] There seem to be residual ambiguities, if not contradictions, in Bernard's teaching, but a general pattern emerges. He teaches the possibility, sometimes even the necessity, of assurance of present forgiveness of sins. This evidence of present calling and justification is a ground for hope concerning the future, but not for certainty since perseverance to the end is not guaranteed. This teaching comes out clearly in one passage:

---

[50]*Inst.* 3.2.7. See A.N.S. Lane, 'Calvin's Doctrine of Assurance', *Vox Evangelica* 11 (1979) 32–54.

[51]Ded 5.7 (SBOp 4:183); Adv 4.2 (SBOp 5:13f.); Ann 1.1 (SBOp 5:344f.); OS 2.3 (SBOp 5:393f.).

[52]SC 16.12; SBOp 1:96.

[53]Ann 1.3; SBOp 5:14f.

[54]Sept 1.1; SBOp 4:345.

[55]Sept 1.1 (SBOp 4:345); O Pasc 2.3 (SBOp 5:119); Ep 107.10 (SBOp 7:274).

[56]Ann 1.3 (SBOp 5:14f.); Ep 107.5, 7, 9 (SBOp 7:270–74).

[57]Ep 107.10; SBOp 7:274.

Who can say, 'I belong to the elect; I am one of those predestined to life; I am of the number of God's children'? Who, I ask, can say this, in the face of the Scripture: 'Man does not know whether he is worthy of love or hatred'? We cannot have certitude. But still the confidence of hope comforts us, lest otherwise the anxiety occasioned by this doubt should become an insufferable torment. Accordingly, we are given certain signs and manifest indications of salvation. It is indubitable that he, in whom they remain, is of the number of the elect. For this reason I say, 'whom God foreknew, he also predestined to be made conformable to the image of his son', in order to give at least the consolation of hope to them from whom—lest they should grow solicitous—he withholds certitude. Hence it is that we are kept always in a state of anxiety, and in fear and trembling have to humble ourselves under the mighty hand of God. For whereas we can know, at least in part, what we are now, what we shall become hereafter it is entirely beyond our power to discern. 'Wherefore, he that thinks that he stands, let him take heed lest he fall'; and let him continue steadfast, yea and make progress in that manner of life which is a sign of salvation and an evidence of predestination.[58]

What follows from all of this? That Bernard's doctrine of justification was protestant? No. Bernard lived before the sixteenth-century controversies, and so it is wrong to expect him to have given consistent answers to questions that had not yet been raised. But there is a strand of his teaching which clearly prefigures the distinctive features of the protestant doctrine noted above. This is to be seen in the debates at the Council of Trent. As has already been stated, there were cardinals and bishops at Trent who did not wish to see the protestant doctrine of justification condemned. They wanted it to be integrated into the framework of catholic theology. These delegates at Trent appealed to Bernard and indeed quoted some of the same passages as did Calvin.[59] They too saw a doctrine of imputed righteousness in Bernard.

What is the significance of all this for today? As has been noted, there has been a radical change of attitude in catholic theology towards the doctrine of justification by faith. During the course of this century Luther's doctrine of justification has changed from being a wicked cloak

---

[58]Sept 1.1 (A. J. Luddy translation); SBOp 4:345.
[59]*Concilium Tridentinum*, ed. Societas Goerresiana (Freiburg, 1901–1976), 5.355, 353, 374, 562; 12.620, 634, 703.

of sin to being a sincere but misguided attempt to resolve his spiritual problems to being a biblical insight. But how can the doctrine be integrated into catholic thought, given its relative absence from the tradition? This is where there is value in a study of Bernard and of those catholic theologians in the sixteenth century who followed him. Bernard can be a meeting ground for catholic-protestant dialogue on this subject.

ABSTRACTS

Tout au long de sa carrière littéraire, Calvin n'a cessé de renvoyer, à propos de nombre de questions, aux écrits de Bernard de Clairvaux. La sage de Genève va jusqu'à revendiquer Bernard comme précurseur (au moins dans une certaine mesure) de la doctrine réformée de la justification. Une telle filiation doctrinale est-elle fondée? En effet, il y a un aspect de l'enseignement de l'abbé cistercien qui préfigure en quelque sort la doctrine protestante, surtout en ce qui concerne l'imputation de la justice du Christ. La chose a été reconnue au XVIe siècle, avant et après le concile de Trente, par les théologiens catholiques qui sympathisaient avec la doctrine protestante de la justification. Leur tentatives de conciliation échouèrent, mais le climat est aujourd'hui différent. Bernard peut offrir un terrain de rencontre pour catholiques et protestants sur ce sujet.

Calvin quoted Bernard many times throughout most of his literary career, on a variety of topics. These include the doctrine of justification, the subject of ecumenical dialogue in Calvin's time and in our own. Calvin claims Bernard as, at least in part, a forerunner of the Reformation doctrine. But how fair is this? There is a strand of Bernard's teaching which prefigures the protestant doctrine, especially concerning the imputation of Christ's righteousness. This was recognised in the sixteenth century by those Roman Catholic theologians, before and at the Council of Trent, who were sympathetic to the protestant doctrine of justification. Their attempts at conciliation failed, but today the climate is different. Bernard can be a meeting ground for Catholic-Protestant dialogue on this subject.

In Laufe seiner literarischen Laufbahn zitierte Calvin Bernhard viele Male zu einer Vielzahl von Themen, einschließlich der Rechtfertigungslehre, die Gegenstand ökumenischer Gespräche zu Zeiten Calvins wie in unserer eigenen Zeit war und ist. Calvin nennt Bernhard zumindest teilweise einen Vorläufer der reformatorischen Lehre. Aber inwieweit ist das gerechtfertigt? Es gibt einen Strang in Bernhards Lehre, der die protestantische Lehre vorzeichnet, speziell in Bezug auf die Zurechnung der Rechtschaffenheit Christi. Dies wurde im 16. Jh. von jenen römisch-katholischen Theologen vor und während des Konzils von Trient anerkannt, die mit der protestantischen Lehre von der Rechtfertigung sympathisierten. Ihre Versöhnungsversuche scheiterten, aber heute ist das Klima anders. Bernhard kann eine gemeinsame Grundlage für den katholisch-protestantischen Dialog zu diesem Thema sein.

BERNARD AND RANCÉ

A. J. Krailsheimer
Oxford University

THE DECEPTIVELY INNOCENT 'and' in such titles as this is in fact loaded with every kind of positive and negative charge, and since neither Bernard nor Rancé is a figure to inspire indifference, it would be disingenuous to claim objectivity in approaching the two of them together. Of the various possibilities created by my allotted title, one I rejected straightaway: a direct comparison between the two men would require far more specialist knowledge of Bernard than I possess and would inevitably lead to value judgements which would be of use to no one. Still less do I want to get involved in the sort of discussion which reads history backwards from the Trappists of today through Dom Lestrange to Rancé's la Trappe in an attempt to identify Bernard's 'true' heirs, as against others presumed to be less true. The purpose of this paper is much simpler: how did Rancé see Bernard, how well did he know his writings, what did he make of him, and what conclusions do the answers to these questions invite?

Chronology is an elementary, but vital, consideration. Rancé's cistercian life extended from 1663, when he entered the novitiate, until 1700, when he died; in the course of that time Mabillon's edition of Bernard appeared and soon became standard. Some 500 years separate Bernard's death from Rancé's entry into the order, and another 500 years lie between Bernard and John Climachus, Rancé's revered monastic authority on penitence. Clearly, there must be a sense in which time is irrelevant in appreciating the spiritual teachings of men and women concerned with eternal truths, as revealed in the Bible, and a life detached from material preoccupations, or at least from materialism, and, in that sense, Climachus, Bernard, and Rancé do not span a thousand years but a single moment. None the less, the seventeenth century in France, the Age of Classicism, consciously looked on the past, or selected aspects of the past, in a way that we have to learn as we would an alien tongue. 'Modern' was not always a term of approval, any more than 'gothic' (as in Goths and Vandals), invented by the Renaissance, remained one of contempt.

The 'classic' mentality believed in the *universal* values of truth and beauty, exemplified in greek and roman antiquity, recovered in the Renaissance and imitated thereafter. *Authority* was an essential part of the doctrine, and matched in the political domain the stabilizing and centralizing policy of Richelieu and then the fifty years of Louis XIV's personal exercise of absolute rule. Authority, in the sense of precedent, was the only effective defense against charges of innovation or singularity, but it was an argument that all respected. It is therefore obvious that while scientific and cultural changes prevented stasis and stagnation, fidelity to the past could be a condition of survival. In those circumstances, no Cistercian bent on a more primitive version of the *Rule* and *Usages*—or a stricter one—than that commonly observed could fail to use Bernard as *the* authority within the order. Toward the end of *De la Sainteté*, Rancé tells his brethren: 'Saint Bernard, who should by himself have more authority for you than a thousand others.'[1]

It is no doubt unjust to the three founding Fathers, but 'bernardin' had long been the name by which Cistercians were generally known, and the importance of the first Clairvaux as an example and ideal was equally widespread. There was an 'image' of Bernard and his life to which constant reference was made—in sermons, for example—and which was popular in a sense that his works could never be. In Rancé's only extant sermon for the feast of Saint Bernard, he takes for his text the verse from Psalm 4:4, *Mirificavit Dominus sanctum suum*, and illustrates it with a range of examples: Bernard's public campaigns against schism, when he dealt with kings and great feudal lords as equals; against heresy, Abelard, Gilbert de la Porrée, and the Cathars; his own detachment from the world and foundation of scores of monasteries where men could follow the call to a life of penitence; his mortification of spirit and

---

[1]References are to the first, 1683, edition of *De la Sainteté*, 2:541; 'S. Bernard, qui doit avoir tout seul auprès de vous plus d'autorité que mille autres.'

senses; his humility.[2] This seems to have been the standard portrait in the seventeenth century, and Bossuet, for instance, in his sermon on Saint Bernard, which antedates his close friendship with Rancé, takes a very similar line.[3] It is noteworthy that the sentimental legends of the later Middle Ages, in particular of the lactation, are not found in either Bossuet or Rancé; they had too much respect for *bienséance*.

In an inevitably idealized way, treatment of Bernard's personality and activity, what I have just called the image, is recognizably distinct from appeals to his authority based on quotation from his work. It is worth stressing at the outset that, for Rancé, Bernard the man and Bernard the authority were inseparable, but their influence is manifested in different ways and different contexts. In Rancé's principal work, *De la Sainteté et des Devoirs de la Vie monastique*, the argument on which all else is based is that the principles of monastic life were laid down by Our Lord himself to the Apostles and that, at the end of the age of persecution, martyrs were replaced by 'solitaries', whose sacrifice was no less complete for being less spectacular and more protracted. The gradual organization of monastic life and the promulgation of rules stands in unbroken continuity and is the work of saints, faithful interpreters of God's will, and not mere compilers of codes for legalistic reasons or motives of convenience. Antiquity thus became, with sanctity, a major criterion for monastic practice; one may compare the imposition of rules supposedly drawn from Aristotle's *Poetics* on seventeenth-century dramatists. These rather obvious facts are reflected directly in the frequency of quotations from particular authorities in *De la Sainteté*; as a further index of importance the aggregate length of quotations is also significant.[4] Bernard comes easily first, with 125 references (twenty-five pages), followed by Benedict, with about 100, and Basil, about the same (twenty-one pages); Climachus with about seventy-five (eleven pages) precedes Augustine and Cassian with about fifty each. No other authority is quoted more than thirty times.

The importance of Benedict and Basil in monastic history is self-evident, but Bernard's primacy demonstrates the specifically cistercian view of monastic life with which Rancé sought to be identified. His book was not meant as a prospectus for the future, but as a report, a defense

---

[2]*Conférences ou Instructions sur les épîtres et évangiles. . .* (2nd ed., Paris: Delaune, 1720) 4:259–99.

[3]J.-B. Bossuet, *Oraisons funèbres, Panégyriques* (Paris: éds de la Pléiade, 1936) pp. 287–314. The sermon was preached at Metz on 20 August 1653.

[4]The two volumes of *De la Sainteté* together comprise rather less than one thousand pages, of twenty-nine lines per page on average.

of a program dismissed as chimerical when first submitted in 1663 to the authorities of the Strict Observance, but twenty years later justified by results. The message is plain: Bernard is *the* authority for the life led at la Trappe, and, though that life falls short of its ideal of perfection, it is neither chimerical nor in any way incompatible with the tradition inaugurated by Bernard at Clairvaux.

The fact of Bernard's authority needs more precise definition if Rancé's knowledge and use of the saint's works is to be properly assessed. For example, it comes as no surprise to find that the fairly brief treatise *De precepto* is mentioned twenty-six times, half of them in Rancé's final, and most provocative, chapter on *Mitigations*, but it would be surprising were it otherwise. More interesting, and more significant, is the range of quotations from other works of Bernard. No fewer than fifty-one quotations from thirty-five *Epistolae*, twenty-six from twenty-one *Sermons*, and nine from other works (*De consideratione* and the *Apologia* three each), to which must be added quotations from the *Vita prima* and letters of Fastrède quoting Bernard. There are several examples of repeated quotations, up to three times, but the text to which Rancé returns most often (five times) is *Epistola 1* to Bernard's nephew Robert, followed by *Epistola 2* to Foulques, used four times. The theme of desertion clearly looms large in Rancé's eyes, and when the motive in two religious as dear to Bernard as these two is—or is stated to be—a preference for comfort and advancement over the hard way of the Cross, the implication for Rancé is all too obvious.

The book *De la Sainteté* demonstrates convincingly that Rancé had an extensive knowledge of Bernard's writings, especially of his letters, and that he was at great pains to justify every contentious aspect of his own teaching and monastic practice by specific reference to those of Bernard. The profusion of authorities cited, the very fact of marginal references to catch the eye, emphasize the formal nature of the case Rancé was presenting. To that extent the spontaneity of Rancé's resort to Bernard, and the others, is prejudged. This is not at all the case in Rancé's own letters, some 2,000 of which survive for a period covering some sixty years in all, and from which some complementary conclusions can be drawn.[5]

---

[5]An edition of Rancé's letters in French is announced for 1992, in four volumes. Apart from a few additions and corrections, reference numbers in this french edition are the same as those in the (partial) english translation published by Cistercian Publications in 1984, and are used throughout this paper to identify letters.

In letters, all but a handful dictated, usually in a hurry, quotations from memory, and thus often inexact, are only to be expected. A complication arises from not immediately identifiable translations, paraphrases, or simply allusions to a text without a name. Thus the statistical findings are far from exhaustive—and this of course applies equally to Bernard and to other authors—but are none the less informative. There are at least twenty-three textual citations plus about the same number again of references to Bernard by name, often implying a quotation, making about fifty identifiable references. Compare this figure with about twenty-three to Benedict and his *Rule* (a frequent topic of discussion with correspondents), twelve each to Augustine and Basil, and seven to Climachus. Scattered so widely through letters which were not intended for publication (and only about a quarter of which have in fact ever been published to date), these relative figures tell us more about Rancé's natural choice of authority than those relating to a carefully edited book on monastic life.

A closer look at the figures suggests a line of inquiry which would repay systematic study. Fifteen of the textual quotations come from twelve of the *Epistolae*, five from various *Sermons*, two from *De precepto*, and one from the *Apologia*. Add to this a quotation from Bernard preserved in a letter by Fastrède, and lengthy translated extracts from the *Vita prima*, amounting to about three pages in all in a single letter, and a picture begins to emerge. *Epistola 2*, incidentally, quoted directly three times, is once again one that clearly impressed Rancé, himself a former archdeacon appointed by his episcopal uncle. Compared with the more concentrated deployment of quotation in *De la Saintetè*, the spread of texts is still wide, and four of the *Epistolae* plus three *Sermons* quoted in Rancé's letters are additional to those quoted in the book, giving a total in the two sources combined of *at least* forty-three *Epistolae* and twenty-three *Sermons* of Bernard.

Inadequate as these statistics are, they show that Rancé had a wide and sound knowledge of Bernard's writings, with an unmistakable preference for the letters. The answers, then, to our first two questions are that Rancé saw Bernard as a saint, active, when called on, in public life and fearless in his dealings with leaders in Church and state, but above all as the man who transformed the modest enterprise of the first Fathers of Cîteaux into an international order, inspired by the ideal realized and lived out at Clairvaux by an abbot and community who imparted new vigor to the benedictine tradition and decisively challenged the monastic values represented by Cluny. In Bernard, Rancé saw an authority and model for any cistercian reform movement which sought to recover the original spirit of Cîteaux. In *De la Sainteté* and subsequent works published in further support of the observance practiced at la Trappe, this is, as one might expect, how Rancé saw Bernard and used him. In Rancé's letters, however, this impression is considerably filled out, and a much closer personal link between the two men begins to appear. As a matter of record, the earliest quotation from Bernard in Rancé's letters comes in a letter of 1661 to his old tutor, Favier, a commendatory abbot like Rancé himself at the time, and concerns the rights and duties of those who derive income from church benefices.[6] The quotation most likely comes at second hand from some compilation dealing with benefices, and cannot be assumed at that date to prove that Rancé was already well acquainted with Bernard. The same quotation is repeated in a letter on the same subject in 1669, to Le Roy, jansenist commendatory abbot of Hautefontaine.

A quite different note is struck in a letter written from Rome to the monks at la Trappe, whom Rancé had not seen for nearly a year, after being with them for barely two months as abbot.[7] Written on the feast of Saint Bernard, this letter quotes verbatim from Bernard (*Epistola 144*) to the effect that he sorely misses his brethren, and again (*Epistola 107*) by way of spiritual encouragement. The much more intimate echo of Bernard, in a letter dating from a frustrating and depressing period of Rancé's life, sounds like a conscious attempt to follow in the saint's footsteps as abbot, and is surely based on serious reading of Bernard's works, especially his letters. In fact, from the summer of 1662, when Rancé stayed at la Trappe (as commendatory abbot) with the reforming monks sent from Perseigne, it is very likely that he began seriously to study Bernard, and, from the date of his entry into the novitiate at Perseigne in May 1663, such reading is certain. Given Rancé's personal distinction, social and intellectual, given the fact that he had never been a member of a regular community under an abbot, and given, moreover, that his conversion led him to regard even the leaders of the contemporary Strict Observance as falling short of his own ideal, one can readily understand that no other model than Bernard was possible

[6]61408, to Favier: 'Quidquid praeter necessarium victum ac simplicem vestitum de altario retines. . . sacrilegium est.' Ep 2, 11, repeated in 69/1 to Le Roy. By 1669, Rancé had, of course, become regular abbot of la Trappe.

[7]650820. Text in L. Dubois, *Histoire de l'abbé de Rancé* (Paris: Bray, 1866) 1:305–307.

in the day to day conduct of a community starting, like la Trappe, from scratch. This implied master-disciple relationship enriched the already systematic acquaintance with Bernard underlying the reformers' case as presented in Rome by Rancé and his fellow delegate. Julien Paris, abbot of Foucarmont, had, in his book *Le Premier Esprit de Cîteaux*, provided a detailed brief, drawing on Bernard in particular,[8] but, in preparing this brief, or even before, Rancé seems to have tried to compensate for his own lack of experience as superior by identifying with the Bernard revealed in the letters.

Just a few months before Rancé wrote to his monks, Bossuet, a theology graduate in the same year as Rancé but not yet his close friend, was pronouncing his second extant panegyric on Saint Benedict.[9] He praised the saint as an example of obedience, and asks the question: 'How did Saint Benedict practice this obedience, he who was always a superior?' and answers: 'When, in spite of his humility, he accepted the position of superior, . . . when he allowed himself to be compelled by charity to leave the peace of his retreat, . . . when he exercised his authority. . . .' Rancé too was always a superior and very sensitive on the score of obedience. It is perhaps for that reason that he always treated criticism of his chosen authorities, especially Bernard and Climachus, as barely short of blasphemy.

Thus, early in 1670, when some nuns of the cistercian abbey of Saint-Antoine in Paris (including cousins of Rancé), tried to secure the more faithful implementation of the brief *In suprema* (1666) in their abbey, they appealed to Rancé for support. Their abbess accused them of insubordination, and she (or her adviser) quoted Bernard on the duty owed by religious to obey their superior in all things. In his reply, Rancé pointed out in the strongest terms, and with ample references, that, in *Epistola 7* to Adam, Bernard had in fact said exactly the opposite, using arguments which fully justified the reforming nuns' refusal to compromise their conscience.[10]

Similarly, a little later, he supported the abbess of Leyme in her attempt to reform her house in accordance with the brief, and bitterly complained that her visitor and other superiors of the Common Observance

---

[8]First edition, 1653; enlarged editions 1664 and 1670.

[9]J.-B. Bossuet, p. 611; sermon preached 21 March 1665: 'Comment est-ce que saint Benoît a pratiqué cette obéissance, lui qui a toujours gouverné? . . . Lorsque, malgré son humilité, il a accepté le commandement . . . lorsqu'il s'est laissé former par la charité à quitter la paix de sa retraite . . . lorsqu'il a exercé son autorité.'

[10]720607.

had twisted Bernard's words to justify themselves: 'They abuse the saints' authority and make them say out of context what they never said or thought.'[11] There then follows a series of lengthy quotations translated from the *Vita prima* to prove that Clairvaux under Bernard's rule was a 'monastery of saints... so submissive to all the views of that great man that there was nothing of which they were less capable than the slightest opposition to his wishes.' The exceptional length and sustained passion of the letter offer convincing proof of Rancé's reverence for Bernard and, implicitly, of the monastic ideal he had before his eyes in his own conduct of the monks of la Trappe.

It appears that Rancé had earned a certain reputation for his reverence for Bernard and knowledge of his work, for, in 1682, Mabillon himself consulted Rancé on the vexed question of Bernard's use of the vernacular in sermons and also on a problem of authenticity. This, of course, was before the publication of *De la Sainteté* and the resultant polemic over monastic studies. If Mabillon's consultation can hardly be ignored as a tactful tribute to Rancé's knowledge, it need not be taken as an endorsement of his judgement.[12]

The conclusions are obvious enough. As a cistercian abbot, Rancé steeped himself in Bernard's writings, particularly the *Epistolae*, and inevitably saw to it that his monks did the same in their *lectio divina*; he took Bernard as his model and justification for the reformed life at la Trappe and fiercely defended Bernard's authority against distortion and attack. Bernard's unique felicity of style cannot have failed to register with the excellent latinist that Rancé was, but, even if Rancé had been capable of similar literary virtuosity, neither the conventions of the seventeenth century nor his own austere temperament encouraged the attempt. Lekai aptly remarks of Rancé's mission to Rome in 1664–1666: 'He instinctively assumed the role of a second St Bernard at the Curia, and tried to give the cardinals of the special congregation lessons in monastic spirituality and reform, though he had made his own monastic profession only a few months before leaving for Rome.'[13] Despite the

---

[11]780307: 'Ils ne manquent pas même de se servir et de l'exemple et des écrits de saint Bernard pour faire croire aux simples que leurs voies sont droites, et qu'ils marchent dans le chemin de la vérité. Cependant ils se mécomptent en tout, ils abusent de l'autorité des saints, et leur font dire mal à propos tout ce qu'ils n'ont jamais dit ni pensé.' This letter also quotes from QH 4 and Ded 3.

[12]For Rancé's answer, see 820830, published by Jean Leclercq in *Revue Mabillon* 45 (1955) 29–35.

[13]Louis J. Lekai, *The Cistercians: Ideals and Reality* ([Kent, Ohio]: The Kent State University Press, [1977]) p. 147.

ironic tone of the distinguished historian, I do not wish to disagree, but when he concludes a little later: 'To some extent the heroic spirit of the first Cistercians had resurged at la Trappe, but for the wonderful vibrancy of St Bernard's contemplative spirit, Rancé substituted the gloom of contemporary rigorism,'[14] the word 'gloom' and indeed the implications of the clearly pejorative word 'rigorism', here defined as contrary to Bernard, do not command my assent. Rancé himself observed extreme reticence with regard to the expression of emotions that classical *bienséance* demanded, and the argument from silence is, in his case, quite unreliable. His constant and enthusiastic reference to Bernard, his insistence that his monks should look to Clairvaux under the saint as their model, and his exhortation to other monks and nuns of the order to do the same, sufficiently witness to his fidelity to the saint. This is not to deny that the Desert Fathers, above all Climachus, misunderstood as they may have been, are at the root of Rancé's post-conversion spirituality, but it is hard to think of any abbot or community in the order by whom Bernard was more honored, studied, and, according to their lights, followed than by Rancé and la Trappe—even after Rancé's death.

ABSTRACTS

En tant que produit de l'époque classique française Rancé se devait de justifier ses idées monastiques controversées en faisant appel à une autorité reconnue. La sainteté personnelle de Bernard et son rôle unique d'influence dans l'histoire cistercienne faisait de lui un choix évident. Dans son principal ouvrage, *De la Sainteté...*, Rancé cite Bernard plus que toute autre autorité, en recourant à un large éventail de ses écrits, mais en marquant une nette préférence pour les *Epistolae*. Dans les lettres de Rancé lui-même, source plus privée et spontanée, Bernard arrive de nouveau en premier, avec également une préférence pour les *Epistolae*. Rancé manifeste une connaissance profonde et étendue des écrits de Bernard, mais l'accent mis sur les *Epistolae* suggère une tentative pour suivre Bernard comme personne et non uniquement comme autorité. La spiritualité des Pères du Désert avait pour Rancé une importance vitale, mais l'autorité de Bernard était suprême à la Trappe et Rancé présentait constamment l'exemple de Clairvaux sous le gouvernement du saint comme idéal pour sa propre communauté (et pour d'autres).

[14]Lekai, p. 151.

As a product of the French Classical Age Rancé needed to justify his controversial monastic ideas by appealing to a recognised authority. Bernard's personal sanctity and uniquely influential role in cistercian history made him the obvious choice. In his principal work, *De la Sainteté*..., Rancé quotes Bernard more than any other authority, using a wide range of his writings, but with a clear preference for the *Epistolae*. Rancé reveals deep and extensive knowledge of Bernard's writings, but the emphasis on the *Epistolae* suggests an attempt to follow Bernard as a person and not just as an authority. The spirituality of the Desert Fathers was vital to Rancé, but the authority of Bernard was supreme at la Trappe and Rancé constantly held out the example of Clairvaux under the saint as an ideal for his own community (and others).

Da er aus dem französischen klassischen Zeitalter hervorgegangen war, mußte Rancé seine kontroversen monastischen Ideen rechtfertigen, indem er an eine anerkannte Autorität appellierte. Bernhards persönliche Heiligkeit und einzigartig einflußreiche Rolle in der zisterziensischen Geschichte waren für ihn die einleuchtende Wahl. In seinem Hauptwerk *De la Sainteté*... zitiert Rancé Bernhard mehr als jede andere Autorität, wobei er einen großen Umfang seiner Schriften benutzte, aber mit einer klaren Vorliebe für die *Epistolae*. In Rancés eigenen Briefen, einer privateren und spontaneren Quelle, kommt Bernhard wieder zuerst, wieder mit einer Vorliebe für die *Epistolae*. Rancé beweist eine tiefe und ausgedehnte Kenntnis der bernhardinischen Schriften, aber die Vorliebe für die *Epistolae* legt den Versuch nahe, Bernhard als Person zu folgen und nicht nur als einer Autorität. Die Spiritualität der Wüstenväter war für Rancé wesentlich, aber die Autorität Bernhards war das Höchste in La Trappe, und Rancé stellte ständig das Beispiel der Gemeinschaft von Clairvaux unter dem Heiligen als ein Ideal für seine eigene Kommunität (und andere) dar.

SAINT BERNARD AND THE TRAPPISTS IN THE NINETEENTH AND TWENTIETH CENTURIES

Colette Friedlander, OCSO
Monastère du Jassonneix

Dedicated to Dom Jean Leclercq

T O PUT THE QUESTION of Saint Bernard's place and influence among the Trappists from the French Revolution to the present day into proper perspective, we must first ask: what was the general view of Saint Bernard during that period, and who were the Trappists? In answer to the first question, we may refer to Jean Leclercq's description of the 'romantic Bernard': on one hand, the man of action, towering over his contemporaries by the sheer force of the spirit; on the other, the 'pious author' whose image had been forged in the Late Middle Ages by the *devotio moderna* school. On the basis of hagiographical legends and apocryphal writings, Bernard the theologian and mystic had been made over into an essentially sentimental figure.[1] If we turn to art, which is always revealing, we see that, in the nineteenth century, 'the theme of honey and bees enriched that of "mellifluity"'—the true meaning of which had been forgotten[2]—'sometimes combined with that of "lactation" in an iconography whose strangeness and complication equaled its poor taste. Never, as regards Saint Bernard, had such a low point been reached.'[3]

---

[1]J. Leclercq, *S. Bernard et l'esprit cistercien* (Paris: Editions du Seuil, 1966) pp. 138 and 130–32.

[2]The medieval meaning of the term *mellifluus* referred to one who extracted the spiritual meaning of Scripture from the letter (Leclercq, p. 120).

[3]Leclercq, p. 139.

As for the nineteenth-century Trappists, their energies at first were largely channeled into the struggle for survival in the political turmoil of the revolutionary and napoleonic periods; later, a life of heroic asceticism continued to make severe demands. This, combined with the mistrust of studies and intellectual endeavor conveyed by an out-of-context reading of Rancé, contributed to a largely 'devotional' spirituality.[4] As a result, the Trappists appear to have been ill-prepared to challenge the contemporary image of Saint Bernard through a rediscovery of his theological stature. That image seems, in fact, to go along well with their dominant traits as we have just outlined them: Bernard the man of action mirrors their spirituality of struggle and effort, whereas the sentimental Bernard reflects their devotional preferences.

So much for background. What evidence can be gleaned from contemporary documents? Two easily available sources come to mind at once: the Acts of the trappist General Chapters,[5] and chronologically arranged bibliographies of works by or about Saint Bernard, the first of which was published by Leopold Janauschek in 1891.[6]

Acts of General Chapters are, of course, a very imperfect mirror of the spiritual and intellectual activity of any religious group. But given the trappist Chapters' preoccupation with regulating minute details of daily life, they might be expected to reflect something of that life. As concerns Saint Bernard, however, the nineteenth-century Acts are quite disappointing. He is referred to only once, in 1854, and then only in reference to his new title, Doctor of the Church, in the various liturgical books.[7] There is not a word about him in connection with studies; the 1861 Chapter of the Congregation of la Trappe, worried about the inadequate intellectual formation many monks were receiving, decided to set up a central *studium*, but its preoccupation with the curriculum goes no further than the choice of a theology manual, and there is no indication whatever that including cistercian sources was even considered.[8] Similarly, Saint Bernard is not referred to when there is question of developing the interior life—a matter with which the nineteenth-century

[4]E. Mikkers, 'Robert de Molesme', in DSp 13:808–809.
[5]*Actes des Chapitres Généraux des Congrégations Trappistes au XIXe siècle, 1835–1891*, ed. V. Hermans (Rome, 1975).
[6]L. Janauschek, *Bibliographia Bernardina*, Xenia Bernardina 4 (Vienna: Hölder, 1891).
[7]*Actes*, p. 81.
[8]*Actes*, p. 314.

trappist Chapters were concerned.[9] Finally, there is no word of the 1890 centenary—although we know from other sources that the trappist abbots did attend the celebration held in Dijon.[10] And from this we may conclude that the nineteenth-century trappist Chapters were not much concerned with promoting 'official devotion' to Saint Bernard. Their main preoccupation was with ensuring that the monks and nuns lived the cistercian life as it had been established by 'our Fathers'.

A study of Janauschek's *Bibliographia Bernardina* yields similarly slim findings. Between 1791 and 1891, the Trappists account for only three entries, one of them uncertain, as against sixteen for the Common Observance, three for the Congregation of Sénanque, and one for the bernardine nuns of Esquermes. Of these three works, two were translated, not authored, by Trappists.[11] The third, a historical study of 'St Bernard, Abelard and modern rationalism', is by Hugues Séjalon,[12] who, as the only nineteenth-century Trappist to have made any contribution to scholarship,[13] must be taken as the exception which confirms the rule.

Why so little? The obvious answer is the distrust for studies already mentioned. It should be added, however, that sacred studies, as the nineteenth century understood them, would have had little chance of developing an appreciation for Saint Bernard. The approach then prevalent was rigidly scholastic and cartesian, with an almost perverse bent for closed systems. As late as 1912, Dom Vital Lehodey, one of the more open minds of his time, expressed regret at Saint Bernard's lack of 'didactic precision'.[14] To this lack of intellectual receptivity must be added the monks' conscious choice in favor of anonymity and self-effacement—something of which Saint Bernard would have approved,

[9]*Actes*, p. 285 (1858) *et passim*.
[10]J. Bouton, *Histoire de l'Ordre*, Fiches cisterciennes (Westmalle, 1960) p. 446. The news bulletin published by the custodians of the shrine at Fontaines-lès-Dijon during the centenary year yields a few revealing insights as to the Trappists' involvement. It is interesting to note, for instance, that none of the preachers at the celebrations were Cistercians (*Bulletin du centenaire de Saint Bernard*, n 11, pp. 6–7, 10–11, 16–18; see also n 9, pp. 13–14; n 12, pp. 10–11). Recounting his community's preparations for the centenary, a cistercian (trappist?) abbot describes various bernardine devotions and a weekly meditation on one of the saint's virtues or maxims (*Bulletin*, n 5, pp. 10–11).
[11]One is a sermon on Saint Bernard, the other a mariological compilation containing many bernardine excerpts (Janauschek, nn. 2533 and 2274, respectively from 1875 and 1858).
[12]Janauschek, n. 2240 (1867).
[13]Mikkers, DSp 13:809.
[14]In a letter quoted by I. Vallery-Radot, *La mission de Dom Vital Lehodey* (Paris: Cerf, 1956) p. 158.

even if he practiced it rather irregularly. As a result, the nineteenth-century Trappists wrote little and published even less.

But did they read Saint Bernard, and, if so, how did they understand him? A full answer would require extensive research in the archives and libraries of those trappist monasteries whose history reaches back into the nineteenth century. The findings might turn out to be both scant and misleading. Early library catalogues are not always extant. The presence on today's shelves of editions and translations of Saint Bernard published in the 1800s or earlier does not necessarily inform us of the nineteenth-century monks or nuns' reading habits; the books in question may have been acquired much later. Furthermore, the altogether detestable custom of destroying old editions when new ones came in makes the absence of such editions equally difficult to interpret.[15]

Vernacular editions were not readily available, however, until the latter third of the century. Two french translations of Saint Bernard's complete works began to appear in 1866, and, by 1877, one of them was into its third edition—a good indication of popularity.[16] Most of the earlier, partial translations had been published in the seventeenth and eighteenth centuries,[17] so that not all monasteries could have owned them. This may account in part for the fact that the authors most read were Saint Alphonsus Liguori and the Jesuit Rodriguez,[18] whose *Perfection chrétienne*

---

[15]An example taken from the monastery of Laval (founded 1816) may serve to illustrate this point. The earliest library catalogue in the archives is dated 1931. Under 'Saint Bernard' it lists ten titles, one of them being the apocryphal *Vigne mystique*, two others the complete works translated by Ravelet (1866)—a marginal note, probably added later, informs us that this series was in the lay sisters' scriptorium—and Charpentier, also 1866. Of the remaining seven titles, three—two collections of extracts and a three-volume set of letters—were published respectively in 1830, 1888, and 1838, to which may be added a *Vie de saint Malachie* translated and printed at Lerins in 1875. But only two of these last four titles figure in the card catalogue begun in the late 1960s, which contains, on the other hand, a *Mois de Marie de saint Bernard* dated 1852, not listed in the 1931 inventory. The Charpentier series catalogued in the 1960s is the standard eight-volume set, with latin text, and there is no trace of the 1866 edition listed in 1931. The conclusion that may be drawn is that the Saint Bernard department of Laval's library between 1931 and 1970 was an evolving one, and this can be taken as a sign of interest; but nothing can be said with any certainty of the state of affairs in the 1800s.

[16]*Oeuvres complètes de saint Bernard*, traduction nouvelle par M. l'abbé Charpentier (Paris: Vivès, 1865 [2nd edition, 1873; 3rd edition, 1877]) vol. 1; *Oeuvres de saint Bernard*, traduites pour la première fois en français par Armand Ravelet (Paris: Palmé, 1865).

[17]For instance, those of Dom Antoine de Saint-Gabriel Desprez, which came out between 1667 and 1684 (see Janauschek, nn. 1151, 1186, 1187, 1204, 1223, 1230, 1250, 1251, 1254, 1261).

[18]Mikkers, DSp 13:808.

was the standard handbook of spirituality in trappist novitiates. Another reason may be the general distrust for mysticism dating back to the condemnation of quietism in the late seventeenth century—and Saint Bernard is quite accurately classified as a mystical, not an ascetical writer in the model catalogue for a monastic library given by the 1869 *Spiritual Directory*.[19] This does not prevent the *Directory* from quoting Saint Bernard rather abundantly, and often intelligently. True, its library catalogue lists none of his works under the heading 'theological and canonical', although that section includes books on mystical theology and although the *Directory* refers often to the *De pracepto et dispensatione*, undoubtedly a canonical treatise. True also, Bernard is cited as a model of observance in such matters as cleanliness and exterior modesty,[20] and called on to justify the more extreme rigors of trappist practice,[21] but also to testify to the beauty, peace, and joy of monastic life[22] and to encourage the monk in trial and temptation.[23] Given the influence exercised by the *Directory*—each postulant received a personal copy on entry, and the book followed him or her to the grave—its reading of Saint Bernard is not without significance. Indeed, if, as Edmund Mikkers asserts regarding the trappist nineteenth century, 'More than authors and their texts, the true witnesses to the spirituality of the strict observance are the many monks and nuns. . . [whose] sanctity, largely hidden and forgotten, was the soul of the Order's renewal',[24] then the same can be said of the Trappists' relation to Saint Bernard; for they doubtless lived the poor, obscure, and unreasonably austere life he had preached more exactly than most if not all Cistercians since the twelfth century. Moreover, if one accepts Jean Baptiste Auberger's thesis, according to which Clairvaux effected a 're-reading' of the earliest Cîteaux as embodied by Saint Stephen Harding—a re-reading stressing precisely poverty and austerity[25]—then nineteenth-century trappist observance had a definitely bernardine coloring. Significantly, this bernardine slant was the result of a conscious intention on the part of Dom Augustin de Lestrange, whose *Règlemens de la Valsainte*

---

[19]*Directoire spirituel à l'usage des Cisterciens Réformés vulgairement dits Trappistes, publié par ordre des Supérieurs* (Paris: C. Douniol, 1869). The author is Dom Benoît Moyne, abbot of Melleray (Mikkers, DSp 13:809).

[20]*Directoire spirituel*, pp. 68, 253, 94, 315.

[21]*Directoire spirituel*, pp. 122, 127, 152, 33–34, 134, *et passim*.

[22]*Directoire spirituel*, pp. 26, 38–39, *et passim*.

[23]*Directoire spirituel*, pp. 74, 78, 79, 81–82, 92.

[24]Mikkers, DSp 13:809.

[25]See J.-B. Auberger, *L'Unanimité cistercienne primitive: Mythe ou réalité?* (Achel: Administration de Cîteaux: Commentarii Cistercienses; Editions Sine Parvulos, 1986).

refer to the stricter regimen they establish as a return to the abbot of Clairvaux beyond the milder reform of Rancé[25a]. Whether living such an observance in a mental perspective divorced from Saint Bernard's doctrinal synthesis made for true fidelity is another question.

The movement towards a spirituality more firmly based in theology and drawing more consciously on early cistercian sources received a decisive impetus with the trappist congregations' reunion into an independent order in 1892. Of the three men whose names are most often associated with this renewal—Dom Jean-Baptiste Chautard, Dom Vital Lehodey, and Dom Anselme Le Bail—two were assiduous readers of Saint Bernard. Quite significantly, Dom Vital Lehodey seems to have discovered him through Saint François de Sales rather than directly; Saint François de Sales' *Traité de l'amour de Dieu* quotes Saint Bernard abundantly, and, more important still, the bishop of Geneva's optimistic conception of human nature and the human will is derived from the *De gratia et libero arbitrio* and meets the vision of the last *Sermones in Cantica*: God's image remains intact in man regardless of his sins, as a root from which the divine likeness can grow afresh.[26] This *theological* discovery was decisive in Dom Lehodey's spiritual development, and ultimately led him to recognize trust and abandonment as the heart of sanctity, in contrast to the anxious asceticism fostered by a view of human nature as essentially depraved. As for Dom Anselme Le Bail, author of the article on Saint Bernard in the *Dictionnaire de Spiritualité*, he excelled in conveying to others a taste for the authors of early Cîteaux.[27] The monks he formed as abbot of Scourmont from 1913 until his death in 1956 have been influential in promoting bernardine studies in the order to the present day.[28]

[25a] '...ces règlements...sont toujours les mêmes [que ceux de Rancé] si on en excepte les points où nous avons cru devoir nous rapprocher de saint Bernard' (*Règlemens de la Maison-Dieu de Notre-Dame de la Trappe...augmentés des usages particuliers de la Maison-Dieu de la Val-Sainte...*, 2 vol. [Fribourg: chez Béat-Louis Piller, 1794], p. IV). See also *Règlemens* 1:V, VI, VII, IX, 87, 88, 100, 102, 129, 444; 2:33, 34, 52, 61, 64, 97, 155, 391–392, 470, 471, 476. All of these passages quote St Bernard as an authority in matters of observance, and that only. Nearly a century later, the rare allusions to Bernard in the letters of a young Trappist named Charles de Foucauld refer to him solely as a model of penance, love and sacrifice; there is no indication of any reading of his works (Charles de Foucauld, '*Cette chère dernière place*'. *Lettres à mes frères de la Trappe*, [Paris, Cerf 1991], p. 37, 102–103, 198).
[26] Vallery-Radot, pp. 50–56.
[27] Mikkers, DSp 13:810.
[28] For instance, Charles Dumont, whose workshops in monasteries and novitiates during the 1970s and 1980s opened up Saint Bernard to a generation of young Cistercians.

If we now turn to sources for the twentieth century such as those used for the nineteenth, a bernardine comeback is immediately apparent. The indices to the Acts of the General Chapters list twelve references to Bernard between 1892 and 1953. Most of these concern such matters as the blessing of Saint Bernard medals or are connected with centenary celebrations,[29] but some refer to publications or aim at encouraging them.[30] The 1924 and 1925 Chapters approved a project for a Cistercian Authors Series fostered by Dom Anselme Le Bail,[31] which unfortunately did not materialize. Both types of mention indicate a growingly conscious, and perhaps self-conscious, relation to Saint Bernard. He is *the* cistercian saint, and as such enjoys official status as an object both of devotion and celebration and of study.[32]

Under the heading 'Studies' in the index to the General Chapter Acts, the findings are rather complex. For one thing, the list of entries is much longer; there is a definite evolution and less distrust. A most interesting document, the account of the retreat held by the members of the 1913 General Chapter,[33] provides a *status quaestionis* for that year. The thirty pages devoted to studies are a distinct encouragement in that direction. They often appeal to Saint Bernard's example as an incentive to center intellectual endeavor on Christ and the spiritual life,[34] but his works are not part of the curriculum sketched out. They are not even included in the list of textbooks recommended for a course in 'ascetic theology', and it seems taken for granted that the students' lifelong 'pious reading' will consist of Mgr. Gay, Rodriguez, Grou, Faber, and the like. However, familiarity with the cistercian authors, first and foremost Saint Bernard, is mentioned as an obvious prerequisite on the part of the professor, and

[29]*Acts of the General Chapter* [AGC] 1913, p. 11; 1920, p. 21; 1921, p. 14; 1927, p. 29; 1932, p. 19; 1946, pp. 7, 31; 1949, p. 9; 1952, pp. 26–27; 1953, p. 33.

[30]AGC 1913, p. 15; 1930, p. 5.

[31]AGC 1924, p. 16; 1925, p. 21.

[32]Not that this dimension was absent in the nineteenth century, but it hardly surfaces at the 'official' order-wide level reflected in Chapter records. Research in the archives of the various monasteries would no doubt be very revealing. At Achel, for instance, confraternity letters were always inscribed 'Bernardus'; the initials 'J.M.J.B.' (Jesus, Mary, Joseph, Bernard) appear as a heading on notes and correspondence; and the main altar of the monastery's first church was consecrated in honor of Mary and of Saint Bernard and bore in its center a sculptured medallion picturing the apparition of Our Lady to Saint Bernard (information communicated by Edmund Mikkers, to whom I am also indebted for many valuable suggestions).

[33]*Compte rendu de la retraite des supérieurs à Cîteaux, 9–10–11 septembre 1913* (Westmalle, 1914). This booklet was widely circulated within the order and exerted a deep influence (Mikkers, DSp 13:310).

[34]*Compte rendu*, pp. 70, 74, 77, 78.

a good grounding in the Church Fathers—among them Saint Bernard—is recommended above all.[35]

Why the dichotomy between the formation thought optimal for professors and that prescribed for their students? It must be remembered that the studies under discussion are clerical studies; the order did not envisage intellectual formation for those not called to ordination, that is, for nuns and laybrothers, until after 1945. Near the other end of the period under discussion, the *Ratio studiorum* approved in 1960 allotted a mere two hours per week for one year to patrology and liturgy together, as against five hours to dogmatic theology and two hours to moral theology throughout the five-year course.[36] This curriculum did not depend on the Trappists; they had to conform to norms set by higher ecclesiastical authorities, among whose theological sources Saint Bernard held no privileged place. The best students—those who later became professors in their monasteries—were sent to the roman universities, which could hardly have been expected to emphasize the Cistercian Fathers. The result was a divorce between formal theological studies, which remained essentially scholastic, and *lectio divina*, to the extent that the latter increasingly centered on cistercian sources. The post-conciliar years brought greater flexibility, but the intellectual climate of that period was largely dominated by the human sciences—to the detriment, again, of the traditional element.[37]

Now for publications. The findings to be gleaned from the *Bibliographie bernardine*[38] covering the years 1891–1957 are in sharp contrast to those of the nineteenth century. The shift did not occur immediately; the Trappists do not account for a single entry between 1891 and 1913— in spite of the 1890 centenary, which gave rise to a sharp increase in

---

[35]*Compte rendu*, p. 73: 'Le professeur évidemment devrait tout d'abord s'être familiarisé avec nos auteurs cisterciens (Migne les donne in extenso)... afin d'en dégager ce qui caractériserait la spiritualité de l'âge d'or de Cîteaux.' And further on: '... Si le professeur a *surtout* pris contact avec les Pères de l'Eglise, notamment St Bernard, St Augustin, St Jean Chrysostome et St Grégoire, quel festin... seront ses classes de théologie' (p. 75, emphasis added).

[36]*Ratio institutionis praesertim studiorum Ordinis Cisterciensium Strictioris Observantiae, ad mentem Constitutionis Apostolicae 'Sedes Sapientiae' atque 'Statuta Generalia'* (Westmalle, 1960) p. 30.

[37]In the early 1970s, the author of the present paper heard Placide Deseille, then in charge of the 'Textes monastiques d'Occident' series of 'Sources Chrétiennes', deplore the difficulty in finding translators for cistercian texts because the Order's best students preferred psychology or sociology as the subject of their dissertations.

[38]J. de la Croix Bouton, *Bibliographie bernardine, 1891–1957*, Commission d'histoire de l'Ordre de Cîteaux 5 (Paris: P. Lethielleux, Editeur, 1958).

bernardine studies within the Common Observance (twenty-seven entries between 1891 and 1910). But the situation changes radically after the latter date: roughly 175 trappist contributions are listed for the years 1913–1957, as against fifty-seven for other Cistercians.[39]

Interestingly enough, nuns are responsible for the first of this long series of entries. In 1913, the Trappistines of Blagnac (now le Rivet) published a small, tastefully presented volume containing selected passages relating to the season of Advent.[40] The introduction which, like the translation, is the work of the nuns, is remarkable for its emphasis—over twenty years before Gilson—on Saint Bernard as a guide to the understanding of the faith—in other words, as a theologian, although the word is not used.[41] With minds undistorted by scholastically oriented clerical studies, the lay members of the order were in a better position to perceive him as such than their priestly counterparts. Only very exceptionally, however, did nuns have the training necessary for even modest publications, and they were even more systematically discouraged than the monks from appearing 'intellectual'. As the level of scholarship in the order rose, the nuns disappeared from the scene until the 1960s. Their interest in Saint Bernard continued, however, and their demand for translations and conferences has had no little influence in stimulating work on the part of monks even in recent years.[42]

Indeed, this element—the living concern of the grassroots monk and nun for Saint Bernard—while the most elusive for the historian, is also

[39]In the *Bibliographie bernardine*, collections of papers by different authors are listed under a single number, but the contents are often detailed; I have counted each paper by a Trappist as one contribution. The figures are somewhat approximate due to the fact that the authors are not always identified as Cistercians; some lesser lights may therefore have escaped my notice. The continuation of the *Bibliographie bernardine* by E. Manning is of little use for our purposes, as the entries are arranged alphabetically rather than chronologically, and especially as the authors' monastic affiliation is not given; hence we have not extended our survey beyond 1957.

[40]*La Suavité des mystères de Jésus-Christ* (Albi: Imprimerie de l'Orphelinat Saint-Jean, 1913). Two other volumes, devoted respectively to the Christmas season and to Passiontide, appeared in 1928 (*Bibliographie bernardine*, n. 334).

[41]'La suavité du Docteur "mellifluus"...comme l'a nommé le moyen-âge, *émane de la profondeur et de la force même de sa doctrine*....Avec lui, *l'intelligence* pénètre davantage dans les mystères sacrés, dont il éclaire et recule les profondeurs' (*La Suavité*, pp. i-i; emphasis added). The texts themselves were chosen for their theological quality (see p. vi).

[42]Not that the nuns themselves have been idle (for instance, a senior member of a french abbey has translated all the works of Saint Bernard), but until very recently they have not been able to acquire the technical skills necessary to produce 'publishable' translations or studies.

the most important, for it is the soil out of which scholarship grows and also the goal toward which cistercian scholarship on the subject primarily aims. Conversely, scholarly production within the order reveals this concern, but scholarship requires certain conditions for its emergence. The contrast between the nineteenth century's 'devotional' and observance-centered relation to Saint Bernard and that of the twentieth century, more concerned with understanding his thought and spiritual vision, is probably due in good part to factors beyond the order's control, such as the general intellectual climate and orientation within the Church.

Obviously this rough and sketchy presentation of the subject raises more questions than it answers. If it stimulates research in the as yet largely uncharted territory of contemporary monastic history, it will have served its purpose.

ABSTRACTS

La vue qu'avaient de saint Bernard les Trappistes du XIXe siècle est assez difficile à saisir. Ils semblent l'avoir envisagé comme objet de dévotion et comme modèle d'observance plutôt que comme source de doctrine, bien que le *Directoire Spirituel* de 1869 le cite souvent et témoigne d'une certaine intelligence de sa perspective spirituelle. Le XXe siècle s'est tourné vers Bernard dans sa recherche d'un renouveau, et a vu un développement signficatif des études bernardines chez les membres de la Stricte Observance. Il est intéressant de noter que la première publication à témoigner d'une perception de Bernard comme théologien a été l'oeuvre de moniales.

The nineteenth-century Trappists' view of Saint Bernard is somewhat elusive. They seem to have considered him an object of devotion and a model of observance rather than a source of doctrine, although the 1869 *Spiritual Directory* quotes him often and witnesses to some understanding of his spiritual perspective. The twentieth century turned to Bernard in its search for renewal, and there has been a significant development of bernardine scholarship among members of the Strict Observance. Interestly enough, the earliest publication to evidence a perception of Bernard as a theologian was the work of nuns.

Das Verständnis, das die Trappisten des 19. Jh. vom hl. Bernhard hatten, ist recht schwer zu bestimmen. Sie scheinen ihn eher als Gegenstand der Verehrung und als Vorbild der Observanz, als als Quelle der Lehre gesehen zu haben, obwohl ihn der 'geistliche Leitfaden' von 1869 oft zitiert und von einem gewissen Verständnis seiner geistlichen Richtung zeugt. Das 20. Jh. hat sich Bernhard zugewandt in seiner Suche nach Erneuerung und hat eine bedeutende Entwicklung der bernhardinischen Studien bei den Mitgliedern der Strengen Observanz zur Folge gehabt. Es ist interessant zu erwähnen, daß die erste Veröffentlichung, die von der Wahrnehmung Bernhards als Theologe zeugt, das Werk von Nonnen gewesen ist.

LIKE FATHER LIKE SON:
BERNARD OF CLAIRVAUX AND THOMAS MERTON

M. Basil Pennington, OCSO
St Joseph's Abbey

IN THIS YEAR when we celebrate the nine-hundredth anniversary of the birth of Bernard of Clairvaux, there is no one of his sons as famous as Thomas Merton, Father M. Louis of Gethsemani. There are many remarkable similarities between these two great men, some more significant than others. First, both were born in France; Bernard at Fontaines-lès-Dijon in 1090 and Merton at Prades on January 31, 1915. Perhaps more important than is readily realized in the life of each is the fact that they both lost their mothers at an early age.

Both went to excess in their early adulthood, in both directions. Merton's excesses are fully reported in his autobiography[1] and successive biographies.[2] Once they entered on the monastic way, both gave themselves to monastic fasts and labor without regard for their relatively weak constitutions. But virtue lies in the middle. Both had to learn, and, before they did, they both managed to do lasting harm to their physical constitution and had to live with the consequences.

Merton came to the cloister a little later than Bernard (Bernard was 23 when he arrived at the gates of Cîteaux; Merton, 26), but both wholeheartedly embraced the monastic life and remained true to it till

---

[1]*The Seven Storey Mountain* (New York: Harcourt Brace Jovanovich, 1948).
[2]Michael Mott's *The Seven Mountains of Thomas Merton* is the biography authorized by the Merton Legacy Trust in accord with the will of Thomas Merton (Boston: Houghton Mifflin, 1984). See also my own complementary study, *Thomas Merton Brother Monk: The Quest of True Freedom* (San Francisco: Harper and Row, 1987).

death in spite of many temptations, if they can be called that. Bernard spurned more than one miter, while Merton steadily declined appeals to come out from the cloister to assume an active leadership role in the causes he championed. Merton did entertain the possibility of a move within the monastic way, with the hope of finding greater solitude, but then Bernard often bemoaned that he was not able to enjoy more fully the peace and solitude of his cloister.

There is no doubt, Bernard and Louis were both men of exceptional genius and well-developed literary talent. Even during their own lifetimes their richly poetic prose was well-known, much in demand, and had significant impact on the Church and society. A much more restricted and christianized society was more affected by the earlier writer. But the later monk reached an extraordinarily large and varied audience, not only within the most powerful nation and linguistic group on earth, but also within many other sectors of human society by virtue of the many published translations of his writings.[3]

Both were moved powerfully by grace to seek the fullness of the mystical life. Both wrote extensively on this search for God. Both saw it as the proper goal of every christian life and, through published writings and personal letters (both were exceptionally good letter writers[4]), sought to encourage the pursuit of it. Their earlier writings were almost exclusively in this vein, along with more specifically monastic themes. The final work of each was decidedly contemplative in its orientation, yet more widely embracing: Bernard's *De consideratione*[5] and Merton's

---

[3]See Marquita E. Breit and Robert E. Daggy, *Thomas Merton: A Comprehensive Bibliography* (2nd ed., New York: Garland, 1986) for a complete listing of the many translations of Merton's works that were published prior to 1986. The *Merton Seasonal*, published by the Thomas Merton Study Center at Bellarmine College, Louisville, Kentucky, continues the listing.

[4]We have a good collection of Bernard's letters, which he himself began to compile for us, in SBOp 7 and 8. The most complete english translation is the collection of Bruno Scott James, *The Letters of St Bernard of Clairvaux* (London: Burns Oates, 1953). Merton's letters are presently being edited and published in five volumes. The first three have appeared: *The Hidden Ground of Love: The Letters of Thomas Merton on Religious Experience and Social Concern*, ed. William H. Shannon (New York: Farrar, Straus, Giroux, 1985); *The Road to Joy: The Letters of Thomas Merton to New and Old Friends*, ed. Robert E. Daggy (New York: Farrar, Straus, Giroux, 1989); and *The School of Charity: The Letters of Thomas Merton on Religious Renewal and Spiritual Direction*, ed. Patrick Hart (New York: Farrar, Straus, Giroux, 1990).

[5]SBOp 3:393–493; trans. John D. Anderson and Elizabeth T. Kennan, *Five Books on Consideration: Advice to a Pope*, CF 37 (Kalamazoo, Michigan: Cistercian Publications, 1976).

Climate of Monastic Prayer.[6] Yet long before they reached these final syntheses, circumstances and the love of Christ urged them to expand their contemplative consciousness to embrace a wounded humanity with its many pressing needs. While the younger Merton who wrote the triumphalistic piety of *The Seven Storey Mountain* might have embraced a crusade, we can hardly conceive of his doing this in the last years of his life. Yet he remained, as did Bernard, a man of his times. Some of today's feminists wish to edit his sexist language and the attitudes it sometimes betrays, rightly judging, I believe, that if he were alive today he would wish to do that himself.

Both, much to the regret of many and to our perduring loss, died at a relatively young age.[7] How much more they could have given us.

While many of the similarities between the two may seem merely coincidental, there is no doubt that the 'Theologian of the Cistercian Order'[8] did exert an important formative influence on his spiritual son.

Fortunately, when the aspiring young writer from New York entered the cloister at Gethsemani in 1941, the community was under the guidance of a wise old abbot[9] who had an appreciation for things literary. While the novice, then young professed, privately wrote his pious poems (which include some of his best) and collected his seeds of contemplation, he was asked to work on a series of translations, which were to be published as The Cistercian Library. For the first volume[10] Merton contented himself with straightforward translation. But, as he approached the third, his creative spirit (which was being exercised at that time in the writing of his famous autobiography) and his deepening contemplative sense led him to do more. In the third volume of The Cistercian Library, which was published in the same year as *The Seven Storey Mountain*, Merton not only translated the report of the General Chapter, *The Spirit of Simplicity*,[11] which dealt largely with exterior simplicity, but he also

[6]CS 1 (Spencer, Massachusetts: Cistercian Publications, 1969).

[7]Bernard died in 1153 at the age of 63; Merton died in 1968, when he was only 53 years old.

[8]See Jean Leclercq, 'The Intentions of the Founders of the Cistercian Order', in M. Basil Pennington (ed.), *The Cistercian Spirit: A Symposium in Memory of Thomas Merton*, CS 3 (Spencer, Massachusetts: Cistercian Publications, 1970) p. 101ff.

[9]Dom Frederic Dunne, who died six years after Merton entered.

[10]Jean-Baptiste Chautard, *The Soul of the Apostolate* (Trappist, Kentucky: Gethsemani, 1946). The second volume in the Cistercian Library series (*An Artist Soul: Roger Durey*) was not translated by Merton.

[11]*The Spirit of Simplicity: Characteristic of the Cistercian Order*, The Cistercian Library 3 (Trappist, Kentucky: Gethsemani, 1948).

added to the volume a second part on interior simplicity.[12] For this part Merton made a judicious choice of texts from the writings of Saint Bernard and commented on them. The choice of texts makes it amply clear that Merton had studied extensively the writings of Saint Bernard and had done so in the original latin, a painstaking task in those days when they were available for the most part only in the poorly printed tomes of Abbé Migne.[13]

The texts which Merton chose were those in which Saint Bernard had set forth most concisely and clearly his theological anthropology, the solid basis for his spiritual doctrine on the dignity and call of the human person. This study, complementing and enriching what Merton had already found in the theology of Saint Thomas Aquinas and in the mystical teaching of Saint John of the Cross, became the basis for his own understanding of the human person and call. Abbot Flavian Burns relates how, when Professor Dan Walsh first read Merton's *The New Man*,[14] he exclaimed: '*The New Man*—the new Merton!' Walsh was not wholly accurate here. In what is Merton's most definitive theological work, he brought forth much of what he had learned from his father, Bernard, earlier in his life. Merton readily acknowledged this.[15] Yet he did not merely repeat the teaching of the abbot of Clairvaux. He gave it powerful new expression in the existential terminology of our times, and perhaps even dared to press it a bit further than did the earlier writer, though this may seem to us to be the case only because of our lack of full comprehension of what the medieval theologian was saying. In any case, Merton set forth our imagining of Christ in our creation and recreation in a way that did not betray Bernard. Rather it challenges us more powerfully in its contemporary expression.

[12]This second part has been reprinted in *Thomas Merton on Saint Bernard*, CS 9 (Kalamazoo, Michigan: Cistercian Publications, 1980) pp. 105–157.

[13]PL 182 and 183.

[14]*The New Man* (New York: Farrar, Straus and Giroux, 1961).

[15]'Without going into great detail, let us sketch out some of the broad outlines of the picture freely, following the thought of St Bernard.' *The New Man*, p. 104. He goes on to quote Bernard's eighty-second sermon on the Song of Songs (p. 111) and cites him a number of times in footnotes. Merton not only uses Saint Bernard but Bernard's sources in Saint Paul and carries their supernatural logic forward to this climatic statement: 'Unlike the mere human individual, Christ is not personalized by the individuation of human nature. His Divine Person can reach out and include all humanity in Himself without ceasing to be individual and distinct and without losing His own transcendent unity. All our personalities, all our individualities are derived from Him and sustained by Him both in what is most personal to each one and in what is common to them all. This not only by grace but also by nature. And this, once again, is all due to the fact that He is the uncreated Image of which we are created images' [p. 139].

In the foundational chapter of *The New Man*, 'Image and Likeness', and elsewhere in the book Merton was dependent on the same bernardine passages he had excerpted in the second part of *The Spirit of Simplicity*.[16] We are made to the very image and likeness of God. Unlike the rest of creation, for us to be is to be alive. Our simplicity is not as complete as that of God, for whom to be is to be alive happily. Our whole being seeks happiness, but it can and has eluded us. Instead of being true to who we are, we have taken on a certain duplicity. In our ignorance we have not known our true selves. Nor have we truly known God. For, if we did, we would know that we are of God and that the goodness of God is such that all is ours as gift. Rather like Prometheus, we seek to steal from God, or, at least, in some way to earn, the happiness for which we long. Instead of, in the truth of our being, embracing wholly the divine will, becoming one in mind and heart with God and thus with our true self, we seek to create a false self. We, who are wholly of God in so far as we are, seek to be something of ourselves. Thus we alienate ourselves not only from ourselves but also from God. We will not find our true self by looking at ourselves. We will find our true selves only in God and in union with him in love. This is love knowledge, something beyond anything the rational intellect can attain, for we are made in the very image and likeness of God, partakers of the divine nature and life. When we love ourselves and others as God loves us, then we have come to our true selves. 'To love like this is to become a god.'[17]

Merton is so filled with the spirit of Bernard and the men of Bernard's time, that like Bernard he reaches for a mythological figure to help bring out the fullness of the biblical teaching. He sets forth a 'promethean theology'[18] using Hesiod's sad figure to image our psychological situation of guilt, rebellion, frustration, insecurity, and self-alienation.

The breakthrough that Bernard made in image theology for his times in his treatise *On Grace and Free Choice*[19] and in his *Sermons on the Songs of Songs*,[20] Thomas Merton made for our times, if we would but

[16]Sermons 81 and 82 on the Song of Songs (*Spirit of Simplicity*, p. 81ff.); SBOp 2:284–302; trans. Irene Edmonds, *On the Song on Songs IV*, CF 40 (Kalamazoo, Michigan: Cistercian Publications, 1980) pp. 157–87.

[17]These are the last words of Saint Bernard that Merton quotes in *The Spirit of Simplicity*, p. 135.

[18]The title of the second chapter in *The New Man*, pp. 21–48.

[19]SBOp 3:165–203; trans. Daniel O'Donovan, *The Works of Bernard of Clairvaux* 7, Treatises III; CF 19 (Kalamazoo, Michigan: Cistercian Publications Inc., 1977) pp. 51–111.

[20]See note 15.

hear him. Like Bernard, Merton grounds a powerful spiritual teaching on profound theological insights. A clear grasp of these insights is a powerful impulsion to live an exciting Christ-centered, Christ-empowered life, the life Saint Paul was speaking about and living. This is not the place to develop the full thesis of *The New Man*,[21] but the modern existential thinker who wants *lectio* that is fully in the spirit of Saint Bernard yet benefits from the subsequent development in human thought and christian doctrine can find no better place to do it than in Thomas Merton and, most especially, in his *New Man*.[22]

Bernard wrote habitually out of his own lived experience. There were few exceptions to this. Merton learned early in his monastic literary career that abstract writing, with an impersonal and more or less scientific approach, did not work for him.[23] His efforts in writing *The Ascent to Truth*[24] brought on his only, though somewhat perduring experience of writer's block. The nervous breakdown he experienced during this same

[21]Merton himself sums up *The New Man* in a letter to his mentor and friend, Mark Van Dorn, dated October 16, 1954: '. . . A book I have been writing this fall, which is all about man being the image and likeness of God. . . .The book is called (so far) "Existential Communion" [eventually published as *The New Man*]. It is about the business of "coming to oneself" and "awakening" out of the inexistential torpor that most people live in, and finding one's real identity—in God. Which is possible because we are His image and likeness, and by our charity we are identified with Him. Thus our knowledge of Him is no longer merely as though it were the knowledge of an "object"! (Who could bear such a thing: and yet religious people do it: just as if the world contained here a chair, there a house, there a hill, and then again God. As though the identity of all were not hidden in Him Who has no name.)' *The Road to Joy*, p. 26.

[22]I would add though that some of Merton's thinking here would have profited from the challenge that the thought of Henri de Lubac (who also had profoundly absorbed Bernard and the other cistercian fathers) set forth in his not yet sufficiently absorbed *The Mystery of the Supernatural*, trans. Rosemary Sheed (New York: Herder and Herder, 1967). In his trinitarian development of the human as the image of God, Merton draws a great deal from Ruysbroeck (p. 141ff.), perhaps not aware of how dependent Ruysbroeck was on Bernard and on Bernard's friend and fellow Cistercian, William of Saint Thierry.

[23]'I have attempted to convey something of a monk's spiritual life and of his thoughts, not in the language of speculation but in terms of personal experience. This is always a little hazardous, because it means leaving the sure plain path of accepted terminology and traveling in byways of poetry and intuition. I found in writing *The Ascent to Truth* that technical language, though it is universal and certain and accepted by theologians, does not reach the average man and does not convey what is most personal and most vital in religious experience. Since my focus is not upon dogmas as such, but only upon their repercussions in the life of a soul in which they begin to find concrete realization, I may be pardoned for using my own words to talk about my own soul.' *The Sign of Jonas* (New York: Harcourt Brace Javanovich, 1953) pp. 8–9.

[24]*The Ascent to Truth* (New York: Harcourt Brace Jovanovich, 1951). Bernard is not absent from this work. There are a sufficient number of references to him through the

period was not brought on solely by this, however. He was still struggling with the integration of himself as a writer and a monk. Merton saw something of this same struggle in Bernard and other early cistercian fathers whom he so greatly admired.

In 1953, on the occasion of the eighth centenary of Saint Bernard's death, Pope Pius XII issued an encyclical honoring the 'Last of the Fathers': *Doctor Mellifluus*.[25] Merton published an english translation of the encyclical with an extensive introduction.[26] As we read what he writes about the Mellifluous Doctor we cannot help but think of how much what he is saying fits the author himself. 'It seems', he writes, 'that one of the things Saint Bernard wanted to get away from when he entered Citeaux was literary ambition.'[27] But 'all sanctity is born of conflict.'[28] He contrasts the rich natural endowments of Bernard and the stark monastic simplicity that the saint sought and goes on: 'Saint Bernard seems to have thought it possible to renounce everything of the first element in his soul and live entirely by the second.'[29] Besides highlighting this conflict that was so much of an element in Merton's own early monastic life, Merton also points to Bernard's widespread influence,[30] noting that

work and a two-page biography at the end. This is not surprising because, while Merton was preparing this work, he published a five-part 'Transforming Union in Saint Bernard and Saint John of the Cross' in Coll. 9 (1948) 107–117, 210–23; 10 (1949) 41–52, 353–61; 11 (1950) 25–38. These articles have been gathered together with other pieces in *Thomas Merton on St Bernard*, pp. 159–239. On the whole, they are a somewhat tedious effort, though rich in content, to prove there is no contradition in the teaching of the two saints on transforming union. In them Merton establishes that Bernard 'provides a strong foundation of tradition for the thoughts developed by the mystics of Carmel' [p. 162].

[25]*Acta Apostolicae Sedis*, 45 (1953) 369–84.

[26]*The Last of the Fathers: Saint Bernard of Clairvaux and the Encyclical Letter, Doctor Mellifluus* (New York: Harcourt Brace, 1954). Besides a six-page preface, Merton has a sixty-eight page introduction. In honor of Bernard's anniversary (1153–1953) Merton also published in three parts 'Action and Contemplation in St Bernard' in Coll. 15 (1953) 26–31, 203–261; 16 (1954) 105–121. This was later published in *Thomas Merton on St Bernard*, pp. 21–104. In this, Merton sums up Bernard's teaching on the matter, mostly from the Song of Songs, showing much concern with demonstrating the superiority of the contemplative life, though trying not to let it become a basis of comparison of the merits of the various religious orders.

[27]*Thomas Merton on St Bernard*, p. 47.

[28]*Thomas Merton on St Bernard*, p. 26.

[29]*Thomas Merton on St Bernard*, p. 25.

[30]'For Bernard was to influence everything from politics to the *roman courtois* and the whole humanistic trend to "courtly love." He left his mark on schools of spirituality, on Gregorian chant, on the clerical life, and on the whole development of Gothic architecture and art.' *The Last of the Fathers*, p. 29.

One of the signs of a spiritual revival that is really spiritual is that it affects every kind of life and activity around it, inspires new kinds of art, awakens a new poetry and a new music, even makes lovers speak to one another in a new language and think about one another with a new kind of respect.[31]

The romantic in Merton perhaps goes a bit far here. Nonetheless, it is true that both Bernard and Merton affected life around them in many ways, inspired poetry and music, and challenged us to have a greater respect for ourselves and for each other.

Toward the end of his life, Merton wrote a significant passage on the literary dimension of Bernard and some of the other early cistercian fathers that not only highlights their struggle but makes us profoundly aware of how much their twentieth-century son is like them. For, as we read the passage, we instinctively say: this could have been written of Merton himself. Permit me to quote it at length:

The rich and elegant vitality of Cistercian prose—most of which is sheer poetry—betrays an overflow of literary productivity which did not even need to strive for its effects: it achieved them, as it were, spontaneously. It seemed to be second nature to St Bernard, William of St Thierry, Adam of Perseigne, Guerric of Igny to write with consummate beauty prose full of sound and color and charm. There were two natural explanations for this. The first is that the prolific Cistercian writers of the Golden Age were men who had already been thoroughly steeped in the secular literary movements of the time before they entered the cloister. All of them had rich experience of the current of humanism that flowered through the twelfth-century renaissance. . . . There is a second explanation for the richness and exuberance of theological prose in twelfth-century monasteries of Citeaux. If contact with classical humanism had stimulated a certain intellectual vitality in these clerics, it also generated a conflict in their souls. The refined natural excitements produced by philosophical speculation, by art, poetry, music, by the companionship of restless, sensitive and intellectual friends merely unsettled their souls. Far from finding peace and satisfaction in all these things, they found war. The only answer to the problem was to make a clean break with everything that stimulated this spiritual uneasiness, to withdraw from the centers in which it was fomented, and get away somewhere, discover some point of vantage from which they could see the whole difficulty in its

[31]*The Last of the Fathers*, p. 29.

proper perspective. This vantage point, of course, was not only the cloister, since Ovid and Tully had already become firmly established there, but the desert—the *terra invia et inaquosa* in which the Cistercian labored and suffered and prayed. . . . The tension generated by the conflict between secular humanism and the Cistercian humanism, which seeks the fulfillment of human nature through ascetic renunciation and mystical union with God, was one of the proximate causes of the powerful mystical writing of the Cistercians. However, once these two natural factors have been considered, we must recognize other and far more decisive influences, belonging to a higher order. . . . It is the relish and savor that only experience can give that communicates to the writings of the twelfth-century Cistercians all the vitality and vividness and impassioned sincerity which are peculiarly their own. . . . The White Monks speak with accents of a more personal and more lyrical conviction that everywhere betrays the influence of an intimate and mystical experience. . . . It is the personal experiential character of Cistercian mysticism that gives the prose of the White Monks its vivid freshness. . . . Since the theology of the Cistercians was so intimately personal and experiential, their exposition of it was bound to take a psychological direction. All that they wrote was directed by their keen awareness of the presence and action of God in their souls. This was their all absorbing interest.[32]

I do not think we would have difficulty in establishing the full validity of this statement in regard to both Bernard of Clairvaux and Thomas Merton. Thomas Merton, Father M. Louis of Gethsemani, is indeed a son of his father, the Mellifluous Doctor, Saint Bernard of Clairvaux.

THOMAS MERTON'S WORKS ON SAINT BERNARD

The Last of the Fathers: *Saint Bernard of Clairvaux and the Encyclical Letter, Doctor Mellifluus*. New York: Harcourt Brace, 1954.

The Spirit of Simplicity: *Characteristic of the Cistercian Order*. The Cistercian Library, 3. Trappist, Kentucky: Gethsemani, 1948.

Thomas Merton on St Bernard. CS 9. Kalamazoo, Michigan: Cistercian Publications, 1980, pp. 159–239.

'Action and Contemplation in St Bernard.' Coll. 15 (1953) 26–31, 203–261; 16 (1954) 105–121.

'Bernard of Clairvaux.' *Jubilee* 1 (August 1953) 33.

---

[32]Quoted in Pennington, *Thomas Merton Brother Monk*, pp. 148–49.

'Foreword' to Bruno Scott James, *St Bernard of Clairvaux*. Chicago: Henry Regnery, 1953, pp. v-viii.

'The Sacrament of Advent in the Spirituality of St Bernard.' In *Seasons of Celebration*. New York: Farrar, Straus, Giroux, 1965, pp. 61–87.

'St Bernard, Monk and Apostle.' *Cross and Crown* 5 (1953) 251-63. Reprinted in *Disputed Questions*. New York: Farrar, Straus & Cudahy, 1960.

'Transforming Union in Saint Bernard and Saint John of the Cross.' Coll. 9 (1948) 107–117, 210–23; 10 (1949) 41–52, 353–61; 11 (1950) 25–38.

ABSTRACTS

Bernard de Clairvaux et Thomas Merton se ressemblent à bien des égards. L'un et l'autre avaient de grands dons littéraires grâce auxquels ils ont exercé une influence considérable. Tous deux recherchaient l'union mystique, mais n'ont pu résister aux appels de l'humanité blessée. Plusieurs écrits-clé de Merton trahissent une influence bernardine, notamment *Le Nouvel Homme*. Leur oeuvre à tous deux doit son impact à la conviction qu'elle véhicule, conviction née d'une expérience spirituelle profondément vécue.

Bernard of Clairvaux and Thomas Merton resemble one another in many ways. Both had great literary gifts thanks to which they exerted considerable influence. Both were in search of mystical union, but were unable to resist the call of wounded mankind. A number of Merton's key writings, particularly *The New Man*, bear the mark of Bernard's influence. The works of both owe their impact to the conviction they convey, a conviction born of deeply lived spiritual experience.

Bernhard von Clairvaux und Thomas Merton ähneln sich in vielerlei Hinsicht. Der eine wie der andere hatten große literarische Begabungen, dank derer sie einen nicht zu verleugnenden Einfluß ausübten. Beide suchten die mystische Einigung, aber konnten den Anfragen der verletzten Menschheit nicht widerstehen. Mehrere Schlüsselschriften von Merton verraten einen bernhardinischen Einfluß, vor allem *Der neue Mensch*. Das Werk von beiden verdankt seine jeweilige Wirkung der Überzeugung, die es trägt, einer Überzeugung, die aus einer tief gelebten geistlichen Erfahrung heraus entstanden ist.